S0-BJF-722

Crucible of Freedom

Crucible of Freedom

Workers' Democracy in the Industrial Heartland, 1914–1960

Eric Leif Davin

Montante Family Library
D'Youville College

FEB 2 5 2011

LEXINGTON BOOKS
A division of
ROWMAN & LITTLEFIELD PUBLISHERS, INC.
Lanham • Boulder • New York • Toronto • Plymouth, UK

Cover photo: "Pittsburgh-area steelworkers on the march, 1936." Photo courtesy of Howard Scott.

Published by Lexington Books
A division of Rowman & Littlefield Publishers, Inc.
A wholly owned subsidary of The Rowman & Littlefield Publishing Group, Inc.
4501 Forbes Boulevard, Suite 200, Lanham, Maryland 20706
http://www.lexingtonbooks.com

Estover Road, Plymouth PL6 7PY, United Kingdom

Copyright © 2010 by Lexington Books

All rights reserved. No part of this book may be reproduced in any form or by any electronic or mechanical means, including information storage and retrieval systems, without written permission from the publisher, except by a reviewer who may quote passages in a review.

British Library Cataloguing in Publication Information Available

Library of Congress Cataloging-in-Publication Data

Davin, Eric Leif.
  Crucible of freedom : workers' democracy in the industrial heartland, 1914-1960 / Eric Leif Davin.
    p. cm.
  Includes bibliographical references and index.
  ISBN 978-0-7391-2238-9 (cloth : alk. paper) -- ISBN 978-0-7391-4572-2 (electronic)
  1. Working class--United States--History--20th century. 2. Labor--United States--History--20th century. 3. Industrial relations--United States--History--20th century. 4. New Deal, 1933-1939. 5. United States--Social conditions--20th century. I. Title.
  HD8072.D277 2010
  331.880973'09041—dc22   2009047067

⊖™ The paper used in this publication meets the minimum requirements of American National Standard for Information Sciences—Permanence of Paper for Printed Library Materials, ANSI/NISO Z39.48-1992.

Printed in the United States of America

HD
8072
.D277
2010

"Freedom is no half-and-half affair. If the average citizen is guaranteed equal opportunity in the polling place, he must have equal opportunity in the market place... I see an America where the workers are really free...where the dignity and security of the working man and woman are guaranteed by their strength, and fortified by the safeguards of law."

President Franklin D. Roosevelt,
Acceptance Speech,
Democratic National Convention, June 27, 1936.

"Looking back over two hundred years, the chronicler sees the American Experiment as a series of planned or unplanned experiments...But the grand experiment that transcended all the others was the effort to expand both individual liberty and real equality of opportunity for all—the supreme promise of the Declaration of Independence, the campaign pledge of the Jeffersonians and Jacksonians and their successors, the subject of Tocqueville's most penetrating observations, the core of the epic struggle of the 1860s, the essence of the twentieth-century philosophical battles over the dynamic tension and interplay between liberty and equality. This experiment was called Freedom, combining as it did liberty and equality."

James MacGregor Burns,
The Crosswinds of Freedom, 1989.

Contents

Acknowledgments

Maurine Greenwald, Jonathan Harris, and Joseph White gave unstintingly of themselves with advice, support, and encouragement over the course of bringing this book to fruition. They have my heartfelt appreciation.

Most of all, however, I am indebted to Richard Oestreicher. Over many long years, Richard was always there for me. His comments and suggestions are reflected on every page. His insights suffuse the book. Even when I despaired, Richard never faltered in his belief in this book, nor in his belief in me. This book would not exist but for him. Thank you, Richard.

Reiko Becker also has my sincere gratitude for preparing the manuscript for publication. Her support was essential in the long slog toward the end.

And Anita Alverio has my deep appreciation for her constant emotional and psychological support through the years. She has always believed in me.

Chapter 1

The Workers' New Deal

The New Deal was an aberration in American culture and politics. It was a time when extreme class consciousness, class solidarity, and class conflict dominated the domestic scene and American politics. This was not true of the eras before that, which had been dominated by ethno-cultural politics. Nor is it true of the present.[1] Perhaps this is why awareness of these intense class antagonisms has faded from our consciousness and now the received wisdom among some political scientists is that they never existed at all. "The American population has *always* been a pragmatic population," claims Harvard University political scientist Morris Fiorina. "They are, by and large, centrist; they don't like extremes."[2]

Despite such claims, the fact is that over the course of the 1930s, the political center almost disappeared as the Democratic New Deal became a litmus test of class, with blue collar workers providing its bedrock of support while white collar workers and those in the upper-income levels opposed it. "The unemployed, relief recipients, low-income households, and blue-collar workers registered overwhelming approval in 1936 and 1940, while business people, professionals, white-collar workers, and upper- and middle-income households all expressed increasing disapproval. In 1936 the difference in the percentage voting Democratic between upper- and lower-income households was 34 percentage points; in 1940, 40 percentage points . . . Over the course of the 1930s [class] sentiment did indeed become translated into political consciousness as the class basis of partisanship became successively more marked from election to election."[3]

By 1948 the class cleavage in American politics was as dramatic as in many Western European countries—such as France, Italy, Germany or Britain—with which we usually associate class politics. This period, then, became "the only era in American political history . . . when class played an important role in determining the prevailing pattern of partisan political preferences."[4]

1

There were also other ways of measuring the increasing class consciousness and class antagonisms of the Thirties. Contemporary social scientists, for example, found a pervasive existence and *consciousness* of class in blue collar America. Sociologists had long investigated aboriginal cultures in the far corners of the earth. In the Thirties, following the lead of academics like W. Lloyd Warner of Harvard, they began to turn their research tools on American society, producing pioneering work on "typical" New England, Midwestern, and Southern towns. They called these towns names such as "Yankee City" (Newburyport, Massachusetts), "Jonesville" or "Elmtown" (Morris, Illinois), "Plainville" (a town in Missouri), or "Old City" (Natchez, Mississippi).

And everywhere they looked they found what Warner found in Newburyport. "The social system of Yankee City," he reported, "was dominated by a class order" based on the kinds of homes people owned, the neighborhoods where they lived, their occupations, and their family backgrounds. And, not only was this rigid class order deeply rooted and widely accepted, there was virtually no movement across class lines.[5] Further, while the language of class used by the people of these towns did not refer to "capitalists," "the bourgeoisie" or "the proletariat," their language revealed their awareness of the class order. They spoke of "society" on the one hand and "good, honest, self-respecting, average, everyday working people . . . who are *all right*" on the other.[6]

It is important to understand why class was so salient in the Thirties, not only so we can glean a clearer understanding of the past, but also so that we can gain a clearer understanding of how the present was created. Central to any understanding of how American society works, argues Walter Dean Burnham, is an understanding of "the mainsprings of American politics," that is, "the mechanisms by which groups not particularly conspicuous for their influence on politics during one era become mobilized in the next or, conversely, how and why it is that groups which are effectively mobilized into the voting system in one era are demobilized or even expelled in the next."[7]

The workers' mobilization during the New Deal Era—their class consciousness and their class solidarity—weren't acts of will. It didn't happen because they were a politically blessed generation, more ideologically "virtuous" than preceding or subsequent generations. Rather, more basic and far-reaching explanations must be sought. "History consists not of erratic and spasmodic fluctuations, of a series of random thoughts and actions," Sam Hays tells us, "but of patterns of activity and change in which people hold thoughts and actions in common and in which there are close connections between sequences of events."[8] To understand the rise and fall of class politics in America, then, we need to understand its social basis, for the class politics of the time emerged from the social, economic, and cultural world of the workers.

Prior to World War I, the world of the ethnic worker was one marked above all by demographic churning, by transience and instability. From the beginning of the Industrial Revolution in America, the American working class was a multiethnic working class. This was especially true of many mass production industries such as the steel industry which, particularly after the turn of the twentieth century, was increasingly built on the backs of imported Southern and Eastern European laborers. Ethnic identity remained strong among these working class immigrants. This very ethnic diversity may have been a major contributing reason for the lack of "class consciousness" in America at this time.[9]

Additionally, however, the creation of this multi-ethnic working class was not something which happened once and for all and then was done with. Rather, it was an on-going process. "Just as in all modernizing countries," Herbert Gutman tells us, "the United States faced the difficult task of industrializing whole cultures, but in this country the process was regularly repeated, each stage of American economic growth and development involving different first-generation factory workers."[10] The American working class was therefore not "made" at any one time, but was constantly being re-made over and over as new waves of immigrants entered the workforce, bringing with them their "alien" customs, beliefs, and values. This constant demographic churning brought to the fore ethnocultural differences and issues, making them—Prohibition, blue laws, religion, et cetera—the cleavage lines of American politics.

A major source of this churning demographic cauldron was removed, however, when World War I and the Johnson Act of 1924 clamped a lid on further European immigration. This contributed to a marked decline in geographic transience, as the settled ethnic enclaves of America solidified into the foundation of a new politics. Without continued injections of foreign elements, both the cities and the workforce—the working class—grew more "Americanized," as the children of the immigrants grew up and joined the world of urban work.

The world of the ethnic worker, then, was a world of aliens becoming Americans. It was a world of both stability and change. On the one hand, an increasingly stable work, neighborhood, and family environment encouraged ties of ethnic solidarity. On the other hand, as the children of these aliens grew up as Americans, they became increasingly conscious of what they had in common with the working class children of other ethnic groups and what America theoretically promised them all, but was not delivering. It was out of their backgrounds of solidarity and their belief in and desire for the promise of America that emerged both the goal and the means to transform America.

By the 1930s, these children of the immigrants had at last come of age. Of the ten largest American cities in 1930, including New York, Chicago, Philadelphia, Detroit, Los Angeles, Cleveland, St. Louis, Baltimore, Boston, and Pittsburgh, only St. Louis and Baltimore had majority native white populations, and that by only 3.4 percent and 3.1 percent respectively.[11] Born and raised in the cities, speaking English instead of a myriad of foreign languages, thinking of themselves as Americans with all the rights of Americans rather than as strangers in a strange land, embedded in a socio-economic network which gave them unprecedented cohesion, these immigrant children were mobilized into the labor movement and electoral arena as their parents had never been.

With their numbers and their solidarity they created the unions of the New Deal Era. These were the workers who provided the backbone of the mass unionization of the steel industry in the Thirties. Louis Smolinski, one of the creators of the steel union in Braddock, outside Pittsburgh, recalled that the foundry and the finishing department of U.S. Steel's Edgar Thomson mill in that town were dominated by Poles and Slavs. Those two departments, especially the finishing department, was where "the organization" came from when the union was organized there in the mid-Thirties. For this reason, Smolinski recalled, "Some of the bosses and other damn things called it a 'Hunky' union. Everybody from the finishing department was in it."[12]

These were the workers who were also crucial to the creation of the New Deal Era itself by forcing the powers-that-be to respond to them and by making the northern wing of the Democratic Party over into "their" party. These workers were, of course, only part (although a vital part) of the New Deal coalition, which also included southern Dixiecrats and big city political machine bosses. Additionally, the New Deal responded to the pressures of other constituencies, as well. Bankers got reform of the banking system and realtors loved the FHA, while Dixiecrats loved the AAA, which rewarded rich farmers and ignored poor tenant farmers.

But Dixiecrats had been loyal Democrats since the Civil War, and there were not enough bankers and realtors in America to install and keep the New Deal in office. Instead, the Democratic Party became the majority party in the 1930s by becoming the party of this vital new majority, the emerging urban, working class, settled children of the immigrants. This can be graphically seen in a city like Pittsburgh. For instance, in looking at the Democratic Party Ward Chairmen and Committeemen in 1934, we find that *not a single one* came from an "American" family of origin. All were ethnics.[13]

By becoming the party of this constituency, the Democratic Party became America's de facto labor party, that is, it occupied the space on the political spectrum which otherwise would have been filled by a labor party, particularly at the state and local levels in the industrial Northeast where these populations were concentrated.[14]

Nor was the "New Deal Social Contract" these workers subsequently forged a "barren marriage" which produced no legitimate offspring. It was a radical and welcome departure from what had existed before the Great Depression. Just in the five years between 1917 and 1922 several court decisions had seriously damaged the labor movement. In 1917 strike activities were severely curtailed by two decisions. In 1919 the courts declared a child labor law invalid and in 1921 picketing was virtually outlawed unless carried out under such restrictions as to cripple its effectiveness. Finally, the 1920s witnessed instance after instance of injunctions being handed down to hamper union activities.[15] The New Deal's Wagner Act of July 1935, and numerous other legal decisions, went far in leveling the legal playing field between labor and capital.

In addition, Democratic administrations instituted various welfare and work relief programs, unemployment and disability compensation, income tax reform, old age pensions, public housing for low income groups, low cost public power, a federal reserve system with all its guarantees for small bank accounts, protection and financial assistance for home owners, as well as financial aid which guaranteed a college education for millions who otherwise would never have gone to college.[16] Moreover, all of this was won in an amazingly short period of time.

These victories were more than what labor scholars at the time believed workers were fighting for. In 1958 Daniel Bell claimed the labor movement was "one of the chief vehicles of social change" in America, even though it was built on the "pale ideology" of "Laborism." This label was given to the ideology of the workers "largely by the 'Wisconsin school' of John R. Commons and Selig Perlman" who argued that Laborism believed in "the limited, day-to-day, expectation of social improvement."[17]

But what ordinary workers wanted and what they actually accomplished in the Thirties was far more than some mere "limited, day-to-day . . . improvement." What they wanted and what they created in a handful of years was a radically different society which at last offered them the respect for which they hungered, the political rights of citizenship promised all Americans in the nation's founding documents and teachings, a more democratic relationship between labor and capital, more of an equal opportunity for workers and their children to prosper, and the economic security which previous eras had denied them.

In the work cited above, Daniel Bell complained about the "End of Ideology," the "Exhaustion of Political Ideas in the Fifties." But there was no "end of ideology" in the Fifties. Rather, there was a "triumph of ideology"—the ideology the workers actually fought for. It is important to emphasize that the workers, in fact, won their struggle of the 1930s. And what they brought forth in the Fifties was exactly the kind of society for which they so militantly fought. The theory and practice of social, political, and economic harmony embodied in the "New Deal Social Contract" which governed American society until recent times was *their* creation.

Leftists seldom actually *listen* to their revered working class to discover what workers truly want and truly fight for. Why should they? Leftists possess the revealed Truth which already tells them what the working class *should* want and *should* be fighting for.

But despite what many on the Left presumed or hoped for, workers in the Thirties were not fighting for something else, for a "socialist revolution" and the abolition of capitalism, perhaps, or for some other vague but "more radical" outcome. They were fighting for what workers, themselves, thought of as a "workers' democracy."[18] And they got it.

Frances Fox Piven and Richard A. Cloward are typical Leftists in expressing their disappointment with the world the workers made in the Thirties. "The years of discontent and disaffection, of protest and possibility, were over," Piven and Cloward sadly claim of the years after the Democratic landslide of 1936. "The people had lined up behind the New Deal. What trouble and turbulence persisted were not sufficient to rock the New Deal or to alter its course."[19]

But workers were still discontented after 1936. Protest continued after 1936. And years of possibility remained—though not for the vague revolution that Piven and Cloward supply no evidence the workers wanted or were ever fighting for. Rock the New Deal? Why should American workers do that? It was *their* New

Deal. They created it—and they had no desire to alter its course. It was giving them exactly what they wanted and had fought for.

It sometimes seems as if Leftists have learned nothing and forgotten nothing, as more recent Leftists, like Piven and Cloward, persist in viewing the New Deal through the same clouded ideological lens as their Thirties' predecessors. In the Thirties, Left intellectuals, infatuated with Marxist dogma, viewed the era as one of a stark apocalyptic choice between fascist capitalism or communist revolution. "Either the nation must put up with the confusion and miseries of an essentially unregulated capitalism," declared the editors of *The New Republic* in 1935, the same year the Wagner Act, the Social Security Act, and the Wealth Tax Act became law, "or it must prepare to supersede capitalism with socialism. There is no longer a feasible middle course." This ideological absolutism prevented such Left intellectuals from clearly seeing how workers were already creating a "workers' democracy" all around them on a daily basis.

Malcolm Cowley was one of the *New Republic* editors who drafted that 1935 declaration that there was no "feasible middle course" between socialism and rough-shod capitalism. While never a member of the Communist Party, he was a Marxist "fellow traveller." In his memoir, *The Dream of the Golden Mountains* (the "Golden Mountains" being the coming communist revolution and subsequent utopian classless society), he explains that, with him and the people he associated with in the Thirties, "There was the notion that capitalism and its culture were in violent decay and on the point of being self-destroyed. There was the idealization of 'the workers' as the vital class, the only one fated to survive. There was the moral imperative: surrender your middle-class identity, merge yourself with the workers, suffer their common hardships, and be born again! . . . Untold numbers of people will be sacrificed in the struggle, but let us be among those victims if the need arises, since history is on our side. All of us joined in brotherhood, our right fists raised in the Red Front salute, let us march forward into the classless society."[20]

Because of Cowley's subservience to the tyranny of this Marxist mirage, he confessed that, at the time, he didn't pay much attention to the New Deal and its dramatic reshaping of American society. "I watched these and other domestic developments with what seems to me now an amazing lack of interest," he said. "They had the defect for us of not fitting into an ideological pattern. We were all ideologists in those days, from Hoover on the right to the Trotskyites on the far left.

"My own country was conducting scores of experiments, based on dozens of theories, and their outcome might determine the shape of Western culture for a hundred years. Like the Russians, however, and like many American intellectuals at the time, I insisted on thinking in terms of either-or: either peace in a world that was ruled by the workers or war between rival imperialisms. I differed from the Communists in being mildly attracted to Roosevelt . . . but still he was defending capitalism; therefore his social experiments were directed toward the wrong goal and they would fail. Assured of what the end must be, I turned to other spectacles as if selecting a more dramatic program. The political struggles in France and

Spain, the foreign invasion and civil war in China, the second Russian Five-Year Plan, the cataclysm in Germany."[21]

And, just as Cowley and his comrades ignored the New Deal, so, too, did they ignore the workers and their struggles. For all their idealization of the workers and their moral imperative to merge with the workers, they didn't bother to actually *listen* to the workers in order to find out what they were fighting for. They already had an ideological understanding of what the workers should be fighting for which precluded any need for actual fieldwork among workers. The workers, their golden dream told them, were fighting for the same communist revolution and classless society they, themselves, yearned for so fervently.

Over the course of time, however, "the golden mountains receded into the mist" as the struggle became muted. As it did, Cowley asked himself if he had truly understood the Thirties he had lived through. He wondered, was the militance of the workers "aroused by anything nobler than the hope of driving a new Buick?"[22] Looking back in 1955 at American Marxists like Cowley and his comrades, Louis Hartz aptly observed that they were "Europeans living in an alien world, unwilling and unable to understand it."[23]

Left intellectuals have continued to bemoan the loss of those golden mountains of radical revolution. One interesting variation on this theme of "radicalism betrayed" is exemplified by Melvyn Dubofsky. This pessimistic variation argues that there never *was* any radicalism to betray, nor did workers accomplish much of any significance in the Thirties. Perhaps the older, wiser, disillusioned Cowley was right. Thirties workers only wanted to drive a new Buick.

Dubofsky comes to this conclusion using as his only measure of a genuinely radical ideology exactly that of Piven and Cloward: "Revolution"—and he just doesn't find it. And because he can't find an acceptable revolutionary ideology among the workers, he views them as "inert masses."

Dubofsky claims that the most important lessons to be learned about the Thirties are, "First, and perhaps obviously, however turbulent were the American 1930s, the depression decade never produced a revolutionary situation. Second, one observes the essential inertia of the working-class masses . . . Most Americans, workers included . . . [had] faith in the 'justness' of the American system and the prospects for improvement without fundamental restructuring . . . As one observer noted of the Flint sit-downers, a group more militant than the majority of auto workers, 'Those strikers have no more idea of "revolution" than pussy cats.'"[24]

Dubofsky then points to some of the social characteristics of ethnics as the reasons for the "essential inertia of the working-class masses." The great mass of industrial workers were, " . . . first- and second-generation immigrant workers, as well as recent migrants from the American countryside, who remained embedded in a culture defined by traditional ties to family, kinship, church, and neighborhood club or tavern. Accustomed to following the rituals of the past, heeding the advice of community leaders, and slow to act, such men and women rarely joined unions prior to a successful strike . . . [and] rarely served as union or political activists and radicals."[25]

John Bodnar reached much the same conclusion. "While Slavs in America were involved in several labor protests for increased wages," he says, "generally their conservative, defensive posture was evidenced soon after their arrival in the industrial milieu. Arriving with a strong traditionalist cultural bent, the tiresome burden of working-class life, sustained by limited mobility through two generations, hastened the emergence of a 'defensive posture.'"[26]

Bodnar elaborates by pointing to what he describes as the "circumscribed world" of the ethnic enclave as the fundamental reason workers sought limited social, economic, or political goals. Workers, he says, had a "realistic assessment of survival," a "fundamental sense of realism," they were "invariably pragmatic," and they knew they had little power to affect anything in the larger "Anglo-Saxon" world which surrounded them. Therefore, they didn't try. They focused simply upon family and group survival, creating a rock-hard social and political conservatism impervious to outside influences and ideologies.

"During the half-century of industrialization after 1890," Bodnar says (i.e., through the 1930s), "a family-oriented culture defined the framework of individual lives . . . If workers agitated for job security more than for social equality, and if they demonstrated a realism that disappointed those who would have preferred a greater ground swell of social idealism in America, it was because equality and even [socio-economic] mobility were largely personal goals, while job security was the key to family sustenance. After all other arguments have been heard, one is left with the belief that for the rank and file in the early twentieth century, labor issues were essentially family issues; culture and economics were simply inseparable . . . Essentially powerless to direct their economic and social well-being, they took refuge in the regularity and predictability of the family and the worker enclave, where they could exercise some power and gain a sense of order. The powerlessness they experienced in their immediate milieu kept them family oriented rather than outward-striving . . . [or] engaging in ideological or economic protest, which seemed quite fruitless in the many instances where resources and power were overwhelmingly in the hands of others. The fact that workers frequently engaged in strikes or protests should not obscure the fact that more often they did not."[27]

The problem with both these characterizations of the world of ethnic workers is that they are static. Neither Dubofsky nor Bodnar see these societies undergoing the throes of transformation, as they were at the time. Ethnic industrial workers in the Thirties were not simply conservative Old World peasants. They were aliens in the process of becoming Americans, and as "Americans" they were assertive and demanding of their "rights"—and their American nature was just as determinative as their Old World nature. The world Dubofsky and Bodnar describe seems to be in a parallel universe from the America of the 1930s that actually happened. If the world Dubofsky and Bodnar describe was all there was—then one would not be able to explain the Thirties, for these "inert masses" are the very ones who transformed America in that decade. They could not have done so if they were simply the conservative, fearful, and isolated people these descriptions evoke.

To illustrate how this model is insufficient to explain the world of ethnic workers in the Thirties, let alone what actually happened in the Thirties, let us look at an example Dubofsky used, that of the Lynds and Muncie, Indiana. In 1929 Robert and Helen Lynd published *Middletown: A Study in Modern American Culture,* an influential study of Muncie. According to the Lynd study, the people of Muncie, mostly native born, divided themselves into two distinct classes defined by occupations. According to the residents, everybody was either "working class" or belonged to an opposing "business class," and the two classes were seen to live in dramatically different social, cultural, and political worlds. When they returned a decade later to see how the Great Depression had changed things in Muncie, they discovered that the city was still divided into two great classes and the business class, led by the Ball family, still ran the city.[28]

Dubofsky uses the Lynds' study of Muncie—and a contemporary study on New Haven—as one of his two primary pieces of evidence to argue for the lack of class consciousness and class militancy in the 1930s. "Surprisingly," he writes, "[the Lynds] found labor organization weaker in 1935 than it had been in 1925, yet the Muncie business class seemed more united and more determined than ever to keep its city open shop (nonunion). The Lynds discovered objectively greater class stratification in 1935 than in 1925 and even less prospect for the individual worker to climb up the ladder of success (see Thernstrom on Boston's depression generation workers for similar findings), yet they characterized Muncie's workers as being influenced by 'drives . . . largely those of the business class . . . Fear, resentment, insecurity and disillusionment has been to Middletown's workers largely an *individual* experience for each worker and not a thing generalized by him into a 'class' experience . . . Such militancy as it generates tends to be sporadic, personal, and flaccid; an expression primarily of personal resentment rather than an act of self-identification with the continuities of a movement or of a rebellion against an economic status regarded as permanently fixed.'"[29]

But Dubofsky's citation of the Lynds is both selective and ahistorical. The "surprising" weakness of Muncie's labor movement in 1935 was because a fierce class war had been fought in Muncie in the early 1930s (of which Dubofsky neglects to inform us) and the workers had been stomped. In 1932 General Motors shut down its local plant and 25 percent of the Muncie workforce was rendered unemployed. Shortly thereafter, the "inert masses" at the Ball glass factory and at the remaining automotive plants—run like dictatorships by the company—petitioned the AFL to send them organizers and rushed to join unions under the NRA. The business class fought back, secretly increasing the size of the police force, arresting anyone who attempted to hand out pro-union literature, and assuring GM of a docile workforce if it returned. The unionization drive was smashed and GM did return, in June 1935, the very month the Lynds arrived back in Muncie.

But, though the union had been smashed, Muncie's "inert masses" could still vote. And, despite what the Lynds described as the greatest effort on the part of the industrialists and bankers in Muncie's history to stampede the electorate for a Republican, in 1936 Muncie went Democratic for the first time since the Civil War. Chortled one happy worker to the Lynds, *"We* certainly licked the big bosses!"[30]

Further, although the Lynds claimed Muncie's workers lacked any "self-identification with the continuities of a movement," thereafter Muncie *stayed* Democratic. Not only that happy worker, but most of Muncie's other "inert" workers seemed to have developed a sense of themselves as a class and acted en masse on that sense in an unprecedented fashion. The result was an enduring political revolution. As Malcolm Cowley noted, "it was a little revolution that amazed and puzzled the authors of *Middletown in Transition.*"[31] And, as Dubofsky himself says, "So much for Muncie," one of the only two pillars of his "inert masses" thesis.[32]

The same development of class consciousness and class cohesion could be seen in Pittsburgh's South Side Wards 16 and 17, which were the "most foreign" wards in the city, with the highest concentration of ethnics, mainly Poles (80 percent of the total) and Lithuanians.[33] According to Dubofsky and Bodnar, these wards should have been the most inert wards in the city—instead, they were the strongest and most militant Democratic wards in Pittsburgh. In the 1932 presidential election, Roosevelt did his best in South Side Polish Wards 16 and 17, where he garnered over 75 percent of the vote.

Following 1932, Democratic margins of victory only climbed in these same wards. Indeed, by one measure, the South Side Polish Wards 16, 17, 18, and 31 (which also became the most militant CIO union wards in Pittsburgh) were the most class conscious wards, not only in Pittsburgh, *but in the entire nation.* Between 1940 and 1954 these Slavic wards ranked among the strongest "labor wards" in America in terms of the percentage of their vote these CIO voters gave to Democrats.[34]

Because he is looking only for "revolutionary" sentiment, Dubofsky is blind to the implications of his own evidence, which indicates a growing, militant, ethnic class consciousness in working class America during the Thirties. For example, Dubofsky admits that, "During the 1930s, it seemed, the United States had developed a true proletariat, more united by its similarities than divided by its differences . . . an altered working-class consciousness [was] part of American reality during the 1930s . . . Despite the continental size and diversity of the American nation, it is possible to glimpse aspects of working-class reality in local settings that disclose uniformities in belief and behavior . . . [Thus,] New Haven's workers . . . did in fact develop a collective sense of class. 'Hell, brother,' a machinist said, 'you don't have to look to know there's a workin' class. We may not say so—But look at what we do. Look at where we live. Nothing there but workers. Look at how we get along. Just like every other damned worker. Hell's bells, of course there's a workin' class, and it's gettin' more so every day.'"[35]

But then Dubofsky dismisses this by saying such class consciousness only brought about trivial changes. "[O]ne must remember," he says, "that during the 1930s ordinary workers, the romanticized rank and file, risked their jobs, their bodies, and their lives to win the contract. And when they won it, as in Flint in February 1937, a sit-down striker rejoiced that it 'was the most wonderful thing that we could think that could possibly happen to people.'"[36]

Further, Dubofsky views working class loyalty to the Democratic Party as futile when he says, "By the end of the 1930s, Roosevelt's Democratic Party had become, in effect, the political expression of America's working class . . . Blacks and whites, Irish and Italian Catholics, Slavic- and Jewish-Americans, uprooted rural Protestants and stable skilled workers joined the Democratic coalition, solidifying the working class vote as never before in American history . . . [but] the one experience during the 1930s that united workers across ethnic, racial, and organizational lines—New Deal politics—[nevertheless] *served to vitiate radicalism.*"[37]

Because the only measure of "radicalism" Dubofsky is looking for is an actual or potential quasi-Marxist "revolution," he misses just how much of a "fundamental restructuring" of the American political economy such developments as unionization actually brought about. "The contract," recognition of the union on the part of management as the workers' bargaining agent, was an essential component of the democratization of labor-management relations.

Nor was this democratization the only thing that workers were fighting for. Contrary to Dubofsky's implications, "the contract" was only one of the things for which the rank and file "risked their jobs, their bodies, and their lives." Taken collectively, these goals radically transformed American society. Given the dramatic and far-reaching changes which actually did take place, an ideologically blind focus on a quasi-Marxist revolution—whether betrayed or never in evidence—diverts us from the significance of what really happened in the Thirties, from what workers actually fought for, and the nature of what they actually accomplished.

Some scholars have energetically searched for these clues and have reached somewhat similar conclusions concerning the desires and ideology which motivated workers to change their society during the Thirties. For example, one major difference about the Thirties from other other periods was that underlying social and cultural changes brought into existence a sufficiently large, coherent, and self-identified community of the dispossessed who had an ideology of revolt which helped mobilize them to enter the political arena on their own behalf. Left intellectuals, enamored as they were, and are, with Marxist ideology, misunderstood, and continue to misunderstand, the nature of this working class ideology of revolt. Gary Gerstle calls this ideology, "Working Class Americanism."

According to Gerstle, the dominant political discourse of the Thirties—and, indeed, even today—was that of "Americanism." The term is ambiguous, "But Americanism was not so amorphous as to resist definition. It can best be understood as a political language, a set of words, phrases, and concepts that individuals used—either by choice or necessity—to articulate their political beliefs and press their political demands." So elastic was the concept that, while Republican capitalists could easily wrap themselves in the flag of Americanism, " . . . for every individual looking to Americanism for comfort and security, we can counterpose another who found in Americanist rhetoric an inspiration for political revolt . . . [Who used] Americanist rhetoric to focus attention directly on the unequal distribution of power between capital and labor that prevailed in the workplace, community, and nation." So dominant was this ideology that it forced, "virtually every group seriously interested in political power—groups as diverse as capitalists, socialists, ghettoized ethnics, and small-town fundamentalists—to couch their programs in the language of Americanism."[38]

For "working-class Americanists," that program was "democratizing relations between capital and labor," as exemplified in the great CIO insurgency which saw itself as, "a grand struggle for freedom and independence."[39]

Among the Catholic French-Canadian textile workers of Woonsocket, Rhode Island, that Gerstle studied, Americanism coalesced in the Thirties to produce an insurgent working class that was both "anticapitalist but anticommunist, patriotic but parochial, militant but devout." Upon this unique foundation the local textile union fashioned a campaign for "industrial democracy" which, in itself, represented a radical rupture with the past. As the union leadership defined it, "Industrial democracy . . . promised workers a very tangible kind of empowerment: control over their hours, their wages, their jobs, their chances for promotion, and even their employers' pricing and investment decisions." As part of this, the primary goal of the working class leaders upon coming to political power in Woonsocket was "a municipal administration that would respect labor's right to organize, picket, and strike, and eventually sponsor municipal welfare and industrial planning programs."[40]

This economic crusade was the axis around which political life spun, not only in Woonsocket, but in America as a whole in the Thirties. To make industrial democracy the nation's political litmus test was "an important achievement" because, "It meant that left-liberal forces had managed to extract from the democratic language of Americanism the words necessary to establish capital-labor relations as a political, even moral, issue of cardinal importance. It meant that radicals and liberals had shifted the balance of ideological power between capital and labor in labor's favor after a long period of unchallenged corporate domination. And, finally, it focused the attention of the American polity squarely on the glaring problem of industrial autocracy in a society ostensibly dedicated to democratic principles."[41]

The establishment of economic independence for wage earners as the nation's—and Woonsocket's—battleground was made possible by an equally radical break from the past: the political empowerment of the ethnic working class. The textile union leaders told their membership that the road to power led through the ballot box—and Woonsocket's long-suppressed workers followed that road to dominance of the city's political affairs by 1938.

"Exercising these electoral rights may appear, in retrospect, a rather tame tactic for radicals to have advocated," Gerstle says. "But ethnic workers in Woonsocket, like their counterparts elsewhere in the North and the West, had only begun to think of themselves as American citizens with the full complement of rights that such citizenship entailed. To them, casting a ballot to determine who would govern and what policies would be implemented constituted a bold, even radical, political act . . . the use of the ballot in the 1920s and 1930s, in cities like Woonsocket, signified a profound political awakening among millions of ethnic Americans. Its significance for national politics was every bit as great as the dramatic growth of black Americans' electoral participation in the 1970s and 1980s."[42]

Lizabeth Cohen, who looked at Chicago workers but argued that she told a national story, also agrees that the workers' New Deal was not as "revolutionary" as most Leftists would like; it was never, Cohen says, anti-capitalist. Nevertheless, it was far more radical than the neo-Marxist theorists would acknowledge.

And, contrary to those who see the New Deal as the triumph of liberal elites, Cohen argues that it was class conscious workers who made the New Deal what it was by "participating in a political movement that was made by, and for, average working people."[43] Whereas the great organizing drives of 1919 had been defeated by the huge ethnic and racial divisions which fragmented the working class, the triumphs of the New Deal were made possible because workers of all ethnic and racial identities had forged a "culture of [class] unity" which created a "common ground" of class consciousness and class-based politics. This class unity—expressed through support of "cross-ethnic working class institutions" such as the Democratic Party and the CIO—was "the big news" of the Thirties.[44]

Thus, Cohen cites a 1936 national conference of ethnic fraternal societies in Pittsburgh which the Steel Workers Organizing Committee (SWOC) organized to support its unionization drive. The success of the conference, trumpeted SWOC, demonstrated that, "a fundamental change . . . has been taking place in American life . . . that some half a million Americans of foreign birth or extraction . . . all agreed to unite for a common purpose, the improvement of the lot of the nation's steel workers by union organization."[45]

Workers used their new-found class unity to accomplish a common goal: the creation of a "moral capitalism." Cohen identifies this moral capitalism as the characteristic workers' ideology, an ideology which turned to "state and union . . . [to] . . . provide the security formerly found through ethnic, religious, and employer affiliation as well as ensure a more just society."[46] Workers, Cohen argues, continued to believe in capitalism, but they no longer trusted capitalists to make it fair. Therefore, through their CIO unions and the Democratic Party, they demanded and created an increasingly interventionist state to make capitalism moral and fair. This "greater expectations for the state" was a fundamental departure from the past and represented a new and symbiotic relationship between the federal government and the working class.[47] Thus—a working class New Deal, created by and for workers.

While Cohen sees the working class creation of an interventionist state as the major accomplishment of the New Deal Era, Karen Orren argues this could not have been accomplished without the prior working class destruction of a feudal past. From the days of Tocqueville and Crevecoeur to Louis Hartz and others, historians and political theorists have viewed America as "exceptional" in that it did not have a feudal past to overcome. And, because of this, Hartz argued, America could also not develop socialism. "One of the central characteristics of a nonfeudal society," he said, "is that it lacks a genuine revolutionary tradition . . . Marx went wrong in his historical analysis, attributing as he did the emergence of the socialist ideology to the objective movement of economic forces. Actually, socialism is largely an ideological phenomenon, arising out of the principles of class and the revolutionary liberal revolt against them which the old European order inspired. It is not accidental that America, which has uniquely lacked a feudal tradition, has uniquely lacked also a socialist tradition. The hidden origin of socialist thought everywhere in the West is to be found in the feudal ethos."[48]

Orren, however, finds the *persistence* of feudalism to be the major factor in the creation of the American polity. And the locus of this feudalism was in the master-servant work relationship inherited from medieval England and protected by a reign of common law beyond the reach of democratic politics. The destruction of this feudalistic master-servant regime by the labor movement— formalized by the 1937 victory of Aliquippa steelworkers over their J & L bosses in the U. S. Supreme Court case, *NLRB vs. Jones & Laughlin*—created modern American liberalism and "accomplished the separation between state and society that since the eighteenth century had been understood, prematurely, to distinguish American liberalism from its feudal antecedents."[49]

Contemporary observers noted that, for example, Pittsburgh's "Slavs sometimes lived a life of near serfdom."[50] For them, feudalism was a reality in the New World, just as much as it had been for them in the Old World. If feudalistic "principles of class" (as Hartz put it) were a necessary pre-condition for the development of an ideology of revolt, then that condition was met in America's industrial heartland.

Orren agrees and says she does not use the term "feudalism" rhetorically. "My argument," she says, "is not that there was a resemblance between late-nineteenth-century employment law and feudal law, or that capitalist employment practices were analogous to feudal practices, but that there was, in actuality, an unbroken line stretching from labor regulation in Tudor England—with strands evident from Plantagenet England and even earlier—to labor regulation in Gilded Age America . . . Thus, when I describe American labor relations in the nineteenth century as feudal, it means that the substance of relations between employers and employees still was under the ultimate jurisdiction of the courts, as was the case in the Middle Ages, and that the old common-law rules of labor governance had been left standing while other institutions had been changed or dissolved."[51]

The dismantling of this literally feudal labor relationship, Orren says—a 60-year struggle which culminated in the 1930s—laid the basis for all further social progress. By bringing the workplace, at last, within the reach of legislative action and legitimizing voluntary collective action, this transformation fundamentally changed the American state and created modern liberal politics. This was not a trivial accomplishment.

And, not only did labor's triumph bring the business corporation under the authority of constitutional law for the first time, it also cleared the way for subsequent social movements, from the civil rights and women's movements to environmentalism and the culture wars of the present. "At the same time that the private sector was opened up by the labor movement as a field of legally sanctioned collective action," Orren says, "the forms of pressure invented by the unions—the picket line, the consumer boycott, the sit-down—were likewise adopted and modified to other ends."[52]

Thus, far from being co-opted and compromised by some dominant and insidious liberalism, as some charge, the labor movement gave birth to that very liberalism out of its own struggle and triumph. "The significance of the labor movement in American politics," says Orren, "lies not in the preemption [creation] of a socialist state, but in the construction of a liberal state. The results of that project have established the basis for subsequent change, both within the framework of liberal politics and beyond it."[53]

****

In this book I seek to explain how and why common working people mobilized in the 1930s to create a more egalitarian America. Western Pennsylvania was one of the major battlegrounds upon which ordinary workers created their New Deal, and it is with the creation of the Steel Valley's "Workers' Democracy" that this radical transformation of America can be most clearly seen. As Elmer J. Maloy, a SWOC organizer who was elected mayor of Duquesne in 1937, said when he declined to run for re-election in 1945, the workers had won everything they set out to win. "All I wanted to do in the first place was to take the place over. The union was strong enough now, so I didn't give a damn."[54]

But, Duquesne and the surrounding industrial heartland did not exist in isolation. They were part of a larger matrix which they both influenced and which they were influenced by. This industrial heartland was only one arena among many in which ordinary Americans fought to make new lives for themselves.

American politics takes place within a federal system with much decentralization. American politics is not just what happens inside the Beltway. Analysts who forget that often do not perceive the true political contours of an age. Politics is also about what happens in the various states. And, within those states, it is also about what happens in the various towns, both large and small.

In the 1930s American workers won unambiguous victories in the mill towns of the industrial heartland. But beyond the industrial heartland there were struggles to be carried on in Pittsburgh, in Allegheny County, the Commonwealth of Pennsylvania, and the nation as a whole. The contestants, though similar, were not always the same in the different arenas, nor were the powers of the antagonists always the same. In some arenas, the workers won outright. In others, they mostly won. In still others they suffered major defeats.

But an accurate evaluation of what happened in America during the New Deal Era demands that we not only evaluate the performances of the antagonists in each arena but also each arena in relation to the other. Only by looking at this entire mosaic can an accurate assessment of the era as a whole be rendered, for the changes which took place in these different arenas were all interrelated with each other, the one affecting the other. By understanding what happened in these multiple arenas during these years—for instance, how the workers won in the industrial heartland but lost the battle over Taft-Hartley or how they lost Taft-

Hartley but elected Harry Truman—we not only come to a better understanding of labor's dynamics in the Thirties, but also to a better understanding how modern America came to be.

And, when the final tally of wins and losses is calculated, we see that, through the struggles of ordinary people themselves, a new political order arose in the 1930s out of the ruins of a repressive past. Ordinary workers dismantled a feudal past which had ruled for centuries and, both in politics and economics, created the modern liberal state and, thus, the basis for all subsequent progress toward equality. In the 1930s, the industrial heartland thus became America's "Crucible of Feedom."

Notes

1. A similar phenomenon seems to have occurred in England where, for instance, Ross McKibbin argues that class consciousness and class conflict reached an intensity in the years 1918-1951 which dramatically distinguished these years from those coming before and after. See Ross McKibbin, *Class and Cultures in England, 1918-1951,* Oxford University Press: New York, 1998.

2. Peter Costa, "A Conversation with Morris Fiorina," *Faculty of Arts and Sciences Gazette,* Harvard University, spring 1993, 10. Emphasis added.

3. Richard Oestreicher, "Urban Working-Class Political Behavior and Theories of American Electoral Politics, 1870-1940," *The Journal of American History,* Vol. 74, No. 4, March 1988, 1283.

4. Oestreicher, "Urban Working-Class Political Behavior," 1285.

5. W. Lloyd Warner and Paul S. Lunt, *The Social Life of a Modern Community,* Yale University Press: New Haven, 1941, 82. Also, see Warner and Lunt, *The Status System of a Modern Community,* Yale University Press: New Haven, 1942; August Hollingshead, *Elmtown's Youth,* John Wiley Sons, Inc.: New York, 1949, rev. ed., 1975 (on Morris, Illinois); James West (pseud. of Carl Withers), *Plainville, USA,* Columbia University Press: New York, 1947; Art Gallaher, Jr., *Plainville Fifteen Years After,* Columbia University Press: New York, 1961; Elin L. Anderson, *We Americans,* Harvard University Press: Cambridge, 1938 (on Burlington, Vermont); and Alfred Winslow Jones, *Life, Liberty, and Property,* Temple University Press: Philadelphia, 1941 (on Akron, Ohio).

6. Allison Davis, et al., *Deep South: A Social Anthropological Study of Caste and Class,* University of Chicago Press: Chicago, 1941, 238, (on Natchez, Mississippi).

7. Walter Dean Burnham, "The Nature of Electoral Change," in his *Critical Elections and the Mainsprings of American Politics,* W.W. Norton & Co.: New York, 1970, 70.

8. Samuel P. Hays, "The Politics of Reform in Municipal Government in the Progressive Era," *Pacific Northwest Quarterly,* No. 55, October 1964, 170.

9. See the useful discussion of this, as well as other possibilities, in Eric Foner, "Why is There No Socialism in the United States?" *History Workshop*, No. 17, spring 1984, 57-80.

10. Herbert G. Gutman, *Work, Culture, and Society in Industrializing America: Essays in American Working-Class and Social History,* Vintage Books: New York, 1977, 14.

11. Bruce M. Stave, *The New Deal and the Last Hurrah: Pittsburgh Machine Politics,* University of Pittsburgh Press: Pittsburgh, 1970, 41, table 5.

12. Louis Smolinski in John Bodnar, *Workers' World: Kinship, Community, and Protest in an Industrial Society, 1900-1940,* The Johns Hopkins University Press: Baltimore, 1982, 136, 139.

13. Stave, *The New Deal and the Last Hurrah,* 180, table 23.

14. J. David Greenstone has made this very point in his comparison of the alliance between organized labor and European labor parties and the alliance between the American labor movement and the Democratic Party. Essentially, the alliances are indistinguishable. "However much it primarily appeals to economic interests in recruiting its members," he says, "the American labor movement has increasingly come to act in national politics less as an economic interest group than as an integral part of one of our two major political parties." See J. David Greenstone, *Labor in American Politics,* Alfred A. Knopf: New York, 1969, xviii.

15. Lewis L. Lorwin, *The American Federation of Labor,* The Brookings Institution: Washington, D.C., 1933, 210-12, 406-407.

16. Greenstone, *Labor in American Politics,* 46-47.

17. Daniel Bell, "The Capitalism of the Proletariat: A Theory of American Trade-Unionism," in *The End of Ideology: On the Exhaustion of Political Ideas in the Fifties,* rev. ed., The Free Press: New York, 1960, 211-212.

18. This phrase was used by the Pittsburgh Central Labor Union (PCLU)—the congress of all AFL unions in the city—in a resolution welcoming and endorsing the 1937 national convention in Pittsburgh of the Peoples Congress for Democracy and Peace. The PCLU endorsed whatever "actions that Congress might take to further advance progressive labor legislation *and the cause of a workers' democracy.*" Pittsburgh Central Labor Union Minutes, November 16 and 18, 1937, in the holdings of the Pittsburgh Typographical Union, Lo. No. 7, Archives of Industrial Society, University of Pittsburgh. Emphasis added.

19. Frances Fox Piven, and Richard A. Cloward, *Regulating the Poor: The Functions of Public Welfare,* Vintage: New York, 1971, 100.

20. Malcolm Cowley, *The Dream of the Golden Mountains: Remembering the 1930s,* The Viking Press: New York, 1980, 315.

21. Cowley, *The Dream of the Golden Mountains,* 216, 218.

22. Cowley, *The Dream of the Golden Mountains,* 314, 316.

23. Louis Hartz, *The Liberal Tradition in America: An Interpretation of American Political Thought Since the Revolution,* Harcourt, Brace & World, Inc.: New York, 1955, 95.

24. Melvyn Dubofsky, "Not So 'Turbulent Years': A New Look at the 1930s," in Charles Stephenson and Robert Asher, Eds., *Life and Labor: Dimensions of American Working Class History,* State University of New York Press: Albany, 1986, 212-13, 219.

25. Dubofsky, "Not So 'Turbulent Years'," 219.

26. John Bodnar, "Immigration and Modernization: The Case of Slavic Peasants in Industrial America," in Milton Cantor, Ed., *American Working Class Culture: Explorations in American Labor and Social History,* Greenwood Press: Westport, Conn., 1979, 349.

27. Bodnar, *Workers' World,* 178-180.

28. Robert S. Lynd and Helen Merrell Lynd, *Middletown in Transition,* Harcourt, Brace, & World: New York, 1937, 77.

29. Dubofsky, "Not So 'Turbulent Years'," 215-16.

30. Lynd and Lynd, *Middletown in Transition*, 450. Emphasis added.

31. Cowley, *The Dream of the Golden Mountains*, 309.

32. Dubofsky, "Not So 'Turbulent Years'," 216.

33. Stave, *The New Deal and the Last Hurrah*, 40-41.

34. See James Caldwell Foster, *The Union Politic: The CIO Political Action Committee*, University of Missouri Press: St. Louis, 1975, Tables 1948D, 1952B, 1954E, 217, 220, 225.

35. Dubofsky, "Not So 'Turbulent Years'," 209, 212, 216-17.

36. Dubofsky, "Not So 'Turbulent Years'," 221.

37. Dubofsky, "Not So 'Turbulent Years'," 221. Emphasis added.

38. Gary Gerstle, *Working-Class Americanism: The Politics of Labor in a Textile City, 1914-1960*, Cambridge University Press: Cambridge, England, 1989, 8.

39. Gerstle, *Working-Class Americanism*, 5, 1.

40. Gerstle, *Working-Class Americanism*, 244.

41. Gerstle, *Working-Class Americanism*, 195, 182, 187, 179.

42. Gerstle, *Working-Class Americanism*, 179-180.

43. Lizabeth Cohen, *Making a New Deal: Industrial Workers in Chicago, 1919-1939*, Cambridge University Press: Cambridge, 1990, 367.

44. Cohen, *Making a New Deal*, 362; Lizabeth Cohen, "Reflections on the Making of *Making a New Deal*," *Labor History*, Vol. 32, No. 4, fall 1991, 598.

45. Quoted by Cohen, *Making a New Deal*, 338.

46. Cohen, *Making a New Deal*, 253.

47. Cohen, *Making a New Deal*, 267.

48. Hartz, *The Liberal Tradition in America*, 5, 6.

49. Karen Orren, *Belated Feudalism: Labor, the Law, and Liberal Development in the United States*, Cambridge University Press: Cambridge, 1991, 215.

50. Writers' Program, Work Projects Administration, *Pennsylvania: A Guide to the Keystone State*, Oxford University Press: New York, 1940, 67.

51. Orren, *Belated Feudalism*, 15-16.

52. Orren, *Belated Feudalism*, 216.

53. Orren, *Belated Feudalism*, 3-4.

54. Elmer J. Maloy Interview, United Steelworkers of America Papers, Historical Collections and Labor Archives, Pattee Library, Pennsylvania State University Libraries, 36.

Chapter 2

The Workers Mobilize

"Revolution, up and down the river!" cried *The Bulletin Index* on its November 11, 1937 cover. That cover of Pittsburgh's *TIME*-like weekly magazine also featured the smiling young face of Elmer J. Maloy, the "C.I.O. Mayor-Elect," as *The Bulletin Index* termed him, of the nearby steel town of Duquesne.

But Maloy, leader of the Steel Workers Organizing Committee (SWOC) in Duquesne, was not, in himself, the "revolution." He was merely the most visible symbol of the revolutionary political transformation of America's industrial heartland comprising the Western Pennsylvania steel towns lining the Allegheny, Monongahela, and Ohio Rivers around Pittsburgh. On November 2, 1937, seventeen of these company-run steel towns swept out long-dominant Republican incumbents and installed in their place labor-oriented Democratic challengers.

These administrations—composed entirely of SWOC members and their close allies—pledged to end the cozy, feudal partnership between local government and the giant steel corporations, "The most Republican of U.S. industries," as the *Index* described them. It was a political revolution, a major party realignment, a lasting transfer of political power.[1] It was the installation of a Workers' New Deal in America's industrial heartland.

A New Orbit of Political Conflict

It is no exaggeration to say that by the 1930s, Pittsburgh was the most Republican city in America. Indeed, the Republican Party was founded in Pittsburgh in the 1850s, with the first organizational meeting of the incipient party taking place in Pittsburgh prior to the party's better-known organizational meeting in Ripon, Wisconsin. In the 1860 presidential election, the Republicans won a higher percentage of the vote (65 percent) in Pittsburgh than in any other American metropolis. This was not because Abolitionism was strong in Pittsburgh. It was not. In the 1850s, Pittsburgh Republicans cared little about the issues of slavery or sectionalism, nor did they have much fear of an aggressive slavocracy. Instead, the primary forces which created the Republican Party in Pittsburgh in the 1850s were anti-immigrant and anti-Catholic sentiment. In their moral crusade against "foreigners," Republican leaders in Pittsburgh allied themselves with the anti-immigrant Know-Nothings to topple and supplant the traditionally dominant Whigs. A triumphant anti-Catholic, anti-immigrant, pro-business Republican Party dominated the city and region thereafter.[2]

By the 1930s, then, the city of Pittsburgh and the Steel Valley in which it is located had, like Pennsylvania and the nation, been dominated by Republicans since the antebellum period. Since the Civil War, only two Democrats, Grover Cleveland and Woodrow Wilson, had been elected to the White House—and Wilson had only won in 1912 because William Howard Taft and Theodore Roosevelt split the Republican majority. The picture was just as bleak for Democrats at the Congressional level. In the eighteen elections between 1894 and 1930, for instance, the Republicans won the majority in the House of Representatives fifteen times.

The Pennsylvania Democratic Party had also been excluded from power since before the Civil War. Indeed, before 1936, the Democrats had not won Pennsylvania in a presidential election since 1852 and before 1928 the city of Pittsburgh had not been won by a Democratic presidential candidate since 1856. Before the election of Democrat George Earle as governor in 1934, the last Democratic governor had been Robert Pattison, elected in 1883 and again in 1890 only because of splits in the Republican Party.

The last time the Democrats controlled either house in the state legislature had been in 1870 and, because of this, then sent the only Democrat to the U.S. Senate from Pennsylvania ever to serve before the 1930s. After the political realignment of the 1890s, the Democratic Party became even more marginalized, as Pennsylvania was converted into a solidly one-party state. For example, "of the 80 statewide contests held from 1894 through 1931, a candidate running with Democratic party endorsement won just one."[3]

What was true of the state at large was also true of the city of Pittsburgh. In the seventy-seven years between 1856 and 1933, only one Democrat—attorney George W. Guthrie, elected for a single term in 1905 at the head of a reform fusion ticket—served as mayor of the city.[4] During the same seventy-seven years, the Democrats did not elect a single City Councillor, local judge, or any other municipal candidate. Only because the law mandated that one of the three Allegheny County Commissioner seats be reserved for the minority party and there be a space reserved for the minority judge of elections did any Democrat ever make it into any office of any kind in the region.

By 1929 Allegheny County, in which Pittsburgh is located, claimed 169,000 registered Republican voters and only 5,200 registered Democrats, virtually all in Pittsburgh itself. Likewise, in the small steel towns clustered tightly around

Pittsburgh, hardly a Democrat was to be found.[5]

The Democratic Party, then, especially in the small steel towns of Western Pennsylvania outside of Pittsburgh, was a hollow shell with a miniscule constituency. A "political simplicity . . . had thus emerged in this industrial heartland of the Northeast by the 1920's [and] . . . It is no exaggeration to say that the political response to . . . industrialism in this American state was the elimination of organized partisan combat, an extremely severe decline in electoral participation, the emergence of a Republican 'coalition of the whole' and—by no means coincidentally—a highly efficient insulation of the controlling industrial-financial elite from effective or sustained countervailing pressures."[6]

Meanwhile, the state's dominant Republican Party drew much of its support and leadership from Western Pennsylvania. The Chairman of the state Republican Party, for instance, William Larimer Mellon, elected in 1926, hailed from Pittsburgh, where his family presided over the city's economic and political life. Meanwhile, Pittsburgh's Andrew W. Mellon was Hoover's Secretary of the Treasury.

What prevailed in the Pittsburgh region and Pennsylvania as a whole was part of a larger political pattern of Republican-corporation rule which had come to dominate the nation around the turn of the century. This was "a political system which was congruent with the hegemony of laissez-faire corporate capitalism over the society as a whole . . . The era of 'normalcy' was one of two noncompetitive party hegemonies: the Democrats in the South and the Republicans throughout much of the North and West."[7]

But, with the presidential election of 1932, that began to change in Pittsburgh. While the rest of the state, for the time being, remained firmly Republican, in the state's industrial heartland Pittsburgh Democrats began a "Long March" through electoral offices, conquering them one-by-one as they came up for election. In 1935, at the end of this "Long March," Pittsburgh became a Democratic bastion, as it has remained up to the present. No Republican presidential or mayoral candidate has carried the city since then, nor has a Republican been elected to any municipal office since 1932. Indeed, Republican Pennsylvania became a competitive two-party state because of the enduring Democratic dominance of Pittsburgh and surrounding Allegheny County which began at this time.

What happened in this industrial heartland in the 1930s is part of the larger story of what happened in America at that time. As Samuel Lubell put it, the Depression era constituted a new "American Revolution," which "rema[de] the politics of our time," as the country went from being "normally" Republican to "normally" and enduringly Democratic.

And, unlike the restoration of Republican power following the Woodrow Wilson presidency, there would be no Republican restoration this time. While Republicans would still be able to win the presidency—as Eisenhower did in 1952—that was not the true measure of the political revolution. Rather, "the significance of the Democratic rise to majority standing lies in the fact that with it has come a wholly new orbit of political conflict—an orbit as controlling upon the Republicans as upon the Democrats, and one which is likely to govern the course of American politics as long as the animosities and loyalties of the New Deal remain in the memories of the bulk of voters."[8]

One measure of this "new orbit of political conflict" is the transformation which occurred at the local level. In this period, Bruce Stave has identified a nationwide "major shift in partisan control" from Republican to Democratic of 92 cities with populations of more than 100,000. "In 1929," he points out, "Republicans . . . controlled 48.9 percent of the city halls in urban America; by 1935 Democratic control equalled that proportion, with Republican strength sliding to 18.4 percent, a figure significantly below the Democrats [30.4 percent] in 1929."[9]

Samuel Lubell also argued that we should look beyond what is now called "the Beltway" to America's cities and towns to fully comprehend the nature and extent of the new political arena. "I have deliberately swung the spotlight away from Washington," he said, "out into the country. It is there, among the people themselves, that the real drama of political realignment is being acted out."[10]

Samuel P. Hays also argues that control of the White House is not the best measure of the transformation wrought by this political revolution. Instead, he says, we should look at Democratic dominance of the U.S. House of Representatives, which was virtually unbroken between 1932 and 1994—with brief Republican resurgences in 1946 and 1952 when, despite Eisenhower's popularity, the Republicans gained only a bare majority. This dominance is "one of the most important phenomena in American political history . . . No party has ever before approached such a long-term dominance of any one branch of the federal government." Indeed, the secular trend was toward increasing Democratic numerical dominance since 1932. "While Truman's Congress averaged 248 Democratic seats, that of Kennedy-Johnson reached 266 and that of Carter 284 . . . To put it rather strikingly, by the Reagan-Bush years the Democratic congressional contingent in a Republican administration had reached a higher level than it had during the Democratic Truman administration."[11]

This political revolution of the Thirties that Lubell and political scientist V. O. Key, Jr. came to identify as a "realignment" of the political universe was elaborated upon by Key in a series of publications in 1952, 1955, and 1959. As Lubell was arguing at the same time, Key saw the era as producing "a major alteration in the pattern of partisan division within the voting population," as the country exchanged traditional Republican dominance for Democratic.[12]

He elaborated this idea further in 1955 when he stated that the political upheaval of the Thirties actually began with the 1928 presidential election— at least in New England—and was part of a larger phenomenon of realigning elections, as was the election of 1896.[13]

Finally, in 1959, he refined the concept of realigning elections by seeing them as part of a larger process of political change which is always gradually evolving into something else. Political change, he argued, " . . . may to some degree be the consequence of trends that perhaps persist over decades and elections may mark only steps in a more or less continuous creation of new loyalties and decay of old . . . other processes operate inexorably, and almost imperceptibly, election after election, to form new party alignments and to build new party groupings."[14]

Thus, the Great Depression was perhaps a culmination of secular trends and "Under the impact of the Great Depression, the Republican following disintegrated and the circumstances were created for the formation of a new Democratic party."[15]

To understand this political revolution which transformed America in the Thirties, we must look at America's Northeastern and Midwestern regions. Since the end of the Civil War, the American South and West had been essentially "colonial" regions of a nation dominated by a Northeastern industrial metropole. The "new party alignments" and "new party groupings" of the Thirties were based upon the mobilization of a new constituency in this Northeastern and Midwestern metropole, the awakening to political activism of a new electorate in this heartland, rather than a conversion of old Republicans into "new" Democrats.

Samuel Lubell and V. O. Key were among the first to note that these "new" Democrats came from a hitherto underrepresented element, the immigrant, urban, industrial population concentrated in the Northeastern metropole. "Industrialization," said Key, "the growth of cities by migration from rural areas, and the gradual assimilation into the political order of the last great wave of immigrants and their children had built a reservoir of potential Democrats."[16] "Overall," then, "the increased [voter] turnout that marked the presidential and off-year realigning elections of the 1930s resulted from new mobilization among immigrant-stock voters, the young, those toward the bottom of the economic ladder, the unemployed, reliefers, and citizens who had chosen to abstain in the 1920s."[17] In other words, the working class of the industrial heartland mobilized politically.

Pennsylvania is a case in point. Although Democratic strength climbed steadily during this period, this was hardly at the expense of Republican registration. Indeed, as the Great Depression began, Republican registration actually increased by almost a third of a million between 1930 and 1932. In 1936, the year of the Roosevelt landslide which finally put Pennsylvania in the Democratic column, Republican registration was actually greater than in 1930 when the state was still considered safely Republican (table 1).

Table 1

Pennsylvania Voter Registration, 1930-1936

Year	Democratic	Republican	Other	Total
1930	675,584	2,659,850	187,076	3,522,510
1932	833,977	2,911,068	167,626	3,912,671
1934	1,401,055	2,624,386	166,850	4,192,241
1936	2,065,697	2,665,697	184,747	4,916,346

Source: Edward F. Cooke and G. Edward Janosik, *Guide to Pennsylvania Politics,*
Greenwood Press: Westport, Ct., 1957, 13.

Similarly, the vote for Pennsylvania's Republican gubernatorial candidates climbed unflaggingly upward throughout the decade of the Thirties, from just over a million in 1930 to over 1,400,000 in 1934 to over two million in 1938.[18] Despite this doubling of the Republican vote, however, the Commonwealth of Pennsylvania had been converted from a stronghold of Republicanism into a fiercely competitive two-party state. The transformation of Pennsylvania in the Thirties, then, was not due to the conversion of Republicans, but to the appearance of an entirely new Democratic electorate.

Based upon this newly mobilized electorate, the "new Democratic party" which came into existence at this time "transformed itself from an institution largely rural in its orientation and leadership to one that embodied the aspirations of the American city dweller—and most notably, the urbanite of immigrant stock."[19] The "new" Democrats of the Thirties were overwhelmingly "concentrated in the industrial cities of the North" where support for the new Democratic party was "far higher among Catholics, Jews, and blacks than among white Protestants." Above all, these "new" Democrats were "predominantly of the working class."[20]

This mobilization into the Democratic Party of the immigrant, urban working class of the industrial heartland, people who were previously outside the political universe, can be strikingly seen at the ward level in Pittsburgh's working class Polish Hill neighborhood (table 2).

Table 2

Voting & Partisanship in Pittsburgh's Polish Hill, Ward Six.

Year	% Dem.	% Rep.	% Other	% Nonvoting
1932	29.7	11.3	0.6	58.4
1936	50.3	09.4	3.1	37.1
1940	61.1	11.2	0.1	27.5

Source: Walter Dean Burnham, *The Current Crisis in American Politics,* Oxford University Press: New York, 1982, Table 11, 146.

Polish Hill "was largely a Polish slum area adjacent to the Allegheny River and some of the area's many steel mills. In 1940, only 6.6 percent of its male labor force was in professional-managerial occupations, while fully 84.0 percent worked in semiskilled or unskilled manual labor occupations."[21] This ward was the Catholic, working class ward over which the labor priest Father James Cox presided from his base at Old St. Patrick's and later his "Good Samaritan" chapel in the adjacent Strip District. It responded enthusiastically to Father Cox's populist appeals and to the appeals of the Democratic Party. From 1932 to 1940, the percentage of the ward's electorate voting Democratic doubled, while the percentage voting Republican remained stagnant. At the same time, the percentage of registered voters who didn't bother to vote at all fell by almost half. Clearly, the Polish Catholic steel workers of Polish Hill had been mobilized to go to the polls and vote Democratic as never before.

And, because these "new" Democrats were "predominantly of the working class," they brought their own unique concerns to the political arena and the new Democratic Party, both of which were transformed by their entry into active political life. Thus, the political realignment of the Thirties brought about by the emergence of this new class of voters was not a value-free realignment. It was a profoundly ideological realignment, made so, not just because of the economic catastrophe of the Great Depression, but also because of the fundamental concerns of the new majority electorate.

As might be expected, these were "working class" concerns, manifested through an intensely class conscious politics which sharply divided the electorate along class lines. When Lubell visited cities and towns across America, he found that where typical rents were below a set level, "pluralities were overwhelming" for Roosevelt, while these pluralities quickly "faded away" once the rents rose above that level. As Lubell also discovered, this new class conscious politics made irrelevant other concerns. Speaking of the 1940 election, he wrote, "When I asked one auto unionist in Detroit why the third-term issue had made so little difference he replied, 'I'll say it even though it doesn't sound nice. We've grown class conscious.'"[22]

Thus, the "electoral upheaval of the 1930s entailed much more than a simple transfer of political control from one majority party to the other. It involved a redefinition of what was salient to the electoral decisions of millions of voters and a consequent transformation of the social-group and attitudinal bases of partisanship ... Among critically sized components of the mass public, perceptual evaluations of the major parties changed drastically. To large numbers of voters, especially the newly mobilized, 'Republican' came to denote hard times, indifference to the plight of the jobless, and opposition to measures aimed at ameliorating the bitter effects of the depression and improving the economic condition of the 'forgotten man.' That new and powerful set of negative evaluations had its positive counterpart, the central focus of which was Franklin D. Roosevelt. It was first Roosevelt, and only later and less completely his party, who came to be perceived as caring about the downtrodden and willing to do battle for their economic security against the amassed forces of 'economic royalists.' These perceptions shaped the cleavage line of the realignment and of the party oppositions that emerged from it."[23]

The political revolution of the Thirties, then, was based upon a new electorate composed of Northeastern and Midwestern, urban, immigrant, working class voters, primarily Southern and Eastern European Catholics, who brought their new concerns to the political arena at the same time they transformed the identity of the combatants in that arena. These were the working class Italians, for instance, of Boston's West End, among whom the sociologist Herbert Gans lived in the late Fifties. "West Enders are Democrats," he observed at that time, and "they would not think of voting Republican." They knew where their political interests resided and "West Enders expect[ed] their politician to develop a public image of them, depicting them as proud citizens fighting for their rights against the hostile outside world. He is encouraged to make fiery speeches that condemn the powerful ... and threaten them with violence or political reprisals by an aroused electorate."[24]

It was class conscious blue collar voters such as Boston's West Enders who put an end to the long-dominant Brahmin Republicanism of Massachusetts and made Calvin Coolidge the last serious Republican presidential contender to come from the Bay State. These are the voters who also made sure that no Republican has been elected to any municipal office in Boston since the 1930s.

And these were the same working class voters who brought workers' democracy to Pennsylvania's industrial heartland in the 1930s.

A New Constituency

Some historians have argued that the New Deal, while representing a dramatic change from the past in that it introduced government as an active "broker state" between labor and business, merely cemented the final triumph of the best elements of that same past. These historians, exemplified by Arthur M. Schlesinger, Jr., have sometimes been termed the "Progressive School" of historians.

In his "Age of Roosevelt" series, Schlesinger argued that the New Deal was a dramatic change from the conservative Republican "normalcy" of the past. The nature of that change, however, was to bring about the triumph of the Progressive liberal tradition of that same past. In the very first paragraph of his first book in the series, Schlesinger stated that, "The nation, in responding to the bitter challenges of depression and war, summoned up the resources, moral and intellectual, of an earlier progressivism, an earlier war effort, and a decade of business leadership. Roosevelt's administration must be understood against this background of a generation's ideas, hopes, and experience."[25]

William E. Leuchtenburg, another much-honored New Deal historian, also viewed the New Deal as a continuation of Progressivism. "Not merely did the New Deal borrow many ideas and institutions from the Progressive Era," he stated, "but the New Dealers and the progressives shared more postulates and values than is commonly supposed." Leuchtenburg is typical of this school in describing the accomplishments of Roosevelt's New Deal as the work of "Heirs of the Enlightenment [who] felt themselves part of a broadly humanistic movement to make man's life on earth more tolerable, a movement that might someday even achieve a co-operative commonwealth."

The Enlightened co-operative commonwealth wasn't reached, he conceded. There was only a "halfway revolution" (which he termed "the Roosevelt Reconstruction"), which was based on the premise "that a just society could be secured by imposing a welfare state on a capitalist foundation." In this way, "The New Deal achieved a more just society by recognizing groups which had been largely unrepresented."[26]

People came to see the federal government for the first time as their friend and protector, a cruel and exploitative industrial system was made more humane, and, most importantly, people who had been left out realized that the benefits of the society were their inalienable heritage. "The New Deal," he said, "assumed the responsibility for guaranteeing every American a minimum standard of subsistence . . . The Roosevelt administration gave such assistance not as a matter of charity but of right. This system of social rights was written into the Social Security Act."[27]

In his many books on Roosevelt and the New Deal, James MacGregor Burns also concentrates intently on the actions of Roosevelt and his administration. Indeed, he opens the last book in his "American Experiment" trilogy with the dramatic picture of Roosevelt, the first presidential candidate to travel in an airplane, flying from his home in Hyde Park to the Democratic Convention in Chicago in 1932 to accept his party's nomination. It was there, in his acceptance speech, that Roosevelt pledged to use the best ideals of the party's past to bring "a new deal to the American people."[28]

More recently, Harvard historian Alan Brinkley has also portrayed the New Deal as something brought about from above by progressive liberal Lady Bountiful elites, such as Roosevelt, not by ordinary voters, workers, and minorities who "became part of the deliberations from time to time, but they rarely shaped the tone or the tenor of the conversation decisively."[29]

According to such historians, New Deal Era was one of triumphant liberal Progressivism dictated from on high by Enlightenment heirs. The reason these historians can advance this argument is because of their focus on President Roosevelt and his coterie of advisers. Once one steps outside the Beltway and begins to look at America, look at the voters who elected and re-elected Roosevelt, one sees a different picture. One begins to see a New Deal shaped not by liberal elites, but by ordinary people whose dreams, desires, and demands, contrary to Dawley, "shaped the tone [and] the tenor of the conversation decisively."

In America's industrial heartland, for example, class conscious rank and file workers moved to take control of local governments in the name of the working class. In Western Pennsylvania this class-based political mobilization was a victory for labor rather than for the Democratic Party, per se.

Outside of Pittsburgh the Democratic Party was a ghost organization boasting only ballot status. But in 1937, steel workers in Western Pennsylvania steel towns, on their own initiative, flooded en masse into the moribund local Democratic parties and made them over in their own image into de facto "labor parties." As George Powers, who lived through these events, noted, "In Duquesne, labor practically took over the local Democratic Party."[30] Local workers then used these local "labor parties" as vehicles to ride to both political and economic power. This was recognized by the local media when, for instance, it referred to "CIO-Democrats" or to Elmer Maloy, not as the "Democratic Mayor-Elect," but as the "CIO Mayor-Elect."

Sustained by the votes of ordinary steel workers and led by local union organizers, these functional equivalents of local labor parties received minimal encouragement or support in their campaigns—either in resources, planning, or execution—from top SWOC-CIO or Democratic Party leaders. Additionally, the early stages of local political mobilization—1933-1935—preceded the most important unionization drives. Taking advantage of previous political victories at the state level, activists used these as leverage to consolidate a political realignment at the local level. In doing so, these de facto "labor party" administrations brought the Bill of Rights to the industrial heartland, made possible the consolidation of the union in the steel industry, and cemented the Roosevelt political realignment at the local level.

These local labor campaigns and subsequent labor administrations therefore not only present a revealing picture of working class street-level political activity and goals during the Great Depression, they also explain how and why the Democratic Party became the dominant party of the time.[31]

These developments revealed a newly awakened electoral cohort of increasingly class conscious, urban, working class voters, overwhelmingly the children of Southern and Eastern European immigrants, who provided the electoral base of FDR's New Deal. Roosevelt never attracted a majority of the WASP vote. His support—like Catholic Al Smith's before him—was in the "ethnic" cities where he attracted not only cross-ethnic, but *working class* loyalty.

This is why Roosevelt "moved to the Left" and attacked "economic royalists" in his 1936 campaign and why the pros and cons of unionization—not the long-time issues of religion, Prohibition or blue laws—dominated the nation's political agenda in the Thirties. The Democratic Party became the majority party in the 1930s by becoming the party of America's Northeastern, urban, ethnic, blue collar proletariat—by occupying the space on the American political spectrum which would otherwise have been filled by a "Labor Party." To put this another way, the Democratic Party became the majority party in the 1930s by responding to the dreams, desires, and demands of the industrial heartland's assertive class conscious workers.

Notes

1. In the wake of the 1937 elections, Democratic Party voter registrations in Allegheny County passed Republican for the first time, *never to be altered up to the present.* Final voter registration figures for the district before the November 1938 elections showed that Pittsburgh, for example, had 334,424 registered voters, with 95,373 more Democrats than Republicans. Registration in Allegheny County as a whole exceeded 662,000, with the Democrats enjoying a 112,355-voter majority. See *The Pittsburgh Press,* October 8, 1938.

2. Michael Fitzgibbon Holt, *Forging a Majority: The Formation of the Republican Party in Pittsburgh, 1848-1860,* Yale University Press: New Haven, 1969.

3. Walter Dean Burnham, "The End of American Party Politics," in Frank Otto Gatell, Paul Goodman, and Allen Weinstein, *The Growth of American Politics, Vol. II, Since the Civil War,* Oxford University Press: New York, 1972, 518. Originally in *Trans-Action,* No. 7, December 1969, 12-23.

4. William T. Martin, "Pittsburgh Figures on 1933 City Voting," *The New York Times,* December 4, 1932.

5. *The Pittsburgh Post-Gazette,* "Initial Day's Registration Sets Record," September 5, 1931, 13.

6. Burnham, "The End of American Party Politics," 518-519.

7. Walter Dean Burnham, *The Current Crisis in American Politics,* Oxford University Press: New York, 1982, 142.

8. Samuel Lubell, *The Future of American Politics,* Harper and Brothers: New York, 1952, 3, 2, 1.

9. Bruce Stave, "The Great Depression and Urban Political Continuity: Bridgeport Chooses Socialism," in Bruce Stave, Ed., *Socialism and the Cities,* Kennikat Press: Port Washington, New York, 1975, 158. The remainder of the nation's city halls were run by non-partisan administrations; Socialist administrations (as in Bridgeport, Conn., Reading, Pa., and Milwaukee, Wis.); or even Farmer-Labor administrations, as in Berlin, New Hampshire and Minneapolis.

10. Lubell, *The Future of American Politics,* 4. Howard W. Allen and Erik W. Austin have also looked at realignment at the Congressional level, identifying Democratic realignment even as far away from the industrial Northeast and Midwest as Washington state—although they argue that Congressional realignment there lagged behind the rest of the nation, not taking place until 1938 or even 1940. See Howard W. Allen and Erik W. Austin, "From the Populist Era to the New Deal: A Study of Partisan Realignment in Washington State, 1889-1950," *Social Science History,* No. 3, 1979, 125-126.

11. Samuel P. Hays, "The Welfare State and Democratic Practice in the United States Since World War II," unpublished paper presented at a history conference at the University of Pittsburgh, 1992, 13, in the author's possession.

12. V. O. Key, Jr., "The Future of the Democratic Party," *Virginia Quarterly Review,* Vol. 28, No. 2, spring 1952, 161, 163.

13. V. O. Key, Jr., "A Theory of Critical Elections," *Journal of Politics,* Vol. 17, No. 1, February 1955.

14. V. O. Key, Jr., "Secular Realignment and the Party System," *Journal of Politics,* Vol. 21, No. 2, May 1959, 198-199. Walter Dean Burnham agreed with Key's concept of "critical elections" redefining the American political universe at certain times and marked out five distinct such "party systems" in our history. Unlike Key, however, he argued that our political institutions don't evolve gradually in response to underlying socioeconomic change. Somewhat like biological evolutionists who have elaborated the concept of "punctuated equilibrium," Burnham argues that the various critical elections in our past have jerked the political universe into overdue equilibrium with the changed socioeconomic structure. See Walter Dean Burnham, *Critical Elections and the Mainsprings of American Politics,* W.W. Norton: New York, 1970.

15. V. O. Key, Jr., *Politics, Parties, & Pressure Groups,* Thomas Y. Crowell: New York, 1964, 187.

16. Key, "The Future of the Democratic Party," 166, 165.

17. Paul Kleppner, *Who Voted? The Dynamics of Electoral Turnout, 1870-1980,* Praeger Publishers: New York, 1982, 89.

18. "Pennsylvania Votes for Governor," *Commonwealth: The Magazine of Pennsylvania,* November 1946, 3.

19. David Burner, *The Politics of Provincialism,* Alfred A. Knopf: New York, 1967, xi.

20. James L. Sundquist, *Dynamics of the Party System,* The Brookings Institution: Washington, D.C., 1973, 200, 203, 202. Similar arguments are made by Everett Carll Ladd, Jr. and Charles D. Hadley, who found that the "submerged, inarticulate urban masses" were central to the creation and consolidation of the new Democratic majority. See Ladd and Hadley, *Transformations of the American Party System,* W.W. Norton: New York, 1975, 31-87.

21. Burnham, *The Current Crisis in American Politics*, 146.

22. Lubell, *The Future of American Politics*, 51, 6.

23. Kleppner, *Who Voted?* 96.

24. Herbert J. Gans, *The Urban Villagers: Group and Class in the Life of Italian-Americans*, The Free Press: New York, 1962, 175.

25. Arthur M. Schlesinger, Jr., *The Age of Roosevelt: The Crisis of the Old Order: 1919-1933*, Houghton Mifflin Co.: Boston, 1957, ix.

26. William E. Leuchtenburg, *Franklin D. Roosevelt and the New Deal, 1932-1940*, Harper & Row: New York, 1963, 345, 347.

27. Leuchtenburg, *Franklin D. Roosevelt*, 332.

28. James MacGregor Burns, *The Crosswinds of Freedom*, Vintage Books: New York, 1990, 3-6.

29. Alan Brinkley, *The End of Reform: New Deal Liberalism in Recession and War*, Alfred A. Knopf: New York, 1995, 13.

30. George Powers, *Cradle of Steel Unionism: Monongahela Valley, PA*, Figueroa Printers, Inc.: E. Chicago, Ind., 1972, 132.

31. This story is a particularly difficult one to recreate as the "SWOC Era" is almost totally lacking in documentation. The current districts of the United Steelworkers of America (USWA) were not established until 1942. Beginning then, and even more so from the mid-40s on, the USWA is fairly well documented at both the local and international level. Most, but not all, of these USWA records can be found in the files of the official depository of the union: the United Steelworkers of America Papers, Historical Collections and Labor Archives, Pattee Library, Pennsylvania State University Libraries. However, explained Peter Gottlieb, Curator of the USWA Papers, "No SWOC collection ever existed. Either SWOC was not the type of organization which generated files, or such files have been lost." This dearth of documentation is one reason we know so little about this period. Interview, conducted by Eric Leif Davin, October 5, 1988.

Chapter 3

The Sources of Solidarity, 1914-1930

The New Deal was above all an "Urban Deal." Despite the attention and dollars lavished upon rural aid programs, the bulk of the New Deal's efforts were directed toward urban problems. More specifically, these efforts were directed to the urban ethnic working class. For the first time in American history these people—used to being disparaged and disdained by politicians—were the federal government's primary focus of concern.

And the urban ethnic working class rewarded the New Deal with its loyalty. By the end of the Thirties, virtually every major American city was producing huge Democratic electoral majorities, even though some, like Pittsburgh, had been dominated by powerful Republican political machines at the beginning of that decade.

This almost inconceivable political transformation was more than just a major realignment of the political universe. That had happened before, as various "party systems" rose and fell in American history. But this was a political aberration unique in American history, never seen before—or since. It was a political transformation based upon the dominance of class politics.

Pollster George Gallup was among the first to realize this phenomenon. Before the New Deal, he said, "There wasn't any real division or stratification on the basis of wealth" when it came to political preferences. However, "With the coming of the New Deal had come a new stratification in the whole body politic, a whole new structure, with the poorer people going Democratic and the people with above-average income going Republican."[1] And enough of these "poorer people" self-consciously voted their class interests to reinvent the political world.

This did not happen just because of the oppressive "Hard Times" of the Great Depression. Indeed, far from making the working class stronger, hard times before and since have often had a crippling effect on union strength and working class interests in general.

Nor was it the somehow "inevitable" final outcome of internally contradictory capitalist development, which Marxist ideology predicted would happen. Both such ideas were discredited by the economic developments of the 1980s and 1990s. The 1980s, for instance, witnessed the only period in American history where double-digit unemployment was *not* accompanied by mass protests movements.

Meanwhile, class inequality *increased* in the 1990s at the same time that class politics—as measured by class-based voting for the Democratic and Republican parties—*decreased*. Obviously, something more than economic developments explains the appearance and maintenance of class politics.

And such was the case in the 1930s. Political analyst Samuel Lubell argued that, "No individual can be said really to vote for the first time. Always he is part of a stream of conditioning that has shaped the political loyalties and antagonisms of his family, his community, the varied groupings to which the voter belongs. When these loyalties do break, they often behave like steams that flow underground, out of sight for a time, only to surface anew."[2]

If this is true, then to understand why the urban ethnic working class voted as it did in the 1930s, we have to look at that underground "stream of conditioning" that "shaped the political loyalties and antagonisms of . . . family . . . community [and] the varied groupings to which the voter belongs." When we do this, we find that the class-based political realignment of the Thirties was made possible by a combination of social factors. These social factors became characteristic of large American cities, especially in the Northeast, from about the beginning of World War I to the coming of the New Deal, approximately 1914-1930.

Foremost among these social factors was simply *stability*. The entire constellation of factors included:

1) Long-term job stability for blue collar workers;

2) Long-term neighborhood stability in blue collar neighborhoods;

3) The consequent growth of a dense social network centered around extended families and ethnic institutions, such as churches and fraternal societies;

and, consequent upon the preceding,

4) The evolution of a working class identity which transcended, but did not replace, ethnic identities. Indeed, as David Brody observed, "Ethnic identity was a shaping force for labor solidarity."[3]

There are classes, but no organized class conflict in an atomized society. Because isolation makes cowards of us all, one of the prerequisites of self-conscious class conflict is community. By the 1930s, urban working class populations witnessed increasing economic and geographic stability and increasing institutional strength in their neighborhoods. Everywhere in urban industrial America these factors resulted in powerful and all-encompassing working class ethnic communities in which ethnic industrial workers were enmeshed.

Community, however, is but one of the legs upon which organized self-conscious class conflict rests. The other leg is an ideology of resistance which mobilizes community strengths. Without such an ideology, community and class solidarity is not political power, but merely potential power.

Antonio Gramsci observed that, "The ruling ideas of an age are the ideas of the ruling class." But this is only true if there are no opposing ideas which effectively resist those ruling ideas. By the 1930s there had arisen a muting of ethnic divisions among the America-born children of the New Immigrants which made them receptive to an ideology of resistance. This was an ideology of "American rights," which meshed with the social changes mentioned above to foster cross-ethnic working class consciousness, solidarity, and resistance, all of which found expression in the Democratic Party.

Pittsburgh and
The Urban-Ethnic Demographic Revolution

The transformation of the political universe in the 1930s was not solely a working class phenomenon. It was also an ethnic phenomenon. Part of the answer to the phenomenon of class conscious political realignment in the Thirties was an intersecting phenomenon, the urban and ethnic demographic revolution. This revolution created what Lubell called a "critically sized component," a critical mass of *potential* Democrats—*if they could be mobilized,* if they could be aroused to vote their class interests through the vehicle of the Democratic Party.

As the 1920 U.S. Census revealed, America finally became an urban nation in the Twenties, as the majority of its population was, for the first time, to be found in the cities. Although the census defined as "urban" all towns with a population over 2,500, this trend nevertheless helps us understand why, after a decade more of growth, "labor's millions" were "on the march" in the 1930s.

The 1936 Presidential election, of course, witnessed the shift of political power at the national level away from the long-dominant Republicans to the Democrats—a trend begun in 1932 (or perhaps 1928 when Democrat Al Smith carried all of the nation's 12 largest cities by appealing to the "immigrant" vote), but cemented in 1936. What made this shift possible was what Samuel Lubell called, "The Revolt of the City."[4]

Not only did America's cities continue to mushroom in the 1920s, but this urban population was also primarily an ethnic population. Of course, these cities had contained ethnic majorities for some time. As the twentieth century progressed, however, this ethnic population took on larger proportions. In 1910, for instance, the great bulk of school-age children in thirty-seven of the nation's largest cities were the children of immigrants. "In cities like Chelsea, Fall River, New Bedford . . . more than *two out of every three* school children were the sons and daughters of immigrants."[5]

But this ethnic majority was a diverse majority, and this very diversity may have been a major contributing reason for the perceived lack of "class consciousness" in America during this period.[6] Unlike the English working class, the American working class was not "made" at any one time, but was constantly being re-made over and over as new waves of immigrants entered the workforce, bringing with them their "alien" customs, beliefs, and values. This constant demographic churning brought to the fore ethno-cultural differences and issues, making them—Prohibition, blue laws, religion, et cetera—the cleavage lines of American politics.

Further, alien workers were thrown into conflict not only with the "natives," but also with other alien workers in an alien land. Owen Zajdel, one of my students at the University of Pittsburgh, told me that around 1930 his Czech grandfather worked with a mixed ethnic crew building the Westinghouse Bridge just east of Pittsburgh. His grandfather had to remove his hat to prove to a fellow worker, a Hungarian, that Czeches did not conceal devil's horns beneath their hats. It was difficult for these polyglot "foreigners" to even understand each other. As for them uniting in common cause, it was just as likely they would finish the Tower of Babel as find common grounds for united political action.

The major source of this churning demographic cauldron was removed, however, when World War I and then the Johnson Act of 1924 clamped the lid on further European immigration. Without continued injections of foreign elements, both the cities and the workforce—the working *class*—grew more "Americanized."

By the 1930s, the children of the immigrants had at last come of age.[7] Born and raised in the cities, speaking English and thinking of themselves as Americans rather than as strangers in a strange land, mobilized into the electoral arena as their parents had not been, they not only shifted the *demographic* gravitational pull decisively away from the countryside, they completed the *political* power shift which had likewise been underway from country to city.

But this political power shift was more than just demographics, as it also changed the long-time *content* of American politics because of *when* it occurred. "The human potential for a revolutionary political change," Lubell noted, "had . . . been brought together in our larger cities when the economic skies caved in."[8] Thus, with the decline of salient ethno-cultural conflict and with the economic crisis of the Depression, class politics, always present but usually submerged by ethno-cultural tensions, became the primary fault line of American political life for the first time.

The political revolution of the Thirties, then, was based upon a new majority electorate composed of Northeastern and Midwestern, urban, immigrant, working class voters, primarily Southern and Eastern European Catholic and Orthodox believers. This new majority electorate brought its new concerns to the political arena at the same time they transformed the identity of the combatants in that arena.

This was especially evident in Pittsburgh. In 1930, Pittsburgh was the tenth largest city in America with 673,800 people and, like all the other top ten— with the single exception of Los Angeles—it was located in the Northeastern-Midwestern industrial heartland of the country. It and its surrounding mill towns were, in fact, the heart of that industrial heartland.

Sitting at the confluence of the Ohio, Monongahela, and Allegheny Rivers, Pittsburgh's steady growth as an industrial center was due to its location in relation to the great coal and oil fields of the surrounding region. The Monongahela tapped the coal fields of West Virginia 100 miles south, while the Allegheny gave access to both coal and oil fields 100 miles north. The Ohio, leading down to the Mississippi River, afforded an ideal shipping outlet seaward for these valleys through the Gulf of Mexico, making Pittsburgh the largest and busiest inland port in the nation.

In the years before World War II a major segment of the American workforce—42 percent in 1940—was engaged in goods-producing blue collar work.[9] Much of that workforce was concentrated in blue collar cities like Pittsburgh. In 1929 the Pittsburgh area produced 8,975,000 gross tons of pig iron while bituminous coal production was 143,516,000 net tons.

Pittsburgh continued to be a major producer during the Depression, though at lower levels. By 1940, reported a contemporary source, Pittsburgh was the "world capital of the steel industry . . . The city accounts for 60 percent of the world's tinplate production, and its output of pig iron amounted to 6,862,000 tons in 1936. That same year Pennsylvania produced 9,433,000 tons of pig iron and more than 9,000,000 tons of raw iron and steel, blooms, billets, and slabs." By 1939, steel and coal production was again almost up to 1929 levels.[10]

Pittsburgh was thus the "capital of the Pennsylvania Ruhr . . . this mighty town is the world's champ, the Paul Bunyan, of heavy industry [which] . . . possesses some thirty-five steel mills and 350 coal mines, some sixty-odd glass factories and more than 100 chemical plants, while some 30,000,000 tons of cargo pass through her river harbor each year. She produces mountainous quantities of electrical equipment and clay products, aluminum, coke by-products and bituminous coal. In most of these, she leads either the nation or the world."[11]

Pittsburgh sits almost exactly in the center of Allegheny County and, in 1930, 48.6 percent of the county's population resided within the Pittsburgh city limits.[12] As a major industrial region and one of the most populous locales in the nation, Allegheny County had a large, immigrant, working class population. The small mill towns sprinkled over the county shared many characteristics with Pittsburgh. Indeed, the factors which made Pittsburgh such a bastion of class politics in the Thirties were perhaps even more salient in the mill towns surrounding it. The people of these "Steel Valley" towns responded readily to the appeals of the "new Democratic party." In fact, the ethnic groups which dominated the Pittsburgh region—the Catholic Irish, along with the Catholic and Orthodox Southern and Eastern Europeans, as well as blacks—have long been recognized as key participants in building the new Democratic majority.

Pittsburgh, and its surrounding region, thus impressed viewers as a bastion of working class solidarity and crucible of class struggle. It was, claimed one observer, "a strike-happy labor town," where "Pittsburgh's extraordinarily powerful Chamber of Commerce, whose membership rolls have contained such names as Andrew Carnegie, Charles M. Schwab, Henry Clay Frick, Andrew Mellon and H.J. Heinz, has been, since the beginning of the Roosevelt labor revolution of 1933, the embattled citadel of 'the interests,' while City Hall has been more or less regarded as GHQ of the liberal-labor junta." At the same time, "Her culture is popularly supposed to be strictly of the mill-end variety . . . To most Americans, Pittsburgh, aside from her great and actual earning and producing power, is a city in which individual man has long since become a particle absorbed in the industrialized, unionized mass."[13]

This negative portrayal, while the view of a visiting middle class journalist, nevertheless touched upon the crucial factor which made Pittsburgh a "labor town"—the blue collar, ethnic workers of Pittsburgh had indeed developed both class consciousness and class solidarity. Both were dependent upon a "mill-end" culture anchored in strong working class ethnic communities which also forged strong ties to the union and to the Democratic Party. Working class consciousness in Pittsburgh and its surrounding mill towns grew out of shared experiences on the job and in the neighborhoods. This working class consciousness found expression in militant mass unionism and in fierce loyalty to the Democratic Party. All of these elements, the work and neighborhood environment, the ethnic identity, the working class identity, and the mobilization into the Democratic Party, were mutually reinforcing.

In conjunction with other major industrial cities of the Northeast and Midwest, then, the Pittsburgh region emerged as a crucial component of the "New Deal coalition," and the forces which transformed the American political universe in the 1930s were particularly acute in Pittsburgh's Steel Valley. It is possible, therefore, that the forces which created the New Deal's new Democratic majority may have been more powerfully at work in Pittsburgh and its Steel Valley than in any other industrial region. As labor historian John R. Commons observed in 1909, "Pittsburgh loom[s] up as the mighty storm mountain of Capital and Labor. Here our modern world achieves its grandest triumph and faces its gravest problem." Perhaps more than any other city, he claimed, Pittsburgh was the focus of "titanic . . . contests for the division of wealth." A quarter of a century later, in the mid-Thirties, other observers of the Pittsburgh scene agreed with this assessment, saying, "[F]or the life of the people of Pittsburgh and its environs the production of wealth on a gigantic scale and the contest for its division are still the basic facts, and that city may yet qualify as the 'storm mountain of Capital and Labor.'"[14]

Steel Valley Peasants

I said previously that two important roots of solidarity in the industrial heartland were: (1) long-term job stability for blue collar workers; and (2) long-term neighborhood stability for blue collar neighborhoods. Let's examine these two social factors.

Job and residential stability had not always been the case in America's ethnic blue collar communities. Indeed, it had not been the case just shortly before this. The period of rapid American industrialization known as the "Second Industrial Revolution," from about 1880 or so to the beginning of World War I, was also a period of people in motion. Massive numbers of unskilled workers were needed for the huge new factories stretching for miles up and down the riverfronts of industrial America. The domestic labor force simply was not sufficient to supply the needed numbers of workers, and so workers were pulled from across the Atlantic.

For indigenous reasons, agricultural societies in Southern Italy, as well as Central and Eastern Europe, were undergoing great turmoil as the on-going industrialization of these societies pushed peasant peoples off their lands. The European Industrial Revolution not only transformed the continent technologically, but also demographically by creating a resulting population boom.

In 1750 the population of Europe had been 144 million. In 1900, just 150 years later, it was 423 million. The main reason for this dramatic increase was a marked decline in the death rate due to medical, nutritional, and sanitation advances, with no corresponding drop in the birth rate. More children were born, more survived infancy, and more reached adulthood. This caused an economic crisis, especially in farming regions where only elder sons inherited the land. There were too many peasants, and they grew increasingly impoverished.

But, it wasn't demographics alone which explained the European "push." Few were leaving Southern Italy and Eastern Europe before the 1880s, despite population pressure. The crucial variables were the growth of new transportation systems, coupled with a resulting commercialization of agriculture. Rural landlords wanted to take advantage of the ability to increase output through mechanization and the ability to ship to the mushrooming cities along the new transportation routes. Mechanization, however, required fewer agricultural workers and was most effective on large-scale farms, so there was increasing pressure to consolidate small farms into large commercial holdings.

The result was the displacement of vast numbers of farm laborers. While the factory cities of Europe swallowed many of the people forced off the land, they could not take them all. Thus, industrial America's need for workers coincided with their need for gainful employment.

In the case of Jews in Eastern Europe and Russian Poland, anti-Semitic persecution also drove whole families across the Atlantic in search of a better life. Official Russian policy was to restrict Jewish economic activity and encourage pogroms—vigilante actions—against Jews. Laws enacted in the 1880s forbade Jews from buying or selling property and established education quotas. Indeed, the Czarist secret police even engaged in the invention of anti-Jewish propaganda, such as the notorious *Protocols of the Elders of Zion,* later popularized by the Nazis, which claimed there was a Jewish conspiracy to conquer the world.[15] Thus, Eastern European Jews had as much reason to look for greener pastures as the hard-pressed peasant farmers of other areas.

America was the Promised Land which pulled many across the Atlantic, and not just because of the plethora of unskilled jobs. There was also the contract labor system, especially prevalent in Southern Europe and particularly in Italy. Under it contractors actively recruited workers for American railroads and corporations.

Such emigration was further facilitated by cheap steamship travel. One-way crossing of the Atlantic fell from three months in the days of sailing ships to 10 days, and was extremely cheap. This encouraged return trips back home when lay-offs in America decreased the demand for labor. And, once back home, such returnees told all their relatives about the American Promised Land, encouraging further emigration.

America thus witnessed the greatest wave of immigration up to that point in its history, as these "New Immigrants" flooded into the country. A million European immigrants per year poured into America for six of the nine years between 1905-1914, with up to three-quarters of them being New Immigrants from Southern and Eastern Europe, while only 14 percent came from Northern Europe.[16] In one year, 1907, nearly 188,000 of these New Immigrants listed Pittsburgh as their final destination.[17]

The peak of this immigration wave was 1910, with the foreign-born accounting for a high of 14.7 percent of the total American population, disproportionately concentrated in the Northeastern industrial cities.[18] In Pittsburgh, for instance, "at one point more than a quarter of the inhabitants had been born in foreign countries . . . They included Poles, Lithuanians, Croatians, Serbians, Slovaks, Magyars, Greeks, Bohemians, Rumanians [sic], and other nationalities and ethnic groups." By some estimates Pittsburghers represented as many as seventy nationalities.[19] And 80 percent of these "foreigners" were Southern and Eastern European.[20]

Although World War I brought immigration to a virtual halt, it quickly picked up again at war's end. "From June 1920, to June 1921, more than 800,000 persons poured into the country, 65 percent of them from southern and eastern Europe, and consuls in Europe reported that millions more were planning to leave."[21]

As late as 1940 such immigrants and, more importantly, their American-born children accounted for more than half the population of 20 large cities, including two-thirds of the population of Cleveland, three-fifths of Newark, NJ., and three-fourths of New York City.[22]

From Peasants to Proletarians

These New Immigrants quickly filled the lower echelons of the American industrial workforce. "They constituted, for example, nearly two thirds of the common labor in a typical large steel plant in 1910. Southern and Eastern Europeans . . . made up 33.4 percent of the total labor force in iron and steel in 1907."[23]

Within a relatively short period of time, therefore, the demographic composition of the American industrial workforce was transformed. The Bethlehem Steel plant in Bethlehem, Pennsylvania, was typical. "Not surprisingly," we are told, "the executive, research, and upper engineering ranks at Bethlehem Steel were predominantly Anglo-Saxon. But, beginning with the importation of skilled Belgian foundrymen in the 1860s, the workforce became more diverse. Shops in the Bethlehem plant became distinctly (though not exclusively) ethnic in flavor and language: Hungarians ran the blast furnaces, Slovaks the specialty mills. Pennsylvania Germans and Windish (German-speakers from Yugoslavia) were shop foremen plant-wide. There were German machinists, Irish plant patrols, Hispanics at the coke works."[24]

By the time of the great failed steel strike of 1919, the majority of America's industrial workers were these New Immigrants. Company accounts of that strike always referred to the strikers as "foreigners," as in a National Tube Co. report that, near the end of the strike, "Hundreds of striking foreigners are leaving for Europe, depleting the strikers' ranks."[25]

On October 10, 1919, U.S. Senator Kenyon and his fact-finding committee visited the steel towns of Homestead, Duquesne, Clairton, and McKeesport to investigate the situation. "Did you see that crowd of 150 strikers at Clairton?" Kenyon asked his committee disdainfully. "Did you notice that when I asked how many of them were citizens, only three raised their hands?"[26]

These "foreign" Pittsburgh-area steelworkers were, John Bodnar discovered in a study of immigrants to the Pittsburgh area between the turn of the century and World War I, "peasants from the most underdeveloped areas of southern and eastern Europe . . . Of those immigrants interviewed, all arrived between 1902 and 1914 from Croatia, Bosnia, Galicia, and the eastern counties of Slovakia. All but one had been agricultural workers or laborers in Europe. Indeed, 82 percent of all Serbians and 70 percent of all Slovaks emigrating from Austria-Hungary were agrarian-peasant workers."[27]

Good Workers in Stable Jobs

Although the social and psychological characteristics of the European peasants who flooded into America in the early twentieth century would eventually mesh with evolving circumstances to create a strong and self-consciously assertive working class, this was not obvious at the time.

For one thing, the new workforce of the Second Industrial Revolution, composed of peasant "New Immigrants," was not, at first, a stable workforce. These New Immigrants were often "birds of passage," who frequently travelled back and forth across the Atlantic because of the cheap travel made possible by falling steamship fares. Thus, yearly turnover rates in a factory workforce could vary from a low of 100 percent to a high of 1,000 percent.

In addition, more than a third of the New Immigrants who came to America returned forever to the Old Country. Depending on ethnic group, these rates could vary from as high as 80 percent in the case of some Balkans to as low as 15 percent in the case of Russian Jews. The transient nature of this population thus made both stable workforces and stable neighborhoods impossible.

This constant demographic churning, however, settled into a pattern of stability after World War I, as immigrants increasingly decided to stay in America rather than return home, and so the flood of new arrivals from Europe ceased. Indeed, the year that war started, 1914, is perhaps a good point at which to suggest the pattern began to change. There were a number of factors which combined to bring order out of demographic chaos.

First, there was the disruption of the Great War itself, plunging the homes of the New Immigrants—Italy, the Austro-Hungarian Empire, the Romanov Empire—into death and destruction. Also, at least until 1917 when it entered the war, America remained a non-belligerent haven, safe from the military draft instituted by the European combatants to meet their gigantic manpower needs.

Following the war there were other reasons to stay in America. Hunger and economic collapse stalked Europe. The Austro-Hungarian and Romanov Empires were sundered. Revolution and bloody civil war devastated Russia. Even Italy, theoretically a "victor," fared poorly in war's aftermath, paving the way for the triumph of Benito Mussolini's fascism. The fascist regimes which came to power in Italy and in the ruins of the Austro-Hungarian Empire were another reason to remain in America.

Meanwhile, in spite of European chaos, there were even fewer fleeing Europe for America because of changed immigration laws in America. In 1924, agitated by the post-war Red Scare and increasingly shrill nativist propaganda, the Republican-dominated Congress sought to preserve the supposedly superior Anglo-Saxon makeup of the population by passing the National Origins [Johnson] Act (co-written by Pennsylvania's Republican U. S. Senator David Aiken Reed, of Pittsburgh, and a founding member of Pittsburgh's foremost legal firm, Reed Smith Shaw and McClay). Such was the anti-immigrant sentiment, that the bill passed overwhelmingly, with not even a single "progressive" vote in Congress cast against it.

Not only did this legislation impose a 100 percent ban on any further Asian immigration, it also greatly restricted further European immigration by establishing a maximum quota of only 150,000 immigrants per year. In addition, immigrants from any country in any year were limited to a maximum of 2 percent of their numbers in the 1890 Census, a time when America was far more WASP. Thus, far fewer Southern and Eastern Europeans were eligible to enter America (only 16 percent of the maximum 150,000 annually), a constraint which would remain in force until the immigration laws were liberalized with the passage of the Hart-Celler Act in 1964.

Thereafter, the percentage of the foreign-born in the general population plummeted, declining in each succeeding decade until the figure reached an all-time low in 1970, to begin climbing again thereafter. In an ironic working of the "law of unintended consequence," the new settlement pattern which this legislation helped create would work to undermine the very WASP-Republican dominance that Congress sought to protect.

Finally, the captains of industry grew to realize how enormous their economic losses were due to the high rates of workforce turnover. They began to institute various packages of "corporate welfare" benefits for their employees, as well as raise wages. One of the most well-known of these wage increases was at the gigantic River Rouge auto plant in Michigan. There, in 1914, at a time when most auto workers were making $5-per-week, Henry Ford instituted his then astoundingly high $5-per-day wage rate in order to retain workers.

Thus, New Immigrant workers settled into what became relatively secure and stable jobs, providing the financial basis for the stable neighborhoods that began to cluster around the factories where they worked. This period of evolving stabilization, from about 1914-1930, laid the foundation for the subsequent pattern of occupational and neighborhood stability which characterized ethnic working class communities in the Thirties and later.

Vincent DeAndrea, an Italian who lived in Bloomfield, a neighborhood known even today as Pittsburgh's "Little Italy," illustrated this job stability. In 1930 he began working at Heppenstalls, a small steel mill in the adjacent neighborhood of Lawrenceville. Except for a stint at Dravo Corporation building LST landing craft during World War II, he put in thirty-six years as a steel cutter at Heppenstalls. He recalled that the entire workforce at Heppenstalls, mostly ethnic, was just as stable. Emphasizing their obsession with economic security, he told me, "Once you got that job, you don't leave."[28]

These industrial workers, who had shortly before been European peasants from the most backward areas, shared certain deeply embedded social and psychological traits. They came from an economy of scarcity in which there was very little wealth, health, or security of any kind. It was, in other words, a world of "limited good," and almost unlimited "bad."[29] Disaster could strike at any moment. Economic advancement, let alone wealth, was considered unachievable.

In such circumstances, job stability and economic security was the overriding goal of life. "Rather than embracing the 'American dream' of personal advancement through education and a career, Slavs sought mainly secure employment . . . In Slavic Europe children were continually taught to work hard; little else seemed available. Not surprisingly, Russian peasants employed one criterion in determining the suitability of their daughter's prospective marriage partner: was the prospective son-in-law a 'good worker.'"[30]

Such "good workers" could be found everywhere in the ethnic communities of Pittsburgh and in the surrounding mill towns for years to come. Angelo DeBone, of Greensburg's Italian Hilltop community, worked stolidly at the local Walworth Co., a manufacturer of brass valves and fittings, for half a century, from the early 1930s to the early 1980s. His friend Anthony Germano was an electrician at the same company for forty years.[31]

John Casciato, of Pittsburgh's Italian Panther Hollow, recalled that Dominic Varratti, a cousin of his, paid for a home in 1965 with cash which he'd saved scrupulously. Similarly, Casciato recalled that Ralph Sciulli, another neighbor, did the same thing, even though he had twelve kids. How was this possible? "No frills," answered Casciato. "They just ate spaghetti without sauce six days a week. All they knew was the Eureka Bank. They got paid, paid their rent, and the rest went in the bank."[32]

Mike Citriniti also exemplified this "good worker" virtue. In 1928 Mike emigrated at age eighteen from Calabria, Italy, to Pittsburgh's Italian Oakland community. Two years later, in 1930, like many other Italians across America, he opened his own cobbler shop.[33] Thereafter he worked six days a week, staying open even on Saturday nights until 10:30 p.m., putting in seventy-five hours per week. He did this month after month, year after year, decade after decade. Indeed, he did this for nearly seven decades, through the administrations of ten American presidents from Hoover to Clinton, finally closing his shop and retiring in 1998 at age eighty-eight.[34] Retirement was fatal. The next year, 1999, Mike Citriniti died in his sleep.[35]

I often visited Mike Citriniti in his shop. Indeed, he was my neighborhood cobbler and repaired my shoes. During one visit he pointed with pride to a photo of him taken in 1934 as he leaned on the brand new Plymouth convertible he'd just bought for $734, which he paid for with cash. He saved the money for his car during the hard times of the Depression by practicing what he preached to everyone who would listen, "If you make a dollar, save a dime."

Cobblers over in the Italian neighborhood of Bloomfield were the same. When Umberto Buccigrossi was eight years old his father apprenticed him to cobbler Henry LeDonne. He shined shoes in LeDonne's shop on Bloomfield's main street, Liberty Avenue, until he graduated from elementary school at the local Immaculate Conception church. Then he began repairing shoes. "From that day to today," he told a reporter, "I never left a hammer." He later apprenticed at a second cobbler shop on nearby Centre Avenue, and then purchased it. He worked in his shop nine hours a day, six days a week, for seventy-five years, during which time, he boasted, he "saved more soles than the pope." When he wasn't saving soles or spending time with his family, he served as the long-time secretary of the Societa' de Beneficenza Ateleta, the fraternal lodge of Bloomfield's Italians, who came from the Italian village of Ateleta.[36]

Frank Trango, Sr., operated his cobbler shop right on Bloomfield's Liberty Avenue. He worked in it only eight hours a day, but he worked in it six days a week for sixty-six years. He lived with his wife and two sons in a two-bedroom apartment above his shop. On his one day off per week, he'd sometimes go to the Ateleta fraternal lodge to play bocce ball with his friends. He worked in his shop until he was ninety-four years old, and only stopped because he fell on an icy sidewalk and hit his head. The resulting brain surgery caused him to loose the use of his hands.[37]

Virtually all of the subjects in Bodnar's study of Slavic immigrants reflected this same traditional European peasant conception of hard and steady work. Zara Werlinich, for instance, was a Serb who immigrated to McKees Rocks, near Pittsburgh, in 1913. "Upon his arrival he conceived a single goal: to get a job. 'We all had to look for work,' he recalled, 'a job don't look for you.' Werlinich was hired as a laborer in the Fort Pitt Foundry and remained a laborer for 20 years until the depression forced him out of work. He was grateful the foundry provided a steady income. Werlinich's aims were shared by the majority of Slavic newcomers who sought steady work as a course of security . . . George Hudock, a Bethlehem [Pa.] Slovak, obtained work operating a crane and rejected subsequent opportunities to earn more because those 'opportunities' seemed less 'steadier.'"[38]

Slavs gravitated especially toward work in the steel mills because it was considered a secure job. "One Pittsburgh Slav emphasized that many of his friends genuinely wanted to work in the steel mills because they disliked outdoor work, which was irregular."[39]

Once Slavs got their jobs in the mills, they clung to them tenaciously. Valerian Duda, a Pole in Bodnar's study, immigrated to McKeesport in 1906 at the age of seventeen. He quickly got a job at U.S. Steel's National Tube Plant in McKeesport among the other Poles already working there. For the next forty-eight years he worked as a tester of galvanized pipe, finally retiring in 1954. Slovak Andrew Bodnar came to Homestead in 1913 where an uncle got him a job in U. S. Steel's Homestead Works. For the next forty-seven years he worked as a "piler" of steel beams, finally retiring in 1960. "The reluctance of Slavs to leave steady work was a pervasive theme," observed Bodnar.[40]

The hard and dangerous nature of the work wasn't as important as the fact that it would always be there. Bill Richter, a maintenance machinist in the foundry at Shenango, Inc., on Neville Island, within sight of Pittsburgh's Downtown Golden Triangle, was the last person out of the plant in 1990 when it closed. "The only thing I can tell you about the foundry," he said, "was that it was hard work. It was dirty work. But it made a good living for a lot of people."[41]

This work ethic made a great impression on the children of the peasant immigrants. As Bodnar noted, "Many children viewed their immigrant fathers as, above all else, hard workers . . . A Polish-American described his parents as individuals who believed in 'work, work, work, and work.' A Serbian son in Pittsburgh remembered his father as a man esteemed by fellow Serbs for his application to his job. The Serbian son claimed his father's characteristics were representative of most Serbs. He clearly explained his father's motives as fear of the loss of his job. He argued: 'Those men were tireless. They did hard work. They stuck with their job; they didn't have to be driven. They were tireless and always feared the loss of their jobs, since they had nothing to fall back on.'"[42]

The amazing persistence of this work ethic is obvious to anyone familiar with Pittsburgh-area workers. Mike Ditka, former coach of the champion Chicago Bears football team and then coach of the New Orleans Saints, was born and raised in Aliquippa, where he graduated from high school in 1957. "To me, it was the ideal American town," Ditka recalled of Aliquippa in the Fifties. "The mills were at their greatest heights and, boy, the work ethic was tremendous."[43]

Kristin Kovacic grew up in the Pittsburgh neighborhood of Carrick during the 1950s. She saw the same steady dependability in her parents. "I come from a family of workers," she said. "We are all (with some much-maligned exceptions) excellent employees. We stay at jobs for lifetimes. Those of us who are not in unions get engraved pens and trivets from our employers. Dependable, our word . . . My father's an electrician, and my mother's a secretary in a public school. I never heard them complain about their jobs. They worried. My mother lost sleep over a new computer she had to master; my father courted heart problems when an efficiency expert eyed the maintenance department. They worked and worried . . . Staying put was a value. A steady paycheck the definition of ambition."[44]

If "staying put was a value," it was also an obstacle to be overcome for those of later generations with ambitions beyond a steady paycheck. Actor Michael Keaton, the megastar of such Hollywood blockbusters as *Batman, Batman Returns,* and *Beetlejuice,* recalled the problems of a kid with ambition growing up in Pittsburgh. "The problem with Pittsburgh," he said, "is . . . they will want to sit on you . . . They will want you not to go far. They will want you not to reach your potential because that's a threat. I don't know if it's some kind of European immigrant thing—don't be too sure of yourself, don't be too cocky, don't ask for too much you shouldn't have, don't go struttin'. They want you to succeed to a point."[45]

A Proper Job for an Ethnic

Not only did ethnic workers stay at their jobs until they dropped, they commonly worked at only particular types of jobs, those jobs already monopolized by their ethnicity. In a wide-ranging survey of findings on American working class occupational structures, John Bodnar found pervasive ethnic occupational clusterings. "By 1911," he noted, "in seven urban areas nearly one-third of all South Italians were categorized as 'general laborers' . . . 65 percent of the Poles were in manufacturing and mechanical pursuits . . . while more than half of all Serbs were general laborers . . . In Indiana oil refineries, Croatians held jobs in only three categories: stillman helper, fireman, and still cleaner . . . Serbs and Croatians in New York City were heavily involved in freight handling . . . By 1900, nearly all of the 3,000 employees in the Peninsular Car Company in Detroit were Polish. By 1909, Polish women in Chicago dominated restaurant and kitchen jobs . . . By 1920, 69 percent of all Slovak males were coal miners, and about half of all Mexican males were blast-furnace laborers."[46]

Thus, virtually everyone in these ethnic enclaves depended on the same type of blue collar jobs and passed these jobs on to their children. "Young workers in [Pittsburgh's] Polish Hill, like their parents before them," for example, "worked at one of the metal plants near the Sixth Ward while those on the [Slavic] South Side performed unskilled tasks at the Jones and Laughlin or the United States Steel works. Some workers, of course, held better jobs but few held white-collar or professional occupations in either community.

"Blue-collar work, frequently in construction, also characterized the Bloomfield and East Liberty Italian districts, although some differences did exist. Bloomfield residents worked as laborers for the Equitable Gas Company, the Pennsylvania Railroad, or the city of Pittsburgh. Nearly two-thirds were unskilled." Both ethnic groups "clung tenaciously" to these jobs and "seldom changed employment locations." In this way, "the ability of both groups to pass along jobs to their children meant that second- and even third-generation Poles and Italians would find their childhood neighborhood as convenient as did their parents. Steady work . . . combined with cooperative family efforts, at the same time enabled both groups to purchase homes in the neighborhood and thus increased the likelihood that they would stay."[47]

A similar story was told to me by my Italian landlord in South Oakland. Vince

DeIuliis (variant spelling of "Diulus"), like most other South Oakland Italians, came from the small Italian village of Gamberale (just as most Bloomfield Italians came from Ateleta). He first came to America with his brothers to work on the construction of the Cathedral of Learning at the University of Pittsburgh. Many of his fellow villagers already worked on this building. After a spell of work, Vince and his brothers returned to Gamberale. They again returned to America, however, bringing more kin, and this time they stayed.

While Italians like Vince and his relatives usually worked in outdoor construction jobs, "In Pittsburgh, Poles established occupational beachheads at the Jones & Laughlin and Oliver mills on the South Side, at Heppenstalls and the Pennsylvania Railroad in Lawrenceville, and at the Armstrong Cork Company [in the Strip District] and the H. J. Heinz plant [on the North Side]." And these ethnic-occupational beachheads were solidified by bringing in relatives, often sons, to work alongside fathers. "According to Stanley Brozek, for instance, fathers spoke to foremen on behalf of their sons to get them jobs at the Edgar Thomson mill in Braddock . . . Every Italian we interviewed in Pittsburgh had relied on kin or friends to persuade foremen or other supervisors to hire them . . . It was not surprising that Leo G. worked for the Pittsburgh Railway Company laying stone foundations for streetcar tracks; his grandfather, father, brother, and uncle all were employed by the company. Similarly, in 1900 Palfilo C. came to the Bloomfield section of Pittsburgh, where his brother-in-law found him a job on a pipe-laying gang.

"A striking example of the Italians' ability to use kinship in order to gain entrance into a particular occupational sector is seen in the accomplishment of newcomers who came to Bloomfield from the village of Ateleta in the province of Abruzzi. From the 1890s to the 1930s, these villagers brought 'paesani' to the pipe construction department of the Equitable Gas Company. One of the first to gain employment was Anthony B., who had been a farmer in Italy; when he found work with the gas company, he informed several friends in Ateleta about job possibilities. Amico L., who initially arrived in 1890, returned to Ateleta three times. Upon each return he recruited a friend or relative for the Pittsburgh pipeline 'gang.' Vincent L. came to the city around 1900 and through an uncle who was already there, obtained his job laying pipe. After two more round trips from Ateleta to Pittsburgh, he returned to Ateleta for good in 1911, but he later sent over one of his sons, who was hired by sewer contractors at the request of friends who were already working with the firm.

"The National Tube Company in McKeesport, Pennsylvania, was reluctant to move its facilities in 1950 because jobs in seamless-type construction had been 'handed down from father to son.' . . . Interviews with Poles in the Lawrenceville section of Pittsburgh revealed that during the 1920s and the 1930s, boys worked alongside their fathers at Heppenstalls, Armour Meats, and other plants in the area."[48]

Like Father, Like Son

As illustrated by the situation at McKeesport's National Tube Company, jobs were not only ethnically homogeneous, they were familial, with sons usually following fathers into the very same jobs. Thus was established a pattern which persisted for decades. "At one point in the 1950s," for instance, "over 4,000 men out of approximately 10,000 in the Homestead Works were father-son combinations."[49]

Employment numbers in Pittsburgh's industries actually climaxed in the decade of the 1920s, then began a long, slow decline. For a long time, however, the decline was so gradual that it was almost invisible. In the meantime, this seemingly permanent level of industrial employment made possible stable occupational patterns, as there were always jobs in the local mill to be handed down from generation to generation. Even as late as the 1960s, "The lives of Pennsylvania's steelworkers seemed so solid . . . that people never had to worry about getting work."[50]

This was true not only of Pittsburgh and environs, but of most steel towns. In 1995, for example, when the last workers on the last shift forever closed the mighty Bethlehem Steel plant in Bethlehem, Pennsylvania, virtually all of them were the sons and grandsons of men who had worked in the mill since the furnaces were turned on at the beginning of the twentieth century. Guillermo Lopez, Jr., a millwright, was the son of a Bethlehem Steel worker. Thomas Beier, who worked in the mill for twenty-two years, was a third-generation steelworker. "My father and grandfather worked here," said Mike Martin, a supervisor at the mill.[51]

The same was also true of other types of jobs. East Pittsburgh resident Frank Pribanic, for instance, remembered that in 1931 his dad pulled him and his brother, Joe, out of 8th grade [which was a common final grade of schooling for ethnic children] to work alongside him dynamiting rock formations in order to build the huge Westinghouse Bridge linking East Pittsburgh with North Versailles. He never went back to school.[52]

In both mining districts and in steel mills it was the fathers who took their sons into the mines and mills to work alongside them, or at least got them their initial adult jobs. Thus, Bodnar notes, "Numerous young men were taught their first job skills by their fathers. Nick Kiak's first job was learning the operation of a crane from his father at the Bethlehem mill. All but seven of over 70 second generation Slavs interviewed in southwestern Pennsylvania coal fields were taken into the mines by their fathers."[53]

And, as George Porvasnik's work career illustrated, once the sons got a steady job, they were as reluctant as their fathers had been to change positions. They'd found what they wanted. Anthony Germano's father had been an electrician at Greensburg's Walworth Co. His father got him a job as an electrician at the same company, and Germano remained at that job for forty years.[54] Frank Horvath, a Hungarian, insisted he never wanted anything other than what he had obtained at the Bethlehem mill. "I just wanted a job," he said, "whether it be a garbage man or an iceman."[55]

The same was true in the small industrial communities which dotted Allegheny County. Mary Rose Bregon, age seventy-four in 1999 and an Italian who was raised in one of them, the coal town of Morgan, recalled that in 1918 her father, age fifteen, followed *his* father into the local mine, where he stayed the rest of his life. Nino Carosone began work in the mines of Morgan in 1930 at age eighteen and remained in the mines until 1950. It was all he knew. "Go out, get a job, make money," he said. "That's the way it was."[56]

Thus, this work ethic was successfully passed on from first generation immigrants to their children, with many sons following their fathers not only into the mills, but into the same jobs—where they remained. "In a quantitative assessment of intergenerational occupational mobility among South Slavic immigrants in Steelton, Pennsylvania," Bodnar reported, "less than one out of four sons was able to attain an occupational status above his father between 1920 and 1940. While a modest amount of occupation advancement occurred, the children were quite similar in their aspirations and accomplishments to their parents."[57]

One major reason for this was the great disdain Slavic peasants had for formal education. They saw no connection between schooling and the all-important job, which was the center of their existence. Therefore they routinely pulled their children out of school at very early ages and got them jobs. Thousands of Slavic boys started work in the glass factories on Pittsburgh's South Side as a prelude to lifetime jobs in the nearby J & L steel mill. Of 115 second generation children interviewed in Bodnar's study, all but two were working by age fourteen.

George Porvasnik was typical. Born in Pittsburgh in 1911, he was the son of a Slovak immigrant. He left school at age fourteen to work at a plant which manufactured chains. Six months later, in 1925, he got a job as a rivet heater at the Pressed Steel company in McKees Rocks, a job at which he remained until he retired in 1965.[58]

Leo Sokol was unusual in that he made it to high school before dropping out in 1935 to begin work at J & L's Eliza plant on Second Avenue in Pittsburgh's Oakland neighborhood. However, he was typical in spending the next forty-three years as a stove tender for the blast furnace before retiring in 1978.[59]

This durable and intimate overlap of family and work was not only one of the most significant aspects of life in the ethnic enclave, but was also of paramount importance for the creation of working class solidarity—because "class" solidarity also meant ethnic, neighborhood, and, more importantly, *family* solidarity. The amazing class solidarity manifested by workers in the Thirties was not due to the fact that workers at that time were somehow more "virtuous" than later generations of workers. Social factors played a large part in creating their class solidarity. As we have seen, as late as the 1950s, 40 percent of the workers in Homestead's U.S. Steel plant were father-son combinations. Thus, to express class solidarity with your fellow workers did not mean embracing strangers. It meant expressing solidarity with your father, your uncles, your brothers, and your fellow Poles or *paesani*. It was hard to say where one kind of solidarity left off and another began.

Buying Homes in Little Worlds

When we speak of an "enclave," we are speaking above all of " . . . a special relationship between a distinctive group of people [in this case, of the same ethnicity] and a place. Thus, an enclave has some characteristics of a subculture, in which a group of people shares common traditions and values that are ordinarily maintained by a high rate of interaction within the group."[60]

In addition to the influence of the job, these high rates of interaction were also fostered by the family, the church, and the many ethnic volunteer organizations in the enclaves. Family kinship, a common religion, a common language, a common home in the "Old Country," and a communal culture tied the residents into a self-contained "little world."

After World War I such ethnic enclaves in the Pittsburgh area began to settle into a pattern of enduring neighborhood stability which reinforced their communal culture for decades to come. Frank Serene documented the turbulent demographic instability of Pittsburgh's New Immigrant neighborhoods in the period before World War I. However, this turbulence subsided after the war, as he found increasing post-war neighborhood stability in his examination of the steady, and even proliferating, numbers of weddings, baptisms, and church memberships in the immigrant churches of the Steel Valley, even during the production declines of 1918-1919 and 1920-1921.[61]

This post-war period witnessed ethnic groups erecting more and more of their own churches, as with the Hungarians of Pittsburgh's Hazelwood neighborhood, which grew up beside a Jones & Laughlin steel mill. In 1919 they erected the small but imposing St. Ann's Roman Catholic Church on Chatsworth Avenue. Just around the corner, on Hazelwood Avenue, Protestant Hungarians erected the First Hungarian Lutheran Church of Pittsburgh in 1925.

Similarly, other scholars have found patterns of exceptional residential and occupational stability among New Immigrant groups during the 1930s.[62] As late as 1989 one observer could write of the Italian neighborhood of Bloomfield that, "It is not uncommon to have three or more generations living cheek to jowl on a narrow street . . . The groceries that dotted Lorgan may be gone now . . . but the people aren't. Houses stay in families, get passed down like Grandpap's Bible."[63]

For example, Vince DeIuliis, my Italian construction laborer-landlord in Oakland, married Elaine, his cousin, whom he met at a wedding. Together they settled in South Oakland, surrounded by their mutual extended kin network. The house I lived in, on Dawson Street, had originally been presented to the newlyweds as a wedding gift by Vince's family, who lived just around the corner on Atwood Street. In 1996, Vince and Elaine continued this tradition by presenting the house I lived in as a gift to their daughter on her wedding—requiring me to move out so the daughter and her new husband could move in. (I moved to Bloomfield, another blue collar Italian neighborhood.)

This communal neighborhood pattern was true even of "Old Immigrant" populations such as Protestant Germans, who had the advantage of starting earlier than the New Immigrants. One such Pittsburgh neighborhood is Allentown, a small village-cum-neighborhood overlooking Downtown from atop Mt. Washington. Even as late as 1991, it was, "An old-fashioned place, its modest houses . . . packed in like molars, flying American flags and stepping up from high curbs . . . Allentown is Pittsburgh writ small . . . 80-percent white, still largely German, it's a village of owner-occupied homes, well kept and handed down through families. The not a-typical Kress family . . . lives in the house grandpap bought in 1903, and coaxed the front-yard evergreen from sapling to 20-foot Christmas tree."[64]

In 1938, when Vincent DeAndrea, then a twenty-eight years old steelworker, bought his home on Bloomfield's Mathilda Street (which he still owned in 2002 when I spoke with him), he said all the workers in the Heppenstalls steel plant where he worked were doing the same. They were always buying property here and there, establishing a patchwork quilt of home ownership. And they were always comparing notes with each other. "How much did you pay for this? How much for that?" Property ownership was a primary topic of conversation among ethnic Pittsburgh's steelworkers in the Thirties.[65]

This characteristic thus gives the lie to Marx and Engels' famous 1848 declaration that, "The proletarians have nothing to lose but their chains."[66] By this they meant that wage laborers would never be able to actually accumulate material possessions, because the capitalist economic system was stacked against them. All workers had was oppression, their chains.

This may or may not have been true in early nineteenth century Europe, when Marx and Engels wrote their *Manifesto*. In early twentieth century America, however, even during the Great Depression, it simply was not true.

Yes, ethnic industrial workers had oppression. But they also had possessions. Indeed, the highest rate of home ownership among the New Immigrants was to be found among those prototypical proletarians, the various Slavic groups. According to Bodnar, because of their peasant quest for security in a world of "limited good" (and perhaps also sparked by a group memory of being dispossessed from the land in Europe), they became almost fanatical buyers of homes. "Denied opportunities for significant occupational mobility, particularly since earlier arrivals such as the Irish and the Germans already held skilled industrial jobs, Slavs turned intensely to home ownership as a means of solidifying their precarious economic status. In nearly every Slavic ethnic community in America, immigrant savings and loan associations were established for the purpose of issuing home mortgages . . . [For example] Slovenes in southwestern Pennsylvania mining towns organized the Slovenian Savings and Loan Association in 1921 with branches in Strabane and Canonsburg . . . [Thereafter] Slavs exceeded nearly every ethnic group in urban America in purchasing homes."[67]

One *gospodar*, the elder head of a Yugoslav *zadruga*, or extended family, explained the connection between such ownership and factory work. "We work in the factory," he said, "so that we can continue to hold onto the land and we hold onto the land because no one knows what is sure."[68] Bloomfield steelworker Vincent DeAndrea gave a similar reason for why he bought a house in 1938. "When you own your own home," he told me, "no one can throw you out if they don't like you, like they can when you rent. You're safe."[69]

This attitude was especially evident when one examined the small steel towns surrounding Pittsburgh where Slavic immigrants were concentrated. "In Pennsylvania mill towns," Bodnar found, "Slavic ownership rates exceeded even the families of native-born whites. Serbs and Croats dominated the rates in Aliquippa, Farrell, and Steelton. Slovaks were the leading owners in Braddock, Duquesne, Homestead, and Munhall. In Homestead, Slovaks bought homes twice as much as native-white families . . . Not surprisingly, in 1930 the foreign-born owned homes at higher rates than the statewide average for all families in Pennsylvania, a state whose immigrant population was primarily southern and eastern European."[70] Table 3 gives the specifics on these ownership rates:

Table 3
Slavic Homeownership in Selected Steel Valley Towns, 1930

	Aliquippa	Braddock	Duquesne	Homestead	Munhall
# of Families	5,271	4,081	4,473	4,346	2,963
% Native White Who Owned	39%	18%	33%	23%	55%
% Foreign Born Who Owned	54%	33%	54%	46%	78%
Largest Ethnic Grp.*	Serbo-Croat	Slovak	Slovak	Slovak	Slovak

* Slavs formed about 50% of the Pennsylvania foreign born population in 1930. Poles and Slovaks accounted for the largest number of Slavs. Source: John Bodnar, "Immigration and Modernization: The Case of Slavic Peasants in Industrial America," in Milton Cantor, Ed., *American Working Class Culture: Explorations in American Labor and Social History,* Greenwood Press: Westport, Conn., 1979, Table 1, 358.

All of these neighborhoods were densely packed, with families often building new houses in their backyards for their grown children, who were now raising families of their own. Dominic Lombardozzi, a first-generation Italian immigrant to Bloomfield, and his wife, Rose, lived and raised their family upstairs from Dominic's parents for twenty-five years, until his parents died. Even as late as 2000, Dominic and Rose continued to live in that same home, while their daughter and three grandchildren (the fourth generation) lived next door.[71]

Thus, we not only see a high level of home ownership among Pittsburgh's ethnic workers, who lived in their homes for twenty, thirty, forty or more years, but we also find a tenacious family grip on such property. Typically, when the parents died, their children continued living in the same homes. Thus, "A member of the original 1930 family continued to reside in the family dwelling in 28 percent of the Italian cases and 24 percent of the Polish cases through 1960. On some streets, such as Edmond and Cedarville in Bloomfield and Eleanor and Leticoe on the South Side, 40 percent of the homes were owned [in 1960] by sons and daughters of the original 1930 residents." And, if the family members weren't living in the same house, most likely they were living just down the block or around the corner. "Nearly half of those who moved within the metropolitan area during each decade stayed in the same census tract neighborhood. The next largest group left the tract but stayed within the particular ward."[72]

Anecdotal accounts confirm this stability. "Over the past 50 years [i.e., since 1921] my family has not moved much within the community," one young Bloomfield resident recalled in 1971. "They have lived on the side streets to the west of Liberty Avenue, on or near Ella Street. Only one place of residence, Carroll Street, was to the east of Liberty Avenue."[73]

Vincent DeAndrea, mentioned above, was the son of an Italian immigrant stonemason. He was born on Pittsburgh's North Side in 1910. In 1913 his family moved to Bloomfield just off Liberty Avenue and, as of 2004, he was still living in Bloomfield in the home he bought sixty-six years before, in 1938, just a few blocks from where the family first settled.[74]

Another man, born in 1930, was found in 1980 to be living on the same lot where he was born, "either in the front house with his mother or in the back house with his wife and kids. 'The family next door,' he jerks a thumb to the right, 'has been here 50 years. The family over there,' a thumb left, 'has been *there* 50 years. I know everybody around here. And they know me. It's all family.'"[75]

La Famiglia

This emphasis upon "family" was another aspect of Slavic peasant life which, when transplanted to America, contributed to remarkable neighborhood stability, once circumstances permitted. Bodnar noted that, "The prevalent family structure among premodern Croats and Serbs was the *zadruga*. Its main components were a communal, joint family which rested upon the supremacy of the older male member and the belief that other males should never leave their home. Sons and their wives and children would remain within the homes of their fathers. Daughters would leave upon marriage to become members of the *zadruga* of their husbands. Sons remained to contribute to the support of the communal family."[76]

For the Condelucis of McKees Rocks, a small town outside Pittsburgh, the neighborhood is literally such a family.[77] About forty-five Condelucis currently live in fourteen homes on a dead-end street leading to "Condeluci Hill." The communal culture of old is still alive on the 4.5 acres of Condeluci Hill, where there is one 20' x 40' communal swimming pool, one snow blower, one stepladder, and one lawn mower which everyone shares. The pool is maintained with funds from intrafamily bake sales and when someone wants to build an addition to a house, everyone pitches in.

The Condeluci patriarch, Antonio, immigrated from Calabria around the turn of the century. In 1911 he brought over his wife, Gennarina, and their first child, Mary. They settled at the foot of the then-barren Condeluci Hill and raised eight more children. In 1917 their son Sinbad was born. "We used to play up here on the hill," he recalled, "and we vowed the day would come when we would buy this hill."

Just before World War II Sinbad and his brother Sam were able to make good on their vow when they pooled their money and bought all forty-five lots on the hill for $3,500. They swore to each other they would never sell except to family. They built a house for Sam out of an old railroad box car. Then they built a home for Sinbad.

In the mid-'40s their brother-in-law won $1,300 in a craps game and they used the money to build a prefabricated Sears home for their sister, Betty Straccia. Slowly the community grew. The children eventually built a home on the crest of the hill for Gennarina and Antonio. Gennarina, who only spoke Italian, would sit on her porch of evenings watching her huge family extend down the hill and whisper, "Questo paradiso"—This is paradise.

Dean Lauria, a grandson of Antonio and Gennarina, moved five minutes away from the hill and finds it hard to like neighbors who aren't family. "For me," he said, "the hill is the center of my universe. I always felt so safe up here. It almost has healing powers . . . I always felt like if I was sick or sad, I could come here and it would heal me. When you have to go out in the world and get dirty, it's tough." When his mother, who lives on the hill, dies, he will inherit her house and return to the hill.

Both the perpetuation of this peasant family structure and the peasant worldview of economic scarcity, which necessitated a dogged pursuit of security, contributed to the enduring cohesion of ethnic enclaves in industrial America.

The Social Web

Previously, we looked at the existence of both long-term job stability and long-term neighborhood stability in the industrial heartland. Both of these contributed to the third factor which I said was also a necessary root of working class solidarity, that being the consequent growth of a dense social network centered around extended families and ethnic institutions, such as churches and fraternal societies. Now let us look more closely at how this strong social web tied workers together in the industrial heartland's working class communities of the Thirties, and for decades thereafter. Even as late as 1960, for example, researchers found that, "The location of one's work, the strength of family relationships, and the effectiveness of certain community organizations all contributed to neighborhood stability."[78]

After World War I, the dense, close, ethnic enclaves of industrial America, tightly woven together by kin networks and an ancient communal culture, became remarkably resistant to out-migration. "Less than one-third of any group from the . . . 1930 neighborhoods left Pittsburgh during the depression era of the 1930s." Thus, strong, enduring, deep bonds of mutual loyalty flourished. "Nearly every individual interviewed for this study spoke of 'pulling together' during the Depression . . . The father of Raymond C., a self-employed Pole, went bankrupt in 1931. Several male members of the family contributed their entire monthly paychecks earned from part-time jobs, to maintain the family . . . Ethnic identity also proved important. An Italian taxicab company dispatcher hired only Bloomfield Italians as drivers during the Depression. At one point the residents of Cedarville Street in the Bloomfield district held community dinners for all the families on the street and nearly all those interviewed for this study could recall numerous instances of mutual aid among neighbors."[79]

Even as, in the 1920s and even the economically depressed 1930s, more and more people were able to afford automobiles, the close tie between jobs and ethnic blue collar communities clustering closely around factories persisted, lessening the pull of out-migration. One reason Vincent DeAndrea liked living in Bloomfield was because it was only a twenty-minute walk to work at the Heppenstalls steel mill, where he was employed for thirty-six years.[80]

In addition, proximity to kin and neighbors made possible employment, something particularly important during the Great Depression. In northeast Philadelphia, for instance, there were 2,000 factories in 1930. The largest industries were textiles and metalwork, both of which were especially susceptible to seasonal variations in the number of workers they needed. Laid-off workers looked for work at other nearby factories which were hiring. Successful job-hunting, however, depended on personal contacts and insider knowledge, on "tavern friendships and gossip . . . Most workers got their jobs because someone they knew 'spoke for them,' or told them on what day to apply at the . . . gate."[81]

The same point was made about the pattern of industrial hiring at the huge Bethlehem Steel plant in Bethlehem, Pennsylvania. "Shop foremen hired from within South Bethlehem neighborhoods," we are told. "Local churches (Sts. Cyril and Methodias Slovak, St. Stanislav Polish) functioned as hiring halls . . . Bethlehem, town and plant, was a honeycomb of interconnected cells."[82] Thus, there were strong job-related reasons to remain in the old neighborhood.

Cheaper housing was also a factor, as well as proximity to "their" churches, fraternal societies, taverns, and extended families. Even in the Fifties, when third-generation grandchildren of the New Immigrants were finally moving out of the old ethnic village neighborhoods, ties to those old neighborhoods remained strong. "Ethnic churches, particularly during the holiday seasons, are crowded with former residents. Many of those interviewed continue to shop, on occasion, in their old neighborhood. The Ateleta Club [named after the Italian Abruzzi village of Ateleta, from whence most Bloomfield Italians originated] in Bloomfield and the Polish Falcon 'nests' on the South Side and Polish Hill still have dues-paying members who no longer reside in the neighborhood of their youth."[83]

Although much attenuated, these patterns seem to have persisted in Pittsburgh much longer than in many other Northeastern cities. As late as the 1990s Pittsburghers moved less frequently than people in any other urban area with a population exceeding one million. At that time, 19.2 percent of Pittsburghers had lived for thirty or more years in the same house. In contrast, only 3 percent of the residents in Riverside, California, and Orlando, Florida, fell into this category. Most Americans fell in between, living eight years in an owned home and two years in a rental.[84]

Similarly, in the neighborhood of South Oakland, where I lived from 1980-96, two extended Italian families have been there since the turn of the twentieth century. These are the Merante and the Diulus families. Like all the other South

Oakland Italians, these two families originated from the small Abruzzi village of Gamberale, population about 1,500. On Semple Street and Bates Street, around the corner, four of the Merante sisters until very recently ran three shops: "Groceria Merante," a corner bodega they inherited from their father and uncle, who trained them, still features ethnic groceries and their mother's homemade sauce and still has a majority Italian clientele; "Dolce Cafe," a bakery-coffee shop; and "Merante's Gifts," an Italian Hallmark-type store, which recently moved to Bloomfield to take advantage of the larger Italian population.

The Merante brothers are also self-employed owners of "Merante Plumbing," a major South Oakland contractor. Additionally, the family owns and manages a number of apartment buildings originally purchased by the now deceased Merante patriarch.

Meanwhile, the Diulus family is so well-established they even have a set of stairs, designated by the city as "Diulus Way," leading from the junction of Bouquet and Dawson Streets down into Panther Hollow. This set of stairs weaves its way down the hillside to No. 44 Boundary Street, where Gaetano Diulus, the progenitor of the Diulus family, once lived.

In 1890, Gaetano was the first Italian to settle in Panther Hollow. Perhaps at that time there were still panthers in Panther Hollow, but not for long, as the last panther in Pennsylvania was killed in 1891. South Oakland was then a mixed Irish and Jewish neighborhood (indeed, it was later the home of Jewish pianist-composer-actor-raconteur Oscar Levant before he left Pittsburgh for fame and fortune). Poles and other Eastern Europeans clustered in the area around Bates Street between what is now the Boulevard of the Allies and the Monongahela River. Panther Hollow was a desolate wasteland given over mainly to B. & O. railway tracks. But, it was available, so Gaetano moved in.

The large and pleasant Schenley Park was being developed at the time (1890-95), and Gaetano had come from Gamberale to work on it. He soon launched his own construction business and prospered. As he prospered, he returned to Gamberale to recruit more immigrants from his family and friends. Much of the later development of Panther Hollow was led by Gaetano's five sons.

By 1914 there were fifty-three families of Gamberale Italians living in Panther Hollow, many of them employed by the DiNardo Construction Co., also located in the Hollow. By 1974 there were 107 South Oakland families which could trace their roots back to Gamberale.

Today the Diulus family owns four homes side-by-side in the Hollow, with two adult daughters and their families living next door to their parents. Eddie Diulus, a descendant of Gaetano's, lives in Gaetano's old house at No. 44. In another part of the same house lives a relative, Bob Casciato, a retired city employee born and raised in the Hollow. The house next door, No. 42, has been occupied by the Casciato family since 1940. John Casciato, who still lives in the Hollow, was born at No. 42 in 1933. Anna Casciato has lived there for fifty years. Today, third and fourth generation Casciatos live in the house. Other members of the Casciato family live just above them on Dawson Street.[85]

Nini DiNardo, of the family which owned DiNardo Construction Co., has lived on Boundary Street all her seventy years. When she married her husband, she moved next door to the house in which she was born. Camille Caliendo, the Hollow's unofficial historian, is the granddaughter of Franchesco Diulus, one of Gaetano's brothers and, in 1914, a founder of the San Lorenzo di Gamberale Mutual Benefit Association. Camille was born at No. 40 Boundary Street in 1925 and, to give an idea of the mingling of family lineage, her grandparents are John Casciato's great grandparents.

Perhaps the most direct descendant of Gaetano Diulus, however, is Nicholas Diulus, a nephew of "Uncle Guy." Nick, a district justice in Oakland since 1969, and his wife Catherine, are the parents of six children. His family owns four houses in a row on Boundary Street. Daughter Cynthia owns two, living in one and renting out the other. Another daughter, Philomena Senko, and her family lives next door to Nick and Catherine.

There's the sentiment in the Hollow that all property should be kept "in the family," rather than being sold to outsiders, for the Hollow is the center of their lives. "I've never, never thought for one minute of leaving Panther Hollow," said Nick Diulus. "If they dropped $300 billion on my doorstep, I'm not leaving. When I was a kid, they talked about Sun Valley, Idaho, and what a beautiful place it was. Well, this is my Sun Valley . . . You don't find neighborhoods like this anymore." Wife Catherine agreed. "As long as we stay here," she said, "we're content."[86]

Two adult Diulus children, Fred and Joe (both long-time members of the Democratic Party Ward Committee), lived with their parents across the street from me when I lived on Dawson Street. The apartment house next door to them was owned by their mother's sister, whose grandchildren were current tenants. This single Diulus family owned a number of apartment buildings in South Oakland, most within a block or two of their home. Their extended family also resided within walking distance. The patriarch's brother was my own landlord, Vincent, who previously lived in my apartment with his wife-cousin, Elaine.

The house to my right on Dawson Street was owned by a son-nephew of the sister and brother living to my left. They were, however, not members of either Diulus or Merante families.

The elderly Italian couple across my back alley, members of the Sciulli extended clan, were also from Gamberale and knew the DeIuliss family "back home." They represented yet a third Italian family which was also well-established in the neighborhood. In my small section of South Oakland, comprising just a few blocks and designated as Ward Four, District [Precinct] 15, by the city, there were 30 Sciullis listed as registered voters in 1996 (all Democrats, of course), including an extended family of seven Sciulli voters residing together at No. 4 Oakland Square.[87] I was thus surrounded by kin networks.

Chain immigration from Gamberale, at least in an attenuated form, seems to have continued up to at least the 1950s. That's when Donato "Danny" Pollice, for instance, moved into this neighborhood at No. 1 Oakland Square. As a young man, Danny fought during World War II for Mussolini in Greece and Yugoslavia. His wife, Gemma, was, like Danny, born in Gamberale, a small and beautiful town of closely packed white plaster homes clustered among cliffs overlooking the Adriatic. Danny has a huge 5' x 5' aerial photo of the town proudly displayed in his den. He showed me the house where he used to live and then pointed to the house where his wife used to live when they both were children. During every summer's San Lorenzo Festival, in honor of Gamberale's patron saint, Danny drives the saint's statue in the bed of his pickup truck through the streets of South Oakland. The rest of the neighbors, some of the women in peasant dresses with jars on their heads, march behind or pin bills to the icon for good luck in the coming year. Thus, Pittsburgh's South Oakland, even at this late date, is like a small Old World village composed of extended kin and lifelong friends. It is a "little world" where everyone knows your name.

Such inbred ethnic enclaves were forming all over industrial America in the years after World War I. John Bregon, age seventy-four in 1999 and a Pole who grew up in Morgan, a small coal town in southwestern Allegheny County, looked at a photograph of the town taken in his childhood and went down the street, naming each family that lived in every company-owned duplex.[88] Because of such social patterns, by the 1920s pioneering sociologists were beginning to view American cities as characteristically composed of "a mosaic of little worlds that touch but do not interpenetrate," where the inhabitants had their most meaningful relationships with those who lived in the "little worlds" with them.[89]

By the 1930s Pittsburghers had " . . . divided the city into a patchwork of ethnic and racial neighborhoods. Italian, Greek, Jewish, Croatian, and Polish communities dotted the hillsides and valleys of the Pittsburgh region. Institutions, kin, and friends within these communities provided social and economic services, assisted in job procurement, and aided both newcomers and young second-generation adults in finding lodging while, at the same time, preserving many premigration attitudes and values."[90]

The stability of these neighborhoods was reinforced by the fact that virtually everyone belonged to the same ethnic group, and came from the same small village in the Old Country, where they'd known each other and perhaps even intermarried. For example, everyone in the Hilltop neighborhood of Greensburg, east of Pittsburgh, was Italian. Not only that, they all came from the same small Italian village of Cercemaggiore, just outside Rome, where the families had known each other before immigrating.[91]

Michael Weber, John Bodnar, and Roger Simon explored the major Italian and Polish neighborhoods of Pittsburgh between 1930 and 1960 and found that most, though not all, of Pittsburgh's Italians lived in Bloomfield and East Liberty while most of the Poles lived in Polish Hill and in South Side neighborhoods clustered around the big Jones & Laughlin steel plant. By 1930, all of these neighborhoods were dominated by second-generation ethnics, the children of the "New Immigrants" of the turn of the century.

And in all of these neighborhoods, dense kinship networks and well-established ethnic religious and social institutions were salient features. "Three of every four families in the Polish Hill district," for instance, "and 80 percent in the South Side neighborhood were first- or second-generation Polish. The two major streets in each neighborhood were more than four-fifths Polish, and the proportion exceeded 90 percent on several streets in each district. Several generations of blood relatives occupied many of the homes. One interviewee, Frank K., told of eight related families all living in the six-block Polish Hill area. On the South Side, as one respondent recalled, 'nearly every family on Mission, Josephine, Leticoe and Kosciusko Streets were Polish. The Wieczorkowskis owned the pharmacy and the Sorocyznskis and the Krismalskis ran grocery stores.'" Meanwhile, in Bloomfield, "Italians now constituted 70 percent of the population. Here, too, kin chains seemed to prevail . . . 34 Donatelli families and 38 Sciullos lived in this six-block area," while East Liberty was also 70 percent Italian.[92]

Within these tenacious ethnic enclaves, rituals, traditions, and beliefs from a previous existence persisted. "Migration to another country," Herbert Gutman observed, speaking of rural European immigrants to the urban centers of industrializing America, " . . . tested but did not shatter what the anthropologist Clifford Geertz has described as primordial (as contrasted to civic) attachments, 'the "assumed" givens . . . of social existence: immediate contiguity and kin connections mainly, but beyond them, the givenness that stems from being born into a particular religious community, speaking a particular language, and following particular social patterns.' Tough familial and kin ties made possible the transmission and adaptation of European working-class cultural patterns and beliefs to industrializing America."[93]

Thus, as in the Old Country, so in the New, where the myriad ethnic enclaves replicated traditional life in which the old-style family model was paramount. As Pittsburgh social workers of the 1930s noted, "In a peasant community most of the families are likely to be related by blood or marriage. The position and satisfaction of each member depends on the strength and property of his family group . . . Each member almost from infancy contributes his labor to the family's good . . . Innumerable records of peasant emigration illustrate the fact that in the communities where emigration becomes a tradition the departure of the individual is less often an assertion of an individualistic will than a part of a family plan through which to solve its problem of poverty . . . In other words, life is corporate, and the corporation is the family. At the head of each family is the father, a sovereign both in rights and in responsibilities."[94]

The little urban villages which the transplanted European peasants founded in the Steel Valley quickly developed a close-knit institutional foundation which served to tie the villagers even more tightly together. As the Italians from Cercemaggiore settled in Greensburg, for instance, they quickly founded a fraternal society, the Hilltop Club. This was followed in 1910 by Our Lady of Grace Church, dedicated to the village's patron saint, La Madonna Della Libera, reputed to have saved Cercemaggiore from destruction at the hands of the Eastern Roman Emperor Constantine in 663 A. D.[95]

Thus, as contemporary observers Philip Klein and his colleagues noted in the 1930s, "Wherever a considerable aggregation of families having the same nationality background succeeds in establishing their homes, there a 'nationality community' has sprung up. Italian, Greek, Polish, whatever the group may be, if it has any social vitality and economic security, its life finds expression in a series of enterprises, individual and corporate, which serve its particular needs—churches, parochial schools, lodges, newspapers, stores—conducted in the language and according to the traditional demands of each group. By means of innumerable interrelations between its members and functionaries such a community develops a coherent and characteristic life of its own."[96] Illustrative of merely one example of such ethnic enterprises, as late as 1940 there were still thirty-eight foreign language newspapers published in Pittsburgh.[97]

The ethnic enclaves thus provided almost everything a person required, from cradle to grave, making most travel outside the neighborhood unnecessary. One Polish resident of the Lawrenceville neighborhood recalled that, in the 1920s, "Most of us never were out of Lawrenceville."[98] The same was true of all the other ethnic groups of Pittsburgh. Many of the Croatians who immigrated to Pittsburgh, for example, came from Jastrebarsko, which residents affectionately called "Jaska," a small town about twenty miles southwest of Zagreb, Croatia. They settled along East Ohio Street in what was once Allegheny City, but which became known as the North Side after it was annexed by a growing Pittsburgh. There, they recreated their homeland and called it "Mala Jaska"—"Little Jaska." Elsie Yuratovich, who grew up there, recalled that, "It used to be like a little Croatian town at one time." And there was never any need to leave it for any reason because, "We had everything in Mala Jaska."[99]

"In those days," John Casciato likewise told me, speaking of Italian Oakland, "everyone stayed in their own neighborhoods. You born in Oakland, East Liberty—you *stayed* in Oakland, East Liberty."[100]

This pattern wasn't just confined to "those days," however. I moved to Pittsburgh in 1978 and was impressed by how "parochial" Pittsburghers seemed to be. While I travelled to all Pittsburgh neighborhoods, I met many natives who had literally never once left the South Side, the North Side, Polish Hill, Lawrenceville, Bloomfield, or Oakland, and who had no idea how to physically get from one neighborhood to another.

At that time I worked as the editor of a small newspaper located in Pittsburgh's Squirrel Hill neighborhood. At one point we needed to hire a new typesetter. We finally found one who, based on her resume and a phone conversation, seemed perfect. Then she asked our location. After I told her we were in Squirrel Hill, she said she couldn't take the job. The reason was that she'd never been to Squirrel Hill. "I can't go anywhere I've never been before," she told me. We finally hired another typesetter who, for the first time in her life, bravely ventured out of Oakland, only about a thirty- to forty-minute walk away (much less by car or bus), to take the job.

The Bonds of Brotherhood

In many of Pittsburgh's ethnic enclaves, the fraternal lodge played a central role. Many of the lodges began as mutual aid societies in which members contributed a few pennies each week out of their paychecks to establish loan or burial funds.

As an observer noted in the 1930s, "These halls are found in every community in Allegheny County where nationality groups live in sufficient numbers to be able to finance the enterprise. As community centers of foreign nationality life these nationality halls are of great importance."[101]

These "community centers" usually held small libraries where one could read the latest newspaper in one's native language, either local or imported; pool rooms where one could engage in friendly games; and bars, where one could drink among compatriots. The hall of the Beneficial Society of North Italy, which the Italians of Pittsburgh's East Liberty neighborhood founded in 1930, was perhaps typical. "It had a dance floor, bar, kitchen and bowling alleys, and a bocce court out back. It was, in many ways, a lot like the small-town clubs in Italy, where members would go to dance and play card games like briscola and scopa."[102]

These halls were, noted the above observer, places where the members could, "feel free from the inhibiting presence of superior-feeling and authoritative Americans." Often they juxtaposed a romanticized nostalgia for the Old Country with a stark reminder of what the members faced in a hostile America. In a Czechoslovak hall in Tarentum, near Pittsburgh, a mural painted on one wall portrayed "a towering feudal castle, a peasant boy and girl on a village street, and a legendary meeting of a knight and the virgin." On the other wall, "a river scene with a 'No hunting, no fishing' sign suggests that the locale is American."[103]

These local fraternal halls and societies slowly joined with similar groups of the same ethnicity in other localities to form a network which linked them to a nationwide community of their ethnicity. Pittsburgh was a national center of such webs, with seventeen ethnic organizations—such as the Polish Falcons, the Croatian Fraternal Union and the American Hungarian Social Association— making the city their national headquarters as late at the 1980s.[104] Indeed, the Croatian Fraternal Union, founded on East Ohio Street in "Mala Jaska" in 1894, was still in the Pittsburgh area in 2000 and boasted a membership of 100,000 in America and Canada.[105]

And, although initially very parochial, the reach of these fraternal societies gradually became more inclusive. Thus, for instance, the National Slovak Society was founded in Pittsburgh in 1890 and welcomed all Slovaks, no matter if they were Catholics, Protestants, or even Freemasons, deemed a suspicious group by many at the time. By 1940 there were almost three million members in such fraternal societies nationwide, representing twenty-five different nationality groups in 32,000 local branches.[106]

The Italians of Oakland founded their own fraternal society, the San Lorenzo di Gamberale Mutual Benefit Association, in Panther Hollow, where they originally settled. Significantly, the year was 1914, when their community, like others throughout the Steel Valley, was beginning to settle into a more permanent neighborhood. At that time, Panther Hollow resident John Casciato told me, "The Club was the only game in town." Among other things, "There was a lot of gambling going on at the San Lorenzo Hall. The men played brisque, a card game. It caused a lot of hollering and fighting."[107]

The fraternal hall was, as the phrase itself implies, "A male bastion," Casciato said. Women were not allowed as members. Such was the case everywhere. Mary Jane Carosone, age eighty-two in 1999, who grew up in the mostly Italian coal mining town of Morgan in southwestern Allegheny County, recalled that, "The men went to the Italian Club, and the women stayed home and watched the kids."[108]

As the decades passed, the Oakland Italian community grew more populous and, in 1938, it built a new and larger fraternal hall for the Association. By this time the Italians had climbed up out of the Hollow to spread into Oakland proper, so the new hall was built above the Hollow, but on its edge, at the junction of Dawson and Bouquet Streets. With its highly religious membership, the Association did not rival the churches of the community, but complemented them. Its very name was that of a patron saint. Many of its festivals, such as the annual August 10th street parade of the statue of San Lorenzo on the saint's day, served not only to remind the community of their common village of origin, but also of their common religious faith, thus reinforcing their cultural solidarity.

The annual August 10th San Lorenzo Festival of Oakland's Italians gradually came to be a community-wide celebration, although for most of its existence it was a strictly Panther Hollow Italian celebration. Hollow residents John Casciato and Camilla Caliendo recalled that the saint's day was the occasion of a huge festival with bands, dancing, and a big fireworks display. The San Lorenzo Hall was decorated with both the American and Italian flags. All the girls between eleven- and thirteen-years-of-age carried donation boxes and the girl who collected the most money won a trophy. Meanwhile, all the men concentrated on playing bocce ball. By the 1930s the Pittsburgh Chief of Police and the mayor of Pittsburgh made a point of being part of the festivities.[109]

Although its membership rolls have shrank with the passage of time, the San Lorenzo di Gamberale fraternal society was still a focus of the community's social life in the 1990s when it had 180 enrolled members and the San Lorenzo Festival was still celebrated. The major event of the celebration was the saint's parade through the streets of South Oakland. Originally the marchers carried a banner with a picture of the saint. However, in the mid-Sixties ("Had to be '65 or '66," John Casciato told me, "because I marched beside it in uniform as a cop before I retired.") the fraternal society acquired a statue of the saint, which it still owns. "Naturally," Casciato said, "it had to come over from Italy to be any good."[110]

Each August 10th the San Lorenzo Association paraded this statue of its patron saint through the streets of Oakland behind aging women dressed in ethnic costumes and carrying water jars on their heads. In the 1980s, I watched the men bear the statue of San Lorenzo in a litter on their shoulders. By the 1990s, as the men got older, San Lorenzo rode in the back of a pickup truck, but the women still preceded the saint in their colorful costumes while marching bands from local schools still followed the saint.

And all residents and on-lookers, not just Italians, were welcome to participate in the ritual by, for example, pinning dollar bills on streamers flowing from the saint, as I did myself. Such devotion was guaranteed to result in prosperity during the coming year.

Oakland's San Lorenzo Festival was similar to such festivals in all other Pittsburgh-area Italian communities. For instance, all the Italians of nearby McKees Rocks came from the village of Villeta Barrela and they honored St. Barbara, their village's "patroness" saint. As recently as the Columbus Day Parade of 2000 they paraded a ten-foot-tall likeness of St. Barbara through the streets of Pittsburgh in what was, by then, a community-wide celebration of Italian culture.[111]

On July 2, the Italians of Greensburg, all from the village of Cercemaggiore, near Rome, still honor their patron saint, La Madonna Della Libera, with a special Mass and banquet in her honor.[112]

The Italians of the steel town of Aliquippa, immigrants from the village of Patrica, honored San Rocco, their own patron saint. Aliquippa began to develop a more stable community in the 1920s and, consequently, began to recreate the rituals of the "Old Country." In 1925 they started the San Rocco festival. As time passed, however, and ethnic boundaries within the working class became attenuated, the San Rocco festival expanded to include other ethnic groups. Eventually, the San Rocco festival became a generalized celebration of the ethic heritage of the vast majority of Aliquippa's population. By the post-World War II years, the San Rocco Festival had thus become a major element in Aliquippa's social life in which even non-Italians participated.[113]

Such religious festivals were replicated in every Italian community across America. Every July throughout the 1930s, for example, the large Italian community in New York's Harlem celebrated the festival of Our Lady of Mt. Carmel with a huge parade of brass bands, clergy, and barefoot penitents carrying a statue of the Virgin. As the procession wound through the streets, people in the crowd gave up donations, which were pinned to streamers on the Madonna.[114]

A Churched Community

As illustrated by the devotion ethnic communities gave to such religious rituals, the church, either Roman Catholic or Orthodox, was even more important than the fraternal society. The Pittsburgh region had the largest Croatian and Slovak populations in the world outside of the Balkans. Not surprisingly, these Slavic populations usually built churches even before fraternal halls. Indeed, America's first Croatian Catholic church, St. Nicholas, the "Mother Croatian Parish," was founded in 1894 on Pittsburgh's East Ohio Street in "Mala Jaska."

Pittsburgh was also the home of America's third largest Polish community. Further, "By the 1930s Pittsburgh ranked fifth in the United States in the percentage of its population that was Catholic (35 percent) and was the seventh largest diocese in the American church."[115] For all of these populations—Croatian, Slovak, Polish, Italian, and so on—the church had been a primary focus of their lives in the small rural villages from whence they came. It was no different in the small urban villages they transplanted to Pittsburgh.

Thus, as Philip Klein and others noted when they studied Pittsburgh in the

1930s, "Among nationality groups in whose tradition the Church has played an important role the Church is likely to be transplanted with great strength and to afford a channel of cultural continuity . . . Among the Greeks, the Poles, the Russians, and to a large extent among the Slovaks, the Church becomes a center of community life, an expression of deep-rooted cultural form, as well as of religious practices. It is likely to draw to itself functions which in the country of origin belonged to the political community. Support of the Church is imposed on all members as a tax, which may be quite heavy. Within the parish societies the activities may vary greatly in value, but at best they conserve habits of cooperation and mutual responsibility . . . Many of the Catholic churches maintain parochial schools. In others a weekly language school is provided to instruct the children in the mother tongue of their parents, thus contributing to the safeguarding of family solidarity."[116]

The church, therefore, was like another family, a home away from home. "Most of them [Poles] lived around their own churches," recalled Pittsburgh worker Joe Rudiak of the 1920s and 1930s. "[They] tried to get as close as possible to their social activities. And the church was part of their social activity." Another Pole, Ray Czachowski, remembered that, "My parents were both Roman Catholics, very staunch Catholics, very strict Catholics. Church was almost a second home to us. I mean we never missed a novena or any service at all. That was it. There were no questions asked. You just went."[117]

Indeed, sometimes the family connection to the church was literal. Novelist and former police officer Joseph Wambaugh, a native of East Pittsburgh, attended the local Catholic St. William's School and recalled that, "My fifth-grade teacher, Sister Blandina, was my mother's first cousin."[118]

A Shop on Every Corner

In addition their churches and fraternal societies, there were many institutions of a commercial nature which also served to knit ethnic working class communities together. Panther Hollow had its own grocery store, candy stores, two banks, and the DiNardo Construction Co., where many of the men worked.

Cobbler Mike Citriniti recalled that when he first came to Oakland from Calabria, in 1928, the neighborhood was a hive of activity. "They used to walk up and down the streets of Oakland and in and out of my shop," he said. On his short block of Semple Street, between Bates Street and Cable Place (the length of which I walked in one or two minutes), there were three butcher shops, a barber shop, a hardware store, and a tailor. None of those shops exist today. "This area is now full of students," Mike said, "but it used to be family. They used to raise their families in Oakland and die in Oakland."[119]

Eleanor Gedunsky Kosterlitz recalls growing up in the 1930s and 1940s in the section of South Oakland along Bates Street between the Boulevard of the Allies and the Monongahela River, where the huge Jones & Laughlin steel mill was located. "There were Polish, Slavic, Hungarian, and Italian families in our neighborhood," she said. "At that time, we were the only Jewish family living on Bates Street . . . My parents, Anna and Isadore (Osher) Gedunsky, owned and operated Gedunsky's Meat Market on Bates Street. Other businesses included Martin Fried's Market, Fred Weinberger's Grocery, Joe Vilella's shoemaker shop, Lasek's Bar, Joe Cohen's dry goods store and Duga's candy store . . . Most of the men worked at J & L Steel. They'd frequent Lasek's or Frank's bar for the card games and the booze. On Sundays, they spent time at St. Michael's Hall, a Polish social club, for more of the same. Our community shared good times and bad. Everyone took care of one another."[120]

Twenty years later, in the 1950s, many of these Bates Street institutions were still there—or had been replaced by similar businesses. Along adjacent Niagara Street there was Gene's Grocery, Leon's Grocery, Wise's Grocery, a meat and fish store, a small discount store, a tailor, and, on the corner of Craft Avenue and the Boulevard, S & B Sandwich Shop. And there was still St. Michael's Hall, the Polish dance hall and drinking club, which "has remained a strong Polish association over the years."[121]

Bars, such as Lasek's and Frank's, were also essential institutions helping to tie the communities together. In addition to Lasek's and Frank's, two other long-lived South Oakland taverns were the Home Plate and the Irish Club. The Home Plate was located on corner of Bouquet and Sennott Streets across from the entrance to Forbes Field, the home stadium of the Pittsburgh Pirates baseball team. It was later purchased by the adjacent University of Pittsburgh and was used for several years as a small theatrical space, where I attended plays. Then the university demolished it to make a parking lot.

Although such taverns began by catering to one ethnicity, over time they began to serve as bridges to other ethnic groups, as all were welcome regardless of ethnicity. Oakland's Irish Club was one such. As its name implies, it was owned by an Irish fraternal society, The Ancient Order of Hibernians. It was located on Oakland Avenue and comprised a large third-floor loft filled with many small square tables and with large windows overlooking Oakland. A long bar filled one side of the space and a small three-piece band often filled the dance floor. "But, it was more than a bar," recalled Lester Goran, a Jew who grew up in Oakland in the 1930s. "It was a kind of unofficial community center, and you were just as likely to find a grandmother or a baby in a stroller as you were to find young men and women courting romance. It was nothing to see three generations at one table. Everyone came to the Irish Club, even neighborhood Jews whose memberships were strictly social."[122]

****

Observers have noted that a strong and coherent sense of community is a necessary prerequisite for political protest.[123] This prerequisite emerged in Pittsburgh, and even more especially in the surrounding mill towns, in the early twentieth century. The people of this industrial heartland were not strangers to each other, drifting through a strange world. They existed in an all-embracing ethnic communal culture in which they were born together, raised together, worked together, worshiped together, played together, and married each other. They lived and they died together. They shared the same values and world-views, hopes, fears, and aspirations. Thus the roots of solidarity grew deep down into the common soil from which working class protest emerged in the 1930s.

The Making of a Working Class

But these people had not always been politically aroused, even as the Great Depression began. Oppression and hard times do not automatically breed revolt. Indeed, the initial response to the onset of the Depression in 1929 by the people who would later make up the new electorate of the Thirties had been political apathy. "Turnout did not increase much in the 1930 and 1932 elections," we are told. "[P]residential turnout in 1932 was 0.9 percentage points below the 1928 level . . . The experience of extreme deprivation and its accompanying perceptions of dissatisfaction are not by themselves sufficient causes of collective political action. To mobilize discontented citizens as an effective political force, these subjectively stressful conditions must be politicized. Individuals have to perceive them both as conditions shared by others and for which government action is somehow relevant."[124]

Something, then, politicized the desperate conditions of the new electorate. Something happened to transform this economically devastated, but as yet politically apathetic, population into an electoral force which changed the face of American politics. Somehow, these dispossessed millions were mobilized into the Democratic Party in the years after 1932 to express their class interests at the ballot box, as well as on the picket line.

But this development was not inevitable. Lubell argued, for example, that this new class conscious constituency of urban, working class immigrant children, coming of age and coming into its own in the 1930s (seven million twenty-one-year-old first-time voters in 1936 alone), with its political loyalty still to be won and cemented, was not yet active and was not yet firmly Democratic. And, indeed, if the inchoate political loyalty of the newly arrived, class conscious, urban working class was up for grabs, it was problematic whether the Democrats, or perhaps some labor or third party movement, would secure and hold it.

How, then, was America's ethnic working class politically mobilized and then won and held for the Democrats? Allegheny County, comprising Pittsburgh and the small mill towns surrounding it, is an appropriate place to look at how this happened. In the 1930s, this industrial heartland changed from a Republican to a Democratic stronghold and has remained so ever since, with a two-to-one Democratic over Republican voter registration even as late as 2000. What kind of changes did the ethnic enclaves of this region go through to make them the wellsprings of revolt?

E Pluribus Unum

It seems that an obvious lesson to be learned from the preceding discussion of Steel Valley peasants and their insular ethnic enclaves is that stolid conservatism and fatalistic inertia toward the larger world surely dominated them, severely limiting any kind of cross-ethnic working class solidarity. Additionally, inter-ethnic antagonisms must have reduced the chances that workers of different ethnicities would discover any larger class solidarity between themselves. "The Pole and the Lithuanian have nothing in common," wrote one local social observer of the time, "and each of them despises the Slovak."[125]

Such, indeed, have been the lessons some historians have learned. John Bodnar, for instance, looked at the various groups and declared that, "The one characteristic they did share was their tendency to be circumscribed, cut off from social and political influences, from those of higher social rank and even from other workers."[126] Because of this, he argued, such communities were passive, inert, and politically conservative.

And yet other observers have found evidence of just the opposite tendency. Such, for example, is the case of the mostly Southern and Eastern European coal miners of Windber in Southwestern Pennsylvania's Somerset County. Divided, as elsewhere, by ethnicity, language, culture and religion, they nevertheless united in cross-ethnic class solidarity and won significant workplace victories through major strikes in 1906, 1922, and 1927.[127]

Indeed, Bodnar himself describes an emerging pan-ethnic class consciousness in the very ethnic enclaves he claims were isolated, conservative, and inward-directed. "Economic exploitation," he reports, "forced immigrants to coalesce around an emerging consciousness which was a blend of working-class status and heightened ethnic identity. Slavs were killed in a united labor protest at Lattimer, Pennsylvania, in 1897. The event evoked widespread criticism in the Slavic press against American officials who fired upon the striking miners. Croatians in Chicago contributed substantially to fellow Croats who struck mines in West Virginia, Colorado, and Pennsylvania."[128]

Even further, "While the peculiar constellation of symbolic traits which derived from Europe, such as religion and ethnic identification, gave the appearance of vast ethnic differences among Slavs, on a structured level the behavior of all Slavic peasants in America was remarkably similar and revealed an ability to integrate their culture with an emerging working-class consciousness."[129]

And, indeed, by the 1930s a pervasive working class consciousness was widespread in America. Although scientific public opinion sampling does not exist for the early Thirties, once it began it clearly identified such "class consciousness." Thus, a University of Chicago survey in the spring of 1936, which interviewed 600 adults in their Chicago homes, found deep suspicion of the "wealthy" among Chicago's lower classes. Fully 80 percent of the men in the "Lower" income category felt that businessmen and people of wealth had too much influence in running the affairs of the nation. In summary, the surveyors found that, "The evidence points clearly to the existence of important attitude differences among income classes."[130]

These "class conscious" attitudes also found expression in class polarized political preferences. For instance, in a May 12, 1940 survey by the American Institute of Public Opinion the question was asked, "If President Roosevelt runs for a third term on the Democratic ticket against Thomas E. Dewey on the Republican ticket, which one would you prefer?" Of those classified as "Upper Income," 69 percent preferred Dewey. Just as starkly, 66 percent of those classified as "Lower Income" and 74 percent of those classified as "Reliefers" preferred Roosevelt.[131]

Such class consciousness and political partisanship was also evident among the Italians of Panther Hollow. "The Republicans never did anything for the little people, for the little class," Camilla Caliendo told me. Her cousin, John Casciato, agreed. "The Republicans are too rich for me," he said. "They're a rich man's party. They're mean people. They don't give a damn for anybody."[132]

Perhaps the reason Bodnar doesn't give full weight to such evident class consciousness is because he gives insufficient weight to the tremendous political power the very features of the tight-knit ethnic enclaves he highlights gave to workers. For this reason, he is unable to adequately explain what happened in the 1930s when these self-contained ethnic enclaves became the bases from which workers transformed American society and politics.

True, he does acknowledge that, "The strong community and workplace ties of the enclave actually facilitated the unionization and organization drives *when they emerged full-blown.* Any reluctance on the part of an individual worker toward organization was usually overcome by the irresistible pressure brought to bear by friends and peers working in the same department."[133]

However, Bodnar's thesis is incapable of explaining how these very same drives "emerged full-blown" from the enclaves, especially since he also argues that the unionization drives of the Thirties *did* emerge from grassroots activists within the enclaves, and not from far-away leaders like John L. Lewis. Somehow, in Bodnar's presentation, *they just happened!* "There was no drive on among the nationality people," he quotes Joe Rudiak as saying, "no drive on by the politicians. You've got to understand that they didn't want these people to vote in the first place. The companies controlled the towns. They controlled the courthouse. They controlled the police. They controlled the state police, the coal mine police . . . So about 1934 was when people would start to talk about voting. 'Let's change the system. Let's change.'"[134]

But why did these supposedly insular ethnics suddenly, out of the blue, begin saying, around 1934, "Let's change the system"? Obviously, by 1934 something dramatic had happened to workers' political consciousness in the ethnic enclaves so that these "powerless" and apathetic people in their "circumscribed worlds" suddenly began saying to each other, "Let's change the system." Bodnar guesses that the reason political and social change emerged from the enclaves in the early Thirties was because the Great Depression was an unprecedented attack upon the economic security of the enclave—so the workers mobilized to rectify the situation.

But this is naive. Oppression is universal and revolt is rare. Hard times do not lead automatically to collective resistance. Indeed, revolutions, Crane Brinton tells us, are not born of despair and total impoverishment. Rather, "Revolutions are born of hope, and their philosophies are formally optimistic ... 'Untouchables' very rarely revolt against a God-given aristocracy."[135]

Further, the specific evidence does not support Bodnar's simplistic explanation. In the years immediately following the onset of the Depression, from 1929 on, there was a significant *decrease* in voter turnout, especially among the ethnic working class. Additionally, the years 1929 to 1933 were the absolute nadir of the Depression, as things continually worsened, and yet worker mobilization at the workplace, as well as working class voter turnout, did not begin to take off until 1934 and later, when things were actually improving economically.

Thus, Bodnar's explanation for worker activism does not fit the facts of the 1930s. His description of a conservative and inert immigrant community does not even explain the "Hunky" explosion of the Great Steel Strike of 1919.

The basic problem with Bodnar's view of the static ethnic enclaves is that his interpretation of them is, itself, static. The Old World peasant traditions he describes are not the whole story. No culture anywhere at any time is completely static. Cultures are always in a process of development and change. Indeed, such was already happening to peasant communities in Southern and Eastern Europe.

And, just as these communities were being transformed in the Old World, they were being transformed in the New. Thus, the seemingly contradictory patterns Bodnar discovers in ethnic communities are themselves evidence of culture in transition. These communities were not exact replicas of the Old World transplanted to the New. America was transforming them into a combination of the two, with newly emerging characteristics co-existing with remnants of the old, as even contemporary observers noted. The " . . . isolated village life is fast disappearing," we are told, "as a result of radio, automobile, and other modern facilities."[136] It's not, therefore, that Bodnar was wrong in what he saw. Rather, he didn't give full weight to the changes taking place in the communities he studied.

For example, it is evident that, besides being imbued with the family ethos, these ethnic communities were also imbued with the ethos of American democracy. They hungered for "American rights" for decades before they were able to gain them in the Thirties. This, then, was that other necessary leg upon which resistance rested, the ideology which permeated these ethnic enclaves and eventually mobilized them to political revolt.

It is also evident, however, that they were indeed powerless to implement this ideology of "American rights" in the decades before the 1930s, though the Great Steel Strike of 1919 was a major effort in this direction. But, by the 1930s, circumstances had fundamentally changed and Bodnar's description of the workers' world falters at this point. By 1934 the workers were no longer powerless, as, indeed, they themselves were beginning to realize. By 1934, the workers' world had been transformed and was now a world of hope—and their ethnic enclaves had become their sources of power.

From Family to Class

What had changed were a number of developments which, working together, changed the "conservative" negatives of the ethnic enclaves into positives. None of these were sufficient unto themselves, but as a constellation of factors working together, they brought about the pan-ethnic class consciousness of blue collar workers that changed American politics in the Thirties.

The first was simply the fact that these ethnic enclaves existed at all. Collective action does not come out of atomized or transient communities. It comes out of strong and stable communities, such as these ethnic enclaves. They did not exist in their coherent form before 1920. In most of America they did not exist after 1960. Thus, far from being a basic on-going fact of American history, they were instead a mere forty-year phenomenon. But, while they lasted, they transformed America.

Second, there was the matter of numbers. Between 1890 and 1910 approximately 14 percent of the total American population was foreign-born. Meanwhile, their second generation children, who had accounted for 14.8 percent of the population in 1870 (the first time the census took note of them), grew to 21.5 percent of the total by 1920. By 1930 the foreign-born population and their children, disproportionately concentrated in the large cities of the Northeast, accounted for about a third of all Americans.[137] Thus, by the 1930s an urban demographic revolution had taken place which transformed America from a largely rural WASP nation into an urban nation with a huge "immigrant" component. Once this component was politically mobilized, its impact was dramatic.

Third, there was the homogenizing influence of industrialization itself. Industrialization created a central place of work where most of one's fellow workers, regardless of ethnicity, were laboring under the same conditions you were. Even as early as 1910, for example, a third of all manufacturing workers in Pittsburgh labored in open hearth furnaces and rolling mills.[138] The same was true of the outlying industrial communities of Allegheny County. Lydia Nemanich, age seventy-six in 1999, recalled of life in coal mining town of Morgan, "Everybody was a miner. It was just a way of life."[139]

Fourth, there was the homogenizing influence of similar lifestyles. Even as late as the 1950s, the largely blue collar Pittsburgh neighborhood of Lawrenceville retained much of this quality, as a Polish Lawrenceville native recalled in a poem: "We didn't sit on decks behind our houses./ We sat on stoops after dinner;/ Played on the street;/ Talked with the neighbors,/ whether we liked them or not./ This was the city—my neighborhood./ Everybody's dad worked in the mills./ Hepenstall. American Bridge./ They always stopped in one of the bars after work./ Everybody knew what everyone else was doing./ Dad . . . mom, they always knew."[140]

More specifically, whether one was Polish, Italian, Ukrainian, Croatian, or Hungarian, one came from a large family in which gender roles were rigidly and similarly defined. The man worked in the mill, where his sons soon joined him, and the woman stayed home and took care of the family and, in many cases, the lodgers. "At the beginning of the twentieth century," we are told, "for women to work for wages outside the home was socially acceptable only for those white married women who had to supplement their family income or for women who were their family's sole support . . . [Even compared to other Midwestern industrial cities] Women in Pittsburgh had fewer options for wage earning and fewer opportunities for civic leadership. In this sense the stereotype of Pittsburgh as a man's town had some relative meaning."[141]

Others have confirmed this conclusion. Thus, we find, for instance, that there is little evidence of Polish or Italian women in Pittsburgh leaving their kitchens and entering the public labor force until the 1950s.[142] Indeed, from 1930 to 1960, "Female offspring were . . . likely to remain in the family home well into adulthood. Few daughters of either Poles or Italians held steady jobs outside the home although many left school at age 14 or 15. Most remained in the parental home until marriage, assisting with the required domestic tasks."[143]

Of course, Old World peasant stereotypes of appropriate gender roles played a large part in this division, but another factor was the great reliance of the Pittsburgh region on male-dominated heavy industry, which left few other job opportunities for women outside the home. Thus, we find that by 1910 only 10 percent of manufacturing workers were women.[144]

If women did work outside the home—usually young and unmarried women—we find that, in keeping with gender expectations, "the most important field of employment for women in Pittsburgh, as elsewhere, was private and public housekeeping. In 1910, 21,147 (41 percent) of the 51,678 women in the Pittsburgh labor force earned their livelihoods as servants, waitresses, charwomen, cleaners, porters, housekeepers, or stewardesses."[145]

Even so, while these occupations would have kept young working women out of the organized labor movement, nevertheless there is evidence that they, as well as their stay-at-home married sisters, became class conscious. From the labor wars in Homestead in 1889 and 1892 to the 1919 steel strike and beyond there is evidence they "strongly defended the rights of organized labor and distinguished themselves as unusually militant during numerous labor conflicts."[146]

The fifth, and perhaps most important, development is that of generational change. It was not primarily the immigrants themselves who fundamentally restructured America in the Thirties. There weren't enough of them. In addition, they were not yet fully assimilated into the culture and society. They may not have been voting citizens, they may not have spoken the language, they may not have identified sufficiently with the cultural symbols and values of the society in which they found themselves.

But their children were another matter. Their children were voting citizens by birth. Regardless of ethnic background they spoke English as the natives they were. And they were immersed in the culture and values of the society in which they came of age. All of this served to mute the intense ethnic rivalry of their parents and bring the children to a common understanding of their status. These, then, the children of the immigrants, are the ones who brought about the restructuring of America.

Sixth, there was the common political oppression that ethnics faced because of their nationality, their religion, their language, their culture—all of which, regardless of how different they may have been from each other, were at odds with the dominant WASP culture.

Seventh, there was, indeed, the economic impact of the Great Depression itself. Regardless of ethnic background, all blue collar workers felt this blow to their economic security.

Next, as contemporary investigators noted, "The growth of labor unions has also promoted a sense of solidarity."[147] This was especially true of CIO unionization after 1935 with its ethos of egalitarianism and class solidarity regardless of ethnicity.

Finally, there was the simple fact that virtually everyone was white. Regardless of ethnic background, race was something all had in common. America was the "whitest" it's ever been during the decade of the 1930s. Blacks, who accounted for 25 percent of the total population at the time of the first census in 1790, declined to their lowest population percentage ever in the Thirties, accounting for only 9.7 percent of the total (three-fourths of whom lived in the South) in both the 1930 and 1940 censuses.[148] In Pennsylvania, the ratio was less than half that, with blacks representing only 4.5 percent of the total population in 1930, with more than half of that 4.5 percent located in Philadelphia.[149]

And, while Pittsburgh had the second largest concentration of blacks in the state (55,000 compared to Philadelphia's 220,000—mostly in their own enclaves, such as the Hill District), the surrounding steel towns were still largely white. The racial composition of Ambridge, for instance, was typical of Steel Valley towns. As late as 1950 there were only 199 blacks in the town of 16,429 people, a mere 1.2 percent of the whole.[150]

Thus, an overlap of identities strengthened "New Immigrant" loyalties to each other. In Pittsburgh, and even more especially in the surrounding mill towns, "Working people lived together in overwhelmingly working-class neighborhoods where they could see the physical similarities in their circumstances."[151]

All of these common life experiences helped create a sense of pan-ethnic community. In the case of the Depression Era Steel Valley, family loyalties, community loyalties, ethnic loyalties, workplace loyalties, and political loyalties went hand-in-hand. The mutualistic ethos of family solidarity (reinforced by the "family economy" where everyone had to work together if the family were to survive) and neighborhood solidarity had mutated into an identification with others who were not of one's family, neighborhood, or ethnicity—indeed, were strangers—but with whom one nevertheless felt a sense of solidarity.

This mutualistic sense of solidarity with strangers could sometimes inspire amazing acts of self-sacrifice. The actions of Mitchell Paige are a case in point. Mitchell Paige was born and raised in the Pittsburgh suburb of Charleroi, the son of a railroad worker who barely made enough to support the family. In 1936, at age eighteen, he joined the Marines to escape Charleroi. Six years later he found himself in command of a thirty-two-man platoon as a sergeant protecting the strategic Henderson air field on the South Pacific island of Guadalcanal. On October 26, 1942, his platoon came under attack by a force of 1,000 Japanese soldiers. The resulting battle left every Marine except Paige dead or incapacitated with wounds. Paige, wounded himself from shrapnel and Japanese bayonets, continued fighting alone, leaping from blazing machine gun to blazing machine gun as each one overheated and jammed in turn. When reinforcements finally arrived, Paige led them in a bayonet charge which secured Henderson Field. The bodies of 920 Japanese soldiers were counted around his platoon's position. Mitchell Paige was awarded the Congressional Medal of Honor and became a Marine Corps legend. Even as late as the 1990s he served as the model for the Hasbro toy company's G. I. Joe action figure.

What made Pittsburgh boy Mitchell Paige do this? How do we account for such bravery? Paige himself deflected such questions by saying that his Medal of Honor really belongs to thirty-three men, every one of the Marines in his unit. Men of his place and generation, he said, naturally sacrificed for others. Millions of them went to war without complaint, giving up jobs, families, their lives for a greater good. "We looked beyond personal interests," he said, "and we looked out for other people and other countries that needed help."[152]

Perhaps it was not necessary to be raised the son of a Pittsburgh railroad worker in the 1930s to do what Mitchell Paige did on Guadalcanal—but there were thousands of Pittsburgh workers who would have completely understood his reasons for doing it. These workers, regardless of ethnic background, tended to think the same way

And, in the voting booth, these workers also voted the same way. Murals of Roosevelt were on the walls of their fraternal and union halls and Roosevelt was on their minds on Election Day. Mike Royko, a Chicago newspaperman who grew up in the Thirties, once described how such loyalties were reinforced in his parents' neighborhood bar and how they came to be identified with Roosevelt and the Democrats. "From the day the place opened," he said, "one work of art was tacked to the wall of the Blue Sky Lounge on Milwaukee Avenue in Chicago—a huge portrait of President Franklin Delano Roosevelt. It had been donated to the tavern's owners—my parents—by a noted patron of the arts, Stanley the Mooch, who was an assistant precinct captain. The same portrait hung in hundreds of taverns in the city's working-class neighborhoods, and this was not insignificant exposure . . . the picture was always there. And even the most addled barfly wouldn't have dreamed of suggesting that FDR was anything less than a living god. Not if he didn't want to be knocked off the bar stool.

"To the patrons of the Blue Sky . . . politics was quite simple. First, Republicans were all rich, greedy, no-good WASP bastards who lived in suburban Lake Forest and owned the factories where the neighborhood guys sweated in low-paying jobs. But Democrats were all hard-working, two-fisted family men. Except for Negroes, but they all lived way out on the South Side and didn't matter. So a traitor who would say anything good about a Republican, much less vote for one, was lower than our spittoons. Growing up in that political atmosphere, it was impossible not to be a Democrat."[153]

In Pittsburgh, these traditions and pressures continued with force well into the 1950s. "We became Democrats because people *told* us to be Democrats,"

John Casciato recalled. "When I was a young man, it didn't matter whether you liked the candidate or not . . . you voted Democratic, regardless." I asked John's brother, Charles, what would have happened in the 1950s if a member of their family registered as a Republican. He smacked his right fist into his left palm and said, "We'd say to him, 'You straighten up, boy, or you're in trouble!'"[154]

How all these elements came together is illustrated by developments in the Mon Valley steel town of Monessen.[155] Like so many industrial towns—from Lowell, Massachusetts, to Homestead, Pennsylvania—Monessen, the industrial capital of the Upper Monongahela Valley, was founded by industrialists seeking new industrial sites. Located on the Monongahela River about thirty miles southeast of Pittsburgh, the town was planted in 1898 as an emulator of the German industrial center, Essen. It was to be Essen on the Mon—Monessen. The two industrial giants of the town were the Page Steel and Wire Company and the Pittsburgh Steel Company, which by 1920 already covered 160 acres and stretched for 2.3 miles along the banks of the Mon River.

Like all other industrial centers in the Steel Valley, Monessen was dominated from its founding by the Republican Party (the party of the businessmen who had the capital required to found industrial corporations). And, as with all other industrial centers in the Steel Valley, this changed in the 1930s. In 1934 the town shifted overnight to the Democratic Party, which has claimed its political loyalty ever since. So stable has been Democratic dominance that one Democratic mayor, Hugo Parente, an Italian, succeeded two previous Democratic mayors of ethnic descent and served for twenty-five years, from 1946-1971.

Like all the other industrial towns of the Steel Valley, Monessen was also peppered with ethnic fraternal clubs representing virtually every nation of Southern and Eastern Europe. In addition, there was a large Finnish population, with its own constellation of clubs. Tyyne Hanninen, born in 1908 in Monessen to Finnish immigrants, recalled that, "We had a great big Finnish hall that we used to call the Finnish Temperance Hall right across the street from where I lived. And then at the other end of the block was what was called the Finnish Socialist Hall. So there was a lot of activity in both of them."[156]

And Stephen Wisyanski, president (1942-44) of the United Steelworkers (USWA) Local 1229 at Pittsburgh Steel, recalled that when the precursor Steel Workers Organizing Committee (SWOC) came to Monessen, it was "in the clubs" that the SWOC organizers signed up their members.[157] No doubt such union organizing was going on in the clubs of all the nationalities, although Stephen Zoretich, a Croatian steelworker at Pittsburgh Steel, recalled that when the SWOC organizers came to town, "a lot of times we had a meeting down at the Croatian Hall. In fact," he continued, "they [the bosses] branded us as communist down here because of that. Anybody that wanted an outside [non-company] union, they branded them as a communist then. They called the Croatian Hall communist and everything else, but it wasn't communist. It was because of the union activities."[158]

Likewise, John Czelen, president in the 1930s and 1940s of USWA Local 1391 at Page Steel and Wire, recalled that little union organizing took place in the plant itself. "Most of the talk of it was very casual inside of the plant because we were watched. A lot of it took place in clubs, taverns, on the street corners, homes."[159]

Thus, there was a large overlap between ethnic clubs and union activities, which can even be seen in the various club memberships people held. Stephen Wisyanski, for instance, USWA Local 1229 president at Pittsburgh Steel, recalled that, "I was president of the Hungarian Beneficial Club for twenty-four years. I'm a member of the Croatian Beneficial Club . . . I helped to organize the Mon Valley Association of Retired Steelworkers, I was president of that for five years. I'm president of the Holy Name Society at St. Leonard's Church."[160]

The fraternal halls—whether the Croatian Hall or the Finnish Socialist Hall—were receptive to union organizers not only because their members were all steelworkers—the steel mills were virtually the only business in town, indeed, the town's very reason for existence—but also because ethnic rivalries between the immigrants were fading among the children of the immigrants. They were coming to realize that they were all "foreigners" together, all similarly mistreated by the "Americans." Wisyanski remembered that the foremen in the plants, all "bluebloods," as he called them, referred to workers under them as, "that 'nigger' out there, or that 'Dago,' or that 'Hunky,' or that 'Wop' or 'Greek.' They weren't too interested in learning the names of their employees. They had other ways of identifying them."[161]

And, no matter what their nationality, all these "foreigners" had to be kept in their place. "There's always discrimination," Croatian Zoretich remembered. "I can't think of any incident but there was always discrimination of foreigners. Any kind of foreigner, not only Croatian, but the Slovak, the Italian, anybody that wasn't educated, there was always discrimination."[162]

And, just as the "bluebloods" saw all the Hunkies and Dagos and Wops as interchangeable "foreigners," even if these "foreigners" were born in Monessen, the "foreigners" were also learning more about each other and slowly coming to accept each other more. Italian Eduardo Furio went to work for Pittsburgh Steel in the years before World War I as a boy picking up scrap in the yard. It was a job performed by many different nationalities and, "We couldn't understand each other," he said. "They used to call me, 'You dirty dago, dirty dago, dirty dago.' And you didn't know what they were saying, but other people told me, the ones I could understand . . . When I got to know them, there was Slavish-Hungarian. All the Slavish, you know, they were called, 'hunky, hunky, hunky.' Somebody called me 'dirty dago.' [I'd yell back] 'Hey you dirty hunky.' Till we got to know each other, then the things got pacified."[163]

And, after the Great War ended, and as time went on, things seemed to get more and more pacified in Monessen, at least among the working class "foreigners." Marianna Maiolini, an Italian, recalled that the mixed neighborhood where she grew up was "Very friendly. Even today we all feel like we're brothers and sisters from the neighborhood. It was a mixture of Russians, Italians, Greeks. We had some Negro families, Hungarians, Croatians, Polish."[164]

Nick Mahalko, Sr., a Ukrainian who worked at Page Steel and Wire, grew up in a mixed Ukrainian and Italian neighborhood, "And everybody got along like one big family. And everybody was learning one another's language. And a buddy of mine—he was Italian and he learned the 'Uke' language faster than I could learn the Italian language . . . he could converse with my mother pretty good. Then we would go over to their home and play records . . . records were a big deal then, and the old player piano . . . and they would have spaghetti, which is Italian food, and wine. Any of them foods with hot sauces. And then they would come over to our home and we would have halubki and pierogi, or something. We got to eat one another's food that way and got better acquainted. We got along pretty much like one family."[165]

By the 1930s, Stephen Wisyanski, president of a Monessen SWOC local, felt the Monessen working class had at last come of age. The great steel strike of 1919 had been broken, Wisyanski said, because "there weren't enough people educated that had command of the English language to be able to put up the kind of a fight that we were able to do in '36. Because our parents couldn't—well, they could analyze the situation but they could not present the cases—did not have the ability to present the cases as their children did after they had their education. Because you take—compare anything, compare myself from fourteen years of age to thirty years of age, thirty-five years of age—you know, younger. The maturity of the working class had a big part in it."[166] The working class had indeed matured and become conscious of itself as a unified class instead of a miscellaneous collection of "foreigners." As Wisyanski said, it had come to see itself as "the working class," regardless of ethnicity.

In retrospect, it is easy to see why pan-ethnic class consciousness was so powerful in the working class at this time. When the working class was overwhelmingly white, Southern and Eastern European Orthodox-Catholic, attended the same churches and fraternal lodges, lived in tight-knit and kin-related urban ethnic villages where everybody was just like everybody else, and everybody engaged in similar industrial occupations with a few, easily identifiable, capitalist enemies thought to be oppressing all equally—it was easy to see what you had in common. It was easy to feel and act upon class solidarity with your fellow workers, who also happened to be your own kin and neighbors. The habits, life, and culture of the ethnic enclave thus became the social basis of class politics in Depression Era America.

Notes

1. George Gallup in Judah L. Graubart and Alice V. Graubart, *Decade of Destiny,* Contemporary Books, Inc.: Chicago, 1978, 302.

2. Samuel Lubell, *The Future While It Happened,* W.W. Norton & Co.: New York, 1973, 141-42.

3. David Brody, "Workers and Work in America: The New Labor History," in James B. Gardner and George Rollie Adams, Eds., *Ordinary People and Everyday Life: Perspectives on the New Social History,* The American Association for State and Local History: Nashville: Tenn, 1983, 147.

4. See his classic description of this trend in chapter 3, "The Revolt of the City," *The Future of American Politics,* Harper and Brothers: New York, 1952.

5. Lubell, *The Future While It Happened,* 29.

6. See the useful discussion of this, as well as other possibilities, in Eric Foner, "Why is There No Socialism in the United States?" *History Workshop,* No. 17, spring 1984, 57-80.

7. Of the ten largest American cities in 1930—including New York, Chicago, Philadelphia, Detroit, Los Angeles, Cleveland, St. Louis, Baltimore, Boston, and Pittsburgh—only St. Louis and Baltimore had majority native white populations, and that by only 3.4 percent and 3.1 percent respectively. See table 5, 41, Bruce M. Stave, *The New Deal and the Last Hurrah: Pittsburgh Machine Politics,* University of Pittsburgh Press: Pittsburgh, 1970.

8. Lubell, *The Future While It Happened,* 32.

9. William Issel, *Social Change in the United States, 1945-1983,* Schocken Books: New York, 1985, 56.

10. Work Projects Administration, Writers' Project, *Pennsylvania: A Guide to the Keystone State,* Oxford University Press: New York, 1940, 301, 74.

11. George Sessions Perry, "The Cities of America: Pittsburgh," *The Saturday Evening Post,* August 3, 1946, 14.

12. Bertram J. Black and Aubrey Mallach, "Population Trends in Pittsburgh and Allegheny County, 1840-1940," Federation of Social Agencies of Pittsburgh and Allegheny County, April 1944, table 1. By 1940, Pittsburgh's percentage of Allegheny County's population had declined only slightly, to 47.6 percent

13. Perry, "Pittsburgh," 46, 14, 15.

14. Philip Klein, et al., *A Social Study of Pittsburgh: Community Problems and Social Services of Allegheny County,* Columbia University Press: New York, 1938, 294. The John R. Commons reference is from "Wage-Earners of Pittsburgh," in *Charities and the Commons,* Vol. 21, 1051.

15. The approximate date for this secret police forgery is 1905, although rumors of such a Jewish conspiracy predated this. See "The Infamous 'Protocols of Zion' Endures," Week in Review, *The New York Times,* July 26, 1987. Also, see the follow-up letter to the editor by Jeffrey L. Sammons, Professor of German at Yale University, *The New York Times,* August 7, 1987. This Czarist concoction was first translated into German in 1920 and appeared in many German editions thereafter. See Lucy S. Dawidowicz, *The War Against the Jews, 1933-1945,* Bantam Books: New York, 1976, 20, 61.

16. Issel, *Social Change,* 157.

17. Patrick J. Kiger, "Ethnic Roots: The Melting Pot Myth," *Pittsburgh Magazine,* October 1983, 18.

18. Issel, *Social Change,* 157.

19. Kiger, "Ethnic Roots," 17.

20. Work Projects Administration, Writers' Project, *Pennsylvania: A Guide to the Keystone State,* 301.

21. William E. Leuchtenburg, *The Perils of Prosperity, 1914-1932,* University of Chicago Press: Chicago, 1958, 207.

22. Richard Polenberg, *One Nation Divisible: Class, Race, and Ethnicity in the United States Since 1938,* The Viking Press: New York, 1980, 35.

23. David Brody, *Labor in Crisis: The Steel Strike of 1919,* J. B. Lippincott Co.: New York, 1965, 39.

24. Roderick J. McIntosh, "Listening to the Mill: Growing up in the Shadow of 'The Steel,'" *Archaeology,* November-December 1999, 55.

25. Anonymous account of the 1919 strike, "Summary of Three Strikes," typed report in National Tube Co. Historical Notes, dated September 19, 1935, Box 3061, L4061, 91:6, 8, Archives of Industrial Society, University of Pittsburgh.

26. National Tube Co. Historical Notes, "Summary of Three Strikes," 9.

27. John Bodnar, "Immigration and Modernization: The Case of Slavic Peasants in Industrial America," in Milton Cantor, Ed., *American Working Class Culture: Explorations in American Labor and Social History,* Greenwood Press: Westport, Conn., 1979, 342. Originally in *Journal of Social History,* No. 9, 1975, 44-71.

28. Vincent DeAndrea interviewed by the author, April 6, 1999.

29. "Limited good" is a phrase and concept originated by George Foster, "Peasant Society and the Image of Limited Good," *American Anthropologist,* No. 67, April 1965, 293-315. Also, see Rudolph M. Bell, "The Transformation of a Rural Village: Istria, 1870-1972," *Journal of Social History,* No. 7, spring 1974, 251-252.

30. Bodnar, "Immigration and Modernization," 342, 343.

31. Anne Cloonan, "Italian Immigrants Found a Home in Greensburg's Hilltop Neighborhood," *The Pittsburgh Post-Gazette,* May 1, 2002, E7.

32. Interview with John Casciato by the author, May 24, 1996.

33. In 1940, 75 percent of the cobbler and shoeshine shops in New York City were owned by Italians. Polenberg, *One Nation Divisible,* 38.

34. Tiffany Pitts, "It's Hard to Heel to Retirement Living: Oakland Cobbler Shutters his Shop After 68 Years," *The Pittsburgh Post-Gazette,* June 22, 1998, B-3.

35. Brian O'Neill, "Cobbler's Life Leaves Behind Footprints," *The Pittsburgh Post-Gazette,* September 27, 1999.

36. Wade Malcolm, "Oakland Cobbler who 'Saved Soles' for 75 Years," *The Pittsburgh Post-Gazette,* June 30, 2005, E-5. As of 2009, the Ateleta fraternal society was still extant and had about 75 members.

37. Kate McCaffrey, "Bloomfield Cobbler for 66 Years," *The Pittsburgh Post-Gazette,* August 19, 2006.

38. Bodnar, "Immigration and Modernization," 343.

39. Bodnar, "Immigration and Modernization," 343. Meanwhile, Italians preferred not to work for others and sought security in owning something. They therefore tended to go into small single-owner businesses, which is how America came to be polka-dotted with pizzarias and cobbler shops.

40. Bodnar, "Immigration and Modernization," 343-4.

41. Bob Batz, Jr., "Memories Flow from Rivers of Steel," *The Pittsburgh Post-Gazette,* April 1, 1998.

42. Bodnar, "Immigration and Modernization," 345-6.

43. Milan Simonich, "Learning a Lesson from Aliquippa Schools," *The Pittsburgh Post-Gazette,* December 21, 1997, A-14.

44. Kristin Kovacic, "Being Pittsburgh," *The Pittsburgh Post-Gazette,* March 24, 1999, Op-Ed Page.

45. "Breakfast With . . . Michael Keaton," *The Pittsburgh Post-Gazette*, October 18, 1999.

46. John Bodnar, *Workers' World: Kinship, Community, and Protest in an Industrial Society, 1900-1940*, The Johns Hopkins University Press: Baltimore, 1982, 168-169.

47. Michael Weber, John Bodnar, and Roger Simon, "Seven Neighborhoods: Stability and Change in Pittsburgh's Ethnic Community, 1930-1960," *The Western Pennsylvania Historical Magazine*, Vol. 64, No. 2, April 1981, 145, 149.

48. Bodnar, *Workers' World*, 172-175.

49. Peter Blair, "Iron Heritage and Steel Dreams," *In Pittsburgh Newsweekly*, October 20-26, 1994, 8.

50. Associated Press, "Bethlehem Steel Sets Closing Timetable; 1,700 To Lose Jobs," *The Tribune-Review*, October 15, 1994, A4.

51. Peter T. Kilborn, "A Pennsylvania City Prepares for Life After Steel," *The New York Times*, December 6, 1994. Len Barcousky, "Bethlehem: Stronger Than Steel," *The Pittsburgh Post-Gazette*, March 3, 1996, G-1. John Holusha, "Farewell to a Mill That Shaped the Modern City," *The New York Times*, October 21, 1995, 19.

52. Pat Dawson, "East Pittsburgh Spans a Century of Ups and Downs," *The Pittsburgh Post-Gazette*, August 24, 1995, E-9.

53. Bodnar, "Immigration and Modernization," 346.

54. Cloonan, "Italian Immigrants Found a Home in Greensburg's Hilltop Neighborhood," E7.

55. Bodnar, "Immigration and Modernization," 345.

56. Kristen Ostendorf, "Women Mine Memories from Life in a Coal Patch," *The Pittsburgh Post-Gazette*, August 19, 1999, 1, for both Bregon and Carosone.

57. Bodnar, "Immigration and Modernization," 344.

58. Bodnar, "Immigration and Modernization," 344-5.

59. Kristen Ostendorf, "Leo Sokol: Steelworker, Cartoonist," obituary in *The Pittsburgh Post-Gazette*, March 21, 1999, E-5.

60. Mark Abrahamson, *Urban Enclaves: Identity and Place in America*, St. Martin's Press: New York, 1996, 2-3.

61. Frank H. Serene, "Immigrant Steelworkers in the Monongahela Valley: Their Communities and the Development of a Labor Class Consciousness," Unpublished Ph.D. dissertation, University of Pittsburgh, 1979, 58-61.

62. John Bodnar, Roger Simon, and Michael P. Weber, *Lives of Their Own: Blacks, Italians, and Poles in Pittsburgh, 1900-1960*, University of Illinois Press: Urbana, 1982, 201-03, 211-33, 237-59.

63. Abby Mendelson, "Invisible Boundaries," *Pittsburgh Magazine*, April 1989, 41.

64. Abby Mendelson, "In Allentown," *Pittsburgh Magazine*, January 1991, 26.

65. Vincent DeAndrea interviewed by the author, April 6, 1999 and January 8, 2002.

66. Karl Marx and Frederick Engels, *The Communist Manifesto*, International Publishers: New York, 1948, 1986, 44.

67. Bodnar, "Immigration and Modernization," 338-9.

68. Bodnar, "Immigration and Modernization," 342.

69. Vincent DeAndrea interviewed by the author, January 8, 2002.

70. Bodnar, "Immigration and Modernization," 339.

71. Deborah Weisberg, "Pupils Gather Tales to Weave Narrative of Bloomfield's History," *Pittsburgh Post-Gazette,* June 15, 2000.

72. Weber, et al., "Seven Neighborhoods," 137, 136.

73. Robert W. Wood, "Community History," unpublished undergraduate paper, University of Pittsburgh, March 18, 1971, copy in the author's possession.

74. Vincent DeAndrea interviewed by the author, April 6, 1999.

75. Abby Mendelson, "Bloomfield," *Pittsburgh Magazine,* June 1980, 29.

76. Bodnar, "Immigration and Modernization," 335.

77. The following information comes from Anna Dubrovsky, "The Ties That Bind," *The Pittsburgh Post-Gazette,* July 25, 1996, and Niki Kapsambelis, "In Pittsburgh, Homes Are Seen as Family Heirlooms," Associated Press story in *The Pittsburgh Tribune-Review,* October 10, 1998.

78. Weber, et al., "Seven Neighborhoods," 123.

79. Weber, et al., "Seven Neighborhoods," 135-136.

80. Vincent DeAndrea interviewed by the author, April 6, 1999.

81. Sam Bass Warner, Jr., *The Private City,* University of Philadelphia Press: Philadelphia, 1968, 181.

82. McIntosh, "Listening to the Mill," 55.

83. Weber, et al., "Seven Neighborhoods," 137-138.

84. Kapsambelis, "In Pittsburgh, Homes Are Seen as Family Heirlooms."

85. Cliff Ham, "Window on the Past: Picture Provides a Look Back," *Oakland,* August 1994. "Valley of Work," Pittsburgh Art Exhibit Teacher's Packet, Westmoreland Museum of Art, Greensburg, Pa.

86. Gary Rotstein, "Panther Hollow's Demise is Feared," *The Pittsburgh Post-Gazette,* March 15, 1993, C-2; K. A. Saunders, "Proud Traditions Keep Neighbors Close," *Oakland,* September 1998.

87. Preliminary Street List for 1996, Pittsburgh Ward 4, District 15, Allegheny County Department of Elections, January 16, 1996. A list of registered voters, however, undercounts the actual number of adult members of these families, as the women were often not registered. Thus, for instance, neither the mother of Fred and Joe Deluliss nor the wife of Danny Pollice were registered voters. Additionally, adult daughters would be listed under their husbands names.

88. Ostendorf, "Women Mine Memories from Life in a Coal Patch."

89. Robert E. Park, "The City," in Robert E. Park, Ernest W. Burgess, and Roderick D. McKenzie, Eds., *The City,* University of Chicago Press: Chicago, 1967, 40, originally published 1925.

90. Weber, et al., "Seven Neighborhoods."

91. Cloonan, "Italian Immigrants Found a Home in Greensburg's Hilltop Neighborhood," E7.

92. Weber, et al., "Seven Neighborhoods," 125-126.

93. Herbert Gutman, "Work, Culture, and Society in Industrializing America, 1815-1919," in *Work, Culture, and Society in Industrializing America: Essays in American Working-Class and Social History,* Vintage Books: New York, 1977, 1966, 43-44.

94. Klein, et al., *A Social Study of Pittsburgh,* 249.

95. Cloonan, "Italian Immigrants Found a Home in Greensburg's Hilltop Neighborhood," E7.

96. Klein, et al., *A Social Study of Pittsburgh,* 249.

97. Polenberg, *One Nation Divisible,* 36.

98. Ray Czachowski in John Bodnar, *Workers' World,* 57.

99. Patricia Lowry, "Saving St. Nicholas," *The Pittsburgh Post-Gazette,* October 10, 2000.

100. Interview with John Casciato by the author, May 24, 1996.

101. Klein, et al., *A Social Study of Pittsburgh,* 251.

102. Patricia Lowry, "Paesani in Pittsburgh," *The Pittsburgh Post-Gazette,* September 29, 1998, G-1. This East Liberty hall closed in 1987 due to declining membership.

103. Klein, et al., *A Social Study of Pittsburgh,* 252-53.

104. Kiger, "Ethnic Roots," 17.

105. Lowry, "Saving St. Nicholas."

106. Polenberg, *One Nation Divisible,* 39.

107. Interview with John Casciato by the author, May 24, 1996.

108. Ostendorf, "Women Mine Memories from Life in a Coal Patch."

109. Interviews with John Casciato and Camilla Caliendo by the author, May 24, 1996.

110. Interview with John Casciato by the author, May 24, 1996.

111. Jeffrey Cohan, "Pittsburgh says, 'Grazie' — Annual parade honors Columbus, Italy," *The Pittsburgh Post-Gazette,* October 8, 2000, B-1.

112. Cloonan, "Italian Immigrants Found a Home in Greensburg's Hilltop Neighborhood."

113. Marcia Chamovitz, "The San Rocco Celebration of Aliquippa: An Italian Saint in an American Setting," seminar paper, History Department, University of Pittsburgh, 1977.

114. Work Projects Administration, Writers' Project, *New York City Guide,* Oxford University Press: New York, 1939, 270.

115. Kenneth J. Heineman, "A Catholic New Deal: Religion and Labor in 1930s Pittsburgh," *The Pennsylvania Magazine of History & Biography,* Vol. 128, No. 4, October 1994, 369-370.

116. Klein, et al., *A Social Study of Pittsburgh,* 250-251.

117. Joe Rudiak and Ray Czachowski in Bodnar, *Workers' World,* 69, 52.

118. Dawson, "East Pittsburgh Spans a Century of Ups and Downs," E-12.

119. Brian O'Neill, "Fading Footsteps: Cobbler Sees Changes in Oakland During 60 Years," *The Pittsburgh Press,* February 21, 1990. Tiffany Pitts, "It's Hard to Heel to Retirement Living."

120. Eleanor Gedunsky Kosterlitz, "Bates Street Memories," *Oakland,* May 1992.

121. Stanley M. Onochowski, "Community History," unpublished undergraduate paper, University of Pittsburgh, March 18, 1971, copy in the author's possession.

122. Mubarak S. Dahir, "Oakland Writ Large," *Pitt Magazine,* June 1998, 23.

123. Others who have made this same point include Edward Shorter and Charles Tilly, *Strikes in France, 1830-1969,* Harvard University Press: Cambridge, 1974; Daniel J. Walkowitz, *Worker City, Company Town,* University of Illinois Press: Urbana, 1978; and John T. Cumbler, *Working-Class Community in Industrial America,* Greenwood Press: Westport, Conn., 1979.

124. Paul Kleppner, *Who Voted? The Dynamics of Electoral Turnout, 1870-1980,* Praeger Publishers: New York, 1982, 85, 97.

125. Kiger, "Ethnic Roots," 18.

126. Bodnar, *Workers' World,* 63.

127. See Mildred Allen Beik, *The Miners of Windber: The Struggles of New Immigrants for Unionization, 1890s-1930s,* Pennsylvania State University Press: University Park, Pa., 1996.

128. Bodnar, "Immigration and Modernization," 341.

129. Bodnar, "Immigration and Modernization," 349.

130. See Arthur W. Kornhauser, "Attitudes of Economic Groups," *The Public Opinion Quarterly,* April 1938, 262, Question 13; 268.

131. See "Gallup and Fortune Polls," *The Public Opinion Quarterly,* September 1940, 537.

132. Interviews with Camilla Caliendo and John Casciato by the author, May 24, 1996.

133. Bodnar, *Workers' World,* 121. Emphasis added.

134. Bodnar, *Workers' World,* 69.

135. Crane Brinton, *The Anatomy of Revolution,* Vintage Books: New York, 1938, 1952, 1965, 250-251.

136. Work Projects Administration, Writers' Project, *Pennsylvania: A Guide to the Keystone State,* 67.

137. Issel, *Social Change,* 8-9.

138. Maurine Weiner Greenwald, "Women and Class in Pittsburgh, 1850-1920," in Samuel P. Hays, Ed., *City at the Point: Essays on the Social History of Pittsburgh,* University of Pittsburgh Press: Pittsburgh, 1989, 35.

139. Ostendorf, "Women Mine Memories from Life in a Coal Patch."

140. Stanley Anthony "Sluggo" Frankowski, "My Lawrenceville," *The [Lawrenceville] Observer,* October 1994.

141. Greenwald, "Women and Class in Pittsburgh," 60, 34.

142. Bodnar, et al., *Lives of Their Own,* 113-151, 241, 254.

143. Weber, et al., "Seven Neighborhoods," 128-129.

144. Greenwald, "Women and Class in Pittsburgh," 35.

145. Greenwald, "Women and Class in Pittsburgh," 39.

146. Greenwald, "Women and Class in Pittsburgh," 49.

147. Work Projects Administration, Writers' Project, *Pennsylvania: A Guide to the Keystone State,* 67.

148. Issel, *Social Change,* 8-9.

149. Work Projects Administration, Writers' Project, *Pennsylvania: A Guide to the Keystone State,* 69.

150. Statistical Abstract of Ambridge, Pennsylvania, 1952.

151. Richard Oestreicher, "Working-Class Formation, Development, and Consciousness in Pittsburgh, 1790-1960," in Samuel P. Hays, Ed., *City at the Point,* 125.

152. Milan Simonich, "The Lessons of World War II," *The Pittsburgh Post-Gazette,* November 11, 1999, 1, A-14.

153. Mike Royko, syndicated column in *The Pittsburgh Post-Gazette,* August 28, 1996.

154. Interviews with John and Charles Casciato by the author, May 24, 1996.

155. Most of this information is taken from Matthew S. Magda, *Monessen: Industrial Boomtown and Steel Community, 1898-1980*, Pennsylvania Historical and Museum Commission: Harrisburg, 1985.

156. Magda, *Monessen*, 75.

157. Magda, *Monessen*, 94.

158. Magda, *Monessen*, 137.

159. Magda, *Monessen*, 110.

160. Magda, *Monessen*, 147.

161. Magda, *Monessen*, 93.

162. Magda, *Monessen*, 135.

163. Magda, *Monessen*, 128.

164. Magda, *Monessen*, 81.

165. Magda, *Monessen*, 72.

166. Magda, *Monessen*, 97.

Chapter 4

From Aliens to Americans
Wishing for a New Deal

The Democratic Party had not always commanded the intense loyalty of the working class that it came to command in the 1930s. Indeed, in 1932 the Democratic Party was not particularly identified with class issues at all, as Roosevelt's only specific campaign promises were that he would balance the budget and repeal Prohibition.

And yet, having the sympathetic Democrats in office was enough to give workers in their myriad ethnic enclaves hope, to inspire them to go to the polls and vote for more Democrats. And, as they flooded into the ranks of the Democratic Party, creating a new mass base for the party, the party became more identified with their concerns, became more the vehicle of their political and economic ambitions. The Democratic Party thus became the party of the working class in the 1930s because it became the vehicle through which ethnic workers found political expression for their most deeply held beliefs of equality and fair play. It became the political manifestation of their pan-ethnic class consciousness.

Already, in the 1920s, many of these workers had come to see the Democratic Party as the primary political vehicle of their desires. This was especially evident in the presidential campaign of Al Smith in 1928. But the emotional and economic impact of the Great Depression solidified their feelings of grievance, of commonality, of group consciousness, and turned increasing numbers of ethnic, Orthodox-Catholic, blue collar urban workers toward politics and toward the Democratic Party. As Italian Monessen steel worker Eduardo Furio remembered, "Everybody was wishing for a New Deal."[1] They found the New Deal they were hoping for in the Democratic Party.

But, the ties binding America's urban blue collar working class to the Democratic Party were ethnic and religious, as well as economic. The Democratic

Party became not only the party of the working class, it also became America's "ethnic" party, a distinction it retains to this day. The party had possessed an urban Catholic constituency for some time in the Irish and South Germans of the Eastern cities. To this core were added other Catholic elements—Poles, Italians, and Croatians—as well as Orthodox blocs—Serbians, Greeks, and Russians. This could clearly be seen in both the make-up and the constituency of the Democratic Party in Pittsburgh.

Pittsburgh was a city composed of about fifty ethnic neighborhoods and was the national headquarters of several Eastern and Southern European fraternal associations, including the Polish Falcons, the National Slovak Society of the USA,[2] and the Italian Sons and Daughters of America. Indeed, the latter published the nationally distributed Italian newspaper *Unione* from its Pittsburgh office. Although *Unione* did not editorially endorse the Democratic ticket in 1932, in 1933 it endorsed the entire Democratic municipal slate as the party and ethnic communities grew closer to each other.

One way the close cooperation between the party and ethnic groups was accomplished was through the care local party leaders took to make sure that these ethnic constituencies were fully represented in the party and in the offices the party began to win after 1932. Indeed, in that 1932 presidential election, Pittsburgh party leader David Lawrence concentrated most of the party's efforts in the most heavily ethnic neighborhoods.

One of these neighborhoods was composed of Wards 16 and 17 on the city's South Side, wards heavily populated by Polish steelworkers in the local Jones & Laughlin mill. These wards had gone for Al Smith in 1928 and Robert LaFollette during his third party campaign in 1924 and would later become two of the strongest CIO and politically "class conscious" wards in the entire nation.[3] Although the majority of Pittsburgh's population was tied to the ethnic community in one way or another in 1930, these two wards, touching on the Monongahela River, were the city's "most foreign wards," composed of large numbers of Poles, as well as foreign-born Lithuanians and Germans. Additionally, "By 1930, and throughout the entire decade, these wards were the lowest rental areas in the city. In 1934 the Seventeenth [South Side] and the Sixth [Polish Hill] ranked among the five wards with the greatest unemployment in the city. By 1940 all three were among the top 40 percent of wards with individuals on the WPA payroll; the Sixth and Seventeenth Wards were also among the four wards housing the greatest proportion of laborers."[4]

Thus, economic interests alone would have impelled them to vote Democratic in 1932, as unemployment was 31.4 percent in Ward 16 and 42 percent in Ward 17. But every cultural and religious imperative was also propelling them in that same direction. "Priests at St. Adalbert's and St. Josephat (Kuncewicz) Polish Catholic Church permitted their church halls to be used for campaign rallies and temporary South Side [Democratic Party] headquarters until a permanent location could be found. Workers were recruited at all of the ethnic parishes. Two Polish and a Croatian fraternal association and several small labor locals provided campaign workers and distributed literature among their membership. While each ward continued to be chaired by a native-born American, mainly Irish, the list of [Democratic Party] committeepersons was liberally dotted with names such as John Karnoski, Peter Dokmanovich, Louise Yarsky and Magdeline Norkiewicz."[5]

The Democratic Party leadership also cultivated a close relationship with every other ethnic neighborhood. In Polish Hill, for example, "[T]he party demonstrated its interest in the Polish vote by assuring that every one of the 16 Democratic committeepersons from the area [Ward 6] were of Polish background. Slightly under one-half of the Republican committeepersons in contrast claimed Polish ancestry."[6]

In the Italian neighborhoods of Bloomfield, East Liberty, and the Lower Hill, all of which had supported Smith in 1928, efforts were made to cement the bonds between the party and that constituency. "An Italian Democratic Committee with branches in the Eighth and Twelfth Wards [Bloomfield and East Liberty] organized to lead the anticipated groundswell toward Roosevelt. Catholic clergy campaigned from their pulpits and fraternal associations became meeting places for the spreading Roosevelt movement."[7]

Sensing that an electoral sea change was in the making in 1932, party leader David Lawrence convinced Roosevelt to campaign in Pittsburgh and reserved 35,000 seats at Oakland's Forbes Field for a rally. "In order to stir enthusiasm for the evening address, Lawrence planned an afternoon tour by the candidate through nearly a dozen of the city's ethnic neighborhoods. Thousands . . . lined the streets to welcome Roosevelt. Public and parochial schools were closed to permit the children to join in the festivities. Several times the Roosevelt caravan was stopped to permit handshaking and picture taking with neighborhood clergy, ward chairmen, and other local ethnic leaders."[8]

That evening, almost 50,000 Pittsburghers jammed into the overcrowded Forbes Field to hear Roosevelt speak. Lawrence warmed up the crowd with the music of half a dozen bands from various fraternal associations and made sure ward politicians from all the important ethnic neighborhoods were seated on the stand next to Roosevelt.

The party's efforts paid off. While losing the state, Roosevelt became the first Democratic presidential candidate to win Pittsburgh and Allegheny County since 1856, carrying Pittsburgh by 27,000 votes (and twenty-six of the city's thirty-two wards) and the county by 37,000.

"Not surprisingly, Roosevelt's greatest support came from the city's working class wards . . . The Eastern European South Side wards gave Roosevelt nearly three-fourths of its votes. The North Side [Ward 24], a mix of second and third generation German and Irish blue collar workers, proved to be the second strongest Roosevelt area with victory margins ranging between 62 percent and 71 percent. The work of Lawrence and his committee also paid dividends in the city's Italian wards . . . Italians in Bloomfield, East Liberty, and the Lower Hill District provided a substantial majority to Roosevelt."[9]

Meanwhile, WASP and upper class wards, such as Squirrel Hill and Shadyside, continued to vote Republican. It was a triumph for ethnic, working class Pittsburgh, as well as for the Democratic Party. From 1932 on, these ethnic

working class wards remained the hard-core bedrock of the Democratic Party in
Pittsburgh (table 4).

Table 4

Demographic Variables in Wards
with Largest Proportion of Foreign Stock and in City

	Wd. 6 Polish Hill	Wd. 16 S. Side	Wd. 17 S. Side	City of Pittsburgh
Foreign stock, '30	65.4%	65.0%	70.0%	51.1%
Unemployment, '34	40.8	31.4	42.0	31.9
Mean Democratic vote, 1932-41 elections	69.4	72.0	70.6	57.6

Source: Bruce M. Stave, *The New Deal and the Last Hurrah: Pittsburgh Machine Politics,*
University of Pittsburgh Press: Pittsburgh, 1970, 42, Table 6.

As the Thirties wore on, this rise to dominance by the city's ethnic elements
presented a problem for the ever-cautious party leader David Lawrence. Although
ethnic Catholics and Orthodox Slavs remained the bedrock foundation of the
party, Lawrence always sought to build bridges to every possible constituency,
including blacks and native-born Protestants.

The problem with Protestants, however, was that there just weren't that many
Protestants the party could turn to as standard bearers. Fred Weir, for instance,
one of the few WASP lawyers close to the party, recalled inadvertently becoming
a Democratic candidate for Allegheny County Court Judge because no one else
of his religion could be found. "Jimmy Kirk [a Lawrence lieutenant] asked me to
come down to the Benedum Trees Building and I went down. He and Lawrence
were there and they said, 'Can you help us find a Protestant candidate?' Believe
it or not, they took out the yellow pages of the phone book under attorneys and
were going through it to see if we could find a candidate out of the phone book . . .
We got down to the W's and they said, 'You're going to have to run.' . . . I didn't
want to run, but I had to.'"[10]

Nevertheless, despite Lawrence's best efforts in this direction, the Democratic
Party in Pittsburgh never made much progress in building bridges to the WASPs
throughout the Great Depression and World War II. In the 1920s and in 1931 the
city had added five western and southern suburban wards. These suburban and less
ethnic new wards, Wards 28-32, (comprising such Pittsburgh neighborhoods as
Fairywood, Westwood, Oakwood, Overbrook, and Gates Manor—the very names
reveal their nature) "continually harassed the Pittsburgh Democratic organization
during its formative years, for each of the five voted below the Democratic city
average for all general elections between 1932 and 1941."[11]

Additionally, the most "Protestant" old wards, such as Squirrel Hill and
Shadyside, also continued to resist the Democratic tide. Shadyside, Ward 7, was

one of the two most resistant (as it remains to this day). Shadyside had the highest proportion of native-white population of any ward and, "Throughout the decade [the Thirties] it was the second highest rental area in the city [after Squirrel Hill, Ward 14]; it had the second lowest unemployment rate for all wards in 1934 [again, after Squirrel Hill] and the seventh lowest proportion of individuals on WPA in 1940. Over 15 percent of its working population held professional jobs in 1940, the highest proportion for any ward in the city, whereas only 2.4 percent served as laborers, the second lowest proportion [once more, after Squirrel Hill] of all wards in Pittsburgh. Only twice during the years between 1930 and 1941 did the voters of the Seventh Ward cast a majority of their ballots in a general election for Democratic candidates. They swung to the Democratic standard bearer in the 1933 mayoralty race and to FDR in 1936. In the latter election all Pittsburgh wards joined in the Roosevelt landslide, with the president garnering 70.6 percent of the city's vote; the Seventh Ward, however, handed Roosevelt a meager 51.4 percent majority. Throughout the decade, it would be the Steel City's most Republican district."[12]

It may have seemed to Eduardo Furio in his blue collar Italian neighborhood in the steel town of Monessen that, "Everybody was wishing for a New Deal." But it wasn't quite true. Even in what became a Democratic citadel like Pittsburgh, there were many—professionals, those with more money, native-born whites, Protestants—who were wishing for no such thing. The New Deal, when it came, came for others, not for them. It came for peasants who'd become blue collar workers, it came for "foreigners," it came for Catholics and for the Orthodox. The New Deal came for "aliens" who were in the process of becoming Americans. And it came because it managed to articulate the deepest dreams, desires, and aspirations of these new Americans. It knew what they were wishing for in their deepest souls.

Four Freedoms

In January 1942, immediately after Pearl Harbor, Roosevelt delivered his annual State of the Union address before Congress. In it he outlined the famous "Four Freedoms" that America was striving for: Every human being, Roosevelt declared, was entitled to freedom of speech, to freedom of religious belief, to freedom from fear, and freedom from material want.

We are perhaps now most familiar with the "Four Freedoms" from the Norman Rockwell poster series later produced by the government and distributed everywhere across the land. "This timeless series," we are told, "perhaps represented the quintessential World War II appeal—the pride in our democratic heritage exemplified through the activities of ordinary Americans."[13] Since it was government-sponsored propaganda, it is perhaps easy to dismiss this poster series as prescriptive preaching by the government, not necessarily representative of popular sentiment at all. But this is belied by the process through which the posters finally became government-sponsored.

Inspired by President Roosevelt's enumeration of the "Four Freedoms," artist Norman Rockwell, on his own initiative, volunteered his services to the government to produce a series of paintings illustrating these "Four Freedoms" to be used in poster format.

The government wasn't interested and turned him down. Rockwell persevered, however, and produced a series of sketches illustrating the "Four Freedoms," which was published as a magazine cover for *The Saturday Evening Post*. Throughout America, readers tore off the cover and taped it on their walls, pinned it to shop floor bulletin boards, posted it in public places.

Responding to the grassroots popularity of the magazine cover, poet Archibald MacLeish, head of the Office of War Information (OWI), belatedly approached Rockwell and asked him to produce the now well-known series of posters for the government, which finally issued them in 1943.[14] That year an astounding 25 million Americans purchased copies of the prints from the OWI.[15] With an estimated population of 136 million in 1943, that means almost 20 percent of all Americans bought these images in that one year alone.[16] Obviously, the images spoke to the hearts and minds of a massive audience.

Coming out as they did during World War II, the tendency has been to see these posters as a counterbalancing of American freedoms versus the international totalitarianism against which the nation was then fighting. The enormous popularity of the images, however, so quickly after Pearl Harbor, suggests an additional interpretation. These images, and Roosevelt's speech itself, represent a short-hand expression of what ordinary people all across the land had already come to believe they were fighting for domestically in the 1930s. These "Four Freedoms" included not only political and religious freedom, but the freedom from material want that they saw as a basic part of the "American Dream."

And, to an astounding degree, ordinary people were successful in creating a New Deal for themselves which guaranteed much of these Four Freedoms, even in the material sphere. Between 1933 and 1937, for example, Roosevelt proposed what he later termed an "Economic Bill of Rights" which, if all the provisions had been enacted, would have created a semi-socialist economy. These proposals would have guaranteed the right to work, the right to adequate food, to housing, a decent education, clothing, and recreation.

Much of this agenda was actually enacted at the local level over the course of the Thirties in the industrial cities of the Northeast and Midwest. There, powerful urban ethnic and working class political organizations implanted political traditions which placed a high priority on expenditures for schools, welfare, and health care.

These developments give us a clue as to the content of the pan-ethnic class consciousness which was evolving in America during the Thirties. This consciousness emerged from a mixture of sources, from both "Old World" and "New World" influences and illustrated how ethnic working class populations were in transition from one culture to another. Neither the attitudes nor the populations were static and unchanging. Their attitudes were dynamic, changing, like the populations themselves. Their strengths came from both old and new wellsprings, merging into a new consciousness.

In its simplest terms, ethnic workers wanted their "rights"—what they felt they were entitled to both as human beings and as American citizens. The sources of their deeply embedded ideas about their "rights" can be found in Jeffersonian republicanism, papal encyclicals—and even a little bit of Debsian socialism, at least as practiced by the Pittsburgh area Socialist Party.

The Church, for instance, preached that, as human beings, they were entitled to what the Church termed "social justice." And the state, in its founding documents and in its pervasive ideology, preached that "all men are created equal." The workers, therefore, felt that, as American citizens, they were entitled to the basic civil liberties supposedly guaranteed "all" Americans by the Constitution. As citizens, they also felt they had a right to do what all "Americans" had a right to do—prosper. Looking at rubber workers in Akron during the Thirties, one observer described this ethnic working class vision as entailing an almost classic Lockean liberalism: "Life, Liberty, and Property."[17]

Meanwhile, the Pittsburgh-area Socialist Party emerged as a militant and persistent advocate of political rights for unpopular ideas and unpopular populations—such as ethnic workers.

Taken together, these influences merged to form what might be termed the American version of European social democracy—what Lizabeth Cohen has called, "moral capitalism."[18] Taken together, these ideas—this social vision—is also what the political struggle of the New Deal was all about. When workers wished for a "New Deal," it was this deal they had in mind.

Ethnic class consciousness, then, contained a mixture of religious and political attitudes derived from both church and state. The workers were embedded in communities in transition from Old World attitudes to New World ones—and the resulting mixture was neither totally one nor the other, but a synthesis influenced by both. When we look at ethnic working class communities in the Thirties as cultures in a process of such change, what we come away with is a picture of peasants becoming proletarians and aliens becoming Americans—and drawing strength from both identities.

Taken together, their attitudes amounted to an agenda for the radical reform of American society and politics as then constituted. These attitudes reveal not only where the New Deal radical reform project was prepared to go—but also where it was not prepared to go.

One place it was not prepared to go was too far toward the Left. If "Life, Liberty, and Property" were major components of the working class vision, then it is obvious that there was never a mass sentiment in America during the Thirties for important parts of the Leftist agenda.

For instance, America was virtually alone among the advanced industrial nations which did not respond to the Depression crisis during the Thirties by nationalizing industries. Despite the severity and length of the Depression, the values of the New Deal constituency itself never supported such a departure from the capitalist free market system. It is because the New Deal constituency itself was not pushing for such structural changes that the Left was never at any time a real threat to FDR and New Deal reform. As Louis Hartz pointed out, "[Socialist Party leader] Norman Thomas wanted the railroads nationalized instead of regulated under the ERA, but Roosevelt did not deliver a fireside chat pointing out how much red tape and how much deadening of initiative nationalization would bring. Thomas wanted the dairy corporations seized by the state, but Roosevelt did not plead against bureaucratizing the American farmer. The face of the New Deal was always turned rightward, where the only real American enemy lay."[19]

When we look more closely at the values and goals of the workers who put the New Deal in office, we can more clearly understand why the Left was never on the verge of power during the Thirties. The workers wanted social justice. And the workers wanted a "moral capitalism." They wanted a democratic capitalism. They did not want what the Left offered them. Socialist revolution was never on the working class agenda in the Thirties.

But both Left and non-Left commentators, blinded by their narrow ideological visions, have been slow to see that there was an alternative to the rampant and rough-handed capitalism of the times other than communism. Therefore, because the working class was not "red," the myth has grown up that not only is America a classless society, but that the mass of people have never been class conscious, nor has class politics ever shaped the course of American political history. "The American population has *always* been a pragmatic population," Harvard University political scientist Morris Fiorina has said. "They are, by and large, centrist; they don't like extremes."[20]

But a closer look at what the working class wanted and what the working class actually did in the Thirties demonstrates that there was a radical, indeed, "extreme," ideology which was neither communism nor rapacious capitalism—an ideology I term "radical reform"—and that the highly class conscious workers of the Thirties opted for this alternative—and thereby reshaped the political universe.

A Liberation Theology

In many ways the strongest traditional institutions of ethnic communities served as bridges from old values to a new worldview. In doing so, what some have viewed as "conservative" aspects of ethnic life became way stations to a new awareness and a new self identity. "Old World" traditions thus became the bastions of a "New World" consciousness.

One example of this phenomenon was the ethnic fraternal hall. Thus, for instance, "In one nationality hall is a small library from which the members may borrow books to be kept by them for several weeks; in another, plans are now under way to raise money for a new book collection. The interest of this group tends toward study of economic problems and radical political theories. One member pointed out that their hall was the center for any enterprise the group wished to consider. Here money had been raised to send to the homeland during the World War. Here also Liberty Bond campaigns were inaugurated . . . In a number of the communities in the Allegheny Valley the nationality halls have mural decorations which are painted by the same artist. One which represents the dual orientation of the members' interests is worthy of note. On both sides of the stage are portraits—on the right, President Roosevelt; on the left, President Masaryk of Czechoslovakia . . . In other halls there were photographs and calendars having pictures of various American presidents. Washington, Lincoln, and Roosevelt seem to have been the favorite choices."[21]

The same political icons would also be found adorning the walls of the steelworker union halls once unions were established—often springing from these very fraternal halls, as with the Croatian Hall in Monessen which gave birth to the USWA local in that town.[22] Thus, even as late as the 1990s, I saw portraits of Presidents Roosevelt and Truman on the walls of USWA Local 1843 (to the end of its existence, the large letters on the front of the union hall identified it as "CIO Local 1843") in the Pittsburgh neighborhood of Hazelwood, where a big Jones & Laughlin mill was located.

Another major example of this synthesis—of something new evolving out of something old—is how the deeply felt religious sensibilities of these communities became sources of revolt. "Catholic influence was always strong in American labor," CIO Publicity Director (and former Wobbly) Len De Caux reminds us. "British and Scandinavian immigrants might fill many skilled jobs, but immigrants from Catholic or largely Catholic countries made up most of the industrial working class. Of AFL members in 1900-1909, almost half were Catholics, according to estimates cited by historian Philip S. Foner. In the CIO, the proportion of Catholic members was undoubtedly higher, and of Catholic leaders still higher again. Priests exerted much influence on their labor parishioners. There were also Catholic labor societies, including the early-century Militia of Christ and, in CIO times, the Association of Catholic Trade Unionists."[23]

By the 1930s, a "social justice" ethos had gained widespread adherence among the Catholic clergy and much of this was passed on to their devout labor parishioners. The origins of this ethos could be found in two papal encyclicals urging Catholics to work for a more just and moral economic order.

The first and most influential was Pope Leo XIII's "The Condition of Labor," (1891), which was—literally—the final word in Catholic thought on social and economic questions for forty years. It advocated what we might call, after Lizabeth Cohen, a "moral capitalism" in which property rights had to take second place to human rights.

The second encyclical was Pope Pius XI's "Reconstructing the Social Order," (1931), which reiterated the principles laid down by Pope Leo and elaborated upon the same theme. As Pius was Christ's Vicar throughout the Thirties and World War II, his views guided the thinking of the Church's leadership throughout this period.

Here in America, in the midst of the great 1919 steel strike, the National Catholic War Council issued the "Bishops' Program of Social Reconstruction," which defended the right of workers to form unions to obtain a "living wage" and urged both industry and the federal government to provide insurance "against illness, invalidity, unemployment, and old age." Many of the authors of the

"Bishops' Program," such as Cleveland Bishop Joseph Schrembs, represented heavily ethnic, industrialized, urban dioceses.[24]

We can get an idea of how the labor movement interpreted Pope Pius' encyclical by looking at its coverage of his later pronouncements. In September 1944, as World War II drew toward its obvious conclusion, Pius contemplated the postwar world and, in a radio broadcast to the world, called for a settlement based upon a "Christian Peace." *Labor,* a national newspaper published by fifteen American railroad unions, pointed out to its membership that the Pope's idea of a "Christian Peace" was based upon a concept of private property that was "a far cry from the idea of the Chamber of Commerce."[25] Private property implies social responsibility, the Pope was quoted as saying, "Whenever capitalism arrogates unlimited right to property without any subordination to the common good, the Church has condemned it, as contrary to the rights of man . . . ever since its origins, the Church has always protected the poor and the weak against the tyranny of the powerful, and has always championed the just claims of workers against any injustice.

"We see an ever-increasing mass of workers going up against concentrations of wealth, often hidden under anonymous forms that succeed in evading their social duties, thereby preventing the worker from building up his own property. We see small and medium property compelled to wage a defensive struggle increasingly arduous and without hope of success.

"On the one hand, we see vast wealth dominate private and public economy, and often civil life. On the other, we see innumerable multitudes of those who are deprived of any direct or indirect security in their lives."

Pope Pius went on to declare that when private property became an obstacle to social betterment, the state had an obligation to intervene to regulate its activities, or even to take it over to protect the common welfare. Observing that individuals had little chance against gigantic aggregations of capital, Pius advised workers that their hope was to be found in organizing or joining "cooperative unions which provide them with some of the advantages of big business." Further, contracts such unions secured with large corporations must take into consideration the social aspirations of workers.

Helping to promote such ideas in America was the National Catholic Welfare Conference, which numbered among its directors the head of the Pittsburgh diocese, Bishop Hugh Boyle. Like many other industrial area bishops, such as Toledo's Bishop Karl Alter, Pittsburgh's Bishop Boyle was pro-CIO and actively supportive of social activism on the part of priests under him. He had also co-authored "The Present Crisis," a 1933 call for American Catholics to teach the message of Pope Pius XI's 1931 encyclical.[26]

Such clerical developments were the background to the formation of Peter Maurin and Dorothy Day's Catholic Worker movement in 1933. The primary ideological sources of the Catholic Worker movement were the papal encyclicals of 1891 and 1931, as well as the lives of Jesus and such saints as Teresa of Avila and Therese of Lisieux, interpreted in the light of the encyclicals.

Basic tenets of the Catholic Worker movement were pacifism, the achievement of social justice through non-violent action, and a belief in individual responsibility to reform society through personal involvement. On May Day, 1933, the movement published the first issue of its tabloid newspaper, *The Catholic Worker,* which continues publication today with a circulation of about 100,000. While peripheral today, the Catholic Worker movement was in the mainstream of Catholic thinking during the Thirties.[27]

In most cases, these voices were preaching to the choir, for the majority of America's Catholic clergy in the Thirties had already taken their Pope's teachings to heart and actively supported most New Deal programs.[28] This active support of the New Deal was also expressed through a vast Catholic communications network which, by 1936, included 134 newspapers and 198 magazines with a combined circulation of 6.9 million.[29]

Many ordinary workers of Catholic origin, in addition to the Catholic clergy, were also deeply influenced by the papal encyclicals. One of these was Patrick T. Fagan, who replaced Pittsburgher Philip Murray as head of United Mine Workers District 5 (Southwestern Pennsylvania) in 1922 after Murray moved on to higher office in the UMW. Fagan served as head of the UMW's District 5 until 1943. He also served as President of the Pittsburgh Central Labor Union (1931-1938) and later the city's CIO "congress," the Steel City Industrial Union Council. Fagan would eventually fill "labor's seat" on the Pittsburgh City Council.

Fagan remembered that, "One of the greatest things that ever happened to labor . . . was the encyclical of Pope Leo XIII. To me it was one of the finest social documents that I've ever seen for social justice, for protecting the worker . . . I became aware of it because of my father's knowledge of the encyclical . . . My father used to read all the encyclicals and talk to us about them . . . Then, of course, I thought that the Pope to me was somebody I was responsible to. He was the vicar of Christ on earth, and he was interested in not only the spiritual and moral, but the material welfare of people that have to work for a living."[30]

Paul Stackhouse was also greatly inspired by Pope Leo's 1891 encyclical. Stackhouse came from a family marinated in both Catholicism and the labor movement. His brother, John, was leader of the Pittsburgh taxi drivers' union, had been the Secretary-Treasurer and de facto head of the Pittsburgh Central Labor Union in the 1920s, and then replaced Patrick Fagan as President of the Central Labor Union in 1938. Raised in Pittsburgh's Lawrenceville neighborhood, in 1930 Paul began working at Scully Steel Supply (later U.S. Steel Supply), a Carnegie Steel warehouse on Pittsburgh's North Side. He was crucial to organizing that facility into the Steel Workers Organizing Committee (SWOC) Lo. 1544, which he co-founded, in 1937.

In 1938 SWOC, the precursor to the United Steelworkers union, hired Paul Stackhouse as an organizer, and he remained on the staff of the steelworkers' union until 1960, ending as Sub-Director of USWA District 19 in the Pittsburgh area. In 1961 he became the Executive Vice President of the Allegheny County Labor Council, the successor to the Pittsburgh Central Labor Union, and in 1974 became, like his brother before him, its President. He served in this office until his death in 1997. From 1972 until his death he was also the Business Agent for

Pittsburgh's Lo. 585 of the Service Employees International Union.[31]

In 1995, when I spoke with Paul Stackhouse, I asked him what had led him to commit his entire life to the labor movement. Without hesitation he told me it was Pope Leo's "The Condition of Labor" encyclical. "The Church preached exactly what I was fighting for," he said.[32]

Catholic social and economic teachings advocating "social justice," then, came to have widespread political influence among Pittsburgh's Catholic workers in the Thirties, perhaps most of all among the most militant and dedicated. For example, when SWOC came into existence, contemporaries described it as a Catholic union. Len De Caux recalled visiting SWOC's Pittsburgh headquarters in the Thirties and finding it "a Catholic setup . . . In national CIO and most other new unions, religion didn't stick out as it did in SWOC . . . Non-Catholics had minority representation in SWOC headquarters. Harold J. Ruttenberg, able research director, and Clinton S. Golden, eastern district director, were of the social reformist rather than Catholic school of unionism. The Left was conspicuously unrepresented."[33]

Perhaps the best remembered example of Catholic political thought and influence at this time was that of "The Radio Priest," Father Charles Coughlin, the parish priest of a small impoverished Detroit suburb. For too many people the image which remains of Coughlin is that of the virulent pro-Nazi anti-Semite and FDR-hater of the late 1930s. If this is all they retain of Coughlin, it is impossible for them to accurately judge the impact of Coughlin among ethnic communities and what he meant to ethnics in the early 1930s—for, in the early Thirties, he represented an entirely different aspiration.

From the time he went on the air in 1930 until 1934 Coughlin was an articulate and unwavering champion of the rights of the poor and of the workers against the rich and the economic elites. During the 1932 presidential campaign he coined the slogan, "Roosevelt or Ruin" and all during 1933 he was a rabid New Dealer. His was a voice which coincided with the spirit of the workers and gave expression to their own beliefs and aspirations.

Coughlin was a poor boy who'd made good. Son of an Irish laborer, he earned a doctorate from the University of Toronto at age twenty-three. In 1930 he began broadcasting sermons on the radio which were infused with large doses of politics. He was an instant success, for he "said the things [workers'] own worries were saying; [he] turned upon the traitors the whole nation was beginning to turn on, denounced the bankers and industrialists who had ruled and ruined the country, the greedy politicians and the money changers in the temple . . . [People's] pointless unrest was suddenly pointed. There were people to blame, things to be done, and there was a leader to follow. Three months from his opening speech on October 30 [1930], Father Coughlin was getting fifty thousand letters a week. Even on the conservative estimate of one letter writer to each two hundred listeners, that meant an audience of ten million, reached over 17 CBS stations plus occasional cut-ins."[34] By 1931 Coughlin was broadcasting over a syndicate of thirty radio stations, including WJAS in Pittsburgh. By 1932 his audience was estimated at between thirty and forty-five million.[35]

Describing himself as, "a simple Catholic priest endeavoring to interject Christianity into the fabric of an economic system woven upon the loom of greed,"[36] he attacked capitalism, Wall Street millionaires such as J. P. Morgan, and Pittsburgh's Andrew Mellon, then President Hoover's Secretary of the Treasury. "To many, his was the only voice that spoke truth. And others approved. *Commonweal,* the liberal Catholic monthly, praised him without stint in 1931. [Detroit] Bishop Gallagher beamed upon his protege. There was reputed to be a letter from the Pope directing thanks to Father Coughlin for spreading the doctrines of social justice first enunciated in the *Rerum Novarum* encyclical of Leo XIII [1891], and amplified by Pius XI himself in 1931."[37]

"For a season," we are told, "Father Coughlin seemed a point of fusion between Populism and the Encyclicals . . . [and his] platform bore many resemblances to that of the Minnesota Farmer-Labor Party."[38] The program of his National Union for Social Justice, which he later formed, was partly derived from the liberal encyclicals of Popes Leo and Pius and called for the nationalization of "important natural resources," the control of private property for the public welfare, a government-controlled bank, and the conscription of wealth as well as men during war.

So powerful was Coughlin's influence in the early Thirties among Northeastern "urban lower-middle class Catholics,"[39] that, when he moved to form a political alliance in 1935 with the equally influential Huey Long of Louisiana, it seemed they might even shake Roosevelt out of the White House with a more "radical" New Deal. "Coughlin," Alan Brinkley claims, "played an important role in shaping popular responses to the Depression . . . [with] a message that reflected some of the oldest and deepest impulses of the American people."

His famous radio sermons, which were entirely political in content after 1930, were "Broadcast around the nation on more than thirty stations [and] attracted an audience estimated as high as forty million. Coughlin received more mail than anyone else in America—more than any film star or sports hero, more than the President . . . When he journeyed from Detroit for appearances in other cities, he drew crowds that were the envy of political candidates. In New York, in the fall of 1933, more than 7,000 enthusiastic followers jammed the Hippodrome to hear him speak, while nearly as many stood in the chilly streets outside listening to his voice over loudspeakers. In Cincinnati, Chicago, Boston, Baltimore, and St. Louis, adoring crowds packed stadiums and auditoriums to hear him or lined his route to and from the train stations just to glimpse him passing by.

" . . . In Brockton, Massachusetts, referees halted schoolboy football games shortly before three o'clock on Sunday afternoons so that parents, coaches, and players could get to a radio in time to hear Father Coughlin . . . In churches around the country, pastors rescheduled Sunday services so they would not conflict with the radio discourses. In urban neighborhoods throughout the East and Midwest— not only Irish communities, but German, Italian, Polish; not only Catholic areas, but Protestant and, for a time, even Jewish—many residents long remembered the familiar experience of walking down streets lined with row houses, triple-deckers, or apartment buildings and hearing out of every window the voice of

Father Coughlin blaring from the radio. You could walk for blocks, they recalled, and never miss a word."[40]

The workers of Pittsburgh also clamored for Coughlin's presence and his message. In early 1931, when CBS temporarily suspended Coughlin's broadcasts, Pittsburgh labor was greatly disturbed. Patrick Fagan, at that time President of District 5 of the United Mine Workers and only a delegate to the Pittsburgh Central Labor Union (PCLU), of which he would shortly become president, introduced a resolution before that body protesting CBS' actions. He wanted organized labor to go on record, "favoring the radio speeches delivered every Sunday evening by the Right Rev. Father Charles E. Coughlin, and urging upon the Columbia Broadcasting Co. to take immediately steps in giving back to Fr. Coughlin the privilege of using its network for his addresses of American truths and economic facts."

The PCLU so voted.[41]

Organized labor also tried repeatedly, but vainly, to get Fr. Coughlin to come to Pittsburgh to inspire the rank and file. For Pittsburgh's second Labor Day celebration in 1932—only revived in 1931—the PCLU urgently requested Coughlin to come and appear as their primary speaker, as "Pittsburgh needs him." Unfortunately, Coughlin was otherwise engaged, so the PCLU reluctantly settled for AFL President William Green and United Mine Workers leader Philip Murray as its Labor Day speakers.[42]

Coughlin turned Pittsburgh workers down again in 1933 when the PCLU once more petitioned him to come to Pittsburgh as its principal Labor Day speaker.[43] The Central Labor Union therefore contented itself with speeches by local labor priests who preached the same message as Fr. Coughlin. At the suggestion of PCLU delegate John J. Kane, President of the Pressman's Union (and later to become the powerful Allegheny County Commissioner), Father James Cox, a charismatic leader of Pittsburgh's unemployed and a local "radio priest" in his own right, came to inspire the labor body.[44]

Meanwhile, the PCLU, now led by UMWA District 5 President Patrick Fagan who had since become Central Labor Union president, participated in local conferences of Coughlin's National Union for Social Justice held at the Irene Kaufmann Settlement House.[45]

Pittsburgh area steelworker Charles G. Gomrick was also one of those who seems to have believed deeply in the principles of Coughlin's Union for Social Justice. Perhaps by looking at those principles Gomrick felt most important, we can gain an insight into what the Pittsburgh labor movement, and particularly Pittsburgh steelworkers, were thinking at this time.

Charles Gomrick grew up in the Steel Valley towns of Braddock and next door Rankin. In the 1930s he worked for a time in both the Open Hearth Division of the U.S. Steel Works at Homestead and in Rankin. In the latter he was a charter member of Lo. 463 of the International Association of Bridge, Structural, and Ornamental Iron Workers. He was also a member of the Rankin lodge of the Amalgamated Association of Iron, Steel, and Tin Workers of North America, the precursor to SWOC and the USWA. When SWOC came into existence, he then became a member of that organization.[46]

Among his possessions which Gomrick bequeathed to us is his copy of *A Series of Lectures on Social Justice* by Father Coughlin, published by the Radio League of the Little Flower, Royal Oak, Michigan, March 1935. This is a collection of Coughlin's radio broadcasts from November 11, 1934 to March 24, 1935, and is heavily marked up by Gomrick. Based upon the pages Gomrick marked, we can glimpse a little of what appealed to Pittsburgh area steelworkers in Father Coughlin's message. In doing so, we can also see that Coughlin's religious message closely coincided with what Lizabeth Cohen terms "moral capitalism."[47]

Reproduced at the front of Coughlin's book of lectures is the Preamble and 16-point Platform of his National Union for Social Justice. Gomrick starred and checked off the points with which he agreed, including, for instance, Number Two, which preached that, " . . . every citizen willing to work and capable of working shall receive a just and living annual wage which will enable him to maintain and educate his family according to the standards of American decency."

Gomrick also agreed with Number Five, which declares, "I believe in upholding the right to private property, but in controlling it for the common good." Gomrick also starred Number Ten, which says, "I believe not only in the right of the laboring man to organize in unions, but also in the duty of the Government, which that laboring man supports, to protect these organizations against the vested interests of wealth and intellect." (This same attitude is found again and again in the minutes of the Pittsburgh Central Labor Union during this period.)

Gomrick also agreed with the final point in Coughlin's Platform, Number 16: "I believe in preferring the sanctity of human rights to the sanctity of property rights, for the chief concern of government shall be for the poor because, as it is witnessed, the rich have ample means of their own to care for themselves."

The lectures which Gomrick then went on to mark up open a further window into his beliefs. In the various broadcasts with which Gomrick agreed, Father Coughlin preached that, "Modern capitalism violates right order because it so employs the working of wage earning classes as to divert business and economic activity to its own advantage without any regard to the human dignity of the workers, the social character of economic life, social justice, and the common good . . . Social Justice seeks and demands a just distribution of the nation's wealth and a just distribution of the profits for the laborers as well as for the industrialist . . . there should be a contract of partnership—partnership not in the ownership of the business, but partnership in the profits of the business by which both laborer and industrialist shall reap their just reward."

And, to make it quite clear where they both stood, Gomrick also marked the passage where Coughlin said, "I call upon every one of you who is weary of drinking the bitter vinegar of sordid capitalism and upon every one who is fearsome of being nailed to the cross of communism to join this Union."[48]

Thus, it is quite clear that what Gomrick found appealing about Father Coughlin's message was that it attempted, as was said somewhat differently in another context, "To put a human face on capitalism." Or, in more technical terms, it sought to overlay a religious-based version of European social democracy on

American capitalism.

Father Coughlin, however, while perhaps the most influential, was not the only Catholic preacher of religious-based "social justice" to whom Pittsburgh area steelworkers were listening. Other such voices included that of Father George Barry O'Toole, who taught philosophy at Pittsburgh's Holy Ghost College (later Duquesne University), and Father Thomas Lappan, director of the St. Vincent de Paul Society of the Pittsburgh diocese.[49]

In Homestead, Father C. J. Hrtanek championed the workers' cause. Mike Zahorsky, a Slovak worker at Aliquippa's Jones & Laughlin plant, recalled that, "We had a pastor [in Aliquippa] at that time by the name of Monsignor Joseph Altany. He's pastor of St. Michael's Church in Munhall [next door to Homestead] now. And he came from the coal fields . . . he was a man's man. He was a humanitarian. He felt that the company owed the people something."[50]

Indeed, at this time so many Pittsburgh priests were agitating on behalf of the workers that it shocked them when they sometimes encountered a priest hostile to their cause. Until 1935 the governor of Pennsylvania was Gifford Pinchot, a moderate Republican often out of step with his party. His wife Cornelia, however, was even more out of step, for she marched to a different drummer entirely—on behalf of civil rights for steelworkers. "She was a son of a bitch when it came to the rights of people," Mike Zahorsky said with admiration, recalling a march of steelworkers in Aliquippa which Mrs. Pinchot led.

In 1934 Louis Smolinski and others in the Braddock U.S. Steel plant who were trying to organize the union locally asked her to come to Braddock to speak on behalf of the workers. "And that's when my parish priest called me up and said, 'What you got this chick in here for?' I said, 'What do you mean?' He told me that I couldn't let her speak here. He started raising hell with me. 'You have to leave her go,' he said, 'and cancel that meeting.' I told him that she was a good organizer and [I said,] 'I ain't canceling nothing.'" Smolinski was astounded that his local parish priest opposed her, especially since, "He was a *Polish* priest . . . I guess the company got after him or some damn thing."[51]

One of the most active of Pittsburgh priests, however, and one who had a great impact on Paul Stackhouse, was Father Charles Owen Rice, who was in turn deeply influenced by the papal encyclicals, which he called social "dynamite." Rice had joined the Catholic Worker movement in 1933 when he visited New York and met Dorothy Day. He returned to Pittsburgh to become a leader in the local Catholic Worker movement, going locally under the name of the "Catholic Radical Alliance." By 1937 he was a regular political columnist for the diocesan newspaper, the Pittsburgh *Catholic,* was commenting on current affairs on three local radio stations, KDKA, WWSW, and WCAE, and was serving as the executive-secretary of the Pittsburgh Catholic Worker School.[52]

In addition, Father Rice joined another priest, Father Carl Hensler, in establishing the St. Joseph House of Hospitality in the Hill District to provide shelter for the homeless and food for the hungry, one of thirty such Catholic Worker "hospitality houses" nationwide. The two "labor priests," as well as the Catholic Radical Alliance, which they led, endorsed the CIO and explicitly engaged in pro-labor political activities in the Pittsburgh area.

Both of these efforts had the blessings of Pittsburgh's Bishop Boyle, who also channeled financial assistance from the Pittsburgh diocese in their direction. "Labor is on the march," Father Rice told his local radio audiences. "On the march to a goal that will bring justice and happiness to all classes of people. Labor's right is everyone's right. It is a fight for decency, justice, and a Christian social order."[53]

In his radio address, "The Dynamite of the Encyclicals," Rice argued that workers have "the right of being treated not like a slave or a machine, but like a human being" and condemned an "unjust economic and social system."[54]

Orville Rice, a founder of the steelworkers' union at Braddock's Edgar Thomson Works, recalled that, "I was first motivated, more or less, to join a union about 1934, '35. Father Rice was touring the district advocating that the young people, as well as the older ones, get interested in [the] union. 'Get interested in organizing your union,' [he said] . . . I heard Father Rice speak at our parish [church] one Sunday afternoon advocating that we get interested, join the union and get interested and inject our voice in the union . . . It [was] shortly afterward that Father Rice started a labor school in Central Catholic High School. A friend of mine and I went down and attended every week. And this is the first that we had learned about unions. We had Father O'Hensley, who was a priest in the diocese of Pittsburgh. He was teaching economics. We had a Father Joyce, who taught us public speaking . . . Father Rice—he was the principal teacher on union tactics. I went to the labor school in 1936 while I was running a crane in the rail mill."[55]

Supposedly, after the passage of the National Recovery Act with its Section 7a, which encouraged the formation of labor unions, UMWA President John L. Lewis sent sound trucks throughout Western Pennsylvania coal districts blaring the message, "The President wants you to join the union." In the Pittsburgh area steel mills, the Catholic Fathers were more directly telling the workers that the Pope wanted them to create and join unions. It was a conjunction of secular and religious imperatives which resonated strongly among the devoutly religious industrial workers of the region.

Equality for Ethnics

Workers in the industrial heartland were aware that class differences existed and that the different classes had conflicting desires, as social workers among the steelworkers of the Pittsburgh region at the time discovered. "There is," they noted, "a consciousness on the part of the laborer that he is capable of recklessness and that there is an ageless score of the poor against the rich."[56]

This ageless score of the poor against the rich was articulated by Pittsburgh-area workers in terms not only of the Church's call for social justice, but also in terms of equal rights, of American liberty and democracy, of American freedoms, of the battle of the "common man," the "citizens," against the "privileged few," of getting what was their just due as "common ordinary Americans."

The identity toward which these "alien" ethnics were evolving was that of

"American." But, even as these ethnics came to see themselves more and more as Americans, and deserving of all the political rights of Americans, they also came up against the hard fact that "the cake eaters," as steelworker Mike Zahorsky in Aliquippa bitterly termed them, did not see them as such and systematically denied them the rights "Americans" were entitled to.[57]

The course of the late 19th century in America might be viewed as a gradual closing down of freedom, especially for subservient populations such as Southern blacks and the emerging ethnic urban industrial working class of the North. While Southern blacks gained a measure of freedom following the Civil War, even that small measure disappeared following the end of Reconstruction. By the 1890s legislation throughout the South had legalized an American apartheid.

Likewise, as the Northern urban working class became increasingly foreign-born over the course of the nineteenth century, that class became more and more circumscribed in its political, economic, and cultural options. Abraham Lincoln noted and criticized this trend as early as mid-century when he wrote to his friend Joshua Speed in 1855, "I am not a Know-Nothing [referring to the nativist, anti-immigrant political party]. How could I be? How can any one who abhors the oppression of negroes, be in favor of degrading classes of white people? Our progress in degeneracy appears to me to be pretty rapid. As a nation, we began by declaring that *'all men are created equal.'* We now practically read it, 'all men are created equal, *except negroes.'* When the Know-Nothings get control, it will read 'all men are created equal, except negroes, *and foreigners, and catholics.'"*[58]

But, though the party faltered, the spirit of the Know-Nothings did take control in America over the course of the nineteenth century. Thus, by 1900 "foreign" (Southern and Eastern European-descended) blue collar workers in the industrial Northeast had joined the list of people deemed inherently inferior by the dominant WASPs.[59]

This development could perhaps be justified by the highly racialized interpretation of Jeffersonian republicanism, America's dominant political ideology, to which many nativist political activists clung. Nevertheless, it was at odds with the perhaps more influential universalist interpretation of Jeffersonian republican equality, most famously expressed in the words of the Declaration of Independence itself, "We hold these truths to be self-evident, that all men are created equal, that they are endowed by their Creator with certain unalienable Rights, that among these, are Life, Liberty, and the pursuit of Happiness."

At least since Lincoln sanctified this ideology in his 1863 Gettysburg Address, "equality" has been the quintessential American ideology. According to this ideology, in America, the "Common Man" was presumed to be the equal to any aristocrat. This was the ideology which shaped and formed American political thought and practice. Thus, Samuel Lubell has argued that the "essential drama of American politics" is the constant struggle for the inclusion of outsiders who want to be part of the egalitarian American Dream.

As an example, the Civil Rights Movement of the late 1950s and early 1960s fought for the inclusion of blacks in American culture and politics as equals, as citizens, as Americans. The political vehicle through which the Civil

Rights Movement realized its agenda of inclusion and equality for blacks was the Democratic Party, to which it was cemented after the mid-1960s.

Similarly, the New Deal was made possible by the struggle of the children of the New Immigrants to be part of an egalitarian American nation. Though not the entire New Deal phenomenon by any means, they were nevertheless an essential new constituency without which neither the New Deal political realignment, nor the mass production unionism of the CIO would have happened. And as even some contemporary observers noted, these ethnic industrial workers didn't want to replace capitalism so much as make it humane and inclusive. The "revolution of 1933," said the *Magazine of Wall Street,* was "undertaken to reconcile capitalism and social justice."[60] Thus, for these workers, the New Deal was above all a populist movement promising equality for a multiethnic "Common Man."

These ethnic workers knew in their guts they weren't "equals" in America, as they were reminded of this over and over in their daily lives. An ethnic racism permeated American society, a racism which espoused attitudes thought to exist only in benighted Europe. Fanned by the arrival of millions of New Immigrants around the turn of the twentieth century, it continued unabated thereafter. "The First World War," we are told, "only interrupted and dampened, but by no means extinguished, in America a rhetoric of 'Nordic,' 'Aryan,' sometimes 'Anglo-Saxon' racial supremacy fully as assured and dogmatic as anything then heard in Germany."[61]

And what was true nationally was certainly true in the Pittsburgh region. Orville Rice, the son of a coal miner, entered Braddock's Edgar Thomson mill in 1929. There he saw his fellow workers, mostly ethnics, treated like cattle. "I was more or less an idealist," he recalled. "I thought fair play should have been exercised. I was surprised by the lack of fair play when there was no union, when I started working there."[62]

Aliquippa steelworker Domenic Del Turco joined his father in the welded-tube department of the local Jones and Laughlin plant in 1924 and remembered how the "cake eaters" in town discriminated against ethnics such as himself. "You had to be a 'fair-haired boy,'" to succeed in Aliquippa, he recalled. "Everything in town was controlled. You could not get a loan unless it was O.K.'d. You couldn't do anything in that town unless it was O.K.'d by higher powers to be. The banks were controlled by the corporation."[63]

Joe Rudiak, a Polish worker at the Standard Steel Car Company in Lyndora, about 25-miles north of Pittsburgh, recalled how everyone left school in their early or mid-teens to go to work. No one finished high school, with most leaving after eighth grade. No one, that is, except "the Anglo-Saxons," who controlled the town.[64]

Those Rudiak called, "the Anglo-Saxons," and Zahorsky called "the cake eaters," Croatian coal miner Tom Luketich called the "Johnny Bulls." Luketich worked in the Mon River mining town of Cokeburg, just up-river from Pittsburgh. There, he recalled, "These guys who were foremen educated their kids and they ran the town . . . The foremen were the only guys with any type of education. They were the 'Johnny Bulls' and they run the town. They were the bosses in the mine, they were on the council, they were on the police force, they were the mayor. They were everything in town."[65]

Ray Czachowski grew up in the heavily-Polish Lawrenceville neighborhood of Pittsburgh and remembered that, "We were in pretty dire need in 1936; we couldn't even raise money for clothes. Let's put it that way. I remember once going for a job at Pittsburgh Railways [the local streetcar company]. I went down there and put in an application, but as soon as they looked at the 'ski' on the back, they tore it up right in front of me and said, 'We'll call you if we need you.' And that sort of stuck with me all my life. It seemed that being a Pole and a Catholic hurt you in some places. That stuck with me. I eventually got a job, but I think you really had to prove yourself. They really give you the 'dirt,' so to speak."[66]

These lives of discrimination and the hunger for equality drove ethnic workers to militant action even before the 1930s. John Czelen, a Polish steelworker in Monessen's Pittsburgh Steel Company, recalled that it was this desire for equality which impelled his father, Casimir, to join the great 1919 steel strike. "I remember the discussions my dad and the others had with the organizer who came into the valley," he said. "They liked it that they could be a member [of the Amalgamated], not for other reasons, but for being a worker. And this was one of the things that sold them. [They were] miserable, [and] telling them that *they were going to be treated with some equality*, this is what they bought. Because up to that point they were looked upon as 'Hunkies,' as 'Polacks,' as 'Dagos,' as foreigners. The boss would say something to you and he'd say, 'Hey, Polack,' or 'Hey, Dago, come here.' Naturally, they resented that. They might not have shown any open resentment, but inwardly they felt hurt that they were treated as secondary citizens. And, incidentally, some of them had their first papers [citizenship]."[67]

Fighting the Ku Klux Klan

Anti-Catholic and anti-ethnic sentiment, however, involved far more than just social and economic discrimination, destructive as those were. It also took an overtly hostile form in the early and mid-1920s in the form of an aggressive Pennsylvania Ku Klux Klan which specifically targeted ethnics.

And ethnics fought back, sometimes in pitched battles between themselves and "the Anglo-Saxon" Klan which took on aspects of a small domestic war in the industrial heartland.

Today we think of the Ku Klux Klan as primarily a racist anti-black organization. And indeed it was in the Twenties, as well, both in the South and in the North. For example, in the Ohio River mill town of Beaver, west of Pittsburgh, Klansmen kidnapped and hanged a black man one night. They cut him down before he died, then beat and kicked him unconscious.[68] But in the north, especially in areas with large Catholic populations, Catholics were the primary focus of the Ku Klux Klan's terrorist hatred.

By 1924, all but two of the state's counties had Klan chapters, there were 250,000 Klan members in Pennsylvania as a whole, and Klan membership in

Western Pennsylvania alone numbered 125,000.[69] The Klan dominated the politics of Indiana, even engineering the election to governor of a sympathizer. Ohio had even more Klansmen, 400,000, making the Ohio KKK the largest in America.[70]

Meanwhile, in 1923, Catholics organized a militant semi-clandestine organization to fight the Klan known variously as "The Red Knights" or the "Knights of the Flaming Circle." Said to have a substantial membership among Pennsylvania's ethnic groups, it welcomed anyone opposed to the Ku Klux Klan and "not a Protestant."[71]

Ethnic opposition to this burgeoning northern Klan also found expression inside the labor movement. The United Mine Workers of America (UMWA), for example, was especially hostile to the KKK, as well as being officially committed to interracial unionism. In 1921, while the American Federation of Labor (AFL) refused to allow a segregated black delegation to that year's national convention to introduce a resolution calling for the suppression of the Klan, the UMWA officially barred from membership any miner who belonged to the Klan. While not entirely successful in ridding the union of Klan members, the Pennsylvania UMWA put union men suspected of Klan membership on trial. At the same time, Oklahoma UMWA members spied on Klan meetings and expelled any union man found to be attending.[72]

The most dramatic conflict between Pittsburgh-area ethnics and the Ku Klux Klan came in the mid-1920s as the Klan stepped up recruitment among "Anglo-Saxons" in Allegheny County. By 1925 the Klan had a membership of nearly 100,000 members in the eastern part of the state alone, with a third of that in Philadelphia. The rest was in the mill and mining counties of Schuylkill, Luzerne, in the Lehigh Valley, and in the "Pennsylvania Dutch" farm country south of Harrisburg.

Meanwhile, in Allegheny County, much of the Klan membership could be found in the same industrial centers where there were large concentrations of ethnics: Homestead, Duquesne, New Kensington, Coraopolis, Vandergrift, Jeanette, Indiana, Connellsville, and Pittsburgh itself. Further afield there were large Klan chapters in Johnstown and Altoona.[73]

The Klan made its presence felt through such terrorist night rider vigilante groups as "The Homestead Wreckers." In Pittsburgh they kidnapped a little girl from her grandparents and they forced the cancellation of a "Defense Day" parade in the Pittsburgh suburb of Wilkinsburg when that community refused to let the Klan march in the parade.[74]

The summer of 1923 brought the domestic war between the Ku Klux Klan and area Catholics to a head. One day that summer 10,000 Klansmen gathered for an initiation ceremony on a hillside overlooking the industrial town of Carnegie, just west of Pittsburgh. The town's mayor would not permit the Klan to march through town, as they wished, and blocked the main bridge into town with cars and trucks. The marching Klansmen shoved the vehicles aside and started down the main street of Carnegie.

They were met by a small army of cursing Carnegie industrial workers, who assailed them with stones and bricks. "The Klansmen in the front ranks shrank back, but those behind pressed them onward into the jostling crowd which overflowed into the street. Hoods were knocked off and robes torn. As the battered marchers struggled on, a shot was fired and a young Klansman, Thomas Abbott, died with a bullet through the temple. The Klan ranks backed up and then turned around, retreating across the bridge."[75] Thomas Abbott became a hero martyr to the local Klan. A booklet, *The Martyred Klansman,* was written about him and memorials and fund-raising events were named after him.

A week later, in the town of Scottdale, southeast of Pittsburgh, the scene was almost repeated. A Catholic gang had waylaid some Klansmen and ripped up their regalia. The Klan decided to teach the Catholics of Scottdale a lesson. "Remember Carnegie and Come Prepared," they told their members.

The local Klan obtained a parade permit and laid out a route which would take them directly past the local parish church. "No masked Klansman will get as far as Pittsburgh Street," declared the Catholics.

Meanwhile, the Klan threatened that if one of their number fell, not a single Catholic would remain alive in Scottdale come morning. As both sides stockpiled guns for the coming battle, the State Police appeared on the scene and calmed tensions. In return for the Klansmen agreeing to unmask, the State Police agreed to escort them through town in their parade. The Klan agreed and the parade took place without further incident.[76]

The next spring the battle narrowly averted in Scottdale erupted in the small Cambria County Irish-German Catholic mining town of Lilly, near Altoona. There was a small Protestant minority among the 2,300 residents of Lilly, and this minority sold the Klan newspaper in town. But, "It also was a strong United Mine Workers town and the Klan's hostility to unions had been increased by the decision of the UMW earlier that year [1924] to expel workers in the local district who were Klan members."[77] In addition, the Catholic miners of Lilly had twice prevented the local Klan from burning crosses on the hills overlooking the town.

Determined to teach the "micks" a lesson, 400 Klansmen from the towns of Indiana, Altoona and Johnstown, as well as Pittsburgh, converged on Lilly in chartered trains on the night of April 5, 1924. As they arrived shortly after 7 p.m., local sympathizers cut electrical power, plunging the valley town into darkness. Debarking armed and fully robed, the Klansmen lined up in front of their trains and marched down the main street to a hill overlooking the town. There they lit the torch to a giant cross which flamed above the town.

As they did so, according to one report, "A mob swept to the foot of the hill where the Klansmen surrounded their blazing cross. A hooded sentry was captured, disrobed, and put on a passing train. When his robes were waved at his assembled brethren, the decision was made to cut things short and return to the station. The crowd turned nasty and began assailing the rear guard of the Klan. A fire hose was used to drench the retreating marchers. As the Klansmen reached their train, those already on board opened fire on the pursuing crowd, which shot back . . . Four men died as a result of the adventure; others were injured and eventually eighteen Klansmen and ten residents of Lilly were sentenced to prison. Klansmen from the Indiana, Pennsylvania, Klavern had been prominent among those arrested at Lilly, and the next year someone set fire to their new $34,000 Klan building."[78]

Another report, based on interviews with locals, concluded that three Lilly men were killed that night, one of them a leader in the attack on the Klan and one of them a Protestant who had helped construct the crosses. In this report, twenty-eight Klansmen and sixteen townspeople were charged with "riot, affray and unlawful assembly." In a joint trial two months later, all of them—invading Klansmen and Lilly residents alike—were sentenced to two years in prison. No one was ever tried for the killings.[79]

This Land Is Your Land

Working class ethnics in the Pittsburgh region, then, were used to being the targets of hatred and discrimination, both from legitimate authorities and illegitimate terrorist gangs. Their resistance to both, and their belief that they should be accepted as equal citizens, would form the basis of more organized action in the 1930s. "I believed in organization," said Stephen Wisyanski, president of the SWOC local at Pittsburgh Steel in Monessen. "I believed that in unity there was enough strength that things can be turned around so that a lot of the companies would be brought to their knees. And that they would have to recognize people as human beings, and not as putting more value into a piece of machinery than into a human being."[80]

For Pittsburgh-area workers, equality and human dignity also meant what we today call "equal opportunity." In preparation for the great 1919 steel strike, organizers flooded into the Steel Valley, including the legendary Mother Jones, who claimed to be eighty-nine-years-old at the time. The first town they targeted was the steel town of Monessen, home of Stephen Wisyanski. Mother Jones was scheduled to speak at an April 1, 1919 rally, along with Phil Murray, then president of the UMWA's District 5. The Republican burgess (mayor) threatened to arrest Mother Jones and anyone who showed up to listen to her. When thousands of mine workers descended upon the town for the rally, the burgess changed his mind and Mother Jones spoke unmolested.[81]

She was not so lucky in Homestead, where she spoke on August 20, 1919. "We are to see whether Pennsylvania belongs to Kaiser Gary [head of U.S. Steel] or Uncle Sam," she told the assembled steelworkers of Homestead. "Our Kaisers sit up and smoke seventy-five cent cigars and have lackeys with knee pants bring them champagne while you starve, while you grow old at forty, stoking their furnaces. You pull in your belts while they banquet. They have stomachs two miles long and two miles wide and you fill them . . . If Gary wants to work twelve hours a day, let him go in the blooming mill and work. What we want is a little leisure, time for music, playgrounds, a decent home, books, and the things that make life worth while."[82]

For uttering such subversive "bread and roses" aspirations, the Homestead police arrested Mother Jones and jailed her. "A great mob of people collected outside the prison," she recalled. "There was angry talk. The jailer got scared. He thought there might be a lynching and he guessed who would be lynched. The mayor was in the jail, too, confering with the jailer. He was scared. He looked out of the office windows and saw hundreds of workers milling around and heard them muttering . . . So the jailer came to me and asked me to speak to the boys outside and ask them to go home. I went outside the jail and told the boys I was going to be released shortly on bond and that they should go home now and not give any trouble. I got them in a good humor and pretty soon they went away. Meanwhile, while I was speaking, the mayor had sneaked out the back way.

"We were ordered to appear in the Pittsburgh court the next morning. A cranky old judge asked me if I had a permit to speak on the streets.

"'Yes, sir,' I said. 'I had a permit.'

"'Who issued it?' he growled.

"'Patrick Henry; Thomas Jefferson; John Adams!' said I . . . He fined us all heavily."[83]

It was, of course, the Declaration of Independence and the promise of American freedoms which inspired Mother Jones and the steelworkers of Homestead and other industrial heartland mill towns to resistance and revolt. But the corporate powers viewed the desire on the part of ethnics to be treated as human beings with the civil rights of citizens and an equal opportunity to succeed as the manifestations of an alien ideology. "Every time one of us opened his mouth and became radical," 1930s Aliquippa steelworker Louis DeSenna told me, *"fighting for his rights,* he was called a Communist."[84] "They [the bosses] called the Croatian Hall communist and everything else," recalled Monessen steelworker Stephen Zoretich, "but it wasn't communist. It was because of the union activities."[85]

The workers' belief in the American rights of freedom and equality is also clearly evident in almost every existing photo we have of labor demonstrations in the 1930s—and even before. In these we see the immigrant workers and the children of the immigrants carrying, like a talisman, the American flag, and sometimes *many* American flags, on their picket lines and on their marches and at their rallies, the flag which promised them freedom and by which they proclaimed that, "We, too, are Americans!"

When Frances Perkins, Roosevelt's Secretary of Labor, toured Homestead in 1933, there was a replay of the Mother Jones episode. Republican Burgess Cavanaugh refused to let her meet with a delegation of steelworkers on the steps of the municipal building. Perkins, however, saw the American flag flying over the post office just down the street. "There is an American flag," she told the tense crowd. "We will go to the post office," which they did, holding their protest meeting under the protection of the American flag.[86]

When steelworkers marched through the streets of Aliquippa in the summer of 1936 with signs urging both unionization and a vote for Roosevelt—they were led by an American flag.[87]

On May 14, 1937, in a major outdoor rally in Aliquippa, the steelworkers of the town rallied for the union and for civil rights under the aegis of a large

American flag.[88]

In 1941 when the Steel Workers Organizing Committee finally triumphed in Johnstown, a Western Pennsylvania steel town dominated by Charlie Schwab's Bethlehem Steel, the photos of their triumphal car caravans winding their way through the heart of Johnstown show them bedecked with American flags.[89] To the steelworkers of the Pittsburgh region, the American flag had become the icon of the freedom for which they hungered.

Similarly, when SWOC members taking part in the Little Steel Strike walked across an open field toward Chicago's Republic Steel plant on May 30, 1937, they were led by a line of union members carrying American flags. About 250 yards from the plant they were met by a line of policemen wielding clubs and guns. "'Stand fast! Stand fast!,' the leaders cried. 'We got our rights! We got our legal rights to picket!' The cops said, 'You got no rights. You red bastards, you got no rights.'"[90]

Reporting on a screening of a film of the occurrence, *The St. Louis Post-Dispatch* wrote, "Suddenly, without apparent warning, there is a terrific roar of pistol shots, and men in the front ranks of the marchers go down like grass before a scythe. The camera catches approximately a dozen falling simultaneously in a heap."[91] The police killed ten and wounded seventy-four in what came to be called the Memorial Day Massacre.

The steelworkers shot down in the Memorial Day Massacre, however, were not "red bastards." The sentiments which motivated them were as American as apple pie and as old as the Declaration of Independence.

In 1931 ethnic steelworker John Czelen was laid off from Page Steel and Wire in Monessen and rode the rails for a year looking for work. Everywhere in America he found that common working people were not being treated as human beings. And he searched for an answer to the despair he saw everywhere around him. The answer he came to was the kind of "moral capitalism" which fueled the struggle of the steelworkers for their "rights."

"I was inquisitive," he said. "And [I asked], what is wrong that a person wanting work can't work? Why are we having a depression? . . . So, along the road I met men who were extremely intelligent. I saw families together. Men who I conversed with—must have had a high education—were riding the rails. I saw as many as two hundred on one freight. I remember I went to a place and begged for something to eat. The woman says, 'Oh, my God, there were so many here.' . . . I've seen human beings who were living in holes. Some of them were sick, and others who were beaten up in the railroad yards. Because the railroad dicks in those days, if they caught you in the yards, they wouldn't evict you. They just used that club and whomp you.

"I learned a lot. I saw what a beautiful country there was, what potential there was. I've seen the metropolis. I've seen the width of our railroads. I would see the potential and I could not understand, why wasn't this in use? It made me think politically. As a young fellow, I tried to understand socialism, the Marxist style. I tried to understand Debs. I read Hegel . . . Debs had the greatest influence on me, his writings. His writings and his example, too—Eugene Debs. I read Marx, but

Marx didn't impress me because I thought Marxism was contrary to man's nature. The extreme left was just as contrary as the extreme right, which at that time was predatory capitalism. I thought, here were two extremes. I looked at it in a kind of modified way, a social democratic way, which I thought Debs was . . . I say, it [Marxism] was kind of counter to man's nature. You know, a man is a squirrel. He wants to accumulate a few nuts. But, the squirrel should not own the forest. I sat down with missionaries, communists, socialists, and Nazis. I read *Mein Kampf*. I'm convinced the extreme left is just as bad as the extreme right.

"If I heard that somebody was to speak on social issues, I'd go to that. I went to the library, I picked up a book. Or I went to a meeting of the unemployed here in Monessen. The Socialists had a meeting here in Monessen advocating the establishment of unemployment compensation. I remember this one guy, he was very articulate. He stood beside an American flag and he talked about why the steelworkers who are unemployed should be receiving a government subsidy, you know. I was so interested because to me it made a lot of sense. Before we know, the cops descended, grabbed him and the American flag, and he went down a set of stairs. They broke up the meeting, and that was the end of it. That further bothered me. I said, 'Why could not a man stand there and say to his people, or the people say, we want to work?'"[92]

After a year riding the rails, John Czelen came back to Monessen. In 1933, long before the coming of SWOC and when local unions were still called "lodges," he and others formed an independent union at Page Steel called the "Honest Deal Lodge"—which lasted three months, he said, before it was "broken by the company."[93] When SWOC later came to Monessen, Czelen became president of the SWOC local at Page Steel and Wire, still looking for an "Honest Deal."

Pete Muselin, a Croatian barber and son of a steel worker in Aliquippa, was also looking for an "Honest Deal." He was also a premature Democrat— Democratic before Roosevelt—when there were perhaps only a dozen Democrats in Aliquippa and the Coal and Iron Police and the J & L police ran everything. Pete was warned that "'If you dare to have a [union] meeting, Pete, we will blow your head off.' . . . Well I had the meetings anyway. So, they'd arrest me. I was arrested so often I could have put my name tag on that cell down in the borough lock-up."[94]

Pete also challenged the Aliquippa City Council, which was then a rubber stamp for the company. "The council would pass these ordinances, and I would defy them on the grounds that they were unconstitutional. They would tell me, and be very emphatic about it, 'We make the rules. This is not the United States. This is Woodlawn [as Aliquippa was sometimes known], and we're going to do what we please.

"Once I went down there and I started reading the Declaration of Independence: 'When in the course of human events, it becomes necessary . . . ' A cop said, 'That's communistic stuff you're reading.' When I got to the part where 'all men are created equal,' he wanted to put me in jail. And he did arrest me. But Charlie Laughlin, the chief of police, just happened to walk in. He said to that cop, 'You dumb so-and-so, he's reading the Declaration of Independence.'"

In 1926 the Aliquippa police raided Pete's Croatian fraternal lodge meeting and arrested him and about thirty others. All but Pete and four others were released. Pete and his friends were tried for violating the Pennsylvania sedition law and sentenced to five years in prison. One of the five died in prison. When Pete was released in 1932, he immediately resumed his activities, becoming a leader of a bloody strike at the American Rolling Mill in Ambridge in 1933, the first strike in the area. That strike was broken by deputized American Legionnaires with tear gas, rifles, and machine guns. When the Legionnaires charged, the man standing next to Pete fell dead, taking a bullet Pete thought was meant for him. Pete and his buddies in Aliquippa were indeed willing to fight for, go to prison for, and to die for the Declaration of Independence and the revolutionary ideology that, "all men are created equal."

Phil McGuigan also believed in that egalitarian American ideal, that "Hunkies" were just as American as any WASP. In 1930 he worked at the McKeesport Tin Plate Company in Port Vue where, he recalled, your nationality was always asked when you were hired. But, he says, "We're all Americans here, and that's all we should have to say. We shouldn't have to say what our ancestry is. In those days, they would ask you your ancestry: Is it Greek, or Italian, things like that."[95]

Perhaps the most eloquent—certainly the most extended—explanation of what the steelworkers were fighting for can be found in the pages of a Braddock novelist who described what the coming of freedom meant to the steelworkers of that mill town. Thomas Bell's *Out of This Furnace* is a novel of the coming of the Steel Workers Organizing Committee—"Swock"—to Pittsburgh's Steel Valley community of Braddock and the unionization of that basic industry in the late Thirties.[96] Written in the late Thirties contemporaneously with the events it describes, and by a son and grandson of Braddock steelworkers, it provides a further clue as to what the workers of the Steel Valley wanted. This novel, "about the acculturation and evolving political consciousness of the immigrant workers of America's steel towns,"[97] expresses a vision of social justice, political and economic democracy, and a deep and abiding faith in egalitarianism.

Much of the vision expressed in Bell's novel came from actual people. "Bell's particular source for much of the novel's inside account of union activities in the thirties appears to have been Louis Smolinski, now retired from U.S. Steel, who in the early thirties was president of the Braddock local of the Amalgamated Association of Iron, Steel and Tin Workers and then a member of both the Employees Representatives at Edgar Thomson and the Steel Workers' Organizing Committee. Smolinski states that the novel's documentary materials concerning union activities—letters, memos, minutes—are essentially verbatim (with some changing of names), passed by Smolinski himself to Bell when he was researching the novel in Braddock in the late thirties."[98]

The first thing which strikes the reader is Bell's description of the "C.I.O. men" who swarmed over Braddock. "They were all sorts of men, Scotch and Irish and Polish and Italian and Slovak and German and Jew, but they didn't talk and act the way the steel towns expected men who were Scotch and Irish and Polish and Italian and Slovak and German and Jew to talk and act.

"They were outspoken, fearlessly so, as though they had never learned to glance around and see who might be listening before they spoke. They were obviously convinced that they were individually as good as any man alive, from Mill Superintendents up or down, as the case might be, and probably better. They assumed that there was one law for the rich and one for the poor, and that it was the same law; and they talked about newspapers and radio chains and law courts and legislative bodies as though these things could be used for the benefit of ordinary people as well as against them; and there was something almost fantastic in their easy, take-it-for-granted air that Braddock burgesses and Pittsburgh police chiefs and Washington congressmen were public servants. And nobody in the steel towns had ever been heard to talk the way they talked—without stumbling over the words, uttering them as though they meant something real right there in Braddock—about liberty and justice and freedom of speech."[99]

Following U.S. Steel's capitulation to SWOC in 1937, Dobie Dobrejcak—a central figure in the novel—thought about the kind of CIO men who brought all the changes to Braddock: "Whatever their ancestry, they had felt the same way about certain things; and because Dobie had been born and raised in a steel town, where the word meant people who were white, Protestant, middle-class Anglo-Saxons, it hadn't occurred to him that the C.I.O. men were thinking and talking *like Americans.*

"'Maybe not the kind of American that came over on the *Mayflower,*' he reflected, 'or the kind that's always shooting off their mouths about Americanism and patriotism . . . but the kind that's got *Made in U.S.A.* stamped all over them, from the kind of grub they like to the things they wouldn't do for all the money in the world.'

"'Made in the U.S.A.,' he thought, 'made in [Braddock's] First Ward . . . If I'm anything at all I'm an American, only I'm not the kind you read about in history books or that they make speeches about on the Fourth of July; anyway, not yet. And a lot of people don't know what to make of it and don't like it. Which is tough on me but is liable to be still tougher on them, because I at least don't have to be told that Braddock ain't Plymouth Rock and this ain't the year 1620.

"'Made in the U.S.A.,' he thought, 'made in the First Ward. But it wasn't where you were born or how you spelled your name or where your father had come from. It was the way you thought and felt about certain things. *About freedom of speech and the equality of men and the importance of having one law—the same law—for rich and poor, for the people you liked and the people you didn't like . . .*

"'I hope it's all in the Declaration of Independence and the Bill of Rights,' Dobie reflected . . . 'All I know is there's certain things I've got to have or I don't want to go on living. I want certain things bad enough to fight for them, bad enough to die for them. Patrick Henry, Junior—that's me. Give me liberty or give me death. But he meant every word of it and by God, I think I do too.'"[100]

This quintessential American civil rights movement by ethnic workers in the industrial heartland was part of a wider "Left Populist" movement all across America in the Thirties for inclusion of the downtrodden in the American Dream. Journalist Bill Moyers recalls that FDR seemed to be the champion of all the

"Forgotten Men" who were "Lost in America," all the dispossessed and tossed aside. Moyers was raised a Baptist in East Texas where his father had left school after the fourth grade to begin life as a cotton picker. His father bought a radio with his meager savings just so he could listen to FDR, "the aristocrat speaking up for common people," during his "Fireside Chats." And the message of FDR and his New Deal, said Moyers, the message his father heard coming over that radio in the East Texas cotton fields was this: "Class and power were not fixed by Nature; inequality was wrong and unemployment humiliating; runaway capitalism could be tamed, privilege checked, monopolies broken up, an end put to government by organized money. To people down and out, broken and feeling betrayed, Roosevelt talked of democracy. He made them think they had a stake in it and a responsibility for it."[101]

The common people who Moyers spoke of embodied a down-to-earth, blue collar, multi-ethnic, democratic ideal we find elsewhere in popular culture during this period. This ideal is found, for instance, in the thousands of photos taken by the photographers sent out across America by the Farm Security Administration (FSA).

From 1935 to 1943 Roy Stryker directed a team of some twenty FSA photographers who produced over 270,000 pictures of the "common people" of America. Some of the iconic images we have of the Great Depression were taken by Stryker's photographers: Dorothea Lange's Okie Madonna broken down somewhere in the California fields; Arthur Rothstein's ruined dust bowl farmers; Walker Evans' images of the hovels and cemeteries of Bethlehem, Pennsylvania, lying in the shadow of the steel mill; Gordon Parks' poor blacks and Ben Shahn's fat sheriffs overseeing picket lines. All of these images—the very images which form our mental image of the Depression—were taken with the instructions of Stryker in mind.

Stryker wanted pictures of "the common people," the hard working survivors who built America. "I think it's significant," Stryker later said, "that in our entire collection we have only one picture of Franklin Roosevelt, the most newsworthy man of the era—this, mind you, in a collection that's sometimes said to have reported the feel and smell and taste of the Thirties even more vividly than the news media . . . you'll find no record of big people or big events in the collection . . . not a single shot of Wall Street, and absolutely no celebrities."[102]

These "common people" were celebrated in 1940 by prominent labor cartoonist Fred Wright in his own favorite cartoon, "The Century of the Common Man!" The cartoon in which Wright portrayed the "Common Man's Century" showed hammer-carrying workers marching out of factories toward the sunlight.

Of course, Fred Wright spoke for Left-wing unionism, being the staff cartoonist for many years for the United Electrical Workers (UE-CIO), who represented the electrical workers at the major Westinghouse factories just outside of Pittsburgh in East Pittsburgh and Wilmerding. But this was not just the ideal of Pittsburgh's more politicized unionists. It was in the air. In 1936, in what he termed his own favorite poem, Carl Sandburg celebrated "The People, Yes!"[103] In 1941, Pulitzer Prize-winning poet Stephen Vincent Benet urged us to "Listen To

The People." These people included, "Paul Bunchick and the Greek who runs the Greek's/ The black-eyed children ouf ot Sicily/ All of them there and all of them a nation./ Our voice is not one voice, but many voices./ Not one man's, not the greatest, but the people's."[104]

In 1942, Aaron Copeland wrote a hymn of praise to "the common man" in his "Lincoln Portrait," the most stirring portion of which is his triumphant beginning, the "Fanfare for the Common Man." In words reminiscent of those Mother Jones spoke at Homestead in 1919, Copeland has a reader quote passages from Abraham Lincoln to the accompaniment of stirring music, passages such as "The spirit of slavery is the same as the spirit that says, 'You work and toil and earn bread, and I'll eat it.' No matter in what shape it comes, whether from a mouth of a king, or from one race of men as an apology for enslaving another race, it is the same tyrannical principle."

This was a theme commonly expressed by radical labor unions in the Thirties, such as the Independent Textile Union of Rhode Island, which had approvingly published the very same Lincoln passage five years before in a 1937 issue of its newspaper.[105]

Perhaps the musical genre which most closely reflected the spirit of the times was folk music. Americans have long composed and sung "traditional" songs such as cowboy laments, Delta blues, Kentucky bluegrass, and the hillbilly songs of Appalachia with its roots in Elizabethan and Scots-Irish ballads. It was not until the twentieth century, however, that such songs came to be identified as "folk songs" of "the people," a populist musical genre which cohered in the 1930s. And it is no accident that the music we most closely identify with the Thirties is folk music.

Folk music describes the lives, loves, and labors of the common people. Meanwhile, the dominant political ideology of dissent in America has always been a "Left Populism" which championed common people against the rich and powerful. It is also no accident, then, that the two periods which witnessed the proliferation of folk songs, the Thirties and the Sixties, were also the only two eras of the twentieth century which witnessed the emergence and flowering of significant populist and oppositional "counter-cultures."

It was in 1935 that the American Communist Party adopted a "Popular Front" strategy which embraced the durable Left Populism of American dissent. The party adopted as its official slogan, "Communism is Twentieth Century Americanism" and the volunteers it sent to fight in Spain against the fascists in that country's civil war did so as members of "The Abraham Lincoln Brigade." At the same time, the Communist-affiliated Composers Collective began including in its *Workers Song Books* indigenous folk music of all types, including songs of farmers, miners, urban workers, and African-Americans.

The most influential folk singer of the Thirties was no doubt Woody Guthrie. He was born into an impoverished Oklahoma dust bowl family and was closely associated with the Communist Party. Guthrie composed more than a thousand songs reflecting the decade's spirit of populist protest and painted "This Machine Kills Fascists" on his guitar. Perhaps his most well-known song is "This Land is Your Land," which declared that "this land belongs to you and me," not, it suggested, to the rich and the corporations.

In 1941 Guthrie joined Pete Seeger, Lee Hays, and others to form the Almanac Singers, a popular folk group which sang for C.I.O. [Congress of Industrial Organizations] organizing campaigns and political rallies. After World War II, as America became more politically conservative, Guthrie, Seeger, and other members of the Almanac Singers kept the populist spirit of folk music alive through such groups as People's Songs. It was at a meeting of the People's Songs Board of Directors that Seeger and Lee Hays wrote "If I Had a Hammer," which gained widespread popularity in the early Sixties. In it, Seeger and Hays proclaimed that they would hammer out justice and freedom "all over this land."

This theme was also echoed in the films of Italian director Frank Capra, perhaps the most popular and successful film director of the 1930s. Born in Sicily in 1897, Capra immigrated to Los Angeles with his parents in 1903. When America entered World War I, he joined the army. After the Armistice, Capra returned to Los Angeles, but was unable to find a job. He bummed around for several years, working at odd jobs, ending up down and out in San Francisco.

It was during those days that this Italian immigrant came to believe that, "The rich have it all, but accomplish little."[106] The essence of Frank Capra's immigrant populism, reflected in his subsequent films, was that it was the decent, hard-working, "little guy" who really represented all that was most American—while the wealthy and the representatives of the powerful represented a venal corruption of the American ideal.

During World War II, this inclusionary sentiment was even evident in the combat films Hollywood churned out. There is a certain tension surrounding these films, as they always portrayed a far more heterogeneous fighting unit than existed at the time. Thus, in 1943's *Bataan,* we find a squad which is a virtual United Nations. There were Filipinos, Southern and Eastern Europeans, a California Mexican played by Desi Arnaz, and even a black soldier. In reality, of course, the military, like America itself, was still racially segregated. Thus, these films reflected the desire, the ideal, more than social reality.

Nevertheless, World War II films witnessed the rise of the democratic platoon, in which ethnic, racial, and class differences were dissolved. The polyglot squad itself was the hero. This can be seen even before America entered the war in a 1940 film such as *The Fighting 69th,* and continued with films like 1943's *Guadalcanal Diary* and *Bataan,* on through to the end of the war with films such as 1945's *A Walk in the Sun,* adapted from the popular Harry Brown novel of the same name. Some of the sentiments portrayed in these democratic platoon films were more than just wish fulfillment. For instance, many American soldiers stationed in England preparing for the Normandy Invasion reportedly hated and resisted the "class" system of their own army, which required them to salute their own officers.[107] Many of these resisting soldiers were also union men. Approximately 20 percent (2,500,000) of the G.I.s who served in World War II were members of labor unions back home.[108]

Thus, we find that one of the pervasive ideas of the period was that the "real"

American was the average, common, hard-working, decent Joe, whose religion or ethnicity no longer mattered. Whatever his background—Homestead or Clairton or Braddock's First Ward—he was 100 percent American with all the equal rights pertaining to citizenship. It was a deeply ingrained ideology which permeated the consciousness of workers, regardless of background.

Fighting for Democracy

This ideology of equal rights was deep-rooted and long-lived in ethnic working class communities. Before the turn of the century, Pittsburgh-area ethnic workers had already imbibed the ideals of Jeffersonian republicanism and were demanding equal rights in pursuit of "the American Dream." A case in point occurred in 1891 (the year before the great Homestead Lockout and Strike and the same year as Pope Leo's encyclical) when a plant guard was slain in an altercation at the Carnegie Corporation's Edgar Thomson Steel Works in Braddock. Sixty workers were charged with the murder, including three Slovaks, who were condemned to death. Not only did the local Slovak Union rally to their cause, but so did Slavic immigrant organizations throughout the country.

Indicative of how a cross-ethnic class consciousness was already emerging, even at that time, clemency petitions, in English and Slovak, signed by thousands of immigrants from various Slavic groups, poured into the Pennsylvania Pardon Board. And each petition protested that Slavic immigrants were barred from participating equally in public affairs and in business in America: "A great majority of us became servants, hewers of wood, drawers of water, workers in the mills, the mines, the fields, and the shops for a compensation which barely allowed us the necessaries of life . . . *We are buying lands, building homes, educating our children* . . . The hanging of these men will be a terrible blow to our people."[109]

Perhaps in another indication of the bias against ethnics—at least in the eyes of the ethnics themselves—this petition campaign to free the three men from condemnation "for a crime they did not commit" failed.

The American experience of participation in World War I reinforced this ideology within the ethnic working class. This "war to make the world safe for democracy" also implanted the ideology of democracy on the home front as never before. "Nowhere," we are told, "not even in the mill towns, could men escape the war propaganda. Chief among the arguments was that the Allies were fighting to make the world safe for democracy. Organized labor found this view particularly congenial, for it justified the painful AFL repudiation of pacifism . . . The American Alliance for Labor and Democracy, created by [AFL president] Gompers in the summer of 1917 . . . became the unofficial [government propaganda] agency for the labor audience."[110]

The labor movement quickly made a connection in its propaganda between the war for democracy abroad and economic and political democracy, "industrial democracy," at home. This meant such things as the eight-hour day and the legalization of unions.

Evidently, this propaganda effort had an effect on the rank and file. After successfully founding a local union in Washington, Pennsylvania, a town just south of Pittsburgh, steelworkers wrote to their *Amalgamated Journal* that they were "victorious in our first fight for democracy over here."[111] Most of the new steelworker local unions founded at this time adopted such names as the "Democracy," "Liberty," or "Old Glory" lodge.[112]

Organized labor's appeals to "democracy" and "liberty" during the Great War were particularly attractive to the ethnic immigrants of the steel towns. "They were the first to crowd the mass meetings and sign up for [union] membership . . . The benefit lists of the Amalgamated Association [of Iron and Steel Workers] show a sharp increase in the number of Slavic names, distributed mainly in new lodges whose officers were also immigrants . . . Frequently held in immigrant [fraternal] society halls, the [union] meetings invariably included speakers in the dominant languages of the communities. The immigrants flocked into the organization. In comparison, the natives were, according to all reports, an unenthusiastic lot."[113]

An Amalgamated organizer in Wheeling, West Virginia, just down the Ohio River from Pittsburgh, wrote to the *Amalgamated Journal* complaining to the apathetic native workers among the journal's readers, "The poorest foreign laborer . . . wants to get organized and you don't . . . They will show you what Americanism really is, one who stands up for his rights."[114]

Standing up for one's "American rights" had come to mean things like free speech and the right to organize. In the months leading up to the great steel strike of 1919 the courts, police, city, and state governments adopted increasingly repressive measures to suppress organizing activity in the steel towns. In February 1919, Pittsburgh-area workers met in a special convention at the Pittsburgh Labor Temple to condemn such actions as not only illegal but "un-American." In nearby Clairton a Hungarian steelworker complained to a visiting Congressional investigative committee, "This is the U.S. and we ought to have the right to belong to the union."[115]

When the 1919 steel strike finally came, it was called the "Hunky Strike," because it was mostly the ethnic immigrants who went out on strike, while the native-born steelworkers scabbed.[116] In contrast, observed the strike committee, the ethnic workers "are proving to have wonderful powers of resistance." One reason for this was because, "The peasant sense of community held the immigrants together." But, also, because the ideals for which the war had been fought had deeply influenced their attitudes. "For why this war?" asked a Polish striker at a Pittsburgh meeting. "For why we buy Liberty Bonds? For mills? No, for freedom and America—for everybody. No more [work like] horse and wagon. For eight-hour day."[117]

This ideology of "freedom" and "American rights" grew into a powerful political language among ethnic industrial workers in the Teens and Twenties for a number of reasons.

First, there were the "Americanization" programs of the Great War and immediately afterward "through which the government sought to enforce an American identity—'100 percent Americanism'—on the nation's cultural dissenters [i.e., ethnics] and political radicals; second, the implementation in the nation's largest firms of a new system of industrial relations—often called Fordism or the American Plan—based on high productivity, high wages, and enlightened schemes of scientific and personnel management; and third, the national diffusion by mass cultural media—movies, radio, and national magazines—of 'American' cultural values and, in the process, of the English language. The combined result of these forces, by the Twenties, was an unprecedented national emphasis on pledging loyalty to American institutions, on defining what it meant to be an American, and on elaborating an American way of life. Such a preoccupation with 'being American' did not in itself procure political or cultural conformity, but it did force virtually every group seriously interested in political power— groups as diverse as capitalists, socialists, ghettoized ethnics, and small-town fundamentalists—to couch their programs in the language of Americanism."[118]

Rights for Reds

There was also the strong presence of political radicals in the Pittsburgh region, which predated the arrival of most of the New Immigrants. From days of old, however, these political radicals had sought to forge links with ethnic working class communities. Thus, for instance, in November 1888, about 300 "anarchists" met in Pittsburgh's Lafayette Hall to hear pro-socialist speeches attacking coke operators for the deaths of workers who were "poor slaves . . . killed for having the nerve to strike."[119]

What we find when we look at this radical presence, especially that of the Pittsburgh-area Socialist Party, is that it often spoke in the language of Americanism, or was at least compatible with the civic patriotism expressed by the immigrants themselves.

For example, in 1909 the overwhelmingly immigrant workers at the Pressed Steel Car Company in McKees Rocks, just outside of Pittsburgh, launched a large, bloody, and ultimately successful strike. Among the company's 5,000 to 8,000 workers were fourteen different nationality groups, the largest being Hungarian. They worked in insufferable plants with names like "Slaughter House" and "Last Chance." On July 10, 1909, 40 "Last Chance" riveters were fired because they demanded to be told what their pay rates were and that former pay cuts be rescinded. In addition, sixty workers in the erection department who'd made similar demands were also fired.

Within forty-eight hours, in an astounding display of cross-ethnic class solidarity, 5,000 leaderless and unorganized workers struck in solidarity. In a scene reminiscent of the 1892 Homestead Lockout and Strike, Pressed Steel loaded scabs onto a riverboat and brought it to the Ohio River landing of the plant, where it was met with rifle fire from the strikers. The riverboat quickly pulled out and fled to the opposite shore to unload the scabs.

The company next called in an army of hundreds of deputy sheriffs and state policemen—the latter a police organization created solely to put down exactly such worker rebellions. Open war broke out. Strikers were evicted from company-owned homes. Lawmen were killed in battle. Pittsburgh area streetcar motormen and railroad men refused to haul scabs into the town.

On August 25, 1909, Socialist Party leader Eugene V. Debs came to McKees Rocks and spoke to 10,000 Pressed Steel Car workers and their families. He told them their struggle was a "harbinger of a new spirit among the unorganized, foreign-born workers in the mass-production industries."[120]

Organizers for the anarcho-syndicalist Industrial Workers of the World (IWW), founded only four years before and speaking a dozen tongues themselves, appeared everywhere among the workers, bringing order out of chaos. The workers responded eagerly to IWW leadership, and on September 7 the company capitulated, agreeing to raise wages by 15 percent, fire all scabs, and rehire all strikers.

This triumph was hailed as an important IWW victory for the new labor organization. And when the IWW-led workers marched afterward in the funeral processions to bury their dead, American flags marched everywhere with the mourners.[121] These "foreign-born" may have been led by the IWW, but they felt they were fighting for something symbolized by the American flag—and there seemed to be no contradiction between the two.

It is clear that socialist organizations put down strong roots among the workers of the Pittsburgh-area in the years thereafter. In 1912, for instance, Socialist Party presidential candidate Eugene V. Debs received 15.5 percent of the vote in Allegheny County and averaged 25 percent of the vote in sixteen Steel Valley towns (as compared to only 4 percent of the vote in Detroit and 5 percent of the vote in New York City).[122]

Additionally, the Steel Valley voted Socialists into office in McKeesport, North Versailles, Pitcairn, New Castle, and Turtle Creek in the years between 1911 and 1917. In 1920 Debs again polled about the same number of votes as in 1912, winning 21.6 percent of the vote in Homestead.[123] This is particularly amazing given the political repression by the dominant Republican oligarchy at the time.

But what was it the ethnic workers felt they were voting for when they voted Socialist? Did this mean they wanted socialism? Or did it mean that they voted for the Socialists because the Socialists spoke up for them when no one else did, and in a language they understood? John Czelen, who became president of a steelworkers local in Monessen in the late Thirties (and who said, "A man is a squirrel. He wants to accumulate a few nuts. But, the squirrel should not own the forest."), said he liked what Debs advocated. Czelen was also greatly impressed by an articulate Socialist Party organizer who spoke in favor of unemployed insurance in a Monessen fraternal hall—all the while clutching an American flag in his hand. It must have seemed to the ethnic audience listening to him that Socialism, unemployed insurance, and Americanism went literally hand-in-hand.

And there were other values the Pittsburgh Socialist Party fought for which must have seemed to ethnic workers to be the very essence of the Americanism they had come to espouse themselves—such as free speech, the first of FDR's

Four Freedoms.

In the summer of 1912 the local Socialist Party staged a massive "free speech" fight in the Homewood neighborhood of Pittsburgh, where it had a large presence. This fight was similar to the free speech fights waged by the IWW all across the West at about the same time. In these free speech fights, militants spoke in public in defiance of legal orders to shut up, and thereafter jammed the jails with their arrests.

Front page headlines in *The Pittsburgh Sunday Post* screamed, "Big Police Corps Makes Onslaught Upon Socialists—Score Are Arrested, Including Women, Out of 10,000 in Homewood—Speakers Martyr Themselves for Free Speech." The story went on to say: "Police and Socialists battled in Homewood last night for two hours. One hundred foot police, 25 mounted members of the famed Black Squadron, and 25 detectives were pitted against 10,000 men, women, and children . . . The meeting was the first attempt of Pittsburgh Socialists to enforce their demand for free speech, the right to hold public meetings without permits. The Socialists have adopted the policy of 'passive resistance.' They did not engage the police in battle except in isolated instances in the crowd, but orator after orator made his way to a small platform erected in Kelly Street, near Homewood Avenue, only to be dragged down by the bluecoats. Women were among the speakers pulled down from the platform.

"The rising of the first speaker was the signal for the reserve of police to swoop down on the meeting. Simultaneously, mounted men galloped from side streets where they had been lurking and drove straight into the crowd.

"A riot call was turned into police headquarters and a moment later policemen darted to the scene in taxicabs, and a large reserve of police centered in the Frankstown police station drove up in two patrol wagons, one of which had been taken from the Squirrel Hill station.

"As soon as the mounted squad made its way to the platform and dragged down the first speaker, a second speaker sprang to his place. The second met the same fate and likewise the third, each being able to get in scarce a sentence, yet the enthusiasts fought for their turn on the platform.

"As though by previous arrangement, many women speakers were waiting, most of them from 18 to 23 years old, and they met the same fate as the men. At the police station they appeared . . . full of fight.

"Even after the platform was cleared and the crowd swept away from it, one old man, thought to be a socialist organizer of Chartiers township, made his way up through a house next door to a second-story balcony, where he harangued the crowd for five minutes. But the police broke into the house, which was locked, beat down the door at his back, and carried him, shouting frantically, to the waiting patrol wagon . . . H. A. Goff, 62 years old, one of the prisoners, after his arrest made an address to the prisoners in the other cells."[124]

The next Saturday, the Socialists returned to the same Homewood street corner, to be met with the same fate. "Arrests Result When Socialists Attempt Meeting," again cried *The Pittsburgh Sunday Post* on page one. "Police Block the Efforts of Speakers to Use Streets of Homewood."

This time there were twice as many Socialists: "Warfare between the police and Socialists in the Homewood district was waged fiercely last night. More than 40 Socialists, men and women, were arrested . . . Twenty thousand men and women, the majority of them wearing the red insignia of Socialism, gathered in the Homewood district. Until far past midnight, Homewood Avenue and surrounding streets were packed with moving, struggling throngs of humanity, intermittently broken up by charges of mounted policemen, only to mass more closely.

"One hundred and fifty foot policemen, 25 mounted men, members of the Black Squadron, and 25 detectives pitted themselves against the Socialists for the second time in eight days. The attempts of two speakers to address the crowd in Kelly Street were frustrated by the police, and later, led by a megaphone man in an auto truck, the crowd moved to a vacant lot on Hamilton Avenue near Homewood Avenue. There the Wilmerding Socialist Band played several airs and the throng sang 'America, The Beautiful.' In the police station, the female prisoners sang patriotic songs.

"At 10 minutes past 8 o'clock a speaker's stand was pushed through the crowd . . . When the first speaker mounted the platform . . . he was pulled from the stand. While being led to a patrol wagon, the speakers and their friends sang the first verse of 'America.'

"An auto patrol wagon was then backed up to the speaker's stand and filled with supposed Socialists. As the patrol wagon was being driven away, a fervent Socialist in the crowd yelled, 'Stop! Wait until I get in!' The wagon stopped and he jumped in. After 25 mounted policemen had cleared the street, an auto truck came out of an alley into Kelly Street containing a man with a megaphone who shouted, 'People, follow me!' The crowd was led to a vacant lot on Hamilton Avenue near Homewood, where a band played . . . and the Socialists and their friends contented themselves with singing 'America.' The mounted police followed the crowd and when orders were given drove it from the lot."[125]

To the reader of these accounts, it appears that the only "riots" which occurred in Homewood on those hot August nights in 1912 were by the police. And the only "crimes" of the Socialists were that they wanted the freedom to speak freely in public and sing "America the Beautiful" on a vacant lot. Surely it must have seemed to ethnic workers that the Socialists and they, themselves, were fighting for the same thing—such basic American rights as freedom of speech and freedom of assembly. And perhaps this is exactly what they were voting for just three months later when Socialist leader Debs got 25 percent of the presidential vote in 16 Steel Valley towns.

Thus, there was a conjunction between every force which had an ideological influence on "alien" ethnic workers who were in the process of becoming "Americans": the Church, their Old World cultural values, the professed ideals of the government and corporations, popular culture, the Great War to make the world safe for democracy—and even the primary oppositional political organization which professed to speak for the workers. All of them preached a political ideology which proclaimed justice, equality, liberty, and fair play for all—an American ideology which seemed to be contradicted by the daily American reality around them.

Notes

1. Matthew S. Magda, *Monessen: Industrial Boomtown and Steel Community, 1898-1980,* Pennsylvania Historical and Museum Commission: Harrisburg, 1985, 86.

2. In 1999 the National Slovak Society still had its headquarters on Pittsburgh's South Side on East Carson Street. Large letters on the building's front boasted, "Fraternal life insurance since 1890."

3. See James Caldwell Foster, *The Union Politic: The CIO Political Action Committee,* University of Missouri Press: St. Louis, 1975, Tables 1948D, 1952B, 1954E, 217, 220, 225.

4. Bruce M. Stave, *The New Deal and the Last Hurrah,* University of Pittsburgh Press: Pittsburgh, 1970, 40-41.

5. Michael P. Weber, "Ethnicity and the Democratic Political Machine in Pittsburgh, 1930-1960," paper delivered at the 1991 annual convention of the Organization of American Historians, 10.

6. Weber, "Ethnicity and the Democratic Political Machine," 10.

7. Weber, "Ethnicity and the Democratic Political Machine," 11.

8. Weber, "Ethnicity and the Democratic Political Machine," 11. It was this visit to Forbes Field in which Roosevelt made his famous, and futile, campaign promise to balance the budget if elected. Four years later FDR returned to Forbes Field for another massive rally in his 1936 campaign for re-election. By that time the federal budget was severely imbalanced through deficit spending. This problem which mattered little to Pittsburghers, but it worried Roosevelt. Bothered by returning to "the scene of the crime" with his 1932 campaign promise unfulfilled, Roosevelt asked Sam Rosenman, his speech writer, for advice on how to finesse the problem. Rosenman answered: "Deny you were ever in Pittsburgh." See Robert Shogan, "50 Years On, FDR Legacy Largely Intact," *Los Angeles Times* story reprinted in *The Pittsburgh Post-Gazette,* April 13, 1995, A-5.

9. Weber, "Ethnicity and the Democratic Political Machine," 12.

10. Recounted in Weber, "Ethnicity and the Democratic Political Machine," 20.

11. Stave, *The New Deal,* 50.

12. Stave, *The New Deal,* 51.

13. G. H. Gregory, Compiler and Editor, *Posters of World War II,* Gramercy Books: New York, 1993, 10.

14. See Andres Martinez, "WW II posters attract baby boomers," *The Pittsburgh Post-Gazette,* August 13, 1995.

15. Peter Plagens, "Norman Rockwell Revisited," *Newsweek,* November 15, 1999, 84.

16. See E. Eastman Irvine, Ed., "Estimated United States Population, July 1, 1943," *The World Almanac and Book of Facts for 1947, The New York World-Telegram,* New York, 1947, 185.

17. Alfred Winslow Jones, *Life, Liberty, and Property,* Temple University Press: Philadelphia, 1941.

18. Lizabeth Cohen, *Making a New Deal: Industrial Workers in Chicago, 1919-1939,* Cambridge University Press: Cambridge, 1990.

19. Louis Hartz, *The Liberal Tradition in America: An Interpretation of American Political Thought Since the Revolution,* Harcourt, Brace & World, Inc.: New York, 1955, 269.

20. Peter Costa, "A Conversation with Morris Fiorina," *Faculty of Arts and Sciences Gazette,* Harvard University, spring 1993, 10. Emphasis added.

21. Philip Klein, et al., *A Social Study of Pittsburgh: Community Problems and Social Services of Allegheny County,* Columbia University Press: New York, 1938, 252-253.

22. "A lot of times we [SWOC] had a meeting down at the Croatian Hall," remembered Monessen steelworker Stephen Zoretich. See Magda, *Monessen,* 137.

23. Len De Caux, *Labor Radical: From the Wobblies to CIO, A Personal History,* Beacon Press: Boston, 1970, 1971, 393.

24. "Bishops' Program of Social Reconstruction," in Raphael M. Huber, Ed., *Our Bishops Speak: National Pastorals and Annual Statements of the Hierarchy of the United States, 1919-1951,* Bruce: Milwaukee, 1952, 243-260.

25. *Labor,* September 9, 1944, 3.

26. "The Present Crisis," in Raphael M. Huber, Ed., *Our Bishops Speak,* 272-300.

27. For more on the Catholic Worker movement, see Patrick G. Coy, Ed., *A Revolution of the Heart: Essays on the Catholic Worker,* Temple University Press: Philadelphia, 1988; Anne Klejment and Alice Klejment, *Dorothy Day and "The Catholic Worker": A Bibliography and Index,* Garland Publications: New York, 1986; William D. Miller, *A Harsh and Dreadful Love: Dorothy Day and the Catholic Worker Movement,* Liveright: New York, 1973; William D. Miller, *Dorothy Day: A Biography,* Harper & Row: San Francisco, 1982; Mel Piehl, *Breaking Bread: The Catholic Worker and the Origin of Catholic Radicalism in America,* Temple University Press: Philadelphia, 1982; Nancy L. Roberts, *Dorothy Day and the "Catholic Worker,"* State University of New York Press: Albany, 1984; and Judith L. Stoughton, *Proud Donkey of Schaerbeeck: Ade Bethune, Catholic Worker Artist,* North Star Press: St. Cloud, Minnesota, 1988.

28. See Monroe Billington and Cal Clark, "Catholic Clergymen, Franklin D. Roosevelt, and the New Deal," *Catholic Historical Review,* 79, 1993, 65-82.

29. Kenneth J. Heineman, "A Catholic New Deal: Religion and Labor in 1930s Pittsburgh," *The Pennsylvania Magazine of History & Biography,* Vol. 128, No. 4, October 1994, 365.

30. Patrick Fagan interviews conducted by Alice M. Hoffman, September 24, October 1, 1968, August 8, 1972, Historical Collections and Labor Archives, Pennsylvania State University, State College, Pa.

31. See, Jim McKay, "A Leader in Area's Labor Movement," Paul Stackhouse obituary, *The Pittsburgh Post-Gazette,* December 18, 1997.

32. Paul Stackhouse interview by the author, October 3, 1995.

33. De Caux, *Labor Radical,* 280-281. Ruttenberg was a Pittsburgh Jew while Golden was the son of a Baptist minister.

34. Wallace Stegner, "The Radio Priest and His Flock," in Isabel Leighton, Ed., *The Aspirin Age, 1919-1941,* Simon & Schuster: New York, 1949, 236.

35. Stegner, "The Radio Priest and His Flock," 236.

36. Quoted in George E. Mowry, *The Urban Nation: 1920-1960,* Hill and Wang: New York, 1965, 105.

37. Stegner, "The Radio Priest and His Flock," 237.

38. Arthur M. Schlesinger, Jr., *The Politics of Upheaval,* Houghton Mifflin Co.: Boston, 1960, 26.

39. Schlesinger, *The Politics of Upheaval,* 26.

40. Alan Brinkley, *Voices of Protest: Huey Long, Father Coughlin, and the Great Depression,* Random House: New York, First Vintage Books Edition, August 1983, 83.

41. Minutes of the Pittsburgh Central Labor Union, January 15, 1931, in the holdings of the Pittsburgh Typographical Union, Lo. No. 7, Archives of Industrial Society, University of Pittsburgh. Hereafter noted as "Minutes of the PCLU."

42. Minutes of the PCLU, May 19, June 16, 1932.

43. Minutes of the PCLU, July 6, 1933.

44. Minutes of the PCLU, February 4 and 18, 1932.

45. Minutes of the PCLU, February 16, 1933.

46. See Gomrick's ID cards and dues books for these organizations in the Charles G. Gomrick Collection, Archives of Industrial Society, University of Pittsburgh.

47. See the Charles G. Gomrick Collection, Archives of Industrial Society, University of Pittsburgh.

48. See pages 43, 55, 27, and 18 in Gomrick's copy of Coughlin's book.

49. See Patrick J. McGeever, *Rev. Charles Owen Rice: Apostle of Contradiction,* Duquesne University Press: Pittsburgh, 1989, 42.

50. Michael Zahorsky in John Bodnar, *Workers' World: Kinship, Community and Protest in an Industrial Society, 1900-1940,* The Johns Hopkins University Press: New York, 1982, 132.

51. Michael Zahorsky and Louis Smolinski in Bodnar, *Workers' World,* 134, 140. Emphasis added.

52. See McGeever, *Rev. Charles Owen Rice.*

53. Charles Owen Rice, "Utica Textile Workers Organizing Committee," radio address, July 19, 1938, WIBX, Utica, New York, Box 27, Rice Papers, Archives of Industrial Society (AIS), University of Pittsburgh.

54. WWSW broadcast, May 15, 1937, Box 27, Rice Papers, AIS.

55. Orville Rice in Bodnar, *Workers' World,* 147, 148.

56. Klein, et al., *A Social Study of Pittsburgh,* 302. This study was made in 1934-36, reflecting attitudes present at that time.

57. Mike Zahorsky termed them "cake eaters" in an interview conducted by Eric Leif Davin and Karen L. Steed, November 23, 1980. Despite the passage of half a century, the bitterness and hatred was evident in his voice.

58. Quoted in Sidney Blumenthal, "Reinventing Lincoln," *The New Yorker,* November 14, 1994, 106.

59. This list would include, of course, blacks, women, Hispanics, American Indians, and even homosexuals.

60. Quoted in Mowry, *The Urban Nation,* 102.

61. Paul A. Carter, *The Twenties in America,* Thomas Y. Crowell Co.: New York, 1968, 89.

62. Orville Rice in Bodnar, *Worker's World,* 150.

63. Domenic Del Turco in Bodnar, *Worker's World,* 125.

64. Joe Rudiak in Bodnar, *Worker's World,* 71.

65. Tom Luketich in Bodnar, *Worker's World,* 102.

66. Ray Czachowski in Bodnar, *Worker's World,* 54.

67. John Czelen in Bodnar, *Worker's World*, 93. Emphasis added.

68. Wyn Craig Wade, *The Fiery Cross: The Ku Klux Klan in America*, Simon and Schuster: New York, 1987, 194.

69. David M. Chalmers, *Hooded Americanism: The History of the Ku Klux Klan*, Duke University Press: Durham, NC, 1987, 236.

70. Patsy Sims, *The Klan*, Stein and Day: New York, 1978, 2.

71. Nancy Maclean, *Behind the Mask of Chivalry: The Making of the Second Ku Klux Klan*, Oxford University Press: New York, 1994, 13.

72. Maclean, *Behind the Mask of Chivalry*, 14.

73. Chalmers, *Hooded Americanism*, 236, 242.

74. Chalmers, *Hooded Americanism*, 237-38.

75. Chalmers, *Hooded Americanism*, 238.

76. Chalmers, *Hooded Americanism*, 239.

77. Lillian Thomas, "The Tiny Town That Fought the Klan," *The Pittsburgh Post-Gazette*, April 11, 2004, F-1.

78. Chalmers, *Hooded Americanism*, 239-240.

79. Thomas, "The Tiny Town That Fought the Klan."

80. Magda, *Monessen*, 95.

81. David Brody, *Labor in Crisis: The Steel Strike of 1919*, J.B. Lippincott Co.: Philadelphia & New York, 1965, 92.

82. Mother Jones, *The Autobiography of Mother Jones*, Charles H. Kerr & Co.: Chicago, 1925, 1972, 212.

83. Mother Jones, *The Autobiography*, 212-213.

84. Interview with Louis DeSenna by the author and Karen L. Steed, November 23, 1980. Emphasis added.

85. Magda, *Monessen*, 137.

86. See George Martin, *Madam Secretary, Frances Perkins*, Boston: Houghton Mifflin, 1976, chapter 24.

87. The author has a photo of this march in his possession.

88. See a photo of this rally in Bodnar, 133.

89. In 1994 the Johnstown Flood Museum—located in what used to be the Andrew Carnegie Public Library of Johnstown—hosted an excellent semi-permanent exhibit on the coming of unionism to the city entitled, "Forging a New Deal: Johnstown and the Great Depression, 1929-1941." The American flag-waving SWOC caravans could be seen in many of the exhibit photos.

90. Howard Fast, "An Occurrence at Republic Steel," in Isabel Leighton, Ed., *The Aspirin Age*, 386.

91. Quoted in Sidney Lens, *The Labor Wars: From the Molly Maguires to the Sitdowns*, Anchor Press/ Doubleday: Garden City, New York, 1974, 374.

92. Magda, *Monessen*, 108-109.

93. Magda, *Monessen*, 109.

94. This and next few paragraphs come from Pete Muselin, "The Steel Fist in a Pennsylvania Company Town," in Bud Schultz and Ruth Schultz, Eds., *It Did Happen Here: Recollections of Political Repression in America*, University of California Press: Berkeley, 1989, 70.

95. Phil McGuigan, interviewed in *Crashin' Out: Hard Times in McKeesport,* prepared by the McKeesport Oral History Project, Mon Valley Unemployed Committee, Pittsburgh, August 1983, 10.

96. Thomas Bell, *Out of This Furnace,* University of Pittsburgh Press: Pittsburgh, 1941, 1976.

97. David P. Demarest, Jr., Afterword, in *Out of This Furnace,* 415.

98. Demarest, Afterword, 421.

99. Bell, *Out of This Furnace,* 384-385.

100. Bell, *Out of This Furnace,* 407-412. Emphasis added.

101. Commentary by Bill Moyers on the NBC Evening News, April 11, 1995, commemorating the 50th anniversary of Roosevelt's death on April 12, 1995.

102. Roy Emerson Stryker and Nancy Wood, *In This Proud Land: America 1935-1943 as Seen in the FSA Photographs,* Galahad Books: New York, 1973, 8.

103. Carl Sandburg, "The People, Yes," in *The American Tradition in Literature, Vol. 2,* Edited by Sculley Bradley, Richmond Croom Beatty, and E. Hudson Long, W.W. Norton & Co.: New York, 1956, 960, 962.

104. Stephen Vincent Benet, "Listen To The People: Independence Day, 1941," in *The Stephen Vincent Benet Pocket Book,* Edited by Robert Van Gelder, Pocket Books: New York, 1946, 367, 379.

105. *ITU News,* May 1937, 5.

106. Jimmie Hicks, "Frank Capra," *Films in Review,* September-October 1992, 291.

107. See David Reynolds, *Rich Relations: The American Occupation of Britain, 1942-1945,* Random House: New York, 1994. See Stanley Frank, "Labor Answers the G.I.," *Collier's,* October 13, 1945, 23.

108. See Frank, "Labor Answers the G.I.," 23.

109. Department of Justice Papers, Board of Pardons, Clemency File, R. G. 56, Pennsylvania Historical and Museum Commission. Emphasis added. The "hewers of wood, drawers of water" is a straightforward biblical quote and is indicative of the religious sensibilities of the petitioners.

110. David Brody, *Steelworkers in America: The Nonunion Era,* Harvard University Press: Cambridge, Mass., 1960; Harper & Row: New York, 1969, 220-221.

111. *Amalgamated Journal,* August 29, 1918, 1, quoted in Brody, *Steelworkers in America,* 221.

112. Brody, *Steelworkers in America,* 223.

113. Brody, *Steelworkers in America,* 223.

114. Quoted in Brody, *Steelworkers in America,* 224.

115. Brody, *Steelworkers in America,* 232, 236.

116. As late as 1980 a retired member of USWA Local 1397 in Homestead, who remembered the strike, still referred to it as "The Hunky Strike" when I interviewed him. Others I interviewed in Homestead at that time also referred to it in these terms.

117. Strike committee quoted in Brody, *Steelworkers in America,* 260. Polish striker originally in *Survey,* November 8, 1919, 91, quoted in Brody, *Steelworkers in America,* 261.

118. Gary Gerstle, *Working-Class Americanism: The Politics of Labor in a Textile City, 1914-1960,* Cambridge University Press: New York; Cambridge, England, 1989, 8.

119. *The Pittsburgh Press,* November 15, 1888.

120. Quoted in Lens, *The Labor Wars,* 188

121. The author has a copy of a picture postcard owned by Mary Beth Schaefer, of Greensburg, Pa., depicting a funeral procession for eight dead McKees Rocks strikers with these American flags in the procession.

122. *The Homestead Daily Messenger,* November 6, 1912.

123. *The Homestead Daily Messenger,* November 5, 1920.

124. *The Pittsburgh Sunday Post,* August 4, 1912, 1, 7.

125. *The Pittsburgh Sunday Post,* August 11, 1912, 1, 2.

Chapter 5

Ambiguous Allies

But, while ethnic industrial workers were steeped in the ideology of equality, their idea of equality had definite limits. At the heart of the New Deal coalition was a powerful centrifugal tension against which the universalist theme of inclusion did constant battle. That tension was the sexism, racism, and lingering ethnic hostility which still permeated American culture at the time. Ethno-cultural tensions had long separated Pole from Italian, Irish from Ukrainian. Those tensions did not entirely disappear in the Thirties, though the CIO and the Left Populism of the times sought to submerge these competing identities within the larger identities of the working class and "the people."

But the ideology of equality is an inherently expansive ideology, and it does not stop at traditionally accepted boundaries between groups. The rallying cry that "all men are created equal" says nothing about the color of a man's skin. And many women have felt that the phrase did not really just refer to "men." Thus, the New Deal banner of equality for all flew over a motley crew of the oppressed, which comprised not only ethnics of all types, but women as well as men, blacks as well as whites.

Blacks had reason to feel optimistic about their inclusion in the common struggle. The Pittsburgh labor movement made a point of officially opposing racial discrimination. For example, at meetings of the AFL-affiliated Pittsburgh Central Labor Union (PCLU) in September 1942, the assembled delegates adopted a "National Unity" program which opposed poll taxes and called for the end of racial discrimination in defense industry jobs.[1]

Women, too, had reasons for optimism. On October 15, 1942, a month after adopting the anti-racist "National Unity" program, the assembled PCLU delegates went on record opposing discrimination based on gender. A representative of Alice Paul's National Woman's Party appeared before the body and asked them to endorse the Equal Rights Amendment to the U.S. Constitution. The membership not only voted to endorse the ERA, but also explicitly stated that, "When we say the 'Brotherhood of Man,' we mean the Brotherhood of Man includes woman."[2]

Even so, women and blacks were seen by ethnic male workers as ambiguous allies in the struggle, and, even with the best intentions, the bridging of gender and racial divisions was not as successful as the muting of ethnic tensions. Especially in the realm of race, ethnic workers remained ambivalent. They were imbued with enough of the ideology of egalitarianism to know that, for example, they *shouldn't* be racist—but this knowledge was at war with their own inner feelings of "us" and "them." Thus, while the CIO was much more sexually and racially egalitarian than the AFL, there still seemed to be little place for women or blacks, at least if that place was the workplace.[3]

Nor was there a place for blacks in the ethnically cohesive enclaves. Nor was there a place for women in such "male bastions" as the San Lorenzo Society of Panther Hollow or the Italian Club of the Allegheny County coal town of Morgan. Even though freedom and equality were in the air of Pittsburgh, and blacks in the Steel Valley were coming to believe that the equality being espoused applied to them as well, the "American Dream" of the ethnic worker was basically a dream of equality for the white, male, Catholic and Orthodox, immigrant-bred, industrial working class. Women and blacks were accepted as supporting players in the on-going drama, but white male workers saw the starring roles as reserved for themselves. How could there not be tensions in the insurgent coalition?

A Woman's Place

Mary Jane Carosone was age eighty-two in 1999. She grew up in the mostly Italian coal mining town of Morgan in southwestern Allegheny County. She recalled that in Morgan, "The men went to the Italian Club, and the women stayed home and watched the kids."[4]

Staying home and watching kids was seen as the full-time job of any respectable wife. And there were always lots of kids. Joseph Dudas, of Monessen, grew up in a family of nine kids. John Czelen, who worked at Page Steel and Wire in Monessen, said there were "just ten" children in his family.

In addition, the wife was expected to contribute to the family economy by taking care of boarders, young bachelor steelworkers who slept and ate with the family. "Most of your foreigners all had boarders," recalled Lester Hunter of Monessen. Dudas remembered that his family had five boarders. "In them days [1900-1920]," remembered Nick Mahalko of growing up in Monessen in a family of nine children, "very few [mothers] ever worked [outside the home]. They were homemakers, believe me. They would produce children and they had their duties to do. Everything was done by hand. Mother had to have supper ready. As a matter of fact . . . they used to have boarders in order to get that extra money. My mother had them. It is very nice, but there was no privacy to start with . . . We didn't have enough room . . . Here's the way they [boarders] operated, too. Guys would work different turns. Maybe Joe would come in the morning at eight o'clock. He knocked off and Bill went in. So you see, they would use the same bed. Believe me when you had to use the privy, there was hell to pay because everybody wanted to go in at the same time. That [privy] was outside. We had a total of, [at] one time in my family, a total of thirteen, that's [with] my grandmother and grandfather." This number included both family and boarders. "You wonder how they done it," concludes Mahalko.[5]

Taking care of the family and boarders at home was where most people wanted married women to be in those Depression years. In a November 1936 national Gallup Poll, 82 percent of the respondents disapproved of a married woman earning money in industry or business if she had a husband capable of supporting her.[6]

True, this reflected the hard times, when jobs were scarce, but it also reflected the prevalent attitude that it was the man's job to earn the family income, not the woman's. If a woman had a man in the home who could support her—then home is where she should be, not out in the workforce. Even in the affluent postwar years, when working women no longer threatened to take scarce jobs away from hard-strapped males, a majority of both women (57 percent) and men (63 percent) in one 1945 survey felt that married women should not be *permitted* to work, regardless of their personal wishes.[7]

In a region like Pittsburgh's Steel Valley, where male-dominated heavy industry commanded the economic scene, there had always been fewer job possibilities for women than in many other places. Ileen DeVault did find that the number of women workers in clerical work increased dramatically in the early years of the twentieth century, accounting for 42 percent of Pittsburgh's clerical workforce by 1920.[8] But this was true only of the city proper and the steel corporation headquarters within the city. Clerical work in the surrounding mill towns and their steel plants remained male preserves until the coming of World War II. The employment situation in Duquesne was typical.

Virtually all available employment in Duquesne was in the local steel mill and in that mill most clerical and typing positions were filled by men. In March 1917, only 11 women were employed in the mill, seven in the plant hospital as nurses, three in clerical positions, and one woman in the metallurgy lab.

A decade later, in March 1927, this number had risen to nineteen women, with six of them being nurses, seven clerks, three stenographers, and three telephone operators. A decade after that, in March 1936, this number had fallen back to ten women, comprising three nurses and seven clerks. As of 1939, in the entire city of Duquesne, only sixty-four women held any kind of either blue collar or white collar industrial job, as compared to 5,527 men in such positions.[9]

What was true of Duquesne was also true throughout the Steel Valley and in the steel industry as a whole. In 1930, for instance, there was not a single woman in U.S. Steel's Homestead mill or in the Carrie Furnaces in Rankin directly across the Monongahela River from Homestead.

At U.S. Steel's Edgar Thomson Works in Braddock, which were much larger than the Duquesne Works, eighteen women could be found, ten of them in clerical positions. Indeed, "Between 1910 and 1939 women consistently accounted for less than 1 percent of the production workforce in iron and steel. Not even the labor shortage associated with World War I made a significant impact on women's employment in steel plants . . . Most women who held steel production jobs were confined to inspecting and sorting tin plate, a job that management considered tailor-made for women's supposed fine sense of touch and keen eyesight." With the increased shortage of male workers after Pearl Harbor, restrictions on female employment in steel production jobs eased. Nevertheless, even a year later, in December of 1942, only twelve women were employed in such jobs at U.S. Steel plants in the entire state of Pennsylvania, and all twelve were at the U.S. Steel's Carnegie-Illinois plant in Clairton in the maintenance and metallurgy departments.[10]

As more and more steelworkers were drafted in 1943 and 1944, this situation slowly began to change. Traditionally, most women who worked outside the home were young and single, and they usually quit their jobs when they married. The decrease in male workers occasioned by the war, however, forced initially reluctant employers to change their antagonism toward married women workers.

Thus, between 1940 and 1944, married women accounted for 74.2 percent of the total increase in the American workforce as, "for the first time in American history, they outnumbered single women in the female labor force." In Detroit, where automakers had been reluctant to hire women at the beginning of the war, "By February 1943, women made up 90.8 percent of the new workers hired in 185 war plants in that city. Elsewhere, they entered shipyard production work; by 1943, they filled 10 percent of those jobs." In the steel industry, female participation in the workforce nationwide climbed to between 8 percent and 12 percent in the years 1943-1945.[11]

Nevertheless, increasing numbers of female workers did not bring increasing acceptance by their male co-workers. Robert Sable, for instance, the grievance committeeman from the open hearth department of USWA Local 1256 at U.S. Steel's Duquesne Works, told a union meeting during World War II, "A woman's place is in the home to raise our next generation of children." He opposed women coming into the mill to replace drafted male steelworkers and advocated throwing all women out of the plant. And, if they *were* going to be thrown out of the plant, James Kane, former president of Duquesne's USWA Local 1256, suggested that the sewer would be a "good place" for such women workers. Many of the rank and file Duquesne steelworkers agreed with the leadership, harassing their female co-workers and attempting to get them fired.[12]

Following the war, these unwanted female workers were quickly flushed out of the plants with the cooperation of the steel union locals. By June 1, 1946, the war-time high of 700 female production workers in the Duquesne plant had been reduced to 125. A month later, on July 1, "only 16 women remained, all located in the chemical laboratory and metallurgical departments. Even these 16 were not entirely secure. The company still sought male replacements for 12 and tentatively decided to keep only four women permanently: a metallographist, a lab assistant, a 'janitress,' and a wash up worker."

USWA Local 1256 in Duquesne defended the firing of these women, all of whom were fellow union members. When U.S. Steel asked the union if seniority rules should be violated to be rid of the women, the local replied that, "women employees should be replaced by veterans and by men," even if those veterans and men had absolutely no seniority at all at the plant.

The USWA locals at Braddock's Edgar Thomson Works and at the Irvin Works were also eager to purge themselves of their female members. So eager was the latter to get rid of women that the U.S. Steel management at the Irvin Works had to caution the local's grievance committees against demanding an immediate expulsion in order to protect management's "interests in not laying off women *before* replacements are ready."[13]

Nevertheless, although the Pittsburgh work world seemed to be overwhelmingly hostile to the presence of women workers, they were there, nonetheless, in the work world. Throughout the Thirties, the ten-member Executive Board of the Pittsburgh Central Labor Union (PCLU), the city's congress of all local unions, always had one token female member. At first this was Cecilia Dixon of the United Garment Workers Local 51. After her death in 1938, Amy Ballinger, Secretary of the Laundry Workers Union Local 141, and twenty-nine-years-old, took her place on the Executive Board.

Amy Ballinger became a popular member of the PCLU (being the third-highest vote-getter in the Executive Board election of 1940, only seven votes behind County Commissioner John J. Kane, and the second-highest in 1941)[14] and continued to be such a presence in the Pittsburgh labor movement that she was eventually elected a member of the nine-person Pittsburgh City Council, serving from 1970-76.[15]

Additionally, the PCLU had a handful of female delegates from such predominantly female unions as the Stenographers and Typists Local 20173, the American Federation of Teachers Lo. 400, the Hotel and Restaurant Employees Alliance Lo. 237, and the Laundry Workers Lo. 14.

If financial sacrifice is one measure of class consciousness and union loyalty, the mostly female Laundry Workers Lo. 141, which Ballinger represented, was perhaps the most militant union in the PCLU. It continually topped the list of donors to union causes, far out of proportion to its membership. For example, in 1941 when the PCLU launched a major fund-raising effort to back labor candidates in the municipal elections, the Laundry Workers were among the top seven financial donors. Only the mostly female Hotel and Restaurant Workers Lo. 237 gave more money than the Laundry Workers.[16]

Similarly, in 1945 when the PCLU launched a local labor newspaper, *Pittsburgh Labor*, the female Laundry Workers were the primary financial supporters. Of 106 local unions affiliated with the PCLU, only the Laundry Workers union bought a subscription for all of its members, 1,302. This figure was not only ten times the number of subscriptions the Laundry Workers were asked to sell, it was also far more than double the number of subscriptions (456) sold by the next highest union, the Teamsters, who had actually originated the idea for a local labor newspaper. The female Laundry Workers alone thus accounted for more than 25 percent of the 4,000 active subscriptions to the PCLU newspaper. This was still short of the goal of 6,000 subscriptions the PCLU desired for the newspaper, but, reported Newspaper Committee Chairman Martin Dixon, "The Laundry Workers Local Union . . . is to be highly commended. Its contribution makes this present showing what it is."[17]

Women workers also organized in ways which were seen as logical extensions of their domestic spheres. Shunned in most male-dominated workplaces, banned from fraternal societies, underrepresented among the union leadership—they yet were seen as the managers of the home and hearth. Their husbands traditionally brought home the pay they earned and turned it over in its entirety to their wives, who then managed the family's finances. This was one avenue of power for working class wives.

Thus, on April 16, 1936, the Pittsburgh Central Labor Union announced to its constituent unions that a "Woman's Union Buyers' Club" was to be organized in Pittsburgh. "All women members of families of Trade Union workers are invited to attend . . . The women spend most of their men's Union wages," the members were told, "and would be glad to help increase those wages and protect them." An organizational meeting was scheduled for the Mayfair Hotel in downtown Pittsburgh on May 5, at which the women officers of the Cleveland, Ohio, Woman's Union Buyers' Club would be present to assist in forming a Pittsburgh Club. The Cleveland club was said to have over 20,000 women members, "who purchase only Union-made goods and patronize only Union stores, restaurants and manufacturers. With the result that every trade in Cleveland and most of the store clerks, are thoroughly Unionized." Women workers, Union wives, and Union daughters were welcome, but "No men are permitted in the business sessions of the club."[18]

Two days later, PCLU Executive Board member Cecilia Dixon reported on the formation of the club, of which she had been elected president, and she invited all women members of union families to join, no dues or initiation fees. "The members," Dixon said, "pledge themselves to spend the Union wages of the family for Union label and Union Made goods."[19] Though not an official auxiliary of the PCLU, and not under its direction or jurisdiction, the women's club saw itself—and was seen as—closely allied to the PCLU.

The club immediately began to organize social events for workers—male as well as female. In June, for instance, "Miss Gardner," a member of the Federation of Musicians and "an agent" of the Woman's Union Buyers Club announced to the PCLU an all day and evening club picnic to be held at West View Park in August, to which all were invited.[20] The PCLU bought a block of tickets to this first event of the club and passed a resolution for a "strong letter of endorsement of the Union Buyers' Club" to be sent to the Pittsburgh Better Business Bureau.[21]

The women's club went on to sponsor a series of social activities over the years, such as card parties and "dinner dances."[22] Four years later the women's club (now called the Women Buyers' League) was still going strong when Rita Boisen, the club Secretary, offered the services of the club to act as hostesses during the annual meeting of the Pennsylvania Federation of Labor to be held in

Pittsburgh.[23]

It thus seems that ancillary union activities and organizations were arenas in which union women could exert some influence. While direct participation in a steelworker union might have been next to impossible, participation on a more egalitarian basis was accepted elsewhere. Therefore, when the first meeting of the Allegheny County chapter of the political organization, Labor's Non-Partisan League, was held, September 27, 1936, women were specifically invited to participate.[24]

Women PCLU delegates were also active in the PCLU's Committee for Political Action, which worked for the re-election of Roosevelt in 1940 and of which Amy Ballinger was Secretary.[25] Ballinger continued to serve as the re-named Political Action Committee's Secretary throughout the 1940s.

Women workers also made their presence felt by organizing community political events. On December 3, 1936, for example, PCLU delegate "Miss Golden" of the Stenographers and Typists Union announced to the membership "an affair" the union was organizing to be held on December 9 at the Carnegie Music Hall in Oakland "under the auspices" of the North American Committee to Aid Spanish Democracy.[26]

Women workers, then, even though they operated under severe constraints, were active participants in the struggle, as wives, daughters—and workers. Though not welcome at all times or in all places, they, too, were fighting for "a workers' democracy."

Black Man's Burden

Another population ethnic male workers saw as ambiguous allies in their struggle for equality were the region's blacks. Like the ethnics, they, too, recalled vivid examples of discrimination against them in Pittsburgh and the Steel Valley. Jim Crow, for instance, had long been a customary way of life, despite the absence of explicit laws mandating racial segregation. Thus, for instance, when the Reformed Presbyterian Synod convened in Pittsburgh in 1888, one of its members, the Rev. G. M. Elliott, of Selma, Alabama, was forced to eat in the basement kitchen of the restaurant they attended because he was black.[27]

Little had changed by the 1930s. The settlement houses sprinkled throughout Pittsburgh's neighborhoods during the Depression were all segregated, to one degree or another, by race. "The Kingsley House excluded blacks entirely, and the Irene Kaufmann settlement, while providing services to the black population, severely restricted their use of its facilities, as did several of the city's YMCAs and YWCAs. Examples of white ethnic hostility toward blacks occurred even before such actions by social agencies. Russpolit Field was established, for instance, by Russians, Poles, and Italians who wished to exclude blacks from their playgrounds . . . One black recalled being denied the right to walk on Herron Avenue . . . Others remembered being excluded from public facilities, particularly swimming pools in Schenley and Highland Parks."[28]

Like the ethnics, however, blacks were also restive and were demanding their rights, their citizenship, their equality, even before the coming of the New Deal. Indeed, black restiveness was also a part of the very coming of the New Deal, as black voters became another vital constituency of the New Deal coalition.

"Equality" and "Freedom," as I said, are part of an expansive ideology. Such ideas do not stop at the color line, and black Americans also wanted some of the "freedom" that was in the air. "The President's Four Freedoms/ Appeal to me," wrote black poet Langston Hughes in a 1943 poem. "I would like to see those Freedoms/ Come to be./ If you believe/ In the Four Freedoms, too,/ Then share'em with me/ Don't keep'em all for you."[29]

In the 1931 Pittsburgh primary election, black dissatisfaction with the status quo was displayed by a widespread black aggressiveness at the polls. Black voters perceived the still-dominant white Republican political machine as attempting to steal the election in black Hill District precincts of Wards Three and Five. At that time, voters could not register at any time of the year. They had to turn up at the polls during a few handful of days to register prior to the later election. When would-be black voters did so at the Letsche School on Bedford Avenue in Ward Three on September 3, 1931, fighting broke out between blacks and whites who also showed up at the same ninth precinct poll to register. "A mob of Negroes," which threatened the two policemen on duty at the poll, was dispersed as police reinforcements arrived and arrested several blacks. Two of these "Hill District Negroes" were later sentenced to thirty days in the county workhouse for "inciting to riot," while one was fined for carrying a revolver without a permit. Meanwhile, the Rev. W. Wade, of Wylie Avenue, the main Hill District street, was acquitted of "voter intimidation," presumably of the white voters.[30]

On the same voter registration day, at precinct 18 of the Hill District's Ward Five, State Police—sent by Governor Gifford Pinchot to police Pittsburgh's elections for the first time in the city's history—curbed a fight between the City Assessor and Harry Lewis, a black candidate for constable opposed by the Republican city administration.[31]

In addition to whites, apparently working for the Republican machine, attempting to register in black Hill District precincts, there also appeared to be an effort to discourage black registration altogether. These efforts resulted in a riot at the Franklin School on September 12, 1931, a subsequent registration day. There, "A crowd estimated at over one thousand jammed the streets in front of the registration headquarters. [Shots were fired into the crowd and] Violence was climaxed by a gas bomb tossed into the line of voters waiting to register. The bomb landed among 40 women who had been waiting four hours to register. The women ran screaming into the street. Shots were fired, followed by bricks, stones, and bottles being tossed into the school building. Abe Miller, one of the registrars, claimed shots were fired at registration board members, and he was hit by a bottle."[32]

Reinforcing the belief that this was a Republican machine effort to discourage black voter registration in the Hill District, there was no further investigation of the incident, nor were questions ever asked by the newspapers or anyone else about where this bomb came from, or who fired the shots and threw the bricks and bottles.

During the 1931 primary election itself, on September 15, eighteen Hill District blacks were arrested as "small riots were frequent in the Hill" and a white poll watcher at the Miller School, precinct six of the Hill's Ward Three, was shot by a black man shortly before the polls opened.

State Police also arrested the entire election board of the Hill's precinct 15 of Ward Five for voter intimidation. Two black voters standing in line to vote at the Moorhead School on Granville Street, the tenth precinct of Ward Three, were also arrested for pushing a white man out of line, claiming he did not belong.[33]

At the same school, John J. Verona, the white Republican political boss who supposedly ran Ward Three, claimed he was attacked by a black man who attempted to stab him at the polls. Verona's claim was "branded as false . . . by Negro leaders, who said the truth was that Verona had beaten a [black] watcher at the Moorhead School polls . . . after the watcher had been arrested and pinioned by police. C. Webster, Negro, President of the Third Ward Voters' Club, charged police and politicians with numerous assaults and attempts at intimidation of Negro voters."[34]

In Pittsburgh in the 1850s, the city's Republican Party had coalesced around anti-immigrant, anti-Catholic sentiment. The local Republican Party had never been overly concerned about slavery or the welfare of blacks before the Civil War. Clearly, these attitudes persisted into the twentieth century and the dominant Republican hierarchy intimidated and disenfranchised blacks just as much as it did Catholic ethnics.

And, also clearly, blacks were fighting just as much as white ethnics for what they perceived to be their legitimate rights of citizenship.

But, they were finding few allies among working class ethnics. Even after they gained a modicum of power, ethnic workers and their leaders discriminated against blacks. Duquesne Mayor Elmer Maloy (elected in 1937 and who was also head of the local steelworkers' union and a major steel union organizer throughout the region) blamed violence on at least one late 1930s picket line at the local Carnegie-Illinois plant on "agitators" who were "Mostly colored people, the majority of them young punks who never had a job—just bums."[35]

Elmer Maloy was an important grassroots leader of the ethnic revolt in the Steel Valley. And, not only was he a leading militant, but I know from looking through his personal papers in the possession of his family that he read Leftist publications. Further, black voters were a major part of the coalition which put him in office as Mayor of Duquesne. Maloy was, it is reasonable to believe, *better* on race issues than most white ethnic workers, and so was the Steel Workers Organizing Committee (SWOC), his union. By 1937 there was a higher percentage of blacks in SWOC than in the steel workforce as a whole. And yet his statement reveals the racialized vision of equality held by him and the ethnic workers he led. It is quite possible the "colored people" who were the "agitators" at the picket line might well have liked to have had a steel mill job, but could not get them. Maloy showed no sympathy with their likely situation.

A telling experience which graphically displays this racist worldview of ethnic workers was recounted by a member of the McKeesport SWOC local. "Rocky" Doratio, born in Italy but raised in Glassport, next door to McKeesport, recalled one all-white meeting of SWOC Local 1408 at the local's union hall. The local had been signing people up left and right at the union hall for the public welfare rolls, for which the only criteria was poverty. "One day a black man came in and Joe Koeval, the president of the local, says, 'What can I do for you?' This black man says, 'I want to get on the welfare.' Joe says, 'Do you belong to the union?'

"'No, sir, I don't belong to the union.'

"'Well, we can't help you.'" And the black man turned and walked out the door.[36]

Perhaps Maloy's "young punks who never had a job" might have wanted a job, but it often seemed that Maloy's union was not so eager to help them. Meanwhile, it is difficult to believe that the McKeesport local SWOC president would have turned away a white kid in the same situation. Without doubt, the president would have instead signed him up for welfare.

This was therefore a Catch-22 situation for blacks. The unions wouldn't help them unless they were members—but the unions also wouldn't let them become members. "A 1940 survey conducted by the Pittsburgh Urban League revealed that only five of 53 labor unions in Pittsburgh had black members. Fifteen of the unions surveyed admitted to constitutional restrictions or 'gentlemen's agreements' to exclude blacks. The remaining 38 responded that they had no black members at present 'because none have applied for membership.' A black construction coalition nearly 30 years later led a demonstration protesting the fact that unions still refused to admit black workers. As labor unions became more powerful in Pittsburgh, exclusion from union membership also excluded one from eligibility for a variety of occupations."[37]

Thus, the Carnegie-Illinois (U.S. Steel) plant in Elmer Maloy's Duquesne, as one example, had few blacks in it. In 1942 (while Maloy was both the town's mayor and also a local union leader), the union's grievance committee for the Duquesne plant, interviewed by a *Fortune* survey team, contained a representative cross section of the plant's workforce—a Hungarian, a Croat, a Slovak—but no black member.

An examination of the records of the Pittsburgh Central Labor Union (PCLU), the AFL umbrella organization for all unions in the city until the coming of the CIO, also reveals not a single mention of black delegates or blacks in any context at any point in the 1930s. Blacks first appear in the record in January 1940, when arrangements were being made by the PCLU to host that year's annual convention of the Pennsylvania Federation of Labor. And, evidently, even as late as 1940, the local AFL branch of the labor movement was still segregating its black union brothers, at least on social occasions. The PCLU delegate in charge of entertainment, for instance, reported that "a special show would be held for the colored delegates."[38]

Such economic discrimination was far more destructive to black aspirations than social discrimination. There had never been many jobs for blacks in the region's steel mills which, of course, dominated the local economy. The exception was during strikes, when the companies routinely imported blacks as scabs, thus fueling already prevalent ethnic racism against them. During one 1888 strike confrontation at the Solar Iron Works in Pittsburgh's Lawrenceville neighborhood, an angry crowd of white steelworkers insulted black scabs as they left the mill. The blacks had come prepared, it seems, and fired pistols into the crowd of white steelworkers, wounding several.[39]

World War I cut off the influx of European immigrants for the duration of the war, which resulted in a very slight increase in the hiring of blacks—but no decrease in the expression of ethnic racism directed against them. Thus, for instance, Abraham Epstein found that, "From a study of colored employees in twenty of the largest industrial plants in the Pittsburgh district, arbitrarily selected, we find that most of the concerns have employed colored labor only since May or June of 1916. Very few of the Pittsburgh industries have used colored labor in capacities other than as janitors and window cleaners. A few of the plants visited had not begun to employ colored people until in the spring of 1917, while a few others had not yet come to employ Negroes . . . The Superintendent of one big steel plant which has not employed colored labor during the past few years admitted that he faced a decided shortage of labor, and that he was in need of men; but he said he would employ Negroes only as a last resort . . . In a big glass plant, the company attempted to use Negro labor last winter, but the white workers ran them out' by swearing at them, calling them 'Nigger' and making conditions so unpleasant for them that they were forced to quit. This company has therefore given up any further attempts at employing colored labor."[40]

Pervasive economic discrimination against blacks continued in the years after World War I. In 1924 a survey of the fifty-nine principal occupations of black males in Pittsburgh found that in every case white workers in the same jobs made significantly higher wages. In some cases, such as with cooks, stenographers, and "inspectors," whites made double or more than blacks in the same jobs.[41]

But it was the systematic exclusion of blacks from the newly emergent labor unions which most powerfully affected black Pittsburghers, as this meant they had no support at all in the economic sphere. In 1918 Epstein questioned a prominent Pittsburgh labor leader who was also a member of the agitational "Alliance for Labor and Democracy," which had been created by AFL chief Samuel Gompers in 1917. The official admitted there were blacks in his trade and that some had applied for membership into his union but, although there had been a growth of 100 percent in his union in the Pittsburgh district over the past six months—there was not a single black member. He also admitted that he personally was aware of complaints of race discrimination against his union by "people of color."[42]

Even during the massive campaign to organize the steel industry in the months just after World War I ended, which culminated in the steel strike of 1919, the mechanical trades unions in the national organizing committee continued to exclude blacks from membership.[43]

It was no wonder, then, that black workers refused to join the strike and looked upon it as a chance to get a much valued job. In late October 1919, "numbers of Negroes began appearing in steel centers," we are told. Over 3,500 blacks were shipped by U.S. Steel into Homestead alone to work as scabs. "They swiftly became an alarming threat to the strike. Chicago leaders reported that it hurt the 'morale of the white men to see blacks crowding into the mills to take their jobs.'"[44]

After the "Hunky Strike" was broken, the companies kept these black workers on. In 1920 they constituted 10.9 percent of the Pennsylvania steel workforce and 14.2 percent of the workforce in Indiana, although their numbers did not increase between 1920 and 1930. And where ethnics and blacks came into contact with each other, "the immigrants disdained their 'inferiors' much as the natives had once disliked them . . . In Gary [Indiana], the Ku Klux Klan flourished."[45]

Little changed in the Pittsburgh labor movement over the succeeding years. Just as there was little help for the black worker in the Thirties, World War II seemed, at first, to be no different throughout the North. "In the West and Northeast, whites, when interviewed, voiced their approval of separate schools, restaurants, and neighborhoods."[46]

As America geared up in 1940 to become the "Arsenal of Democracy," blacks were shut out of the burgeoning factory jobs. Even in 1940, for instance, "only 240 of the 100,000 workers in the aircraft industry were black."[47] Perhaps prompted by the egalitarian ethos which was permeating Pittsburgh and the Steel Valley at this time, *The Pittsburgh Courier,* the influential nationally-distributed black newspaper, called for a "Double V" campaign, "Victory over our enemies at home and victory over our enemies on the battlefields abroad."[48]

Only after A. Philip Randolph, leader of the all-black Sleeping Car Porters' Union, called for a massive "March on Washington" in 1941 to highlight job discrimination against blacks in the expanding war economy did Roosevelt issue an executive order banning racial discrimination in war industries.

The dream, then, of freedom and equality for "all" left some people out. Ethnic class consciousness, it appeared, was basically for the white, ethnic, male, industrial worker. As Barton Bernstein noted, this left out "sharecroppers, tenant farmers, migratory workers and farm laborers, slum dwellers, unskilled workers, and the unemployed Negroes." Their dream would have to wait for a later day.

Thus, within Joe Magarac's dream of social justice and full citizenship there were already the makings of a nightmare for Joe—a nightmare of John Henry and Rosie the Riveter sweating next to him and demanding their just due, demanding their rights and their citizenship.

And this would come, as the ideology of equality is contagious. First one wants equality, then everybody wants equality. During the 1930s, the struggle of the Common Man for equality came to be seen by blacks as their struggle, as well.

"We colored people of the Second Ward," said a black voter in Homestead just before the 1936 election, "led by Rev. Soloman . . . are better off now than we've ever been. Mr. Roosevelt is for the worker and for the poor classes while Landon is a tool for the bankers and those who have money."[49]

The Rev. S.H. Soloman, himself, who was leading Homestead's black citizens into the Democratic Party, declared, "Didn't God of the Universe send President Roosevelt and give him a plan to take care of the needy? Are we going to let the enemy, which is the Republican Party, deceive us? I am asking the Negroes who belong to the Second Ward Democratic Club to be sure to come to the meeting Monday night . . . Because together we stand, but divided we fall."[50]

An Aliquippa "Colored Voter" said that the "citizens" of Aliquippa had "long realized that *there has come into this community a feeling that every man and woman has certain inalienable rights* and he who surrenders them is less than a man . . . Our citizens are determined to test whether the principles of democracy shall be applied in Aliquippa or whether the selfish interest of a favored few political bosses shall continue to triumph against the will of our citizens . . . This is simply the will of an oppressed and aroused citizenry bent upon the execution of those national symbols which are embodied in the articles of our Constitutional guarantee."[51]

Blacks in the Steel Valley had come to believe that the egalitarian ideal which workers everywhere in the industrial heartland were espousing applied to them as well, that they, too, were "Americans" who deserved their freedom. The Republican-controlled Duquesne newspaper complained that the ethnic coalition which was the foundation of Democratic victory looked upon FDR "like unto Moses." But, it wasn't just the ethnics who saw FDR and the Democratic Party he led in this light. Joseph Barton, a black steelworker at the Pittsburgh Steel Company in Monessen, also felt that FDR was a Moses for the oppressed, "a God-sent man . . . That man, he just got the poor people, you know. Heaven for the poor people . . . I tell you the truth, that Roosevelt Administration was just a heaven—and [he was a] God-sent man. Anything that Roosevelt ever did was always for the little man."[52]

Thus, the "colored" were part of the coalition of "below the tracks" steel workers who put SWOC leaders in office throughout the Steel Valley in 1937. Because of this, many SWOC officials emulated Elmer Maloy in Duquesne who, despite his expressed disdain for black "young punks who never held a job," nevertheless made a point of improving municipal services for "below the tracks" black neighborhoods as mayor. The atmosphere of change in the Steel Valley, of equality for all, seems to have been a heady one, which eventually also brought great changes for the black population *as* blacks.

And, even though the concept of ethnic equality didn't include blacks specifically, it is significant that Elmer Maloy *did* make a point of improving municipal services for blacks, which the Republicans never did. And, half a century after it happened, "Rocky" Doratio vividly remembered the McKeesport SWOC president turning away the black welfare applicant because it offended his own sense of equality and fair-play. Ethnic steelworkers seemed to be struggling in a state of what psychologists call "cognitive dissonance," a state of fervently believing two opposing and contradictory ideas at the same time. At some level, Maloy and Doratio believed in their own professed ideology of equality. Blacks weren't "us," and therefore weren't equal—but blacks were human beings, too, and therefore equal.

It is because ethnic workers believed, at some level, in their own ideology of equality that a more receptive legal environment for blacks emerged in the mid-Thirties. The change really began after the Democrats gained control of the Pennsylvania State House and elected George Earle governor in 1934. One of the few Democratic accomplishments of the years before the true beginning of the Little New Deal in 1936 (years in which the Republicans still controlled the State Senate and stymied much progressive legislation) was the revision of the Pennsylvania Civil Rights Act of 1887. On September 1, 1935, the Democrats amended the Act to grant all people "within the jurisdiction of the Commonwealth full and equal accommodations, advantages, facilities and privileges of places of public accommodation, resort or amusement."

Actions such as this, amid the general atmosphere of freedom and equality on the march, greatly emboldened the black community. Before 1935, few civil rights cases were ever heard in Allegheny County courts. After the revision of the law, civil rights cases reached the Allegheny County courts virtually every year, with twenty-seven cases being tried between 1938 and 1949, while many more were settled before ever reaching court.[53]

Further, it was in 1937 in Pittsburgh and 1938 in the Steel Valley, after the new SWOC administrations came into office, that de facto Jim Crow policies began to fall. In 1937, in Pittsburgh proper, black teachers for the first time successfully integrated the public school teaching staff.

Meanwhile, black residents of Homestead recall that blacks could not eat inside the "white" department stores and restaurants during the Thirties. They had to buy their ice cream cones, for instance, and eat them outside. Likewise, the Leona Theater, Homestead's principal picture palace—which, indeed, was the major one for the entire Mon Valley—required blacks to sit in the balcony, segregated from the white audience on the main floor.

This changed, with relatively little resistance, in 1938 after SWOC captured Homestead's City Hall and all things seemed possible. A sit-in movement started. Dee Filipe, whose parents refused to let her participate in the movement because of her youth, remembers that her friends went in and sat on the main floor of the Leona Theater, in the white section. When they refused to move, the police hauled them off to jail.

However, in the wake of this single sit-in (and no doubt in part because of the 1935 revision of the state Civil Rights Act), the Leona changed its policy of racial segregation—a change which was followed soon afterwards by the department and drug stores of Homestead.

Evelyn Brooks was another black woman who remembers sitting upstairs in the Leona's segregated balcony. She used the word, "revolution," to describe what happened to Homestead race relations in 1938.[54]

Over in Clairton, where local SWOC leader John Mullen was elected mayor in 1937, 3,000 black residents threatened to swim in the city's whites-only swimming pool when it opened for the summer of 1939, eventually forcing its desegregation.[55]

Nor was this movement confined to small towns in the Mon Valley, for black protestors also de-segregated the picture palaces of Pittsburgh at this same time, although in many other areas of race relations Pittsburgh itself lagged behind the SWOC-dominated milltowns of the Mon Valley. Pittsburgh's Highland Park swimming pool, for instance, would not be desegregated until the early 1960s.

Perhaps the relative ease with which the public facilities of SWOC-controlled towns in the Steel Valley were racially desegregated in 1938 and 1939—fifteen to twenty years before the black Civil Rights Movement of the 1950s and early 1960s—has obscured the significance of the changes in attitudes and values taking place in the industrial heartland at this time. The belief that "all men are created equal" was an expansionist doctrine which, set in motion, didn't stop at the color line. This was true for both blacks and whites. Blacks were emboldened to sit in at the Leona Theater. But part of their new-found boldness came from the fact that white legislators *had* passed the Civil Rights Act of 1935. In addition, white SWOC leaders and members pledged to an ideology of equality now controlled the governments of Duquesne, Clairton, and Homestead.

In a sense, then, the first stirrings of the black Civil Rights Movement, which many historians have seen in the egalitarian ethos of the fight against fascism in World War II, might instead be found in the values championed by the working class political revolution which transformed the Steel Valley and other industrial regions of the Northeast in the 1930s. There was a Civil Rights Movement of the 1930s and 1940s simultaneous with the ethnic revolt taking place. Herein was the origin of the ideological fight against fascism in World War II and herein was also the political shape of things to come in the Fifties and Sixties.

Herein, also, however, was the future of political reaction. The incorporation of both these civil rights movements—one racial and the other ethnic and class— into the multi-racial and multi-class Democratic Party was problematic and had fateful repercussions, perhaps not yet resolved. The mass entrance of the Northern, urban, ethnic, Catholic, working class into the Democratic Party alienated the large Southern, rural, native-stock, Protestant wing of the party, which had been the party's backbone heretofore. In reaction, many of the conservative Southern Congressmen who represented this wing of the party joined forces with Republicans to stymie the New Deal agenda after 1938.

Likewise, the entrance of a vastly enlarged black electorate into the Democratic Party, especially in the South, after the mid-1960s alienated huge numbers of white Southerners who deserted the party for the Republicans. This reaction was the grounds upon which some saw an "emerging Republican majority" at the time and was both the basis of Nixon's "Southern strategy" and one of the sources of "Reagan's Democrats."

Thus, by the 1990s, the South—meaning the white Southern voter—had become the Republican happy hunting ground, the new bedrock of the Republican party. In the 1994 mid-term elections, when Newt Gingrich's Republicans seized control of the House of Representatives, the South elected more Republican Congressmen than Democratic for the first time since the end of Reconstruction, including both senators from Tennessee and Jamie Whitten's northeastern Mississippi House seat, which had not had a Republican Representative since the

1870s. The Republican tide which swept across the South in the 1994 elections was propelled by the massive desertion of the Democratic Party by white voters. While Democrats got a strong black vote, "exit polls showed 68 percent of whites voted GOP. Among Southern men, 73 percent voted Republican."[56]

The truly great and amazing thing about the New Deal phenomenon, however, was the extent to which major and enduring racial and gender hostilities were muted by a universalist ethos which made possible even the "supporting role" participation of blacks and working class women in the political triumph of the "white man's" New Deal. That this was possible at all was due to an abiding ethical sense of fair play for "the common man" which found its political home in the Democratic Party.

"The ideal of the ethical society," we are reminded, "safe, decent, egalitarian, fair—was the animating force behind great advances from the New Deal to the civil-rights movement. The Democratic Party's ability to articulate and legislatively enact this ideal made it for nearly half a century the nation's dominant party, and liberalism the majority philosophy in American politics."[57]

At the same time, the ability of the Democratic Party to become the home of this ethos meant the "Last Hurrah" for the Labor Party tradition in American politics.

Notes

1. Minutes of the Pittsburgh Central Labor Union, and the holdings of the Pittsburgh Typographical Union, Local 7, Archives of Industrial Society, University of Pittsburgh. Hereafter notes as "Minutes of the PCLU." September 17, 29, 1942.

2. Minutes of the PCLU, October 15, 1942.

3. Suggestive of the exclusion of blacks from public discourse during this period is the absence of any survey on race relations in George Gallup's *Public Opinion Quarterly* for the years 1936, when the journal was launched, up until 1941.

4. Kristen Ostendorf, "Women Mine Memories from Life in a Coal Patch," *The Pittsburgh Post-Gazette,* August 19, 1999, 1.

5. Matthew S. Magda, *Monessen: Industrial Boomtown and Steel Community, 1898-1980,* Pennsylvania Historical and Museum Commission: Harrisburg, 1985. Dudas and Czelen, 68, 100. Hunter, 76. Mahalko, 69-70.

6. George Gallup and Claude Robinson, "American Institute of Public Opinion—Surveys, 1935-38," *The Public Opinion Quarterly,* July 1938, 392.

7. "Justice for All," *LIFE Celebrates 1945,* June 5, 1995, 58.

8. Ileen DeVault, *Sons and Daughters of Labor: Class and Clerical Work in Turn-of-the-Century Pittsburgh,* Cornell University Press: Ithaca, 1990, 12.

9. Jim Rose, "'The Problem Every Supervisor Dreads': Women Workers at the U.S. Steel Duquesne Works During World War II," *Labor History,* Vol. 36, No. 1, winter 1995, 26-27.

10. Rose, "The Problem Every Supervisor Dreads," 25, 32.

11. Allan M. Winkler, *Home Front U.S.A.: America During World War II,* Harlan Davidson, Inc.: Arlington Heights, Ill., 1986, 50-51. Rose, "The Problem Every Supervisor Dreads," 37.

12. Rose, "The Problem Every Supervisor Dreads," 41-42.

13. Rose, "The Problem Every Supervisor Dreads," 44, 46.

14. Minutes of the PCLU, February 15, 1940, February 20, 1941.

15. When she retired in 1976, Amy Ballinger was replaced on the City Council by Sophie Masloff, who'd also worked herself up through the local labor and Democratic Party hierarchy. Masloff would go on to become Pittsburgh's first female (and Jewish) mayor. In 2009, Amy Ballinger was living in retirement in Florida, swimming daily at age one hundred.

16. Minutes of the PCLU, December 4, 1941.

17. Minutes of the PCLU, July 5, 1945.

18. Minutes of the PCLU, April 16, 1936.

19. Minutes of the PCLU, May 7, 1936.

20. Minutes of the PCLU, June 4, 1936.

21. Minutes of the PCLU, August 6, 1936.

22. Minutes of the PCLU, June 2, 1938; November 19, 1938.

23. Minutes of the PCLU, March 7, 1940.

24. Minutes of the PCLU, September 17, 1936.

25. Minutes of the PCLU, October 17, 1940.

26. Minutes of the PCLU, December 3, 1936.

27. *The Pittsburgh Press,* June 1, 1888.

28. Michael Weber, John Bodnar, and Roger Simon, "Seven Neighborhoods: Stability and Change in Pittsburgh's Ethnic Community, 1930-1960," *The Western Pennsylvania Historical Magazine,* Vol. 64, No. 2, April 1981, 130-131.

29. Langston Hughes, "How About It, Dixie?" in *Jim Crow's Last Stand,* Race and Culture Series No. 2, Negro Publication Society of America: New York, 1943, 9.

30. *The Pittsburgh Post-Gazette,* "Troopers Quell Disorders in Tense Registration Day," September 4, 1931, 1; March 17, 1932, 4.

31. *The Pittsburgh Post-Gazette,* "Troopers Quell Disorders," September 4, 1931, 1.

32. *The Pittsburgh Post-Gazette,* September 14, 1931, 3.

33. *The Pittsburgh Post-Gazette,* "Gunplay, Riots Mark Primary," September 16, 1931, 1, 3.

34. *The Pittsburgh Post-Gazette,* "Claim Verona Not Attacked," September 16, 1931, 2.

35. *Pittsburgh Press,* October 15, 1940, 1.

36. "Rocky" Doratio, interviewed in *Crashin' Out: Hard Times in McKeesport,* prepared by the McKeesport Oral History Project, Mon Valley Unemployed Committee, Pittsburgh, August 1983, 20.

37. Weber, et al., "Seven Neighborhoods," 131.

38. Minutes of the PCLU, January 23, 1940. There was also separate entertainment for the "lady delegates."

39. *The Pittsburgh Press,* February 5, 1888.

40. Abraham Epstein, *The Negro Migrant in Pittsburgh,* University of Pittsburgh School of Economics: Pittsburgh, 1918, 30.

41. Report of J. Carter Robinson, State Department of Labor Placement Secretary for Pittsburgh's Hill District office, to Forrester B. Washington, Director, State Department of Labor's Negro Survey, December 1924. Copy in author's possession.

42. Epstein, *The Negro Migrant in Pittsburgh*, 38-39.

43. Brody, *Steelworkers in America: The Non-Union Era,* Harvard University Press: Cambridge, Mass., 1960; Harper & Row: New York, 1969, 224.

44. Brody, *Steelworkers in America,* 254.

45. Brody, *Steelworkers in America,* 266, 267.

46. Winkler, *Homefront USA,* 59.

47. Winkler, *Homefront USA,* 58.

48. Quoted in John Morton Blum, *V Was For Victory: Politics and American Culture During World War II,* Harcourt Brace Jovanovich: New York, 1977, 208.

49. Letter to the Editor, *The Homestead Daily Messenger,* October 3, 1936.

50. Rev. S. H. Soloman, Letter to the Editor, *The Homestead Daily Messenger,* September 19, 1936.

51. *The Union Press,* October 1937, emphasis in the original.

52. Magda, *Monessen,* 83-84.

53. Martha E. Foy, "The Negro in the Courts: A Study in Race Relations," Ph.D. dissertation, University of Pittsburgh, 1953, 88.

54. Dee Filipe and Evelyn Brooks in interviews conducted by Eric Leif Davin and Anita Alverio, 1980.

55. See *The Pittsburgh Press,* June 23, 30, 1939.

56. See William M. Welch, "'A sea change' in character of the House," *USA Today,* November 9, 1994, 3A.

57. Michael Kelly, "The Man of the Minute," *The New Yorker,* July 17, 1995, 28.

Chapter 6

A Choice of Champions

"With thousands of other workers of the Homestead district,
I believe it is to the best interests of the common man to
place Franklin Delano Roosevelt back in the White House."

– A Fourth Warder
Letter to the Editor
The Homestead Daily Messenger
October 8, 1936

Almost from its birth the American labor movement harbored a strong desire for what came to be called "independent political action." This phrase was generally understood to mean a political party separate from all others—a labor party.

The first example of this tendency was the Working Men's Party of Philadelphia, founded by that city's Mechanics Union of Trade Associations to contest the municipal elections of 1828. Indeed, this was not only America's first labor party, but the world's first labor party, providing inspiration, for instance, to England's soon-to-emerge Chartist movement. A score of the party's candidates were elected that year and again the next. Workingmen in other Pennsylvania cities also began to organize politically and by 1830 it seemed a statewide Working Men's Party would be formed. Internal dissension, however, tore the incipient movement apart by 1831.

Nevertheless, between 1828-1834 similar municipal labor parties were organized in sixty-one cities and towns from Burlington, Burlington, Vt., to Washington, D.C., and as far west as Pittsburgh and Ohio.[1] Throughout the nineteenth century other such municipal and statewide efforts were made from time to time to establish labor parties around the country. By the 1880s a number of these local labor parties had come to power in many localities, as in Scranton, Pennsylvania, where Terence Powderly, leader of America's first truly national

145

labor union, the Knights of Labor, served as mayor from 1878 to 1884.[2]

The efforts on the part of labor toward "independent political action" were not identical with the efforts of Socialists to form their own parties friendly to labor. The first of these was probably the Social Party of New York City, formed in 1868 by a merger of two German organizations, the Lassallean German Workingmen's Union and the Marxist Communist Club.

In 1874 the Labor Party of Illinois garnered nearly a thousand votes in the Chicago municipal elections, enough to encourage it to continue agitation. In 1876 this party merged with the International Workingmen's Association and the Social Democratic Workingmen's Party to form the Workingmen's Party of the United States. After undergoing various permutations, this party became Daniel DeLeon's Socialist Labor Party, which is still in existence. The failure of this party to win the allegiance of the American labor movement, however, gave rise to the Socialist Party of Debs. Still later came the Communist Party, the Socialist Workers Party, and all the other sectarian grouplets on the Left which appealed for labor's love—and lost.

The rise to dominance of the American Federation of Labor (AFL) under Samuel Gompers meant that the Gompers policy of political neutrality—of "rewarding one's friends and punishing one's enemies," regardless of party—also came to characterize the political orientation, at least rhetorically, of a large part of the labor movement. After 1906, while still proclaiming political neutrality, the AFL began to tilt toward the Democratic Party.

But the Gompers policy was never the sole political tendency within the movement and the desire for a party of labor's own remained strong within certain sections.[3] This was especially true following the "Red Scare" of 1919. In the wake of that hysteria, and with increasingly hard times for labor as the Twenties began, labor party sentiment flared anew. Local Labor and Farmer-Labor Parties coalesced across the country, while the Non-Partisan League successfully contended for office as a third party in the upper Great Plains.

Additionally, some liberals and unionists formed the Workers' Education Bureau, which the AFL Executive Council supported until 1928, despite the Bureau's advocacy of "independent political action." Other sources of labor party agitation were the "labor colleges" which labor activists and progressive intellectuals founded, the most notable being A.J. Muste's Brookwood Labor College in Katonah, New York, launched in 1921.[4]

In 1924, even the AFL halfheartedly surrendered to this tendency when it endorsed (and then abandoned) the Presidential candidacy of Robert M. LaFollette under the banner of the Progressive Party. With LaFollette's defeat, however, the labor party upsurge faltered and most of the local parties faded, leaving only the Minnesota Farmer-Labor Party as a viable remnant.[5]

Even then, however, the flame was tended by on-going coalitions of unionists and progressives such as the League for Independent Political Action, the Conference for Progressive Political Action, and, later, the Farmer Labor Political Federation, which kept the idea alive in hopes of more propitious times ahead.[6] Then, with the coming of the Great Depression in 1929, local labor parties again sprang up all across America like mushrooms in a meadow after a warm summer rain.[7]

Even today, some unions, such as the United Electrical Workers (UE), call for the formation of a labor party at every annual convention. On June 26, 1985, Richard Trumka, then president of the United Mine Workers (UMW), called for the formation of an independent labor party at the annual convention of The Newspaper Guild in Pittsburgh. America has "one party with two branches," said Trumka, "both apparently subservient to the interests of big money and the power of multinational corporations. All of us in the labor movement must consider the possibility that we are not going to establish a government of the people in this country as long as we remain so closely tied to the Democratic Party."[8]

But the ritualistic convention mandates of unions such as UE and the rhetoric of leaders like Trumka are mere lip service to the nostalgic dream of an independent labor party, not meant to be seriously acted upon. Even Trumka, while attacking the two-party system, disclaimed any interest in leading a genuine third party effort. Much more indicative of organized labor's attitude today is former AFL-CIO president Lane Kirkland's belief that labor is a "natural constituency" of the Democratic Party and the Democratic Party is the natural home of the labor movement.[9] Indeed, echoed United Steelworkers (USW) past president Lynn Williams, "If you took the labor movement out of the Democratic Party, what's left? It's the heart and soul of the Democratic Party."[10]

So close is this alliance today that by the mid-1980s, the AFL-CIO had already been guaranteed forty voting seats on the Democratic National Committee, the governing body of the Democratic Party. Labor's political neutrality died in the Great Depression of the Thirties. So, also, did the old dream of "independent political action"—the dream of a labor party. Since the great realigning election of 1936, organized labor has been somewhat shakily married to the Democratic Party.[11]

This transferral of partisan loyalty can be strikingly seen in the Pittsburgh region, in which a tradition of radical third-party voting had emerged. In the 1912 presidential election, for instance, Socialist candidate Eugene V. Debs averaged 25 percent of the vote in sixteen Western Pennsylvania steel towns, while Socialist Party candidates swept the local elections that year in Allegheny County's North Versailles. The small steel town of Homestead was typical.

In 1892, James B. Weaver, the Populist presidential candidate, got 15 percent of the vote in Homestead. Meanwhile, Populist State Assembly and Congressional candidates got 28 percent and 25 percent of the vote, respectively.[12] In the 1912 election, 26.8 percent of the Homestead District (Homestead, West Homestead, and Munhall) vote went to Debs. At the same time, he took 43 percent and 67.6 percent of the vote in nearby Lincoln Place and Whitaker.[13] That same year Socialist Party vice presidential candidate Emil Seidel spoke at a massive Labor Day parade in Homestead, along with Charlotte Perkins Gilman, one of the nation's leading feminists.[14] As late as 1920, Debs still got 21.6 percent of the Homestead vote.[15]

In 1924 Robert M. LaFollette (on the ballot as a "Socialist-Labor" candidate) won 25 percent of the Homestead vote, while he carried West Homestead and Whitaker. Meanwhile, in Pittsburgh LaFollette got 36 percent of the vote.[16] In Polish Hill, one of Pittsburgh's myriad ethnic neighborhoods, La Follette's vote ran closely behind the Republican candidate, and was nine times larger than the Democratic vote.[17]

In the Thirties, this class-conscious support for socialist third parties transferred to the Democratic Party, as the latter came to be seen as a more viable vehicle for working class aspirations. To illustrate, I said that Robert M. LaFollette won 36 percent of the Pittsburgh vote in 1924 on a "Socialist-Labor" ticket. The wards (such as Polish Hill) that supported LaFollette, which we might call the most highly class conscious, were the same immigrant, working class wards which voted for Socialist Eugene V. Debs in 1912—and voted for Democrat Franklin D. Roosevelt in 1932 and thereafter. The Debs-LaFollette vote became the Roosevelt vote.

At the same time, John W. Davis, the 1924 Democratic presidential candidate, garnered only 8 percent of the Pittsburgh vote, and that vote came from wards "poles apart" from the wards that supported Debs, LaFollette, and later Roosevelt. The "new" Democratic vote, therefore, was very different from the "old" Democratic vote of just a decade before. The "new" Democratic vote was based in the very "third party" wards which had spurned the Democrats of 1924 and had, instead, been the strongholds of Debs and LaFollette. This allegiance shift of the class conscious working class vote from Socialist or "Socialist-Laborite" to Democratic in a period of eight years was the foundation of Democratic dominance in the Thirties.[18]

Furthermore, this working class and class conscious "new" Democratic vote grew much larger over time, as more and more working class voters mobilized. In 1924, Socialist-Laborite LaFollette received 25 percent of the Homestead vote. But in 1928, the Homestead vote cast for Catholic Democratic presidential candidate Al Smith was 68 percent higher than the *total* voter turnout of 1924.

In nearby Pittsburgh, where by 1934 *all* of the Democratic Party ward chairmen and Committeemen were of non-WASP origin, the WASPs continued to vote Republican in the same numbers they always had. For example, 95.3 percent of Pittsburgh voters in 1930 were Republican, while only 4.7 percent were Democrats. By 1936 Republican registration had dropped to 43.9 percent of the total, while Democratic registration climbed to 56.1 percent. *Numerically, however, the Republican vote was as high as ever.* The political universe had changed, but not because there had been any change in the hearts and minds of the Republican electorate. The political universe had been transformed by a tremendous expansion of the electorate—mostly working class and mostly in favor of the Democrats.[19]

The expansion of the Democratic electorate in the areas most loyal to Debs and LaFollette raises an interesting question: What was there about the appeals of the Socialist Party, LaFollette, and the Democratic Party of the Thirties such that the working class voters who supported them saw a clear line of continuity between them? What did they think they were voting for when they first voted for

Debs and LaFollette and then voted for Roosevelt? What was the promise which motivated them, which resonated in their hearts?

Only by looking at the local, face-to-face, level will we fully understand the political mobilizations of the New Deal Era and how Debs' workers became "the heart and soul" of the Democratic Party. And, once we place this realigning phenomenon under the microscope, we find an impressive and unprecedented grassroots, working class, political mobilization which was not simply an amorphous response to FDR and the Wagner Act, nor simply a result of the machinations of national labor leaders, though these certainly provided maneuvering room and encouragement. Fundamentally, the political mobilization of the working class in the Thirties was a class war for political and economic equality.

The call to this class war was issued, not from the top down, but from the bottom up by a myriad of self-starting local working class leaders responding to local imperatives. Collectively, the actions of these class conscious, street-level leaders brought about the political realignment of the Thirties, the triumph of the Democratic Party, and the creation of a new America built around the concept of a "Workers' Democracy."

These local leaders, and the workers they led, were motivated by the most basic promises of American politics. "Give me liberty or give me death." "All men are created equal." Freedom. Equality. Democracy. These were the revolutionary words of promise which resonated in the hearts and minds of the workers.

And the flag of revolution which waved over every picket line, demonstration, and funeral for slain strikers was the American flag, "Old Glory," with its promise of equal rights for all. This is what "class consciousness" meant to the children of the immigrants, to be Orthodox or a Catholic, to be an industrial worker, to be from Pittsburgh or Homestead or Braddock—and still to truly be "free Americans."

And, as with the Civil Rights Movement which would follow it twenty years later, the political vehicle through which this movement realized its agenda of inclusion and equality was the Democratic Party, to which it was cemented after the mid-1930s. To working class ethnic voters, it seemed the Democratic Party was the one which cared about them, not the Republicans.

Camilla Caliendo is a Democratic Judge of Elections for the 14th Precinct of Ward Four in Pittsburgh's South Oakland neighborhood. Born a Diulus in the Panther Hollow family home in 1925, she was six when her father died in 1931. Her mother, who came over from Italy in 1922, was left a widow with seven children. When Camilla was nine, in 1934, Democrat William McNair was elected mayor of Pittsburgh. Camilla remembered that her mother was strongly supportive of the new Democratic mayor. "He was for the little class," she recalled, "the poor, those with no income, like my mother. If the Democrats were in office, you always made money. If the Republicans were in office, we had to go on the bread lines. It's a proven fact. The Republicans never did anything for the little people." John Casciato, born in Panther Hollow in 1933 and a distant relative of Camilla's, agreed. "The Republicans are too rich for me," he said. "They're a rich man's party. They're mean people. They don't give a damn for anybody."[20]

One of the reasons for this close identification of ethnic workers with the Democratic Party was that Roosevelt spoke their language when he articulated what he and his party stood for in attempting a "New Deal." "We who support this New Deal do so because it is a square deal," he told an audience in Green Bay, Wisconsin. "Man is fighting those forces which disregard human co-operation and human rights in seeking that kind of individual profit which is gained at the expense of his fellows . . . It [the New Deal] seeks to cement our society . . . into a voluntary brotherhood of freemen, standing together, striving together, for the common good of all."[21]

Also, as Aliquippa steelworker Mike Zahorsky put it, "The Democratic Party promised labor that they were going to get them some freedom."[22] And the Democratic Party delivered on its promise of freedom.

Indicative of the crucial changes the Democratic Party brought to the industrial heartland was the headline in *The American Guardian,* September 18, 1936, "Troops Won't Slay Strikers Earle Asserts." At a massive Labor Day rally at Pittsburgh's Forbes Field in Oakland, attended by 150,000 workers and their families, the new Democratic Pennsylvania Governor George Earle also pledged that striking steelworkers would be able to get public relief. "I give you my solemn pledge that the Pennsylvania National Guard will not be used to break strikes," he said. "Our National Guard is not a company police system and will not be used as such. And the relief authorities will not at any time be used as strike breakers . . . The weapon of starvation to coerce workers has been taken away." The newspaper went on to report that this pledge was "regarded of high significance to the steel organizing campaign" then underway.[23]

And, in return, the working class pledged its unwavering loyalty to the Democratic Party. Many at the time, who should have known better, never truly realized the depth of this commitment. Thus, when Father Coughlin turned on the New Deal in 1934 and attacked FDR in vicious terms, his popularity plummeted. The Pittsburgh Central Labor Union, which had repeatedly begged him to come to Pittsburgh before this, never again invited him to Pittsburgh and there is never again a mention of Father Coughlin in the meeting minutes of the Pittsburgh Central Labor Union. The National Union Party, the third party Coughlin organized to run North Dakota Congressman William Lemke for president in 1936, turned out to be a paper tiger. Lemke received less than a million votes scattered across the nation. Coughlin, albeit temporarily, retired in chagrin from the airwaves.

Similarly, CIO President John L. Lewis turned on FDR in the waning years of the Thirties and endorsed the Republican presidential candidate Wendell Willkie in 1940. Further, he made it personal. In a nationwide radio broadcast, he told his faithful legions that the election would be a referendum upon his own, Lewis', wisdom and leadership. It was deemed a close race for the presidency, and if Roosevelt won, Lewis said, it would be clear that the working class vote elected him. He would interpret that as a vote of no confidence in himself and resign as their leader.

The revered Lewis did not get the reaction he hoped for. His followers immediately branded their leader a traitor, a Judas Iscariot. Roosevelt returned to the White House and an analysis of election returns made it clear that working class communities had voted overwhelmingly for him. John L. Lewis resigned in disgrace from the CIO presidency, to be replaced by his lieutenant, Philip Murray.

In 1948 the entire nation—or at least the nation's media and all those whose opinions counted—felt that the hour of the elephant had at long last come. Roosevelt was dead. Truman was an unelected president everyone deemed a loser. The purely personal loyalty the ethnic working class was supposed to have had for FDR would not carry over to Truman.

In addition, former Vice President Henry Wallace, one of the fiercest of the New Dealers, was challenging Truman and the Democrats for the allegiance of the working class with his own run for the presidency as the candidate of the Progressive Party. In this effort he was enthusiastically backed by the Communist Party, which also felt that the time had come for a more Leftist "labor party," now that Roosevelt was dead.

But on the day after the election, it was the triumphant Truman who laughingly held up the premature newspaper headlines proclaiming Dewey the victor. The CIO had remained loyal to Truman and the Democratic Party. And election returns showed that the ethnic industrial voter had remained loyal to Truman and the Democratic Party. These loyalties were enough to assure Truman's victory.

Like Father Coughlin, like John L. Lewis, and like so many others, it seems that Dewey, Wallace, the Communists, and the pundits had misjudged the depth of working class loyalty and commitment to the Democratic Party, which had become the workers' party. Over the course of the 1930s and 1940s, the Democratic Party had become the party which most faithfully expressed and responded to the dreams, desires, hopes and aspirations of the working class.

Let us now see how this was accomplished in America's industrial heartland.

Notes

1. See, e.g., Gordon Berg, "The Workingmen's Party—A First in Labor Politics," *Worklife*, No. 1, March 1976, 23-26. An excellent overview of these early efforts can be found in Alden Whitman, *Labor Parties, 1827-1834*, International Publishers: New York, 1943. Also, see Nathan Fine, *Labor and Farmer Parties in the United States, 1828-1928*, Rand School: New York, 1928.

2. See, e.g., "The Workingmen's Party of California, 1877-1882," *California Historical Quarterly*, 55, 1976, 58-71 (no author listed), and Neil Larry Shumsky, *The Evolution of Political Protest and the Workingmen's Party of California*, Ohio State University Press: Columbus, 1991. The rise and fall of the local labor parties of the 1880s can be traced in Leon Fink's *Workingmen's Democracy: The Knights of Labor and American Politics*, University of Illinois Press: Urbana, 1983.

3. Indicative of this on-going struggle is Samuel Gompers' polemic against the enduring labor party idea, *Should A Political Labor Party Be Formed?* pamphlet published by the AFL, 1918.

4. On farmer-labor party movements of the Twenties, see, e.g., Hamilton Cravens, "The Emergence of the Farmer-Labor Party in Washington Politics, 1919-1920," *Pacific North West Quarterly,* No. 57, 1966, 148-157; Wayne Flynt, "Florida Labor and Political 'Radicalism,' 1919-1920," *Labor History,* No. 9, 1968, 73-90; Stuart A. Rice, *Farmers and Workers in American Politics,* Columbia University Press: New York, 1924; Hayes Robbins, *The Labor Movement and the Farmer,* Harcourt Brace: New York, 1922; Stanley Shapiro, "'Hand and Brain': The Farmer-Labor Party of 1920," *Labor History,* No. 26, summer 1985, 405-422 and Murray S. Stedman and Susan W. Stedman, *Discontent at the Polls: A Study of Farmer and Labor Parties, 1827-1948,* Columbia University Press: New York, 1950.

An interesting article dealing with the Non-Partisan League is William C. Pratt, "Socialism on the Northern Plains, 1900-1924," *South Dakota History,* 18, spring/summer 1988, 1-35.

For an overview of the educational efforts, see Susan I. Wong, "Workers Education, 1921-1951," Ph.D. dissertation, Columbia University, 1976. Also, Peter E. Van DeWater, "The Workers' Education Service," *Michigan History,* 60, 1976, 99-113 and Richard Dwyer, "Workers' Education, Labor Education, Labor Studies: An Historical Delineation," *Review of Educational Research,* 47, winter 1977, 179-207.

The Bryn Mawr Summer School for Women Workers, which lasted from 1921-1938, was another example of a successful "labor college." During its existence, 1,700 working class women were recruited from blue-collar jobs for an intensive two-month program in left-wing trade unionism. See Lucille A. Maddalena, "The Goals of the Bryn Mawr Summer School for Women Workers as Established During its First Five Years," Ph. D. dissertation, Rutgers University, 1979, *Dissertation Abstracts International,* 40, 76-A. A fine film documentary on this school is, "The Women of Summer," written, produced, and directed by Suzanne Bauman and distributed by Filmakers Library.

In 1923, philosopher Will Durant, later famous for *The Story of Philosophy,* was the Director of New York's Labor Temple School. Meanwhile, Bertram D. Wolfe directed The Workers School in New York City, which was militantly class-conscious and supportive of a labor party. See its announcement of classes for 1926-1927, "Training for the Class Struggle," The Workers School: New York, 1926.

An interesting labor college of the time was the Commonwealth College. On it, see William H. Cobb, "From Utopian Isolation to Radical Activism: Commonwealth College, 1925-1935," *Arkansas Historical Quarterly,* 32, 1973, 132-147. On Brookwood Labor College, see Richard Altenbaugh, "Forming the Structure of a New Society Within the Shell of the Old: A Study of Three Labor Colleges and Their Contributions to the American Labor Movement," Ph. D. dissertation, University of Pittsburgh, 1980, *Dissertations Abstracts International* 41, 565-A (a study of Brookwood, Commonwealth College, and Work People's College); Charles F. Howlett, "Brookwood Labor College and Work Commitment to Social Reform," *Mid-America,* 61, 1979, 47-66; Charles F. Howlett, "Brookwood Labor College: Voice of Support for Black Workers," *Negro History Bulletin,* 45, 1982, 38-39; and James W. Robinson, "The Expulsion of Brookwood Labor College from the Workers' Education Bureau," *Labour History* [Canberra, Australia], No. 15, 1968, 64-69.

The story of Brookwood's decline and fall is told by Jonathan D. Bloom, "Brookwood Labor College: The Final Years, 1933-1937," *Labor's Heritage,* Vol. 2, No. 2, April 1990, 24-43. From reading the account by Bloom we glean the answer to a puzzling question: Why should Brookwood, the most successful of the labor colleges, collapse in 1937 at the very height of labor's insurgency, after having survived the "lean years" of the Twenties so well? The answer is Brookwood's continued advocacy of a Labor Party while the unions which were its major financial support—principally Sidney Hillman's Amalgamated Clothing Workers and David Dubinsky's International Ladies Garment Workers Union— abandoned their long-held support for a Labor Party in favor of Roosevelt and the Democrats. When these unions pulled the financial plug on Brookwood, it was unable to go on, despite a last desperate attempt to form an alliance with the United Auto Workers, where Labor Party sentiment remained high. Roy Reuther, brother to Walter and Victor and, like them, a Labor Party champion, was a Brookwood faculty member during these final years and was seen as a link to the UAW.

5. I recommend two interesting studies on the Minnesota Farmer-Labor Party. The first is Millard L. Gieske's *Minnesota Farmer-Laborism: The Third-Party Alternative,* University of Minnesota Press: Minneapolis, 1979. The other, more provocative in its argument for the viability of localized radical political movements, is Richard M. Valelly's *Radicalism in the States: The Minnesota Farmer-Labor Party and the American Political Economy,* University of Chicago Press: Chicago, 1989.

6. See, e.g., Karel Denis Bicha, "Liberalism Frustrated: The League for Independent Political Action, 1928-1933," *Mid-America,* No. 47, 1966, 19-28, and Richard J. Brown, "John Dewey and The League for Independent Political Action," *Social Studies,* No. 59, 1968, 156-161.

7. For a history of one such local labor party, which dominated the city of Berlin, New Hampshire, from 1934-1943, see Eric Leif Davin and Staughton Lynd, "Picket Line and Ballot Box: The Forgotten Legacy of the Local Labor Party Movement, 1932-1936," *Radical History Review,* 22, winter 1979-80, 43-63. See, also, David J. Pivar, "The Hosiery Workers and the Philadelphia Third Party Impulse, 1929-1935," *Labor History,* winter 1964. For a study of the United Rubber Workers' efforts to create a labor party, see Richard W. Shrake, II, "Working Class Politics in Akron, Ohio, 1936: The United Rubber Workers and the Failure of the Farmer-Labor Party," unpublished M.A. thesis, University of Akron, 1974. Daniel Nelson treats, superficially, the United Rubber Workers' labor party efforts in "The CIO at Bay: Labor Militancy and Politics in Akron, 1936-1938," *The Journal of American History,* 71, December 1984.

Hugh Lovin has done much work on the Midwest and Pacific Northwest efforts to form a labor or farmer-labor party during this period. His work includes: "The Fall of the Farmer-Labor Parties, 1936-1938," *Pacific North West Quarterly,* 62, January 1971; "Toward A Farmer-Labor Party in Oregon, 1933-1938, *Oregon Historical Quarterly,* Vol. 76, 2, June 1975; "The Persistence of Third Party Dreams in the American Labor Movement, 1930-1938," *Mid-America,* 58, October 1976; "The Ohio Farmer-Labor Movement in the 1930s," *Ohio History,* 87, Autumn, 1978; "The Farmer-Labor Movement in Idaho, 1933-1938," *Journal of the West,* Vol. 18, 2, April 1979; "The Automobile Workers Unions and the Fight for Labor Parties in the 1930s," *Indiana Magazine of History,* 77, 1981; and "CIO Innovators, Labor Party Ideologues, and Organized Labor's Muddles in the 1937 Detroit Elections," *The Old Northwest,* 8, fall 1982.

For a contemporary and somewhat comprehensive survey of labor party efforts nationwide, see the special issue on the subject in *Industrial Democracy*, Vol. 5, No. 11, February 1938 by Harry W. Laidler, "Toward a Farmer-Labor Party."

An additional argument for and survey of contemporary labor party building efforts may be found in Brookwood Labor College instructor Joel Seidman's booklet, *A Labor Party for America?*, published by the Education Department, United Automobile Workers of America, Detroit, 1937; and the book by Brookwood instructors Katherine H. Pollak and David J. Saposs, *How Should Labor Vote?* Brookwood Labor College Publications: Katonah, New York, 1932. (This latter was considered the organizational blueprint by many local labor parties at the time.)

Also, see Paul H. Douglas, *The Coming of A New Party*, McGraw-Hill: New York, 1932, and Morris Hillquit and Matthew Woll, *Should The American Workers Form A Political Party of Their Own?* Rand School: New York, 1932. The latter is a debate on the subject between Hillquit and Woll, with Hillquit (of the Socialist Party) in favor and Woll representing traditional AFL opposition to the idea.

8. *The Pittsburgh Post-Gazette,* June 27, 1985.

9. *The New York Times,* April 29, 1985.

10. Author's notes of a speech to a labor/academic luncheon, Pittsburgh, September 19, 1986.

11. For an extensive overview and history of the Labor Party Movement of the 1930s, definitive, in my opinion, see Eric Leif Davin, "The Very Last Hurrah: The Defeat of the Labor Party Idea, 1934-1936," in Staughton Lynd, Ed., *"We Are All Leaders": The Alternative Unionism of the Early 1930s,* University of Illinois Press: Urbana, 1996. A condensed account of the movement is Eric Leif Davin, "The Labor Party Movement of the 1930s," in Ronald Hayduk and Immanuel Ness, Eds., *The Encyclopedia of Third Parties in America*, M. E. Sharpe Publications: New York, 1999.

12. Ann Marie Draham, et al., "People, Power, and Profits: The Struggle of U.S. Steel Workers for Economic Democracy, 1882-1985," unpublished manuscript, n.d., 39, in the author's possession.

13. *Homestead Daily Messenger,* November 6, 1912.

14. *Homestead Daily Messenger,* September 2, 1912.

15. *Homestead Daily Messenger,* November 5, 1920.

16. *Homestead Daily Messenger,* November 5, 1924.

17. See Walter Dean Burnham, *The Current Crisis in American Politics,* Oxford University Press: New York, 1982, Table 11, 146.

18. See Bruce M. Stave, *The New Deal and the Last Hurrah: Pittsburgh Machine Politics,* University of Pittsburgh Press: Pittsburgh, 1970, 36, 37.

19. Stave, *The New Deal and the Last Hurrah,* 180, 181.

20. Interviews by the author, May 24, 1996.

21. Quoted with approval in *Sam Clark's Red Ink: Volleys of Truth,* September 1934, 48. *Red Ink* was a small independent political journal published in North Dakota.

22. Michael Zahorsky in John Bodnar, *Workers' World: Kinship, Community, and Protest in an Industrial Society, 1900-1940,* The Johns Hopkins University Press: Baltimore, 1982, 131.

23. *The American Guardian,* September 18, 1936, 1. This was Oscar Ameringer's weekly newspaper.

Chapter 7

Storming the Bastille, 1930-1934

Storm's Prelude

The first struggle of the workers was for the right to struggle. And this struggle, during long years of repression, helped nurture an assertive class consciousness among these workers.

English labor historian E. P. Thompson has described the decade of the 1820s in England as the period in which the English working class became *class conscious*. By this phrase he meant that, "working men formed a picture of the organization of society, out of their own experience . . . which was above all a political picture. They learned to see their own lives as part of a general history of conflict between the loosely defined 'industrious classes' on the one hand, and the unreformed House of Commons on the other."[1]

We see evidence of a similar evolution of class consciousness in the Pennsylvania steel towns. Since Andrew Carnegie and Henry Clay Frick's destruction of unionism in steel at the 1892 Battle of Homestead, a common experience of oppression had led workers of various ethnicities to a clear awareness of their own interests, as workers, in distinction to those of others, in this case the steel companies, the Republicans, and what workers called "the Republican police," the "cossacks."

At the beginning of the twentieth century, the workers of the industrial heartland lived and worked in feudal servitude. Many, however, because of the solidarity arising from their strong working class ethnic enclaves, remained steadfast in their opposition to corporation dominance. "Repeatedly," John Fitch reported in his 1907 investigation of the Steel Valley, "I was told that workmen have been discharged at Duquesne for refusing to vote the way the company wished."²

Despite the threats of discharge, the surveillance, and the complete political and economic dominance of "the steel trust," Fitch still found that, "In spite of the period that has elapsed since there was any form of union activity in the steel mills, there is still a firm belief on the part of a great many that some day the mills will be all unionized. A majority of the workmen feel that it is only through their efforts, and that of the community at large, together launched against the opposing powers, that their industrial freedom is to be won."³

Even at that time, however, many felt that they had to move *beyond* workplace organizing if they wanted to gain their freedom. Already, in 1907, Fitch discovered that, "Not all of the socially hopeful workmen look to trade unionism to secure to them what they consider their rights. As the years have gone by since unionism was overthrown, and each year has seen the control of the employers grow more certain, and nearly absolute, many have turned to politics as the way out ... There is a deep unrest among the voters in the mill towns with regard to things political ... Most of the Pittsburgh steel workers vote the Republican ticket, because they see no immediate hope of success through a workingmen's party; but they are ready to accept any political theory that promises something worthwhile to labor. If the workmen in the mills were once convinced that in an approaching election there existed a possibility of election of the socialist candidates, there would follow what could not adequately be termed a landslide; it would be an avalanche."⁴

Until the Thirties, however, the possibility of such political success was frustrated by an omnipresent Republican-corporate control. David Brody has detailed the "sources of stability" in the mill towns which contributed to an enduring status quo of steel corporation rule.⁵ The smaller communities were one-industry towns which depended totally upon the local steel mill for their continuing existence, sometimes even for their birth. Even in a large city like Pittsburgh, half of its industry was steel production in the early years of the century. Local business elites, therefore, as well as newspapers, and even the churches, were quick to ally with the company in any labor dispute.

There were also the ethnic divisions among the steel workers themselves, both on the job in segregated occupations and in the surrounding communities. In a steel town as tightly controlled as Aliquippa, for instance, these divisions were carried to such an extent that Jones & Laughlin Steel (the major renter) assigned each ethnic group, including sub-divisions of Eastern and Southern Europeans, to different parts of town.

But perhaps most importantly there was company control of municipal government, which guaranteed an unyielding hostility on the part of local officials to workers' grievances in general and to strikes in particular. When all else failed, the local police force could always be counted upon to break any strike or stifle any organizing campaign before it gained momentum.

By the time of the 1919 steel strike, local government in the Steel Valley belonged completely to the corporations. The Sheriff of Allegheny County, which encompassed Pittsburgh and its surrounding steel towns, was the brother of a United States Steel plant manager. The President of the Homestead Borough Council was an official in U.S. Steel's Homestead plant. Indeed, virtually every Homestead Burgess between 1894 and 1921 was either a member of the mill's top management or a close company ally from the town's business elite.

The Burgess of Munhall, where most of the Homestead facility was actually located, was the plant superintendent. Likewise, the Burgess of Clairton was an official in the U.S. Steel mill in that town. George Wilson, the "labor-Democrat" candidate for Burgess of Midland in 1937, pointed out during the campaign that, "For years . . . this little Steel Town has been ruthlessly mismanaged by the hirelings of a great steel corporation. Coercion, discrimination and terrorism in general has been the lot of the great majority of the people here . . . The Steel corporation had their flunkies and still have them in the school board and in the town council. The majority of these men are mill superintendents elected to do the company's bidding."[6]

Where the local political establishment was not actually employed by the corporations, it nevertheless protected the interests of the corporations. Mayor Lysle in McKeesport and Mayor Crawford in Duquesne, brother of a steel company president, forbade union meetings in their towns. Mayor Cavanaugh in Homestead had forbidden U.S. Secretary of Labor Frances Perkins from meeting with Homestead steel workers. Steel Valley mayors and councils everywhere followed their lead. In Aliquippa, remembered union organizer Louis DeSenna, "The Burgess and the Council were all appointed by the company. No one dared run against them, so you may as well say they were appointed. They ran the town for the company."[7] The Duquesne experience is illustrative of this feudal condition.

Duquesne had a population of about 20,000 throughout the Thirties.[8] The largest employer, dominating the town, was the Carnegie-Illinois mill, a subsidiary of United States Steel, where virtually everyone worked.[9]

Closely allied to the steel corporation was the town government, headed by Mayor James C. Crawford. The Crawford family had dominated the community, economically and politically, since its genesis as an incorporated town. Crawford's father, John, had been elected the original Burgess of the town in 1896 and son James had taken over the reins of government in 1917, just in time to crush the 1919 steel strike in Duquesne. Crawford was president of Duquesne's only bank. His brother was president of the huge McKeesport Tinplate Corporation.

The Crawford administration—and virtually the entire electorate—was Republican. "It was all Republican," remembered Elmer Maloy. "They controlled the politics of the town and the school and everything else . . . by 1933, when Roosevelt came in, here was a town that had been practically 100 percent Republican. I don't think there were over 50 Democrats as voters in that town . . . There were a few families that didn't work in the mill, businessmen and other ones, that stayed Democratic, but outside of that, everybody was a Republican."[10]

This Republican administration routinely marshalled the town's police to suppress demonstrations of worker dissatisfaction, but Mayor Crawford's police force was not directed *only* against the workers. Elmer Maloy remembered that when the relatively pro-labor Gifford Pinchot was the Republican Governor of Pennsylvania in the early Thirties, neither he nor his activist wife, Cornelia Bryce Pinchot, were allowed to speak in Duquesne. Like Frances Perkins in Homestead, Mrs. Pinchot had to resort to federal territory if she wanted to speak: "She had to go down to the federal building, the post office, and speak from the post office steps. That's the only way she could speak in the town without getting arrested. And he was the governor of the state!"[11]

In Aliquippa it was perhaps even worse.[12] Mike Zahorsky, who began working in the Aliquippa Jones & Laughlin (J & L) mill in 1921 at age thirteen, was Catholic and worked for Democrat Al Smith in the presidential election of 1928 because Smith was Catholic. But, he recalled, almost no one actually dared register as a Democrat. There were then only thirty-five registered Democrats in Aliquippa, and about 10,000 Republicans.[13]

"You couldn't get a job if you were a Democrat," Zahorsky recalled. "It was like living in Russia, Siberia . . . The company had their stooges out and you didn't know who you were talking to . . . You couldn't trust a fellow you knew for 25 or 30 years. They'd come up to a guy in the mill and they'd say, 'Hey, Mike, what the hell were you talking about up at the Slovak picnic the other day? Word got to us you made a derogatory comment about the company. How many years do you have in the mill? Do you like your job?' You start to quake."[14]

In the 1930s (and until 1978), J & L was the fourth-largest steel producer in America, employing 45,000 workers. Its principal products were structural steel and sheet metal, although at the Aliquippa Works in Beaver County it manufactured steel for tubes, barrels, and pipes.[15]

And Aliquippa was the place where, in 1933, J. & L. organized a private army of American Legionnaires and detectives from the Bergoff Detective Agency. This private army charged with submachine guns and tear gas bombs over the bridge spanning the Ohio River into neighboring Ambridge to break a strike which Ambridge Burgess Philip J. Caul refused to crush. The invading army did it for him, killing one striker and wounding scores.

In 1934, George Isasky, an Aliquippa rank and file leader, was railroaded into a state insane asylum for trying to organize a union in the town. It took thirty-five days before the workers were able to induce a gubernatorial investigation which found him sane and released him.

Although his wealth came out of Aliquippa—and other J & L mills such as the ones in Pittsburgh's South Side and Hazelwood neighborhoods—James Laughlin, III, who owned and ran the company in the 1920s and 1930s, did not live in Aliquippa. He lived on Woodland Road in Pittsburgh's Squirrel Hill neighborhood, the wealthiest street in the city's wealthiest neighborhood.[16] He left Aliquippa and his mill there in the hands of one he trusted: J.A.C. Ruffner.

Ruling Aliquippa as his personal fiefdom, though in thrall to J. & L., J.A.C. Ruffner was publisher of *The Aliquippa Gazette*, the town's only newspaper. He had also been School District and Borough Tax Collector since 1914, Chairman of the local Republican Party since 1916, Director of The Woodlawn Building and

Loan as well as the Woodlawn Trust Company, and Director and Vice President of the First National Bank of Aliquippa.

When asked about the 1933 charge over the Ohio into Ambridge by the army of Tommy Gun-wielding strike breakers, Ruffner said, "That was one of the most wonderful things that ever happened in this valley . . . We won't see the law thrown aside because certain authorities [such as Ambridge Burgess Caul] fear the mob."

"Where was the mob, the throwing aside of law?" he was asked.

"Why, they were picketing!" he answered. "Whenever three or four men gather and make remarks that could be resented by another person, they are inciting to riot."[17]

Croatian barber Pete Muselin, son of a mill worker and a World War I vet, said that, "The J. & L. police carried their guns openly wherever they went. Their purpose was to intimidate people throughout the town . . . The coal and iron police were domiciled right next to the J. & L. main office . . . They had all their machine guns . . . and tear gas . . . in there, and they had a shooting range right next door. Every day we could see them off of mom's dining room window, practicing with pistols, rifles, and so on.

"[J. & L. Police Chief] Harry G. Mauk was the fellow behind the political scene for J. & L. The borough council was composed of strictly Jones & Laughlin people and the town's professionals. Mauk would direct Dr. Stevens, the physician, and Bud Scott, the dentist, and others . . . Bud Scott was my dentist. A long time afterward he told me, 'Pete . . . I hated that Mauk. He ordered me to be a councilman and told me, "You will do at these council meetings what I tell you to do, and you will vote the way I tell you."'"[18]

What that council did was to make sure the Bill of Rights did not apply to Aliquippa. "The council would pass these ordinances," Muselin remembered, "and I would defy them on the grounds that they were unconstitutional. They would tell me, and be very emphatic about it, 'We make the rules. This is not the United States. This is [Aliquippa].'"

Pete Muselin, being a barber and not directly employed by the mill, was one of the few in Aliquippa who dared to register as a Democrat in the Twenties and continued to call union meetings, despite being "arrested so often I could have put my name tag on that cell down in the borough lock-up." What motivated him to do this was a deep belief in the concept of political equality, the basic promise of America.

"Once I went [to the city council]," he said, "and I started reading the Declaration of Independence . . . a cop said 'That's communistic stuff you're reading.' When I got to the part where, 'all men are created equal,' he arrested me."[19]

While Mauk was chief of the J. & L. police, Mike Kane, Aliquippa Police Chief and Squire (magistrate), was his right hand man. Kane was the State Chairman of the Constitutional Defense League, an anti-union strike force created by the Americanism Committee of the American Legion in 1935. He was perhaps even more vicious than Mauk. He patrolled Aliquippa's "Hunkeytown" on a motorcycle, which was also an instrument of terror. He'd roar into backyards on his motorcycle, gunning it up onto porches and smashing into people's kitchens.

"With a *motorcycle* he'd go into the kitchen," said Muselin, "dispersing the men who were there, and shout, 'Break it up, you Hunkies!' And do you know what the men had been doing? They were either playing Ferbel, a card game, or they had a glass of wine in front of them, or maybe they were singing a little bit . . . When two people met peacefully [on the street] and might have been talking about who knows what, according to the . . . police they were inciting to riot: 'Break it up, Hunkies.'"

Mike Kane and Harry Mauk were just the most prominent of these "Republican Police," as the local steel workers called them. All the police acted as a private police force enforcing a private police state. "Every once in a while," Muselin said, "the cops came to my home and just raided the place—no warrant, no nothing. They would take every book, every periodical, every bulletin; they'd just dump them in a pile and throw them in the police cruiser and they would never return them. A policeman used to attend our Croatian fraternal lodge meetings. He stood in the back there, big guns strapped to his side, his arms crossed, with a club dangling down . . . He just wanted to make sure he didn't hear the word 'union.' . . . [Aliquippa] was a typical cossack town."

In 1926 the police raided Pete Muselin's Croatian lodge meeting and arrested him and thirty others. Muselin and another four were charged with sedition under Pennsylvania's state anti-sedition law. Prosecuted by J. & L.'s long-time attorney, they were found guilty in 1927 and sentenced to five years in the Allegheny County workhouse. Their convictions were upheld on all appeals until they reached the United States Supreme Court—which refused to review them. The five Aliquippa workers served out their five-year sedition sentences. One of them died in prison and the other four were released in February 1932.

Pete Muselin, returning from prison, then resumed his activities. He became one of the leaders of the 1933 Ambridge strike crushed by the army of American Legionnaires and Bergoff detectives from Aliquippa. By 1933, however, there were many more workers like Pete Muselin, not only in Aliquippa, but throughout the Pittsburgh region.

That had not been the case in the 1920s, nor, indeed, even at the beginning of the Depression. Indeed, the initial response by most workers to the Great Depression had been despair and political apathy. "Turnout did not increase much in the 1930 and 1932 elections," we are told. "[P]residential turnout in 1932 was 0.9 percentage points below the 1928 level . . . The experience of extreme deprivation and its accompanying perceptions of dissatisfaction are not by themselves sufficient causes of collective political action. To mobilize discontented citizens as an effective political force, these subjectively stressful conditions must be politicized. Individuals have to perceive them both as conditions shared by others and for which government action is somehow relevant."[20]

Something happened, then, to transform this oppressed and economically devastated, yet politically apathetic, population into a powerful electoral force, a force which changed the nature of American politics. Somehow, these people mobilized in the years after 1932 to express their class interests at the ballot box, as well as on the picket line. What caused this amazing transformation?

We have seen how their strong and stable communities and stable work situations contributed to their group strength. We have also seen how their religious values and adherence to basic American civic ideals fostered a culture of resistance among them. An additional factor in the political assertion of the industrial heartland's workers was the revival of the long-dormant labor movement.

For the Union Makes Us Strong

As 1932 began, Pittsburgh workers were literally under attack. In the early morning hours of March 10, a powerful bomb ripped apart the headquarters of the Harmarville United Mine Workers (UMWA) just outside Pittsburgh. The Republican county sheriff blamed "reds" and vowed to investigate. Throwing doubt on "reds" as the bombers, however, no investigation of any kind was forthcoming, as surely would have been the case had the authorities sincerely suspected "reds."[21]

But the times were changing. Labor was becoming more assertive, more sure of itself, less of a victim. Suggestive of this was the revival of Labor Day. During the 1920s, the tradition of observing Labor Day had lapsed in the Pittsburgh region. However, on June 4, 1931, John J. Kane, Business Representative of the city's Pressmen's Union Lo. 9, State Representative of the International Printing Pressmen and Assistants Union of North America, and a member of the Executive Board of the Pittsburgh Central Labor Union (PCLU), proposed to that body that Labor Day be revived. He advocated a large rally. Other members thought it a good idea, but argued instead for a parade.

Kane's preference carried and West View Park was retained as the site of the first revived Labor Day celebration in the Pittsburgh region. "It is urgently requested of all Union Labor," the PCLU moved, "to demonstrate that labor is still a factor by patronizing West View Park on next Labor Day." The event turned out to be such a success that the following year, 1932, West View Park offered a bribe of $100 to the PCLU for them to sponsor another Labor Day celebration there.[22]

The increasing requests by political candidates for the PCLU's endorsement also indicated labor's new importance. On February 4, 1932, for example, attorney Henry Ellenbogen, a supporter and close ally of Father Cox, "delivered a splendid address" before the body seeking its endorsement for his U.S. Congressional candidacy. Ellenbogen won the labor body's endorsement.[23]

However, as a "Cox candidate," Ellenbogen did not win the endorsement of Pittsburgh's Democratic Party boss, David Lawrence, nor that of the Democratic Party organization.[24] It didn't matter. Ellenbogen had labor's support, and he went on to trounce the party's endorsed candidate in the Democratic primary. In the general election in November 1932, the PCLU's candidate became the next U.S. Congressman to represent the Slavic South Side's 33rd Congressional District.

It was clear there was a new power broker in town, which had to be taken into consideration.

Even more indicative of how times were changing was the endorsements extended at the February 18, 1932, meeting of the PCLU. At that meeting, at which "labor priest" Father Cox also spoke about the economic trials of the time, three local union leaders were endorsed as Democratic candidates for the State House of Representatives. These included Executive Board members John J. Kane, of the Web Pressmen's Union, and Thomas J. Gallagher, of the Flint Glass Workers, as well as N. J. Grady of the Electrical Workers. "It behooves every Union man and woman to do all in their power to elect these three candidates," said the PCLU.[25]

The next month, the PCLU unanimously endorsed three more Democratic union men for the State House: James Sipe, a member of the Moving Picture Operators, William McMillen, a member of the Plumbers Union, and Albert B. Davidson, a former streetcar motorman. Because more and more candidates were asking for the PCLU's endorsement, it occurred to the body that some kind of formal procedure ought to be developed to process endorsement requests.

So the Executive Board was directed to "draw up suitable questionnaires to be given candidates for their signature of approval before receiving an endorsement."[26] This marked the first official procedure for granting political endorsements and was a sign of the times. Labor's approval was becoming valuable.

It was also evident that the labor body was beginning to show an increasing preference for Democrats. In April of 1932 American Federation of Labor (AFL) President William Green wrote to the PCLU urging—in the Sam Gompers tradition of rewarding one's friends (while punishing one's enemies), regardless of party affiliation—they they endorse incumbent Republican U.S. Senator James J. Davis in the upcoming 1932 election. Despite the fact that Davis had been friendly toward organized labor, and so had support among some PCLU delegates, this request "brought on quite a discussion in opposition." Too many delegates argued that Republicans should be opposed on principle, regardless of the candidate, so the body voted to table Green's letter and take no action.[27]

And, although it was becoming more politically active, the labor body was not receptive to the idea of forming or helping an incipient Labor Party. When the Full Fashioned Hosiery Workers of Philadelphia wrote the PCLU in July, asking the body to join them in launching a Pennsylvania Labor Party, the request was referred to the Executive Board, where it died.[28]

The body did, however, send a representative to an August political conference of the nascent Labor Party held in Harrisburg, the state capitol. This may have been, though, because the state Federation of Labor was co-sponsoring the conference and specifically requested the participation of the PCLU.

At that Harrisburg meeting, statewide Labor Party candidates were endorsed, including Pittsburgh's John J. Kane and Thomas Gallagher, who were actually already running as Democratic candidates. The PCLU delegate also reported back to the PCLU that local labor candidate N. J. Grady, of the Electrical Workers, would also be endorsed by the Labor Party. Thus, all three would appear on the ballot as both Democratic and Labor Party candidates.

These three candidates seemingly accepted their endorsements, as they were given, more out of labor solidarity than as any sign of real support for a Labor Party. Thus, when the newly formed Pennsylvania Labor Party later requested help in obtaining signatures on the nominating petition for its U.S. Senate candidate, the PCLU merely received the request as information, without taking action on it. This was even though a Labor Party endorsed candidate, John J. Kane, was on the PCLU Executive Board.[29]

The increasing preference of the PCLU for the Democratic Party was made more blatant in the spring of 1933 when a "Communication and Resolution" was received from the union of the Pittsburgh Post Office Clerks requesting the PCLU's endorsement of their efforts to launch a local labor party in the Pittsburgh region. Instead, the PCLU voted that it did not concur with their efforts.

Patrick Fagan, President of the PCLU, as well as of the local District 5 of the United Mine Workers, then announced at that same meeting that there would be a "Testimonial to the Democratic Party" held in the Ft. Pitt Hotel on May 22, to which everyone was invited for free food and free drinks.[30] With this entry, any further agitation for a local labor party which there might have been disappears from the PCLU record.

In 1931, the PCLU had sponsored a Labor Day rally. On May 5, 1932, the PCLU voted to sponsor the first modern Labor Day parade in Pittsburgh. This was to be a "Vehicle Labor Day Parade," in which each local organization was to have one or more floats with banners denoting the numerical strength of that organization. "There was a splendid enthusiastic gathering at the meeting," we are told, "and all showed great interest in the question. Everybody displayed an enthusiastic spirit and vowed they would do all in their power to make their Labor Day demonstration a success."

Two weeks later it was reported that, although the PCLU preferred Father Charles Coughlin as its primary Labor Day speaker, he had declined to appear in Pittsburgh. Instead, AFL President William Green had agreed to be the primary speaker at the event. A little later UMW chieftain Philip Murray also agreed to come to Pittsburgh for Labor Day.[31]

A large reviewing stand was built in the North Side along the parade's route and local churches urged their parishioners to attend. The massive parade was "a huge success," the PCLU reported, and President Fagan congratulated local unions in once more making their presence so visible in Pittsburgh.[32]

The Pittsburgh labor movement was also literally making itself heard more throughout the region with its weekly Sunday broadcasts over radio station WJAS. In addition to the "voice of labor," the broadcasts of Fathers Coughlin and local labor priest James Cox could be heard on the station the same day.

And organized labor was becoming more vocal in championing the "non-labor" concerns of its primarily ethnic constituency. Prohibition was still the law, and at the May 19, 1932 meeting of the PCLU, "Brother Greer" of the Musicians' Union reported that they had endorsed a proposition for a big "We Want Beer" demonstration in the near future, to which all members of organized labor were invited to participate.[33]

Thus, as organized labor in Pittsburgh was becoming more restive, it is evident that it was also forging closer ties to the Democratic Party, as well as to the Catholic Church, and to the ethnic communities which comprised the membership of all three institutions.

Rejecting the Reds

There was another group, however, which was competing with the labor movement and the Catholic Church for the loyalties of the Steel Valley's ethnic workers. That was the Communist Party. But, although there was a fairly large cadre of energetic and dedicated party workers in the Pittsburgh region, the Communists had difficulty putting down roots in the ethnic communities.

Initially, the Communist Party had targeted the Pittsburgh region for high-priority agitation following the 1929 Stock Market Crash. This was in keeping with their Marxist belief that the industrial proletariat was destined to lead the way in destroying capitalism and establishing the classless society. Obviously, the destined day had dawned.

The Communists were still in their ultra-sectarian "Third Period," which had begun in 1928. As part of their ultra-sectarianism, they attempted to build up their own Trade Union Unity League (TUUL) as an alternative congress of radical labor unions to rival the American Federation of Labor.

One of TUUL's constituent unions was the Metal Workers Industrial League (MWIL), which attempted to build bridges between part-time workers and the Unemployed Councils also being organized under Communist auspices. The MWIL helped organize the big Communist-led Hunger March on the nation's capitol in March 1930. In June 1931, it also helped organize and lead the first Allegheny County Hunger March, in which thousands of steel workers and striking miners marched on the City-County Building on Pittsburgh's Downtown Grant Street demanding greater expenditures on relief.[34]

Subsequently, the MWIL participated in a February 4, 1932 demonstration of the unemployed and part-time workers in McKeesport, which resulted in a street battle involving thousands of workers and city police. In August 1932 the MWIL held its National Convention in Pittsburgh and changed its name to the Steel and Metal Workers Industrial Union (SMWIU). Under the latter name they seem to have generated something of a following in the steel town of Ambridge, where they played a role in the big labor confrontation there in 1932.[35]

However, the Communists themselves admitted that they were having trouble putting down roots in much of the Steel Valley. Their August National Convention of the MWIL in Pittsburgh noted that, " . . . in spite of these actions [noted above] we had taken nothing like full advantage of the opportunity to firmly entrench our union organizations, either unemployed or mill branches, nor had we succeeded in building permanent broad united front unemployed movements in these towns."

One reason for this Communist failure was the "Lack of trained workers to send out as full-time organizers into the Monongahela River and Ohio River Valleys," which has "hampered the work." Nevertheless, they chastised themselves, "there can be no excuse for our failure to lead more struggles of the workers in these hunger-stricken steel towns."

They pointed to the nearby town of New Castle as illustrative of their failures throughout the industrial heartland. Their work in New Castle was composed solely of calling for demonstrations, "with little or no organizational follow-up in the neighborhoods, and no connection with the work of the union inside the mill. The result is decline of demonstrations, falling off of attendance at mass meetings, until a few months ago we let a 50 percent cut in relief go through without any struggle against it."[36]

But, it was not just in the mill towns of the Steel Valley in which the Communists were failing to put down roots. They confessed they were inactive even on Pittsburgh's Polish South Side, perhaps Pittsburgh's most volatile and class conscious neighborhood, with some of the highest unemployment rates in the city.[37]

Given the status of the region's industrial workers as an oppressed population, it might be presumed that they would have been more receptive to the Communist message, that they would be more "radical," more "revolutionary," would have sought to overthrow American society rather than struggle to become part of it.

But there is no evidence in the language or actions of the mass of the region's workers to support these presumptions. The Steel Valley's workers did not speak in terms of "the proletariat" or "socialism," and they vehemently denied they were "reds" when accused of being so. Indeed, many Pittsburgh-area workers were aggressively anti-Communist, not surprising in a population which comprised such a high percentage of deeply religious homeowners struggling to prosper.

Aliquippa steelworker Domenic Del Turco recalled that Communists tried to recruit him into the party in 1934 and he rebuffed them saying, "Communism and unionism doesn't mix. 'I'm a union man [Amalgamated Association of Iron and Tin Workers at this time], and I'm going to stay a union man. I don't want no part of communism . . . I'm a labor man and I'll stay that way. And I'm a Christian. I don't believe in communism.' . . . 'We're trying to establish democracy,' [the Communists told him]. I said, 'Your kind of democracy, not mine.'"[38]

Over at Braddock's Edgar Thomson steel mill, Stanley Brozek, a founder of SWOC in the plant, recalled that the men who founded the union had very few among them who were sympathetic to communism. "We weren't Communists," he declared. "We only had a few—you could count them on your fingers—that would really claim to be a Communist . . . I wasn't interested in their setup. I just felt that they have a program where the end justifies the means, you understand? And they will lie and cheat. And they don't give a damn what happens to you as long as their aims are satisfied. Their ideals are satisfied. No religion at all."[39]

Braddock's Orville Rice, another founder of the union local at the Edgar Thomson plant, agreed, saying, "I knew enough about socialism to realize that it was, first of all, anti-Catholic. It was against my religion. I'm a Catholic. That in itself . . . And then I realized, too, from what we had read up to this time, that what we had studied [was true], that socialism can't be entirely successful, although we have our doubts about capitalism."[40]

Thomas Brown, a General Electric worker up in Erie, Pennsylvania, who helped found the "Leftist" United Electrical Workers union there, recalled that, later, "In the 1940s, when we got so big and powerful, a 'Red-scare' came into the picture. They dragged us through all the mud and slime and everything they could think of. What they did to the electrical workers from the Atlantic to the Pacific you could never replace. Many guys went to their graves condemned. They crucified the guys . . . I went through that Red smear. I know what it was like. Christ, you come out of church on a Sunday morning and the priest would say, 'Hey, you still with the Red union? Why don't you think it over?' . . . this stuff of trying to be Communists was from people who were out of their minds. None of us were Communists."[41]

Stephen Zoretich, a Croatian steelworker at Pittsburgh Steel in Monessen, agreed. He recalled that when the SWOC organizers came to Monessen, "a lot of times we had a meeting down at the Croatian Hall. In fact," he continued, "they branded us as communist down here because of that. Anybody that wanted an outside union, they branded them as a communist then. They called the Croatian Hall communist and everything else, but it wasn't communist. It was because of the union activities."[42]

John Czelen, later president of the SWOC local at Monessen's Page Steel and Wire, helped organize an independent union at his plant long before the coming of SWOC. In 1933, when local unions were still called "lodges," he and others formed the "Honest Deal Lodge" at Page Steel—which lasted three months, he said, before it was "broken by the company."[43] Czelen said, "As a young fellow . . . I read Marx, but Marx didn't impress me because I thought Marxism was contrary to man's nature. The extreme left was just as contrary as the extreme right, which at that time was predatory capitalism."[44]

So, instead of turning to the Communists and their Marxist ideology in those hard times, the industrial heartland's workers turned to the Catholic Church and its liberation theology.

And, where the Communists confessed that they were inactive on Pittsburgh's South Side, the Catholic Church and its priests were everywhere.

Similarly, the most active presence in the massive "Hooverville" in Pittsburgh's Strip District was not that of Communist organizers of the unemployed. Rather, it was that of the Catholic Church in the person of Father James R. Cox.

Cox's Army

Although Father Charles Owen Rice has had the longest career as a prominent Pittsburgh "labor priest," in the early Thirties Father James R. Cox, pastor of Old St. Patrick's Church, was the city's foremost activist priest. Father Cox's career resembled that of Coughlin's so closely it might have been cut from the same sacramental cloth. Father Cox seems to have had the same power to inspire large numbers and, because of this, played a crucial role in catalyzing the initial political mobilization of Pittsburgh's working class, Catholic, ethnic community in the early Thirties.

James R. Cox, like many of the "labor priests," was born poor. Further, he had worked in a steel mill before becoming a priest. He knew what it meant to be a struggling working man. Born in 1886, Cox came from a long line of Pittsburgh Irish Catholics and had been educated in Catholic parochial schools all his life. This continued when he went on to study at Pittsburgh's Holy Ghost College (now Duquesne University).

Upon graduation, he entered the seminary at St. Vincent's in nearby Latrobe. Following his studies, he was ordained into the priesthood and assigned as the parish priest at St. Mary's on 46th Street in Lawrenceville and, soon thereafter, at Pittsburgh's Old St. Patrick's in Downtown Pittsburgh, the oldest Catholic parish in the city.[45]

Like Father Rice, Father Cox had been deeply influenced by the papal encyclicals of Popes Leo and Pius. And, like Father Rice, Father Cox was also a "radio priest," with a weekly thirty-minute broadcast, first on local station WJAS beginning in 1925 (the same station which later broadcast Father Coughlin and the PCLU), and later on WMBJ, where he continued broadcasting until 1951. Like Father Coughlin, he had a bombastic radio speaking style, as if he were shouting into a public address system to a large crowd.[46]

And like Father Rice, Father Cox also established a labor school for trade union organizers, aided by, among others, United Mine Workers leader John Brophy. There, students were taught Pope Leo's encyclical "The Condition of Labor," as well as the "Bishops' Program of Social Reconstruction" which grew out of it.[47]

And, again like Father Rice, Father Cox presided over a program which provided shelter and food for the homeless and unemployed. Industrial cities like Pittsburgh had been particularly hard-hit by the Depression. By 1933, 80,000 Pittsburgh workers were still unemployed, with 15.7 percent of the white and 43.4 percent of the black workforce on the relief rolls. A "Hooverville" of the homeless engulfed the Strip District, one of three such, presided over by Father Cox, in whose parish it was.

By the fall of 1930, St. Patrick's soup kitchen, abutting Polish Hill at the Strip's Fourteenth Street and Penn Avenue, was serving a thousand meals a day. Meanwhile, hundreds were offered shelter in the basement of the church.[48] Old St. Patrick's, like the city's other religious and social agencies, was overwhelmed by the demands of the needy.

The city government wasn't doing much better. As in other cities, the Depression had hit Pittsburgh hard. Business activity had fallen to less than half of the 1929 volume. As of January 1931, 20 percent of the workforce, over 100,000 Pittsburghers, had lost their jobs.[49] That same month Pittsburgh exhausted its state relief allocation of $200,000 and called on its wealthier citizens to respond to the crisis. The business elite, led by Richard B. Mellon and Howard Heinz, did so, forming the Allegheny County Emergency Association. Despite the efforts of the Emergency Association, which raised five million dollars and channelled direct relief to 30,000 recipients in 1931 and 1932, conditions worsened.[50]

Father Cox, like many others, became increasingly frustrated with the worsening conditions and the inability of local charity or government agencies to adequately address the situation. Therefore, he decided to lead a march of the Pittsburgh-area unemployed and homeless on Washington to demand job-creating action from President Hoover.[51]

Forty-five thousand men, refugees from both blue- and white-collar jobs, answered his call and set out on January 5, 1932 in a truck caravan of 978 trucks and cars for Washington, D.C. By the time the procession reached Johnstown, east of Pittsburgh, 20,000 had to be left behind due to a lack of transportation. Many of those, however, continued on foot, determined to walk to Washington.

When the column had reached Johnstown on the afternoon of January 5th, it was met by Mayor Eddie McCloskey, who joined Father Cox in demanding government relief action. Later that day the caravan reached Harrisburg, the state capitol. This time it was Pennsylvania Governor Gifford Pinchot, an old Teddy Roosevelt "Progressive" Republican, who welcomed them, declaring that "civilized government is a failure if men who are able and willing to support their families cannot get the chance."[52]

After an overnight stay at the Huntingdon, Pennsylvania, fairgrounds, the marchers, now numbering between 15,000-20,000, reached Washington the following day, where they camped in an open field, like the Bonus Army marchers would do later that same year.

Then, on January 7, 1932, Father Cox led his own "army" to the steps of the U.S. Capitol where he presented a "Resolution of the Jobless" to Pennsylvania Representative Clyde Kelly and Pennsylvania Senator James J. Davis. Demonstrating the patriotic nature of the petitioners, part of "Cox's Army" comprised a band playing martial airs, a hundred World War I veterans were dressed in their military uniforms, and one marcher was dressed as Uncle Sam. Clearly, these religious-led marchers also viewed their "petition in boots" as being in the best traditions of Americanism.

Father Cox's "Resolution of the Jobless" called for Congress to stimulate the economy through an appropriation of five billion dollars for public works programs and farm loans, to be financed by taxing the rich through higher income and gift taxes. After presenting his petition to Congress, Father Cox and a dozen representatives, including attorney Henry Ellenbogen, not yet elected to Congress, visited the White House. They were cordially received by President Hoover, although he termed the petition "inappropriate." He already had a proposal before Congress, he claimed, which would soon adequately deal with the Depression.

Still, Father Cox was pleased with the friendly reception his marchers received at both the White House and at the Capitol, and felt the march had essentially accomplished its purpose. He led his followers to Arlington National Cemetery, where he delivered a victory speech.

Back in Pittsburgh, the marchers were welcomed home as heroes, as if they had actually accomplished something, and a huge rally in their honor was held for them at the University of Pittsburgh's Oakland stadium. In a show of support, Governor Pinchot sent Pennsylvania Federation of Labor President John Phillips to represent him at the rally.

Despite the January cold and dampness, 55,000 excited Pittsburghers turned out to cheer Father Cox and his "army." Proclaiming that "Ours is a battle against Wall Street and Smithfield Street [Pittsburgh's equivalent]," Father Cox denounced the Republican-dominated state legislature for its callous inaction and promised that his "Main Street" protest "will grow and expand throughout the nation."[53]

Organized labor responded enthusiastically to Father Cox's message and the Pittsburgh Central Labor Union invited him to deliver his message before them. "All officers of the various local organizations are urgently requested to attend," the PCLU told its constituent unions, "as we feel an address by Fr. Cox will be greatly appreciated." On February 18, Father Cox appeared before the Central Labor Union's assembled union delegates, " . . . and delivered a splendid address, which was well received by the meeting. He also received a rousing ovation."[54]

The march of Father Cox's "Jobless Army" on Washington made him even more of a hero to Pittsburgh workers than he had been before. A typical response was that of Joseph LoCascio, a worker in nearby Etna, who took it upon himself to paint a 5' x 7' oil painting of Father Cox leading his Army on the Capitol. The painting portrayed a field of American flags flapping over Father Cox's marchers, who were led by a man dressed as Uncle Sam. The painting was hung in St. Patrick's parochial school at Penn Avenue and 14th Street, along with a plaque giving the text of Father Cox's jobless resolution underneath, "so that future generations will see what was done in January 1932."[55]

Also typical was a letter to the editor from R. Brooks, of nearby Donora, who praised Father Cox's march and appealed for aid for the unemployed. "Prosperity was made by these individuals," Brooks wrote. "They earned their money and spent it, putting it into the hands of the few, who seem to stand by and give no help . . . [We must] take government control of profits, whatever is a legitimate profit . . . and insure equality for every man."[56]

In an attempt to expand his protest "throughout the nation," Father Cox launched a whirlwind speaking tour of the country, declaring to the desperate thousands who flocked to hear him that, "We have come to the end of an economic era. As a nation we are groping in the dark, awaiting the dawn of a new day. When that dawn comes, it must bring a better era than that which has passed." Speaking to the hopes and aspirations of his working class listeners, Father Cox declared that this coming new era, "must provide equal opportunities to all men, regardless of wealth."[57]

On March 29 he announced that a national convention to launch a "Jobless Party" would be held August 17 in St. Louis. "We promise," he said, "to give every citizen his divine and natural right to a job."[58]

However, that "divine right to a job" was not fulfilled, for Father Cox's dramatic march met with no material success, either in securing congressional passage of the "Resolution of the Jobless," or in leading to permanent organization of Pittsburgh's unemployed workers, while his "Jobless Party" fizzled.

Thus, the anger and discontent which had given birth to Cox's Army remained. Some called for workers themselves to solve their problems through broad-based unity. "Only by the united efforts of every man and every woman will we be able to solve our problems," declared James A. Davin of Connellsville. "We should all make a united effort and endeavor to eradicate all forms of hatred and bigotry so that we as citizens could demand proper representation from a social, political, and industrial standpoint . . . What we need are men [as elected leaders] who will fight for the common good of all citizens and not politicians who will bow to special interests."[59] That November, Franklin Delano Roosevelt would become the beneficiary of such desires.

A New Hope

In 1930, before the full impact of the Depression had hit home, the Pittsburgh electorate was still a Republican electorate. The Democratic Party, with only 4.7 percent of the registered voters, was essentially a joke, as the remaining 95.3 percent of voters were all Republicans. Six years later, in 1936, the electorate had become majority Democratic, 56.1 percent, while the Republican percentage of registered voters fell to 43.9 percent.[60]

Numerically, however, the Republican vote was as high as ever. For the most part, then, Roosevelt's success was due not to any major conversion of Republican hearts and minds in Pittsburgh, but to a dramatic expansion of the size of the city's electorate—all in the Democrats' favor. As in other industrial cities across the Northeast and Midwest, this expansion of the Democratic electorate in Pittsburgh was principally brought about by the political mobilization of a previously inert population. This population was simultaneously ethnic, Orthodox-Catholic, and working class. In a city such as Boston, this ethnic, Catholic, working class electorate was overwhelmingly Irish. The steel industry, however, was dominated by Eastern and Southern Europeans—and so in Pittsburgh this population was the the one which provided the base for the Democratic realignment.

Thus, it is no surprise that Roosevelt's main support in the city came from the working class ethnic wards. These included the Slavic South Side, the German North Side, Italian Bloomfield and East Liberty, and Polish Hill, which had already shown a history of supporting both Democrats and pro-labor candidates. As voter registration and turn-out climbed in these wards, so, too, did the Democratic vote.

In 1930, the majority of Pittsburgh's population, like most other large American cities, was mainly immigrants and the children of immigrants.[61] These immigrants and the children of immigrants, overwhelmingly Catholic and working class, were, for the most part, politically inert and did not vote.

However, when they did vote, they had shown a tendency to vote Democratic and for candidates who championed the cause of the working class. In the 1928 presidential election, for instance, Catholic Al Smith, the Democratic candidate from New York City, carried all of the nation's twelve largest cities, including Pittsburgh. Before that, in 1924, the Progressive Party presidential candidate, Robert M. LaFollette, also did well in the cities, garnering 36 percent of the Pittsburgh vote, for instance, even though running locally on the ballot as a "Socialist-Labor" candidate.

A ward-level comparison of LaFollette's 1924 Pittsburgh vote with Roosevelt's 1932 Pittsburgh vote reveals not only that LaFollette's support came from the "foreign, lower economic classes of the city," but that "both La Follette and Roosevelt drew their support from much the same wards."

Additionally, the wards which supported Roosevelt in 1932 and LaFollette in 1924 were the very same wards which had supported Socialist Eugene V. Debs in 1912, "indicating a firm connection between the support for the Progressive candidate in 1924 and the Socialist standard-bearer of a dozen years earlier."[62] The Debs-LaFollette vote, then, became the Roosevelt vote. The big difference between 1932, however, and the previous election years of 1928, 1924 and 1912, was that the vote from these ethnic working class wards was so much larger. The ethnic workers in these wards had become more highly motivated to vote—and to vote Democratic.

The Democratic Party leadership, both at the state level and the city level, worked hard to win the potentially majority ethnic working class vote for their party and their presidential candidate. State Democratic Party leader Joseph F. Guffey, for instance, who came from Pittsburgh and realized the potential of the city's ethnic working class wards, "Perceived with clarity that the future [of the Democratic Party] lay with labor and the minority groups."[63] Much of the coordination of this effort in Pittsburgh, however, was carried out by the city's Democratic Party boss, David L. Lawrence.

Just as the later Civil Rights Movement of the 1950s and 1960s would be based in Southern black Baptist churches, Catholic churches were a crucial base for the Northern ethnic working class "civil rights movement." Thus, on the Slavic South Side, David Lawrence was able to obtain not only ethnic fraternal associations for political meeting sites, but also the community's Catholic churches.

In the Sixth Ward, Polish Hill, where 90 percent of the population was Polish and Catholic, Father Cox was a valuable ally, as many of the residents were his parishioners. Father Cox, who had briefly toyed with a presidential bid of his own at the head of his nascent "Jobless Party," spoke six times during the closing days of the campaign at the Falcon's Nest Hall, Polish Hill's main fraternal association, urging a solid vote for Roosevelt. Additionally, Lawrence made sure the Democratic Ward Committee for Polish Hill was 100 percent Polish.[64]

Italian Bloomfield and East Liberty, which had voted for Catholic Al Smith in 1928 and where unemployment was higher than the city average, also appeared ripe for Democratic inroads. Lawrence formed an Italian Democratic Committee to work in those neighborhoods and—as on the South Side—enlisted willing Catholic priests and fraternal organizations in his effort.

In addition to the promising response from these ethnic working class neighborhoods, the Pittsburgh Democratic Party gained a major financial angel who put the local organization on a solvent footing for the very first time. Michael Benedum, a millionaire oil baron long associated with the Republican Party, but appalled by the economic collapse of the country, defected to the Democrats. He donated a total of $50,000 to the Pittsburgh Democratic organization that year, thus giving Lawrence an unprecedentedly huge war chest.

Buoyed by these developments, Lawrence wrote to New York Governor Franklin D. Roosevelt at Hyde Park, the Democratic nominee for President of the United States. Lawrence begged him to come to Pittsburgh to campaign. Lawrence was a savvy politician and was certain that Pennsylvania was undergoing a political sea change and that the state could be carried by a healthy margin, going Democratic for the first time since before the Civil War. All that was needed, he felt, was a dramatic local appearance by Roosevelt to mobilize and cement the loyalty of the region's ethnic working class voters.

Roosevelt finally agreed to deliver a major radio address to the nation from Pittsburgh on Wednesday, October 19th. As the baseball season had recently ended, Lawrence quickly made arrangements to rent Oakland's now-available Forbes Field. The Field had been the home of the Pittsburgh Pirates since it was built in 1909. One side of it loomed over Pittsburgh's Italian working class neighborhood of Panther Hollow. The other sides towered over the rest of South Oakland. Even though October 19th was in the middle of the work week, Lawrence was certain the Democratic organization would be able to fill the seven-acre ballpark.

Governor Roosevelt arrived at the South Side's Pittsburgh and Lake Erie Railroad Station on the morning of October 19th. Everywhere, Pittsburghers greeted the New York governor as a conquering hero, lining the streets from the station into downtown Pittsburgh to cheer his motorcade.[65] He then drove on to Wheeling, West Virginia, 40-miles down the Ohio River, to deliver a quick address. He returned to Pittsburgh that evening to meet with local Democratic Party officials before his appearance at Forbes Field.

Forbes Field had been designed for 35,000, but well over 50,000 crowded into the bleachers and into the aisles to catch a glimpse of Roosevelt and to hear his address. Organized by Lawrence, the event was a masterpiece of political theater and the capstone of Roosevelt's 1932 campaign.

Giving every ethnic group its due recognition, Lawrence arranged for six bands from six different ethnic fraternal organizations to march onto the field and entertain the crowd as night fell. In addition, there were four "colored" bands from the all-black Allied Roosevelt Clubs of Western Pennsylvania, as well as a patriotic band from the American Legion.

A parade of local Democratic leaders warmed up the listeners as cheerleaders dressed as Democratic donkeys coaxed roaring ovations from the stands. Father Cox exhorted Catholics in attendance to vote for Roosevelt. Robert Vann, owner of *The Pittsburgh Courier,* the city's influential black newspaper, joined ethnic leaders on the podium and pledged the continued support of his newspaper for Roosevelt and urged blacks, heretofore mostly Republican, to join the Democratic campaign. Statewide Democratic candidates, Lawrence himself, and well-known local ethnic leaders also spoke on behalf of the governor from New York.

Then, at 10 p.m., as roars echoed out over the surrounding homes of Italian Oakland, Roosevelt appeared. The center field gates opened and through them marched the Greentree Fife and Drum Corps, followed by an automobile in which sat a single passenger. Cheers rolled over the field as Roosevelt waved his hat to the crowd and his car slowly approached home plate, where Lawrence awaited the governor at the stage. When Roosevelt was ready, one last speaker approached the microphone. The honor of introducing the New York governor was that of the local party's financial angel, Michael Benedum.

In his live radio address to America that night from Forbes Field, Roosevelt savaged Republican lack of concern for the unemployed and the soaring federal budget deficit. Attacking "Republican death-bed repentance on the subject of the economy," Roosevelt pledged to those straining to catch his words that, "If men or women or children are starving in the United States, I regard it as a positive duty of government to raise by taxes whatever sum may be necessary to keep them from starvation."[66] It was what Pittsburghers wanted to hear. They cheered wildly for Roosevelt and then went home afterward confident that their champion would win the White House.

On Election Day, however, Roosevelt did not win Pennsylvania, as Lawrence had predicted. Philadelphia and the rest of Pennsylvania remained strongly Republican. Nevertheless, he carried "Republican" Pittsburgh by a margin of 27,000, winning twenty-six of the city's thirty-two wards. And he won heavily in the ethnic working class wards. He carried Polish Hill 2,348 votes to 951. On the Slavic South Side, Roosevelt had vote totals over 75 percent. On the German-Irish North Side he won with vote totals representing 62 percent-71 percent. He carried Italian Bloomfield (Ward Eight, 3,270 to 1,987) and East Liberty (divided into different wards), while making deep inroads into the black wards. Only in the well-to-do Squirrel Hill (Ward 14) did Roosevelt lose by a sizeable majority.

Indicative of how Republican control was beginning to waver in the Steel Valley as a whole, Roosevelt also carried all the principal steel towns of Allegheny County, including Braddock, Clairton, Duquesne, East Pittsburgh, Etna, Homestead, McKeesport, McKees Rocks, Millvale, Munhall, Rankin, Turtle Creek, and West Homestead.[67] The combined vote of Pittsburgh and these towns gave Roosevelt a 37,000 vote majority in what had been a Republican county.

Roosevelt also proved to have long coattails. Pittsburgh elected six Democratic candidates to the state legislature, including local union leaders and PCLU members John J. Kane and Thomas Gallagher, running as both Democratic and Labor Party candidates. Before the election, Pennsylvania had only three Democratic Congressmen out of a statewide delegation of thirty-six. But now Pittsburgh and the surrounding Allegheny County sent four new Democratic U.S. Representatives to Congress, including PCLU-endorsed Henry Ellenbogen, who had accompanied Father Cox on his march to Washington. Ellenbogen, along with another successful Democratic Congressional candidate, M. A. Dunn, had run on Father Cox's "Jobless Party" ticket, as well as the Democratic ticket. They joined seven other Democratic Congressmen statewide as part of the "traditionally almost solid Republican" thirty-four-strong (down two due to reapportionment) Pennsylvania delegation in Washington.

Because of Prohibition, the WASP crusade against drinking, alcohol had, by this time, become a potent symbol of ethnic identity. Thus, indicative of the increasing clout of the ethnic vote, was the defeat of the state's foremost advocate of Protestant Prohibition. "Upsets were general," reported *The Pittsburgh Post-Gazette,* "with possibly the most surprising reversal in the Washington-Greene district. There, Henry W. Temple, dean of the Pennsylvania delegation, was defeated by Charles I. Faddis, a Democrat and opponent of Prohibition. Temple was one of the House's most militant advocates of Prohibition, a neighbor of General Edward Martin, state Republican Chairman, and widely known."[68]

These Democratic victories, reported *The Post-Gazette,* were all part of "a political tornado which swept into Allegheny County." The politically moribund majority—the ethnic, Catholic, working class "minorities" who were the bulk of Pittsburgh's population—had risen and began their mass movement into the Democratic Party.[69]

Leaving Lincoln

I said earlier that the emergence of a Democratic majority in the previously Republican industrial heartland was not due to the winning of Republican hearts and minds. There was, however, an exception to this, as one segment of Republican voters did transfer its long-held Republican allegiance to Roosevelt and the Democrats: the black electorate. Accounting for almost 10 percent of the Pittsburgh electorate, this breakthrough was a major Democratic triumph locally.

But this, like the mobilization of ethnic workers, was also part of a national transformation of the electorate. Voters divided along class lines more and more over the course of the Thirties, with the affluent becoming ever more Republican, while the workers became ever more loyal Democrats. Even so, "Perhaps the most dramatic switch," argues Michael Goldfield, "took place among African-American voters, whose traditional Republican allegiances gave way to overwhelming Democratic Party support."[70] And Pittsburgh played a major role in this national transformation.

Since the Civil War, black voters in Pittsburgh, as in the nation at large, had been Republicans out of a lingering loyalty to Lincoln. They routinely delivering the Third and Fifth Wards (the Hill District), the Twelfth Ward (Lincoln-Lemington on the Allegheny River), and the Twentieth Ward (the West End).[71] Indeed, just as the Republicans had long-since come to take for granted the loyalty of the black vote, Pittsburgh's Republican Party had also come to expect the customary loyalty of the voters in Pittsburgh's black neighborhoods.

In exchange, however, black voters received little return on their investment of political loyalty. This was true both nationally and locally. At the national level, the Republican Party had initially obtained the political allegiance of blacks because it was the party which had abolished slavery and, during Reconstruction, had attempted to better the lives of the former slaves. Since the defeat of Reconstruction, however, black voters had become the forgotten step-children of the Republicans.

But the Pittsburgh Republican Party had never deserved even this initial loyalty. As Michael F. Holt has shown, the Pittsburgh Republican Party coalesced before the Civil War on the basis of anti-immigrant, anti-Catholic sentiment, not hatred of slavery or beneficence toward blacks. Therefore, there had never been any logical reason for Pittsburgh blacks to be politically loyal to the local Republican oligarchy. Then, as economic conditions worsened during the onset of the Depression, the city's Republican bosses scaled back even the few patronage jobs which they had tossed to blacks.

This was galling to many local black leaders, but especially so to Robert L. Vann, editor of the influential and nationally distributed black newspaper, *The Pittsburgh Courier*. Vann had moved to Pittsburgh from rural North Carolina to attend the University of Pittsburgh Law School, from which he graduated in 1909 at age thirty-one. From then until 1936 he was a practicing attorney, but in 1910 he also helped found the *Courier*, which he then edited.

The *Courier* was needed because Pittsburgh newspapers, like newspapers nationally, did not carry news of the black community. The *Courier* filled this gap both locally and, along with a handful of other black newspapers like the *Chicago Defender*, at the national level, as well. It grew to a weekly Pittsburgh circulation of 30,000 copies and, by the 1930s, a national circulation of 250,000, making it the most influential black weekly in the United States. By 1947 its national circulation would hit 400,000 and a dozen editions of the *Courier* were distributed across the United States and in Canada, Europe, the Virgin Islands, Cuba, and the Philippines.[72]

Robert Vann had become a Republican in 1903 and had labored diligently for the party. As a reward, he was named an alternate delegate to the party's national convention in 1924. He also served the dominant Republican administration in Pittsburgh as an assistant city solicitor from 1917 to 1921.

But by 1932 Vann had become restive with the Republican powers. While no doubt troubled by the economic conditions in the black community—which faced unemployment and relief rolls three times higher than in the white community— there was also a personal aspect to Vann's dissatisfaction. After working hard to deliver the black vote to the previous three Republican presidents, both in Pittsburgh and nationally, Vann had hoped for appointment to some federal office. It had not been forthcoming. As the 1932 presidential campaign got underway, therefore, Vann began to look toward the Democratic Party as a more hospitable home. Toward this end, he sent out feelers.

Thus, one day in 1932, while a black manicurist in Pittsburgh was working on the nails of Emma Guffey Miller, a Democratic National Committeewoman, she casually mentioned that Robert Vann would like to meet with Mrs. Miller's brother, state Democratic Party leader Joseph F. Guffey, who also lived in Pittsburgh. Mrs. Miller delivered the message to her brother, who quickly called Robert Vann and arranged a meeting. When the two met, Vann made clear his willingness to help bring Pennsylvania's 280,000 black voters into the Democratic fold.[73]

Guffey wasted little time. At his urging, Governor Roosevelt, by then the Democratic presidential nominee, invited Robert Vann to visit him at his Hyde Park, New York, residence. Vann left the meeting with Roosevelt assured that he would be more highly valued in Roosevelt's administration than he had been in Hoover's. Changes were soon forthcoming in national Democratic circles. "It was hard work," Guffey later reported, "but I finally persuaded [Democratic National Committee chief] Jim Farley and Louis McHenry Howe to establish the first really effective Negro division a Democratic campaign committee ever had"—of which Pittsburgh's Robert Vann was placed in charge.[74]

Thereafter, *The Pittsburgh Courier* pounded away ceaselessly on the need to support the Democratic campaign. At the same time, Vann founded black Democratic Clubs all across Pennsylvania as part of his work at the head of the "Negro" section of the Democratic National Committee. These auxiliary Democratic clubs numbered 1,000 members in Pittsburgh's Allegheny County alone.

Robert Vann's efforts were climaxed by a famous speech he delivered before a Cleveland Democratic audience on October 7, 1932. After chronicling the failures of recent Republican administrations in their relations with blacks, Vann concluded that in the upcoming election, "millions of Negroes [would be] turning the picture of Lincoln to the wall."[75] The Civil War-era Emancipation debt blacks owed the Republican Party, Vann implied, had been paid in full.

Of course, all of Robert Vann's efforts would have been for naught had a new spirit not been moving among his readers and listeners. Vann was merely giving voice to this spirit and helping to direct it. But, while full conversion of Pittsburgh's black electorate would not come until the 1934 elections, the breach in solid black Republicanism had been made. On Election Day, Roosevelt ran better than any previous Democrat ever had in Pittsburgh's black wards, with Hoover carrying the Hill District's Fifth Ward, for instance, two-thirds black, by only a slight majority.[76] Black voters had begun to turn Lincoln's picture to the wall.

Hope in a Hopeless Land

Despite carrying Pittsburgh's Allegheny County by 37,000 votes in the 1932 election, Roosevelt lost the state to Hoover. Indeed, Pennsylvania as a whole remained under Republican control until 1935.

However, in the state's two major cities, Philadelphia and Pittsburgh, realignment was already evident at the municipal level. Although the Democrats would not totally control Philadelphia until 1951, nevertheless, "It was the municipal election of 1933 that marked the beginning of the revival of permanent two-party politics. That election . . . witnessed the rejuvenation of the Philadelphia Democratic Party. The minority party took on new leaders and new spirit. By the end of 1933, the Philadelphia Democrats had become a formidable opposition party."[77]

But, while Philadelphia might be seen as a case of delayed realignment, the city of Pittsburgh was another matter. There, realignment went faster and further, resulting in dramatic transformations of the local political universe in the 1933 elections for a mayor and city councillors.

Local Republicans, having learned little from Hoover's debacle, still did little to address the city's economic collapse. So, as one disaffected voter put it, "Perhaps a Democratic Mayor will give Pittsburgh a New Deal."[78] Making sure continuing discontent like this was channelled into the Democratic Party was local party boss David Lawrence's task in the 1933 municipal election. In this, his strategy was essentially the same as the year before: appeal to the city's ethnic, Catholic, working class majority, hitherto politically subservient to the "native American" Republicans.

Municipal elections in Pittsburgh and the rest of Western Pennsylvania occur every four years. The previous municipal election, in November of 1929, had taken place only days after the October 29th stock market crash which launched the Great Depression. At that time, which seemed now an almost ancient era, the Republican Party counted for everything in Pittsburgh politics, as the Democrats hardly existed. Indeed, as noted earlier, even by 1930 Democrats still numbered only 4.7 percent of Pittsburgh's registered voters. Thus, the 1929 Republican candidate for mayor—Charles Kline, a champion of the party's old-line organization—had no trouble winning election.

Kline, however, was forced to resign in the wake of a conviction for corruption and John S. Herron, City Council president, replaced him. As the incumbent, Herron received the Republican party organization's backing for the 1933 mayoralty primary. Republican dissidents, including leading local businessmen like Howard Heinz, "the pickle man," and steel magnate Ernest T. Weir, owner of Weirton Steel, sought a "cleaner" administration. Therefore, they backed City Councillor P.J. McArdle for the primary, as did the upper class and Republican-dominated League of Women Voters, while Register of Wills Joseph N. Mackrell also sought to run as a "reform" Republican.

Meanwhile, the Democratic mayoralty nomination at last seemed worth having. A Democrat in the White House helped. Shortly after taking office, Roosevelt put Pennsylvania Democratic Party State Committee Chairman Joseph Guffey in charge of all federal patronage jobs in the state. Guffey then gave Lawrence, Chairman of the Pittsburgh Democratic organization, control of all federal patronage appointments in Western Pennsylvania. Lawrence also gained a sinecure of his own, that of district collector of internal revenue, freeing him to devote all his energies to the party. Being a Democrat, it seemed, was worth something after all. For this reason, a primary battle also shaped up for the Democrats.

First to declare was John M. Henry, a local lawyer and long-time Democrat. Henry had been fired from a state commission by Republican Governor Gifford Pinchot as part of a patronage-for-support deal between Pinchot and Lawrence. Smarting from that slight, he hoped to find revenge against the local party organization in the newly competitive times.

For his part, Party Chairman David Lawrence had seemed an obvious candidate as a result of his losing 1931 race for Allegheny County Commissioner, during which he had actually carried the city of Pittsburgh. However, in that race he had been supported by the same faction of the local Republican organization—headed by powerful State Senator James J. Coyne—now tainted with charges of corruption. Lawrence therefore thought it advisable not to seek the mayoralty. Instead, he anointed attorney William N. McNair as the party's champion.

The choice of McNair suggests that Lawrence was not altogether aware of just how much the Pittsburgh electorate had actually changed, as Lawrence chose McNair for his "Republican" pedigree. Among his presumed virtues was that, while a life-long Democrat, McNair was nevertheless of native stock with deep roots in Pennsylvania's colonial past. Thus, while Lawrence was an Irish Catholic, McNair was a Protestant, another factor still presumed to be in McNair's favor.

Additionally, McNair had some name recognition, as he had run and lost as the Democratic standard bearer in five different campaigns, most recently the 1928 U.S. Senate contest. He had also managed Lawrence's 1931 county commissioner campaign, so he was deemed to have some administrative ability.

McNair was initially reluctant to run, having lost so many previous campaigns for various offices. However, Lawrence finally persuaded him to be the party's candidate. Reversing roles, this time Lawrence ran McNair's campaign, master-minding all aspects, although the official campaign manager was Cornelius D. Scully, another party stalwart.

This arrangement, however, made McNair vulnerable to charges of being a Lawrence puppet, accusations opponent John Henry soon raised in the primary campaign. Electing McNair as Mayor, Henry charged, would be simply to "install in the city of Pittsburgh the Guffey-Lawrence machine."[79]

Much of John Henry's primary campaign, though, centered around the role of "privilege" in the city's political life. This represented a theme which ran to the heart of the newly polarized class politics fast coming to dominate the political arena. All political "bosses," he charged, whether the Democrat Lawrence or the Republican Coyne, were subservient to privileged interests, represented by such as Michael Benedum, the local Republican millionaire oilman who had defected to Roosevelt in the 1932 campaign. "If you vote for Guffey's man," John Henry said of McNair, "who is also Benedum's man, you have voted to continue the rule of utilities and the oil, coal, and steel barons. You have voted to continue the rule of the same crowd of money changers that Franklin Roosevelt drove out of Washington. That is not the New Deal. It's the same old deal, dressed up in a new deck."[80]

Sensing the changed concerns of the electorate, the Lawrence-orchestrated McNair campaign fired back in the same vein. It was not John Henry, it said, but McNair who represented true "Roosevelt Democracy." Indeed, John Henry had been opposed to Roosevelt's nomination prior to the 1932 Democratic national convention and had been active in attempting to block it. Thus, McNair—always pictured next to Roosevelt in newspaper political ads—was the real Democrat who represented an attack on privilege, giant utilities, and the "power of such reactionary interests and political industrialists as Andrew Mellon."[81]

At the same time, the Lawrence organization continued its campaign to woo black voters away from the Republican party, an effort greatly aided by the on-going support of Robert Vann's *Courier.* Lawrence echoed Vann's 1932 charge that the Negro debt to Abraham Lincoln's Republicans had been paid in full. It was now time to join the Democrats, a party which, McNair promised black audiences, offered "a square deal for all the people."[82] While McNair eventually lost Pittsburgh's black wards in the general election, he won them against John Henry in the primary, with the campaign as a whole serving to further erode black allegiance to the Republican Party.

Indeed, McNair, the nominee of the "real" Democrats, won every Pittsburgh ward in the September primary, with 88 percent of the 26,325 Democratic votes. So, too, did the five City Council candidates backed by the official Democratic Party organization. Pittsburgh's Democrats, it seemed, had a clear idea of who the true champion's of "Roosevelt Democracy" were. McNair, like Roosevelt himself, was perceived to be the candidate of "those who are sick of the old order, who want a New Deal for Pittsburgh as well as the nation."[83]

On the Republican side, indicative of their obliviousness to the onset of class politics, the campaign issues were not so much questions of privilege, as with the Democrats, as with clean government versus the corruption of the Coyne machine, represented by Acting Mayor John Herron. Indeed, James Coyne himself, along with his brother, twenty-two Republican officials, and the police officers who helped them, were indicted that August on voting fraud charges. Additionally, scandal swirled around the exposure of Republican "macing" of city employees. (Macing was the practice of forcing city workers to contribute to a campaign on peril of losing their jobs.)

Nevertheless, backed by the machine's ward organization (which delivered both legitimate and fraudulent votes) and funded by lavish infusions of Mellon family money, John Herron trounced his divided rivals, McArdle and Mackrell. The stage was set for the November showdown between the old-line Republican rulers of Pittsburgh and the champion of Roosevelt's New Deal, a showdown which highlighted the new salience of class in the city's political life.

Dawn of a New Day

While privilege versus "the common good" of the great majority would also be a dominant theme in the post-primary campaign, the Democratic Party was helped by the standard, but this time widely-publicized, fraudulent campaign tactics of the Republicans. In a clear effort to discourage participation, the Coyne-run Republican city government assessed a poll tax on almost 20,000 potential voters in the Fifth Ward, the Republican black Hill District, although less then 6,500 families resided in the ward.

In the Second Ward, which included the Strip District along the Allegheny

River, 268 newly registered voters, some registered more than once, were discovered to be registered as living in speakeasies, flop houses, gas stations, empty lots, warehouses, and even at the address of a billboard. One "voter" turned out to be a bronze statue. The *Pittsburgh Press* ran a series of photographs of the alleged residences of these dubious voters—and also charges of continued macing of city employees.

Republican City Council candidates, for this reason and perhaps also because they belatedly sensed a changed mood in the electorate, thereafter attempted to distance themselves as much as possible from the party, seldom acknowledging in their literature or ads that they were Republicans.

A sense of doom seemed to grip the Republicans. For example, the dissident Republicans, defeated in the primary campaign and perhaps anticipating Republican defeat, did not return to the Republican fold as the general election neared. Indeed, local newspapers publicized a steady stream of prominent Republican defections to the Democrats over the course of the campaign: losing Republican mayoralty candidate Mackrell, former City Council President James F. Malone, League of Women Voters head Mrs. R. Templeton Smith, Tenth Ward (Stanton Heights-Morningside) Republican Chairman John Huston.

Perhaps the most telling defection, however, indicative of shifting political currents of major proportions, was that of powerful former Mayor William Magee, who had won one of the five City Council nominations in the Republican primary. A nephew of Christopher Magee, the nineteenth century founder of Pittsburgh's Republican Party, William Magee personified the local Republican Party. But, when David Lawrence offered to drop one of the Democratic Council candidates and replace him with Magee, the former Republican mayor readily accepted the hitherto worthless Democratic line on the ballot machine.

The Republican-dominated City Council countered these defections by finding another $300,000 for relief funds and calling back to work those laid off from relief work projects after the primary. Democrats responded by pointing out that the city had to borrow $250,000 to meet its payroll and had accumulated a $1.5 million deficit at the end of the previous year.

Meanwhile, suggestive of its new support in the electorate and the grassroots character of its appeal, the Democratic campaign showed more energy and popular enthusiasm than had ever before been the case. Indeed, in some cases, the party organization had to work hard to establish control over what was essentially an independent insurgent movement in ethnic working class wards. In several wards—such as those comprising the Slavic South Side 16th Ward and Hazelwood's largely Hungarian 15th Ward, site of a Jones & Laughlin steel mill—younger, newly mobilized recruits to the New Deal banner founded Democratic political clubs outside the regular party structure and threatened—sometimes successfully—to shove aside Democratic old-timers. Because of this influx, Lawrence sometimes sacrificed long-time Democratic ward bosses to accommodate the insurgent ethnic and working class "New Democratic" activists taking over the party at the ward level.[84]

There was also another reason for such ethnic voters to take increased interest in the upcoming election. There were referendum questions on the ballot which called for the repeal of Protestant Prohibition and the repeal of a ban on Sunday sports. The latter was championed by the Pittsburgh Pirates and the Pittsburgh Steelers. Both eventually passed by huge margins, with Pittsburghers voting six to one to allow Sunday sports and seven to one to repeal Prohibition (the huge headline in *The Pittsburgh Post-Gazette* after the election read, "McNair Elected Mayor-Sunday Sports Win Here").[85] The repeal of Prohibition also carried statewide, and thus Pennsylvania, along with Ohio and Utah, killed Prohibition, becoming the final states needed to annul the 18th Amendment to the Constitution.

Surprisingly, however, neither were issues in the city campaign. Neither Herron or McNair once mentioned these referenda in their speeches. That both passed by such huge margins, and with so little controversy, however, also says much about the nature of the new Pittsburgh electorate. Both Prohibition and Sunday "Blue Laws" were long central efforts of native stock Protestants to control the moral lives of the urban immigrant masses. As "drink" had thus become tightly interwoven in American culture with ethnic identity in reaction to the Protestant crusade against it, this victory over Protestant Prohibition was a powerful sign of the emergence of a powerful new ethnic electorate.[86]

David Lawrence launched the Democrats' general election campaign with a massive rally at Oakland's Frick School on Fifth Avenue, the Fourth Ward home base of Republican boss James Coyne. He then oversaw a non-stop campaign which organized a multitude of well-attended campaign rallies for every rally the Republicans held. "The Republicans would hold one big meeting per night," said Fred Weir, a senior campaign aide, "while we held half a dozen . . . On the night, for example, that Herron . . . held a big meeting at the Duquesne Gardens [a popular Oakland skating rink on the corner of Fifth Avenue and Craig Street] . . . McNair talked to more people than Herron did . . . We would just run in and say a few words and they would roar and we would leave. There was nothing significant said."[87]

Nothing needed to be said. The election wasn't really about McNair and Herron, anyway. It was about class, not about personalities. It was about ousting the elitist Republican status quo and bringing Roosevelt's working class New Deal to Pittsburgh. The images and rhetoric of the campaign emphasized the class nature of the new political era. Repeated full-page ads in the newspapers pictured McNair as the "Roosevelt Candidate for Mayor of Pittsburgh." McNair himself attacked the entrenched interests of privilege represented by Republican boss James Coyne and William L. Mellon, the Republican financier, as did Lawrence.

At a campaign rally at Kennywood Park, a popular amusement park on the Monongahela River just east of Pittsburgh, Lawrence savaged the "seemingly bottomless man-made abyss dug by avarice, deepened by gold-mad Morgans and Mellons."[88] Only Roosevelt and his local supporters, Lawrence said, could lead Pittsburgh out of such depths. Roosevelt, noted *The New York Times*, seemed to be the Democratic candidate for Mayor of Pittsburgh and the election was essentially a plebiscite on the New Deal.[89]

Nor were the Democrats amiss in tying their campaign so closely to Roosevelt, for Roosevelt was seen as a savior of the common man throughout the industrial region of southwestern Pennsylvania. Commenting on a September campaign rally in Uniontown, a coal town not far from Pittsburgh, Republican—but pro-New Deal—Governor Gifford Pinchot was surprised that 15,000 to 20,000 miners turned out in the pouring rain to demonstrate their support for the president.

"You would have been deeply touched to see how these people believe in you," he wrote Roosevelt. "They had a parade four miles long, and it was dotted all over with pictures of you as the miner's friend. They trust you and they all believe that you are working to get them recognition of the United Mine Workers of America."[90]

With increased contributions creating an unprecedentedly huge war chest, local Democratic Party leaders were able to mount a lavish campaign, open a permanent office for the first time, and put out a newspaper, the *New Deal News*, which served to reinforce the linkage of the local party with the New Deal.

They also continued the campaign to woo black voters to the Democracy. Through their connections with Democratic National Committee chief James A. Farley, they obtained the appointment of five well-known blacks to the Pittsburgh office of the Home Owners Loan Corporation. The *New Deal News* then widely publicized this action and pointed out that, while blacks accounted for 13 percent of Pittsburgh's electorate in 1933 (up from 10 percent in 1932 and indicative, also, of the mobilization of new black voters), the Republicans allowed them only 3 percent of the city's patronage appointments. Under a Democratic municipal administration, they promised, this would change. Meanwhile, *Courier* publisher Robert Vann appeared with both Lawrence and McNair in their numerous appearances before black audiences.[91]

The party, however, did not neglect its ethnic base. It especially made overtures to the Italian community, which comprised 19 percent of Pittsburgh's population, the largest single ethnic bloc. In one notable appearance before a large and excited Italian standing-room-only audience at the Carnegie Library's Music Hall on the North Side, McNair solicited their votes in a way no former mayoralty candidate ever had—*in Italian!* This Democratic Party rally was the first political event in Pittsburgh ever organized by and addressed to Italians. Eventually, though it had earlier supported the Republican mayoralty candidate and had refused to back Roosevelt in 1932, the influential local Italian newspaper *Unione* also endorsed McNair for Mayor.

Meanwhile, the organized labor vote was sought in the persons of John J. Kane, former president of the Web Pressmen's Union, and Thomas J. Gallagher, a popular Irish-Catholic leader of the Flint Glass Workers Union who had risen through the ranks. Both had been elected State Representatives the previous November and both were on the Executive Board of the Pittsburgh Central Labor Union.

Gallagher had begun his political career in 1924 as head of the Robert LaFollette Progressive Party campaign committee in Pittsburgh's Sixteenth and Seventeenth South Side Wards and personified the gravitation of "third party" labor leaders toward the Democratic Party.[92] Suggesting the local Democratic

Party's acknowledgement of its expanded working class constituency, it had nominated Gallagher and Kane as two of its Democratic City Council candidates.

So popular was the Democratic campaign beginning to appear that even Republican John Herron began to align himself with FDR's New Deal. After Allegheny County Republican Party Committee Chairman William H. Coleman attacked Roosevelt and the NRA in a speech to party ward heelers at the Republican headquarters, Herron frantically attempted damage control. "The N.R.A. deserves the support of every man and woman in Pittsburgh interested in Recovery," he proclaimed, and pointed out that he was the honorary chairman of the Pittsburgh NRA committee.[93]

Still, Lawrence was certain the Republicans would attempt to win the election in their time-honored fashion, as "the Republican machine has been planning to make a super effort to steal the election."[94] On election day, the well-financed and revitalized Democratic organization fielded a small army of trained poll watchers to guard against the expected and traditional Republican fraud and intimidation of voters. Lawrence also assigned lawyers to Democratic campaign headquarters, ready to take cases of fraud instantly to court. He also requested judges to be available all night long to hear petitions for impounding ballot boxes, and he established a fund to cover the $50 fee required to impound each ballot box. Finally, the Democrats demanded, and received, State Police surveillance of the polls.

Nevertheless, the Republicans fielded an army of workers twice as large and reports of fraud poured in. Voters were bribed, poll overseers were intimidated into validating fraudulent ballots, and unlawful assistance was rendered voters in marking their ballots.

But, such typical Republican tactics weren't enough to offset the Democratic tide in Pennsylvania. On the other side of the state, in Philadelphia, there were no elections for mayor or city council that year. Instead, the highest offices up for election were the so-called "row offices" such as City Controller, City Treasurer, Coroner, and Register of Wills, as well as magistrates (justices of peace). The Democrats swept all row offices and most of the magistrates. In thirty of Philadelphia's forty-eight wards, the Democratic ticket trounced the Republicans.

At the same time, the numbers of those actually registering as Democrats also increased greatly. "The number of registered Democrats, which had never exceeded 40,000 in municipal election years, soared to almost 180,000 in 1933. The highest previous number of registered Democrats had been in 1928, when the figure was 102,000." Although complete Democratic hegemony in Philadelphia had to wait a while longer, Democratic vote totals in the former one-party city never again fell below 40 percent in any municipal, state, or national election after 1933.[95]

In Pittsburgh, despite a 122,000 Republican majority among registered voters, McNair and the entire Democratic City Council slate carried three fourths of the city's wards and 57 percent of the vote, only one percentage point lower than Roosevelt the previous year. Two of the new Democratic City Councillors were State Representatives Thomas J. Gallagher and John J. Kane, PCLU Executive

Board members who would hold what would henceforth come to be known informally as "labor's Council seats."

In addition to the clean sweep of all city offices up for election, the Democrats also won the sheriff's office, a newly created juvenile court judgeship, and another seat in the state legislature.[96] Any office which could be won, was won. It was an unprecedented, unimaginable defeat for the Republicans who had ruled the city since before the Civil War. State Democratic Chairman Joseph Guffey claimed that the election was an endorsement of "the gospel of government laid down by Roosevelt."[97] McNair agreed, saying, "I have promised the people of this community a New Deal at city hall." He later acknowledged, "They were voting for Roosevelt, they didn't care anything about me."[98]

Pittsburgh Republicans never recovered from their defeat and would never again, not even unto the present, be elected to any Pittsburgh office. As premonitions of things to come in the next round of municipal elections in 1937, the Republicans also lost some of their first elections out in the small mill towns surrounding Pittsburgh. In Wilmerding, home of both the Westinghouse Corporation and the militant Local 610 of the Left-leaning United Electrical Workers (UE), a Socialist was elected mayor over a fusion Republican-Democratic opponent. Elsewhere it was Democrats who were defeating Republicans. Democrats swept Millvale and a Democrat, James Gold, replaced the incumbent Republican mayor of Monessen.[99] In Braddock, site of Carnegie-Steel's giant Edgar Thompson Works, the Republicans had only one clear-cut victory, with a winning Council candidate. The other Council seats, as well as the other offices, were won by Democrats.

The most impressive Democratic victory, however, was in McKees Rocks, site of the notorious IWW-led Pressed Steel Strike of 1909. There the candidates of Miles Bryan, the Republican boss who'd run the town as his fiefdom for two generations, won only two of eight offices up for election. The new mayor was a Democrat.

The triumphant Democrats celebrated with a huge parade. "Old residents could scarcely believe that it was a Democratic parade passing them," the *Post-Gazette* reported. "No Democrat had ever set match to a red fire in McKees Rocks in the memory of the borough's oldest inhabitant. But it was true. Bryan—the same Bryan who had laughed amusedly at every timid flowering of independence for years—had not only been beaten, but was now being flouted in defeat by those who overthrew him. From the new bridge across the Ohio down into the heart of town, the Democrats, led by the long-eared symbol of their party, vociferously informed the town from 'The Bottoms' to the hilltops that the 'New Deal' had arrived. Bryan himself, the silver-haired cigar-profferring handshaker of an earlier day of politics, was not in evidence as the parade stormed through the borough."[100]

On the front page of the *Post-Gazette* issue which reported this parade in McKees Rocks there appeared a large photograph of what would become a common sight in the Steel Valley: steelworkers leading a donkey in a victory parade down a city's main street. And a representative of the Democratic Party, in this case T. J. Donahoe, chairman of the McKees Rocks Democratic Party, riding the donkey. And all about the triumphant marching McKees Rocks workers fluttered huge American flags.

In 1909, during their bloody strike, during their battles with the "Republican police," Socialist leader Eugene V. Debs had come to McKees Rocks to rally the struggling workers. He told them their struggle was a "harbinger of a new spirit among the unorganized, foreign-born workers in the mass-production industries."[101]

Debs was right. There *was* a new spirit among the workers. And, at long last, they had won. And no Republican would ever again be elected to any office in McKees Rocks. The future, it seemed, now belonged to workers such as these.

Still Waiting for the New Deal

Although giving victory to the Democrats, it was not yet clear to observers that the Pittsburgh-area electorate had undergone a thorough-going sea change. Was this second Democratic landslide in a row a temporary phenomenon, or was it, in truth, the harbinger of permanent partisan realignment? Voters had voted for change and promises and hope. The question now was: Would these hopes be fulfilled?

Some parts of the electorate remained unconvinced of the Democratic promise. Despite the best efforts of Robert Vann and the Democratic Party, Wards Three and Five—the city's black Hill District wards—still voted Republican, although by slimmer margins than in 1932. Indeed, the Democrat McNair even carried some precincts in these wards, which no Democrat had ever done previously. To build on this, black Democrats launched a permanent party organization in Ward Three two weeks after the election.[102]

In spite of such inroads, the Democrats had failed to carry any of the first six wards, the city's original wards extending from "The Point" downtown, where the Allegheny and Monongahela Rivers converged to form the Ohio River, up to the Duquesne Bluffs, including the Hill District and Oakland. While the city's Republican organization had done little to retain these wards in the 1932 presidential campaign, that had not been the case in 1933. In the municipal campaign, the organization fought desperately, by any means necessary, to hold on to its control of these wards, and in this it succeeded.

There was also only soft support for the Democrats among the city's native Protestant wards, such as Shadyside and Squirrel Hill, although there was an increasing Jewish population in the latter. These neighborhoods voted Democratic in 1933, but their vote was perceived as more of a vote against the corruption of Pittsburgh's incumbent Republican Party than it was a "class vote" for the Democrats.

Another area the Democrats were still in the process of winning over were the Italian wards. A majority of Italian voters supported the Democratic ticket, but this Italian vote was weaker for McNair than it had been for Roosevelt the previous year.

All of these areas, therefore, represented problems that David Lawrence's Democratic organization had to address as it attempted to consolidate its victory. In this effort the Democrats would eventually succeed as, by 1936, the black and all ethnic wards formed the solid base of the local Democratic organization.

That 1936 election, too, would witness for the first time the numerical superiority of the Democratic electorate in the once solidly Republican stronghold of Pittsburgh. In 1929, Democrats numbered only 5,200 out of an electorate of 175,000. By the time of the 1936 general election, Democrats finally outnumbered Republicans by 172,179 to 136,451.[103] Democrats remained the majority of the electorate ever after.

Thus, it seemed that with Pittsburgh's 1933 municipal election, the city had started on a new political path after eighty years of iron clad Republican rule. And so it had.

This new dawn, however, was not so clear as it might have seemed. There was still the problem of cementing the ideological loyalty of the newly mobilized ethnic working class voters to the Democratic Party. In this task, the newly-elected Democratic Mayor was of no help at all.

David Lawrence had chosen William McNair as the party's standard bearer because of his perceived "Republican" qualities. But those very qualities created a poor fit between the new mayor and the electorate which had put him into office. As it turned out, he had little understanding of the dynamics transforming the city and region, nor sympathy for the agenda of his own political base.

William McNair had run as "Roosevelt's" candidate for mayor, and immediately after the election David Lawrence and Joe Guffey escorted him to Washington to meet his supposed leader. The meeting with Roosevelt was friendly and McNair returned to Pittsburgh with kinds words for the president.

Before long, however, McNair began criticizing both the president and the local Democratic organization. As Philadelphia and the state government were still controlled by the Republicans, McNair was the most prominent elected Democrat in Pennsylvania, and it seems this went to his head. He felt he'd been elected due to his own personal virtues and reputation, and that this entitled him to call his own shots. A year after his election, he was offering his services to the leaders of the right wing Liberty League in defiance of Roosevelt.[104] With these actions, McNair clearly did not heed his own election night analysis that the electorate had voted for Roosevelt, and didn't care for him at all.

Particularly distressing to local Democratic leaders was McNair's opposition to the local implementation of various New Deal programs. This served to quickly alienate him from the essential Democratic constituencies, such as blacks and ethnic working class voters. Black jobs were especially slow in forthcoming from the McNair Administration, moving one black voter at a church meeting to tell McNair, "We knew little of you when your name came up for election, but we understood that you were an exponent of the New Deal. And we are waiting for that New Deal to materialize."[105]

They had to wait a bit longer, as McNair proceeded to name the Republican President of the League of Women Voters, Mrs. R. Templeton Smith, as his

Budget Director. He then played musical chairs with the important patronage post of Public Safety Director, rejecting the Democratic organization's candidate and naming a succession of his own men. In the important patronage office of Director of Public Works, he appointed Leslie Johnston, the Republican president of the good government Citizens' League.

McNair thus shut the Democratic organization out of the most powerful city positions which, between them, controlled most of the patronage jobs in Pittsburgh. The Department of Public Safety, which oversaw the Police and Fire Bureaus, controlled a four million dollar payroll, while most of the rest of Pittsburgh's 1934 budget of $21,252,549 also went for salaries. In the mayor's cabinet, only City Treasurer James P. Kirk and City Solicitor Cornelius D. Scully, who had been McNair's nominal campaign committee chairman in the election, represented the Democratic organization.

Lack of access to city jobs was clearly intolerable to Lawrence and the Democratic organization, while demoralizing to the working class voters who had hoped for so much from Pittsburgh's promised New Deal. Speaking before a rally of the party faithful in the nearby town of Washington, however, state party chief Joseph Guffey implored them, "Do not lose faith if some Democratic officeholder should fail to measure up to his responsibilities . . . We will, perhaps, at times elect the wrong man to public office."[106]

In choosing William McNair as the New Deal's local standard bearer, David Lawrence had made a grievous error, and the newly mobilized Democratic coalition had indeed elected the wrong man to office. Pittsburgh workers would have to wait just a bit longer for a New Deal.

A Referendum on the New Deal

Like the ethnics and blacks of Pittsburgh, there were others who were also still waiting for a New Deal as 1934 began. Change had come—but it was piecemeal, haphazard, as yet inchoate. The future beckoned, but the past lingered on.

Nationally, the presidential election of 1932 had not reshaped the fault lines of political combat. This was because it was not yet so much an example of class politics as much as it was a rejection of Republican Hooverism by all categories of voters. Indeed, although this had not been the case in the Pittsburgh region, nationally there had even been a slight decline in voter turnout over 1928, as those most economically devastated simply abstained from political activity, devoid of hope and resigned to their fate. "It was only by the next pair of elections, 1934 and 1936, that economic discontent had become politicized. Consequently, turnout increased more noticeably and new and durable party coalitions took shape." Workers flooded to the polls nationwide to vote their class interests and "in 1934 turnout was 9.1 percentage points higher than in 1930, and presidential turnout in 1936 was 4.2 percentage points above the 1932 level . . . In 1936 (and perhaps as well in 1934, when the political alternatives were sharply delineated, as they had not been in 1932), extraordinary numbers of lower income voters were stimulated to cast their ballots."[107]

Thus, it seems that the Pittsburgh region was ahead of the nation in the forthcoming political transformations, as it was only by 1934 that large enough numbers of the economically devastated nationwide were mobilized sufficiently to reshape the electoral universe.

Indicative of this coming transformation was the salience of strident, uncompromising political rhetoric on both sides which called their constituencies to fierce class combat as 1934 began. Wealthy Democrats abandoned their party in August 1934, to found the Liberty League. These renegade Democrats engaged in unceasing anti-New Deal vitriol, which attracted "old style" Democrats like the Protestant William McNair.

Republican leaders were doing the same. "In 1934 and 1936, Republican state platforms regularly denounced the New Deal as a peril 'to the very foundation of our free government,' and attacked Roosevelt for having assumed 'dictatorial powers unheard of in America.' The party's national leaders were no less unequivocal in castigating the New Deal for having 'dishonored American traditions' by attempting to replace the American system of government with 'one that is alien to everything this country has ever before known.'"[108]

The class lines of partisanship were equally evident in the actions of office holders. "Shifts in rhetoric and behavior since the early 1940s have obscured the extent to which the Republican party in the 1930s behaved and characterized itself as a staunchly and steadfastly anti-New-Deal party. In the Seventy-third House (1933-34), Republicans may have been disorganized and impressed by Roosevelt's popularity, but they still cast a majority of their roll-call votes against his proposals. During that Congress, 73 percent of the roll calls pitted a majority of Democrats against a majority of Republicans, a much higher level of party voting than had occurred in any House since the Sixty-first (1909-11)."[109]

Also indicative of the saliency of class politics was the fact that the Democratic Party had to appeal to organized labor, the new core of its strength, because, "The organizational alliance between unions and the Democrats had a mobilizing impact that extended beyond the behavior of union members. To win elections, parties must at least mobilize their own supporters. Apart from the few bailiwicks of their urban machines, the Democrats lacked the necessary organizational capability, especially in places [like Western Pennsylvania] where the Republicans had been entrenched and virtually unchallenged for over a decade. Adaptation of the union infrastructure helped to offset that deficiency, to sustain the intensity of the Democratic appeal, and to mobilize the party's constituency in heavily urban areas where union political activity was concentrated."[110]

By just such means, however, the emerging working class constituency was transforming the Democratic Party to represent its own interests. This can easily be seen in the role given to organized labor in the Pennsylvania Democratic gubernatorial campaign of 1934. Democratic rhetoric in this campaign featured heightened appeals to the newly powerful labor vote. In addition, and for the first time, the Democrats formulated a campaign especially designed to appeal to labor interests. Two years before, Roosevelt had run a vague Democratic campaign which had specifically promised only to repeal Prohibition and balance the budget. In the 1934 Pennsylvania campaign, however, the Democratic Party for the first time ran quite explicitly as "labor's party." The campaign, therefore, clearly posed the question as to whether the political climate had changed enough to make "labor's party" viable in Republican Pennsylvania.

Besides state offices, a U.S. Senate seat, that of Pittsburgher David A. Reed, was also up for election in 1934. Pennsylvania had been one of six states to go for Hoover in 1932, and Pittsburgh and Allegheny County were as yet the only significant Democratic islands in a statewide Republican ocean.[111] If Democratic influence was to be enlarged beyond Allegheny County to the rest of the state, then an organization had to be built which could win statewide offices.

Already it seemed there was the basis for such an organization. The same mobilization which had brought previously inactive voters into the ranks of the Pittsburgh Democratic Party was also happening statewide. While Democrats were a majority of registered voters in only eleven of the state's sixty-seven counties, some of them small counties, nevertheless statewide Democratic voter registration had climbed to 1,401,563 in 1934.[112] Pennsylvania's Democrats were still heavily out-numbered by the state's 2,625,238 Republicans. Even so, this represented an increase of 300,000 new Democratic registrants since 1933 and 850,000 since 1932. Perhaps something was happening and perhaps there was a momentum to build upon.[113]

Also, there were reasons to believe that, after a dry spell of forty years, Democratic victories might be possible in at least a few statewide races. Just as class politics, exacerbated by economic troubles, had presaged Democratic victories in Pittsburgh, the same seemed to be occurring in Pennsylvania as a whole. Unemployment lingered at just under 25 percent. Over a third of a million people were on the relief roles, with another 1,350,000 dependent on relief payments. Hundreds of thousands more were working half- or part-time. As in Pittsburgh in 1933, and the nation in 1932, the Republican state administration was seen as responsible for the economic conditions. Thus, despite an almost a two to one Republican advantage among registered voters, the state election looked competitive.

Further, Gifford Pinchot, the popular and relatively moderate Republican Governor (who was often out of step with his own party), was forbidden by law from succeeding himself. Therefore, he was stepping down to run for the U.S. Senate in the Republican primary against the conservative incumbent, anti-New Dealer and prominent Pittsburgh attorney David A. Reed. Senator Reed was a partner of the influential Pittsburgh law firm of Reed Smith Shaw and McClay and the senator who had sponsored the immigration restriction legislation of 1924.

To replace Pinchot as governor, the Republican organization, pressured by such Republican financial angels as William L. Mellon and Joseph Grundy (President of the Pennsylvania Manufacturers' Association), Republican State Committee Chairman Edward Martin, and Pinchot himself, supported William A. Schnader, Pinchot's Attorney General. Schnader was opposed in the Republican primary by Charles Margiotti, a Pittsburgh Italian-American attorney popular in labor as well as Italian circles.

Organization endorsement, however, was tantamount to election in Pennsylvania at that time, and Schnader easily carried the Republican gubernatorial primary. Pinchot, on the other hand, did not win such endorsement, and lost the senatorial nomination to Reed by just under 100,000 votes.

Thus it was incumbent Senator David Reed, of Pittsburgh, who faced off against Pennsylvania's Democratic state party chairman Joseph Guffey, also from Pittsburgh, who'd easily won the Democratic senatorial nomination. Following Roosevelt's victory in 1932, the new president had placed all federal patronage jobs in Pennsylvania under Guffey's control, and at least the Philadelphia *Inquirer* thought these tens of thousands of federal job holders were decisive in Guffey's primary victory.[114] It's more likely, though, that this association was more useful in closely linking Guffey with Roosevelt's New Deal in the minds of the voters than in actual votes from federal job holders.

For governor, the Democratic state leadership, at Guffey's behest, backed a Philadelphia Main Line Republican, George Earle, III, who was then Roosevelt's ambassador to Austria. Like Lawrence, Joe Guffey was still unsure of the strength of the new ethnic working class electorate. Only eight years earlier, in the 1926 gubernatorial election, Republican John S. Fisher had won election with 75 percent of the vote, the biggest victory margin in Pennsylvania history. The legacy of such crushing defeats yet loomed large in the minds of Democratic leaders. Thus, Guffey felt that a liberal Republican, with ties to Roosevelt, might be the best way to woo independent and liberal Republican voters, while retaining Democratic voters.

George Earle came from a wealthy Philadelphia business family and was a Harvard graduate. At age twenty-six he had served in Pershing's futile 1916 pursuit into Mexico after revolutionary leader Pancho Villa. When America entered World War I in 1917, he joined the Navy and captained the submarine *U.S.S. Victor,* earning the Navy Cross for his service. After the war he returned to the family business empire, serving on several boards of directors, and proceeded to lead the life of a leisured Main Line Republican gentleman.

However, Earle had become disturbed by Hoover's lack of response to the Depression and so became a financial backer of both Roosevelt and the Pennsylvania Democrats in the 1932 election, contributing $35,000 to each.[115] When FDR took office in 1933, he rewarded Earle with the ambassadorship to Austria. There Earle garnered a fair amount of American media attention when he supported Chancellor Engelbert Dollfuss—assassinated in July 1934 by Austrian Nazis—in what was to be an ultimately losing battle against Austrian Nazism.

Party leaders also hoped that, being independently wealthy, Earle would finance his own campaign, as well as a large part of the general Democratic campaign. This he later did, contributing $175,000 to the 1934 campaign.[116] Thus, this enthusiastic convert to the New Deal seemed to be a good choice for the Democratic gubernatorial nomination in what was still an overwhelmingly Republican state.[117]

The Democratic Party leadership had hoped for a smooth primary campaign in order to present a united front to the Republicans. Pittsburgh's Mayor McNair, however, would have none of that. Convinced of his own popularity, McNair entered the Democratic gubernatorial primary in yet another act of defiance toward the Democratic leadership.

A group of dissident rural Democratic committeemen also made life difficult for the party leadership by objecting to Republican Earle as the party's nominee for governor. Meeting in Harrisburg a week after the Democratic State Committee which endorsed Earle and Guffey, these dissidents nominated Judge Charles D. Copeland of Western Pennsylvania's Westmoreland County for governor and Roland S. Morris, a former ambassador to Japan, for the senate.

In the primary campaign, both the dissident Morris-Copeland and the leadership-backed Guffey-Earle slates claimed to be the true Democrats. Both, also, proclaimed their loyalty to Roosevelt and the New Deal.[118] Thus, what seemed to be happening within the party was not an ideological conflict as something else. According to one analyst, it was more a reaction by "The faction of the old party with solid Pennsylvania German antecedents . . . [who] *were being pushed aside by labor leaders,* brain trusters, and Republicans-turned-Democratic."[119] Urban-based, ethnic political leaders like Pittsburgh-based Guffey and Lawrence were shoving out the old party stalwarts in the state organization. Significantly, however, even the older, rural Democrats, while resisting the newly arrived ethnic and urban elements within the state's Democratic Party, pledged allegiance to the class politics which the new urban arrivals symbolized.

Even so, the future of the Pennsylvania Democratic Party belonged to those Lawrence and Guffey represented, and Earle won an easy primary victory, with a four to one margin over his opponents. Indeed, in Allegheny County this Philadelphia-area candidate even beat Pittsburgh Mayor William McNair two to one on his home turf, reinforcing the impression that McNair's 1933 mayoralty triumph had been a victory for a "new deal," and not for him personally. In a spiteful move which did not endear him to the Pittsburgh Democratic leadership, nor, surely, to his own constituency, McNair responded by endorsing the Republican, William Schnader, for governor.

It was George Earle, then, who carried the Democratic banner into the general election. Indicative of the new importance of the working class vote, his running mate for Lt. Governor was one of those labor leaders the old-line rural Democrats reluctantly made room for, Thomas Kennedy, of Hazelton. Kennedy was the Secretary-Treasurer of the United Mine Workers of America and a close ally of UMWA President John L. Lewis.

Already aware of the increasing strength of the urban, ethnic, working class vote, Pittsburgh's Democratic boss Davy Lawrence had been courting organized labor since 1928. Even by 1934, however, this courtship had not yet been consummated, either in Pittsburgh or the state. The anointing of UMWA leader Thomas Kennedy as the Democratic candidate for Lt. Governor, however, went far in furthering the ties between organized labor and the Democratic Party in Pennsylvania.

Additionally, even while the Republicans still held the governorship and controlled the state legislature, by 1933 Pennsylvania Democrats had already begun emulating the pro-labor programs of FDR's New Deal with their own proposed "Little New Deal." The 1934 Democratic state platform took this further by being almost entirely devoted to the cause of labor, with the first eight points prominently addressing labor issues.[120]

Following the May primary, Joseph Guffey, who was now a candidate for the U.S. Senate, backed David Lawrence for the uncontested post of Democratic Party State Committee Chairman, to which the party elected him on June 9, 1934.[121] Lawrence's ascension to power was reinforced when Guffey next ceded him his control over all federal patronage jobs in Pennsylvania, informing the state's Congressmen they now had to deal with Lawrence. This benefited Guffey by distancing him from a brewing patronage scandal before the general election really got underway. Still, Guffey would hardly have relinquished his primary power base had he not been confident he would soon be moving on to greener pastures in the Senate.

While the Republican candidates remained relatively dormant during the months following the May primary, the Democratic slate campaigned aggressively throughout the summer. Once more, class issues were principal themes of the campaign. Lawrence, the day before his election as Democratic State Committee Chairman, attacked Mellon and Grundy as wealthy financiers who thought their money could buy the state. But, he said, "There is not enough money in all the Mellon banks or in the treasury of the Pennsylvania Manufacturers' Association [which Grundy led] to pay for another U.S. Senatorship for the reactionary David A. Reed . . . nor for a Governorship for Joe Grundy's attorney Bill Schnader . . . I say there is not enough Mellon money or Grundy Greenbacks in Pennsylvania to buy this election . . . [I]n our platform we make a solemn covenant with the people of Pennsylvania that if the Democratic Party of Pennsylvania is given the mandate it asks it will bring the New Deal into our state Government."[122]

George Earle continued to espouse this attack upon the wealthy even after the campaign ended. In August 1935, when critics charged that the intensifying tone of class warfare emanating from the FDR's New Deal had to be the work of Communists or their sympathizers in Roosevelt's administration, Earle denied it. Venturing brazenly into the lion's den to denounce the incipient witch hunt, Earle told a convention of the American Legion that the real enemies of America were the rich. We should, he warned, beware of "our men of wealth [sending] us on a wild-goose chase after so-called radicals while they continue to plunder the people."[123]

Besides attacking "men of wealth," Pennsylvania's Democratic candidates also unabashedly "sang the glories of the New Deal which had saved the banks, revived employment, *placed human rights before property rights,* and brought an end to industrial serfdom," promising to bring that New Deal home to Pennsylvania if elected.[124] There would be a New Deal for the state's farmers, promised Earle, a New Deal for miners, a New Deal for the unemployed through the implementation of unemployment insurance, and a New Deal for Pennsylvania's urban ethnic industrial workers through the abolition of private police forces (such as the notorious Coal and Iron Police) and the introduction of minimum wage and maximum hours legislation.[125]

The Democratic Party's platform also called for the abolition of child labor, an end to sweat shops, and "the absolute right of collective bargaining for labor." These were major policy differences from the Republican Party and offered the voters of Pennsylvania a stark and clear choice between explicit alternatives.

Republican newspapers in Philadelphia quickly ridiculed these promises as a "Little New Deal," and the name stuck. Indeed, the election, said Earle, was essentially a referendum on New Deal policies and on President Roosevelt. "Tell him you know he's for you," Earle told the voters, "and that you're for him. Franklin Roosevelt hasn't failed you. Don't you fail him."[126]

Evidently, many working class voters of Pennsylvania agreed with this framing of the election as a New Deal referendum. Shortly before the election, a political reporter for the Pittsburgh *Press* picked up a hitch-hiking coal miner and engaged him in conversation about the up-coming election. The miner had no idea who George Earle was, but said "All of us" in the mines are Democrats and all planned to vote for "President Roosevelt's party."[127]

This decision was no doubt aided by the fact that one of their union leaders, UMW Secretary-Treasurer Tom Kennedy, was on the ticket of "Roosevelt's party" as the Lt. Governor candidate. But this was not just the sentiment among the state's coal miners. Throughout Pennsylvania, reported one journalist who interviewed voters from the New Jersey to the Ohio borders, "They are talking about only one man and that man is Franklin D. Roosevelt . . . It was expressed to me by farmers, soda clerks, waitresses, barbers, hotel desk clerks, laborers, unemployed, hitch-hikers and skilled union workers."[128]

Indicative of how prevalent this mass sentiment was in the Pittsburgh region was the unusual event which took place at Kennywood Park that summer. Then, as now, Kennywood Park was the largest amusement park in the area. It has survived for decades by sensing exactly what its patrons want. Evidently, what its customers wanted in the summer of 1934 was a "Roosevelt Day," for that was what Kennywood Park sponsored. For their "Roosevelt Day," the park constructed a huge central monument composed of an open book displaying Roosevelt's image and biographical facts as the text. At the same time, and for the first time, Kennywood began sponsoring various ethnic nationality days at the park.

Also suggestive of popular sentiment was a new restaurant which opened at the main intersection in the Steel Valley town of Turtle Creek. Located on the prominent corners of Braddock Avenue and Penn Avenue was "The New Deal Restaurant," which remained a salient fixture in the town's cityscape until at least 1996.[129]

As had been done in Pittsburgh's municipal campaign, Democratic Party leaders also made efforts to woo the traditionally Republican black voters. Of course, the general nature of the New Deal's egalitarian aura appealed to blacks, but Guffey also made deliberate attempts to bring them into the Democratic coalition.

So did Earle, inviting the entire membership of the Negro Citizen's

Democratic Committee of One Hundred to an elegant soiree at his home on the Main Line.[130] Earle also emphasized his family's long championship of black rights. It seems his great grandfather, Thomas Earle, was a Quaker who had financed an underground railroad for runaway slaves and had supported the rights of blacks to vote in state elections.

Robert Vann, publisher of the *Pittsburgh Courier*, was again pressed into service. He had received the federal job as a special assistant U.S. Attorney that Lawrence and Guffey had promised him, and so campaigned across the state in support of the Democratic ticket. In addition, a special edition of the *Courier* was published listing the myriad jobs blacks had received from Guffey's patronage pot, with the promise that blacks would share in the spoils of future Democratic victories.

And, indeed, blacks would benefit from the coming election. Running as a Democrat, Homer S. Brown would be elected to the State House as Pittsburgh's first black State Representative. In 1935 Brown would lead the Democrats in revamping the state's 1887 Civil Rights Act to greatly expand citizenship rights for black Pennsylvanians. Thus, as with labor, the Democratic Party promised—and would enact—major policy differences from the Republicans on issues of concern to black voters.

The effort to woo more of the large Italian vote into the Democratic coalition also continued. David Lawrence approached Charles Margiotti, the Italian attorney from Pittsburgh who'd lost the Republican gubernatorial primary to William Schnader. In return for his endorsement and active campaigning, Lawrence guaranteed him a position in Earle's cabinet should the Democrats win.

Margiotti agreed to this. Picking up on the class themes of the campaign, Margiotti denounced the wealth of Mellon and Grundy, proclaiming that victory for the Democratic Party was, "[T]he only practical way of securing to the people of Pennsylvania the decent social and economic relief to which they are entitled."[131] Margiotti then carried this message to the regions which had voted strongly for him in the primary: Italian South Philadelphia, Pittsburgh's Italian Bloomfield and East Liberty, sections of Western Pennsylvania where the labor vote had gone for him, and in his home town of Punxsutawney, where he was greeted by a 500-car caravan when he brought Earle there with him for a rally.[132]

Meanwhile, after some hedging, Gifford Pinchot, the losing senatorial candidate in the Republican primary, endorsed the Republican ticket. Even among the Republicans, however, respect had to be paid to the new reality of class politics. Thus, Pinchot endorsed the Republican candidate, yet pledged allegiance to the New Deal, claiming that Guffey and the "greenhorn playboy" Earle would actually hinder the implementation of New Deal programs in Pennsylvania.[133] Schnader, on the other hand, not daring to attack the New Deal, decided to ignore it, claiming it and Roosevelt were non-issues, irrelevant to a state campaign.[134]

In this regard, however, it appeared Schnader was out of step with what many voters felt. For them, the contest was nothing less than a showdown between what the *Pittsburgh Press* later called the "unpopular Republican Raw Deal" and the promise of a better life with a Democratic New Deal.[135]

For anthracite coal miners in the town of Kelayres, it was even more than that. It was a matter of life and death. A "laborers' village" of around 700 people, "partially surrounded by slag heaps" in Pennsylvania's northeastern Schuylkill County, Kelayres was only a few miles from UMW leader Thomas Kennedy's home town of Hazelton. Nothing so highlighted the open class warfare that Pennsylvania politics had become than the battles in Schuylkill County that summer between the coal miners and the coal companies.[136]

Schuylkill County was the center of widespread bootleg coal mining by freelance miners. Beginning in the late 1920s the county's largest coal producers had begun to cut back production and disinvest in the region due to a stagnant market. By 1933, coal production had been cut by a third and almost 65,000 miners had been thrown out of work, with unemployment running at around 50 percent in the county.[137]

In response, people in local mining communities had begun mining coal on their own in "illegal" operations known as "bootleg" mines, thereby surviving the hard times. A state of continuous low-level armed guerrilla warfare soon developed in Pennsylvania's anthracite region. The Coal and Iron Police, a statewide, state-supported, police force used by corporations to control workers in coal and steel communities, dynamited bootleg mines. In response, the miners forcibly drove these company police out of the region when they could.

In July 1934, with the State Police (which had been formed in the nineteenth century specifically to repress such miner rebellions) backing up their own Coal and Iron Police, the coal companies launched a major offensive to wipe out bootleg mining in Schuylkill County. Their pre-dawn raids blasted bootleg mines into rubble throughout the county, but armed confrontations with massed miners and their families finally forced the raiding parties to abandon the campaign.

But, there was also an electoral dimension to this on-going war in the coal fields. The guerrilla war in Schuylkill County thus came to a head in the town of Kelayres on Election Eve.

Like many other mining towns in the state, Kelayres was run by a Republican boss, in this case Joseph Bruno, in close alliance with the coal companies. The efforts of the miners to organize politically under the banner of the opposition Democratic Party had already resulted in a major gun battle between them and Bruno's Republican organization that summer.[138] Sensing victory, though, after the defeat of the companies' dynamiting campaign of the summer, several hundred miners and their families staged an Election Eve Democratic Party rally beside the huge slag heap at the western end of the main street. As the rally broke up, the miners decided to parade through the town behind Carl Vacante, an Italian miner carrying the American flag, and a group of children.

As the miners paraded past Bruno's house, perhaps taunting him, gunfire from what the State Police later described as a "veritable arsenal of revolvers, shotguns, rifles, and pistols" erupted from the house, decimating the miners. Carl Vacante crumpled, both him and the American flag riddled with bullets.[139] Sixty-five-year-old Frank Fiorella's head "was shattered by a shotgun blast . . . [as] Rifle and shotgun fire began to pour onto [the streets] . . . John Galosky, thirty, a miner . . . went to Fiorella's aid and was shot down immediately. Dominic Perna, thirty-seven, a leading Kelayres Democrat, was blown off his feet near Fiorella and Galosky . . . Edward Vespucci, an unemployed colliery worker and Democratic orator, was shot in the head . . . Andrew Kostishion, thirty-six . . . raced to the intersection to find his daughter. He was shot in the stomach . . . This was not a brief, sudden spasm of gunfire. It was a deliberate slaughter, and it went on and on."[140] In all, five miners, Fiorella, Perna, Galosky, Kostishion and William Forke, were killed and twenty-six men, women, and children, were wounded by the hail of gunfire from Republican boss Bruno's house.

The Schuylkill County Democratic Chairman got on the phone and news of the massacre flashed around the state. Every newspaper in Pennsylvania featured the story on Election Day. Further, "John B. Kelly, Philadelphia County [Democratic] chairman, who was on the radio making a statewide broadcast, told his audience about the cold-blooded killing of patriotic Democrats by murderous Republicans, and [David] Lawrence repeated the story at intervals on the radio throughout election day."[141]

For many, this "ultimate in Republican persuasiveness," as the Scranton *Times* called it, symbolized the life and death class struggle in the election, as "machine gunners operating in the interests of 'Wee Willie' Schnader'" murdered their working class Democratic opponents at the behest of the Republican corporations.[142] As far as many Pennsylvania Democrats were concerned, "the Kelayres massacre was simply Republican politics carried to its logical conclusion: a monstrous attack on the New Deal at the grassroots level."[143]

The town of Kelayres swept out the Republicans in a 10-1 landslide. Democratic victories elsewhere weren't nearly so lop-sided, yet nevertheless the Democratic triumph was spectacular. Allegheny County, still dominated outside Pittsburgh by Republican administrations, nevertheless went for Earle by 75,000 votes, almost double Roosevelt's 1932 victory margin. Schnader came out of Philadelphia, which had been expected to give him a 100,000 vote lead, with a lead shaved to 20,000 votes. Even Bristol County, home of Republican State Committee boss Joseph Grundy, went Democratic. In a major upset, Earle beat Schnader statewide by more than 66,000 votes, with the final count being 1,476,467 to Schnader's 1,410,138.[144] He thus became Pennsylvania's first Democratic governor since Robert Pattison had been elected in 1890, and only the second since 1860.

In the U.S. Senate race, Joseph Guffey did even better, beating incumbent Republican David Reed by 128,000 votes, thereby becoming the first Democratic U.S. Senator from Pennsylvania since 1875.

While the entire top of the Democratic ticket swept into office, Democrats lower down the ticket did almost as well. The Democrats won all contested Pennsylvania-wide offices and captured a majority of the lower house of the General Assembly, 116 seats out of 206 contested seats. This gave the Democrats their first majority in the State House in half a century.

In addition, the Democrats, who had only three State Senate seats before the election, won sixteen of the twenty-five contested State Senate seats (although

Republicans retained a majority in the State Senate of thirty-one to nineteen). They also took twenty-three of the thirty-four U.S. Congressional seats, giving them the first Democratic majority in the state's Congressional delegation in the twentieth century. This was a dramatic change from the situation before the 1932 elections, in which Democrats held only three of thirty-six Pennsylvania Congressional seats.

In Allegheny County, every single Democratic State House and State Senate candidate triumphed. It was an astounding victory. "For the people of Pennsylvania," proclaimed David Lawrence, it was "a red letter day marking the emancipation of millions from the yoke of the Mellon-Grundy industrial and financial autocracy."[145]

Just as the 1934 elections had been a referendum on the New Deal in Pennsylvania, so they had been nationally, as well. And, just as in Pennsylvania, the New Deal had won.

Since the Civil War and Reconstruction, only three presidents have won off-year gains in Congress: Franklin D. Roosevelt in 1934, Bill Clinton in 1998, and George W. Bush in 2002. Of these, Roosevelt's was the largest. When he was elected in 1932, a year of general dissatisfaction with Republicans, he carried into office with him a gain of ninety seats in the House and thirteen in the Senate. One might have expected many of the freshmen Representatives to be vulnerable two years later. Such was not the case. Not only did all of the Democratic freshmen legislators of 1932 retain their seats, but nine more Democrats joined them in the House, and nine more Democrats were elected to the Senate.

But nowhere was Roosevelt's gains more remarkable than in Pennsylvania. While the national media had paid little attention to Pennsylvania before the election—the class politics of Democrat Upton Sinclair's End Poverty In California (EPIC) campaign for governor of California and Democrat Huey Long's "Share Our Wealth" rhetoric in Louisiana seemed much more dramatic that year—the startling and unexpected breath of Pennsylvania's Democratic victories finally captured their attention. *Newsweek* called the Republican defeat in Pennsylvania, "The biggest crash of all," while *The Literary Digest* declared that, "The rout of the Republicans in Pennsylvania, their citadel, will serve as a symbol of what occurred in most of the nation."[146]

And, just as the Democrats had made inroads that year into traditionally Republican strongholds such as Philadelphia and Pittsburgh's surrounding Allegheny County, so they had made progress among targeted constituencies which retained significant Republican sentiments. The Italian and black vote were cases in point. Although only 22.6 percent of the South Philadelphia Italian vote had gone Democratic in the 1932 presidential election, Earle captured a majority of this vote, 52.2 percent, in 1934.

Meanwhile, although a majority of Pittsburgh's black voters had remained Republican in the 1933 municipal election, this time the majority voted Democratic. They would remain majority Democratic ever after. While the particulars differ, the same trend was evident elsewhere in the nation. In 1934, the "traditionally Republican Negro vote shifted and elected a Democratic mayor and congressman" in Louisville. Even more dramatically, "In Chicago, Oscar De Priest fell before a Democratic Negro, Arthur W. Mitchell, who himself had been a Republican a few years back."[147]

Back in Pennsylvania, black voters sent Pennsylvania's first black to the State House of Representatives, Democrat Homer S. Brown, president of the Pittsburgh chapter of the NAACP. Brown would go on to serve a long tenure in the state legislature. His tenure would begin with a dramatic series of hearings in the State House (now controlled by the Democrats) on the refusal of the Pittsburgh Board of Education to hire black teachers. Things were beginning to change.

Meanwhile, 41 percent of black voters statewide—an estimated 170,000—went Democratic in the 1934 election. Although this was still a minority of Pennsylvania's black electorate, it was nevertheless higher than ever before. By 1936, a solid majority of the Pennsylvania black vote would be Democratic. Indeed, blacks would then be voting Democratic in larger percentages than the general electorate, as they have ever since.[148]

Thus, Pennsylvania's 1934 "New Deal referendum" election was a milestone in the transfer of black political loyalty statewide and the culmination of this transfer in Pittsburgh.[149] This transformation of the political loyalties of Pittsburgh's black electorate was not only enduring, but the process of switching loyalties burned itself into the minds of many black voters. Viola Dandridge, a resident of Pittsburgh's mainly black Brushton neighborhood and a voter in the 1930s, was typical of black Pittsburghers in this regard. When asked in 1990 which of the eighteen presidents whose terms she had lived through did the most for blacks, she quickly answered, "Franklin Roosevelt did more for black people than anyone before or after him."[150]

There remained, however, dark corners of the state which yet remained unchanged. In Pittsburgh, with the election of William McNair, the New Deal had only made a false start. In the steel towns surrounding Pittsburgh, where local Republican administrations allied to the steel corporations remained entrenched, a start was yet to be made. And, despite the width of Democratic victories, the 1934 elections had been close, with the Democrats winning approximately 51 percent to the Republicans' 49 percent of the vote.

Nevertheless, it was clear that a major part of the Pennsylvania electorate, more than ever composed of urban, black, ethnic, working class voters, wanted the New Deal and the class politics championed by the new Democratic Party. Thus, the Democratic victory was not so much a victory for Guffey or Lawrence or the almost unknown Earle. It was a victory for Roosevelt, the champion of the dispossessed, and "Roosevelt's party," which was coming to be identified with the aspirations of the newly mobilized black and ethnic working class.

Certainly, this was the opinion of the pundits and political leaders of the day, as they were virtually unanimous in agreeing that the election was won by the Democrats because of the great popularity of Roosevelt.[151] Indeed, George Earle echoed William McNair's comments of the year before when he joked with political reporter Joseph Alsop, "They say we rode in on Roosevelt's coattails. Hell, he carried us in piggy-back."[152]

****

Four days after the 1934 election, on November 9th, 20,000 workers and "Almost every state Democratic leader, from George Earle on down," attended a collective funeral for the five coal miners murdered by the Republicans in Kelayres. "An enormous motorcade escorted the five hearses (where possible, all abreast) . . . to the men's final resting places . . . This dramatic affair conveyed the solidarity of those murdered, *ethnically diverse but uniformly working-class,* even in death. It also portrayed them as clients of the New Deal, senselessly slaughtered by its reactionary enemies. Lest there be any doubt, Democratic politicians made their point verbally. George Earle announced that 'they died in the trenches of the New Deal.'"[153]

In Pennsylvania, class politics was class war.

Notes

1. E. P. Thompson, *The Making of the English Working Class,* Vintage Books: New York, 1963, 712.

2. John A. Fitch, *The Steel Workers,* The Russell Sage Foundation, 1910; The University of Pittsburgh Press: Pittsburgh, 1989, 229.

3. Fitch, *The Steel Workers,* 234-235.

4. Fitch, *The Steel Workers,* 235-236.

5. David Brody, *Steelworkers in America: The Nonunion Era,* Harvard University Press, 1960, 112-124.

6. *The Union Press,* No. 11.

7. Interview by Eric Leif Davin and Karen L. Steed, November 23, 1980.

8. The 1930 U.S. Census listed the population at 21,396, while the 1940 U.S. Census listed it at 20,661. Duquesne was thus the third largest community in Steeltown after McKeesport and Aliquippa.

9. Separate figures are not available, but the combined employment in 1937 at the four Allegheny County U.S. Steel facilities—Duquesne, Clairton, Homestead, and Braddock—was 22,981. See *Ninth Industrial Directory of the Commonwealth of Pennsylvania,* 1938. In 1940, 8,000 men were working in the Duquesne facility, which was comprised of six blast furnaces and 32 open hearths. See *The Bulletin Index,* September 19, 1940. "At one period during the Depression," said the *Index,* "when all six blast furnaces and 28 of the open hearths were shut down, a mere 4,000 men were employed."

10. Elmer Maloy Interview, United Steelworkers of America Papers, Historical Collections and Labor Archives, Pattee Library, Pennsylvania State University Libraries, 6, 8. Hereafter cited as USWA Papers.

11. Maloy Interview, USWA Papers, 32.

12. The 1930 U.S. Census placed Aliquippa's population at 27,116. The 1940 U.S. Census put the population at 27,021, making Aliquippa the second largest community in Steeltown after McKeesport. In 1937 there were 9,388 workers in Aliquippa's Jones & Laughlin Steel facility, making it the primary employer. See *Ninth Industrial Directory.*

13. According to *The Beaver Valley Labor History Journal,* Vol. 1, No. 2, June 1979, 6, Democratic registration in Aliquippa hovered between 50 and 100 throughout the Twenties.

14. Interview conducted by Eric Leif Davin and Karen L. Steed, November 23, 1980.

15. Julie A. Reddig, "Steel plant inspires trail of history," *The Pittsburgh Post-Gazette,* October 11, 2000; Craig Lambert, "Cantos and The Stem Christie," *Harvard Magazine,* January-February 1995, 59.

16. Lambert, "Cantos and the Stem Christie," 60.

17. Marguerite Young, "Ruffner Led Vigilante Committee," *The Union Press,* No. 10, October 20, 1937, 2.

18. All Muselin statements from Pete Muselin, "The Steel Fist in a Pennsylvania Company Town," in Bud Schultz and Ruth Schultz, *It Did Happen Here: Recollections of Political Repression in America,* Berkeley: University of California Press, 1989, 69, 70, 71.

19. Muselin, "The Steel Fist," 70.

20. Paul Kleppner, *Who Voted? The Dynamics of Electoral Turnout, 1870-1980,* Praeger Publishers: New York, 1982, 85, 97.

21. *The Pittsburgh Post-Gazette,* March 11, 1932, 1; March 14, 1932, 4.

22. Minutes of the Pittsburgh Central Labor Union, June 4, 18, and July 2, 1931, and March 17, 1932, in the holdings of the Pittsburgh Typographical Union, Lo. No. 7, Archives of Industrial Society, University of Pittsburgh. Hereafter, "Minutes of the PCLU."

23. Minutes of the PCLU, February 4, 1932.

24. *The Pittsburgh Post-Gazette,* March 28, 1932, 4.

25. Minutes of the PCLU, February 18, 1932.

26. Minutes of the PCLU, March 17, 1932.

27. Minutes of the PCLU, April 21, 1932.

28. Minutes of the PCLU, August 4, 1932. For background on the attempt of Philadelphia's Hosiery Workers to form a Labor Party at this time, see David J. Pivar, "The Hosiery Workers and the Philadelphia Third Party Impulse, 1929-1935," *Labor History,* No. 5, winter 1964, 18-28.

29. Minutes of the PCLU, August 4, 18, September 1, 1932.

30. Minutes of the PCLU, May 18, 1933.

31. Minutes of the PCLU, May 5, 19, June 16, 1932.

32. Minutes of the PCLU, September 1, 15, 1932. Suggestive of the close relations between organized labor and the Church, at the September 15 meeting a letter from Bishop Mann, head of the Pittsburgh Diocese, was read thanking the PCLU for participating in services at his church the Sunday evening preceding their huge Labor Day parade.

33. Minutes of the PCLU, June 2, May 19, 1932.

34. Joe Dallet, "The Steel Workers Fight for Unemployment Relief," *Labor Unity,* December 1932, 13. *Labor Unity* was the "official organ" of the TUUL.

35. Dallet, "The Steel Workers Fight," 14, 13.

36. Dallet, "The Steel Workers Fight," 13-15.

37. Dallet, "The Steel Workers Fight," 15.

38. Domenic Del Turco in John Bodnar, *Workers' World: Kinship, Community, and Protest in an Industrial Society, 1900-1940,* The Johns Hopkins University Press: Baltimore, 1982, 125, 126.

39. Stanley Brozek in Bodnar, *Workers' World,* 141, 142.

40. Orville Rice in Bodnar, *Workers' World,* 152.

41. Thomas Brown in Bodnar, *Workers' World,* 155, 156.

42. Matthew S. Magda, *Monessen: Industrial Boomtown and Steel Community, 1898-1980,* Pennsylvania Historical and Museum Commission: Harrisburg, 1985, 137.

43. Magda, *Monessen,* 109.

44. Magda, *Monessen,* 108-109.

45. Years later Cox returned to school and become the first Catholic priest to earn a Ph.D. from the University of Pittsburgh.

46. Of his thousands of radio speeches, 101 recordings survive, mostly from the 1940s, and are stored in the Archives of Industrial Society, University of Pittsburgh.

47. John Brophy, *A Miner's Life,* University of Wisconsin Press: Madison, 1964, 9, 100, 127, 223.

48. See Thomas H. Coode and John D. Petrarulo, "The Odyssey of Pittsburgh's Father Cox," *The Western Pennsylvania Historical Magazine,* Vol. 55, No. 3, July 1972, 219.

49. *The Pittsburgh Press,* January 21, 1931.

50. See Wilson Warren, "Behind the Radical Veil of an Unemployed Organization: An Examination of Working-Class Consciousness During the Great Depression," seminar paper, University of Pittsburgh, 4.

51. See Coode and Petrarulo, "The Odyssey of Pittsburgh's Father Cox," 220 ff.

52. *The Pittsburgh Press,* January 6, 1932.

53. *The New York Times,* January 17, 1932, quoted in Coode and Petrarulo, "The Odyssey of Pittsburgh's Father Cox," 224-225.

54. Minutes of the PCLU, February 4 and 18, 1932.

55. *The Pittsburgh Post-Gazette,* "Painting of Jobless Army Given to Father Cox," March 18, 1932, 4. This story contains a photo of the painting.

56. *The Pittsburgh Post-Gazette,* March 19, 1932.

57. Andrew J. Krupnick, Campaign Diary of Father James Cox, 1932, James Cox Papers, Historical Archives of the Diocese of Pittsburgh.

58. *The Pittsburgh Post-Gazette,* March 29, 1932, 13.

59. *The Pittsburgh Post-Gazette,* Letter to the Editor, March 15, 1932.

60. Bruce M. Stave, *The New Deal and the Last Hurrah: Pittsburgh Machine Politics,* University of Pittsburgh Press: Pittsburgh, 1970, 181.

61. Of the ten largest American cities in 1930—including Pittsburgh, New York, Chicago, Philadelphia, Detroit, Los Angeles, Cleveland, St. Louis, Baltimore, and Boston—only St. Louis and Baltimore had majority native white populations, and that by only 3.4 percent and 3.1 percent respectively. See table 5, 41, Stave, *The New Deal and the Last Hurrah.* By 1940, the Italian-born comprised 19 percent of the foreign-born population in Pittsburgh, making them the largest single ethnic group, a designation they also held in 1930. See "Vital Facts—Countries of Origin of Leading Foreign Born Groups in Pittsburgh," *The Federator,* 19, June 1944, 19-20. This, however, undercounts the Italian (and ethnic) population, as it ignores the second-generation children of the immigrants.

62. See Stave, *The New Deal and the Last Hurrah,* 36, 37. LaFollette's 36 percent of the vote in Pittsburgh more than doubled the 16 percent he received nationally, suggesting the saliency of class politics in Pittsburgh even before the New Deal era brought such politics to dominance.

63. Arthur M. Schlesinger, Jr., *The Politics of Upheaval,* Houghton Mifflin Co.: Boston, 1960, 335.

64. Michael P. Weber, *Don't Call Me Boss: David L. Lawrence, Pittsburgh's Rennaissance Mayor,* University of Pittsburgh Press: Pittsburgh, 1988, 50.

65. Following Roosevelt's visit, PCLU President Patrick Fagan gave "an interesting talk" to that body about "the tremendous crowds that turned out to greet Governor Roosevelt on the various routes taken by him while on his visit to speak at Forbes Field." See Minutes of the PCLU, October 20, 1932.

66. *The Pittsburgh Post-Gazette,* October 20, 1932.

67. *Pittsburgh Post-Gazette* November 9, 1932.

68. *Pittsburgh Post-Gazette* November 9, 1932.

69. And once in office, State Representatives John Kane and Thomas Gallagher also worked to bond labor and the Democratic Party tighter together. Typical of these efforts was Kane's invitation to state Federation of Labor President Phillips to meet with the Democratic Caucus of the state legislature to discuss joint work on issues of mutual interest. See Minutes of the PCLU, March 16, 1933.

Pittsburgh labor also viewed the work of Democrats at the national level as being in their best interests, particularly the soon-to-be passed National Industrial Recovery Act with its Section 7(a), endorsing labor's right to organize. At a June 1933, meeting of the PCLU, there was much discussion about the NIRA "and the benefits therein to labor. Several delegates . . . stated that labor should take advantage of this opportunity of organizing their men, as it is the best opportunity given us for many years." See Minutes of the PCLU, June 15, 1933.

70. Michael Goldfield, *The Color of Politics: Race and the Mainsprings of American Politics,* The New Press: New York, 1997, 179.

71. See Weber, *Don't Call Me Boss,* 49.

72. See Jim McKay, "Under its editor Courier grew to be nation's top black paper," *The Pittsburgh Post-Gazette,* February 6, 1995, B1.

73 . Joseph F. Guffey, *Seventy Years on the Red-Fire Wagon,* privately printed, 1952, 170.

74. Joseph Alsop and Robert Kintner, "The Guffey, Biography of a Boss, New Style," *The Saturday Evening Post,* March 26, 1938.

75. *The Pittsburgh Courier,* October 8, 1932.

76. Weber, *Don't Call Me Boss,* 54. FDR rewarded Vann by appointing him a special assistant U.S. Attorney in 1933, a position in which Vann served until 1936. He died of cancer on October 14, 1940, age 61. See Jim McKay, "Under its Editor, Courier Grew."

77. Irwin F. Greenberg, "Philadelphia Democrats Get a New Deal: The Election of 1933," *The Pennsylvania Magazine of History and Biography,* April 1973, 210.

78. Letter to the Editor from "A Disgusted Republican," *Pittsburgh Press,* August 31, 1933. Indeed, this shortly became the dominant campaign theme of Democrats both locally and on the other side of the state, where that year's Democratic candidates in the City of Brotherly Love also promised to "bring the New Deal to Philadelphia." See Greenberg, "Philadelphia Democrats Get a New Deal," 223.

79. *Pittsburgh Post-Gazette,* September 1, 1933.

80. *Pittsburgh Press,* August 31, 1933.

81. *Pittsburgh Sun-Telegraph,* August 25, 1933.

82. *Pittsburgh Post-Gazette,* September 6, 1933; *Pittsburgh Courier,* September 16, 1933.

83. *Pittsburgh Press,* September 22, 1933, editorial.

84. See Stave, *The New Deal and the Last Hurrah,* 72. New leadership also flooded into the Philadelphia Democratic Party and it is with this election that Jack Kelly, the father of actress Grace Kelly, emerged to become party leader in Philadelphia.

85. *The Pittsburgh Post-Gazette,* November 8, 1933. "Majority in Many Pittsburgh Areas is 20 to 1," said a sub-headline.

86. See Andrew Barr, *Drink: A Social History of America,* Carroll & Graf: New York, 1999.

87. Interview by Michael P. Weber, quoted in *Don't Call Me Boss,* 58-59.

88. Quoted in Weber, *Don't Call Me Boss,* 59.

89. *The New York Times,* November 5, 1933.

90. Gifford Pinchot to Franklin D. Roosevelt, September 5, 1933, Franklin D. Roosevelt Papers, Official File 175, Box 1, Franklin D. Roosevelt Library, Hyde Park, New York.

91. The Philadelphia Democratic Party was equally successful in wooing black voters away from the equally unresponsive Republican Party. There, Edward W. Henry, a magistrate and the city's only black elected official, as well as the city's only ward chairman as Republican leader of the the 30th Ward, defected to the Democrats. In the general election, Henry, running as a Democrat, received more votes than any other magistrate candidate. "In the voting divisions where blacks accounted for over 90 percent of the voters, Roosevelt had received only 26 percent of the votes in 1932. In 1933, these same voting divisions cast 45 percent of their votes for the Democratic candidate for treasurer." See Greenberg, "Philadelphia Democrats Get a New Deal," 228.

92. See unidentified newspaper clippings on Gallagher in the Gallagher File, Pennsylvania Division, Carnegie Library of Pittsburgh.

93. *The Pittsburgh Press,* October 26, 1933.

94. *The Pittsburgh Post-Gazette,* November 3, 1933.

95. See Greenberg, "Philadelphia Democrats Get a New Deal," footnote No. 38 on 222, 231.

96. The offices included all five of the nine City Council seats up for election. However, incumbent Republican Councillor P. J. McArdle was re-elected on both the Democratic and Republican tickets. In the new Council, he continued to vote with the four hold-over Republican Councillors, usually giving them a five-four majority.

97. *Pittsburgh Sun-Times,* October 23, 1933.

98. *The Pittsburgh Post-Gazette,* November 8, 1933. *The Pittsburgh Post-Gazette,* February 20, 1933.

99. Gold would serve as "burgess" (mayor) until 1942. He was replaced by another Democrat, Joseph Lescanac, who served until 1946. Lescanac was replaced by another Democrat, Italian Hugo Parente, who served until 1971. And so it went.

100. *The Pittsburgh Post-Gazette,* November 10, 1933.

101. Quoted in Sidney Lens, *The Labor Wars: From the Molly Maguires to the Sitdowns,* Anchor Press/ Doubleday: Garden City, New York, 1974, 188.

2. *The Pittsburgh Courier,* November 11, 18, 1933.

103. This gave a total electorate of 308,630, as compared to a 1929 electorate of 182,200. Additionally, there was a decline of only 38,549 in the Republican total. If we assume these Republicans defected to the Democrats, that means the Democrats still had to pick up 133,630 newly registered voters. If we look at Republican totals in the small steeltowns surrounding Pittsburgh, we find that there was virtually no decline in Republican registration at all. Thus, Democratic hegemony was won not through the conversion of Republican hearts and minds, but through a tremendous expansion of the political universe, all in the Democrats' favor.

104. *The Pittsburgh Sun-Telegraph,* September 5, 1934.

105. *The Pittsburgh Courier,* February 3, 1934.

106. *The Pittsburgh Sun-Telegraph,* January 30, 1934.

107. Kleppner, *Who Voted?* 98, 85, 105.

108. Kleppner, *Who Voted?* 102.

109. Kleppner, *Who Voted?* 101-102.

110. Kleppner, *Who Voted?* 109.

111. In 1933 a Republican-turned-Democrat had been elected mayor of Scranton, some county offices had been won by Democrats in Lackawanna County, and, despite an increased Democratic vote, only two Democrats had been elected to minor offices in Philadelphia.

112. *The Pennsylvania Manual,* 1935-1936, 420-421.

113. *The New York Times,* October 21, 1934, 24; *The Pittsburgh Press,* October 21, 1934, 10.

114. *The Philadelphia Inquirer,* May 16, 1934.

115. Paul Beers, *Pennsylvania Politics: Yesterday and Today,* Pennsylvania State University Press: University Park, Pa., 1980, 119; Bruce Bliven, Jr., "Pennsylvania Under Earle," *The New Republic,* August 18, 1937, 38.

116. Ray Sprigle, "Lord Guffey of Pennsylvania," *The American Mercury,* November 1936, 284.

117. After his tenure in state politics, Earle returned to the world of foreign diplomacy when Roosevelt appointed him ambassador to Turkey. While in that post, Roosevelt asked him to determine responsibility for the Katyn Forest Massacre of Polish Army officers. Earle concluded that the Soviets were the likely perpetrators. Roosevelt was unhappy with these findings, as they implicated a war-time ally. Earle persisted in his conclusion and Roosevelt retaliated by reassigning him as assistant head of the Somoan Defense Group in the South Pacific, far from Washington and reporters. This effectively ended his diplomatic career. See Laurence Rees, *World War II Behind Closed Doors,* Random House: New York, 2009.

118. See the York, Pennsylvania, *Gazette & Daily,* May 2, 1934 and the York *Dispatch,* May 14, 1934.

119. Edwin B. Bronner, "The New Deal Comes to Pennsylvania: The Gubernatorial Election of 1934," *Pennsylvania History,* Vol. 27, No. 1, January 1960, 52. Emphasis mine.

120. Richard C. Keller, "Pennsylvania's Little New Deal," *Pennsylvania History,* Vol. 29, No. 4, October 1962, 400.

121. The details of this arrangement come from an interview with James Law, Luzerne Democratic County Chairman, conducted by Michael P. Weber. See Weber, *Don't Call Me Boss*, 93.

122. *The Pittsburgh Press*, June 9, 1934.

123. Schlesinger, Jr., *The Politics of Upheaval*, 92.

124. Bronner, "The New Deal Comes to Pennsylvania," 55. Emphasis mine.

125. The Wilkes-Barre *Record*, October 26, 1934, 5; October 31, 1934, 13; the Scranton *Times*, September 4, 1934, 1.

126. *The Philadelphia Inquirer*, November 6, 1934, 6.

127. *The Pittsburgh Press*, October 21, 1934, 11.

128. Kermit McFarland in *The Pittsburgh Press*, October 2, 1934.

129. Charles J. Jacques, Jr., *Kennywood: Roller Coaster Capital of the World*, Vestal Press Ltd.: New York, 1982, 83, 86, 78. See painting by Kathleen Ferri, "Braddock and Penn Ave., Turtle Creek, PA," in collection of Westmoreland County Museum of Art, Greensburg, Pa..

130. The Philadelphia *Record*, November 5, 1934, 7. On Joseph Guffey, see Alsop and Kintner, "The Guffey, Biography of a Boss, New Style."

131. Chester Harris, *Tiger at the Bar: The Life Story of Charles J. Margiotti*, Vantage Press: New York, 1956, 324-325.

132. Harris, *Tiger at the Bar*, 326.

133. The Wilkes-Barre *Record*, October 5, 1934, 1.

134. The Reading, Pennsylvania, *Eagle*, October 23, 1934, 2; October 30, 1934, 1.

135. *The Pittsburgh Press*, November 9, 1934, 22.

136. John Cerullo and Gennaro Delena, "The Kelayres Massacre," *The Pennsylvania Magazine of History and Biography*, Vol. 107, No. 3, July 1983, 332.

137. *Report of the Anthracite Coal Industry Commission*, Murelle Printing Co.: Harrisburg, Pa., 1938, 67; "The Employment Situation in the Pennsylvania Anthracite Region," Works Progress Administration, Washington, D.C., 1935, A-1 to A-6.

138. The Philadelphia *Record*, September 1, 1934, 1.

139. *The New York Times*, November 6, 1934, 1.

140. Cerullo and Delena, "The Kelayres Massacre," 334.

141. Interviews with Kelly and Lawrence by Edwin B. Bronner, in Bronner, 64.

142. The Scranton *Times*, November 6, 1934, 6.

143. Cerullo and Delena, "The Kelayres Massacre," 337.

144. *The Pennsylvania Manual*, 1935-1936, 422.

145. *The Pittsburgh Press*, November 7, 1934.

146. *Newsweek*, November 17, 1934, 9; *The Literary Digest*, November 17, 1934, 5.

147. Schlesinger, Jr., *The Politics of Upheaval*, 436.

148. See Ruth Louise Simmons, "The Negro in Recent Pittsburgh Politics," unpublished M.A. thesis, University of Pittsburgh, 1945, 16-18; and James E. Miller, "The Negro in Pennsylvania Politics, with Special Reference to Philadelphia, Since 1932," unpublished Ph.D. dissertation, University of Pennsylvania, 1945, 228, 234.

149. Richard Keller, *Pennsylvania's Little New Deal*, Garland Publications: New York, 1982, 154.

150. Patrick Evans, "Black in the Old Days," *In Pittsburgh,* January 31-February 6, 1990.

151. These leaders included David Lawrence, George Earle, John B. Kelly (Chairman of the Philadelphia Democratic Committee), and many others interviewed by Edwin B. Bronner. Losing Republican Schnader was alone in denying the election was a referendum on the New Deal. See Bronner's footnote No. 114.

152. Joseph Alsop and Robert Kintner, "The Guffey, The Capture of Pennsylvania," *The Saturday Evening Post,* April 16, 1938, 16.

153. Cerullo and Delena, "The Kelayres Massacre," 337. Emphasis added.

Chapter 8

The Workers' Real Deal, 1935-1937

Increasingly in the mid-1930s, the northern wing of the Democratic Party—an uneasy multi-class, multi-ethnic, multi-racial coalition of sometimes competing interests—came to fill the space on the political spectrum, particularly at the state and local level in the heavily industrial Northeast, which would have been filled by a "true" labor party or a social democratic party in a parliamentary system.[1]

Part of the reason for this is that the Democratic Party came to espouse a new, more tolerant ideology, which made it receptive to previously excluded ethnic and black citizens. In addition, powerful gravitational forces, from President Roosevelt to the top leadership of many major unions, worked to pull America's increasingly class conscious working class into the Democratic Party.

Typical of Roosevelt's stated goals which must have resonated with the working class were those voiced in his January 1935 address to that year's first Congressional session. The New Deal had not yet "weeded out the overprivileged" or "effectively lifted up the underprivileged," he mourned, but nevertheless it was pledged to fight against those of great wealth, who had both "undue private power over private affairs and, to our misfortune, over public affairs, as well."[2]

The legislation which soon followed was in some ways more important for "the underprivileged" than the legislative whirlwind of the "First Hundred Days" in 1933. The watershed legislation of 1935 was made possible by a large enough liberal majority in Congress in the wake of the astoundingly successful 1934 mid-term elections that it could pass progressive legislation without the need of conservative Southern Democratic votes.

In quick secession the Democratic administration passed the Social Security Act, the Wagner Act guaranteeing labor's right to organize and bargain collectively, and the Wealth Tax Act, which increased income and inheritance taxes on private wealth, coupled with a graduated tax on corporations to replace their former flat rate taxes. These were features of the New Deal's "radical reform" which served to reinforce working class belief that their faith in the Democratic Party as "their party" was not misplaced.

Perhaps nowhere was this more dramatically evident than in Pennsylvania, the most Republican state in the nation. Especially in Pittsburgh and the rest of Western Pennsylvania, the Democratic Party—long a fellow victim of the dominant, corporation-oriented, Republican regime—seemed a natural political home for a newly aroused working class battling a common enemy.

And it is perhaps also in Western Pennsylvania that we see the most radical manifestations of the "Workers' Real Deal." Western Pennsylvania shows us just how far the New Deal could possibly have gone, because its radical reform agenda was shaped by the hopes and aspirations of working class voters like those in the Steel Valley.

In like manner, Western Pennsylvania also shows us the limits beyond which the New Deal's radical reform agenda could not have gone. Workers in the Steel Valley did not get a "revolution" in the Marxist sense—but, then, they never wanted one.

However, Steel Valley workers did get a "Real Deal"—which was exactly what they wanted.

Ripping the Mayor

The 1934 gubernatorial election had shown what a congenial home the Democratic Party could be for organized labor at the state level. In Pittsburgh, that marriage was still in the process of evolving. It was hampered, however, because the antagonism of Mayor William McNair kept a local labor-oriented "New Deal" from taking root in the city after the 1933 Democratic municipal triumph. Thus, the first time organized labor clearly emerged as the decisive element within the new Democratic Party locally was in the 1935 campaign to capture the elected offices of the surrounding Allegheny County.

In the meantime, although Democrats won every municipal office up for election in 1933, because of staggered terms the Republicans still controlled the nine-member City Council by five to four (and therefore also held the powerful post of President of the City Council). It would thus take more municipal elections before Pittsburgh's version of the New Deal would be able to sweep the last vestige of Republicanism from office.

In the interim, though, the intransigent office holder who most had to be swept out was the very man who had seemed to herald the changing of the guard, Democratic Mayor William McNair. Now that Democrat George Earle was the new governor, and with Democrats controlling the State House, Democrats had the potential power in the state legislature and in the Governor's mansion to "rip" any local office holder from office through the introduction of what was known as a "ripper" bill. Indeed, a Pittsburgh mayor had been removed from office in 1902 by just such means, as well as lesser officials in the 1920s. The vacancy thus created would then be filled directly by the governor through appointment.

Impeachment was also a possibility, but this had a severe drawback. If the mayor were to be impeached and removed from office in that manner, the vacancy would then be filled by the President of the City Council, in this case long-time Republican Councillor Robert Garland.[3] Impeachment would thus replace one Republican-in-all-but-name with a real Republican. If the Democrats were to quickly gain control over City Hall, therefore, William McNair had to be ripped from office.

To some, it looked as if representative government was being violated as long as McNair stayed, as he increasingly seemed to represent all that the electorate had repudiated in the 1933 election. "There is nothing in City Hall but the old Republicans who were here before we were elected," declared John Huston, a newly-elected Democratic City Councillor. "Let McNair go back to Jimmy Coyne [Chairman of the Pittsburgh Republican Party] and the Republicans. That's where he belongs."[4] McNair only strengthened this impression when he later ordered all municipal employees to change their party registration from Democratic to Republican.[5]

If, for instance, Pittsburgh's New Deal was meant to usher in an administration which was more pro-labor than the Republicans had been, that was not what Mayor McNair was delivering. Indeed, he made clear his anti-labor attitudes by denouncing the 1934 San Francisco General Strike as a civil war and called upon workers to abandon their unions rather than engage in such activity.[6]

He also failed to provide local labor with the support it had anticipated. Shortly after the 1933 election, the Pittsburgh Central Labor Union (PCLU) passed a resolution requesting Mayor-Elect McNair "to recognize Organized Labor when making his appointments for the different [municipal] departments."[7] Not only did McNair ignore this request, he proceeded to staff his administration with anti-labor Republicans.

Further, however, McNair did nothing to restrain on-going anti-strike activities by the Pittsburgh Police Department. In September 1934, PCLU delegates from the Teamsters Union requested that the PCLU protest the practice of police riding in trucks and protecting strike breakers at the Swift & Co. and the St. Louis Packing Co., where the Teamsters were conducting strikes.[8] The PCLU complied with this request, but the practice continued, resulting in an October City Council meeting called by the Democratic members on "strikes, picketing, free speech, and free assemblage" and packed by the PCLU.[9]

Nothing changed, however, and that December the PCLU sent a "strong resolution of protest" to McNair for the assistance McNair was giving to strike breakers at the Teamster-struck P. H. Butler Co.[10]

By February 1935, the rupture between McNair and the Pittsburgh labor movement was irreparable. On February 21st the PCLU unanimously passed an angry resolution calling for the ouster of Mayor William McNair from office and sent copies to McNair, the newspapers, and every member of the Pennsylvania

House and Senate.

The resolution stated that McNair had "insulted the intelligence of representatives of organized labor" when the PCLU went to meet with him, had "not lost an opportunity to harass, heckle and embarrass" the Democratic members of the City Council, and, worst of all, since becoming Mayor he had "openly aided and abetted strike-breakers hired to break the ranks of organized workers." Therefore, the PCLU endorsed "any method that may be used to remove the said William N. McNair from the office of Mayor of Pittsburgh as soon as possible."[11]

Thus, it was no surprise that, when the Committee on Cities of the now Democratic-dominated State House of Representatives actually did begin hearings on a ripper bill, one of the angriest witnesses to testify against the mayor was Patrick Fagan, President of the Pittsburgh Central Labor Union (as well as President of Western Pennsylvania's District 5 of the United Mine Workers).[12] McNair then further alienated organized labor by attacking its idol, Franklin D. Roosevelt, as being the mastermind behind the ripper maneuvering.[13]

McNair also alienated the ethnic and black constituencies which had elected him. For example, although both the Italian and black voting blocs had been assiduously wooed during McNair's mayoralty campaign, he now shut them out from what they felt was their just due of city jobs. This was particularly galling to the black community at a time when they suffered a 60 percent unemployment rate.[14]

Even worse, in the view of the increasingly class conscious electorate, McNair and his Director of Public Workers, Leslie M. Johnston, former head of the "good government" Citizens' League and "the banker's plant in the McNair Administration," kept Pittsburgh from participating fully in both state and federal work relief programs.[15] McNair repeatedly vetoed City Council votes to participate in or supplement federal relief programs and attacked the Works Progress Administration (WPA)—which had allocated 57,000 jobs and $47 million for Allegheny County—as a "wholesale bribery of the electorate."[16] Indeed, because of McNair's opposition, Allegheny County had the lowest WPA placement rate of any Pennsylvania county and the Democratic organization had no access to the 3,500 government patronage positions and relief-funded jobs on county bridges, roads, and parks.[17]

Given this rising cry by Democratic constituents to oust McNair, Democratic Party head David Lawrence finally moved. Following his election, Governor Earle immediately chose Lawrence as Secretary of the Commonwealth, his chief cabinet official. As such, Lawrence became the primary architect of Pennsylvania's Little New Deal, with the politically inexperienced Earle serving essentially as public figurehead and cheerleader.

Additionally, with Joe Guffey moving on to Washington as Pennsylvania's new Democratic U.S. Senator, Lawrence also inherited his position as head of the Democratic Party in Pennsylvania. Lawrence also retained his local leadership of the Pittsburgh Democratic Party. These combined positions made him the single most powerful Democrat in the state.

In mid-February 1935, Lawrence chaired a caucus of the Democratic House members to consider a ripper bill aimed at McNair. There was overwhelming support among the Democratic Representatives, with twenty-four of the twenty-five Allegheny County representatives supporting the bill.[18] On March 6, with only two Democrats opposed, the State House voted to rip out Mayor McNair and replace him with an interim city commissioner to be appointed by Governor Earle.[19]

Despite passage of the ripper bill by the State House, the Republican-controlled State Senate was another matter. Here, McNair's fate was determined by Republican State Senator James J. Coyne, who also headed the Allegheny County Republican Party. Coyne sat on the Senate Committee on Municipal Government, which had jurisdiction over the bill, thus determining whether it would be reported out of committee to the full senate for action. Despite intense lobbying from Governor Earle, his cabinet, and Lawrence, the Senate Committee on Municipal Government, dominated twelve to five by Republicans and led by Coyne, voted not to report the bill out of committee.

And so the ripper bill died in the Republican-dominated committee, leaving William McNair in control of Pittsburgh's City Hall. More than ever, McNair seemed to be allied with the very Republican machine Pittsburgh's voters had sought to overthrow in the 1933 municipal election.

The Capture of the County

But, with upcoming elections for county government, attention quickly turned to the Allegheny County Commissioners' race. County government in Pennsylvania has far more power and financial responsibilities than in many states. Further, Allegheny County government was run by three partisanly elected and all-powerful Commissioners. Of these, only two could be elected from either major party, thus guaranteeing minority representation to the other party.

The incumbent Allegheny County Commissioners in 1935, however, were actually three Republicans, reflecting the overwhelming dominance of the party at the time of the last county election in 1931. These included former State Senator William Mansfield and long-time incumbent Charles C. McGovern, both of whom had been elected as the official Republican candidates, along with Republican Caldwalder Barr, who had won the third seat as a titular independent, defeating David Lawrence, the Democratic champion in 1931.

Frustrated in its relations with the mayor, organized labor turned to the other powerful—indeed, perhaps more powerful—office in the region, that of Allegheny County Commissioner. At its July 18, 1935 meeting, "By unanimous rising vote, the secretary [of the PCLU] was instructed to draft a resolution requesting Brother John J. Kane to be Organized Labor's candidate for County Commissioner of Allegheny County. The name of every delegate to the Central Labor Union was ordered affixed to the resolution." The PCLU then invited all members to West View Park on July 30 for a rally honoring Kane, at which President Patrick Fagan, "labor judge" Michael Musmanno, and others would speak.[20]

John J. Kane was greatly popular in Pittsburgh's labor movement and had impressive credentials. He was a member of the Pittsburgh Central Labor Union Executive Board and the former president and current Business Representative of Pittsburgh Local 9 of the International Printing Pressmen and Assistants Union of North America. In 1932 he had been elected, with PCLU endorsement, a State Representative and had used his position in Harrisburg, the state capital, to cement relations between the Pennsylvania Federation of Labor and the Democratic Party. In 1933 the PCLU endorsed him in his successful run for the Pittsburgh City Council, where he became the leading advocate of participation in federal relief programs on the Council, a role which put him in constant conflict with Mayor McNair.

When John J. Kane spoke, organized labor listened. It was Kane, for instance, who was the original advocate, in 1931, of reviving the celebration of Labor Day in Pittsburgh. It was also Kane who had suggested inviting Father Cox to address the Central Labor Union after the latter's return from his jobless march on Washington in 1932.[21] Labor was beginning to have many champions in Pittsburgh—but none stood above Kane in respect. Indicative of the increasing influence of organized labor in both the region and the party, the Democratic organization promptly endorsed Kane and State Senator George Rankin, Jr. (also endorsed by the PCLU), as its two Commissioner candidates for 1935.

The other major candidate in the Democratic primary for County Commissioner was Mayor McNair. In 1934, he'd run for the Democratic gubernatorial nomination, only to be bested by Earle. Perhaps he felt that, if he couldn't run the state, at least he could run a county.

McNair's decision to run for County Commissioner threw into high relief the very question of relief and class politics, as McNair had become the bulwark of the Republican status quo ante. Kane angrily attacked McNair for attempting to "starve the needy and the jobless" while obtaining the "aid and comfort of those reactionary Tories who would like to see the unemployed starve."[22]

Meanwhile, in the Republican primary for County Commissioner, McNair endorsed the county's Republican Party boss and State Senator James J. Coyne, the man who had saved him by blocking the ripper bill in the State Senate. In their primary, Coyne and incumbent Republican Commissioner Charles C. McGovern won their primaries easily. Not surprisingly, given the new political constituencies which now dominated the Democratic Party, McNair lost overwhelmingly to Kane.

McNair then cemented his alliance with the Republicans by renewing his endorsement of James Coyne for the November general election and attempting to rally the municipal employees under his control for the Republican leader. Part of this effort was a letter entitled "Rip the Rippers!" from an "Employees Committee" mailed to all 6,000 city workers urging them to "back the Mayor wholeheartedly in his stand against our common enemy," the Democratic Party.[23]

Not surprisingly, this effort failed, with the Democratic candidates swamping Coyne and the Republicans that November, with Kane being the number one vote getter in the county. Henceforth, for the next sixty years, into the 1990s,

Democrats would control Allegheny County government. But the man who would immediately control the county payroll and relief efforts would be City Councillor John J. Kane, President of the Printing Pressmen's Union.

As an added bonus, the Democrats picked up more seats on the Pittsburgh City Council, finally giving them a majority. One of the new City Councillors was Thomas J. Gallagher, leader of the Flint Glass Workers, who had previously been elected State Representative along with Kane.

And, for the first time, the Hill District's Ward Three, one of the two main black wards in the city, voted Democratic. Although registered Republicans still outnumbered Democrats in Ward Three, this Democratic victory nevertheless indicated that the process of Democratic realignment at the grassroots level was continuing, as targeted constituencies returned increasing votes for the Democrats.[24]

The labor movement was ecstatic over Kane's victory. Immediately following the election, the Pittsburgh Allied Printing Trades Council called upon the PCLU to organize a testimonial dinner in honor of "our worthy and esteemed friend—Labor's drafted candidate—John J. Kane."

The PCLU happily complied, scheduling the dinner for December 28 at the Downtown William Penn Hotel, one of the most prestigious hotels in the city. "While the space is large," the PCLU noted, "the demand for reservations for their testimonial to Organized Labor's champion in Allegheny County will permit the admission of only those who apply first." Speakers honoring Kane included U.S. Senator Joseph Guffey, Lieutenant Governor Thomas Kennedy, and Pennsylvania Federation of Labor President John A. Phillips. "A rousing reception by Organized Labor to the outstandingly successful candidate from the ranks of Organized Labor is assured."[25]

From an electoral point of view, the capture of Allegheny County government was crucial to the further consolidation of both the Democratic Party and the electoral influence of ordinary workers. Control of county government went far in guaranteeing electoral democracy throughout the county, because the county government was (and is) responsible for conducting and supervising every election in the more than 100 municipalities in the county, including Pittsburgh city elections.

It was (and is) also responsible for registering voters in every Steel Valley municipality, except in Pittsburgh itself. From now on, voter registration in steel towns like Homestead, Clairton, Duquesne, Braddock, and McKeesport would be controlled by labor-oriented Democratic county officials.

And, on election day, it would be labor-oriented Democratic county workers who would be responsible for staffing the polls and counting the ballots everywhere in the Steel Valley. Phantom Republican voters and stolen ballot boxes, long a tradition in Allegheny County elections, became a thing of the past. Not only could steelworkers in towns up and down the Steel Valley now find a friendly face when they came to register to vote—they could be assured that their votes would actually be counted.

The primary election of 1931 was typical of past elections. In that election,

Governor Gifford Pinchot had sent State Police to guard the polls in Pittsburgh, Homestead, Braddock, McKees Rocks, "and other places where the police are under the domination of one of the opposing political factions."[26]

Nevertheless, that election was marked by "Political terrorism and intimidation, kidnappings, shootings and sluggings, arrests and reprisals. Disorders were widespread over the city and county as rival political factions fought with fists, clubs, and guns. Scores were arrested, including an Oakland magistrate, fifteen deputy sheriffs, other peace officers, and members of election boards. Voters were intimidated and the work of election boards interfered with as police answered alarm after alarm. One board sought shelter in the sheriff's office, where the count was completed. Disorders continued from early morning until early [the next day] when riot calls still were pouring into police stations."[27]

The election was a litany of horrors. The Homestead Fire Chief was kidnapped during "spirited clashes among deputy sheriffs, election workers, and borough police and was found later in the Hazelwood police station." The entire election board of one Homestead precinct was arrested for violating election laws, while three members of the election board in another Homestead precinct were arrested on charges of intimidating voters. A Homestead police lieutenant was charged with intimidating voters in yet another precinct.

The entire election board of precinct 15 in the Hill District's Ward 5 was arrested for the intimidation of voters. The election board of Pittsburgh's precinct 9, Ward 9, was rounded up and brought into court and ordered to honor the certificates of watchers and overseers. There was a police kidnapping and police beatings in Pittsburgh's Ward 25. In East Liberty a constable candidate and eight of his supporters were arrested for "riding through East Liberty creating a disturbance." There were arrests for fighting at another Pittsburgh poll in the Mt. Washington neighborhood. There was rioting in Duquesne and a constable candidate was arrested for firing his gun during the melee. The aid of forty State Troopers was requested in sections of Allegheny County where conditions were "entirely out of control." They were also badly needed in Wilmerding and other areas. At the Bedford School at S. 10th Street and Bingham Street in Pittsburgh's South Side Ward 17, two armed men entered the poll after it closed and made off with ballots which were being counted.[28]

In McKees Rocks, which in 1931 was still run by Republican boss Miles Bryan just as ruthlessly as he had run the town since 1891, the home of an opposition candidate was bombed. Gangs of Bryan henchmen terrorized voters by parading through the town, intimidating one and all. They entered one poll and drove the watchers away. The constable who led the thugs told the watchers, "Go home. We'll count the ballots to suit ourselves. The old man [Bryan] is waiting."[29]

On the day before the election, the courts had stricken 7,500 "phantom" voters from the rolls as non-existent voters. Two hours before the polls closed, however, the order came over the police radio that, "All radio cars are to go to every election district and notify the boards that any person stricken from the rolls by the board is permitted to vote." The order overruling the courts came directly from the Pittsburgh Police Superintendent. Thousands of illegitimate Republican voters flooded into the polls to vote at the last minute. No wonder David Lawrence lost that election for County Commissioner![30]

But what a difference Democratic control of the county's election machinery made. In the election of November 1936, the first general election to be supervised by the new Democratic Commissioners elected in 1935, it was reported that, "Judges, sitting in Common Pleas and Criminal Courts with the grand jury nearby to investigate cases of election law violations, found their task less formidable than in any previous election year. There were few attempts to tamper with the vote. Common Pleas Court adjourned less than an hour after the polls closed. With state troopers, deputy sheriffs, county police, and an unnumbered army of watchers, overseers, and other election officials swarming through the county, election violence and fraud apparently was at a new low in the most important election in decades."[31]

Once in office, John J. Kane immediately staffed county offices with loyal party members. These included not only Italians, blacks, and good union men, but also members of another element just coming into visibility as a separate Democratic constituency: women.

Just as women, as a separately identified group, were beginning to be mobilized into the new Democratic coalition at the national level by Eleanor Roosevelt, Frances Perkins, and their women's club allies, so was this happening at the local level in Pittsburgh. The local Democratic Party had an on-going Women's Democratic Club led by Mrs. J. Wood Clark, which worked to mobilize women voters and sponsored regular lectures by noted politicians, such as Progressive Montana U.S. Senator Burton Wheeler.[32] Kane rewarded many of these female Democrats with county jobs.

Typical of the new employees—and "a study in the contrasts that forged their party, their nation"[33]—were two teenage girls who were already active in the party as members of the Young Democrats. Rita Wilson was an Irish Catholic who had just graduated from South Catholic High School. Placed next to her in the county tax office to run an addressograph was Sophie Friedman, a Romanian Jew who had just graduated from Fifth Avenue High School in Pittsburgh's Soho District, which was home to a significant Jewish population.

Rita Wilson eventually left her job when she married Kane's son, John J. Kane, Jr., but stayed in close touch with her new-found friend, who moved on to become receptionist for Commissioner Kane and then a clerk in the Court of Common Pleas. Both became early members of the Pennsylvania Federation of Democratic Women, where they took turns in various top posts. "I remember once," Rita recalled, "Sophie and I went to Penn Hills [a wealthy Pittsburgh suburb] to organize a Democratic women's group, and there were [only] eight women in the group. It was horrible!"[34] In 1960, with Sophie's help, Rita Wilson Kane won the office of Allegheny County Register of Wills, a position she retained until she retired in 1992.

Sophie Friedman married Jack Masloff, who did not have the political lineage of Rita's husband, but she eventually rose further in the ranks of the local Democratic Party. She became Chief Clerk of the Court of Common Pleas. Then, in 1976, with Rita's help, Allegheny County Democratic Committee members rewarded her for forty years of loyal service to the party by nominating her to fill the Pittsburgh City Council seat vacated by another labor union woman, Amy Ballinger, who was retiring after six years on the Pittsburgh City Council.

With the party's backing, she won the special election for that seat and went on to win re-election to the Council in 1977, 1981, and 1985. Following the 1985 election, her colleagues made her President of the City Council. Thus, on May 6, 1988, after Mayor Richard Caliguiri died in office, Sophie Masloff, a Jewish grandmother from Squirrel Hill, succeeded to the mayor's office, thus becoming the first female mayor of Pittsburgh, an office she held until 1994.

Meanwhile, John J. Kane, "Labor's drafted candidate," and fellow Democratic Commissioner George Rankin used their new power to implement other aspirations of their constituency. And they had a lot of power to do so. In a report to their constituency published almost a dozen years later, Kane and Rankin highlighted what it meant to run Allegheny County.[35]

The 745-square-mile county, they said, had a 1947 population of one and a half million people, a larger (in some cases much larger) population than fifteen states, including Maine, New Hampshire, Vermont, Rhode Island, Delaware, Colorado, Wyoming, South Dakota, North Dakota, Montana, Idaho, Oregon, Nevada, Arizona, and New Mexico.

As what they termed "the real center of industrial America" Allegheny County had "more than 2,600 manufacturing establishments, of which 20 are the world's largest in their fields. In Allegheny County are the home offices and (in most cases) plants of such nationally known companies as Carnegie-Illinois Steel [U.S. Steel], Mesta Machine, Westinghouse Electric and Manufacturing, Aluminum Company of America [ALCOA], Gulf Oil, H. J. Heinz, Rockwell Manufacturing, Koppers, Jones and Laughlin Steel, Pittsburgh Consolidation Coal Co., Standard Sanitary and Manufacturing, Pittsburgh Plate Glass [PPG], and others."

In addition, the county was the world's largest manufacturer of forged steel sheets, air brakes, plate glass, steel rolls, window glass, safety equipment, plumbing fixtures, and rolling-mill machinery. It had the world's largest tinplate mill, by-product coke plant, food products company, independent wire manufacturing plant, radium and vanadium reduction plants, manufacturing company of lifting forks, and operating unit in the steel industry, as well as the world's second-largest electrical equipment company and independent steel company.

The county also contained America's largest stainless steel company and independent oil company, and was America's largest commercial coal producer, bituminous coal producer, primary aluminum producer, and largest manufacturer of nuts, bolts, rivets, and wrought-iron pipes. Not surprisingly, in 1940 35 percent of the county's labor force was employed in manufacturing, as compared to 24 percent of the nation's labor force as a whole.[36]

In addition to overseeing all elections in the county, the Commissioners were also responsible for assessing and levying county taxes, appropriating county funds, initiating and building roads and highways, building bridges, maintaining a large system of parks (the largest of which were 2,260 acre North Park and the

1,985 acre South Park), and building and running all airports in the county. The two largest of these were the Allegheny County Airport and the Greater Pittsburgh Airport, for which the county purchased 1,458 acres in 1941.

The county also had its own police force and ran a county jail, a nursing home, and, eventually, the John J. Kane Hospital to provide medical care for those unable to afford other hospitals or who (as time went by) relied on medical assistance for payment.[37]

The county also dispersed money to other agencies as it saw fit. In 1947, for instance, it appropriated $15,000 to the Carnegie Free [Public] Library of Pittsburgh, resuming a practice of county aid to the library which had been abandoned in 1932, as the Depression intensified.

Finally, the county was responsible for coordinating all sewage projects among the county's 100+ municipalities and had the authority to control smoke from all sources, including the railroads, and "empowered to require general compliance, without exception."[38]

As Kane and Rankin saw it, their primary responsibilities were "the construction and operation of public works," because "we must not lose sight of the fact that people are now inclined to expect more and more services from their government."[39]

Above all, they felt, "the average man wants to know, 'What security can I expect for myself and my family?'" Because "Our average citizen now considers himself an active participant in community movements, community action based on community planning [guaranteed that] the prospects of the average family are better than average in Allegheny County."[40]

The Democratic Commissioners provided these services and security through, initially, a ten-year plan of strategic economic development, such as the construction of a network of highways throughout the county, "thereby facilitating the accessibility for many industries to locate at points in the County that were never previously considered as industrial sites. As an added complement to these new industrial sites, modern residential districts would spring up."[41]

Ironically, the construction of these new highways and industrial and residential districts would contribute to the suburbanization of the county which, in turn, would help lead to the economic and political decline of the very Steel Valley municipalities upon which the Democratic commissioners based their power.

The commissioners also launched a "selective program of industrial development" designed to encourage a diversified regional economy. This would help "secure the maximum employment of the available labor supply and reduce seasonal and cyclical payroll fluctuations to a minimum. We can have a stable labor supply, increased population, increased production, and increased capacity to consume."[42]

However, these changes were not to come at the expense of the "average guy." "First of all," they said, "we do not believe that taxation drives industry out of any prosperous area, other factors being favorable." Therefore, they advocated a reduction of the county real estate taxes, because, "Taxes on the homes of workers and other modest real estate owners should never be called upon to finance some of the governmental functions to which they are at present applied. [Thus,] the Commissioners have sought during the past 11 years to relieve real estate taxpayers as much as possible."

In place of these taxes, the Commissioners favored taxation on "other forms of wealth," such as "capital stock, bank shares, and corporate loans."[43] These were to be the sources of revenue that were to provide the funds for the ambitious program of infrastructure improvements the Commissioners were soon to launch.

Another major area of economic development which the Commissioners made sure did not come at the expense of the "workers" was bridge building. Three major rivers—the Ohio, Allegheny, and Monongahela—trisected the county and the huge network of highways the Commissioners envisioned also demanded a huge program of bridge building. "In 1936, when first taking office," Kane and Rankin wrote, "the Commissioners were confronted with the problem of developing a continuing, long-range program of public works [so] a program was set up for the improvement of the County's physical plant, with construction of roads, bridges, highways, tunnels, airport improvements and additions, and other phases of modern works development.

"At the time we took office, however, there existed a body known as the Allegheny County Authority, which had been authorized by the Legislature in 1933 and incorporated January 2, 1934. The Authority had plans to construct improvements and defray the cost by levying tolls on the users of these needed improvements. We were not in sympathy with the idea. We felt that tolls would represent a form of double taxation for the residents of certain areas of the County. For example, plans for four major bridges would have made them toll bridges. These were the Homestead High Level Bridge [connecting Homestead with Pittsburgh across the Monongahela], the Highland Park High Level Bridge [connecting Pittsburgh with the north across the Allegheny], the Jerome Street Bridge into McKeesport, all built and in use, and the Rankin Bridge [for the towns of Rankin and Braddock] which is soon to be under construction. And agreements had been concluded with the [Republican administration of the] City of McKeesport under which the Third Avenue Bridge would have been torn down, thus forcing use of the proposed toll bridge by many [Monongahela River] residents of Glassport, Port Vue, and Dravosburg, as well as the residents of McKeesport themselves.

"Since we felt the program could be accomplished and facilities furnished on a more equitable basis, we abolished the Authority and adopted a policy of 'toll-free' improvements. To be exact, the plan was adopted in November 1936," and was the philosophy which, over the years, guided all further county development projects under Kane and Rankin.[44]

Finally, as the county-wide government, Kane and Rankin had been given much authority to control smoke pollution in Allegheny County due to the Anti-Pollution Act of 1937 passed by Governor Earle's Little New Deal in Harrisburg. "From time to time in promoting the general welfare of our citizens," the duo wrote, "and to assure them a healthier and more beneficial life, it is necessary for business to suffer inconveniences. For example, we in Allegheny County are on the threshold of a smokeless era. In abating this unhealthy and dirty condition it is necessary for all of us to suffer the inconveniences and the cost of making such a program effective. Smoke control for Allegheny County is no different from any other modern improvement for the welfare of the people," and polluting businesses must be forced to comply with new regulations designed to bring about a "purified atmosphere."[45]

Because of all these developments, Kane and Rankin concluded, the future looked almost utopian. "It is our belief that the people of the County of Allegheny enjoy unlimited opportunity to attain the security and prosperity so ardently desired by every family. We now have radar, rocket bombs, rocket ships, atomic energy, penicillin, blood plasma, and scores of other accomplishments which a few years ago would have been scoffed at as some of the fantasy of Jules Verne or the Buck Rogers comic strip. It seems quite reasonable, then, to expect that we can actually clean the air we breathe, rid our streams of pollution, and rearrange our physical set-up in more happy conformance with modern invention and progress.

"More persons in the County of Allegheny are looking to the future with justified optimism. But, more importantly, the so-called 'little people,' the average man and woman, are considering their home location with faith and a sound conviction that they can expect to live out their lives here, and that *their children will enjoy an equal opportunity to do so in prosperity.*"[46]

"A Democracy of Opportunity"

But in 1936, when Allegheny County Commissioners Kane and Rankin took office, the "equal opportunity" for the "little people" which these labor leaders promised was still to come. In the meantime, Pennsylvania's Little New Deal had stalled in Harrisburg after the 1934 gubernatorial election. Although the labor-oriented Democrats had carried all the top state offices and a majority of the State House, as well as a majority of the State Senate seats up for election—they had failed to gain outright control of the State Senate due to staggered elections.

Holdover Republicans, therefore, continued to dominate the State Senate and, in this fashion, stymie virtually the entire Little New Deal legislative program. Just as, for example, the Republican majority never allowed the anti-McNair ripper bill to emerge from committee, so it similarly bottled up almost all of the labor legislation on which Earle had successfully campaigned.

Under David Lawrence's guidance, a package of labor laws identical to the 1934 Democratic state platform on labor had been quickly introduced and passed by the Democratic-dominated House—only to fail in the Republican-dominated Senate. By 1936, the Democrats had only a handful of accomplishments they could point to after two years in office, important though these few were.

They had been able to abolish the detested Coal and Iron Police, the state-supported corporation police force which had dynamited the bootleg mines in Schuylkill County and had terrorized mining and steel towns throughout the state on behalf of the corporations for so many decades.

They had appointed Lt. Governor Thomas Kennedy, Secretary-Treasurer of the United Mine Workers (UMWA), as commander of the Pennsylvania State Police. This body had been originally created in 1905 specifically to suppress worker rebellions in mining and manufacturing communities, such as McKees Rocks. It was there, fighting the striking workers at the Pressed Steel Car Co. in 1909, that the first State Police officers had died in the line of their mandated duty.

And they had passed a provision for state financial aid to strikers. All of these 1936 accomplishments went far in redressing the balance of power between labor and capital and in encouraging workers in Western Pennsylvania to push for more.[47]

Additionally, the Democrats revised the Pennsylvania Civil Rights Act of 1887, thereby launching a "Little New Deal" specifically for the black citizens of Pennsylvania. On September 1, 1935, the 1887 Act was amended to grant all people "within the jurisdiction of the Commonwealth full and equal accommodations, advantages, facilities and privileges of places of public accommodation, resort or amusement." This action symbolized the fact that even in the absence of significant black pressure, there had developed among white Democrats a greater feeling of social justice and egalitarianism for all Pennsylvania citizens.

Actions such as this, amid the general atmosphere of freedom and equality on the march, greatly emboldened the black community. Before 1935, for example, few civil rights cases were ever heard in Allegheny County courts. After the revision of the law, civil rights cases reached the Allegheny County courts virtually every year, with twenty-seven cases being tried between 1938 and 1949, while many more were settled before ever reaching court.[48]

But these changes merely served to whet the appetite of the new labor-black Democratic constituency for yet more far-reaching change. Such change, however, remained stymied by the remaining Republicans in the State Senate. If this governmental road block were to end, therefore, the Democrats had to conquer the Pennsylvania State Senate in the upcoming 1936 election.

In this, organized labor agreed, and toward this end UMWA President John L. Lewis contributed $40,000 in union funds to the Democrats, earmarked specifically for their State Senate campaign. This seemed to be money well invested, for it appeared that gaining control of the Senate was indeed a real possibility in 1936. Of the twenty-five seats up for election, only three were held by Democrats, giving the Republicans the most chances to lose. What was even worse for the Republicans was that the Democrats needed to win less than half that number to gain a Senate majority.

Meanwhile, realignment continued apace as the electorate continued to swell in the Democrats' favor. Since 1932, Pennsylvania Democrats had gained on the Republicans by almost one and a half million new voters, with 375,000 new Democratic voters registering in 1936 alone, as opposed to only 30,000 new Republicans. In this regard, Pittsburgh witnessed two turning points in 1936.

For the April primary season, the first elections to be conducted under the supervision of Democratic County Commissioners Kane and Rankin, more new

Democratic voters registered than Republicans for the first time since the Civil War.

Then, on October 10, David Lawrence announced that registered Democrats outnumbered registered Republicans in the Pittsburgh electorate for the first time in history, 172,179 to 136,451. It was a power shift which has not been reversed down to the present day.

Additionally, 1936 was a presidential election year and Roosevelt, wildly popular in Pennsylvania's industrial and mining regions, was running for re-election. The president's election in 1932 and the passage of the Wagner Act in 1935 had made possible not only the 1935 creation of the Committee on Industrial Organization (CIO), but also its initial drives in steel and other mass production industries, a job which was, of course, incomplete. John L. Lewis and other high CIO leaders, therefore, deemed the re-election of Roosevelt in 1936 essential to the continued success of their efforts.

Despite the popularity of Roosevelt in Pittsburgh and Allegheny County, in the 1932 election Pennsylvania as a whole had given its thirty-six electoral votes to Hoover. Lewis hoped to help reverse that decision in 1936. His main vehicle, in Pennsylvania as elsewhere, was Labor's Non-Partisan League (LNPL). Lewis appointed Patrick T. Fagan, president of the Pittsburgh Central Labor Union and president of southwestern Pennsylvania's District 5 of the United Mine Workers, as chairman of the Pennsylvania chapter the League.

From the beginning, the League was primarily designed to re-elect Roosevelt, with little attention, other than the $40,000 contribution to the State Senate campaign, given to the Democratic ticket at lower levels. With this goal in mind, the League worked hard to carry Pennsylvania for the president. During the campaign, for instance, "Seventeen thousand five-hundred one sheet posters were supplied to county chairmen along with large quantities of window cards and Roosevelt buttons."[49]

In addition, the Pennsylvania Non-Partisan League organized large Roosevelt rallies, distributed half a million copies of its four-page newspaper, *The Labor Voter*, and "enrolled 150,000 members [into the League] from various trade unions in the state and collected over $81,000 in union contributions."[50]

In the meantime, the CIO's Steel Workers Organizing Committee (SWOC), formed on June 16, 1936 with Lewis lieutenant Phillip Murray in charge, was active on Roosevelt's behalf independently of the League. "The union announced that a vote for the New Deal was a vote for collective bargaining," and "The time and energy of many [SWOC] organizers and staff members were diverted toward the political campaign."[51]

The Pittsburgh labor movement was just as active locally in working to guarantee a large voter turnout for Roosevelt among its union constituency. The Pittsburgh Central Labor Union (PCLU) had been a champion of Roosevelt since before the 1932 election. In January 1933, it had initiated an annual birthday party for the President which had come to rival Labor Day on the local calender of labor celebrations. The 1936 FDR birthday party was held at the Ft. Pitt Hotel and, "In this year," the PCLU admonished, "when the industrial and financial opponents of

Organized Labor are striving to their utmost to check and throw back the advance of the humanitarian objects of Labor Unions, all members of Labor Unions should assemble and show their strength at their Labor celebration of the birthday of the man who is championing their cause in the highest legislative and executive chambers of the country—President Franklin D. Roosevelt. Labor should show the reactionaries of the district that Union workers are back of the President."[52]

For the night of Saturday, June 27th, the PCLU organized a "mass meeting" of union men at the huge county-owned South Park to hear the radioed nomination acceptance speech of Roosevelt at the Democratic National Convention. Not only would this be a public endorsement of the President, it would also serve to encourage a mass enthusiasm for the President's words. Constituent unions cooperated and "a splendid crowd" of workers massed in South Park to listen to Roosevelt.[53]

The Democrats helped fuel this local enthusiasm by holding their presidential nominating convention in Philadelphia, where the state's leading Democrats—Earle, Guffey, Lawrence, and others—were prominently displayed. Democratic National Committee Chairman James Farley, who engineered the convention, noted that "An excellent platform was adopted, full of ringing New Deal phrases, pledging a continuation of the humanitarian legislation of the Roosevelt administration."[54]

Then the Democrats re-nominated Roosevelt by acclamation. In his acceptance speech, Roosevelt issued a clarion call to class war. His words echoed exactly the dreams and aspirations of Pittsburgh workers. In this he was no doubt an astute politician in touch with what his constituency wanted to hear. Ever since his election, the "forgotten man" had been writing "Father" Roosevelt and his wife, "Mother" Eleanor, millions of long and heart-breaking letters filled with their problems and pleas. Several recurrent and pervasive motifs dominated these millions of letters, most prominently an emphasis on equality and fairness.[55] The briefest acquaintance with these millions of letters would give any insightful politician myriad clues at to what his constituency wanted to hear. And Roosevelt responded.

Roosevelt made it clear in his speech that he sought not just to win an election, but to win a victory over poverty and greed, as he intended to master the "forces of selfishness and lust for power." Speaking to the convention delegates, and to a nationwide radio audience which included the assembled workers of Allegheny County at South Park, he defined the terms of combat.

"Economic royalists," said Roosevelt, had "carved [out] new dynasties, built upon concentration of control over material things." This "new industrial dictatorship" enriched itself and solidified its power at the expense of the common man, crushing him as it turned free enterprise into "privileged enterprise," rendering political equality meaningless because economic equality did not exist. Freedom, said Roosevelt, could not exist in halfway measures. The ordinary American, "guaranteed equal opportunity in the polling place must have equal opportunity in the market place." To combat the "new despotism," the Democrats pledged a "democracy of opportunity, and aid to those overtaken by disaster."

But, warned Roosevelt, "the resolute enemy within our gates" must first be overcome. "These economic royalists," Roosevelt continued, "complain that we seek to overthrow the institutions of America. What they really complain of is that we seek to take away their power. In vain they seek to hide behind the Flag and the Constitution. In their blindness they forget what the Flag and Constitution stand for. Now, as always, they stand for democracy, not tyranny; for freedom, not subjection; and against a dictatorship by mob rule and the overprivileged alike."

Roosevelt ended his speech by calling for "this generation of Americans" to meet their "rendezvous with destiny" by joining him in a great reform crusade.[56]

After Roosevelt's call to arms in Philadelphia, Pennsylvania's Democratic leadership took advantage of the post-convention momentum by immediately launching a "Roosevelt Caravan" of their candidates across the breath of the state. This rolling, on-going political rally, befitting its labor orientation, suddenly appeared at factory gates, mine entrances, and city squares without let-up into the fall. Perhaps the greatest gathering of all took place on Labor Day, September 7, in Pittsburgh, which both the Democratic Party and its ally, Labor's Non-Partisan League helped build. On that Labor Day, over a quarter of a million workers rallied and marched through the streets of Pittsburgh in what its organizers boasted was, "the largest gathering of labor people, or for that matter any other public meeting, ever held in the nation."[57]

Meanwhile, on August 6th, the PCLU unanimously endorsed Roosevelt for re-election and on August 20th targeted Republican State Senators for labor's wrath. "The Republican controlled Pennsylvania Senate," the PCLU thundered, "long the barrier to all social and labor legislation, has once again turned its back on every wage and salary earner in this Commonwealth. Through its domination by a half dozen Republican Senators, all of whom are puppets of the utilities, the sweatshops, and big business, the Republican majority prevented the passage of the Unemployment Insurance Bill [passed by the Democratic-controlled House]. Labor had a right to expect passage of legislation to comply with the requirements of the Social Security Act. Old Age Pensions and Unemployment Insurance are obligations of society to workers. They are the foundation stones of the structure for social justice and economic security. Labor demanded that security replace anxiety and fear; that unemployment insurance replace the dole.

"Labor was disappointed, but not surprised. From past experience it could expect nothing better from the Grundy dominated State Senate, which has been a consistently effective slaughterhouse of all social legislation. The Senate at this session did not cast off the vicious control of the enemies of the wage earners. The Republican majority are still Punch and Judy actors of the Mellon-Grundy-Pew circus.

"The responsibility for failure to pass the unemployment insurance bill must be placed on the Republican leadership of this state. The administration of Governor Earle did valiant service in Labor's behalf. The Democrats sponsored and fought for a real unemployment bill. [This bill] complied fully with the Federal Social Security Act and passed the Democratic House of Representatives, May 19th. The bill was on its way to victory until it reached the State Senate.

There it met the fate of all other measures in the interests of labor and the people.

"The reactionary industrial and financial pirates who control certain members of the State Senate commanded that the unemployment insurance bill be killed and their Senate puppets obeyed. The Republican leadership of this Commonwealth is so blind and stupid that it compels this state to lose millions of dollars in federal grants rather than permit the enactment of any social legislation, as a precedent for the enactment of other labor measures."

The PCLU then singled out State Senator James J. Coyne, head of the Allegheny County Republican Party, as "Pittsburgh's No. 1 Labor enemy, leader of the battered remnants of the corrupt and discredited Republican gang," who was responsible for burying the bill in committee. Therefore, the PCLU resolved "That the Central Labor Union specifically and emphatically denounce the action of Senator James J. Coyne in assuming leadership in the mutilation of the unemployment insurance bill and that the Central Labor Union hereby pledge its energies and resources to bring about the defeat of James J. Coyne."[58]

At the same time, the PCLU threw itself entirely behind Labor's Non-Partisan League (LNPL) efforts to re-elect Roosevelt, contributing funds from its treasury to the cause. While PCLU president Patrick T. Fagan continued to head up the statewide efforts of the League, D. A. Harshbarger of the Railroad Switchmen's Union No. 62, and an active and influential member of the PCLU, became Chairman of the Allegheny County chapter of the LNPL. He opened LNPL headquarters in Downtown Pittsburgh at 211 Smithfield Street and held a first mass meeting there on September 27. "Meetings every afternoon between now and election are planned," noted the PCLU. "Come and bring the family. A vote of thanks was given to Brother Harshbarger and his co-workers for the fine work they did in fixing up the elaborate quarters of Labor's Non-Partisan League. It is planned to make the League's headquarters a permanent meeting place for Labor. Membership in the League is being solicited with dues ranging from 10 cents a month upwards—according to the member's inclination and ability to contribute."[59] The League HQ quickly became a major way-station for visiting politicians sympathetic to labor, such as New York City Mayor Fiorello LaGuardia, who spoke to a meeting there on October 17.[60]

In addition to the League, the CIO was also backing another new labor organization in Pennsylvania that summer: the Steel Workers Organizing Committee (SWOC). Founded (as was the CIO in 1935) in Pittsburgh on June 17th, ten days before Roosevelt's Philadelphia acceptance speech, it was headed by the UMWA's Philip Murray and included Patrick Fagan as one of the two official UMWA representatives. With headquarters in Downtown Pittsburgh's Grant Building and half a million dollars from the UMWA, it launched the first serious attempt to unionize the steel industry since the Great Steel Strike of 1919.

In what the union termed, "The opening gun," an organizing rally was held four days later in McKeesport on the banks of the Monongahela River, Sunday, June 21. Using a coal truck as a platform and bracketed by large American flags, local "labor judge" Michael Musmanno and SWOC chief Murray announced to a crowd of mostly coal miners that the drive to unionize steel was at long last launched. The presence of a sympathetic judge on the platform, a judge endorsed by the PCLU and elected with labor votes, was evidently intended to assure the workers that this time, the courts would not be uniformly against them.[61]

A few days later, on July 5, SWOC took its organizing campaign across the Monongahela River for its first meeting in Homestead. "State Guards Steel Labor's Civil Rights," declared the *Pittsburgh Press,* as the State Police escorted their chief, Lt. Governor and UMWA Secretary-Treasurer Thomas Kennedy, into Homestead to be the main speaker, and then "filtered through the crowd as insurance against interference by company-dominated municipal police."[62]

At a three-hour open-air meeting at the 17th Street Playgrounds, a crowd of 4,000 Homestead-area workers joyfully celebrated the Fourth of July, as well as the July 6, 1892 "Battle of Homestead" against Frick's army of Pinkertons. They also declared their own independence from the "lords of steel." Charles Scharbo, a pipe-fitter in the Homestead mill, invoked a powerful and evocative symbol of American freedom when he read to his fellow workers a "Declaration of Independence," which the Homestead workers themselves had drawn up.

"The lords of steel try to rule us as did the royalists against whom our fathers rebelled," Scharbo read from the Declaration. "We steel workers today solemnly publish and declare our independence. We say to the world: We are Americans!"[63]

Scharbo went on to declare that, "Through this union we shall win higher wages, shorter hours, and a better standard of living. We shall win leisure for ourselves, and *opportunity for our children.* We shall abolish industrial despotism. We shall make real the dreams of the pioneers who pictured America as a land where all might live in comfort and happiness."

At the conclusion of the meeting, the crowd marched to the local cemetery to honor the Homestead steelworkers killed in the 1892 Battle of Homestead. PCLU president Patrick T. Fagan delivered a eulogy, declaring "Let the blood of those labor pioneers who were massacred here be the seed of this new organization in 1936."[64]

The hunger for equality and equal opportunity which the Homestead steelworkers expressed in their "Declaration of Independence" can also be seen in much other language used by Homestead steelworkers in the days just before the highly polarized election of 1936. "Landon," declared a twenty-year-old Homesteader, referring to the Republican presidential candidate, "is fighting against the people."[65] "Notice all the Landon buttons in town," pointed out another. "The men and women [who wear them] are all pretty well-dressed and look prosperous."[66]

"Labor is for Roosevelt," said another, "because it has everything to gain and nothing to lose. It has nothing to lose, because under Republican administrations, labor had nothing. What it has gained in rights and liberties has been gathered in the last four years. Is that not reason enough for my vote, and yours, for Roosevelt?"[67] "Mr. Roosevelt and his administration," said yet another, "have had an uphill battle against the combined forces of Capitalism on all sides. But he gave the workman a break."[68]

Paraphrasing Tom Paine, another Homestead worker said, "Capitalism makes a wide swath in the rights of men."[69] "I'm for Franklin Delano Roosevelt," declared one, "because he was a strong adherent to the Utilitarian Principle: 'The greatest good for the greatest number,' and the greatest number were the poor, the unemployed, the aged. Thank God we have a leader—one who has been unafraid of Wall Street!"[70]

"To return the Republicans to power," said another Homesteader, "would be to place money over humanity. The principles held and the policies advocated by the real leaders of the Republicans are narrow and reactionary and primarily intended for the benefit of the privileged few and that if translated into law would limit social and economic justice, true liberty, and real democracy in the United States. Roosevelt stands for the interests of the people as a whole. The Hoover leadership *did nothing for humanity*. The policy of considering the wants of the whole people is called, 'The New Deal.' It means that human rights are entitled to legislative consideration. The fight for social and economic justice and security for the people has not yet been fully won, the people will continue to fight in the typically American way (with ballots) *for their fair share of the social and economic benefits inherent in our American democracy*."[71]

"I believe I'd vote for Roosevelt," declared a Homeville resident, "because every banker is against him. I'm no red—just a common ordinary American."[72]

Roosevelt added to the enthusiasm for him expressed by Pittsburgh area workers by announcing that he would return to Pittsburgh for a major campaign address at Oakland's Forbes Field, as he had done in 1932. He greatly wanted to carry Pennsylvania in 1936 and it seemed he might, although James Farley, his campaign manager, was far more confident of doing so than Roosevelt himself. Farley noted that, "in Pennsylvania we were informed of cases where Republican Clubs, with memberships running up into the thousands, formally abandoned the national ticket of their party and declared for Roosevelt and [Vice President] Garner."[73]

Indeed, Farley went so far as to predict that the president would not only carry Pennsylvania, but every state in America except for Maine and Vermont, a fantastically wild prediction with which Democratic Pennsylvania U.S. Senator Joseph Guffey agreed. They would turn out to be right.[74]

Roosevelt delayed entering the fray until late September, at which point he engaged in a "one month on the stump" whirlwind of activity. He opened his campaign in New York and then took it to Pennsylvania. For a week prior to his scheduled October 2 appearance at Forbes Field, Pittsburgh's excited newspapers spoke of little else but the coming visit of the president and of "his friend," David Lawrence.

"Democratic" Mayor McNair, on the other hand, was ignored by the media, excluded from the pre-rally receptions with the president, and pointedly not invited to appear beside Roosevelt at the Forbes Field event itself. Perhaps in a pique, perhaps in order to grab the spotlight back from Roosevelt and Lawrence, on October 1, the very night Lawrence was introducing Roosevelt to the party faithful at a private reception, McNair fired the last Democrat remaining in his administration. The unlucky official was James P. Kirk, the City Treasurer.

Lawrence consoled Jim Kirk by stepping aside to make him head of the Democratic Party in Allegheny County. After all, he could afford to do so, as Lawrence remained head of the state Democratic Party.

But, this remained a sideshow to the October 2 appearance of Roosevelt himself at Oakland's Forbes Field, the ballpark overlooking the Italian community of Panther Hollow. This 1936 campaign represents perhaps the climax of the New Deal Era's class politics at the presidential level, as Roosevelt and other Democrats savagely attacked the Republican "economic royalists" who oppressed the working man. Nowhere in Roosevelt's fevered barnstorming through the Northeast and Midwest that autumn was this more evident than during his Pittsburgh rally at Oakland's Forbes Field.

Political attitudes in Pittsburgh had become highly charged and class consciousness was intensifying among workers, especially the younger workers. This was evident in a 1934-35 survey of union attitudes among the steelworkers, who accounted for 20 percent of the total workforce in Allegheny County at that time. While both native white and older foreign-born workers favored unionization, especially alternative unions to the "company unions" then represented by the Employee Representation Plan promoted by the companies, "Younger foreign-born workers were *violently* pro-union." Even "Younger Negro workers cast their lot with the outside unions" because a *"more uniform outlook seemed to be developing as the old foreign-born and Negro backgrounds were replaced by an industrial background common to all."*

Thus, even before the coming of the CIO and the Steel Workers Organizing Committee, investigators had found that Pittsburgh's steelworkers, black and white, were "organizable" into a union free of corporation dominance. "This organizability sprang from the urge for freedom of expression, an urge made doubly powerful by the repression which most of the iron and steel companies had exercised in the conduct of their welfare and labor control activities."[75]

"The workers' frame of mind," added others, was that of "fear coupled with hatred. There is a consciousness on the part of the laborer that he is capable of recklessness and that there is an ageless score of the poor against the rich."[76]

The political rhetoric in Pittsburgh reflected this class hatred. The night of October 2, claimed the *Pittsburgh Press,* Pittsburgh was "the political capitol of the United States." It might well have said that the neighborhood of Oakland was the political capitol of the United States. At the very time President Roosevelt was addressing frenzied workers at Forbes Field, Republican Vice Presidential candidate Col. Frank Knox was exhorting a crowd of 8,000 party faithful at Oakland's Duquesne Gardens. This was an ice skating rink on the corner of Craig Street and Forbes Avenue, close enough to Forbes Field for the assembled Republicans to hear the angry Democratic roars echoing over Oakland from the ball park.[77]

Some estimates put the crowd jammed into Forbes Field at 70,000 that night, 20,000 more than the crowd which had cheered him at the ball park in 1932. Many of these had come from the small steel towns ringing Pittsburgh in huge honking car caravans which turned the municipalities left behind into ghost towns. A 100-car caravan of steelworkers from Homestead left that steel center "practically deserted last night, what with almost everyone and his little brother in the Oakland section of Pittsburgh to hear the leaders of the Republican and Democratic ranks."[78]

A reporter who followed Roosevelt's campaign from the beginning left a vivid description of the rally at Forbes Field. "To me," he wrote, "the whole political story of the country was epitomized in the jubilant night meeting for President Roosevelt in the baseball park. As I picked my way through the mad throng, I saw a plump little old woman, nearly as broad as long, run cackling and screeching merrily through the crowd. She was just buoyant with animal spirits. All by herself she was having one magnificent time. Crushed on her head, a bit onesided in a gesture of bravado, was a red, white, and blue hat. It did not stand up properly and erect, like the other souvenir hats you spotted here and there in the jostling, merry crowd. (Across the front of the hats was a picture of the President.) It looked for all the world like the tricolored cockade which other women wore once so many years ago. Gaily and nonchalantly she dashed away and was lost in the crowd. She was the crowd.

"Before the President arrived, before the convoy of motorcycle policemen put-putted slowly through a gate in the far corner of the park, before the Deliverer appeared in his open car to wave his hat and set off a great burst of human joy and delirium that swept across the field and thundered back from the grandstand— they had their Danton, one of their own. State Senator Warren R. Roberts [of Bethlehem, home of Bethlehem Steel, and a champion of the New Deal in the Pennsylvania Senate], he was, a stern-faced, square sort of fellow, who knew the common touch. He gave them their enemies and they spat out their names—Andy Mellon (poor, poor Andy, he said, and they tittered); Textile Joe Grundy, Pew (the oil man), Rockefeller (the still bigger oil man). 'Boo' came the swelling chorus after each name. (You could almost hear the swish of the guillotine blade as it fell.)"

In the nineteenth century, the slogan, "equal opportunity for all, special privileges for none," was often invoked by working people. State Senator Roberts of Bethlehem seemed to realize that this same egalitarian ideology was the basis of working class anger that night. "*'The President,' he said, 'has decreed that your children shall enjoy equal opportunity with the sons of the rich!,'* and the crowd went into hysteria as he continued to attack the 'smug complacence of the pseudo-aristocracy.' They also roared their approval when Governor Earle marched to the podium to denounce their class enemies, 'There are the Mellons—who have grown fabulously wealthy from the toil of the men of iron and steel, the men whose brain and brawn have made this great city; Grundy—whose sweatshop operators have been the shame and disgrace of Pennsylvania for a generation; Pew—who strives to build a political and economic empire with himself as dictator; the du Ponts—whose dollars were earned with the blood of American soldiers; Morgan—financier of war.'"

The workers of Pittsburgh knew their enemies well. At the mention of each villain's name, Gov. Earle was forced to pause until the chorus of anger rolling back from the bleachers ("like the whine of the hurricane before it strikes") abated. "He stood, smiling and confident," the journalist wrote, "enjoying the tempest he produced. Again, you could almost hear the swish of the guillotine blade as it fell. The mob was whipped into a frenzy ready for the Deliverer. He entered in an open car. It might have been the chariot of a Roman Emperor. They drowned him with paeans of joy."[79]

Back in Homestead later that same October night, thousands of returning steelworkers assembled for the largest Democratic Party parade and rally in the history of that town. As October darkness fell over Homestead, three hundred cars and trucks jammed with 2,000 cheering and waving passengers rolled slowly and majestically five abreast down Eighth Avenue, the town's main street, and into the neighboring town of West Homestead. In the hands of each of the 2,000 madly screaming passengers were brilliant blood-red flares luridly illuminating the Homestead night. It looked like a river of fire through the heart of Homestead.

After snaking its way through the adjacent town, the long torch-lit procession ended up at Homestead's Elks Hall, where Democratic State Senate candidate P. J. Henney (the Burgess [mayor] of neighboring McKees Rocks, which back in 1933 had tossed out the Republican boss who'd ruled McKees Rocks since 1891) brought the loudest and longest cheers with a revised parable of the biblical Good Samaritan.

"The rich merchants," Henney said, "rode past the sickly man at the side of the road. But Roosevelt, the Good Samaritan, came along riding his Democratic Party donkey and placed him on that donkey, taking him to the next inn for food and shelter." To roars of approval from Homestead workers, local Catholic priest Father C. J. Hrtanek followed up by declaring that, "If Roosevelt's a Communist, then I'm one too! Roosevelt proved to the satisfaction of the workingman that all men are created equal."[80]

Roosevelt himself continued with variations on this theme for the remainder of the month. On October 31 he spoke to a gigantic Democratic rally in New York's Madison Square Garden. Political historian William Manchester was a fourteen-year-old volunteer working for Roosevelt's campaign in Springfield, Massachusetts that night. He begged his nineteen-year-old supervisor, future Democratic National Committee Chairman Lawrence E. O'Brien, to free him so he could hitchhike to New York for the speech, but O'Brien said he could not be spared. Manchester regretted missing what he called "FDR's greatest political philippic" for the rest of his life. Decades later he described that night:

"Nearly fifteen minutes passed before [FDR] could say a word. The band was playing 'Happy Days Are Here Again,' and the sound of the audience—packed to the roof of the huge hall—was earsplitting. Roosevelt finally raised his arms, like a biblical patriarch, and a hush fell. He turned up that great organ of a voice, identifying his 'old enemies': 'Business and financial monopoly, speculation, reckless banking, class antagonism,' and 'organized money,' adding 'Government by organized money is just as dangerous as Government by organized mob.' The crowd, on its feet throughout, ringing cowbells, howled its approval. In an edged voice he said: 'Never before in all our history have these forces been so united against one candidate as they stand today. They are unanimous in their hate for me—and I welcome their hatred.' *The New York Times* compared the applause to 'roars which rose and fell like the sound of waves pounding in the surf.' The President declared: 'I should like to have it said of my first Administration that in it the forces of selfishness met their match.' Now his voice swelled: 'I should like to have it said.' He had to pause, the ovation had begun; he raised his arms again and the din abated: 'I should like to have it said of my second Administration that *in it these forces met their master."* The cheering surged and continued long after his departure."[81]

So pervasive was the popular feeling that the election was a class crusade against the forces of privilege and discrimination that blacks back in Pittsburgh's Steel Valley clearly identified with the ethnic workers' crusade and saw it as a battle to better their own class condition, as well. "We colored people of the Second Ward," said a black voter in Homestead, "led by Rev. Soloman, are better off now than we've ever been. Mr. Roosevelt is for the worker and for the poor classes, while Landon is a tool for the bankers and those who have money."[82]

The Rev. S. H. Soloman, himself, who was leading Homestead's black citizens into the Democratic Party, declared, "Didn't God of the Universe send President Roosevelt and give him a plan to take care of the needy? Are we going to let the enemy, which is the Republican Party, deceive us? I am asking the Negroes who belong to the Second Ward Democratic Club to be sure to come to the meeting Monday night. Because together we stand, but divided we fall."[83]

Meanwhile, the firing of City Treasurer James Kirk proved to be McNair's final folly. As Roosevelt spoke to the over-flowing Forbes Field, the city of Pittsburgh ground to a halt, and not just because all eyes were on Roosevelt. With Kirk gone there was no one to sign the city's checks. The City Council, now dominated by Democrats since the 1935 election, refused to seat McNair's replacement, and the Treasurer's Office remained vacant.

On October 6, in an impetuous flash of anger typical of the mayor, McNair submitted a one-line letter of resignation. The Council immediately accepted the resignation and quickly swore in close Lawrence ally Cornelius Scully as acting mayor. McNair had fired Scully as City Solicitor in 1934 and Lawrence retaliated by tapping him for the City Council to fill the Democratic vacancy created when John J. Kane left in January of 1936 to become Allegheny County Commissioner. The new Democratic majority which existed after the 1935 election then elected him Council President, one of the functions of which was to take over as mayor if and when a vacancy occurred. When McNair changed his mind a few days later and attempted to rescind his resignation, he found it was too late. Pittsburgh had a new mayor.

One of the first actions of Mayor Scully was to fire Citizen's League president and Republican Leslie Johnston as the city's recalcitrant Public Works Director, who had long resisted participating in WPA programs. On the eve of the 1936 November election, the Democratic Party at last controlled both the mayor's office and a majority on the City Council. Mayor Scully telegraphed President

Roosevelt saying, "The city administration of Pittsburgh will line up four-square with you."[84]

The New Deal had finally come to Pittsburgh.

The Little New Deal

Similarly, Pennsylvania's long-delayed Little New Deal finally came to pass. As Farley had predicted, FDR carried formerly Republican Pennsylvania—in a 600,000 vote majority landslide. In doing so, he became the first Democrat to carry Pennsylvania since 1856 when a native son, James Buchanan, defeated the Republican Fremont. Every significant city in the state went for Roosevelt, with Pittsburgh contributing a 190,000 vote majority and Philadelphia a 210,000 vote majority. This time, not only did every Italian and black ward in Philadelphia in the east go for the president, but every last ward in Pittsburgh in the west, regardless of composition, went Democratic as well.

There was a drenching rain throughout Western Pennsylvania on that election day, but nothing could stop the Democratic votes from pouring in. In a record turnout of more than a half million votes, Roosevelt took Allegheny County by almost 300,000 votes. The turnout swamped that of 1935, which, in turn, had been a record turnout. "Rain and lowering clouds could not deter them," reported *The Pittsburgh Post-Gazette*. "It was like a picture of crusading armies on the march. Rain broke upon the district early in the afternoon, but it could not keep the crowds away. So huge was the vote that ballot boxes were overflowing long before closing time."[85]

In Braddock FDR won by five-to-one. In Clairton the victory margin was three-to-one. In Duquesne it was four-to-one. In McKeesport, the second largest city in the county, it was two-to-one. Roosevelt took both of Pittsburgh's South Side Wards of 16 and 17 by more than six-to-one. Polish Hill went five-to-one for Roosevelt. Oakland went two-to-one for the President. In the black Hill District, Ward 3 went nine-to-one for FDR (his best showing) while Ward 5 went for him by more than three-to-one. Meanwhile, the wealthy Republican ward of Shadyside went for Roosevelt by a slim margin.[86]

In lesser populated Beaver County, which Roosevelt carried by only 54 votes in 1932 and where the steeltowns of Aliquippa, Ambridge, and Midland are located, Roosevelt had a nearly 17,000-vote margin of victory. Roosevelt carried Johnstown and the coal county of Cambria by two-to-one. Greene County went for Roosevelt two-to-one. Greensburg and Westmoreland County was Roosevelt's by two-to-one.

But the victory was not just for Roosevelt. The Democratic tide swept everything before it and the swish of the guillotine claimed Pennsylvania Republicans in unprecedented numbers, completing the Democratic revolution at the state level begun in 1934. All Republican State Representative candidates in Beaver County went down in defeat, as did the county's single State Senator, against whom Governor Earle had campaigned.

Roosevelt also carried nearby Fayette County, where every Democratic State Representative candidate was also elected. Lawrence County sent every Democratic candidate to victory due to a tremendous vote in the industrial districts of New Castle, which went five-to-one for Roosevelt. In Westmoreland County the former local WPA administrator would be the county's new Democratic Congressman in Washington.[87] A Democrat also replaced the Republican State Senator from Erie. Likewise, across the state in Philadelphia, Democrats swept all Congressional seats in their county and took forty-three out of forty-five State Senate and State Representative seats.[88]

Not a single Republican won election to any office all of Allegheny County. Republicans in the county's five U.S. Congressional districts were "Buried Under A Landslide of Ballots." All twenty-seven of Allegheny County's Democratic State Representative candidates won, flushing out hold-over Republican incumbents.

And both of the county's Republican State Senators also went down in flames. In a vote indicative of the clash between the Steel Valley mill towns and more rural Republican municipalities, McKees Rocks Burgess P. J. Henny defeated the incumbent Republican State Senator in his district by 7,000 votes, despite the latter rolling up large majorities in the safely Republican southern suburbs of Dormont and Mt. Lebanon (both of which also went for Landon).

However, foremost among the defeated Republicans—losing by a two-to-one margin—was Pittsburgh's State Senator, James J. Coyne, "a dominant factor in Republican politics for 15 years,"[89] head of the Allegheny County Republican Party, the chief architect of labor-Democratic defeats in the State Senate, and, according to the PCLU in targeting him for defeat, "Pittsburgh's No. 1 Labor enemy."

It was the end of Republican power in Pittsburgh, the most Republican city in America. It was never to recover.

The long-ruling Republican machine in Homestead was stunned by the outcome. "Huge majorities were rolled up in Munhall, Homestead, West Homestead, Whitaker, the Thirty-first ward [of Pittsburgh, across the Monongahela from Hazelwood and adjacent to Homestead] and the township by the Democratic Party. Republican headquarters in Homestead was a sad, neglected place last night as returns started to indicate which way the wind was blowing. The few that gloomily sat about the office and watched the weather shed tears in their behalf silently reached to lapels and dropped Landon sunflowers, and at the same time their hopes and aspirations, to the floor."[90]

The Democratic tidal wave, however, also swept out of office Pennsylvania's only two Socialist State Senators, both from Berks County near Philadelphia. One of them was militant Socialist leader Darlington Hoopes, who was also the City Solicitor of Reading. Their constituents, it seemed, now preferred Democrats to Socialist representatives.[91]

Thus, for the first time in almost 100 years, Democrats controlled all government branches of the Commonwealth of Pennsylvania, as well as claiming the overwhelming majority of the U.S. Representatives, winning twenty-six of the state's thirty-three Congressional seats. (Eight years before, in 1928, Republicans claimed 100 percent of the Congressional seats). Not only did the Democrats capture the only two statewide offices Republicans still held—that of State Treasurer and Auditor General, the latter won by State Senator Warren R. Roberts of Bethlehem, who'd introduced FDR at the Forbes Field rally—but the Democratic majority in the State House was increased to a staggering 154 to 54.

And, finally, Democrats took control of the State Senate, the last barrier to the implementation of the state's Little New Deal. Democrats had needed to gain only ten of the contested twenty-five Senate seats to control the body. They instead took eighteen, giving them a two-thirds Senate majority.

Almost as an after-thought to their campaign to re-elect the president, Labor's Non-Partisan League had targeted fourteen anti-Little New Deal Republican State Senators for defeat in an edition of *The Labor Voter*. Of these fourteen Republicans, ten were defeated. Thus, Labor's Non-Partisan League, justifiably or not, claimed a major share of the credit for swinging Pennsylvania into the Democratic camp.

Two days after the election, D. A. Harshbarger, Chairman of the Allegheny County LNPL, "made a glowing and flowing report of the work of the League during the recent political campaign" to the PCLU, while that body's president, Patrick Fagan, who was also state chairman of the League, reported on plans to make the League a permanent organization. By unanimous vote, the PCLU delegates gave a "rising vote of thanks" to Fagan and Harshbarger for their "splendid work."[92]

Governor Earle declared that the Democratic victory was "proof that human welfare was paramount."[93] He viewed the vote as "a mandate to proceed with many of the measures which the Republican controlled Senate either pickled or defeated. The election marks the turning over of a new leaf in our government to the cause of humanity instead of special privilege." First on his agenda was the unemployment insurance legislation Pittsburgh's State Senator James Coyne had helped kill earlier in 1936. He also promised "to abolish sweatshops and the exploitation of women in industry."

Meanwhile, Democratic State Chairman David Lawrence declared that, "With Democratic control of the Senate, the people of Pennsylvania can rest assured that legislation in their interest can no longer be blocked by reactionary influences."[94]

****

Based on these sweeping 1936 victories, "The Little New Deal was now completed as Governor Earle exhorted the legislators: 'We have before us a tremendous responsibility and an unprecedented opportunity. Liberal forces control both Executive and Legislative branches of our state government for the first time in 91 years. It is now our duty to translate that liberalism into positive effective action.' The legislature responded with the most sweeping reform program in

Pennsylvania's history."[95]

Pennsylvania's Little New Deal, fashioned after FDR's New Deal, quickly caught up with its model and, in some cases, surpassed it. "Used at first as an epithet by unfriendly newsmen, the term 'Little New Deal' caught on as a description of the Earle administration and was soon accepted by friend and foe alike. For the next few years, news stories publicized the Little Wagner Act, the Little A.A.A., the Little Brain Trust, and Little Fireside Chats."[96]

The new Democratic-dominated state legislature worked at a furious pace of non-stop twelve- and fourteen-hour days and, over the next two years, from early 1937 to late 1938, the entire Democratic pro-labor platform of 1934 was swiftly enacted into law. These two years of the "Little New Deal" saw more legislative activity in Pennsylvania than at any other time in its history. The very first piece of legislation to be passed into law was the unemployment insurance bill which Senator Coyne had blocked. It at last brought Pennsylvania into compliance with the federal government's social security legislation on the same issue.

The Little New Deal was also a "Real Deal" for workers in other ways. The Pennsylvania Anti-Injunction Act of 1937 severely curtailed the use of court injunctions to halt strikes during labor-management disputes.

Company stores in company mining and industrial towns were banned, as were company-paid city police officers.

The Pennsylvania Labor Relations Board was created to oversee the "Little Wagner Act," which for the first time legalized the right of Pennsylvania workers to organize into unions and collectively bargain with their employers. This was accompanied by legally mandated penalties for recalcitrant employers which were far harsher than those called for under the New Deal's federal Wagner Act.

A Workingmen's Compensation Act covering on-the-job injuries and work-related diseases also went much further than anything proposed in Washington.

In the wake of the 1936 election Governor Earle had promised to abolish sweatshops and the exploitation of female workers—and so a minimum wage for women and children was mandated, as well as a maximum work week of forty-four-hours—although the Earle administration originally introduced legislation for a thirty-five-hour work week.

Of 371 bills introduced to the state legislature by the Earle administration over the first five months of the 1937 session, only six failed to pass. In June 1937, the Pennsylvania Federation of Labor issued a pamphlet, "Labor Legislation," detailing all the beneficial labor and social legislation passed by the state legislature in the first session of the Little New Deal. In Pittsburgh, the Central Labor Union thought it an important synopsis of the legislation and purchased 1,000 copies to distribute to its delegate members.[97] PCLU President Patrick Fagan pointedly called attention to the great advances labor had made in electing friendly Democratic office holders and to the favorable labor legislation they had passed.[98] As far as organized labor in both Pittsburgh and the state were concerned, the faith working class voters had placed in the Democratic Party in the 1936 elections was well justified.

****

The Little New Deal was also a Real Deal for Pennsylvania's black citizens. They had moved quickly into the Democratic Party infrastructure in both Pittsburgh and Philadelphia. In the latter city alone there were 330 black Democratic Committee members in 1938. There were also six black State Representatives, all Democrats. In addition, the Democratic administration had passed substantial legislation directly affecting the status of blacks, proving, claimed black leaders, that the promises of the New Deal "were not mere idle words, but a new creed of government."[99]

Perhaps foremost among this legislation—at least in the estimation of blacks themselves—had been the 1935 "Equal Rights" amendment to Pennsylvania's 1887 civil rights law.[100] This civil rights law was drafted by Homer S. Brown, a black Democratic State Representative from Pittsburgh, the son of a North Side minister. It outlawed discrimination in "any places of public accommodation, resort or amusement," regardless of "race, creed or color." In a state where de facto Jim Crow practices were common and which had a racially segregated state university system, this was a crucial first step, even though enforcement was usually lacking.

Black leaders pointed to Governor Earle's signing of this bill into law as an act of courage and recounted how it came about. After it was introduced in the Democratic controlled State House during Earle's first term, it had passed without a single dissenting vote. The Democratic leadership then "rushed it through the [Republican controlled] Senate before prejudiced white opponents knew the real import of the measure. It was not until it was on Governor Earle's desk for his signature that a number of prejudiced white proprietors became aware of its benefits to the Negro people. It was then that the fight against this measure began. Thousands of telegrams were sent to the members of the legislature from all parts of Pennsylvania, most of them seething with race prejudice. Some of the members of the legislature, becoming concerned about re-election, decided to recall the measure from the Governor's desk. Led by Republican senators and representatives, a motion was made to recall the act in order that it might be killed by the Republican Senate. The Negro legislators became alarmed and went personally to Governor Earle, [who] showed these colored legislators stacks of telegrams which he and his wife had received threatening to oppose his political advancement if he dared to sign the bill.

"He immediately sent to the Attorney General's office and had the bill brought to him and affixed his signature in their presence, at the same time saying, 'No one by threats or intimidation can prevent me from doing justice to a race which has suffered so much injustice.' The passage of the Equal Rights Bill is the most far-reaching benefit which we as a people have ever received from a public official, for it effects us on a thousand fronts in our daily life. It is more important than jobs and positions; it has lifted the Negro people to a new level of manhood and womanhood and made possible a new era of racial advancement, all of which is due to the courage, manhood, and sense of justice of the man who is now the governor of the state of Pennsylvania—George H. Earle. It is to be remembered that for 45 years the Republican Party had been in control of the state government, and that they had received more than 99 percent of the Negro vote during all this period. Yet they were deaf to this just demand of the colored people."[101]

Black leaders also looked to the "Little Wagner Act" of 1937—which forced employers to accept binding arbitration in labor disputes with duly authorized unions—with much hope that it would also be a "New Deal for Negro Labor." When the Little Wagner Act was under consideration, black representatives were concerned, as there were twenty-eight labor unions in the Commonwealth of Pennsylvania which barred blacks from membership. "Consequently, if any of these unions were given the bargaining power for any industry, it might forever bar Negroes from an opportunity to work in such industries."

Therefore, Democratic leaders inserted a provision into the Little Wagner Act stating that, "no labor union could take advantage of the benefits of this act which by ritualistic practice, constitutional or by-law proscription, by tacit agreement among its members or otherwise, denies a person or persons membership in its organization on account of race, creed, or color."

Because of this provision, black labor leaders now "confidently expected that the labor unions of Pennsylvania by the pressure of this act will give the Negroes a new deal. Since labor in Pennsylvania must largely rely upon this law to strengthen its hand in its fight with capital, it is expected that all of these labor unions which heretofore discriminated against Negroes will put an end to this practice, rather than forego the benefit of this law."

Black leaders also highlighted both the federal WPA and state work relief programs as of particular importance to them. Claiming that the Depression "struck us harder than any other group in America," they stated that in 1933 in Pennsylvania's large cities, 35.1 percent of blacks were on such relief programs, as compared to only 11.7 percent of whites. At one point, 90,000 of Philadelphia's 250,000 blacks were on relief.

Since 1934, they said, the Earle administration had contributed $250 million in state funds for direct relief payments, of which $41,250,000 (approximately one-sixth) went to black recipients. Both the New Deal and the Little New Deal, they concluded, "has been a life saver to the Negro people."

They also praised WPA health care work as of special concern to blacks. "In hundreds of communities, WPA doctors, nurses, and teachers are spreading the gospel of better health to thousands of colored workers, housewives, and children." In Pennsylvania, the Little New Deal established venereal disease clinics for the poor throughout the state and also provided pneumonia vaccines for those unable to pay. "The Negro has suffered from these two classes of ailments probably more than any other group because the cost of properly treating these diseases is most expensive. This humane attitude on the part of the Democratic controlled state government should find an appreciative response in the hearts of all fair-minded citizens."

As to housing, black leaders estimated that 60 percent of all Negroes lived in slums. Indeed, 50 percent of all urban slums, they said, were "colored" slums. But in 1937 the Little New Deal passed the Housing Authority Act which established and funded state agencies to build low-cost "New Deal apartments" to house the ill-housed. Under this act, the Pittsburgh Housing Authority was established in October 1937. Appointed to its five-person board of directors was State Representative Homer S. Brown, who lived in an affluent part of Pittsburgh's black Hill District known as "Sugar Top." The Housing Authority's very first project was the "Bedford Dwellings," in Representative Brown's Hill District. "It is expected that approximately 421 modern, sanitary dwellings, at low rent, will be available on this site to former dwellers in slum houses."

Law after law passed by the Little New Deal guaranteed "More Money For Injured Negroes," "Compensation for Negro Unemployed," "Money for Blind, Children, and Aged." In 1937 black Representatives Homer S. Brown and Marshall Shepard introduced a bill granting an appropriation of $50,000 to Lincoln University, a black state college in Oxford, about 45 miles southwest of Philadelphia.

"Governor Earle personally interested himself in securing the passage of the bill," we are told. "Nearly 100 scholarships have been given to deserving Negro students for study at Lincoln University. This is the first time in the history of Pennsylvania that this institution for the education of our youth has received aid from the Commonwealth of Pennsylvania." Such state aid continues to this day, with Lincoln University now a state-affiliated university.

The passage of the Magistrate Court Act of 1937 was cited as the law which broke the stranglehold Republican magistrates had on the black population of Philadelphia and "Liberates 225,000 Negroes From 40-Year Political Bondage." Hundreds of blacks were appointed to positions in government statewide and tens of thousands were benefitting from new jobs due to "fair and unbiased appointments under the State Civil Service laws."

At the county level, Democratic Allegheny County Sheriff John Heinz, a union man in good standing with Firemen's Local No. 1 in Pittsburgh, had appointed three black Deputy Sheriffs for the county shortly after the Democrats captured the county government in 1935. P. J. Henney, the former Democratic Burgess of McKees Rocks who was elected to the State Senate in 1936, was elected Allegheny County Coroner in 1937 and appointed the county's first black Deputy County Coroner. The Democratic Allegheny County Treasurer was appointing blacks to jobs in the County Treasurer's Office. The Democratic County Register of Wills was appointing blacks to jobs in his office. County Commissioners John J. Kane and George Rankin were appointing blacks to jobs in the Bureau of Registration, the Bureau of Claims and Investigation, and the Board for Assessment and Revision of Taxes, as well as hiring 125 blacks for jobs as utilitymen, teamsters, caretakers, and chauffeurs. A high point of this process came when Homer S. Brown became the first black judge in Allegheny County.

Meanwhile, the Democrats who now controlled Pittsburgh appointed that city's first black policemen, firemen, and detectives. The Democratic city administration also appointed blacks as nurses at Mayview Hospital in the

Department of Public Welfare, a black building inspector, a black city assessor, a black Assistant City Solicitor, a black engineer in the Department of Public Works, black social workers, a black referee to the Workmen's Compensation Board, black court officers, and black clerks and stenographers to six different departments.

The city's Democratic administration also promised "sympathetic co-operation with efforts to include Negro teachers in the Public School System" and "Fair and unbiased appointments under the new Municipal Civil Service Law."

All in all, it was "A New Deal and A New Day for a New Negro." Unlike the Republicans, the Democratic Party had given "Performance, Not Promises." Therefore, blacks throughout the state were encouraged to support the party because, among other things, "A majority of the Negroes belong to the laboring classes and the Democratic Party is a Party for the laboring masses."

Political scientists Philip A. Klinkner and Rogers M. Smith, of Hamilton College and Yale University, respectively, have argued that black Americans have never progressed toward racial equality or fairness throughout our entire history except during time of war.[102] Indeed, they claim such periods of progress are "relatively rare" and, "Thus far in our history, [they have] occurred only during the Revolution, the Civil War, and the era of World War II and the Cold War."[103]

As we have seen, however, black Americans won a number of victories in both the Pittsburgh region and, because of the Little New Deal, in Pennsylvania as a whole at this time. This peace time progress toward racial equality ended de facto Jim Crow practices and laid the legislative ground work for a more assertive Civil Rights Movement yet to come. If we accept that Klinkner and Smith are correct about the other periods of racial improvement, then these Little New Deal efforts toward racial fairness are truly unique in American history and suggest the social conditions—other than hot or cold war—through which progress in race relations might be obtained.

****

The Democratic Party may have been a "Party for the laboring masses," but there was also a large portion of the Little New Deal program which was of a generally progressive, public improvement nature. For instance, it launched America's first superhighway, the 200-mile Pennsylvania Turnpike from Pittsburgh to Harrisburg. It passed slum clearance and public housing laws. It enacted a graduated state income tax. It instituted prison and court reform. The myriad local poor boards which administered public relief funds in sometimes arbitrary fashion were summarily abolished via a ripper bill and replaced by the state's present Department of Public Assistance.

The Little New Deal created Pennsylvania's present Public Utilities Commission to regulate public utilities and it passed regulatory legislation to keep consumer utility costs under control. A Fair Trades Practices Act forbade "dumping" of goods at below cost. The Anti-Pollution Act of 1937 began the process of banishing the environmental scourge of smoke and smog which had hovered eternally over the state's industrial regions. The abolition of capital punishment was proposed, but failed to pass.

Finally, the Little New Deal enacted electoral reform aimed at levelling the playing field between the urban-based Democrats and the rural-based Republicans. Between 1906 and 1937 the Republican-dominated Pennsylvania legislature had enacted a series of voter registration laws which required personal voter registration in the state's cities, but not in rural areas or in small towns. These were Progressive Era "reforms" which had the cumulative effect of disenfranchising large numbers of voters in urban and working class areas.[104]

David Lawrence and the urban-based Democrats now in control of the state legislature were much aware of the adverse impact of Pennsylvania's electoral laws. However, as with so many other such anti-working class "reforms" of the Progressive Era, it was not politically feasible to abolish these statutes. However, they were determined to redress the balance.

Therefore, in 1937, as part of a complete overhaul of the state's election laws, they imposed mandatory personal registration requirements on all rural areas of the state, as well. "Indeed," declares Walter Dean Burnham, "one of the more interesting fruits of the 1935-38 'Little New Deal' in Pennsylvania was this complete revamping of the state's elections laws, including the extension of personal registration requirements to all jurisdictions in the state."[105]

****

By November 1938, the radical reform project of Pennsylvania's Little New Deal had transformed the status of labor and of its primarily ethnic and black constituencies. Through laws such as the Little Wagner Act, state funding for strikers, the abolition of the hated Coal and Iron Police, and the use of the State Police to protect the civil rights of labor organizers, it had helped democratize labor-capital relations in the state. It had bettered the lives of workers by passing unemployment insurance and workmen's compensation legislation. It had raised minimum wages and shortened maximum hours. It had provided new jobs, new homes, and new hope for Pennsylvania's black citizens.

And what was true at the state level was also true at the county and local level in the Steel Valley. For both blacks and ethnic workers the Democratic Party had delivered on its promise of "equal opportunity," which these constituencies saw as the heart and soul of the New Deal.

The "Party for the laboring masses" had delivered a "Real Deal."

Now, the changes of the New Deal at the national level, and the Little New Deal at the state and county levels, had to be brought down to New Deals in the littlest jurisdictions of all, the myriad steel towns of the industrial heartland.

Steel Valley Resistance, 1932-1937

Things had already begun to change in the myriad mill towns of the Steel Valley after the election of Roosevelt in 1932. FDR provided a psychological umbrella which empowered the steelworkers of Pennsylvania to begin to move en masse. Duquesne steelworker Elmer Maloy remembered the tidal wave nature of political change his town: "In 1932, when Roosevelt was elected, there was a wave, when the Democratic votes started to hit, pretty soon everybody started to change their registration to Democrat. (The company couldn't stop them), it was too late, they couldn't do anything with them, they just changed, the whole lot of them."[106]

Louis DeSenna, who started working at Aliquippa's J. & L. mill in 1934, recalls that, "In 1932 we had some Democrats, but not too many. You'd lose your job real quick. They'd put you on a train. But then Roosevelt gave us the freedom to vote. Then, in 1937, we had a revolution and every one turned Democrat. Before that, it was a dangerous thing to say anything for either "Pappy" Roosevelt or the union."[107]

Aliquippa's Mike Zahorsky agreed. "It was Roosevelt," he said. "He was the father. Before that people were too fearful. But when Roosevelt was elected in 1932, nobody was fearful any more. We had no fears."[108]

The psychological and political impact of Roosevelt moved them in the direction of aggressive action even in the days of the old Amalgamated. The previously mentioned 1933 Frances Perkins incident in Homestead illustrates how unruly the workers quickly became.[109] Several hundred angry workers descended on the Homestead City Hall to speak with her following a tour of U.S. Steel's Homestead Works. When she asked Republican Burgess Cavanaugh if she could use the City Hall to meet with the workers, he refused, saying, "These men are no good. They are undesirable Reds."

Nevertheless, Perkins met them on the steps of the City Hall. Cavanaugh appeared at the head of a police contingent and told her, "You can't talk here! You are not permitted to make a speech here!" Perkins then saw the American flag flying over the post office just down the street. "We will go to the post office," she told the tense crowd. "There is an American flag."

She led the workers to the federal building, over which Burgess Cavanaugh had no jurisdiction, and held the meeting there under the protection of the American flag. "Twenty or thirty men" from the crowd accepted her invitation to speak up and "they said they wished the government would free them from the domination of the steel trust. We ended the meeting with handshaking and expressions of rejoicing that the New Deal wasn't afraid of the steel trust."

Notice that several hundred angry steelworkers had stormed the City Hall, demanding to see her *despite* Burgess Cavanaugh (Perkins described him as the "nervous Burgess") and his police. Further, at the subsequent meeting at the post office, over twenty workers were not afraid to step forth and speak publicly against "the steel trust." It had commonly been said before this that, "If you want to talk in Homestead, you have to talk to yourself," as anyone, even your best friend, could be a company spy. This fear quickly dissipated. Only the "nervous

Burgess" displayed any fear in this incident. John A. Fitch had discovered the workers' new confidence after a 1935 visit to Homestead.[110] The Perkins incident makes it clear, however, that workers were "talking union" even earlier.

Labor historian Edward Levinson claimed that the first union meeting to occur in Homestead was the one previously mentioned, the one which took place on July 5, 1936 under the auspices of the newly-formed SWOC, the one where the workers read their "Declaration of Independence."[111] Perhaps this claim was meant to glorify the "coming of SWOC" as something which finally gave the Homestead steelworkers the courage to speak up.

But prior to this, in 1933, the steelworkers of Homestead had already organized a local of the Amalgamated Association of Iron and Steel Workers. They did so three years to the day before SWOC was founded on June 16, 1936. The election of Roosevelt had encouraged workers in Homestead, as elsewhere, to take action on their own. Thus, on June 16, 1933, the very day the National Industrial Recovery Act was passed, a truck with loudspeakers boldly prowled the streets of Homestead announcing a public union meeting to be held that night at Turner Hall, in lower Homestead near the mill. Over a thousand Homestead steelworkers jammed into the hall to found the "Spirit of 1892" lodge of the Amalgamated.[112] *This* was the first official union meeting of the Thirties in Homestead, taking place even before the CIO was born.

Such working class restiveness also found an expression in the "new" labor-oriented Democratic Party as the Homestead municipal election of 1935 neared. That election was for three seats on the five member school board and seven seats on the fifteen-member borough council. It was the workers' first serious challenge to Republican rule at the local level in Homestead, a challenge met by police terror and fraudulent voter rolls.

Responding to pleas from Homestead workers, on Election Eve Lieutenant Governor Tom Kennedy, commander of the State Police, sent two detachments of the State Police to ensure a fair election. Even so, Election Day witnessed brutal street battles between workers and Cavanaugh's "Republican police," as the latter beat and attempted to intimidate Democratic candidates and voters.

Nevertheless, the worker-Democrats won all three seats on the School Board and four of the seven seats on the Council. The tide was beginning to turn in Homestead.

****

Workers were also becoming more restive in nearby Duquesne. On May 31, 1935, for example, the Ft. Dukane Lodge of the Amalgamated, led by William "Bill" Spang, attempted to strike in support of strikers in Canton, Ohio. Mayor Crawford ordered the police to suppress this effort by arresting and jailing Spang and the other lodge officers for parading without a permit.

This, however, failed to intimidate Spang and the Ft. Dukane Lodge membership. Following the release of the local union officers from jail, a mass meeting of Duquesne steelworkers called for a solidarity strike at all U.S. Steel facilities within two weeks, on June 16, 1935, to coincide with a projected United Mine Workers strike (which Lewis later cancelled).[113]

But instances of police repression such as this reminded the Ft. Dukane membership of the necessity for political, as well as workplace, action. Thus, the lodge passed a resolution calling for the formation of an independent, "anti-capitalist Labor Party."[114] Already, in 1930, the coal miners of Western Pennsylvania's Cambria County had actually launched such a Labor Party.[115] These actions indicate how strong the third party-labor party sentiment, an indication of class sentiment, remained among Western Pennsylvania mine and steelworkers only a short time before they began heavily voting Democratic.

More commonly, however, Duquesne's rebellious steelworkers were coming to see the Democratic Party as a more promising political vehicle. One of those who did so was Elmer J. Maloy, a World War I veteran and forty-five-year-old electrician in Duquesne's Carnegie-Illinois plant.

Maloy's father, an Irish-Catholic coal miner and member of the Knights of Labor, brought the family to Duquesne in 1911, at which time Maloy began working as a water boy in the mill. Over the next seven years he worked his way up through cover boy in the soaking pits, to craneman, to electrical millwright, before leaving to fight in Europe in 1918. Demobilized and back in Duquesne in time to be idled by the 1919 steel strike, he returned to the mill after the strike ended, working as a craneman on a stripper for the next fourteen years.[116]

In May 1935, the same time the Ft. Dukane Lodge of the Amalgamated was agitating under the leadership of Bill Spang, elections were held for a rival "company union" called the Employee Representation Plan (ERP). The ERPs were responses to increasing worker militancy through which management hoped to domesticate discontent.

With twenty-six years in the mill, Maloy had become popular with his workmates and was elected to head the Duquesne ERP almost without trying. As he described it, the workers themselves engineered his election and thrust him into prominence as their spokesman: "I wasn't even in the mill [on election day, but] I had told all these fellows, dinkmen, cranemen and the men who worked around the open hearth that I thought I'd run for employee representative, just to see if I could do something. They all got together, and when I came out I never saw such a thing. All the walks were painted with my check number and name, the water tower, clear up for 50 feet in the air, and down in the open hearth and all the buildings and everything. Well, I got twice as many votes as the two old representatives."[117]

Shortly thereafter, Maloy was elected to head the association of ERPs in all the Carnegie-Illinois plants of the Pittsburgh District. He immediately began making trouble, demanding a wage increase, for instance, the very day after his election in Duquesne. Charging company domination of the ERPs, he led a revolt of the company unions, which resulted in his ouster by the plant management on the grounds that he was covertly helping to organize the nascent Steelworkers Organizing Committee—though he was not a member of SWOC at the time.

Nevertheless, Maloy soon joined SWOC after it was founded on June 16, 1936, and was made National Grievance Chairman and President of Duquesne's SWOC Lodge No. 1256 once it organized.[118]

****

Police repression of organizing activity, such as that of the Ft. Dukane Lodge of the Amalgamated, was also the reason Louis DeSenna gave as why Aliquippa's steelworkers finally decided to organize politically. "If you're going to fight the company on a union basis," he said, "the cops in town are going to harass you to stop you from organizing. They'll raid your house and plant moonshine in your house, something of that nature. So, we had to go into politics."[119]

Mike Zahorsky echoed DeSenna's feeling that if the workers of Aliquippa couldn't gain some measure of political power, they would never be able to carry out the activities necessary to organize the mill: "We found out that whenever the sheriff came down with his deputies and he brought 150 people with guns and all we had were clubs—why, we felt we had to get into those offices where we could control that."[120]

Therefore, as in Homestead and Clairton the same year, steelworkers in Aliquippa entered the 1935 municipal elections. In that first political campaign, three of their candidates won minor offices, which were then abolished in retaliation. Seeking to gain some power over the police, Angelo Volpe, Vice President of the local Amalgamated Lodge No. 200, ran for constable and received 3,293 votes to the winning Republican's 4,690—the most votes ever received by a Democrat in Aliquippa.

A surge of Democratic registration accompanied this increase in Democratic votes. While Aliquippa's Democratic registration hovered between 50 and 100 throughout the 1920s, by early 1935 Aliquippa's Beaver County already had 20,960 registered Democrats to 45,675 Republicans, only a little more than a two-to-one edge for the Republicans.[121] Reminiscent of Maloy's rationale for the explosion of Democratic registrations in Duquesne, Zahorsky explained this mushrooming growth on the grounds that, "There were so many that they couldn't fire everyone."[122]

This political groundswell began to undermine the ruling powers. Indeed, even as early as 1934, political leverage had begun to crack open Aliquippa. In his chapter on the unionization campaign in Aliquippa, Robert R.R. Brooks recreates a conversation between Joseph Timko and SWOC Regional Director Clint Golden on June 18, 1936, two days after SWOC had been created by John L. Lewis' fiat.[123] Timko, a veteran UMW organizer in Harlan County, Kentucky, had just been brought to Pittsburgh to become Sub-Regional Director for the Beaver Valley, which included Aliquippa, Ambridge, and Midland. Golden gave Timko a capsule history of Aliquippa before sending him in.

Aliquippa and Midland had not joined in the 1919 strike because of the tight control the corporations and their Republican allies had over the towns.

"Aliquippa," in particular, said Golden, "is a dark town. Even Bill [William Z.] Foster's organizers couldn't get near it back in 1919. Company and city police barred the roads and watched the railroad station. When strangers couldn't give a good account of themselves, they were hustled to jail overnight and then out of town."

On October 4, 1934, Republican Governor Gifford Pinchot, a relative progressive, had sent in the State Police after J. & L. railroaded union organizer George Isasky into an insane asylum. Golden remembered that the State Police "Opened up the town and on October 14, Cornelia Bryce Pinchot spoke at the first labor meeting the town had ever seen. There were more than four thousand there. Men began to sign union cards [to join the Amalgamated] right and left and in a month or so there were over three thousand members."

Later SWOC President Philip Murray was himself more explicit and more dramatic in describing the self-organization of Aliquippa steelworkers in 1934. Speaking to the October 1935 AFL annual convention in Atlantic City in favor of the resolution calling for industrial unionism, Murray recalled that, "I was invited to a meeting in the town of Aliquippa eighteen months ago [around April 1934], at the great plant of the Jones & Laughlin Steel Company, where some 8,000 men are employed. The workers employed in that plant, *of their own volition, of their own motion, without an organizer attending the meeting in its initial stages,* called meetings. And those workers operating under their own motion, without any assistance from any international union, without any assistance from the American Federation of Labor, at that time organized 6,500 of the 8,000 workers at the Aliquippa plant into an independent union."[124]

But, it seems that the pace of unionization, even the ability to sustain union gains, ebbed and flowed with available political support. The State Police could not remain as a permanent occupation force and, when they left, the status quo ante reasserted itself: "The company kept right at it with discharges, discrimination, evictions, and so on," Golden asserted. "The union began to melt away and continued to drop off even after charges were brought under the National Labor Relations Act."

Then Golden sent Timko on his way. He advised Timko to set the SWOC office up in neighboring Ambridge, across the Ohio River, because Philip J. Caul, the Democratic Burgess (and a member of the carpenters' union there), would protect him. Timko did so. When he held his first SWOC organizational meeting in Aliquippa itself, it was in the local Democratic Party headquarters—which the steelworkers of Aliquippa had already taken over with steelworker Angelo Volpe serving as President.

During the late summer of 1936 Timko launched the SWOC organizational campaign in Aliquippa with mass outdoor meetings held in vacant lots. That these initial SWOC meetings were possible at all was because they had some political clout on their side. As he had done in Homestead in 1935, Lieutenant Governor and UMW Secretary-Treasurer Tom Kennedy sent state troopers to stand guard over them.[125]

In this, Kennedy was being true to his word. At the mass meeting of

Homestead steelworkers on July 5, 1936, where they had read their "Declaration of Independence," Kennedy had pledged State Police protection and financial aid in case of a strike. "If the steel magnates throw people out in the streets as a result of organization activities, they will be entitled to relief," he said. Further, he assured the workers that the National Guard or the State Police would not be called in to break their strikes, as had happened in 1892 and 1919. "Governor Earle," he told them, "as commander-in-chief of the military and police organizations of the state, will see that workers get their constitutional rights, the captains of steel can't get away with the stuff they got away with before. The government of the United States is now in Washington, not New York, and the government of Pennsylvania is now in Harrisburg, not Pittsburgh."[126]

But, it was still up to the workers of the Steel Valley to take control of their local governments. As early as 1907, John Fitch had felt that, "The Pittsburgh steelworkers are very nearly ready for a political movement. They are inwardly seething with discontent. The workingmen of Pittsburgh or any other American community could not be roused over night to the point of serious, premeditated, revolutionary violence. Revolutions, however, do not necessarily involve violence. And through either the trade union or the political movement, there is bound to be a revolution erelong that shall have as its goal the restoration of democracy to the steelworkers."[127]

****

In early 1937, Elmer Maloy made an apparently independent decision to run for Mayor of Duquesne against Burgess James Crawford. The reason he gave, however, was the same as that given by the union activists elsewhere. "I was mad at Jim Crawford and the Chief of Police," he remembered. "I wanted to get him out of office and I wanted to control the city; the police force especially."[128]

The catalyst seems to have been the denial by Crawford and the Police Chief of Maloy's request for a permit to hold a union meeting. Maloy decided to hold the meeting anyway and rented the Croatian Hall for $30.

But, he said, "Then the bank [of which Crawford was president] put the screws on the Croatian Hall, because they had a mortgage on the place. They told them they were going to foreclose the mortgage unless they withdrew their rental of the hall to me. And then I had gone to every hall that there was in the place and some of them told me, 'We're being subsidized by the company, paying so much rent a month to not rent the hall to you, or any labor organizations.' Well, I got sort of peeved about this, so I said, 'Damn it. I know what I'll do. I'll run for Mayor. Then I know that we can hold a meeting, and the first meeting we're going to hold, we'll hold right up in the City Council chambers!'"[129]

This decision on Maloy's part was not part of any strategy devised by the top SWOC leadership, nor did the national leadership even seem to care about it. When asked if John L. Lewis or Phil Murray endorsed him or helped in any way, Maloy emphatically denied their involvement. "They didn't endorse us," he said, "either me or [John] Mullen [in Clairton]. They didn't put a dime into the campaign. They had absolutely nothing to do with it. I understood that Mullen received a very small sum of money, like $300 or $400, you know, something that couldn't be used very well in a political campaign. But I received absolutely nothing."[130]

Nor did what passed for the local Democratic Party welcome Maloy's candidacy. The "old" Democrats endorsed another candidate for the primary election. To overcome his lack of money and official endorsement, Maloy relied upon the same steelworkers who had elected him president of the local ERP: "I figured that with the vote I had in the open hearths alone I had a nucleus. There were about 700 guys, not counting their wives, enough to swing the primary. At the time I ran, there were a good thousand union members, mostly foreigners [i.e., ethnics]."[131]

And, while Maloy's decision to run was his alone—just as his decision to run for ERP representative was his alone—once made it seemed to unleash a torrent of steelworker energy. In John Fitch's words, they were "ready for a political movement." Workers swarmed to Maloy's impoverished campaign and made his campaign their own. "All of these people that worked for us," Maloy recalled, "were a whole indiscriminate group of Croatians, Serbians, Hungarians, and colored. They were real workers. Nobody could bribe them. They didn't get any pay. They didn't *want* any pay. They even contributed money, you know, to run the campaign. They lost work, they laid off, they went to every meeting, they campaigned door-to-door, they did the most efficient job. In fact, I was told later by John Kane, the County Commissioner, that it was the most efficient political organization he had ever seen."[132]

Borne on the backs of these workers, Maloy smashed the candidate of the "old" Democrats in the primary. Now Maloy and his "indiscriminate group" of ethnic and colored steelworkers *were* the Democratic Party in Duquesne.

Meanwhile, Mayor Crawford had decided to step down after sixteen years in office and anointed as his successor in the Republican primary R.W. Schriber, owner of the Duquesne Bus Company and the town's largest shipping garage. At the same time, the "old" Democrats who had been shoved aside in the primary by the steelworker campaign refused to accept Maloy as their candidate. "The local Democrats," said one report, "virtually deserted their candidate and worked for the election of the Republican candidate."[133]

Maloy ignored that "official" Republican candidate and campaigned against Crawford himself, who remained the power behind the throne. It was a logical decision. Ex-Mayor James C. Crawford was the president of the town's only bank and brother of the former president of the McKeesport Tinplate Corp. Crawford had been the only mayor in Duquesne's twenty-year history as an incorporated third-class city and was notorious for crushing the 1919 steel strike in his town during which he declared that "Jesus Christ himself could not hold a union meeting in Duquesne."

Maloy attacked Crawford for arranging to have his mid-town mansion, surrounded by a quarter-mile stone wall, assessed as a farm. He lashed Crawford for keeping Duquesne "in chronic bankruptcy since 1917 through such maneuvers as placing $300,000 of the city's funds in his own bank at no interest, then lending the city $1,500,000 at 6 percent."[134]

Maloy chastised Crawford for ignoring the material infrastructure of the city and for refusing to accept any of the New Deal's relief programs for Duquesne's needy. But most of all he challenged Crawford's anti-union stance which prevented union organizers from exercising their basic civil liberties of free speech, free association, and freedom from coercion.

An indication of the hope and enthusiasm ignited by Elmer Maloy's campaign may be gleaned from an account of Democratic Governor George Earle's visit to Duquesne to stump for Maloy and urge the defeat of local Republicans "hostile to Roosevelt's program."[135] Over 1,500 "wildly cheering Duquesne voters jammed the city high school auditorium and grounds" to hear Maloy, Earle, Pat Fagin, President of District 5 (Pittsburgh region) of the United Mine Workers, Democratic Congressman Henry Ellenbogen [who represented Pittsburgh's South Side], and others blast the Crawford administration.

The auditorium had been jammed beyond capacity with not even packed standing room left fully an hour and a half before the arrival of the speakers. For the benefit of the "hundreds who were not able to get even standing room," a public address system was hastily erected so that the speeches could be broadcast to those milling around outside the building.

A caravan of "blaring bands" and honking cars escorted Elmer Maloy and the other dignitaries up to the auditorium entrance where they received a hero's welcome as they made their triumphal way through the wildly cheering throng. Once inside, Maloy was introduced by Congressman Ellenbogen as, "A man risen from the ranks of labor and one who knows its problems." Maloy then "assailed the present city administration, charging it with being reactionary and always hostile to labor." He called for a "liberalization of Duquesne" because, "We've been called the most reactionary city in the United States, simply because of the domination of the Republicans."

Maloy's candidacy lit a match in a gas-filled room and the resulting explosion swept out Crawford and his cronies. Maloy carried the working class neighborhoods of Duquesne in a convincing demonstration of the power of the "new" Democratic vote. "Oh, hell," remembered Maloy, "they went solid. My brother [who was Chairman of the Democratic City Committee] had been down in the first ward (on election day) where all these Croatians, Hungarians, Serbs, and all the colored lived (and knew how they'd voted). When the vote came in, I won without any problem at all."[136]

The entire "new" Democratic slate, with the single exception of the office of City Controller, also won with no problem at all.

****

In explaining Aliquippa labor's 1937 re-entry into politics (workers had already contested the 1935 municipal elections, winning some victories), Manuel Wood, who had by then replaced Timko as the top SWOC organizer in town, explained that political power was a necessary first step toward unionization. In an August 8, 1937 speech to J. & L. workers at Aliquippa's Polish Hall he said, "The present Republican administration has sided with employers against labor again and again, using its police powers to harass and oppress union men and terrorize the town in an effort to prevent the union from getting a foothold here. It has always been an enemy of the people, and we must throw it out of office."[137]

The steelworkers of Aliquippa proceeded to do this first by challenging the "old" Democrats in the September Democratic primary. They had already taken over the party organization, known as the Democratic Social Club, with their 1935 constable candidate, Angelo Volpe, as president. This worker-dominated Democratic Social Club named a full primary slate of candidates for all offices, headed by George Keifer, a pro-union druggist, as their Burgess candidate.

Keifer's main platform promise was, "We will have but one Chief of Police and one Police Force. Their duties will be to police the town of Aliquippa, keep law and order and meddle with nothing else. The Police Department will be under the direct supervision of the Burgess with the approval of Council. The entire Police Force will take orders from nobody else [such as J. & L.]"[138]

Six of the ten "new" labor-Democratic candidates running with Keifer were union members. They included Council candidate Peter P. Haubner, a Grievance Committeeman for the tin mill and a member of the Socialist Party; Council candidate Michael O'Connor, member of the Railroad Brotherhood; Auditor candidate Michael J. Wallace, a Grievance Committeeman for the welded tube mill; School Director candidate Harrison Kirkwood, hot mill shop steward; and School Director candidate Paul Luger, an officer in the local meat cutters' union. Even the precinct level candidates included members of labor unions for the offices of Judge and Inspector of Elections in the various wards.

Leading the "new" Democratic slate of City Council candidates was Paul Normile, who had replaced Volpe as President of Aliquippa's SWOC lodge. Normile pledged to bring in New Deal programs such as the WPA and PWA, which the current "Republican rule" refused to do.

But above all else was the pledge to do something about the police. First and foremost, the "importation" of outsiders to staff the Aliquippa police force had to end. Of thirty-five police officers, only three lived in Aliquippa, seeming to guarantee a hostility on the part of the "occupation force" toward Aliquippa workers. "We pledge ourselves," swore Normile, "that in the selection of police officers, we will first select local residents."[139]

The message of independence was also repeated by the "new" Democratic candidates for Justices of the Peace. Speaking to a rally of Aliquippa steelworkers at the Serbian Hall on September 12, just before the primary, R. J. McLanahan "promised that in his capacity as Justice of the Peace he would accept orders from no one," while Ivor L. Jones "promised to uphold the American rights of Democracy."

The workers of Aliquippa, it seemed, wanted these "American rights of Democracy" more than anything. In the September 14 primary, their slate of "True Roosevelt Democrats" trounced the "old" Democrats to become the official standard bearers of the party, with Keifer defeating his "old" Democratic opponent five to one. The steelworkers and their leaders were now the Democratic Party in Aliquippa.

Next they attacked the Republican-Corporation hegemony. There was a spirit of euphoria in the air. It seemed the entire population of Aliquippa was united in opposition to an alien occupation army. All things—even American Democracy—seemed possible.

"A Colored Voter" reflected the spirit of the movement in a letter written to *The Union Press* shortly before the election. In words reminiscent of the Declaration of Independence, he not only tells us what the "revolutionary ideology" of the workers was, but also illustrates how that ideology tended to be all-inclusive, turning the crusade into a multi-racial crusade, as well as multi-ethnic.

"Our citizens have long realized," he wrote, "that *there has come into this community a feeling that every man and woman has certain inalienable rights* and he who surrenders them is less than a man. Our citizens are determined to test whether the principles of democracy shall be applied in Aliquippa or whether the selfish interest of a favored few political bosses shall continue to triumph against the will of our citizens. In this election every right and privilege that our citizens yearned for will be at stake. This is simply the will of an oppressed and aroused citizenry bent upon the execution of those national symbols which are embodied in the articles of our Constitutional guarantee. During their many years of official tyranny imposed upon our citizens their long train of abuses pursued invariably an objective designed to reduce us to absolute serfdom. Now it is our right and our duty to throw off the yoke of Republicanism."[140]

The sentiments of this "Colored Voter" seemed to be widespread, for the "new" labor-Democrats dominated the November elections, electing Keifer as Burgess and winning all but one Council seat. It was the first political defeat for the Republican-Corporation alliance in all of Aliquippa's history.

The Angry Cry of the Dispossessed

These steelworker victories in the 1937 municipal elections in the steel towns surrounding Pittsburgh are perhaps the most dramatic examples of how much had changed. The victories weren't just in Duquesne and Aliquippa. They were everywhere.

Stretching for miles up and down the Monongahela, Allegheny, and Ohio Rivers, the grimy steel towns of Western Pennsylvania represented perhaps the largest concentration of industrial might in the world. Described collectively by

The Bulletin Index as "Steeltown," these small communities were emblematic both of the country's industrial heartland and of the business-oriented Republican grip upon that heart:

"As a composite," *The Index* said, "Steeltown has had a grim, long-publicized history of adamant, walled opposition against labor unionism, rough treatment of 'alien' agitators, undisguised steel company domination. No more solid symbol of rock-ribbed Republicanism was there in the U.S. prior to 1932 than Steeltown." Thus, the *Bulletin Index* described the municipal elections of 1937 in the Steel Valley as being "of transcendent significance."[141]

Of all the component communities comprising Steeltown, the largest was McKeesport, just east of Pittsburgh and home of the huge McKeesport Tinplate Corporation and the National Tube Company. There, seventy-year-old Mayor George H. Lysle, who had been in office for twenty-seven years, survived the unprecedented challenge of "Democratic Laborite" Carl Bechtol, a worker at the National Tube Co., who would be elected to the City Council in the next election. But Lysle's was a solitary victory.

"The day after election, Lysle could look out over the string of steel towns that flank McKeesport and see not one familiar face in the mayoral chairs of Steeltown. Before him stretched a lonely term as the last of Steeltown's Old Guard."[142] He was, said *The Pittsburgh Post-Gazette,* virtually the sole exception to the "mighty wave of Democratic victory which rolled over Allegheny County yesterday."[143]

Duquesne was directly across the Monongahela River from McKeesport and the third largest community in Steeltown after McKeesport and Aliquippa. There the new Burgess would be "C.I.O.-Democrat" Elmer J. Maloy, a twenty-six-year veteran in the local Carnegie-Illinois mill and chief of the local SWOC lodge. The defeat of his designated heir was viewed as a crushing repudiation of ex-Burgess James Crawford himself.[144]

John J. Mullen was the new Mayor-elect in Clairton which, according to the *Post-Gazette,* did not go Democratic; it "went CIO," reflecting the popular impression that this was a triumph for the CIO local unions more than a Democratic Party victory.[145] Clairton was, said the *Index,* "long rated with Aliquippa as the two most typical company-dominated steel towns in the U.S."[146]

Mullen, the local Sub-District Director for the Steel Workers Organizing Committee (SWOC), defeated a Clairton policeman to become the first Democrat ever elected to any office in the town's history. Unlike the situation in every other Steeltown campaign (and perhaps because Mullen was on the SWOC headquarters staff), SWOC chief Philip Murray had a reluctant SWOC Treasurer David McDonald contribute some small funds out of the SWOC treasury to Mullen's campaign.[147]

Despite this, Mullen's campaign (like those of other Steeltown candidates who coincidentally happened to be SWOC members) was very much a venture independent of SWOC—and the Clairton Democratic organization as well. As in Duquesne, the regular Democrats endorsed one of their own in the primary. Mullen, however, was the Democrat calling for class war and his candidacy tapped into a tidal wave of popular sentiment. He rolled over the old-line Democrat in the primary.

Then, despite a "four-to-one Republican registration lead in this town, strictly because of mill dominance,"[148] Mullen led the Democratic slate to complete victory in the November elections, not even allowing the Republicans a single office, as they had won in Duquesne. "I took it as a showing that our people were tired of suppression," Mullen said. "If they were really allowed to voice their hopes and their thoughts, they would vote Democratic and vote for a union, too. I ran on the basis that a vote for me was a vote for unionism, that's how I became the mayor."[149]

In Aliquippa, west of Pittsburgh on the Ohio River and long controlled by the Jones & Laughlin Steel Corporation, all but one of the CIO-Democratic candidates swept into offices ranging from Mayor and Council down to Tax Collector and Inspector of Elections. This ended the twenty-three-year reign of J.A.C. Ruffner. Ruffner had been Tax Collector since 1914, Chairman of the local Republican Party since 1916, was Director and First Vice-President of the town's only bank, director of the sole building and loan company, director of the community's major trust company, and owner of *The Aliquippa Gazette,* the town's only newspaper. Replacing him was a CIO-Democratic administration whose leading member was Paul Normile, President of the Aliquippa SWOC lodge.

Directly across the Ohio from Aliquippa in Ambridge, a town named after a U.S. Steel subsidiary, the American Bridge Corporation, Democratic Burgess (Mayor) Philip J. Caul, an AFL plasterer, was elected, along with his entire slate, due to massive support from the local SWOC lodge.

Caul had earlier served as the Ambridge Chief of Police and *The Union Press,* weekly newspaper of the Aliquippa SWOC lodge, praised him before the election for his pro-labor orientation in that office. "During the earlier days when he first occupied the office of Chief of Police," it said, "he waged a relentless fight against the encroachments of Coal and Iron Police within the territorial limits of the Borough and succeeded in eliminating the nefarious practice of industrial police patrolling the streets of the Borough and spying upon the private affairs of the citizens."[150]

Every other part of Steeltown repeated the story. In Homestead, a labor-based slate of candidates, "sweeping every Republican before it," ended the sixteen-year incumbency of local Republican Party boss and Burgess John Cavanaugh, the "nervous burgess."[151] Along with a new Burgess, eight Democratic Councillors, four Democratic School Board members, a Democratic Tax Collector, and a Democratic Justice of the Peace were installed.

A thousand steelworkers celebrated Cavanaugh's defeat with a honking 100-car caravan down Eighth Avenue, Homestead's main street. Bearing a coffin emblazoned with Cavanaugh's name and led, appropriately, by a "Democratic" donkey ridden by a Homestead steelworker, "mourners" forced themselves to weep by squeezing freshly cut onions under their eyes.

Of the many Republican defeats in the various communities of Steeltown on that election day, the *Pittsburgh Post-Gazette* thought the "Most outstanding of these was the overwhelming defeat of Burgess John J. Cavanaugh. Many years during his regime he ruled the borough with an iron hand, controlling the naming of many borough and county office holders."[152]

In Donora, home of a large American Steel & Wire facility, Democrat Michael J. Sweeney, a high school math teacher and son of an Irish coal miner, was elected Burgess with labor backing.

New Kensington, run by the Pittsburgh-based Aluminum Company of America (ALCOA), "saw its Republican ribs broken by a thirty-four-year-old Reliance Life Insuranceman named Dick Miller Reeser."[153] Reeser, a drummer and a member of the AFL's American Federation of Musicians, was backed by the local SWOC lodge to become the first Democrat ever elected to any office in the town.

In Monessen, Democratic Mayor and SWOC member James C. Gold, a twenty-nine-year veteran of the open hearth furnace, was elected.

The CIO-Democrats cleaned out the entire Republican Council in Rankin, across the Monongahela from Homestead, along with the 12-year incumbent Burgess. The new burgess was John Martcshek, a laborer at Union Switch & Signal and a member of the CIO's United Electrical Workers, Local 610.

Returns in next door Braddock, home of U.S. Steel's behemoth Edgar Thomson Works, revealed "a clean sweep" for the CIO-Democrats. In North Braddock, up in the "American" hills overlooking "Hunky" dominated Braddock, only the Republican Burgess survived "an avalanche of votes" that elected five CIO-Democratic Councillors.[154]

In McKees Rocks, the CIO-Democrats finished the job begun in 1933, sweeping out the last holdover Republican officials and taking all borough offices, with the CIO-Democratic Burgess candidate leading his Republican opponent by five-to-one.

There was "complete victory" for the CIO-Democrats in the race for five City Council seats in East Pittsburgh.[155]

"The impossible happened in Glassport," said the *Post-Gazette,* "where a Democratic slate that was not given a chance in a thousand swept into power, ousting a Republican rule that had existed beyond the memory of the oldest residents." Joseph Faix, Jr., a local glassworker, was the new Burgess, with CIO-Democrats filling every other office in the city. Even though the Glassport vote was still laboriously hand-counted, "The vote was so top heavy, the Republican slate conceded defeat an hour after the count began."[156]

Some soon afterwards hailed this political earthquake as a triumph for Labor's Non-Partisan League, which had remained in existence after having been formed the previous year by CIO-leader John L. Lewis to aid in the re-election of President Roosevelt.[157]

Others described it as a centralized SWOC headquarters initiative. Yale professor Robert R.R. Brooks, in an almost contemporary history of the unionization of steel, viewed the 1937 political transformation of Steeltown as vital in the success of unionizing the steel industry. "Such formerly 'closed' towns or boroughs as Clairton, Duquesne, Brackenridge, Aliquippa, Ambridge, and

Midland," he said, "are now either completely controlled or powerfully influenced by union members. This fact is of considerable significance in connection with the permanent establishment of unionism in steel communities."

However, he also incorrectly described it as a top-down strategy. "S.W.O.C. encouraged lodge leaders in the 'company' towns of Pennsylvania and Ohio to enter contests for such offices as those of mayor, burgess, constable, and town or borough council," he said.[158]

On the other hand, George Powers, a labor champion who lived through these dramatic events, highlighted the fact that these were not victories of Labor's Non-Partisan League or even SWOC headquarters, but of local union lodges acting on their own. He also declared that the significance of these 1937 Steeltown victories was not just in establishing unionism in steel, but also in introducing political democracy to America's industrial heartland.

"For the first time in the history of the Monongahela Valley," he said, "people were free to exercise their vote as they saw fit, no longer cowed by the pressure of the mill superintendent. There was a new freedom over the land."[159]

Workers in Power

Elmer Maloy, the new Mayor of Duquesne, immediately promised a "New Deal for Duquesne." "The banks have made enough off of Duquesne," he declared. "That will end." There had never been a single WPA project in Duquesne. "Well, that is something we will have," he vowed.[160]

A month later, both Maloy and John Mullen, the new Clairton Mayor, were in Washington, D.C., to testify before Congress about labor conditions. A Washington newspaper noted that, "The fact that these two CIO organizers became mayors last month was pointed to as evidence in itself of some kind of a New Deal in their communities."[161]

The "New Deal" which Maloy instituted in Duquesne was, first and foremost, a labor-oriented New Deal, a "Workers' Democracy." True to his promise, SWOC President Elmer Maloy held the first post-election meeting of the local SWOC lodge in the Duquesne City Council chambers—at the invitation of Mayor Elmer Maloy.

Virtually his first official act was to appoint his brother Bill, already the Chairman of Duquesne's Democratic City Committee and a twenty-year veteran of the police force, as the new Chief of Police. His next act was to disarm the company's private police force. Maloy recalled the importance of this act: "In Allegheny County, they used to deputize all the mill police when there was labor trouble, so you didn't have a chance, see? When I became mayor, I took away all their guns, made them leave them in the plant. They weren't allowed to go out of the plant without a gun permit. The only one who could give it to them was me and I just refused to permit them to have a gun."[162]

As far as the SWOC organizing efforts were concerned, disarming the company police and putting the city police under the control of his brother made all the difference in the world. One magazine featured a photo, for instance, of a SWOC member handing out leaflets at the plant gates in Duquesne and noted in the caption, "Today, leaflets can be distributed without restriction at factory gates. Before Mayor Maloy's time, this was unheard of."[163]

Within two weeks of taking office, Mayor Maloy had facilitated the enrollment of all city employees into the CIO's State, County, and Municipal Workers of America and reduced the Fire Department from a seventy-two- to a forty-hour work week.[164]

He then set up a relief office in the SWOC hall and began interviewing applicants personally. Mayor Crawford had not allowed federal relief programs to be implemented in Duquesne, so there was a large reservoir of need. Over 1,000 were quickly entered into the newly established relief rolls.

Maloy also welcomed the WPA to Duquesne for the first time. Using WPA funds, Maloy built and repaired roads, constructed a "modern red-brick school house," and instituted WPA work projects, which garnered wide support. As Ben Kirschbaum, a "credit jeweler," said, "I'm for the mayor on principle. He is for progressive things like housing and sewing projects."[165]

These initiatives were accomplished without raising taxes or going into debt. "Economy in administration is a Maloy slogan," reported one source, and it seemed to be true. Working with Dominic Genito, "Special Fireman" in charge of public improvements, Maloy installed a traffic light system, police and fire boxes, and laid new cables for the city's power lines at nominal cost. "Dominic and Mayor Maloy made most improvements out of scrap materials from mills," and the scrap pipe for the traffic light stands cost $20 for the entire city.[166]

Maloy's frugality was coupled with new sources of revenue. For instance, the city's account was transferred out of Crawford's bank and to a bank which began paying interest on the deposits. Also, within two weeks of taking office, Maloy had reduced the annual municipal budget by $6,000 when he "sliced the salaries of higher ups."[167]

Duquesne's "Workers' Democracy" also meant a New Deal for the "colored," who were part of Maloy's "new" Democratic coalition. Maloy made a point of improving municipal services for "below the tracks" black neighborhoods. But the political revolution in the Steel Valley also brought great changes for blacks *as* blacks. It was in 1938, for example, after the "new" Democratic administrations came into office, that Jim Crow policies started to topple in Homestead, Clairton, and throughout the Steel Valley.

The change for blacks had already begun after the Democrats gained control of the State House and elected George Earle governor in 1934. As we have seen, with the 1935 revision of Pennsylvania's Civil Rights Act of 1887, racial discrimination was outlawed at all public facilities in Pennsylvania.

But laws do not enforce themselves. Someone has to be willing to enforce them. And it was in 1937 in Pittsburgh and 1938 in the Steel Valley, after the new SWOC administrations came into office, that Jim Crow policies really started to fall. In 1937, black teachers for the first time successfully integrated the Pittsburgh public school teaching staff.

Meanwhile, black Homestead residents successfully challenged, and abolished, the customary Jim Crow segregation of that town's theaters and businesses in 1938, after the new SWOC administration came into office.

In John Mullen's Clairton, 3,000 black residents threatened to swim in the city's whites-only swimming pool when it opened for the summer of 1939, quickly forcing its de-segregation.[168]

This Civil Rights Movement continued in the region into the 1940s. It was in the 1940s, for instance, that K. Leroy Irvis, then an Urban League staff member, later a long-time State Representative from Pittsburgh, led the picket lines at department stores in Downtown Pittsburgh which resulted in the hiring of black salesclerks—reputedly "the first such incident in the nation."[169]

Duquesne's "Workers' Democracy" proved popular and Maloy was pressured to run for a second four-year term in 1941, even though he felt he'd accomplished everything he set out to do. "I really didn't want to run a second time," he said. "I never wanted the mayor's job. All I wanted to do in the first place was to take the place over. The union was strong enough now, so I didn't give a damn." Nevertheless, he allowed himself to be acclaimed as the Democratic candidate, although "I was too busy [with union business] to be bothered with campaigning."[170]

Maloy didn't need to. Although he recalled that he was hardly in town during the campaign, others—the same ones who had carried him to victory on their backs the first time—did it for him. Maloy returned to the Mayor's seat for another four years entirely because, complained *The Duquesne Times,* he had an "army" of "former residents of below the tracks," ethnic and colored "Roosevelt followers" who believed "the Democratic Party is on a level with Moses."[171]

Workers' Democracy in Duquesne, it seemed, had a life of its own, entirely independent of Maloy.

****

Although not all the City Council seats in Aliquippa had been up for election in 1937, and so the Republicans still retained a majority on the Council, never again would Aliquippa be run as a company town.

When the new municipal government was sworn in on January 3, 1938, the new labor-Democratic City Councillors and Burgess introduced a motion to fire six of the most vicious town policemen. The resulting battle over control of the police force grew into what *The Aliquippa Gazette* termed a "Burgess-Council War," the eventual culmination of which was neither a complete purge of the police nor a return to the status quo ante of unrestrained police terror.[172] The political atmosphere of the town had been irrevocably altered and "The use of repressive political force in the company's interest abated. Incidents of police use or denied meeting permits to stifle union activity became less common."[173]

Workers' Democracy in Aliquippa was a force even Republican Party boss J.A.C. Ruffner felt that, at long last, he must come to terms with. In a 1939

anniversary issue of Ruffner's previously anti-SWOC *Aliquippa Gazette,* the
paper carried a full-page article on SWOC written by the local lodge recording
secretary and "No hint of antiunionism appeared in the issue."[174]

Indeed, in order to survive in Aliquippa's transformed political environment,
even the Republicans had to become pro-union. In the 1941 mayoralty election,
Republican candidate Charles O'Laughlin, former head of J. & L.'s private police
force, did his best to out-SWOC the "new" Democratic leaders. Speaking at a
SWOC-sponsored rally of J. & L. workers, he told them to, "spread the philosophy
of 100 percent unionism, go to meetings, pay your dues, follow your leadership,
and fight for your rights and against wrong."

His statements electrified his audience. "This," said the local newspaper,
"represented a complete reversal in Republican tactics in handling the borough's
10-20,000 workers."[175] Indeed, such comments illustrated how solidly the New
Deal political realignment and Workers' Democracy had been hammered home at
the most local level by rank and file workers themselves.

Thus, Workers' Democracy meant more than the coming of the union. It also
meant that the Bill of Rights, that democracy itself, had finally come to America's
industrial heartland. Robert Brooks asked an Aliquippa steelworker and SWOC
leader what he thought the labor movement's greatest contribution had been. "To
be able to walk down the main street of Aliquippa," the worker answered, "[and]
talk to anyone you want about anything you lke, and feel that you are a citizen."[176]

Notes

1. This was the opinion, for example, of socialist Michael Harrington and many others.
See Michael Harrington, *Socialism,* Saturday Review Press: New York, 1972, 260, and J.
David Greenstone, *Labor in American Politics,* Knopf: New York, 1969, 4, 6-7, and 50-51.

2. Quoted in George E. Mowry, *The Urban Nation: 1920-1960,* Hill and Wang: New
York, 1965, 110.

3. Robert Garland was the Grand Old Man of the Council, having served continuously
since 1911 when the nine-member at-large Council was created. Outside of Pittsburgh, he
was known as the man who persuaded Woodrow Wilson to adopt daylight saving time.

4. *Post-Gazette,* October 11, 1934. James Coyne was head of the Allegheny County
Republican Party.

5. *Pittsburgh Press,* February 19, 1935.

6. *Pittsburgh Press,* July 18, 1934, and *The New York Times,* July 19, 1934, 1.

7. Minutes of the Pittsburgh Central Labor Union, December 21, 1933, in the holdings of
the Pittsburgh Typographical Union, Lo. No. 7, Archives of Industrial Society, University
of Pittsburgh. Hereafter, "Minutes of the PCLU."

8. Minutes of the PCLU, September 6 and 20, 1934.

9. Minutes of the PCLU, October 18, 1934.

10. Minutes of the PCLU, December 6, 1934.

11. Minutes of the PCLU, February 14, 21, 1935.

12. *Pittsburgh Press,* February 24, February 27, 1935.

13. *Pittsburgh Press,* February 26, 1935.

14. *Pittsburgh Press,* February 7, 1935.

15. Accusation made by Edward Jones, Pennsylvania State WPA Administrator, *Pittsburgh Sun-Telegraph,* October 7, 1935.

16. *Pittsburgh Press,* March 16, 1935.

17. See Allegheny County Employment Records, 1930-35, City-County Building, Pittsburgh.

18. See *Pittsburgh Press,* February 11, and *Pittsburgh Sun-Telegraph,* February 11, 1935. Also, *Legislative Journal,* Commonwealth of Pennsylvania, 1935, 417 and 446.

19. *Pittsburgh Press,* March 7, 1935.

20. Minutes of the PCLU, July 18, 1935.

21. Minutes of the PCLU, June 4, 1931, February 4 and 18, 1932.

22. Speech by John J. Kane, September 15, 1935, found in the David L. Lawrence Speech Folder, Allegheny County Democratic Committee Headquarters.

23. Letter in the Publicity File, Allegheny County Democratic Committee Headquarters, Pittsburgh.

24. The 1935 election is also interesting for what was happening across the state in Philadelphia. Virtually alone among big Northeastern cities, Philadelphia did not succumb to Democratic control in the Thirties. Yet, it might not be accurate to view this as a case of "failed realignment," for the realignment process was also at work there in the increasing Democratic vote totals. The mayoralty election of 1935 is a case in point. The Democratic candidate, John B. Kelly, a local leader of the party, garnered a third of a million votes while losing to Republican S. Davis Wilson in a close election, 330,000 to 370,000. However, it is possible that Kelly—the father of screen star Grace Kelly—did not lose at all. "There is general agreement today," we are told, "that [Kelly] was 'counted out' by Republican-controlled boards of election." See James Reichley, *The Art of Government: Reform and Organization Politics in Philadelphia,* New York, 1959, 6.

Additionally, this "Republican" victory was ambiguous in that Wilson had been elected Philadelphia City Controller in 1933 as a reform Democrat and as this "Republican" mayor he was closer to Lawrence's state Democratic Party than he was to the state Republican Party. In 1938, Mayor Wilson would run in the Democratic primary for the party's U.S. Senate nomination as a defender of the New Deal.

John L. Shover argued that what was happening in Philadelphia during this period was not an instance of a single "critical election," but a "critical period," which nevertheless gave clear signs of a Democratic realignment by 1936. Thus, "[W]hat appears in Philadelphia is a period of political fluctuation, beginning in 1928 and extending at least to 1936. Electoral allegiances were vacillating and the Republican machine was fighting for self-preservation. Tendencies toward stabilization can be detected in 1934; the election of 1936 marked not only the advent of a New Deal coalition but culminated a process of transition that had been under way since 1928." See John L. Shover, "The Emergence of a Two-Party System in Republican Philadelphia, 1924-1936," *The Journal of American History,* Vol. 60, No. 4, March 1974, 1000.

25. Minutes of the PCLU, November 7 and 21, December 19, 1935.

26. *The Pittsburgh Post-Gazette,* September 15, 1931, 3.

27. *The Pittsburgh Post-Gazette,* "Gunplay, Riots Mark Primary," September 16, 1931, 1.

28. *The Pittsburgh Post-Gazette,* "Gunplay, Riots Mark Primary," September 16, 1931, 3.

29. *The Pittsburgh Post-Gazette,* "McKees Rocks Fraud Charged-Voters Intimidated," September 16, 1931, 2.

30. *The Pittsburgh Post-Gazette,* "Police Vote 'Phantoms' in Final Hours," September 16, 1931, 4.

31. *The Pittsburgh Post-Gazette,* November 4, 1936.

32. *The Pittsburgh Post-Gazette,* April 13, 1932.

33. Dennis B. Roddy, "Rita Wilson Kane, Her Longtime Alter Ego, Was Shoulder To Lean On," *Pittsburgh Post-Gazette,* February 3, 1993.

34. Mary Breasted, "The Eveready Mayor," *Pittsburgh,* July 1992, 30.

35. John J. Kane and George Rankin, Jr., *Your Future in Allegheny County,* North River Press: New York, 1947.

36. Kane and Rankin, *Your Future in Allegheny County,* 12, 7, 8, 10-11.

37. The John J. Kane Hospital eventually closed and, in the mid-1980s, the county replaced it with a network of four 360-bed nursing homes for the elderly—known as John J. Kane Regional Centers—located in McKeesport, Glen Hazel, Scott, and Ross Townships. See Mark Belko, "Competition Bending Kanes," *The Pittsburgh Post-Gazette,* October 11, 1999.

38. Kane and Rankin, *Your Future in Allegheny County,* 32.

39. Kane and Rankin, *Your Future in Allegheny County,* 13, 4.

40. Kane and Rankin, *Your Future in Allegheny County,* 1, 2, 4.

41. Kane and Rankin, *Your Future in Allegheny County,* 29.

42. Kane and Rankin, *Your Future in Allegheny County,* 27, 39.

43. Kane and Rankin, *Your Future in Allegheny County,* 28-29.

44. Kane and Rankin, *Your Future in Allegheny County,* 22-23.

45. Kane and Rankin, *Your Future in Allegheny County,* 32.

46. Kane and Rankin, *Your Future in Allegheny County,* 39, 49. Emphasis added.

47. Additionally, the Earle administration aided local unionization drives in ways that it could. For example, when the *Harrisburg Telegraph Press* locked out the Printing Trades Union, Earle and his cabinet were "of great assistance" in winning a "complete victory" for the locked out union. Minutes of the PCLU, May 7, 1936.

48. Martha E. Foy, "The Negro in the Courts: A Study in Race Relations," unpublished Ph.D. dissertation, University of Pittsburgh, 1953, 88.

49. Thomas T. Spencer, "'Labor is with Roosevelt!': The Pennsylvania Non-Partisan League and the Election of 1936," *Pennsylvania History,* Vol. 46, No. 1, January 1979, 7. The continuing presence in Pennsylvania flea markets and antique stores of Philadelphia-manufactured Non-Partisan League buttons urging Roosevelt's re-election, some of which I have purchased, corroborate this effort.

50. Spencer, "Labor is with Roosevelt!" 14.

51. Robert R. R. Brooks, *As Steel Goes, . . . Unionism in a Basic Industry,* Yale University Press: New Haven, 1940, 119.

52. Minutes of the PCLU, January 16, 2, 1936.

53. Minutes of the PCLU, June 4, 12, 18, July 2, 1936. Both of the large and centrally located county-run parks, North and South, would henceforth be the scene of many labor oriented "mass meetings."

54. James A. Farley, *Behind the Ballots: The Personal History of a Politician,* Harcourt, Brace & Co.: New York, 1938, 307.

55. See *Down & Out in the Great Depression: Letters from the "Forgotten Man,"* Robert S. McElvaine, Ed., University of North Carolina Press: Chapel Hill, 1982.

56. Franklin D. Roosevelt, "Acceptance of Renomination for the Presidency," Philadelphia, Pa., June 27, 1936, in Samuel I. Rosenman, Ed., *The Public Papers and Addresses of Franklin D. Roosevelt,* Random House: New York, 1938-1950, Vol. 5, 230-236.

57. Labor's Non-Partisan League of Pennsylvania, "Report on September 12th, 1936," in Pennsylvania Federation of Labor, Election Materials, Labor's Non-Partisan League, Box 1, Historical Collections and Labor Archives, Pattee Library, Pennsylvania State University.

58. Minutes of the PCLU, August 6, 20, 1936.

59. Minutes of the PCLU, September 17, 1936.

60. Minutes of the PCLU, October 15, 1936.

61. Vincent D. Sweeney, *The United Steelworkers of America . . . The First 10 Years,* booklet published by the USWA, Pittsburgh, 1946, 4-7. Photo of the McKeesport rally on 7. Sweeney was the original SWOC Publicity Director and one of the founders of the union at the June 17, 1936 meeting.

62. *The Pittsburgh Press,* July 6, 1936. Sweeney, 10.

63. "State Guards Steel Labor's Civil Rights," *The Pittsburgh Press,* July 6, 1936. The promise of American freedom embodied in the Declaration of Independence permeated the American working class almost from the beginning and there is a long tradition of such "alternative" Declarations of Independence by labor. Philip Foner has published an anthology of twenty-two such declarations of independence, beginning with "The Working Men's Declaration of Independence" of 1829. He missed the Homestead Declaration of Independence of July 5, 1936, however. See Philip S. Foner, Editor, *We, the Other People: Alternative Declarations of Independence by Labor Groups, Farmers, Woman's Rights Advocates, Socialists, and Blacks, 1829-1975,* University of Illinois Press: Urbana, 1976.

64. Sweeney, *The United Steelworkers of America,* 11. Emphasis added.

65. "M.P.M.," Letter to the Editor, *The Homestead Daily Messenger,* October 19, 1936.

66. "Unchanged," Letter to the Editor, *The Homestead Daily Messenger,* October 9, 1936.

67. "R.M.," Letter to the Editor, *The Homestead Daily Messenger,* October 7, 1936.

68. "A Fourth Warder," Letter to the Editor, *The Homestead Daily Messenger,* October 8, 1936.

69. "R.W.D.," Letter to the Editor, *The Homestead Daily Messenger,* October 9, 1936.

70. Thomas A. Havican, Letter to the Editor, *The Homestead Daily Messenger,* October 9, 1936.

71. P. H. McGuire, Letters to the Editor, *The Homestead Daily Messenger,* October 27, 6, 1936. Emphasis in boldface type in the original.

72. "Homeville Resident," Letter to the Editor, *The Homestead Daily Messenger,* October 3, 1936.

73. Farley, *Behind the Ballots,* 322.

74. Farley, *Behind the Ballots,* 323-325.

75. Carroll R. Daugherty, Melvin G. de Chazeau, & Samuel Stratton. *The Economics of the Iron and Steel Industry,* Bureau of Business Research, 1937, 936-941, emphasis added.

76. Philip Klein, et al. *A Social Study of Pittsburgh: Community Problems and Social Services of Allegheny County,* Columbia University Press: New York, 1938, 302. (This study was made in 1934-36, reflecting attitudes present at the time of the '36 presidential campaign.)

77. *The Pittsburgh Press*, October 1, 3, 1936.

78. *The Homestead Daily Messenger*, October 1, 2, 1936.

79. Thomas L. Stokes, *Chip Off My Shoulder*, Princeton University Press: Princeton, NJ, 1940, 458-460. Emphasis added.

80. *The Homestead Daily Messenger*, October 30, 1936, 1, 9. Such attitudes would persist among "old-timers" for decades to come. In 1997 a former steelworker at U. S. Steel's Duquesne Works recalled that "several years ago" he worked along side "this older gentleman" who told him, "'Jimmy, the government and the rich people in this country don't want you'—by *you* he was talking about the working man—'to own anything or to fly on airlines on vacations alongside them. They (the rich) think of us (the working man) as being lowlifes, who, by buying nice things, will cause their prices to go up, thus digging into their greedy pockets.' He then said that they—the government and the rich—would fix it so we the working class could no longer enjoy some of the finer things in life. When this older gentleman told me this, I laughed at him. Well, I'm not laughing anymore. It seems the government is working very hard to keep us down. We, the working people, are the majority and should be dictating to the government policies to be followed, not the rich." Letter to the Editor by Gardner J. Walters, Coraopolis, *The Pittsburgh Post-Gazette*, November 18, 1997.

81. William Manchester, "FDR Thunders," in *A Sense of History: The Best Writing from the Pages of American Heritage*, American Heritage: New York, 1985, 33. Originally in the thirtieth anniversary issue of *American Heritage*, December 1984, in which the editors asked eminent scholars to describe the one moment in American history they would like to have witnessed.

82. Letter to the Editor, *The Homestead Daily Messenger*, October 3, 1936.

83. Rev. S. H. Soloman, Letter to the Editor, *The Homestead Daily Messenger*, September 19, 1936.

84. *The Pittsburgh Post-Gazette*, November 5, 1936.

85. *The Pittsburgh Post-Gazette*, November 4, 1936.

86. *The Pittsburgh Post-Gazette*, November 4, 1936.

87. *The Pittsburgh Post-Gazette*, November 4, 1936.

88. *The Pittsburgh Post-Gazette*, November 4, 5, 1936.

89. *The Pittsburgh Post-Gazette*, November 4, 1936.

90. "Defeat Here Stuns Republican Party," *The Homestead Daily Messenger*, November 4, 1936, 1.

91. *The Pittsburgh Post-Gazette*, November 5, 1936.

92. Minutes of the PCLU, November 5, 1936.

93. *The Pittsburgh Post-Gazette*, November 4, 1936.

94. *The Pittsburgh Post-Gazette*, November 5, 1936.

95. Richard C. Keller, "Pennsylvania's Little New Deal," *Pennsylvania History*, Vol. 29, No. 4, October 1962, 404-406.

96. Keller, "Pennsylvania's Little New Deal," 401.

97. Minutes of the PCLU, July 1, 1937.

98. Minutes of the PCLU, July 15, 1937.

99. "The Story of the New Deal and the Negro," published by the Colored Democratic [Pennsylvania] State Campaign Committee, 1938, 1, in the author's possession.

100. Such is the argument, at any rate, presented in "The Story of the New Deal and the Negro."

101. "The Story of the New Deal and the Negro," 4. The rest of this section is based upon this fifteen-page publication.

102. Philip A. Klinkner, with Rogers M. Smith, *The Unsteady March: The Rise and Decline of Racial Equality in America,* University of Chicago Press: Chicago, 1999.

103. Philip A. Klinkner, interviewed by Peter Monaghan, *The Chronicle of Higher Education,* November 19, 1999, A30.

104. For a seminal discussion of how Progressive Era municipal reforms—such as the elimination of ward-based governmental bodies and the imposition of at-large municipal elections—served to shrink the electorate by disenfranchising immigrant, working class voters which used Pittsburgh as a case in point, see Samuel P. Hays, "The Politics of Reform in Municipal Government," *The Pacific Northwest Quarterly,* 55, October 1965, 157-169.

105. Walter Dean Burnham, *Critical Elections and the Mainsprings of American Politics,* W.W. Norton & Co.: New York, 1970, 87.

106. Elmer J. Maloy Interview, United Steelworkers of America Papers, Historical Collections and Labor Archives, Pattee Library, Pennsylvania State University, State College, Pa. Hereafter referred to as USWA Papers, 8. Parentheses in the original.

107. Interview conducted by Eric Leif Davin and Karen L. Steed, November 23, 1980.

108. Interview conducted by Eric Leif Davin and Karen L. Steed, November 23, 1980.

109. See George Martin, *Madam Secretary, Frances Perkins,* Boston: Houghton Mifflin, 1976, chapter 24.

110. John A. Fitch, "A Man Can Talk in Homestead," *Survey Graphic,* Vol. 25, No. 2, February 1936.

111. Edward Levinson, *Labor on the March,* Harper & Bros.: New York, 1938, 188.

112. *Homestead Daily Messenger,* June 17, 1933.

113. Staughton Lynd, "The Possibility of Radicalism in the Early 1930s: The Case of Steel," *Radical America,* Vol. 6, No. 6, November-December 1972, 56.

114. Lynd, "The Possibility of Radicalism," 58.

115. Some of their ephemera, including leaflets and convention delegate credentials, are in the possession of the author.

116. *The McKeesport Daily News,* January 4, 1938, 20.

117. Maloy Interview, USWA Papers, 11.

118. *The McKeesport Daily News,* January 4, 1938, 20.

119. Interview by Eric Leif Davin and Karen L. Steed, November 23, 1980.

120. Interview by Davin and Steed, November 23, 1980. Reinforcement of idea that police actions had an important influence on whether or not organized labor turned to electoral politics can be gleaned from other accounts, as well. See, e.g., Alan Dawley, *Class and Community: The Industrial Revolution in Lynn,* Harvard University Press, Cambridge, 1976, 226: "It is said that history does not repeat itself, but the history of Lynn between 1860 and 1890 contradicts that axiom, because a certain sequence of events that occurred first in 1860 recurred with uncanny similarity in 1878 and again in 1890. Each time there were three steps in the sequence: (1) a strike occurred, (2) bringing out the police, (3) causing the strikers to mount a political campaign to unseat the incumbent officials and dismiss the police chief."

Also, see Eric Leif Davin and Staughton Lynd, "Picket Line and Ballot Box: The Forgotten Legacy of the Local Labor Party Movement, 1932-1936," *Radical History Review,* No. 22, winter 1979-80, which details how the labor movement of Berlin, New Hampshire, entered politics as a result of state force used against strikers. And the same thing happened in New Bedford and Akron. See Eric Leif Davin, "The Very Last Hurrah: The Defeat of the Labor Party Idea, 1934-1936," in Staughton Lynd, Ed., *We Are All Leaders: The Alternative Unionism of the Early 1930s,* University of Illinois Press: Urbana, 1996.

121. *Aliquippa Gazette,* April 3, 1936.

122. Interview conducted by Eric Leif Davin and Karen L. Steed, November 23,1980.

123. Brooks, *As Steel Goes,* 111ff.

124. Philip Murray's account is found in the 1935 Office Files of AFL President William Green, AFL Papers. The copy is badly damaged and there are no page identifications. Emphasis added.

125. Brooks, *As Steel Goes,* 117.

126. *The Pittsburgh Press,* July 6, 1936.

127. Fitch, "A Man Can Talk in Homestead," 243.

128. Maloy Interview, USWA Papers, 33, 36.

129. Maloy Interview, USWA Papers, 33, 34. Tom Striegel, Maloy's son-in-law, recalled that the company also supplied free electricity to all Duquesne churches from its private power plant, which insured church hostility to SWOC. Interview conducted by Eric Leif Davin, June 6, 1989.

130. Maloy Interview, USWA Papers, 34.

131. Maloy Interview, USWA Papers, 35.

132. Maloy Interview, USWA Papers, 35.

133. "Union Mayor, Union Town," *Friday,* December 27, 1940, Vol. 1, No. 42.

134. "Union Mayor, Union Town."

135. The following account comes from undated, unidentified newspaper clippings in the personal papers of Elmer J. Maloy. Now in the possession of his daughter, Jean Striegel, they are hereafter designated Maloy Papers.

136. Maloy Interview, USWA Papers, 35.

137. *The Union Press,* No. 4, September 8, 1937, 3.

138. *The Union Press,* No. 4, 2.

139. *The Union Press,* No. 4, 2.

140. *The Union Press,* No. 10.

141. *The Bulletin Index,* November 11, 1937.

142. *The Bulletin Index,* November 11, 1937.

143. *The Pittsburgh Post-Gazette,* November 3, 1937.

144. *The Pittsburgh Post-Gazette,* November 3, 1937. Crawford quote in David Brody, *Labor in Crisis: The Steel Strike of 1919,* J. B. Lippincott Co.: Philadelphia and New York, 1965, 94.

145. *The Pittsburgh Post-Gazette,* November 3, 1937.

146. *The Bulletin Index,* November 11, 1937.

147. Mullen remembered that McDonald "fooled around" and finally came up with $425. "Am I supposed to run a political campaign for mayor on $425?" Mullen complained. "That's all I have," McDonald answered. John J. Mullen Interview, United Steelworkers of America Papers, Historical Collections and Labor Archives, Pattee Library, Pennsylvania State University Libraries, 15, hereafter cited as USWA Papers.

There is no account of this event in McDonald's autobiography. See David J. McDonald, *Union Man,* E.P. Dutton & Co., Inc., New York, 1969. This suggests that Mullen's Clairton campaign was not an official policy of the top SWOC leadership and was of no great interest to McDonald, personally.

148. Mullen Interview, USWA Papers, 15.

149. Mullen Interview, USWA Papers, 15-16.

150. *The Union Press,* Vol. 1, No. 11, October 29, 1937.

151. *The Pittsburgh Post-Gazette,* November 3, 1937.

152. *The Pittsburgh Post-Gazette,* November 3, 1937.

153. *The Bulletin Index,* November 11, 1937.

154. *The Pittsburgh Post-Gazette,* November 3, 1937.

155. *The Pittsburgh Post-Gazette,* November 3, 1937.

156. *The Pittsburgh Post-Gazette,* November 3, 1937.

157 . Joel Seidman, "Organized Labor in Political Campaigns," *The Public Opinion Quarterly,* October 1939, 650-651.

158. Brooks, *As Steel Goes,* 251, 252.

159. George Powers, *Cradle of Steel Unionism: Monongahela Valley, PA,* Figueroa Printers, Inc.: E. Chicago, Ind., 1972, 134, 142.

160. Maloy Papers.

161. Maloy Papers.

162. Maloy Interview, USWA Papers, 32.

163. "Union Mayor, Union Town," *Friday.*

164. It also seems that Maloy used the Fire Dept. as an ancillary to the Police Dept. in protecting SWOC organizers. In October 1940, Maloy's jurisdiction over the Fire Dept. was transferred to Republican City Councillor Frank Kopriver (later to be his losing mayoralty opponent in 1941). The reason given was that Maloy "called on the firemen to help quell a disturbance at the main entrance to the Duquesne Steel Works during a dues picketing drive by the local CIO union, of which Mayor Maloy is a member." Maloy Papers.

165. "Union Mayor, Union Town," *Friday.*

166. "Union Mayor, Union Town," *Friday.*

167. Maloy Papers.

168. See *The Pittsburgh Press,* June 23, 30, 1939.

169. Laurence Glasco, "Double Burden: The Black Experience in Pittsburgh," in Samuel P. Hays, Ed., *City at the Point: Essays in the Social History of Pittsburgh,* University of Pittsburgh Press: Pittsburgh, 1989, 93.

170. Maloy Interview, USWA Papers, 36.

171. *The Duquesne Times,* November 7, 1941. *The Duquesne Times* was the only newspaper in town and was closely identified with both the Republicans and with the steel corporation. In fact, the U.S. Steel logo was emblazoned to the left and right of the masthead at the top of page one.

172. February 25, 1938.

173. Karen L. Steed, "Unionization and the Turn to Politics: Aliquippa and the Jones and Laughlin Steel Works, 1937-1941," graduate seminar paper, University of Pittsburgh, 1982, 18.

174. Brooks, *As Steel Goes,* 129.

175. *The Aliquippa News,* November 19, December 10, 1941.

176. Brooks, *As Steel Goes,* 129.

Chapter 9

Thermidor, Deadlock, and Consolidation, 1938-1940

By 1938 ethnic industrial workers and their allies had politically transformed both the Steel Valley and Pennsylvania. A despised and powerless people had come into power and into the respect that power brings.

However, in politics there are no permanent victories. The New Deal nationally, the Little New Deal in Pennsylvania, and what might be called the "Littlest New Deal" in Pittsburgh and the Steel Valley had gone as far as they could. One reason for this was that the political mobilization of the working class and its allies engendered a counter-mobilization of the Republican constituency.

Nationally, much of the resistance to the New Deal came from southern and rural Democrats allied with increasingly mobilized northern and midwestern Republicans. In Pennsylvania the resistance came from those areas outside major urban industrial centers.

However, even in Allegheny County, now dominated—as it would be for the next sixty years—by the Democrats, this dominance was continually contested. In 1940, for example, the county's Republican presidential vote was 41.7 percent and in 1944 it was 42.7 percent.[1]

Even in Pittsburgh itself Democratic rule (based in working class ethnic wards such as those on the Slavic South Side, in Italian Bloomfield and in Polish Hill, and in the black Hill District) met unceasing Republican resistance from well-to-do and WASP wards, such as Shadyside and Squirrel Hill, the latter the most populous ward in the city. In 1930, Shadyside, Ward 7, had the city's largest proportion of native whites, 59.4 percent, while in 1940 Squirrel Hill, Ward 14, had the lowest percentage of people on WPA payrolls, 1.1 percent, and the lowest

265

percentage of laborers in its workforce, 1.6 percent, with Shadyside close behind in these categories.[2] And both of these wards voted for Republicans Wendell Willkie in 1940 and Thomas Dewey in 1948.

What resulted from this working class mobilization and WASP-affluent counter-mobilization was an intensification of class conflict in the electoral arena. Over the course of the Thirties and Forties, subsequent elections witnessing increased levels of class-based partisanship as the electorate became steadily more polarized along class lines, climaxing in the 1948 presidential election.

As part of this process, organized labor's partisan role grew steadily, especially in the mid-1940s. The presidential elections of 1944 and 1948 marked organized labor's complete entry into the national party system as a Democratic Party campaign organization.[3]

Thus, by 1948 the Democratic Party—both because of grassroots working class identification with it, and because of institutional ties between it and organized labor—had become America's de facto "labor party." In the meantime, the increasing opposition to these developments coalesced around the Republican Party, making it America's de facto "Tory" party.

This resulted in a political stalemate, which was one of the primary obstacles which prevented the further advance of the working class radical reform agenda.

Republican Thermidor

While the reconstituted "CIO-Democratic Party" dominated Western Pennsylvania after 1937, such was not the case with the state as a whole. At the state level, what emerged after 1937 was not Democratic dominance, but Democratic viability in what had once been America's most Republican state.

Nevertheless, class politics *was* dominant, for it was on the basis of class polarization and calls to ideological combat that the struggle now turned. Inspired by such calls for an ideological crusade against the surging Democratic tide, the Republicans rallied in 1938.

The catalyst for Pennsylvania's Republican Thermidor might have been the great CIO-Democratic victories in the Steel Valley in 1937, but there was also much happening nationally which served to mobilize Republicans, both in Pennsylvania and across the country.

In April 1937, the U.S. Supreme Court upheld the legality of the Wagner Act, giving a tremendous boost to organized labor's cause. Labor was on the move as never before. There was, for example, the capitulation of U.S. Steel to SWOC in March, followed by the surrender of Jones & Laughlin Steel in May, both signing unprecedented contracts with the union. There was also the violent Little Steel Strike of 1937, which turned industrial communities like Cleveland and Ohio's Mahoning Valley into vast battlefields and which resulted in death at Chicago's Memorial Day Massacre.

But steelworkers were only part of the story. Nearly five million workers went on strike in 1937 in all types of industries. Nor were these entirely traditional strikes. A new element had been introduced to the labor struggle of the Thirties, an escalation of the class war at the point of production: the sit-down.

Sit-down strikes, in which strikers "sat down" where they were and refused to leave the plants, began in late 1936 and reached a crescendo in the first few months of 1937. By the end of that year, more than 400,000 workers had participated in this "seizure" of their employers' property.[4] The CIO, of course, made gigantic gains through these sit-downs, most notably, perhaps, being the March 1937, triumph over General Motors (GM) in the great Flint, Michigan, auto strike.

But these CIO triumphs also frightened Republicans, corporate leaders, and many Americans beyond those industrial communities. Not only did Republican politicians and business spokesmen launch an intense rhetorical counter-offensive,[5] but this union militancy also intensified anti-union feelings among many voters nationwide.

In February 1937, during the GM strike itself, 56 percent of the respondents to one Gallup Poll said their sympathies were with GM. Once GM capitulated in March, another Gallup survey found that 67 percent of the respondents said sit-down strikes should be outlawed. In April 65 percent said that state and local authorities should use force to remove sit-down strikers.

By June, almost half of the respondents to a Gallup survey said their attitudes toward labor unions had become more negative since the beginning of 1937, and in August, 76 percent of the respondents to a further poll said they approved of the vigilante groups which had lately sprung up in strike areas to combat strikers. In early 1938, a big majority of respondents further said they sided with Henry Ford against the United Auto Workers in the strike then underway.[6]

And, since organized labor had by now come to be identified with the Democratic Party—Walter Lippmann, for instance, attacked Roosevelt for encouraging illegal activities by strikers and "paralyzing the enforcement of law by public officials"[7]—this anti-union sentiment found its voice in the Republican Party. Support for the Republican Party surged.

But, this Republican resurgence, both nationally and in Pennsylvania in 1938, was not based solely upon an intensification of anti-union sentiment. It was also based upon a reaction against Democratic Party proposals in general, thus establishing the basic ideological postures of the two parties which have existed ever since.

Because of Democratic Party responsiveness to urban working class concerns, the New Deal launched the era of government intervention into the economy in an effort to solve essentially urban industrial problems. The Democratic Party has remained the champion of new programs ever since, the gas pedal propelling us into the future.

The Republican Party, on the other hand, has evolved into the brake, the party of opposition and resistance, the party of the status quo. This has been true even when it has controlled the White House. At those times, the Republican Party continued to act in opposition to initiatives coming from the Democratic Party leadership in the House of Representatives, which controlled the House from 1930 to 1994, with only two brief interruptions in the Fifties. A look at the constituencies of the two parties helps in understanding why this political stance evolved.

The Democratic surge to power during this period was due to the loyalty and aggressiveness of the urban, ethnic, working class. By 1938-40, the primary foundation of the New Deal coalition was in the nation's cities. Already the more rural-oriented South, despite continued loyalty dating back to Reconstruction, was starting to doubt its allegiance to the first party in America's history to be dominated by an urban-oriented ideology.

Meanwhile, despite pockets of urban support, such as Pittsburgh's Shadyside and Squirrel Hill neighborhoods, Republican strength resided mainly in the countryside, where Democratic strength declined even as it surged in the cities. "[I]n entirely rural areas throughout the Non-south, the Democratic share of the eligible electorate declined between 1932 and 1936, and the Republican share increased . . . After 1936, that pattern became more marked in the rural areas and extended as well to other groups of counties, except the most heavily urban category."[8]

After 1936, fewer than 100 U.S. Congressmen were Republicans. These House Republicans were the principal survivors of the Democratic juggernaut, and so became the main leaders of the party. These Republican Congressmen were protected from the Democratic tide because most of them came from safe rural areas. This rural and WASP electoral base set the tone of their resistance to the New Deal and the ideological tone of the party as a whole. They were rural, anti-urban, anti-ethnic, anti-labor, and anti-New Deal. Thus, they formulated a reactionary—literally—political philosophy based upon this stance.

But, while the powerful conservative coalition which formed in Congress after 1937 was composed of surviving rural Republicans, it also had its fair share of conservative southern Democrats. Expressing this continuing reality, in the 1990s political consultant James Carville looked at Pennsylvania and described it as, "Pittsburgh and Philadelphia with Alabama in between."

However, this perceived "southern" political difference is, and was, not so much southern as rural. As in the North, so in the South after 1937 we find the the same urban-rural breakdown, as "most conservative congressmen after 1936 were from rural districts or states . . . The [conservative] coalition was composed not so much of Republicans and *southern* Democrats as of Republicans and *rural* Democrats; *urban* Southerners were often more favorably disposed to administration programs than their rural counterparts."[9]

Thus, many New Deal stalwarts could be found in the South, such as Senators Hugo Black of Alabama, Claude Pepper of Florida, and Alben W. Barkley of Kentucky, and Representatives such as Sam Rayburn of Texas.

Nevertheless, there were many of these rural southern Democrats from safe seats in the countryside who allied themselves with the surviving rural Republicans. "The existence of this urban-rural split upon many economic issues after 1936 was indisputable," declared one observer. In breaking down only *Democratic* votes in the House *contrary* to the position of the Democratic leadership in the 1937-1939 period, this scholar found that of those Democrats who voted to investigate the sit-down strikes, 82 percent were rural; of those who voted to recommit fair labor standards, 74 percent were rural; of those who voted to investigate the National Labor Relations Board, 77 percent were rural; 69 percent of the Democrats opposing the lending bill were rural; and 83 percent of the Democrats opposed to the housing bill were rural. Since 54 percent of all Democratic Representatives represented rural districts in 1937 and 57 percent of all House Democrats represented rural districts in 1939, rural Democratic opposition on these bills was politically powerful.[10]

This urban-rural breakdown also played itself out in Pennsylvania. The difference, however, was that while the Democratic Party—for historical reasons going back to the Civil War and Reconstruction—had a rural constituency in the South, it never had one in heavily Republican northern states like Pennsylvania.

Thus, when the Democratic Party came to power in Pennsylvania, as elsewhere in the Northeast, it came as an urban-based party, while the hinterlands largely remained—as they'd always been—Republican. Although there were small coal towns such as Winber, and small industrial centers such as Johnstown, Scranton, Bethlehem, and Allentown, which voted Democratic, what finally tipped the scales and made the Democratic Party competitive in Pennsylvania were its urban bases in Allegheny County and Philadelphia. In 1940, Philadelphia and Allegheny County combined comprised 34 percent of the state's population and, in 1944, cast 39 percent of the major party vote. This combined Philadelphia-Allegheny County vote was 58.2 percent Democratic.[11] As one Democratic activist told me, "There's nothing between Pittsburgh and Philadelphia but trees . . . and every one of them votes Republican."

This political division, however, was based upon more than just geography. Much of this vote was simply the traditional WASP-ethnic breakdown—and ethnics (as well as blacks) tended to live in larger urban industrial centers, while WASPs dominated the countryside. Texas Democratic Representative Martin Dies—soon to become notorious as head of the Communist-hunting "Dies Committee"—colorfully, but nonetheless accurately, described the nature of the conservative coalition of which he was a leading member. It should not be thought of as a *Southern* bloc, he said. Rather, it had "the support of nearly all small-town and rural Congressmen." who were jointly allied against "the men from the big cities, which . . . are politically controlled by foreigners and transplanted Negroes."[12]

Walter Dean Burnham described the opposing coalitions, which continue to this day, along similar lines, though less colorfully. Burnham looked closely at political developments in Pennsylvania because, among other reasons, "In the case of Pennsylvania . . . discontinuities [in the political universe] tend to appear at the same time as they do nationally."[13]

What he discovered was that the realignment of the 1890s had "immeasurably solidified the ascendancy of the Republican-industrialist political complex, in Pennsylvania even more completely than in the nation at large. [But] the realignment of the 1930s may be viewed as involving the development of structures of countervailing power . . . through the unionization of labor in the coal and steel industries, the ending of the grossest forms of company-town feudalism, and the mobilization of new immigrants and their children into a reconstituted Democratic Party."[14]

These countervailing Republican and Democratic powers fractured along lines which are now familiar to us. "[T]he Republican electoral base has remained in the familiar pattern established in the 1930s: native-stock elements living in rural areas, small towns, and suburbs; people with advantages of wealth and education; and people of 'obsolescent' social strata, particularly those of traditionalist socioreligious perspectives who tend to resist changes which seem to threaten their traditions.

"The Democratic electoral base has included disproportionate support among the electorally active poor, Negroes, Jews, Catholics, trade-unionists, and residents of the central city in metropolitan areas." Furthermore, "This well-known coalitional structure has remained quite durable in Pennsylvania . . . even into the 1960s, elections continued to be structured to a considerable extent in terms of the polarizations laid down thirty years before."[15]

Additionally, Gallup Polls conducted in the summer of 1938 revealed the same class polarization in major party loyalty nationally as in Pennsylvania. When asked, for example, "Are you for or against President Roosevelt today?" a 48 percent *minority* of property or home owners said they approved of the president, while 65 percent of the *non-property owners* supported him. The difference was more dramatic between investors and non-investors, with only 35 percent of investors supporting Roosevelt against 62 percent of the non-investors.[16]

This class polarization can also be seen within Pittsburgh itself—as well as the counter-mobilization of the Republican vote. Reference has already been made to the Democratic mobilization of Pittsburgh's working class Polish Hill neighborhood. At the opposite end of the socioeconomic spectrum was Pittsburgh's Ward 14, the Squirrel Hill neighborhood.

In 1940, when Squirrel Hill voted Republican, 49.6 percent of the male workforce was engaged in professional or managerial occupations, while 21.0 percent was engaged in semi-skilled and unskilled manual work (with only 1.6 percent being laborers and only 1.1 percent of the ward's population employed on WPA jobs).[17] What we see happening in this largely white collar neighborhood over the decade of the Thirties is both the mobilization of the Democratic vote as well as the counter-mobilization of the Republican vote (table 5).

Table 5

Voting & Partisanship in Pittsburgh's Squirrel Hill, Ward Fourteen.

Year	% Dem.	% GOP	% Other	% Nonvoting
1932	18.0	22.8	1.1	57.6
1936	36.8	29.6	0.4	32.5
1940	36.4	39.4	0.2	23.8

Source: Walter Dean Burnham, *The Current Crisis in American Politics*, Oxford University Press: New York, 1982, Table 11, 146.

As we see, the Democratic vote in Squirrel Hill doubled over the course of Thirties, *but the Republican vote almost doubled as well,* so that, although Ward 14 voted for FDR in 1936, by 1940 Squirrel Hill was once again a majority Republican ward, as the Republican vote had started from a slightly higher base. Both of these partisan mobilizations came at the expense of non-voters, whose numbers dropped by more than half over the same period.

What happened in Squirrel Hill also happened in the nation at large. Indeed, by some measures, these parallel mobilizations reached their apex nationally in the off-year elections of 1938 (when voter turnout in the North and West reached 58.6 percent) and the presidential election of 1940 (when turnout reached 73.7 percent), as voter turnout not only reached unprecedented levels—but reached levels which, outside the South, *have never been equalled since.*[18]

The intensity of class politics, then, as well as the mobilizations of both the Democratic and Republican constituencies, seems to have reached a fever pitch in the last years of the Thirties. The climax of this electoral class war, however, was perhaps the presidential election of 1948 when class tensions were at their highest and the realignment pattern of the Thirties had solidified, although turnout was lower than in 1940. Nevertheless, in Pennsylvania the first stage of the Republican Thermidor came with the gubernatorial election of 1938.

Divisions Within

The gubernatorial election of 1938 revealed the limits on the working class radical reform agenda imposed from both within the New Deal coalition itself, and externally from the Republican counter-mobilization.

Democratic victory in 1934 had made the Democratic gubernatorial nomination in 1938 desirable. The most viable candidate no doubt would have been Governor George Earle himself, but the state constitution prevented him from a second consecutive term. Earle therefore announced for the U.S. Senate seat then held by Republican James J. Davis.

Senator Davis was a former iron worker who'd started as a breaker boy at a young age in the coal mines. He entered politics and worked his way up the political ladder, serving as Secretary of Labor in the administrations of Harding, Coolidge, and Hoover before turning to the Senate. Befitting his labor background, he was actually a moderate Republican who had supported most of Roosevelt's New Deal programs and who, moreover, had good relations with the American Federation of Labor (AFL).[19]

As 1938 began it seemed debatable whether or not Earle could beat Davis, as the Democratic Party was still the minority party in the state in terms of registrants. Democratic victory in 1934 had depended upon a feverish mobilization of previously inactive voters. In the four years since then, however, that very mobilization had brought forth a Republican counter-mobilization. Thus, in 1938 Democratic voters in Pennsylvania numbered 2,209,276 while Republicans numbered 2,372,528, a Republican advantage of 163,252 more voters.[20]

Nevertheless, this was better than two years previously, in 1936, when Roosevelt carried the state and there were myriad Democratic victories, despite a 400,000 deficit in Democratic registrants. And it was also better than in 1934, when Earle had been elected governor at a time when the Republicans still out-numbered Democrats in Pennsylvania by the amazing figure of over 1,200,000 registrants.[21]

Thus, despite the Republican edge, the shrinking registration gap made Democratic prospects seem better than at any previous time, and if anyone could beat the incumbent Republican senator, it was the incumbent Democratic governor. Indeed, Earle was even being touted as the prospective Democratic presidential nominee for 1940, if Roosevelt did not run for a third term. In a poll asking voters about possible Democratic presidential candidates in the summer of 1937, Earle had ranked third in popularity among Democratic voters nationally, just behind Vice President John Nance Garner and Democratic Party Chairman James Farley. By the spring of 1938, Earle had fallen to fourth among Democrats nationally, but he remained a strong presidential contender.[22] Earle was, then, the logical Democratic senatorial nominee.

Attention, therefore, focused on who would be the Democratic nominee for the open governor's seat. It was with this question that the internal limits imposed upon the radical reform agenda were thrown into high relief.

The first to be heard from was UMWA and CIO president John L. Lewis. Organized labor was now a power in the Pennsylvania Democratic Party, its voice not to be ignored lightly. Lewis had loaned $40,000 in UMWA money to the state party in 1936, earmarked for the successful campaign to wrest control of the State Senate, and labor's support had been crucial to the party's 1934 victories.[23] Indeed, Lewis's Secretary-Treasurer in the United Mine Workers, Thomas Kennedy, had been elected Lieutenant Governor in 1934 and was now the appointed commander of the State Police, another sign of labor's increased political clout in the state.

Thus, it was now Kennedy that Lewis wanted as the Democratic gubernatorial candidate, making known his desires a year ahead of time, in the summer of 1937. The *Philadelphia Evening Ledger* denounced this as, "the CIO invasion of Pennsylvania politics," and saying that, "Mr. Lewis will get [the nomination] for him—or else."[24]

This "CIO invasion of Pennsylvania politics," however, was not the dire threat Republican newspapers made it out to be. This reality highlights another reason there were limits to the working class reform agenda. The Democratic Party may have filled the "labor party" vacuum in the American political spectrum, but even in Pennsylvania—where the working class electoral influence seemed so spectacularly successful—the labor constituency was still just part (although a crucial part) of a larger coalition of forces under the Democratic umbrella.

Thus, Democratic leaders at the highest levels put a brake on labor's influence within the party, and balanced labor's demands against those of others. In this case, the man with his hand on the brakes was state party chief and Pennsylvania Secretary of the Commonwealth David Lawrence.

Lawrence had already shown a willingness to rebuff labor's demands.

Following the 1935 elections, John J. Kane resigned his seat on the Pittsburgh City Council in order to devote all his attention to his new job as Allegheny County Commissioner. The Pittsburgh Central Labor Union (PCLU) felt the seat Kane vacated on the Council was rightly a "labor seat" and should be filled by another union man.

As the seats were filled on a partisan basis, the party which held that seat was entitled to name someone to it when a vacancy occurred. It therefore fell to David Lawrence, as head of the Allegheny County Democratic Party, to anoint someone to fill Kane's seat. The PCLU felt that organized labor had shown both its clout and its loyalty to the Democratic Party in the 1935 election. Therefore, it had earned the right to have its men sit at the table of power.

Immediately after the election, on November 7, 1935, the PCLU nominated George L. Riley, the Labor Director of the Pittsburgh office of the WPA and a leader of the Stereotypers Local Union 56, as its candidate for Kane's seat and "demanded" he be seated. On November 14 the PCLU Executive Board (of which Kane was a member) voted to send a letter to the City Council and to Lawrence saying that Riley was labor's choice to replace Kane and that, in any event, a PCLU member should be named to the vacancy.[25]

Lawrence did not agree, and appointed a loyal party man with no ties to organized labor. On January 13, 1936, PCLU President Pat Fagan, of the Mine Workers, and the rest of the PCLU Executive Board (minus Kane, "who was engaged at the office of the County Commissioners") met with Lawrence in his office in the Downtown Benedum-Trees Building to discuss "the matter of having no Organized Labor member appointed a member of the City Council."

At that meeting, "Lawrence informed the Board of the policy of the Democratic organization toward Organized Labor and made several suggestions as to the manner in which Organized Labor might present its pleas." Much as we would like to know the details of this policy, the official relationship between organized labor and the Democratic organization can only be guessed at, as the record is silent. Evidently, however, Lawrence felt secure enough to view labor's "demands" as merely "pleas" for inclusion, which could be safely ignored.

It also seems Lawrence deflected labor's demands by advising that they speak to him with a more unified voice. As a result of the meeting with Lawrence (and evidently at his suggestion), the Executive Board created a five-man sub-committee to "act as directed by the Board on civic matters." Despite the creation of this civic affairs sub-committee, there is no indication Lawrence gave its opinions much weight in his own direction of civic matters.[26] This was one indication of the limits the Democratic organization placed on labor within its own councils.

Now, just as he had turned aside labor's candidate for the Pittsburgh City Council, Lawrence also rejected the CIO's candidate for governor. In Lawrence's estimation there were a number of drawbacks to Kennedy's nomination.

First, he was an Irish Catholic, as was Lawrence himself. It was only a decade after the defeat of Catholic Al Smith for the presidency and Lawrence viewed Catholicism as still too much of a handicap for a viable candidate facing a predominantly Protestant electorate, as was the case in Pennsylvania. This consideration had kept Lawrence himself from coming forth as a gubernatorial candidate that year. Lawrence and the rest of the Democratic leadership saw it as no less a handicap for Kennedy.

Second, however, was the fact that the CIO was not the only labor voice in town. There was also the American Federation of Labor, and now that the labor vote was so crucial to Democratic prospects, the party leadership was wary of alienating one wing of the labor movement by being too closely identified with the other. William Green, AFL national president, adamantly objected to Kennedy's selection as an "attempt of C.I.O. dictator John L. Lewis to seize political control of the state," and demanded an equal say in the state party's decisions.[27] Indeed, Green even appeared before a Harrisburg convention of the Pennsylvania Federation of Labor where, in a "fist-flailing speech," he attacked John L. Lewis as a "dictator, a Hitler, and an autocrat," and Tom Kennedy as his "Charlie McCarthy" puppet.[28]

This hysterical AFL opposition to Kennedy presented the Democratic leadership with a dilemma, for AFL voters were almost as fanatical Democrats as were CIO voters. In the summer of 1938, for example, 79 percent of all CIO members nationally told Gallup pollsters they were for Roosevelt—but so did 70 percent of all AFL members.[29] The AFL, therefore, could not be ignored. The party, both nationally and in Pennsylvania, had to walk a tight rope of neutrality between the two competing labor factions.

Therefore, the party leadership decided against John L. Lewis's candidate. At a nominating meeting on February 17, Lawrence and the party leaders selected their man: Protestant Charles Alvin Jones, a Pittsburgh lawyer and Allegheny County Solicitor.

Charles Jones was a party stalwart who had always been a Democrat—even in the long years of Republican rule in Allegheny County. He had the added virtue of bringing geographical balance to the ticket, as Earle was from the Philadelphia suburb of Haverford. And, in addition to being Lawrence's choice, he was also supported by John B. Kelly, who led the party in Philadelphia. This decision was ratified at a Democratic State Committee meeting on February 25.

Joseph Guffey, however, objected to this decision. Despite having handed over formal state party leadership to Lawrence after he was elected to the U.S. Senate in 1934, Guffey still retained much influence in the party, especially in Philadelphia. He felt the party's only hope for success was to nominate a man closer to the labor movement. Therefore, he backed Tom Kennedy. Perhaps emboldened by this, Kennedy announced for the gubernatorial nomination, despite the absence of the party leadership's endorsement.[30]

Thus, the Democratic primary became a three-way race: Democratic Party Chairman Lawrence, Philadelphia leader Kelly, and the Pennsylvania Federation of Labor supported Jones; Guffey and the state's CIO leadership backed Kennedy; meanwhile State Attorney General Charles J. Margiotti, a popular Italian-American criminal lawyer from Pittsburgh, ran on his own with no endorsers. Four years earlier, in 1934, Margiotti had unsuccessfully sought the gubernatorial nomination as a Republican in that year's Republican primary. Since then he'd switched to the Democrats, and now he wanted the Democratic gubernatorial nomination.

The list of endorsers expanded on March 17 when Earle—close to Lawrence who, as Secretary of the Commonwealth, had pushed through much of his "Little New Deal" programs—came out in favor of Lawrence's man, Jones.[31] Then, on March 28, S. Davis Wilson, the liberal mayor of Philadelphia, nominally a Republican, joined the fray when he announced for the Democratic Senate nomination in opposition to Earle, declared his support for the New Deal, and aligned himself with Guffey, Kennedy, and the CIO.[32]

When the Congress of Industrial Organizations (CIO) broke with the American Federation of Labor (AFL), all Pittsburgh-area industrial unions belonging to the CIO had left the AFL-affiliated Pittsburgh Central Labor Union. They established an umbrella organization of all CIO-affiliated unions in the Pittsburgh region, the Steel City Industrial Union Council, with a membership of 100,000 CIO unionists. This new labor body was headed by UMWA leader Patrick Fagan—who had been forced to resign from his presidency of the PCLU after the national AFL expelled CIO-affiliated unions—with Elmer J. Maloy, the CIO-Mayor of Duquesne, as Vice President. This CIO body had endorsed Tom Kennedy for governor.

On April 21st the Executive Board of the Pittsburgh Central Labor Union recommended to its membership that it concur in the action previously taken by the State Federation of Labor and endorse Jones for governor over the CIO-backed Tom Kennedy.[33] The PCLU also attacked the rival Steel City Industrial Union Council as "a labor-splitting, treasonable betrayal of organized labor" because it had "quit the American Federation of Labor and set up a destructive dual labor movement."[34]

The PCLU also noted that the "Earle-Jones-AFL Labor Committee" was sending speakers to various AFL unions and urged local bodies to make time in their meetings for these representatives to speak in favor of the Earle-Jones ticket. It then voted to contribute financially to the Pennsylvania Federation of Labor's Committee for Political Action, which was working to defeat the CIO-backed Kennedy.[35]

Ideologically, it may have seemed that there was little to chose from, as all the candidates, including Margiotti and "Republican" Wilson, championed the New Deal and pledged to defend it. Suggesting that candidates from both labor factions were acceptable to the highest Democratic leadership was the endorsement by Democratic National Committee Chairman James Farley of both Earle (AFL's man for the Senate) and Kennedy (the CIO's man for governor).[36]

However, if we look upon the CIO's man, Tom Kennedy, as a proxie for the most "extreme" manifestation of the radical reform agenda, this contest is a useful barometer for measuring the strength of that agenda's support within the newly revitalized Pennsylvania New Deal coalition itself. Already, from the fact that the party leadership had refused to endorse the CIO candidate, we can see the friction between the various elements of the party's constituencies. The primary election took that contest to a wider sphere, the party constituency statewide.

In the primary election on May 17, Earle buried Wilson two-to-one in the expected landslide for the party's senatorial nomination. The gubernatorial vote, however, was much closer. Despite being opposed by the Democratic Party leaders of Philadelphia and Pittsburgh and the Democratic State Committee, as well as both the state and national AFL, the CIO almost pulled it off for Tom Kennedy among the voters themselves. Margiotti garnered only 13 percent of the vote and carried only one county. On the other hand, Tom Kennedy carried a majority of the state's counties and over a half-million Democrats—517,101, or 40 percent of the total—voted for the CIO-backed UMWA union leader.

However, party- and AFL-backed Charles Jones edged him out with 591,546, or 46 percent of the total. The "CIO invasion of Pennsylvania politics" had the support of a large and significant number of the state's Democratic adherents— but not a majority.

Further, it was Allegheny and Philadelphia counties which put the leadership-endorsed Jones over the top, with leads over Kennedy of 34,000 in Allegheny and 64,000 in Philadelphia. Of course, Jones was well-known in Allegheny County, being the County Solicitor, and in Philadelphia he was backed by party leader John Kelly. In addition, the PCLU—as well as AFL unions throughout the state— bitterly opposed the CIO candidate and helped kill the CIO's best bid to elect a governor of Pennsylvania.

The vote, then, perhaps indicates both the influence of the party organization in these locales and also the extent of divisions within the labor movement itself.[37] At the same time, it also suggests the limits of the CIO version of the radical reform agenda even within heavily industrial Allegheny County, where its influence might be considered most powerful.

Reaction Without

Following the primary, attention turned to the November general election, which would reveal the external limits political circumstances were placing on further radical reform. Incumbent Republican Senator James Davis had won his primary handily and campaigned in the general election as a friend of labor and supporter of the New Deal, a stance his record supported.

The Republican gubernatorial primary had featured an attempted come-back by seventy-two-year-old Gifford Pinchot, Republican governor twice before. He ran in the primary as a New Deal supporter and opponent of the party leadership, comprised mainly of the Philadelphia trio of Joseph Grundy, Joseph N. Pew, Jr., a wealthy manufacturer, and Pew's ally Moses Annenberg, publisher of the *Philadelphia Inquirer.*[38] This trio backed State Superior Court Judge Arthur H. James, age fifty-four, who had previously served as the Lieutenant Governor from 1927-1931.

James was from Plymouth, near Wilkes-Barre in the northeastern coal mining region of Luzerne County. He liked to style himself as a former miner, but in fact he only worked in the mines his father managed during his summer school vacations.[39] Where Pinchot styled himself as a supporter of the New Deal, James attacked both the New Deal and Pinchot viciously. He accused Pinchot of being a friend of John L. Lewis and likened the New Deal to Hitler's Nazi dictatorship. He promised a law and order government against the lawless labor movement and pledged to lower taxes on business.[40]

It must have been balm to Republican ears. James buried Pinchot in a two-to-one landslide, winning 66 percent of the primary vote to Pinchot's 32 percent.[41] Having found a winning theme, James continued to rally the Republican electorate with this message as he began the general campaign. The central—indeed, sole—issue in the campaign was the New Deal, the continuation of the Little New Deal, and the rights of organized labor.[42]

Meanwhile, the Democrats pulled themselves together and ran a united labor-oriented campaign against the Republicans. Guffey signed on as the state campaign manager and both Tom Kennedy and John L. Lewis loyally urged a straight Democratic vote.

National AFL President William Green, however, urged local AFL bodies to support the labor-friendly Republican Senator James Davis, as well as other Republicans, and a letter from Green to that effect was received by the PCLU on September 15. At the same time, however, the PCLU received official notice from the Pennsylvania Federation of Labor that it had in convention unanimously endorsed Earle.[43] These rival endorsements from AFL leadership circles represented yet another debilitating civil war within the labor movement.

In early 1938 William Green had dismissed the entire Pennsylvania Federation of Labor leadership because the state body had refused to expel CIO-affiliated locals, which constituted 75 percent of the Pennsylvania membership. He then installed a new and presumably more loyal body of officers. But, in defiance of William Green and the national AFL leadership, this new "loyal" state AFL leadership endorsed the entire Democratic campaign, while derogating Green as an outsider who was "so gullible that a . . . kind word from a president of the Chamber of Commerce has more effect on him than the interests of those wage earners who are paying his salary."[44]

On October 20 the PCLU received an angry letter from Green, as well as a second one from AFL Director of Organization Lewis G. Hines, criticizing the PCLU for endorsing the Democratic ticket in the upcoming election. At the same time a joint communication was read from James L. McDevitt, President, and David Williams, Secretary-Treasurer, of the Pennsylvania Federation of Labor, rejecting Green's actions.

The PCLU evidently agreed with the state officers in their critique of Green, for they immediately voted unanimously to support the state federation's endorsement of Earle and the rest of the Democratic ticket.[45] A united Pennsylvania AFL-CIO labor front for the Democratic Party was thus presented. AFL President Green countered this rejection by issuing his personal endorsement of Republican Senator Davis.[46] It was all very confusing.

In the gubernatorial race, both Democrat Jones and Republican James turned out to be barroom brawlers, fighting an aggressive campaign against each other. Under the slogan "James and Jobs," the Republican championed business interests in general and called for fewer taxes on business as a way of spurring industry. He attacked what he termed "anti-business laws" and what he saw as the general tendency of the New Deal toward government centralization, Nazi-style dictatorship, and class hatred.[47]

Democrat Charles Jones called for a continuation of the Little New Deal, support for FDR's New Deal, and the defeat of the manufacturing, banking, and utilities interests which backed the Republican campaign.[48] Essentially, he issued the same calls to ideological combat that the Democrats had issued in 1934 and 1936, only now he could point to the accomplishments of the Little New Deal during the interim: Unemployment relief, the protection and extension of labor's legal rights, legal advances for blacks, taxation of wealthy corporations, public works programs—the whole panoply of "Real Deal" reform measures Democrats had installed over the previous two years in power. The basic issue, declared both Jones and Earle, was "Democratic liberalism versus Republican reaction— the New Deal versus the old." Meanwhile, the Republicans branded much of the Pennsylvania's Little New Deal legislation "bonfire material."[49]

It was the most intense, heated, hotly contested state campaign in Pennsylvania history, as both parties mobilized their respective constituencies. "The candidates criss-crossed the state a number of times, repeating their themes to enthusiastic audiences wherever they went . . . interest had never been greater for a state election . . . Each party had drawn three-fifths of its registrants to the primary polls; the turnout on November 8, 1938, was an astronomical 82 percent, exceeded only by the 84 percent who voted in 1936."[50]

Indeed, indicative of the increasing mobilization of both Democratic and Republican constituencies, this was the highest voter turnout Pennsylvania has ever had for a state election, even to this date, despite a severe winter storm which blanketed most of Pennsylvania. It represented 39 percent of the state's total population, close to the highest ever turnout for a presidential election, 42 percent in 1936.[51]

And, in an unprecedentedly strong showing, Democrat Jones received almost one and three-quarter million votes—*almost a third of a million more votes than Earle had won in 1934* and more than any gubernatorial candidate, Democrat or Republican, had ever before received in Pennsylvania history. No doubt the Democrats mobilized every possible Democratic vote in the state.

Despite this astounding increase in the Democratic vote, however, the Democrats just did not have enough numbers to win further victories. The Republican James received even more votes, beating the Democrat by almost 300,000 votes. Incumbent Republican Senator Davis also beat back Earle's challenge by 400,000 votes. In addition, the Republicans took back control of both the State House by a wide margin and the State Senate by a narrow margin, while regaining a majority of the state's Congressional representation, 19-15.[52]

Both the urban-rural political division of Pennsylvania, as well as the class nature of the vote, manifested itself in the breakdown of the returns. "The

Republicans piled up large majorities in the rural, small-town, and small-city areas, as well as in the affluent suburbs outside of Philadelphia."[53]

In Allegheny County, the vote broke down along now-familiar lines. Industrial communities like Homestead, Braddock, and Duquesne voted Democratic by large margins, while more affluent Republican suburbs like Dormont, Mt. Lebanon, and Fox Chapel returned lopsided votes for the Republican slate. Even so, both Jones and Earle carried Allegheny County and Pittsburgh, while losing Philadelphia by only 10,000 and 14,000, respectively.[54]

In addition, the mining counties around Allegheny County—Fayette, Greene, Washington, and Westmoreland—all went for Democrat Jones while two went for Democrat Earle. Meanwhile, the northeastern coal counties of Lackawanna and Luzerne went for Jones and Earle, respectively.

Nevertheless, the drive to extend and enlarge the radical reform agenda of Pennsylvania's Little New Deal had been stopped. "In the post-election analysis . . . The Republicans put . . . emphasis on the issue of the New Deal itself and saw their victory as a repudiation of Governor Earle and President Roosevelt."[55]

This was indeed the case for, despite an unprecedented mobilization of the Democratic constituency, the Republican electorate—still the majority in Pennsylvania—had also mobilized in unprecedented numbers to repudiate Governor Earle and President Roosevelt.

It was the end of the Little New Deal, the most progressive, pro-labor period of government in Pennsylvania's history.

Democracy's Deadlock

It was also the end of the "Big" New Deal, for the same pattern was evident all across the country that November. In Congress, the Democrats lost eighty House seats and eight Senate seats, increasing Republican strength to 169 and 23 respectively. "Since unreliable [rural] Democrats already numbered some forty in the House and twenty in the Senate, the administration faced a divided Congress before the session began. The President's achievements in 1939 were negligible; the domestic New Deal, for all intents and purposes, made no more striking gains."[56] Over the next few years, Republicans and rural Southern Democrats forged a conservative coalition in Congress which routinely blocked New Deal legislation. The New Deal had lost the political initiative of the early Thirties and went on the defensive thereafter.

Some labor historians—citing just such set-backs—have pointed to 1938 as a year when the workers supposedly turned toward the Right, politically, and have searched for the reasons. "Rooseveltian Democracy," says Mike Davis in one influential account, was "openly in crisis, and seemingly propitious conditions again existed for the further growth of local labor or farmer-labor movements and their eventual coalescence. The traditional view of certain Marxist currents has been that 1938 was the most advantageous opportunity for revolutionary politics in the twentieth century. The puzzle, however, is how to explain why 1938 was actually a year of unmitigated disaster for third-party and labor party hopes, which instead of growing at the expense of the New Deal's crisis, virtually collapsed." Not only did the Wisconsin Progressive Party and the Minnesota Farmer-Labor Party suffer "devastating losses" in 1938, but "in California, the EPIC movement quietly disappeared from the scene."[57]

Mike Davis finds the answer to this enduring puzzle within the labor movement itself. "The key to this paradox," he claims, "was the veritable 'civil war' which broke out between the AFL and the new unions in 1937-38," explicitly pointing to the fact that, " . . . the AFL worked to defeat Mineworkers' leader Tom Kennedy in his gubernatorial bid in Pennsylvania." This resulted not only in "labor disunity," but also "an extraordinary resurgence of right-wing trade unionism."[58]

A look at the record, however, at least in Pennsylvania (which Davis uses as one support for his thesis), does not support Davis's argument. Judging by the number of votes the Democrats received and where those votes came from, the New Deal was not in crisis at all. Not only were industrial working class towns, districts, and regions still supporting the Democrats—*they were supporting the Democrats in far larger numbers than ever before!* There is absolutely no evidence that workers were turning to the Right.

Nor is there any great puzzle as to why third party hopes—as embodied in the Wisconsin Progressive Party or the Minnesota Farmer-Labor Party—foundered in 1938. The answer is that workers were more closely identified with the Democratic Party, which they increasingly saw as *their* party, than ever before.

Also, Mike Davis' claim that the Republican Thermidor of 1938 was due to divisions within the labor movement itself distorts Pennsylvania events. Davis neglects to inform us that the AFL opposition to Tom Kennedy was in the primary, not in the general election, as his account would have us believe. And, as we have seen, that rift was healed, at least within the Pennsylvania labor movement itself, by the time of the general election. Thus, the Pennsylvania labor movement presented a united AFL-CIO front against the Republicans in the general election.

And, indeed, that general election witnessed a literally unprecedented mobilization of the working class vote behind the Democratic candidates, with Jones receiving more votes than any gubernatorial candidate—Democratic or Republican—had ever before received in Pennsylvania history.

The problem in Pennsylvania, then, was not debilitating AFL-CIO divisiveness, which Davis lays such stress upon in order to support his thesis of "New Deal in crisis." Rather, it was an equally unprecedented Republican counter-mobilization to defeat the Little New Deal in a state that was still majority Republican.

Likewise, Davis is correct that EPIC "quietly disappeared from the scene" in 1938, but his statement distorts and obscures what actually happened in California that year. EPIC "quietly disappeared from the scene" because in the 1938 election an EPIC supporter was elected the first Democratic governor of California in the twentieth century, along with an extreme left-wing CIO advocate as his Lieutenant Governor. These "EPIC" Democrats then launched California's pro-labor "Little New Deal," thus bringing the New Deal, at long last, to California.[59] Through them, the agenda of the failed EPIC crusade of 1934 became the agenda of the victorious Democratic crusade of 1938, with the Democratic Party becoming the repository of the hopes of "labor's new millions," in California as elsewhere.

Thus, Mike Davis draws false conclusions from incomplete data, and in doing so misinterprets what happened in 1938. There was no diminution of working class support for the Democrats in 1938, thus presenting some kind of opening for "radical" third party or labor party activism. Rather, the breakdown of the vote which I presented above tells us that working class support for the Democrats was strengthened and mobilized as never before in 1938. This was because workers felt they'd gotten a "Real Deal" from the New Deal, and therefore had something real to lose in a Republican Thermidor.

Locally, in Pittsburgh, the official representatives of the working class were also becoming more firmly committed to the Democratic Party and the New Deal. For example, the minutes of the PCLU reveal that it was continually infiltrating more and more of its members into all the infrastructure levels of the local Democratic Party and local government. They placed their members in the local WPA, in the local National Labor Relations Board, in the Workmen's Compensation Board, as inspectors for the Pennsylvania Department of Labor and Industry, in the Fire Department, as constables, magistrates, and justices of the peace, all of which gave them more influence and also more of a commitment to the evolving structure. The events of January 1939 were typical.

On January 5, the PCLU endorsed Executive Board member George J. Walters, President of the Pittsburgh Building Trades Council (the AFL umbrella organization of the city's myriad construction unions) and Business Representative of Bricklayers Local No. 2, for appointment to the Pittsburgh Board of Education, an appointment made by the judges of the Court of Common Pleas. On January 19 PCLU President Leo Abernathy (who had replaced Pat Fagan), reported that he and PCLU Secretary John Stackhouse contacted the Court of Common Pleas judges on behalf of Brother Walters. As a result, the judges on their first ballot appointed Brother Walters to the Board of Education.[60] Such appointments of union men to positions in the local government happened on a regular basis.

Yet another example of the increasingly close relationship between the Democratic Party, government, and the labor movement occurred in July when D. R. Rogers, Superintendent of Property for the City of Pittsburgh, wrote to the PCLU informing them that he was coordinating the national convention of the Young Democrats, which would be held in Pittsburgh in early August. He requested that the PCLU purchase ads in the convention booklet to help finance the party convention. The PCLU did so because, among other things, Superintendent Rogers was also President of the United Brotherhood of Carpenters and Joiners, Local No. 142, and a member in good standing of the PCLU.

Even Pennsylvania Democratic Party chief David Lawrence showed that he was not totally opposed to appointing labor leaders to political office. In July of 1939 a vacancy appeared on the Pittsburgh City Council when one of the Councillors died. Although PCLU member Thomas J. Gallagher was already a "labor" representative on the Council, the PCLU still felt they deserved another one to replace the departed John J. Kane. They therefore endorsed Executive Board member Edward Leonard for the vacant seat.

Leonard was a plasterer, born and raised in the working class neighborhood of East Liberty. In the 1920s he'd been elected the business representative for Local 31 of the Plasterers' union and in 1930 he became Secretary of the Pittsburgh Building Trades Council. Leonard had campaigned hard for Roosevelt in 1932, both among his union colleagues and in his East Liberty neighborhood. In 1935 he also worked hard to elect another union man, John Kane, then head of the Pressmen's Union, as Commissioner of Allegheny County. The PCLU felt he was a logical candidate for "Kane's" City Council seat.[61]

This time, it seems, Lawrence agreed. He appointed Leonard to fill out the unexpired term on the nine-member City Council. Leonard then went on to win that year's primary and general elections for a full term on the City Council. Following his victory in the November election, Leonard spoke to the PCLU thanking it for its support in his original appointment to the Council and in the primary and general elections. "He further stated that the Honorable John J. Kane had set a precedent . . . by proving that he could represent labor and the public honestly and sincerely."[62]

Evidently representing both labor and the public "honestly and sincerely" would mean crossing swords with Lawrence himself, as a decade later Councillor Leonard would mount the last serious challenge to Lawrence's power in Pittsburgh.

Thus, judging from both election returns and from the increasingly intimate relationship between organized labor and the Democratic Party, there was no working class diminution of support for the party and the New Deal it represented in 1938. Instead, working class support for the Democratic Party and the New Deal was reaching even greater heights of intensity.

Because of this heightened intensity, the Republican Thermidor of 1938, while it put an end to both Pennsylvania's Little New Deal and Roosevelt's New Deal, did not mean a return to Republican dominance, in Pennsylvania or nationally. As Gary Gerstle has shown us in his study of the textile workers of Woonsocket, Rhode Island, it was only in 1938 that the workers of that city came to dominate municipal politics. And they did so through the vehicle of the Democratic Party.

Thus, what was said of Connecticut politics after 1938 was just as true of Pennsylvania politics after 1938. "[T]he Democrats rose from the inept and hopeless minority party of the mid-1920s to the powerful majority party of the mid-1930s . . . Events of the late 1930s, however, proved that Democrats could not presume an easy dominance of the state's politics. Although the changes in Connecticut politics proved lasting . . . Connecticut had left a period of Republican hegemony not for one of undisputed Democratic control, but rather for one of competitiveness."[63]

So, too, did the Pennsylvania Democratic and Republican parties vie after 1938 in a seesaw battle for control, in itself something unprecedented since the Civil War. Again, this toe-to-toe slugfest between roughly evenly matched opponents reflected the political sentiment of the nation at large. In the summer of 1938, for instance, one national Gallup poll asked registered voters which party they would join if there were only two parties in America, "one for conservatives and the other for liberals." The response was an an exact 50-50 breakdown.[64]

According to Samuel Lubell, it should have been expected that this political stalemate would emerge in 1938 and be anchored in a Congressional conservative coalition. "Under our system of separation of powers," he noted, "whoever loses the Presidency continues the battle for control of the government through Congress. It is not surprising that the anti-Roosevelt coalition in Congress took form in 1938, at the very next election after the formation of the Roosevelt coalition in 1936. The year 1938 opened with the Southern filibuster against the proposed anti-lynching law; 1938 also marked Roosevelt's unsuccessful purge of the more conservative Democratic Senators. It was the year in which John L. Lewis tried to capture control of the Democratic Party in Pennsylvania and lost; and of the CIO's unsuccessful battle to win control of the Ohio Democratic Party. It was also the year in which the old alliance of isolationism and economic liberalism was shattered, and, with it, both the Wisconsin Progressives and the Minnesota Farmer-Laborites. By 1938, in short, the alignment of issues and forces which have held the nation in deadlock since had taken form."[65]

In Pennsylvania this deadlock persisted on roughly equal terms throughout the Forties and Fifties, despite the intervening World War and the McCarthy Era witch hunts of suspected Communists, of which Pittsburgh was a major storm center. Indeed, it was the very saliency of class issues in Pittsburgh's politics which led the Federal Bureau of Investigation to Pittsburgh in search of radical agitators after the war, under the assumption that "the reds" were responsible for Pittsburgh's politics.

This Cold War hunt for subversives, however, had little impact on either the class support for the Democratic Party in Pittsburgh, or in the Commonwealth as a whole, or upon the viability of the party. Indeed, in the decade of the Fifties the Democratic Party won just as many statewide contests as it did in the Thirties, and its mean percentage of the total vote was even slightly higher than in the Thirties. The durability of this political duel can be seen in a glance at the voting patterns in Pennsylvania since the coming of class politics in 1932 (table 6).

Table 6
Pennsylvania Voting Patterns, 1932-1968

Period	No. of State Offices	Dem. Wins	Mean % Dem. of Total Vote	Mean % GOP of Total Vote	Mean % Dem. of State House
1932-1940	21	12	49.0	48.6	52.4
1942-1950	25	6	46.5	52.7	37.6
1952-1960	24	12	49.4	50.3	48.7
1962-1968	19	10	50.9	48.0	51.3

Source: Walter Dean Burnham, *Critical Elections and the Mainsprings of American Politics*, W.W. Norton & Co.: N.Y., 1970, Table 3.6, 52.

Essentially, it was a decades-long electoral stalemate, reflecting a similar stalemate at the national level. This electoral stasis was made possible in Pennsylvania and elsewhere by an enduring Republican appeal to traditional WASP elements (including some workers of modest means), as well as educated and upper-income voters, balanced against continuing Democratic dominance of the urban black and ethnic industrial regions.

For example, after 1932 the Western Pennsylvania regions of "Allegheny, Washington, Westmoreland, Cambria, and Fayette counties subsequently went Democratic and, by and large, stayed Democratic. These counties have supplied from 35 percent to 50 percent of the total Democratic representation in the [state] General Assembly and over half the Democratic representation in Congress."[66] It was the continuing Democratic dominance of these areas—as well as, later, Philadelphia—which made it possible for the Democratic Party to rebound in 1940 in a see-saw electoral battle which continues to this day. Pittsburgh and the Steel Valley, especially, remained the capitol of the laborite wing of Pennsylvania's Democratic Party.

Thus, it was entirely appropriate that, less than a week after the 1938 election, a new national labor organization was officially founded in an ethnic fraternal hall on Pittsburgh's working class North Side. Pittsburgh's Democratic Mayor Cornelius Scully warmly welcomed delegates from all over America who, from November 14-18, founded the Congress of Industrial Organizations. The CIO was no longer simply an "organizing committee." It had at last taken the decisive step of transforming itself into a permanent federation of industrial unions to rival the AFL. Appropriately, it did this in the very city—"the most completely organized city of any in the country" declared John L. Lewis in his opening remarks—where Gompers had helped found the AFL fifty-seven years before almost to the day.

The proceedings were opened by a benediction from a local Catholic Worker priest active in the Pittsburgh labor movement. This was the young Rev. Charles Owen Rice, pastor of the Holy Rosary Catholic Church, who was already on his way to superseding Father Cox as a legendary Pittsburgh "labor priest."

"O Lord and Savior, Jesus Christ," he prayed, "You who were a worker Yourself . . . We pray for the victory of the worker in this country, O Almighty God, because his victory is Your victory, his cause is Your cause. A victory for labor in its struggles for decent conditions is a victory for Americanism and for Christianity. Amen."[67]

To which the assembled CIO delegates responded with loud "Amens."

And, with these words as inspiration, the Congress of Industrial Organizations was officially founded in 1938 in the Steel City.

The Class Line in American Politics

But, despite the claims of John L. Lewis, Pittsburgh was not entirely organized. The struggle for that continued, although now made easier because it was taking place in a political context favorable to the labor movement.

The political context of Pennsylvania at large, however, and many other important Northeastern industrial states, was not so favorable in the aftermath of the Republican Thermidor of 1938. Political mobilization along class lines remained at high levels, and it was not at all clear that labor and the Democrats could triumph in the upcoming 1940 presidential election, or even win those states where Democratic revitalization had taken place. In a Gallup survey of registered voters conducted in the summer of 1939, Republican sentiment was the majority sentiment in several crucial industrial states. In Massachusetts, 55 percent of the electorate said they'd like to see a Republican victory in 1940. In Pennsylvania, Michigan, and Illinois, 54 percent hoped for a Republican victory. In New York, 53 percent looked forward to a Republican triumph and even 52 percent of the voters in "Progressive" Wisconsin wanted to see a Democratic defeat. Much higher numbers in those same states said they definitely would not be voting for Roosevelt in 1940 if he ran for a third term. Even 64 percent of the voters in California, which had elected a labor-backed Democrat as governor in 1938, said they would not vote for Roosevelt.[68]

And yet, during the summer of 1939, various city bosses and key Democratic Party leaders came to the conclusion—as other potential contenders like John Nance Garner, party chairman James A. Farley, and even Harry Hopkins fell by the wayside—that only Roosevelt could hold together the still-fragile New Deal coalition which had brought victory in 1936.[69] Labor's political battles, then, were evidently far from over. Victory would require an even greater mobilization of workers in 1940.

Realizing this, the delegates to the CIO's 1938 founding convention in Pittsburgh endorsed political action to elect Democratic candidates in 1940. Delegates called for organized labor to move into the political arena "[I]n every industrial state, in every congressional district, down into the wards and precincts, so when these future election days come, labor will be able to give a steadily better account of itself, and finally win the recognition which is its due upon the political as upon the industrial field."

The Resolutions Committee then introduced Resolution No. 40, dealing with "Political Action." It endorsed President Roosevelt and called upon him "to continue his determined fight to maintain the gains of labor and of the common people and to forge ahead to achieve a program of economic and social reform." It then declared that "[L]abor cannot be just hewers of wood and drawers of water . . . Labor in the United States must have an increasing participation in the functions of government . . . [because] The preservation of political democracy and the extension of legislative democracy requires vigorous participation by organized labor in the political life of the nation." Therefore, it called upon the CIO Executive Board to "take appropriate action to coordinate political and legislative activities of each of its affiliates" to bring this about.

Mike Quill, Left-leaning leader of the New York City Transport Workers Union and an American Labor Party member of the New York City Council, rose to speak in favor of the resolution. "I ask you to raise the question of political action in every trade union hall you are connected with throughout the length and breadth of the United States," he told the delegates, "and put over this resolution with a tremendous vote." And so it was.[70] Among other things, the CIO then authorized the creation and distribution of a booklet to all its locals entitled, "How to Organize and Conduct a Local Political Campaign."

The evolution of the CIO (as well as the AFL) into increasingly intimate political relations with the Democratic Party was dictated not only by New Deal policies which had benefited organized labor, but also by the overlap in constituencies. "The social composition of the CIO's locals especially bore a remarkable resemblance to the constituency that the Democrats mobilized politically in 1934 and 1936: both were heavily urban, immigrant stock, and lower income groups. Involvement in such a class-exclusive infrastructure [as the CIO] reinforced party commitments and sustained the partisan cleavage structure well beyond the crisis of the 1930s."[71]

Thus, it was only natural that, as the presidential election of 1940 neared, those local CIO political campaigns would be conducted on behalf of Franklin D. Roosevelt for an unprecedented third term. Indeed, "In many localities the union leadership virtually took over the Democratic campaign, as Van Bittner did in West Virginia."[72]

Nor was the AFL idle on FDR's behalf. In September 1940, the AFL-affiliated Pittsburgh Central Labor Union voted unanimously to launch its own independent campaign to elect Roosevelt "and friends of labor" and open its own office for that purpose. It requested all affiliated unions to contribute financially and, at the beginning of October, opened the "Pittsburgh Central Labor Union Roosevelt Labor Headquarters" at 411 Grant Street, Downtown.

On October 17 the Pennsylvania Federation of Labor wrote to the PCLU reminding them that the state AFL body had also endorsed FDR for re-election at its last convention and "urged all members to extend every possible effort to bring victory to the forces of Organized Labor and thus assure a continuation of liberal government by returning that great Humanitarian, Franklin D. Roosevelt, to the White House." At that same meeting the PCLU gave a warm reception to New York City Mayor Fiorello LaGuardia, who was visiting the city urging the re-election of Roosevelt.[73]

On October 24, the PCLU's Committee for Political Action held a mass meeting for Pittsburgh area workers at Oakland's Syria Mosque auditorium. The purpose of the meeting was to urge all workers to vote for Roosevelt and "the Democracy." The principal speaker was the national Teamsters union president Dan Tobin.[74]

Also typical of organized labor's attitude was the stance of David Dubinsky's International Ladies' Garment Workers Union (ILGWU), which passed a resolution endorsing Roosevelt at its 1940 annual convention. After the resolution passed, delegates from twenty-six states danced through the aisles of New York's Carnegie Hall chanting "We Want Roosevelt."

Events in Europe also seemed to encourage support for a Roosevelt third-term. In August 1939, polls showed that only 40 percent of the electorate favored a third term. However, after the fall of France to the Nazis in June 1940,

57 percent of the electorate favored a continuation of the incumbent president.[75]

Meanwhile, Roosevelt shored up his strongholds of urban strength with "nonpolitical" visits to key locales. Typical was his October 11th visit to Pittsburgh to dedicate Terrace Village, Pennsylvania's first low-rent federally-subsidized housing complex. The housing was built by the Allegheny County Housing Authority, now headed by Pittsburgh City Councillor Edward Leonard, and was located on the hills overlooking Oakland.

The President's visit, combined with Republican presidential candidate Wendell Willkie's rally at Forbes Field a week before, on October 3rd, seemed to stir up an "all-time peak in political interest." Pittsburgh's Democratic Mayor Cornelius Scully proclaimed the day one of "public celebration" and gave all 5,000 city employees a half day off to greet the president.[76]

After touring flood control projects in Johnstown, Roosevelt arrived at East Liberty's train station on his special train. Accompanied by Democratic U.S. Senator Joseph Guffey and Pittsburgh's Democratic Representative (and PCLU-endorsed) Joseph McArdle—both up for re-election also—Roosevelt's entourage made a round-about tour of selected Mon Valley steel towns.

Driving through the communities of Edgewood, Swissvale, and Whitaker on Pittsburgh's eastern border, "FDR [was] given a tumultuous and exciting welcome in the well-known Democratic hotbeds of Rankin and Homestead." Roosevelt toured the 310-acre Homestead Works of the Carnegie-Illinois mill—part of U.S. Steel—where he saw armor plate being manufactured for a dozen warships. Homestead was already becoming a crucial part of the "Arsenal for Democracy." Huge and enthusiastic crowds lined both sides of Homestead's main street, Eighth Avenue, to cheer the president as his open convertible glided slowly through the town to the giant Mesta plant in West Homestead, where the president also toured that huge steel mill.

Then it was back across the Mon River to Pittsburgh to dedicate the opening of Terrace Village, the ostensible reason for Roosevelt's visit, where the Housing Authority had already prepared space for 100,000 to greet the president.

Terrace Village was—and is—located on Ruch's Hill overlooking the Oakland neighborhood. Today the University of Pittsburgh's Trees Hall swimming pool and stadium stand next to it. "One of the biggest of the New Deal housing projects," Terrace Village—like the massive Roosevelt Towers in Cambridge, Massachusetts, and many similar sites elsewhere—was "seen as a symbol of optimism to a country exiting the Depression and as nothing less than basic heat and shelter to thousands of local residents living in tenements."

Divided into two sections—Addison Terrace and Allequippa Terrace—the $12,800,000 complex was designed to house 2,653 families and "was viewed as a godsend in a city where officials found more than 78,000 homes needed major repairs or were substandard. 'We were in a bad house—a *terrible* house,'" remembered Elease Marsh, who turned out for Roosevelt's appearance and who moved into Terrace Village three months later. "At that time, people were glad to get a decent home,'" she recalled. "We were in slum houses. This was nice, warm and comfortable.'"[77]

After being welcomed by Democratic Party chief David Lawrence, City Councillor Edward Leonard, and "labor priest" Father Charles Owen Rice, Roosevelt told the crowd that, "'Not only this section, but every other section of the Union, is richer for having antiquated, squalid shacks replaced by these bright decent houses.'"[78]

Then Roosevelt's triumphal parade wound slowly down the hill and along Oakland's Fifth Avenue and then along Liberty Avenue through the heart of downtown Pittsburgh. The entire Pittsburgh Police Department—900 officers— plus another 150 firemen dragooned into crowd control duty, strained to hold back frenzied, cheering thousands of Pittsburghers as FDR's cavalcade rolled sedately to the Pennsylvania Railroad Station, where the president departed for a similar jubilant welcome in Akron.[79]

This intensity of adulation and devotion to Roosevelt was vividly experienced by ten-year-old Walter Dean Burnham on a bus trip to Pittsburgh that same year. "I grew up," Burnham said, "during the Great Depression and the Second World War, in the Pittsburgh area," where unemployment in 1934 stood at a third of the workforce and where it remained high until America became the world's "Arsenal of Democracy" as World War II began.

"The town in which I grew up gave Wendell Willkie 85 percent of its vote in the 1940 election. As with the parents and the milieu, so with the son . . . One day in the fall of 1940 I took the bus to downtown Pittsburgh, arrayed with several Willkie buttons . . . No sooner had I gotten off at my destination than I was surrounded by several men, far more shabbily dressed than my father. They gave me to understand very clearly that my Willkie buttons were not welcome. I removed them, put them in my pocket, and the scene dissolved without further incident. But this encounter made a vivid and life-long impression. When, later, I read *The People's Choice* and learned from Robert Alford's *Party and Society* that the index of class polarization reached an all-time high in the 1940 election, the arguments of both works fitted readily into this remembered experience."[80]

Ironically, although Roosevelt, like most politicians, knew in his gut where his strength resided, like most politicians he nevertheless denied the reality of this class polarization in 1940. At the very time that the class alignment of the political parties and class-based political loyalties were more intense than ever before, Roosevelt observed that, "The growing independence of voters, after all, has been proved by the votes in every presidential election since my childhood—and the tendency, frankly, is on the increase." In truth, the tendency, frankly, was on the decrease, and had been for years, as voters aligned with the parties more and more based entirely on class membership.[81]

Fearing their more traditional candidates might not overcome Roosevelt's tremendous popularity, the Republicans turned in desperation to Indiana businessman-turned-politician Wendell Willkie. He was an amateur politician who'd never been elected to anything. Rather, he was a Wall Street lawyer and had recently been president of the Commonwealth and Southern Corporation, a giant utilities holding company which had been broken up by the New Deal in 1939 as a monopoly.

This inflamed Willkie's opposition to the New Deal's perceived zeal for regulating big business although, except for his fiscal conservatism, on many other issues he was a liberal. For instance, while the Republican Party was dominated by isolationists, Willkie was a fervent internationalist who had championed the League of Nations as a Wilson Democrat. In addition, he had been a socialist in college and opposed the Ku Klux Klan in his native Indiana when it virtually ran the government of that state in the 1920s. Further, he remained a registered Democrat until after he actually received the Republican presidential nomination.

For all these reasons, there had been some opposition to Willkie from conservative Pennsylvania Republicans, especially Philadelphia-based Sun Oil Company Vice President Joseph N. Pew, who was displacing Grundy as leader of the Pennsylvania party. These Pennsylvania Republicans felt Willkie wasn't anti-New Deal enough for their liking. So, at Pew's direction, the Pennsylvania delegation to the Republican national convention had cast all of its seventy-two votes on the first ballot and even sixty-five votes on the second ballot for their "favorite son," Arthur James, Pennsylvania's new Republican governor and Democratic dragon slayer.

Nevertheless, there were powerful elements within the Republican Party, especially Republican media moguls, who saw Willkie as the ideal candidate to run against Roosevelt. Henry Luce, publisher of *Time*, shared Willkie's internationalist outlook. Ogden Reid, owner of *The New York Herald Tribune*, and the Cowles brothers, publishers of *Look* magazine and influential Midwestern newspapers, also liked his anti-Fascism and used their outlets to champion Willkie's cause. As Hitler's armies advanced across Europe in the fall of 1940, Willkie's interventionist stance gained popularity within the party. In the end, the choice was Willkie in a stunning party convention upset on the sixth ballot over Ohio Senator Robert Taft and New York City District Attorney Thomas E. Dewey.

Willkie campaigned vigorously and, "As the 1940 political campaign went into its penultimate week, the result of the presidential election became increasingly doubtful. The re-election of President Roosevelt, which a month before had seemed certain, now hung in the balance. The political experts and the polls were virtually unanimous in proclaiming that this would be the closest election since 1916 . . . Into this setting came the voice of John L. Lewis on the night of October 25."[82]

By 1940, both the working class in general and organized labor in particular, and especially the CIO, had become so closely identified with Roosevelt and the Democratic Party that it seemed nothing could shake the alliance. Yet CIO leader John L. Lewis attempted to do exactly that in the most dramatic act of political suicide since Father Coughlin had turned against the New Deal in the mid-Thirties.

Lewis had become increasingly disillusioned with Roosevelt during the president's second term. At the height of the 1937 Little Steel Strike, Roosevelt, no doubt sensing the increasing hostility toward the CIO in the public at large, had distanced himself from the conflict by declaring, "a plague on both your houses."[83] The president had been equally cool toward Lewis and the UAW during the Flint sit-down strike.

Lewis thundered his disapproval at this betrayal by someone who had "supped at labor's table," and grew increasingly distant from the president. As war loomed larger in Europe, Roosevelt's sympathy for Britain's struggle also alienated Lewis' isolationist sentiments. In the spring of 1940 Lewis had endorsed Senator Burton Wheeler, an isolationist, for the Democratic nomination. But, when Roosevelt made the decision to run for a third term—and won the Democratic nomination—Lewis began searching for alternatives outside the party.

Knowing this, Willkie began wooing Lewis and, in a midnight New York City meeting, promised him that, if he won, he would not roll back labor's gains under the New Deal. Additionally, he promised that the Secretary of Labor would be chosen from among the leaders of organized labor—perhaps hinting that Lewis would be that man. "Lewis volunteered his support if Willkie agreed to repeat that statement publicly in his labor speech scheduled for Pittsburgh on October 3. Willkie agreed, and their midnight session ended. The Republican candidate's address before a Forbes Field audience of thirty thousand did repeat his assurances to labor . . . He also announced his intention of having a labor man represented in his Cabinet."[84]

John L. Lewis then kept his part of the bargain. On the night of October 25, Lewis delivered a major radio address to his millions of CIO followers. In the looming close election, it was obvious that Roosevelt's re-election hopes depended upon the loyalty of CIO voters. Lewis knew this. "The direct and affiliated membership of these several [CIO] organizations," he said, organizations of which he was the spokesman and representative, "amounts to substantially ten million men and women. Adding to this number the numerical strength of their dependent families, there is achieved a sum-total of human beings amounting to approximately one-fourth of the total population of our nation." Moreover, this one-fourth was heavily concentrated in the industrial swing states of the Northeast and Midwest which Roosevelt had to carry to win.

Therefore, Lewis tested the loyalty of this working class constituency. Were they more loyal to him or the president? Could he swing them to Willkie? Lewis bet that he could. He told his millions of followers to abandon the Democrats and vote Republican in the upcoming election.

Then he made the stakes as high as he could. After telling his followers that a vote for Roosevelt meant a vote for war in Europe, he threw down the gauntlet. The presidential vote would be a vote of confidence in Lewis himself. "Sustain me now, or repudiate me," he said. "It is obvious that President Roosevelt will not be re-elected for the third term unless he has the overwhelming support of the men and women of labor. If he is, therefore, re-elected it will mean that the members of the Congress of Industrial Organizations have rejected my advice and recommendation. I will accept the result as being the equivalent of a vote of no-confidence, and will retire as President of the Congress of Industrial Organizations at its convention in November."[85]

His followers were shocked and appalled. Instead of rallying to the side of their leader, they erupted in outrage at what they considered to be a betrayal by the new Judas of the labor movement. Many of Lewis' followers had gathered expectantly in CIO union halls across the nation to listen to their leader endorse Roosevelt. Walter and Victor Reuther heard the address at Detroit's West Side UAW Local, along with many of that local's 26,000 "stunned" members. "[W]e saw many veterans of the sit-down strikes, tears streaming down their faces, leave the hall in anger and bewilderment," Victor Reuther recalled.[86]

John L. Lewis had misjudged the loyalties of his followers. Very few of the constituent CIO unions followed Lewis' lead. All of the major CIO unions—except the United Mine Workers, which Lewis directly controlled—quickly repudiated their leader and reaffirmed their loyalty to the president, urging their membership to re-double their efforts on behalf of Roosevelt's re-election in the face of this betrayal. These unions included the Textile Workers, the Amalgamated Clothing Workers, the United Auto Workers, the Steel Workers Organizing Committee, the United Rubber Workers, and the United Electrical Workers.

All of the CIO's six Vice Presidents—including Philip Murray of SWOC, R.J. Thomas of the UAW, Sherman Dalrymple of the URW, Emile Rieve of the Textile Workers, and Reid Robinson of the Mine, Mill, and Smelter Workers—continued to work hard for Roosevelt. Where local union officials—such as Harry Bridges of the West Coast longshoremen's union—joined Lewis in this "betrayal," the rank and file angrily demanded the resignation of their own leaders as traitors to the working class. The San Francisco Warehousemen, the Longshoremen of San Francisco, Portland, San Pedro, Stockton, and Aberdeen quickly issued declarations of support for the president, as did the National Maritime Union and the Shipbuilding Workers.

In Pittsburgh, a local SWOC leader laughed off Lewis' influence on Steel Valley voters, declaring, "he isn't going to hurt Roosevelt at all," while the president of a SWOC local in Beaver Falls repudiated Lewis by telling a reporter, "Let Lewis support Willkie . . . He'll do us more good on the other side."[87] There was talk of impeaching Lewis even among his own otherwise fanatically loyal UMW members. The coal fields around Pittsburgh were especially "seething with rank-and-file demands for Mr. Lewis' UMW scalp."[88]

Indeed, the prediction of the Beaver Falls SWOC leader proved prophetic, for Lewis' "betrayal" actually did do more good for the president than Lewis might have done by endorsing him. It stirred the union membership nationwide into a fever pitch of activity for the president—in order to counter Lewis' possible influence—which it might otherwise have been more difficult to inspire. In many places, "It also spurred the unity idea and many meetings were organized jointly by the CIO, the AFL, and the railway brotherhoods."[89] No doubt these fierce actions had a part in creating the largest voter turnout America has witnessed in the last sixty years.

And Roosevelt won a third term easily, carried to victory on the backs of the workers. With 55 percent of the popular vote—27 million votes to Willkie's 22 million—he swept all of the country's largest cities except for Cincinnati. Roosevelt's vote in the blue collar cities was "with majorities that were sufficient to overwhelm the Willkie vote in the rural areas. Willkie, for example, carried upstate New York by half a million but lost New York City by seven hundred thousand."[90] Roosevelt carried the big pivotal states, including Illinois, Ohio, and the two with the most electoral votes in the nation, New York and Pennsylvania, although Willkie polled substantially higher totals in all four states than did Landon in 1936.

Even so, Willkie's greatest strength was in the farm states of the Midwest, especially Kansas, Nebraska, and Iowa. Where Roosevelt's urban vote wasn't large enough to overcome the rural Republican vote, the loss was often by narrow margins. He lost Willkie's home state of Indiana by only 25,000 votes and Michigan by only 7,000 votes.

Indicative of the mobilization of voters on both sides of this class war, Wendell Willkie's 22 million votes was the largest number of votes ever cast for a losing presidential candidate in the history of America up to that time, and 300,000 more than any Republican—even a winning Republican—had ever garnered. At any other time, the Republican turnout would have been enough to make Wendell Willkie president. And, given Willkie's liberal and Democratic Party credentials, this record-high Republican vote can only be seen as a loyal rural and class-based vote for the party, not for the candidate.

The Democratic vote was just as polarized. In state after state, it was the urban industrial regions which gave Roosevelt his victory. Roosevelt carried New Jersey because of his strength in "the strong Democratic counties—Hudson, where Mayor Frank Hague of Jersey City, Vice Chairman of the Democratic National Committee, piled up a big Roosevelt vote, and Camden and Middlesex, where big industries with strong Roosevelt labor strength are located."

In formerly Republican Massachusetts, Roosevelt's victory was based upon that same vote. "President Roosevelt was strongest in the industrial cities outside Boston. He carried Lynn by almost 6,000 votes and New Bedford by a ratio of nearly 2 to 1. It was estimated that Roosevelt's margin in Boston would approach 100,000. He carried Somerville by 4,100 votes."

Similarly, *The New York Times* reported that, "Aided by impressive strength in the industrial areas, President Roosevelt apparently duplicated his feat of 1936 and won the 36 electoral votes of traditionally Republican Pennsylvania in yesterday's election," despite the Democrats having a minority of registered voters in Pennsylvania.[91] The Steeltown communities around Pittsburgh were typical of this trend. Roosevelt took McKeesport by 5,000 votes. He took Duquesne, Clairton, and Aliquippa by two-to-one margins, Braddock by three-to-one, and Homestead by four-to-one. Lewis' own mine workers in the coal fields surrounding Pittsburgh gave Roosevelt a 48,000 vote victory margin.[92]

Other Pennsylvania Democrats shared in the sweet glow of triumph. The Republican-oriented *Pittsburgh Post-Gazette* had particularly targeted incumbent Democratic U.S. Senator Joseph Guffey, elected in the class referendum vote of 1934, for defeat. "He represents all the things which are worst in the New Deal," said the newspaper. His defeat will help in "finishing the job of eliminating the rubber-stamp New Deal Congressional delegation from this state," which was begun in 1938.[93]

Perhaps such an attack on Guffey by a Republican newspaper was considered an endorsement by working class voters. In any case, Guffey was easily re-elected, as was the entire Democratic slate for statewide offices, including the re-election of the incumbent Democratic State Treasurer and Auditor General.

The Democrats also surged back in other races. They gained thirty-nine seats in the state House of Representatives, which they'd lost in 1938, thus giving them control of that body once more. In some State Representative districts the Democratic vote was overwhelming. In Pittsburgh's First District, for example, which included Downtown and the black Hill District, black Democratic State Representative Homer S. Brown was re-elected by a four-to-one margin over his Republican challenger.[94]

Democrats also picked up four seats in the U.S. House of Representatives, thus regaining a majority of U.S. Congressmen from the state. In Allegheny County the Republican Party Congressional delegation almost ceased to exist. The Democrats took all five of the county's Congressional seats, defeating two incumbent Republicans. They took both State Senate seats up for election. One of the seats was won by Joseph M. Barr, the Executive Secretary of the Democratic County Committee. David Lawrence had appointed Barr to fill the State Senate seat vacated by Thomas Kilgallen. In turn, Lawrence had appointed Kilgallen to fill the Pittsburgh City Council seat which became vacant following the death of Councillor P. J. McArdle. Now Barr won a full State Senate term on his own. He would eventually go on to follow his patron, Lawrence, into the Pittsburgh mayor's office in the 1950s.

Finally, Allegheny County Democrats took twenty-two of the county's twenty-seven State House seats. Roosevelt came out of Allegheny County with a 105,599 vote majority over Willkie, which gave him and the Democratic ticket enough of a margin to insure its election throughout Pennsylvania. The record turnout of 630,000 county voters was about 90,000 more than in 1936—which had been the previous all-time high voter turnout. "The turnout of voters," said *The Post-Gazette*, "represented more than 86 percent of the enrollment—astounding in view of the fact that a heavy rain fell during the last few hours of voting time."[95]

The county vote featured the usual heavy Republican majorities in well-to-do suburbs such as Fox Chapel, Dormont, and Mt. Lebanon, as well as the affluent Pittsburgh neighborhoods of Shadyside and Squirrel Hill. It also featured the even heavier Democratic majorities in the steel towns and Pittsburgh's working class neighborhoods of the Hill District, Polish Hill, and the Slavic South Side. In one of those South Side polling places, a young mother who had come to vote held up her baby son before a laughing, cheering crowd of steelworkers. "Vote for Roosevelt, the friend of the people!" the boy "chirped" to his enthusiastic audience.[96]

Indicative of the close identification between labor voters and Democratic voters was what *The Post-Gazette* called, "The most formidable array of Democratic leaders to vote in any one district," the 24th precinct of Ward 19. The "Democratic leaders" it referred to were actually all labor union leaders who lived in that neighborhood. They included SWOC chief Philip Murray, County

Commissioner John J. Kane of the Pressmen's Union and PCLU Executive Board, local UMWA and Steel City Industrial Union Council chief Pat Fagan, and City Councillor Thomas J. Gallagher of the Flint Glass Workers.[97]

Prior to the election, pundits had made much of the third term factor and of Roosevelt's aid for England, then standing alone against a Nazi-conquered Europe. These were negatives which would detract from Roosevelt's vote, they opined. In retrospect, these proved to be total non-issues for the electorate, on both sides. The issue was the New Deal radical reform agenda, and nothing else. "For the Republican party itself, personal letters of both the prominent and the so-called 'grassroots' voters confirmed that the real issue was getting rid of the New Deal and FDR. They could disagree among themselves about how much the United States should risk by helping England, but there was complete harmony in believing that the Administration was an enemy of private enterprise, which they were still fond of calling 'free' enterprise. Even the issue of the third term was subordinate to this factor. As a Gallup poll showed, those who wanted to get rid of Roosevelt for other reasons liked to offer the third term as an excuse, while New Deal supporters minimized its importance. As a real issue, it never became basic."[98]

What was basic was workers' unwavering support for what they saw as the class politics of the New Deal—and Republican opposition to the New Deal for the same reason. Indeed, the aftermath of the 1940 election was, "a wider difference between . . . rich and poor, indicative of continuing and perhaps even somewhat increased class consciousness."[99]

Among every category of worker, the Democratic Party polled huge margins of support: 79 percent among CIO members, 71 percent among AFL members, and even 64 percent among non-union workers.[100] "Republican hopes were blacked out in factory smoke," declared Samuel Lubell in his post-election analysis. "The New Deal accomplished what the Socialists, the I.W.W., and the Communists never could approach. *It has drawn a class line across the face of American politics* . . . [with] a class-conscious vote for the first time in American history."[101]

This class line in politics, which actually was not being drawn for the first time, was clearly evident East and West, North and South, in every industrial center of the nation. In 1938 in North Carolina, a sometime textile mill worker and union organizer had said, "Sure, I'm for this administration. I'm with Roosevelt right up to the hilt. I don't know whether Roosevelt'll have a third term or not, but if he doesn't . . . God help this country! I'm dealin' with the workers every day and I know what they say. They've got more from this administration than ever before and they're not gonna stand for anybody takin' it away from'em."[102]

This intensity of class partisanship could also be seen in the Steel Valley election returns. In a close post mortem of the election, Irving Bernstein examined sixty-three counties and fourteen towns in twelve states where CIO membership was salient in order to determine how the workers voted. Bernstein concluded that, "Roosevelt ran well ahead of his national position in the CIO regions," carrying all fourteen towns (as he had in 1936) and fifty-five of the sixty-three counties.[103]

Because "Pennsylvania is the heart of the CIO country," with half a million CIO members, Bernstein looked particularly closely at Pennsylvania, and even harder at the steel towns surrounding Pittsburgh where SWOC-CIO membership was concentrated. Allegheny County, with a CIO membership estimated at 25-30 percent of the population, went for Roosevelt with a 58.3 percent Democratic vote over-all. This vote was even higher, however, in some of Allegheny County's steel towns. Bernstein looked closely at McKeesport, Clairton, and Duquesne, "all heavily CIO in their composition, much more so than Pittsburgh. Almost one-half of the voters in McKeesport are CIO workers and the mayors of both Clairton and Duquesne [John Mullen and Elmer Maloy] are CIO officials. Of the 22 election districts in these two towns, only one went to Willkie, that one in Duquesne."

Of the total vote in these three towns, the Democratic share was 60.1 percent in McKeesport, 67.3 percent in Clairton, and 68.5 percent in Duquesne. "The conclusion," Bernstein said, "is that the workers voted for Roosevelt overwhelmingly . . . [Despite Lewis] Roosevelt not only held the CIO group but may even have slightly increased his share of it . . . The fundamental factor in the re-election of President Roosevelt was his hold on the labor vote. Without it he could not have won. In the strategic industrial states, the industrial unions were the sheet anchor of Roosevelt victory."[104]

Thus, claimed Samuel Lubell, "the third term election brought the crucial trial by fire and water which demonstrated the coalition's durability."[105] That this coalition was profoundly urban was at last clear to all after 1940. "In both 1932 and 1936," Lubell pointed out, "Roosevelt would still have been elected without his heavy urban pluralities. In 1940, however . . . the margin of victory that accounted for at least 212 electoral votes was supplied by the dozen largest cities in the country."[106]

That the New Deal coalition was also profoundly working class was also clear. "In Pittsburgh," said Lubell, "Roosevelt got three fourths of the vote in wards whose rentals averaged under $40 a month and only four tenths of the vote where rentals were above $60 a month. Minneapolis, whose social make-up contrasts sharply with Pittsburgh, showed much the same results—about 40 percent of the vote for Roosevelt in the highest income ward, but seven of every ten voters in the lower rental areas.

"When I asked one auto unionist in Detroit why the third-term issue had made so little difference he replied, 'I'll say it even though it doesn't sound nice. We've grown class conscious.' With other unions there may have been less bitterness, but the division between worker and 'economic royalist' was as sharply drawn. In a Minneapolis ward, inhabited largely by teamsters, the pastor of one church had been outspoken in condemning the third term. He admitted bitterly, 'I don't suppose I changed a single vote.' John Lewis, who had endorsed Willkie, could have echoed him."[107]

Indeed, Lubell recognized the suicidal futility of Lewis trying to lead his "followers" out of their new home in "the workers' party," and not just for economic reasons. "[I]t is questionable whether the leaders of labor could move the bulk of the workers out of the Democratic party today," he said. *The ties binding the laboring masses to the Democratic emblem . . . are ethnic and religious as well as economic.* The strength of the Democratic appeal reflects the many different ways through which Roosevelt touched and lifted the aspirations of the urban masses. Any attempt to lead them out of the Democratic fold would run against insurmountable psychological barriers."[108]

Thus, the 1940 election starkly revealed that America's ethnic urban working class viewed the Democratic Party as *their* party, the worker's party, labor's party. Labor "leaders" who failed to recognize the loyalties of their "followers" were simply flailing in futility, as Lewis discovered. He had himself forgotten that the slogan his sound trucks had blared throughout the coal fields when building the labor movement was not, "John L. Lewis wants you to join the union!" It had been, "The *President* wants you to join the union!"

The day after the election, Roosevelt ventured out to lay the cornerstone of a new post office in his Hyde Park neighborhood. As reporters and photographers crowded around him at the post office ceremonies, he admonished them to turn their cameras away from him and look at the union men parading around the post office with their signs. *"There's* your story," Roosevelt told the reporters. They turned and read the signs the workers carried: "Not Lewis, but unity." "When Lewis resigns, labor will have peace." "Our champ, Franklin D. Roosevelt."[109]

Rank and file American workers had now completely embraced the Democratic Party as their own. The result was a permanent restructuring of Pennsylvania—and the nation's—politics. Based on the outcome, Luther Harr, Pennsylvania Democratic State Campaign Manager, predicted that Pennsylvania would eventually be classed as "traditionally Democratic," rather than traditionally Republican. "The election has shown that Pennsylvania is a truly liberal state," he said, with "more victories to come."[110]

However, *The Pittsburgh Post-Gazette* was more accurate in its editorial following the election when it looked at the divided state government and said, "Once before in recent history the same thing happened, in the 1935 regular and 1936 special sessions, when administration and House were Democratic and the Senate Republican. And that period was productive of some of the bitterest legislative sessions in the history of the Commonwealth . . . There will be political warfare in the state capital again, as a result of the 1940 election."[111]

The Democrats had not replaced Republican hegemony in the state at large, but the state had become politically competitive. And in Pittsburgh and the industrial communities surrounding it, Republican power was gone forever, replaced by a blue collar, class-based, Democratic Party.

This close identification of the Democratic Party with the working class was to persist nationwide for decades to come. "From the 1930s through 1960, at least, lower income groups gave disproportionate electoral support to the Democratic Party . . . Within a political context marked by unusually clear party cues, voter turnout increased [in the Thirties], new mobilization exhibited a distinctly pro-Democratic bias, and a new majority was forged. In the process, the social group and attitudinal bases of partisanship shifted from an older ethno-religious focus to a newer . . . economic-group alignment. The symbiotic and structural relationships between organized labor and the Democrats operated to sustain the new alignment."[112]

Further, the intensity of this class-based partisanship was evident to everyone at the time. Following the election, the Republican-oriented *Pittsburgh Post-Gazette* appealed to Roosevelt to do something to alleviate the class war roiling society. "The administration," said the newspaper, "has the renewed opportunity to undo, so far as possible, the class consciousness and the class bitterness which have been created in the last few years."[113]

****

Two weeks after the 1940 presidential election, John L. Lewis, a crippled "misleader" of labor and a pariah outside of his own union, a man who had begun to march out of step with the social movement he seemingly led, resigned as president of the CIO. He had fatally misjudged his power and his influence over the tidal forces which had transformed America in the Thirties.

He was replaced by his lieutenant, SWOC President Philip Murray, who thenceforth led the CIO from his Pittsburgh headquarters. Evidently feeling that Murray should have refused the proffered leadership of the CIO, Lewis peevishly called together a kangaroo court of UMWA allies who dutifully expelled Murray from the union for his disloyalty.

****

On Labor Day, September 1, 1941, SWOC locals from as far away as Johnstown gathered in Homestead to dedicate a four-ton granite monument on Eighth Avenue, the town's main street. The monument commemorated the workers killed in the Homestead Lockout of 1892, the lockout which broke unionism in the steel industry until the 1930s.

Drum and bugle corps and marching bands from Homestead, Munhall, and "industrial communities scattered throughout Western Pennsylvania" led a big parade through the streets of Homestead and neighboring Munhall to highlight the ceremony. The burgesses (mayors) of Homestead, Munhall, and West Homestead—all elected to their positions as champions of the steelworkers and with steelworker support—were part of the festivities.

The climax of the occasion was an address from ailing SWOC President Philip Murray, read by SWOC Secretary-Treasurer David J. McDonald. "For nearly 50 years," Murray's message declared, "the name of Homestead has stood for . . . the home of non-unionism . . . from now on, Homestead will symbolize— not the home of non-unionism, but the citadel of true unionism."

Indeed, the Homestead monument dedicated that day did symbolize triumphant unionism and the righting of past wrongs. But it also symbolized a new political order which now dominated the industrial heartland, a political order built around a new Democratic Party with inextricable ties to the working class. That new Democratic "Labor" Party had come to stay in Homestead and throughout Western Pennsylvania.

Class politics was the only politics in the Steel Valley.[114]

Notes

1. *The Gallup Political Almanac for 1946,* American Institute of Public Opinion, Princeton: N.J., 153.

2. Bruce M. Stave, *The New Deal and the Last Hurrah: Pittsburgh Machine Politics,* University of Pittsburgh Press: Pittsburgh, 1970, 49, Map 7; 48, Map 6, and 47, Map 5.

3. J. David Greenstone, *Labor in American Politics,* Knopf: New York, 1969, xiv.

4. Sidney Fine, *Sit-Down: The General Motors Strike of 1936-1937,* University of Michigan Press: Ann Arbor, 1969, 330-31.

5. Fine, *Sit-Down,* 334-38.

6. George Gallup and Claude Robinson, "American Institute of Public Opinion— Surveys, 1935-1938," *The Public Opinion Quarterly,* July 1938, 379-380; American Institute of Public Opinion survey 87, June 14, 1937.

7. Walter Lippmann's nationally syndicated column, "Today and Tomorrow," March 25, 1937.

8. Paul Kleppner, *Who Voted? The Dynamics of Electoral Turnout, 1870-1980,* Praeger Publishers: New York, 1982, 110.

9. James T. Patterson, "A Conservative Coalition Forms in Congress," in *The Growth of American Politics, Vol. II, Since the Civil War,* Frank Otto Gatell, Paul Goodman, and Allen Weinstein, Editors, Oxford University Press: New York, 1972, 358. First published in the *Journal of American History,* 52, March 1966, 757-772. Emphasis added.

10. Patterson, "A Conservative Coalition Forms in Congress," 358. Emphasis added.

11. *The Gallup Political Almanac for 1946,* American Institute of Public Opinion, Princeton: N.J., 153. In the 1940 and 1944 presidential elections, Philadelphia voted even more heavily Democratic than did Allegheny County, 60.0 percent vs. 58.3 percent and 58.9 percent vs. 57.3 percent, respectively.

12. Quoted in George E. Mowry, *The Urban Nation: 1920-1960,* Hill and Wang: New York, 1965, 121.

13. Walter Dean Burnham, *Critical Elections and the Mainsprings of American Politics,* W.W. Norton & Co.: New York, 1970, 67.

14. Burnham, *Critical Elections,* 68.

15. Burnham, *Critical Elections,* 59.

16. "American Institute of Public Opinion—Surveys, 1938-1939," *The Public Opinion Quarterly,* October 1939, Question No. 4, 583.

17. Walter Dean Burnham, *The Current Crisis in American Politics,* Oxford University Press: New York, 1982, 145-146; Stave, *The New Deal and the Last Hurrah,* 49, Map 7; 48, Map 6, and 47, Map 5.

18. Burnham, *The Current Crisis,* 148. Although Squirrel Hill would tilt Democratic in 1944 during World War II, it would return to the Republican fold in 1948. See Samuel Lubell, *The Future of American Politics,* Third Edition, Revised, Harper & Row: New York, 1965, 198. After 1952, however, Squirrel Hill became increasingly Democratic and has remained so to the present. There are two shifts which may help explain this ward's more recent tilt toward the Democratic Party, despite the continuing high socioeconomic status of the ward's population.

The first is that the ward became increasingly Jewish over this period. In the 1930s, a big portion of Pittsburgh's Jewish population was in the Lower Hill District. This population migrated almost entirely out of the Lower Hill in the Forties and Fifties into Squirrel Hill, making the latter the major Jewish population district in Pittsburgh at present.

The second factor is that the Jewish population itself became increasingly Democratic over time. Harvard political scientist V. O. Key, for example, noted the partisan shift of Jewish votes in Boston's predominantly Jewish Ward 14 from Republican to Democratic during the years 1928 to 1952. In 1928, about 80 percent of the Jewish voters in Boston's Ward 14 were registered Republicans. By 1952, 90 percent of the Jewish voters were registered Democrats. This was a shift as dramatic as that among black voters. A similar partisan shift among Jewish voters may well have taken place in Pittsburgh's Ward 14, explaining its shift to the Democrats after 1952, despite the neighborhood's wealth, as the ward became increasingly Jewish. See V. O. Key, "Secular Realignment and the Party System," *The Journal of Politics,* Vol. 21, 1959, 207.

19. On Davis' career, see Robert H. Zieger, "The Career of James J. Davis," *Pennsylvania Magazine of History and Biography,* 97, 1974, 67-89.

20. *The Pennsylvania Manual,* Vol. 81, 1939, 151.

21. See table 2.

22. George Gallup and Claude Robinson, "American Institute of Public Opinion—Surveys, 1935-1938," *The Public Opinion Quarterly,* July 1938, 383.

23. See the testimony of Frank Taylor, Chief Clerk, Democratic State Committee, Commonwealth of Pennsylvania vs. David L. Lawrence in the Court of Quarter Sessions of Dauphin County, Pa., February 26, 1940, Vol. 4, 1787.

24. "Pennsylvania Democrats and Mr. Lewis," *Philadelphia Evening Ledger,* March 12, 1938.

25. Minutes of the Pittsburgh Central Labor Union, November 7, 14, 1935, in the holdings of the Pittsburgh Typographical Union, Lo. No. 7, Archives of Industrial Society, University of Pittsburgh. Hereafter, "Minutes of the PCLU."

26. Minutes of the PCLU, January 2, 14, 1936.

27. Guy V. Miller, "Pennsylvania's Scrambled Politics," *The Nation,* May 14, 1938, 555; Green quote in *The Pittsburgh Press,* May 18, 1938.

28. Report of the Proceedings of the Special Convention of the Pennsylvania State Federation of Labor Held at Harrisburgh, Pennsylvania on April 7th, 8th, 9th, 1938, 60, Historical Collections and Labor Archives, Pattee Library, Pennsylvania State University, and "Green Urges A.F.L. to Smash Ticket Headed by Kennedy," *Philadelphia Record,* April 8, 1938.

29. "American Institute of Public Opinion—Surveys, 1938-1939," *The Public Opinion Quarterly,* October 1939, Question No. 4, 583.

30. Joseph F. Guffey, *Seventy Years on the Red-Fire Wagon,* privately published, 1952, 108, 109.

31. *The Philadelphia Record,* March 18, 1938.

32. *The Philadelphia Record,* March 29, April 1, 1938.

33. Minutes of the PCLU, April 21, 1938.

34. Minutes of the PCLU, May 5, 1938.

35. Minutes of the PCLU, May 5, 9, June 2, 1938.

36. *The Philadelphia Record,* May 17, 1938.

37. *The Pennsylvania Manual,* 84, 1939, 148-150.

38. See *The New York Times,* May 16, 1938.

39. See Philip S. Klein and Ari Hoogenboom, *A History of Pennsylvania,* New York, 1973, 422-423.

40. See *The Philadelphia Record,* April 7, 12, 20, May 10, 1938; *The New York Times,* May 17, 1938.

41. *The Pennsylvania Manual,* 84, 1939, 147-150.

42. *The Philadelphia Record,* September 3, 5, 17, 18, October 4, 25, November 8, 1938.

43. Minutes of the PCLU, September 15, 1938.

44. *The Philadelphia Record,* September 21, 1938 and "P.F.L. Continues Feud With Green," unidentified newspaper clipping in the Pennsylvania Federation of Labor Papers, Labor's Non-Partisan League materials, Box 1, Pattee Library, Pennsylvania State University. The AFL had vowed at its 1937 national convention to oppose any candidate "who would in any way favor, encourage or support the CIO," even if that candidate had a perfect pro-labor voting record and was friendly to the AFL. This was no idle threat. In the 1937 Detroit mayoralty election, the AFL opposed Patrick H. O'Brien, the CIO candidate, helping to bring about his defeat. In the 1938 Seattle mayoralty election, a CIO-backed candidate won the Democratic nomination. The AFL then endorsed the business-oriented Republican candidate, helping to defeat the CIO-Democrat. The AFL national headquarters ordered the Pennsylvania AFL to follow this same policy and oppose the Democratic ticket, as it was endorsed by Lewis and the CIO. As did the California AFL in elections that year, however, the Pennsylvania AFL ignored this order and opted for labor unity within the Democratic Party. See Joel Seidman, "Organized Labor in Political Campaigns," *The Public Opinion Quarterly,* October 1939, 651.

45. Minutes of the PCLU, October 20, 1938.

46. *The New York Times,* September 10, 1938.

47. *The Philadelphia Record,* September 11, 1938; *The New York Times,* October 16, 1938.

48. *The Philadelphia Record,* September 17, October 1, November 8, 1938.

49. *The Pittsburgh Post-Gazette,* November 9, 1938, 6. The Pennsylvania Communist Party was supportive of the Democratic Party by this time and issued a pamphlet attacking the Republicans which reiterated this point. Its cover showed a bonfire into which Republican James was tossing scrolls labelled with the names of all the Little New Deal programs, such as "Little Wagner Act." See "Gov. James Kept His Promises . . . To the Bankers! Put Out the Bonfire! Unite to Win the 1939-1940 Elections!," issued by the Communist Party, Pittsburgh Branch, copy in author's possession.

50. Alfred L. Morgan, "The Significance of Pennsylvania's 1938 Gubernatorial Election," *The Pennsylvania Magazine of History and Biography,* April 1978, 207.

51. "Pennsylvania Votes for Governor," *Commonwealth: The Magazine for Pennsylvania,* November 1946, 6.

52. The precise totals for governor were, James, 2,035,340 and Jones, 1,756,192. For senator, the vote was Davis, 2,086,931, and Earle, 1,694,367. *The Pennsylvania Manual,* 84, 1939, 152, 157-173.

53. Morgan, "The Significance of Pennsylvania's 1938 Gubernatorial Election," 208.

54. *The Pennsylvania Manual,* 84, 1939, 153, 154.

55. Morgan, "The Significance of Pennsylvania's 1938 Gubernatorial Election," 208. Jones would go on to serve as Chief Justice of the Pennsylvania Supreme Court. Governor James was not able to live up to his pledge to cut taxes, although he did hold the line on them by cutting relief expenses. Despite being pro-business and anti-labor, he was not able to bring business activity back, as promised, until World War II turned the country into the "Arsenal for Democracy" near the end of his term.

56. Patterson, "A Conservative Coalition Forms in Congress," 360.

57. Mike Davis, *Prisoners of the American Dream: Politics and Economy in the History of the U.S. Working Class,* Verso: London, 1986, 68-69.

58. Davis, *Prisoners of the American Dream,* 69, 70.

59. See Robert E. Burke, *Olson's New Deal for California,* University of California Press: Berkeley, 1953.

60. Minutes of the PCLU, January 5, 19, 1939.

61. Minutes of the PCLU, July 6, 20, August 3, 1939.

62. Minutes of the PCLU, November 16, 1939. Leonard quickly showed an interest in housing problems in the city and county and shortly became Chairman of the Allegheny County Housing Authority, charged with building low-cost housing throughout the county. See PCLU minutes, January 16, 1941.

Again, however, it seems Lawrence was not willing to grant any more to the labor movement than he felt he had to. In December 1939, City Councillor P. J. McArdle died in office. The Carpenters and Joiners immediately enlisted the PCLU behind their President, City of Pittsburgh Superintendent of Property D. R. Rogers, to fill the vacancy. On January 5, 1940, representatives of the PCLU, the Building Trades Council, and the Teamsters Joint Council voted to meet with Lawrence to back Rogers for the Council. When they met with Lawrence the next day, he informed them he had decided to appoint State Senator Thomas Kilgallen to fill McArdle's seat. Apparently, he felt two labor representatives on the nine-member City Council were enough. Although angered by his actions, the PCLU Executive Board recommended that no more action be taken regarding McArdle's seat and further recommended "that it be a closed incident." Minutes of the PCLU, January 4, 5, 16, 1940.

63. John W. Jeffries, *Testing the Roosevelt Coalition: Connecticut Society and Politics in the Era of World War II,* The University of Tennessee Press: Knoxville, 1979, 4.

64. "American Institute of Public Opinion—Surveys, 1938-1939," *The Public Opinion Quarterly,* October 1939, Question No. 37, 594.

65. Lubell, *Future of American Politics,* 195.

66. Edward F. Cooke and G. Edward Janosik, *Guide to Pennsylvania Politics,* Greenwood Press: Westport, Conn, 1957, 17.

67. *Proceedings of the First Constitutional Convention of the Congress of Industrial Organizations, Held in the City of Pittsburgh, Pennsylvania, November 14 to November 18, 1938, Inclusive,* Lewis' comment on 9, Rev. Rice's benediction on 8.

68. "American Institute of Public Opinion—Surveys, 1938-1939," *The Public Opinion Quarterly,* October 1939, Question No. 6, 584.

69. See Bernard F. Donahoe, *Private Plans and Public Dangers: The Story of FDR's Third Nomination,* University of Notre Dame Press: Notre Dame, Indiana, 1965.

70. *Proceedings of the First Constitutional Convention of the Congress of Industrial Organizations,* 230-231.

71. Kleppner, *Who Voted?* 107.

72. Irving Bernstein, "John L. Lewis and the Voting Behavior of the C.I.O.," *Public Opinion Quarterly,* June 1941, 238.

73. Minutes of the PCLU, September 19, October 1, 3, 17, 1940.

74. Minutes of the PCLU, October 17, 1940.

75. Herbert S. Parmet and Marie B. Hecht, *Never Again: A President Runs for a Third Term,* The Macmillan Co.: New York, 1968, 40-41.

76. *The Pittsburgh Press,* October 12, 1940, 2, October 9, 1940, 1, 16.

77. *The Pittsburgh Press,* October 12, 1940, 2; Mark S. Warnick, "FDR's Legacy on the Hill," *The Pittsburgh Press,* October 9, 1990.

78. Warnick, "FDR's Legacy on the Hill."

79. *The Pittsburgh Press,* October 12, 1940.

80. Burnham, *The Current Crisis,* 4. He is referring to Paul Lazarsfeld, et al., *The People's Choice: How the Voter Makes Up His Mind in a Presidential Campaign,* Duell, Sloan, & Pearce: New York, 1944, and Robert Alford, *Party and Society,* Rand McNally: Chicago, 1963.

81. Quoted in Arthur M. Schlesinger, Jr., "Not the People's Choice: How To Democratize American Democracy," *The American Prospect,* March 25, 2002, 26. Schlesinger used FDR's supposedly expert observation to justify his own judgment that, by 1940, "Party loyalty became tenuous; party identification, casual." The reality, of course, was just the opposite. It is amazing that Schlesinger, a noted historian of the Thirties, could make such a comment as late as 2002.

82. Bernstein, "John L. Lewis and the Voting Behavior of the C.I.O.," 233-234.

83. Quoted in Melvyn Dubofsky and Warren Van Tine, *John L. Lewis: A Biography,* Quadrangle-The New York Times Book Company: New York, 1977, 314.

84. Parmet and Hecht, *Never Again,* 234.

85. Quoted in Bernstein, "John L. Lewis and the Voting Behavior of the C.I.O.," 234.

86. Victor Reuther, *The Brothers Reuther and the Story of the UAW: A Memoir,* Houghton Mifflin: Boston, 1976, 222.

87. *The Pittsburgh Press,* October 27, 1940, 10.

88. *The Pittsburgh Press,* November 6, 1940, 1.

89. Bernstein, "John L. Lewis and the Voting Behavior of the C.I.O.," 239.

90. Parmet and Hecht, *Never Again,* 276.

91. *The New York Times,* November 6, 1940, 1.

92. *The Pittsburgh Press,* November 6, 1940, 1, 16; Bernstein, "John L. Lewis and the Voting Behavior of the C.I.O.," 242-244.

93. *The Pittsburgh Post-Gazette,* editorial, November 1, 1940.

94. *The Pittsburgh Post-Gazette,* November 6, 1940.

95. *The Pittsburgh Post-Gazette,* November 7, 1940.

96. *The Pittsburgh Post-Gazette,* November 6, 1940.

97. *The Pittsburgh Post-Gazette,* November 7, 1940.

98. Parmet and Hecht, *Never Again,* 277.

99. Jeffries, *Testing the Roosevelt Coalition,* 86-88.

100. Bernstein, "John L. Lewis and the Voting Behavior of the C.I.O.," 241.

101. Samuel Lubell, "Post Mortem: Who Elected Roosevelt?," *The Saturday Evening Post,* January 25, 1941, 9. Emphasis added.

102. Anonymous worker quoted in *These Are Our Lives: As Told by the People and Written by Members of the Federal Writers' Project of the Works Progress Administration in North Carolina, Tennessee, and Georgia,* University of North Carolina Press: Chapel Hill, 1939; first paperback publication by W.W. Norton & Co.: New York, 1975, chapter entitled, "I Couldn't Be What I Wanted To Be," 409.

103. Bernstein, "John L. Lewis and the Voting Behavior of the C.I.O.," 241.

104. Bernstein, "John L. Lewis and the Voting Behavior of the C.I.O.," 241-244, 249.

105. Lubell, *The Future of the American Politics,* 54.

106. Lubell, *The Future of the American Politics,* 54.

107. Lubell, *The Future of the American Politics,* 54-55.

108. Lubell, *The Future of the American Politics,* 197.

109. *The Pittsburgh Post-Gazette,* November 7, 1940, reported by a *Post-Gazette* staff writer on the scene.

110. *The Pittsburgh Post-Gazette,* November 7, 1940.

111. *The Pittsburgh Post-Gazette,* November 7, 1940.

112. Kleppner, *Who Voted?* 107, 110-111.

113. *The Pittsburgh Post-Gazette,* editorial, November 7, 1940.

114. This account of the dedication ceremonies and excerpt from Murray's speech is taken from *The Homestead Daily Messenger,* September 2, 1941.

Chapter 10

Equality, Solidarity, and A Fair Deal, 1940-1948

Equality and Justice for All

In 1942, the first full war year and a year of increasing employment, *Fortune* magazine sent a survey team into the steel mills of Pittsburgh, the symbolic capitol of the American working class, to answer the question, "What's Itching Labor?"

The answer, they found, was "Basically, a strong, unsatisfied equalitarian [sic] urge." While no sensational labor turmoil was currently roiling Pittsburgh, they nevertheless found that "its workers are not happy yet." Despite their increasingly secure jobs, workers in America's industrial heartland remained dissatisfied and restive. Although "Franklin D. Roosevelt's administration is about the closest thing to a 'labor government' the U.S. has had since 1787 . . . many a worker seems to be sincerely convinced that U.S. Steel is running Washington . . . At the bottom of almost every conflict is the same underlying issue: these workers resent the fact that they are not full partners."[1]

Steelworker union leaders, claimed the *Fortune* survey team, were "undoubtedly motivated by visions of a 'reformed' society and a controlled economy . . . Checked against the opinions of dozens of individual steelworkers in Pittsburgh, [these ideas] proved to express a group attitude."[2]

Additionally, a nearly universal desire for "justice" seemed to motivate "the grumbling workers of Pittsburgh." The survey team conducted a group interview with the grievance committee at Duquesne's U.S. Steel subsidiary, Carnegie-Illinois. This grievance committee, we are told, not only represented every major division of the Duquesne plant, but also "a fair cross section of Duquesne's working population: an Irishman, a Hungarian, a Scot, a Croat, a Slovak." (Significantly, there was no black member on Duquesne's grievance committee.) The surveyors found that, "at the base of most arguments, contradictions, and demands is an acute and overriding desire for equality, an ever-present resentment against 'being played for a sucker.' . . . this leitmotif goes through all conversations with the workers of Pittsburgh . . . [T]hey get really excited only when it comes to what they feel to be a basic violation of fair play."[3] At basis, then, Pittsburgh workers were motivated by the same egalitarian ideology which often moved working people in the nineteenth century when they had frequently invoked the slogan, "Equal opportunity for all, special privileges for none."

In addition to their "overriding desire for equality," the workers of Pittsburgh were also almost fanatically patriotic and fervid in their sense of citizenship. "In general," the survey found, "Pittsburgh workers have a distinct set of favorites and dislikes. Most popular with them are, in this order: the United States, Franklin D. Roosevelt, the unions, the U.S. Army."

The Pittsburgh workers' "love affair" with the United States seemed to be bound up with what they thought America stood for: Equality and justice for all. Thus, "[t]heir faith in this nation's ultimate genius for fair play is as unlimited as their self-identification with the country."

"Something of a love affair is also their relationship with Franklin D. Roosevelt," for in him they see "the real leader of this country's labor. Phil Murray [president of the steelworkers union] and, with some of the men, John L. Lewis are O.K.—but the boss is, of course, F.D.R."

Then there was their loyalty to the union. "They are for their union, and they mean it. But it's rational recognition of services rendered rather than emotion . . . Since the unions invaded [sic] Pittsburgh, wages and working conditions have been extensively and undeniably improved."

Finally there was the immensely popular United States Army. "There is in Pittsburgh's industrial villages," the surveyors found, "hardly a block without substantial representation in the armed forces." One of the great reasons Pittsburgh's workers liked the army, besides their patriotism, was the egalitarian draft, of which they approved immensely. They "insist on a rather literal interpretation of equality of sacrifice," and the military draft—which played no favorites—guaranteed that all would sacrifice equally.[4]

This approval of the egalitarian nature of the military draft was perhaps a major reason for its widespread acceptance even during the "peaceful" Fifties. A Pittsburgh Korean War veteran, who was drafted for service, recalled that, "For us the draft was an obligation which, being fairly imposed and widely shared, flattened out differences of origin, class and race and created a single company of purpose."[5]

Thus, the overriding themes of this survey of Pittsburgh's workers were Justice and Equality. Moreover, they felt that justice *demanded* equality, which—regardless of ethnic background—they felt they were being denied by "them," U.S. Steel and the millionaire class.

The "grumbling workers of Pittsburgh," like so many others, also believed that America was not yet sufficiently egalitarian. However, they seemed intent upon making it so. "At the end of the war," *Fortune*'s survey team predicted following their 1942 survey, "labor will be poised to submit its own ideas of 'an industrial democracy'—a type of society that gives everybody a voice not only in running the state, but also in running the plants. Labor, in short, is bidding for high stakes after the war."[6]

Pittsburgh's workers, then, wanted "a type of society that gives everybody a voice." They had cheered in frenzy at Forbes Field in 1936 when the speaker who introduced Roosevelt told them, "The President has decreed that your children shall enjoy equal opportunity with the sons of the rich!"

Part of that "equal opportunity" implied a greater measure of economic security than they had experienced heretofore. Many of them were the children of European peasants, recently removed. Whether real or imagined, the threat of financial disaster hovered eternally over them. This was why they clung so tenaciously to their jobs, why the work ethic was so strong within them. "A fair shake," then, meant more security for them and their children. That was part of the American promise.

But the rich, they felt, still ran everything and were determined to deny them that promise—as they had since time immemorial. And in this class war of the rich against the poor, all that workers had with which to fight back was their numbers. And their solidarity. And at long last, it seemed, they were poised to take what was rightfully theirs—so long as they stuck together.

The history of the 1940s is therefore the history of their intensifying drive—through solidarity and militancy—to realize that perceived egalitarian promise of America. And there were two vehicles by which they hoped to realize that promise. The first vehicle was the Democratic Party. The second vehicle was the union.

Solidarity Forever

When the 1940s began, it seemed the major part of the American promise workers still needed to achieve was economic security. This meant the consolidation of the union in the mass production industries, for even in steel the union was just beginning to make in-roads. And for that purpose, solidarity and militancy were necessary. Their actions spoke as loudly as any words. In 1941, for example, as the economy improved, four times as many workers went out on strike across the country as in 1940.

The task of union consolidation was made easier by the massive industrial build-up from 1939-41 as Hitler conquered Western Europe and America began to emerge as the "Arsenal of Democracy." Millions of unemployed and under-employed were put to work and shortages of skilled workers began to appear. "By December 1941, unemployment, which had stood at over 10 million in 1939 and 8.5 million as late as June 1940, had ebbed to around 4 million . . . Recalled a Pennsylvania worker in a plant producing shell casings: 'By mid-December [1940] we were on a seven day ten hour schedule . . . All I did was sleep and eat.'"[7]

And yet, while working longer hours due to full-time (in place of part-time) employment and overtime, few of these auto, steel, and rubber workers had received hourly rate wage increases since 1937. Indeed, some had even agreed to wage cutbacks.[8] Thus, they saw this as the moment to finish the task of organizing the core industries of the nation and to strengthen existing contracts. The situation in Duquesne and Aliquippa was typical of labor's militant upsurge around the country.

By October 1940, only 3,500 of the 6,000 steelworkers at Duquesne's U.S. Steel subsidiary, Carnegie-Illinois Steel, were enrolled in SWOC. The fight to consolidate SWOC in the plant, therefore, continued apace. This push was now aided by the fact that the Mayor of Duquesne, Elmer Maloy, was also leading the SWOC organizing drive.

On the evening of October 14th, just days after FDR's triumphal visit to Pittsburgh's Terrace Village housing project, "Night-riding dues pickets of the CIO-SWOC massed at the gates of the Carnegie-Illinois Steel Company's Duquesne Steel Works [and] traded blows and brickbats with a crowd of 1,500 spectators," beating up a foreman in the process. Mayor Maloy blamed all the trouble on company "agitators" attempting to break up the dues picketing.

That same night, dues pickets at the J & L plant in Aliquippa also beat up a foreman and only the arrival of State Police troopers—now controlled by the Republican state government—dispersed the SWOC militants. State Police Lt. Andrew Hudock warned Aliquippa's Acting Mayor, local SWOC leader Paul Normile, that his SWOC pickets would not be allowed to "stop traffic into the plant."[9]

Nevertheless, the next month, November of 1940, Philip Murray, the CIO's new president, announced that such labor actions would continue throughout the industrial heartland as the CIO planned to initiate the "most vigorous, far-reaching organization drive that has ever been put on."[10]

Thus, the class war continued. Now, however, the tide in the Pittsburgh area was running in favor of the workers. In a city which only a decade before had been a citadel of corporate anti-unionism, angry and aggressive union members were everywhere on the assault, determined to make Pittsburgh and the surrounding communities 100 percent union towns.

The amazing solidarity and self-confidence in their new strength was evident on November 22, 1940, for instance, when 7,500 workers at the Aluminum Company of America (ALCOA) plant in nearby New Kensington spontaneously walked off their jobs. They struck, not over wage, hours, or working conditions— but to protest the employment of a single ALCOA employee who refused to pay union dues. The workers of ALCOA weren't satisfied with a workplace union membership of 7,499-to-1. It had to be absolutely total.[11]

This consolidation of the union continued into the next year and "The general tempo of summer-fall, 1941 . . . was a strong upbeat of rank-and-file energy with clear refrains of the 'spirit of '37.'"[12] Overall, about 2,360,000 workers— 70 percent of them CIO members—were on strike in 1941. "The 4,200 strikes represented one of the highest totals in American history. During the first four months of the year, steel, auto, electrical, and agricultural implement workers struck corporations that had resisted the earlier CIO drive of 1936-37."[13]

Of these thousands of strikes in 1941, the two most important were those at Bethlehem Steel's plants in Eastern Pennsylvania and at Ford's River Rouge plant in Michigan, which finally brought these obdurate holdouts under the sway of the CIO. Both of these strikes illustrated how rank and file workers were directing events.

With a major plant in the small town of Bethlehem, Pennsylvania, near Allentown, Bethlehem Steel was one of the "Little Steel" companies which, along with Republic Steel, had resisted the 1937 SWOC unionization drive, to which U.S. Steel and Jones & Laughlin Steel had succumbed. (The term "Little Steel" refers to the collection of steel companies other than U.S. Steel, which was known as "Big Steel.") Of the town's 75,000 inhabitants, well over 20,000 worked in the local steel mill, which the corporation ran—as it did the town—with an iron fist.

On March 25, 1941, 19,000 of the plant's 20,000 workers walked out to protest the company's promotion of an in-house union, an ERP. Management was more willing to concede to union demands than in the past because it now had lucrative war-related contracts to fulfill and could not afford to see production interrupted due to work stoppages. Thus, after a period of confrontation which saw the usual tactics of corporate intimidation fail, the company agreed to elections supervised by the National Labor Relations Board. Of the corporation's 28,500 workers in its myriad mills in and around Bethlehem, 21,500 (c. 75 percent) voted for SWOC representation.[14]

The situation was much the same in Johnstown, a Western Pennsylvania town about 40-miles east of Pittsburgh, also dominated by Bethlehem Steel. In the battle to unionize the Bethlehem Steel plants in Johnstown during the "Little Steel" Strike of 1937, SWOC had been brutally crushed by Republican Mayor Dan Shields and the company's private police force. Since then, however, the workers of Johnstown had replaced Mayor Shields with a Democrat.

On April 16, 1941, virtually the entire 15,000-man workforce at Johnstown's Cambria Plant walked out to also protest the imposition of the ERP union upon them. Former Mayor Shields was arrested by the city police and jailed when he showed up near the picket lines.

In May, on their own and in solidarity with the on-going strikes in Bethlehem and Johnstown by the steelworkers, 2,700 coal miners at three mines owned by Bethlehem Steel Co. shut down their mines and vowed no coal would be dug until John Bragg, a black coal miner who had resisted joining the UMW for six years, joined the union. Bragg finally signed a union card, making Bethlehem's mines 100 percent unionized—and the miners went back to work.[15]

Faced with such widespread rank and file solidarity and determination, Bethlehem Steel finally also acquiesced to plant-wide representation elections in Johnstown, presided over by the NLRB. On June 25, 80 percent of Johnstown's steelworkers—8,940 to 2,108—voted for SWOC as their bargaining agent. Thereafter, Bethlehem Steel signed its first union contract in Johnstown. Due to their solidarity, their determination, and their initiative, rank and file steelworkers finally brought the New Deal to Johnstown, Bethlehem, and the remaining industrial regions of Pennsylvania.[16]

Soon thereafter, the other members of "Little Steel" recognized the inevitable and fell into line. Without the necessity of an NLRB election, Youngstown Sheet and Tube and Inland Steel, both of Ohio, recognized SWOC. Then Tom Girdler, head of Republic Steel, at which the Memorial Day Massacre of 1937 had occurred, acknowledged the union's authority when he discovered that 70 percent of his 40,600 employees had pledged their loyalty to the union.[17]

In mid-September 100 SWOC steelworkers at U.S. Steel's Clairton Coke Works staged a sit-down strike in the plant, refusing to work alongside of hold-out non-union workers. The action of these 100 Clairton workers idled 2,500 others—not only at the Clairton Works, but also at U.S. Steel's Homestead and Irvin Works (the latter opened in West Mifflin in 1938)—until the recalcitrants joined up.[18] The unionization of the steel industry was complete. But union security in other industries remained to be gained.

                    ****

The unionization of the auto industry was accomplished a few weeks after Bethlehem Steel capitulated. The decisive factor at the Ford Motor Co.'s massive River Rouge plant was also the self-initiative and solidarity of rank and file workers. Henry Ford had been the great hold-out against the 1937 tide of unionization in the auto industry. Nevertheless, the UAW had maintained a presence in Ford's plants, including his River Rouge plant outside of Detroit.

On April 1, 1941, when Ford's notorious Service Department, an in-house police force, began a purge of union organizers, thousands of rolling-mill workers spontaneously struck in solidarity. Other workers quickly joined them, and the wildcat strike mushroomed into a massive confrontation. Caught by surprise, the UAW rushed to endorse the rank and file action and gain leadership of it. On April 10, Ford—who had war-related contracts to fulfill, just as did Bethlehem Steel—agreed to an NLRB recognition election to be held the next month. In that election, 70 percent of the 74,000 workers at River Rouge voted to join the CIO, with the rest voting for a rival AFL union.

The following month, June of 1941, Ford negotiated a contract with the UAW which "astounded everyone by re-establishing Ford as the industry wage leader and granting the UAW sweeping union security, dues collection, and seniority benefits."[19] The contract also called for a closed shop (union members only), the first of its kind in the auto industry. This brought the 100,000 workers at all Ford plants into the union. The battle for union recognition in the auto industry was now also over.

****

Successful CIO unionization drives were then launched at Allis-Chalmers, International Harvester, and Weyerhaeuser. "In all, during the peak fifteen-month period of defense production (June 1940-December 1941) the unions gained about 1.5 million new members."[20]

Such was the intensity of feeling among angry workers in 1941 that even "non-combatants" were not safe. When Dr. E. M. Baker of Pittsburgh attempted to buy some medicine he needed for an emergency call at the strike-bound Zemmer Chemical Co. near Forbes Field in Oakland, eighteen strikers pulled him from his car and beat him for trying to cross their picket line.[21]

Indeed, as this incident indicates, "strike fever" had infected even workers outside of the basic heavy industries. In late August 1941, a four-month strike by service employees at the West Penn Hospital in Pittsburgh's Italian Bloomfield neighborhood ended in victory when hospital officials agreed to increase their wages from $38 to $45 per month and allowed them to form a grievance committee.[22]

That same August clerical workers for the National Tube Co., a subsidiary of U.S. Steel, became the first white collar workers in the steel industry with a union contract. Their contract, negotiated by SWOC, gave 1,700 office workers a $17 per month raise.[23]

In late September, over 2,400 service workers at the city's major hotels—the William Penn, the Ft. Pitt, the Roosevelt, the Schenley, the Keystone, the Pittsburgher, and Webster Hall—launched a city-wide strike.[24]

Even Pittsburgh city employees were on strike against "their" Democratic city government. In September, 450 garbage truck drivers and their helpers decided to join a strike already in progress by Pittsburgh's road crews and began picketing the City-County Building.[25]

Nor did concern for America's role as the "Arsenal of Democracy" seem to temper the angry strike wave. That June, as Hitler's Panzer divisions plunged deep into Russia, Pittsburgh's General Teamsters Union Local 249 shut down 179 freight companies in the region for the entire month over a demand for a ten-cent per hour raise.

The Pittsburgh Chamber of Commerce complained that the teamster strike was crippling the district's defense production and the Pennsylvania Railroad alone had 80,000 shipments to local consignees stored in its warehouses and yards. But the union members remained on strike, and won. On June 27, the teamsters settled for a six cents per hour raise.[26]

The teamsters were not the only ones, by far, who shut down defense production that summer in the Pittsburgh region. In late August, 2,500 workers at the Pressed Steel Car Co. in nearby Stowe—a company which produced armor plate for the U.S. Navy and shell forgings for the U.S. Army—laid down their tools and walked off their jobs in a demand for union recognition as a part of SWOC.[27]

In late October 1941, a dues inspection picket line closed the Carnegie-Illinois (U.S. Steel) Irvin Works in West Mifflin while 240 cranemen at the company's Homestead Works spontaneously closed down production there, as well, in order to enforce collection of dues. Both plants were working on defense contracts.[28] At West Homestead's Mesta Machine, 3,000 workers were making plans to walk off their jobs beginning on December 9, 1941.[29]

Because of job actions such as these, the U.S. Army's 107th Field Artillery Division began training at the army's Ft. Indiantown Gap barracks in central Pennsylvania in "riot quelching tactics." Their mandate was to guard strike-bound defense plants in the event of labor disputes.[30]

This feverish strike activity in the Pittsburgh region's defense-related industries was part of a national strike phenomenon which was threatening to disrupt the war mobilization Roosevelt was then in the process of orchestrating. In all, around two million workers just in defense-related industries alone struck nationwide in the fifteen months after June 1, 1940.[31]

The mine workers were particularly vehement in demanding union recognition and security in the so-called "captive mines" owned by the steel companies and a small war to push home this demand had erupted in the weeks before Pearl Harbor.

In the Pittsburgh region, a six-day strike in late November 1941 idled more than 200,000 miners, even at the mines owned by the Duquesne Light Co., Jones & Laughlin, and Hillman, which had already recognized the UMW and signed contracts with the union.[32] Car caravans of as many as 300 striking miners roamed the region's coal fields to shut down all local mines, resulting in fierce battles at the Red Lion, Grindstone, Ralph and Ronco mines.[33]

On November 20th, in neighboring Fayette County, armed union miners suddenly appeared and laid siege to the Henry Clay Frick Company's non-union Edinboro mine. During the resulting furious three-hour gun battle between them and armed non-union miners, twelve of the attacking union miners were wounded.[34] The next day, an agreement was reached with the mine owners and the strike ended with the mines being unionized.[35]

While many of the work stoppages in the Pittsburgh area were economic and union recognition strikes, many were also due to the "all for one and one for all" mentality which permeated the Pittsburgh workforce. For instance, on February 25, 1942, about 1,000 workers at the Crucible Co. steel plant on Pittsburgh's North Side laid their tools down and walked out after a fellow employee was fired for refusing to take an eye examination.[36]

Instances of such solidarity strikes continued in Pittsburgh throughout the war, despite the insistence of the leaders of organized labor on no strikes for the war's duration. An example of one such occurred on March 17, 1944. At that time, all the drivers, terminal employees, and maintenance workers at the Pittsburgh Greyhound Line facility, numbering 400, went into an "extended meeting" to discuss the March 6 firing of two bus drivers who had refused to work. The unofficial work stoppage shut down all busses operating out of Pittsburgh, a major east-west hub, and stranded thousands of hapless passengers. When Greyhound agreed to rehire the two drivers, the "extended meeting" adjourned and the 400 employees returned to work.[37]

****

Meanwhile, President Franklin D. Roosevelt was already turning away from domestic reform to face the growing international crisis. He joined with business leaders, the military, and Congressional conservatives to condemn such strikes and call for an end to such conflicts.

Roosevelt had already co-opted an important American Federation of Labor (AFL) leader, Amalgamated Clothing Workers head Sidney Hillman, by appointing him to a leading position at the Office of Production Management. Thereafter, Hillman gave the AFL exclusive bargaining rights for all government war-related construction contracts. By 1944, this meant that AFL carpenters would double their membership; boilermakers grew from a 1938 union membership of 28,000 to 336,900; plumbers from 37,7000 to 130,000; and electrical workers from 175,000 to 312,9000. In all, AFL building trades unions added 1.25 million new members by 1944.

And, like President Woodrow Wilson during the previous war, Roosevelt also moved to intervene in labor-management disputes. In March 1941, in the wake of a violent strike at a Milwaukee defense plant, Roosevelt established the eleven-member National Defense Mediation Board, later to become the National War Labor Board (NWLB). Roosevelt brought in CIO chief Philip Murray, who quickly pledged CIO cooperation with the administration's goals, as one of the Mediation Board's four labor representatives. The remaining three labor representatives were United Mine Workers Secretary-Treasurer Thomas Kennedy; George Meany, Secretary-Treasurer of the AFL; and George Harrison, president of the Brotherhood of Railway Clerks, unaffiliated with either the AFL or CIO. The remaining seats were divided between employer and government representatives.

The Mediation and War Labor Boards established industry-wide wage patterns for the first time and helped shape the internal workings of many new industrial unions. They formalized a pattern of government management of the economy and "normal" and bureaucratic labor-management relations. Labor's acceptance of their decisions was made more likely by making the union leadership itself part of the decision-making process.

By June 1941, the federal government demanded that all big labor-management disputes be settled by the Board. Since the Mediation Board called for the end to a particular strike as soon as a dispute was brought before the Board for mediation, this essentially amounted to a policy of no strikes at all.

The country's entire union hierarchy agreed with this (except for the United Mine Workers, led by John L. Lewis), and this "no-strike pledge" soon became mandatory and more explicit than the implicit one asked of labor during World War I. In addition, the Board now had the authority to issue binding decisions in labor disputes and to establish work conditions and pay scales. It thus became the final arbiter in labor-management disagreements.

In order to reconcile the labor movement to these developments, the Board initiated a "maintenance of membership" policy, which, more than anything else, created the huge growth in labor unions during the war years. The Board mandated that any new worker who began working at a unionized shop (and all defense-related industries were, by then, unionized) was to be automatically enrolled in and pay dues to the union. New workers had two weeks in which to "opt out." If they did not do so, membership in the union was "maintained" and workers could not resign. Thus, as industrial production expanded throughout the war, so, too, did union membership. By war's end, total union membership in America had grown by 50 percent.

In addition, and as part of this policy, companies in all these unionized war industries initiated a "dues checkoff" in which union membership dues were automatically deducted from a worker's paycheck and given to the union. This radically changed the financial situation of unions. According to Nelson Lichtenstein, "The practical impact . . . dramatically increased the size and financial stability of wartime industrial unions . . . In the United Steel Workers, the dues picket lines came down and the union's net worth grew sevenfold between May 1942 and November 1943 . . . Years later, the USW's accountant described the NWLB's dues checkoff policy as 'manna from heaven' that finally resolved the union's chronic financial problems . . . as factories and mills expanded, new workers were automatically enrolled, increasing the steady flow of dues . . . Excluding the UMW, which left in 1942, CIO membership almost doubled during the war. Overall, the unionized sector of the workforce increased . . . from 9.5 to 14.8 million. Most new union members were covered by government-sponsored maintenance-of-membership contracts."[38]

Even with the official "no strike" pledge, however, unauthorized "wildcat" strikes continued. A major reason for this was the priority the Board set on keeping inflation under control. Therefore, wage hikes were largely curtailed by government regulation for the duration of the war. The key to the War Labor Board's approach was its "Little Steel" wage policy.

In a July 1942 decision, the Board increased wages for workers at the "Little Steel" companies 15 percent above what they had been January 1, 1941, corresponding to what they argued was the cost of living increase during that time. Since most unionized steelworkers had already won a wage increase of 15 percent in the spring of 1941, this meant there would be no further wage increases for the war's duration. This "Little Steel Formula," based on industry-appropriate wage levels in January 1941, was then extended to all other sectors of the economy. Because of this unprecedented governmental intervention in the economy, no one was to get a larger wage increase until the war ended.

Thus, wage resentment lingered and production intensified, while safety conditions deteriorated. Wages were low, profits were high, and workers were angry. The Board, however, made it clear that strikes were no longer an option. The clearest example of this policy came in June 1941, when a strike broke out at the Inglewood, California plant of North American Aviation, which produced training planes for the Army Air Corps. Mediation Board member and CIO-President Phillip Murray pressured the CIO-affiliated United Auto Workers, which represented the workers, to declare the strike unauthorized, illegal, and Communist-motivated. (This was just before Hitler's invasion of the Soviet Union, and so the Communist Party opposed U.S. involvement in the "imperialist" war.)

But workers refused UAW-leadership orders to return to work. Roosevelt then ordered 2,500 Army troops to the plant, where they dispersed picket lines and banned all worker meetings within a one-mile radius of the plant. The strike was soon broken, which established the power of the Mediation Board's directives; its orders would be backed up by military force. Such strikes would not be tolerated "for the duration." But, the stick was balanced with the carrot; in July, the Board ordered big wage hikes for workers at North American Aviation, which the UAW took credit for.

Localized dissatisfaction continued elsewhere. Wildcat strikes over shop floor control, work assignments, piece-rate wages, and production schedules remained endemic and, in fact, increased from 1942 until the end of the war. In January 1944, a national railway strike was narrowly avoided.

But there was no avoiding confrontation with the pugnacious John L. Lewis and his United Mine Workers. Neither Lewis nor his followers had ever accepted the "Little Steel Formula," and coal miners clamored for higher wages. Lewis declared war on the formula and, in an effort to demolish it, led his union out on strike four times in 1943.

Lewis and his union were vilified and an angry Congress retaliated. In mid-June 1943, following the third UMW strike in just six weeks, Congress passed (over Roosevelt's veto) the Smith-Connally War Labor Disputes Act, which authorized the use military force to seize struck mines and factories and provided for fines and jail terms for strike leaders. It became a crime to advocate a work stoppage in defense industries. The new law also mandated a thirty-day "cooling off" period in other industries, followed by a secret National Labor Relations Board-supervised strike vote by union members, before a strike could be launched. Finally, it banned labor unions from contributing financially to political campaigns, something Republicans had long desired.

This powerful anti-union legislation did not intimidate Lewis and his union. On November 1, 1943, the UMW struck a fourth time and all of the nation's 530,000 bituminous miners walked out on strike. Using his new powers, Roosevelt sent in troops and seized strike-bound coal mines. He also threatened to draft striking miners. Lewis replied that the president "could not dig coal with bayonets" and refused to back down.

Instead, it was the president who retreated. Roosevelt ordered Secretary of the Interior Harold Ickes to bypass the War Labor Board (which had a policy of not negotiating with a striking union) and negotiate a contract acceptable to the mine workers. The resulting wage increases of 25 percent essentially abolished the "Little Steel Formula" for the coal industry, although it remained in place elsewhere. Next to the creation of the CIO itself, this was perhaps the greatest victory of Lewis' career. He had faced down a wartime president and won.

Inspired by this example, wildcat strikes by at least 150,000 steelworkers broke out on Christmas Eve, 1943, as steelworkers also demanded wage hikes. Again, Roosevelt personally intervened and ordered the War Labor Board to grant benefits to the strikers and to consider their wage demands.

For the most part, however, the "Little Steel Formula" remained in force for the remainder of the war and the top union leaders neither challenged the wage policy nor deviated from their no-strike pledge. But the Smith-Connally Act had proven ineffective as a war-time anti-strike weapon when used against powerful unions determined to resist. Its lasting legacy was to give the government increased authority to curtail labor's political rights and it represented the first rollback of labor's legislative gains. Many aspects of Smith-Connally would be revived in the postwar Taft-Hartley Act of 1947.

****

In the mean time, industrial workers were still struggling for other aspects of their lives to be given the respect and consideration they wanted. In the 1933 municipal election, Pittsburghers had voted overwhelmingly to repeal both the "Blue Law" ban on Sunday sports as well as Protestant Prohibition. Such "Protestant" bans, however, remained on the books for other activities and in other communities. Just as alcohol had become a powerful symbol of ethnic identity in reaction to the Protestant crusade against it, so, too, did opposition to Sunday "Blue Laws" come to be seen as an ethnic crusade. And so ethnic industrial workers continued the drive to repeal such laws.

In the November 1941, municipal elections, referenda to repeal the laws banning Sunday movies were on ballots of many communities around Pittsburgh. In some places, the laws were repealed. In others, the ban was upheld. Indicative of how fierce the struggle over this social issue was, however, was the battle in Uniontown, southwest of Pittsburgh. This battle also seemed eerily prophetic of the type of social issue campaigns to come.

"In one of the most bitter and intensive campaigns ever conducted in Uniontown," reported the *Post-Gazette,* "Local churches spent hundreds of dollars in newspaper advertisements and committees were named either to telephone or visit homes of every voter in the city. Sunday films were denounced from all the local pulpits and collections were taken to defray expenses of the campaign. Church workers appeared at each polling place in the city and thousands of 'Vote No' stickers and cards were handed out. Chimes in downtown churches pealed all day with sacred music being broadcast to influence the voters against the project."[39] And it worked. The ban on Sunday movies was upheld.

But in other places, ethnic voters prevailed. Mayor George Lysle, of McKeesport, who had been virtually the sole Republican survivor in the last Steel Valley municipal elections of 1937, was finally pulled down in the 1941 elections. "Upheaval Deemed Impossible on Election Eve," reported the *Post-Gazette.* But, after twenty-eight years in office, the "Grand Old Man" was defeated by an unknown first-time Democratic candidate. Meanwhile, steelworker Carl Bechtol, who'd lost to Lysle in 1937, was simultaneously elected to the City Council.

"It used to be Maine, Vermont, and McKeesport [which voted Republican]," said the *Post-Gazette*. "Now it's just Maine and Vermont." The novice Democrat who defeated Lysle had cast his first presidential vote for LaFollette in 1924, who'd been on the ballot in the Pittsburgh region as a "Progressive-Socialist" candidate. Now, he was a Democrat because, he said, "I'm a New Dealer at heart."[40]

Thus, while workers looked increasingly secure in the workplace, the political battles continued. "Even the enormous patriotic pressures of global conflict could not reverse the fundamentally contentious and conflictual nature of labor relations in the United States," Robert Zieger tells us. "The war dampened and redirected the ongoing struggle, but it did not eliminate conflict."[41]

In the November 1942, Congressional elections, the Pittsburgh-area AFL and CIO workers felt enough common cause in the face of Republican hostility to unite on the political front. While the national leadership of the rival union movements continued to feud, the Pittsburgh region representatives of these two bodies joined hands in solidarity. On September 1, 1942, Pat Fagan and other leaders of the CIO's Steel City Industrial Union Council (SCIUC) attended a meeting of the AFL's Pittsburgh Central Labor Union (PCLU) Executive Board to discuss "joint AFL-CIO endorsement and support of candidates for the upcoming election."

The PCLU recommended a joint political action committee comprised of equal representation from both bodies. This committee would draw up a program of joint action and "call a mass meeting of all unionists to support joint endorsees."[42] On September 17 the joint committee presented its plan for united AFL-CIO political action to the PCLU. The Pittsburgh unions declared they could unite around a demand for a "War Economic Program," which included "Labor's just wage demands, price controls, limitation of profits, and taxes placed on those able to pay."

They also called for a "National Unity" program based on opposition to poll taxes and opposition to racial discrimination in industry and the armed forces. They also agreed on opposition to all anti-labor bills in Congress and "Adequate representation of labor men on national and local boards dealing with the war effort." Finally, they agreed on all candidates to be endorsed by labor. All were, of course, Democrats. Among the endorsees as arbitrators on the local National War Labor Board were the local labor priests, Rev. James R. Cox and Rev. Charles Owen Rice.[43]

Then there occurred an event which highlighted the premium Pittsburgh workers placed on solidarity. While the PCLU (like the SCIUC) had voted to endorse Democrat F. Clair Ross for Governor in the 1942 election, for some unknown reason PCLU President Leo Abernathy (a popular hero to the Pittsburgh labor movement) had other ideas. In political ads appearing in Pittsburgh's morning newspapers on October 26 and in a radio appearance that night, Abernathy allowed himself to be identified as President of the PCLU and as Chairman of the "Labor for Martin [the Republican gubernatorial candidate] Committee." Abernathy did not indicate that he was speaking personally. Rather, he suggested he was speaking in an official capacity when he endorsed the Republican for governor.

The PCLU was enraged. The afternoon following Abernathy's radio appearance, a special meeting of the PCLU Executive Board (absent Abernathy) took place. They drew up a statement which they presented to Abernathy and the local media. Despite his past services, Abernathy was "in flagrant defiance" of the labor movement and had "proven himself unworthy and unfit to preside over the PCLU and to attend its functions and business. He is, therefore, requested to remove from his shoulders the presidential mantle of respectability under which he has paraded himself politically in the outside world. Mr. Abernathy's resignation is requested as a formality to give him an opportunity to affirmatively get out of the organization from which he has already removed himself automatically."[44]

At a full PCLU meeting on November 5, the union delegate members voted 128 to 49 to concur with the Executive Board call for Abernathy's resignation. Despite the vote, Abernathy declared that he refused to resign as president.[45] Following an Executive Board trial of Abernathy, as called for by the PCLU by-laws, on November 18 the Executive Board voted 17-to-1 to expel Leo Abernathy from his position as their President and from membership in the PCLU. The next night, the PCLU membership as a whole voted to uphold the Executive Board expulsion.[46] President Leo Abernathy, like Lewis before him, became a leader repudiated by his followers for violating the political solidarity they valued so highly.

Despite labor militancy and solidarity—such as that displayed by the Pittsburgh AFL and CIO councils—the still-mobilizing Republicans and anti-New Deal Democrats won resounding victories nationwide in the 1942 elections, handing them control of Congress. Alarmed at this set-back, the labor movement next formally became part of the Democratic Party campaign infrastructure.

On July 8, 1943, CIO union leaders formed the CIO Political Action Committee (CIO-PAC) to help insure the re-election of Roosevelt in 1944. Designed to create a formal political presence allied to the Democratic Party at every level of the labor movement, it collected huge contributions directly from the members of affiliated unions. The Smith-Connally Act, passed in the summer of 1943 by a conservative Congress fearful of just such a labor-Democratic alliance, had made it illegal for any trade union to make political contributions to any candidate or party from its treasury.[47] But the CIO-PAC could collect and spend union funds because it was not, itself, a trade union and was officially separate from the CIO. Thus, PACs came into existence to circumvent this electoral "reform" law.

This new labor organization "churned out an impressive series of pamphlets for distribution to union members and their families, graphically explaining the CIO economic and social program. It targeted appeals to women workers, union members' wives, black workers, and other minorities and groups. PAC bought time on radio stations, organized rallies, conducted door-to-door canvassing, and worked closely with local party leaders—usually Democrats—to get out the vote and to support liberal candidates."[48]

In the Pittsburgh region, close working relations continued between the AFL-affiliated PCLU, which represented 250,000 union members, and the CIO-affiliated SCIUC, which represented another 100,000 union members.[49] When SCIUC chief Pat Fagan was appointed to the War Manpower Commission for the Pittsburgh Area in April 1943, the PCLU sent a telegram of hearty congratulations.[50]

As the spring primary season of 1944 got underway, the PCLU again voted to continue its joint political work with the SCIUC, and this time include the Railroad Brotherhoods.[51] Solidarity among all workers was needed as much as ever, as the Republicans had won the governorship again in 1942 and were in the process of dismantling the "Little Wagner Act." Among other things, two succeeding Republican governors had staffed the state Labor Relations Board with so many members hostile to labor that the Act was becoming a charade.[52] In addition, Pennsylvania's Republican-controlled legislature passed the Farrell Bill, similar to the Smith-Connally Act, which banned unions, as such, from actively participating in state or local primary or general elections.[53]

The labor movement also continued to encourage solidarity between the races. In October 1943, Brother Boykin F. Gibson, of the Hotel and Restaurant Workers Alliance, Local 237, submitted a resolution on race relations, which the PCLU endorsed. It called upon the PCLU to "convey to the Board of Judges of Common Pleas Court of Allegheny County that no qualified person should be rejected as a member of the Board of Public Education because or race or religion. This organization is of the opinion that the Board of Public Education will more adequately serve the needs of the school system if and when its members are composed of persons of different races and creeds."[54]

The PCLU then endorsed long-time black State Representative Homer S. Brown, of the Hill District, for the school board. Following his endorsement, Brown became the first black appointed to the Pittsburgh Board of Public Education, for which he thanked the PCLU.[55]

Like the AFL-affiliated PCLU, the CIO-affiliated United Steelworkers was also attempting to live the principles of racial solidarity. In November of 1944, District 19—the Pittsburgh region—of the USWA sponsored "A Day of Fun" for local steelworkers. Over 5,000 men and women from all USWA locals in Allegheny County gathered at Sportsmen's Park in Tarentum, near Pittsburgh, for fun and games. Among the festivities was the crowning of "Miss War Worker," selected by those in attendance. Two women, one black and one white, were jointly elected and bedecked with the "Miss War Worker" ribbon. Both were pictured smiling side-by-side in a subsequent issue of the union newspaper. The photo is the only evidence of these selections and the lack of commentary on this dual selection could suggest that this was not a unique occurrence.[56]

As the 1944 elections approached, AFL unions across the country were following the lead of the CIO-PAC and forming Political Action Committees of their own. Pittsburgh was no exception. On August 11 the PCLU officially launched its own PAC. The workhorse Secretary of the new PAC was long-time Executive Board member Amy Ballinger, who had represented the Laundry Workers in the PCLU throughout the Thirties and who was the only woman on the Executive Board. As noted previously, "Sister" Ballinger would rise through the ranks of the labor movement and go on to serve on the Pittsburgh City Council from 1970-76.[57]

The PCLU-PAC raised "voluntary" contributions (and thus legal under the Smith-Connally Act and Pennsylvania's Farrell Bill) from every Pittsburgh union, whether affiliated with the PCLU or not. It also launched voter registration drives in every union local as well as political education drives in every local.[58] At its September 13 meeting, $73 was raised on the spot from delegates in order to purchase 2,000 posters encouraging union members to register, all of which were to be ready in a week for distribution in local union halls.[59]

Nationally, organized labor also launched a "popular front" PAC called the "National Citizens PAC," headed by Sidney Hillman of the Amalgamated Clothing Workers; Freda Kirchwey, publisher and editor of *The Nation;* Clark Foreman of the Southern Conference for Human Welfare; and James G. Patton, head of the National Farmers' Union. "While CIO PAC expresses the will of the 5,500,000 CIO members," explained the United Steelworkers to its members, "the National Citizens PAC speaks for all progressive Americans, in and out of the labor movement. Both PACs have common objectives."

These common objectives were evident in the two domestic planks in the National Citizens PAC: "1) Full production and full employment after the war. 2) Equality of opportunity and full security for all Americans, regardless of race, color, or creed." These dual domestic goals could only be won, of course, by supporting Roosevelt, for only "Under FDR's administration came economic and social freedom to the workers."[60]

And it was not just for workers, as workers, that Roosevelt's administration was bringing "economic freedom." In his January 1944, State of the Union Address to the nation, Roosevelt had outlined the future domestic programs his Administration would fight for in the coming year, and he once more proved that his finger was on the pulse of his constituency. In his address, Roosevelt pronounced an "Economic Bill of Rights" to which all citizens were entitled as much as they were to the political Bill of Rights attached to the Constitution. These "economic rights" included a right to a job, to a decent home, to "adequate protection from the economic fears of old age," and a right to a good education.

Coincidentally, the day before FDR's State of the Union Address, Missouri Democratic Senator Joel Bennett Clark introduced legislation for a "Bill of Rights for G.I. Joe and G.I. Jane." In June, Roosevelt signed into law this "G.I. Bill of Rights," which entitled millions of Americans to guaranteed home mortgages and financial support for college education.[61]

In the past, from the Revolutionary War to the Civil War and beyond, America had always rewarded the veterans of its wars with either free farm land in the West, a pension, or, in the case of World War I "Doughboys," with a "bonus." During World War II, however, it had become obvious that the veterans who would soon be returning to an urbanized economy didn't need farm land and a "bonus" wouldn't go far. A modern economy mandated that they needed an education, the functional equivalent of farm land.

And so the G.I. Bill was enacted to enable veterans to go to college. This was the kind of security the Democratic constituency was yearning for and the kind of security Roosevelt promised in his "Economic Bill of Rights." This kind of security would have massive social repercussions in the post-war years.

And, of course, on Election Day Roosevelt won, yet again, with his usual huge majorities in the nation's industrial regions. In 1944 he carried Pennsylvania for the third time, with a lead of 132,000 in Philadelphia alone over Republican Thomas E. Dewey. In addition, Democrat Francis J. Myers did what Earle could not do in 1938. He retired incumbent Republican U.S. Senator James Davis. Joining incumbent Democrat Joseph Guffey, this meant that for the first time in its history, Pennsylvania had two Democratic U.S. Senators simultaneously. The Democrats also re-elected their incumbent State Treasurer and Auditor General and won three additional seats on the State Supreme and Superior Courts. They also recaptured the State House of Representatives.

John L. Lewis was just as adamantly opposed to Roosevelt in 1944 as he had been in 1940, but in the voting booth rank and file mine workers paid him no more heed than they had previously. "The returns showed that once again the soft coal miners in western Pennsylvania and the anthracite miners in the East repudiated John L. Lewis, president of the United Mine Workers of America, by turning in thumping pluralities for Mr. Roosevelt."[62] Even among Lewis' mine workers, it was loyalty to "their" party and "their" president which mattered.

Tomorrow's Security

The coming of peace in 1945 brought a changed global economy. All other major industrial powers were devastated and America, her economy stimulated out of Depression by the war, bestrode a ruined world. And as the world segued into the Cold War, America's war-time economy continued to boom.

Despite this, however, the workers of the industrial heartland were fearful there would be a return to the hard times of the Depression and were increasingly concerned about the economic security which had always been a cornerstone of their demands. Typical of both the economic status and yearnings of Pittsburgh-area workers in the immediate post-war years was Homestead steelworker Henry J. Mikula.

The son of a Slavic immigrant and one of 14,000 workers in U.S. Steel's Homestead Works, *The New York Times* thought Mikula was "A symbol of the industrial wage-earner" nationwide.[63] Mikula was born, raised, and lived in Homestead, which was, in turn, dominated by the steel mills which ran for 22-miles along the "industrial river valley."

As late as the 1950s, 40 percent of the Homestead steelworkers were father-son combinations, and Mikula fit that pattern. His father and his step-father had previously worked in the Homestead mill, as did currently his five brothers-in-law, while his oldest son planned to. Mikula was only thirty-six-years-old, but had already worked in the Homestead mill for twenty years. Like most of his fellow workers, in 1929 he had followed his father into the mill at age sixteen and had worked beside his father there throughout the Thirties and the war years.

Mikula was also a registered Democrat, as were three-quarters of all voters in Homestead, and he had run unsuccessfully for Homestead borough council in 1947. In addition to being politically active, he was also a good union man, serving as assistant grievance chairman of Homestead's USWA Local 1397 and, as a conscientious Catholic, he was the head trustee of his church. In any social role, Mikula was a pillar of his community.

By no means flush economically, Mikula was still doing much better than in either his personal past, or the historical past of the town and industry. He earned roughly $56/week, which was less than the industry average, but compared favorably with the national average for industrial workers. He owned his own home, a four-room bungalow he had sacrificed to buy in the recession year of 1938 and on which he did all the maintenance. In being a homeowner Mikula was, again, typical of Homestead steelworkers, half of whom, according to union estimates, owned the homes they lived in.

In 1948 he bought a used 1935 auto for $50. "By meticulous budgeting, making many of the children's clothes, keeping a garden, and 'making out the grocery order with a pruning knife,' the Mikulas have been able to get by and still have a little left for an occasional trip to the movies or a ball game. But there is nothing for savings and the war bonds which Henry bought regularly during the flush period when the mill worked overtime have long since been cashed in."

It is understandable why Henry Mikula would have been so concerned about his family's economic situation—and not because of economics, alone. Henry Mikula was the son of a Slavic immigrant. As we discovered in chapter 3, Southern and Eastern European immigrants came to America from a culture of profound material scarcity. The resulting never-ending economic anxiety is what created their legendary work ethic, which caused them to work in a mill for fifty years, work as a cobbler for seventy-five years, work relentlessly until they dropped.

The children of these immigrants, men like Henry Mikula, the men who created a Workers' Democracy in the industrial heartland in the Thirties, inherited their fathers' work ethic—and their fathers' compulsive desire for economic security. Thus, it is not surprising that *The New York Times* discovered that Henry Mikula was concerned not so much with "today's wage," as with "tomorrow's security." It was clear that, "The most important thing about Henry Mikula is the conviction that what is to him a fairly decent way of life can be made even better." This could be accomplished not by wages alone, but, more importantly, with more social welfare and economic security.

Henry Mikula had been active in the three-month steel strike of 1946, which had been primarily over wage increases. Now, in 1949, the steelworkers' union was planning another strike. However, "the present dispute is not primarily over wages—which are reasonably good for a non-craft industry—but the less immediate factors of better pensions, more sick benefits, and other aspects of social security . . . If he goes on strike, it will not be out of hunger or desperation, but for the new principle of welfare that has been added to labor's arsenal of demands, now that the basic wage-hours fight has been largely won."

Indeed, "It is security that has become the touchstone of Henry's world . . . Until recent years most union demands centered on a fuller lunch pail. Today they are being extended to include the concept of a fuller life . . . emphasis has been shifted from the hearth to the hearthside."

Mikula, like many other steelworkers, was beginning to look to his personal future as a retiree. "'When a man gives forty or fifty years of his life to a job,' Henry says, 'he should be able to retire in comfort—a little comfort, anyway.' Thirty years ago, in Homestead at least, this attitude would have been considered an impertinence by many. Today, to a generation of workers that has grown up in the midst of an increasing drive toward the 'welfare state,' Henry's point of view strikes him as anything but revolutionary."

A Republican Renaissance

But, while their overriding desire for economic security may have struck the industrial workers of Pittsburgh and vicinity as "anything but revolutionary," it was alien enough to the leading Democratic politician of the region, David Lawrence, when he finally chose to run for office. Ever a bridesmaid but never a bride, Lawrence had never been elected to public office in his thirty-year political career. Even as Secretary of the Commonwealth under Earle, he had been appointed.

That now changed, as Lawrence was given the party's endorsement to replace Cornelius Scully as mayor of Pittsburgh in 1945. His nomination and subsequent election marked a decisive turn in the direction of local events. Like many Democratic politicians of the New Deal Era, from FDR and Harry Truman on down, Lawrence benefitted from the social movements of the period by gaining a public reputation for political sagacity and deep insight into the psyche of the electorate, supposed virtues which in turn made possible his stunning political victories.

But, too often, the political beneficiaries of the massive tidal shifts in American society during the Thirties—men like Father Coughlin and John L. Lewis—had little understanding of the social basis of their success. David Lawrence seems to have also been one such. While a far-reaching urban social reform agenda was being enacted in most other Northeastern industrial centers, an agenda congruent with the hopes and aspirations of men like Homestead's Henry Mikula, Lawrence concentrated, instead, upon an ambitious civic improvement program which was the dream child of the city's corporate elites.[64]

Thus, it was under Lawrence's post-war stewardship that the Democratic Party hierarchy began to undermine the very social foundations which had made possible their political dominance. Lawrence himself was a primary actor in this transformation.

Lawrence was an Irish Catholic from a working class family, comfortable in church groups and fraternal halls and union headquarters. However, as an elected official he ultimately proved to be more of a civic reformer than a social reformer, more of a disappointment to labor than a champion of labor.

Moreover, as a politician shaped by long years in the exile of minority party status, he never seems to have quite realized that—at least in Pittsburgh—a "real" Democrat who appealed to the ethnic working class could easily win. This was why Lawrence consistently backed blue-blooded Protestant aristocrats for mayor of Pittsburgh. His disastrous choice of McNair in 1933 was because he hoped McNair would appeal to Republicans, doubting there were enough Democrats to get him elected.

This was the same reason he backed Cornelius Scully to replace McNair in 1937. Despite being a Democrat from the days in which it was unpopular to be a Democrat, Scully was an Episcopalian, a member of the city's most prestigious social clubs and circles, an aristocrat from a family of aristocrats going back into Pittsburgh's ancient past. He was just the man to appeal to the Republicans in Shadyside and Squirrel Hill whom Lawrence hoped to woo.

But, an analysis of the vote reveals that Scully never did what Lawrence had picked him to do. In Scully's 1941 re-election, for instance, it was the loyal Democratic vote which sent him back to city hall, as he carried all the black, blue collar, industrial, and ethnic wards which had become the party's backbone. Meanwhile, he lost all of the Republican wards like Shadyside, Squirrel Hill and other "suburban" wards in the East and West Ends and the South Hills.

But even the loyal Democratic voters were obviously unhappy with their blue-blood Episcopalian candidate, as Scully won by only 3,163 votes, despite a Democratic registration advantage of over 81,000.[65] Thus, Lawrence's "astute" strategy to woo Republicans not only failed, it also alienated his own blue collar Democratic constituency, only narrowly averting defeat.

So it was obvious to all, even to David Lawrence, that Scully could not be the party's candidate for a third term as mayor at the end of the war in 1945. The problem, however, was that Lawrence still did not comprehend that the problem was not with the candidate, but with his own failed strategy. Thus, he looked around for similar quasi-Republican candidates, but saw no clear replacement. He turned first to Judge John J. Kennedy of the Court of Common Pleas. Judge Kennedy was a former city solicitor and much in the style of the past respectable blue bloods Lawrence had backed in his role as king-maker. But Kennedy rebuffed him when Lawrence offered him the keys to the city.

While Lawrence dithered, Patrick Fagan—former president of both the AFL-affiliated Pittsburgh Central Labor Union and the CIO-affiliated Steel City Industrial Union Council, a founder of SWOC, and local district director of the United Mine Workers—declared his candidacy. True to his practice, Lawrence refused to back such an obvious Catholic and strong champion of labor. His own reputation within the party was such that he could have had the nomination for the asking, but—also true to his practice—he was reluctant to put forth any Catholic, even himself, for elective office, even in Pittsburgh, even in 1945, as he feared a Catholic could not possibly be elected.

Other men, however, such as Allegheny County Commissioner John J. Kane, the second most powerful Democrat in Western Pennsylvania, were more perceptive than Lawrence. They realized that there had been a political revolution in Pittsburgh, realized that Lawrence's caution was uncalled for, as Democrats now out-numbered Republicans two-to-one in the city with a 100,000 vote majority (many of them Catholic), and realized that Lawrence could therefore win. They appealed to Lawrence to become the candidate and, lacking any other acceptable nominee, Lawrence reluctantly agreed to run. Once he announced for the nomination, Patrick Fagan and the few other hopefuls dropped their candidacies and united behind the party chairman.

But, despite the huge Democratic majority now existing in Pittsburgh, Lawrence still seemed unwilling to trust that Democrats alone could elect him. Still a minority politician in exile, if only in his own mind, Lawrence crafted a pro-business campaign designed to appeal almost solely to Republicans.

There was also another reason Lawrence turned to the Republican business community: Pittsburgh problems which concerned Lawrence more than working class economic security. These were the urban decline and population loss (coupled with suburban growth) which was already becoming perceptible in the immediate post-war period.[66]

Lawrence's response was to try to turn Pittsburgh into a city which would attract and hold businesses and population, even if this was at the expense of the ethnic working class communities which were the basis of his power. His resulting plan to build buildings, highways, and parks would radically reshape the "Smoky City" into the mid-1960s. And his approach to urban renewal would be subsequently emulated by big city Democratic mayors throughout the Northeast faced with the same problems.[67]

On April 20, 1945, Lawrence announced a campaign platform of civic improvements which he hoped would garner support from the city's Republican business and professional communities. These included calls for conferences between the future mayor and businessmen; the creation of an "industrial expansion committee"; public infrastructure improvements advocated by the Allegheny Conference on Community Development (ACCD); residential rezoning; new residential construction; and improvements on the central business district.[68]

Later, he called for the construction of a huge new civic auditorium. This would become the city's Civic Arena, which devastated the now-Democratic Hill District and forced a diaspora of blacks from the area.

He wanted new highway construction, which would soon destroy much of the solidly-Democratic North Side and force another diaspora, this time of working class whites.

He planned to "redevelop" the city's downtown business district where the Ohio and Monongahela Rivers met to form a triangle, a district christened after the make-over as, "The Golden Triangle." This rejuvenation, which would benefit only the business elite, would be financed by public taxes, a form of "corporate welfare," in which money would taken from the poor to enrich the rich.

He wanted to demolish the Downtown slums of the Point Irish, from which he himself had emerged. They would be replaced by a large and grassy park at the Point, where the rivers met, which would become Point State Park. It is today a pleasant green playground, with a picturesque fountain spraying the air. But no one lives there.

This blueprint for a Republican-business "Renaissance" (as it was later dubbed) became the one which David Lawrence implemented as he restructured Pittsburgh over the next sixteen years.[69] And it was a message he took to groups of businessmen, engineers, lawyers, and teachers—audiences very different from the black and ethnic industrial workers who were his natural constituency. Their opinions were neither sought, nor needed.

Shortly before the 1945 election, Lawrence called for the establishment of a "business-labor-professional committee" to advise the new mayor on how best to transform the city's urban environment. Evidently, Lawrence made a more persuasive Republican than did Scully, for in the subsequent election he recorded large gains over Scully's 1941 vote in the Republican middle and upper class neighborhoods of Shadyside, Squirrel Hill, the South Hills, and Carrick, although he failed to carry any of these Republican wards outright.

But Lawrence's Republican Renaissance failed to address the social welfare and economic security concerns of Pittsburgh's blue collar voters. And, because it offered nothing to such voters, Lawrence paid a price in otherwise strong Democratic wards. While Republican turnout increased in Republican wards, the Democratic vote plummeted in former Democratic strongholds such as the majority-black Hill District, Homewood-Brushton, blue collar Lawrenceville, and the heavily working class central North Side, as well as other once-dependable Democratic wards. David Lawrence carried just over half of the city's thirty-two wards and, despite a lopsided Democratic voter registration advantage of 100,000, he squeaked into office with a meager victory margin of just 14,000 votes, not that much better than Scully did in 1941.[70]

It is clear that there was no enthusiasm among Pittsburgh's blue collar, black, and ethnic voters for his grand schemes of civic restructuring. If Lawrence's objective was, as his biographer Michael Weber claimed, "to broaden the party's traditional New Deal coalition," he failed. Instead, master politician David Lawrence came perilously close to dissolving Pittsburgh's traditional New Deal coalition. But residual party loyalty among the Democratic faithful, and sheer overwhelming two-to-one registration numbers, gave Lawrence his paltry victory.

And, just as the blue collar Democrats of Pittsburgh showed no enthusiasm for Lawrence's Republican Renaissance, neither did Mayor Lawrence show much interest in their concerns. In his inauguration speech presented in the City Council chambers on January 7, 1946, the new mayor said nothing about the labor turmoil then rocking Pittsburgh and the nation. Instead, he reiterated his call for a business-oriented Republican Renaissance. "We are all partners in Pittsburgh," he declared, "everyone of us." And together, this partnership could build a new Pittsburgh and bring about "miracles undreamed of."[71]

Commenting on the changing of the guard at Pittsburgh's City Hall, *The Saturday Evening Post* observed that, "Pittsburgh's extraordinarily powerful Chamber of Commerce . . . has been, since the beginning of the Roosevelt labor revolution in 1933, the embattled citadel of 'the interests,' while City Hall has been more or less regarded as GHQ of the liberal-labor junta. But that fissure has begun to heal . . . There is . . . good reason to believe that Pittsburgh is in the beginning stages of one of the most dramatic periods of municipal renaissance that any great American city is likely to undergo in the next decade."[72]

It was an accurate observation.

Bread and Roses, Too

While that prediction would indeed prove to be true, it was of little immediate interest to the industrial workers of Pittsburgh. These workers could not be long ignored by the new mayor and, instead of urban restructuring, the blue collar Democrats of the region were much more interested in changes that would benefit them directly. In 1945-46, in the immediate aftermath of the war, wages— something Lawrence never touched upon in his campaign, even for city workers— were high on their list. Moreover, they felt they had the numbers and the solidarity to get what they wanted. Their demands, therefore, set Pittsburgh's public agenda.

Thus, in 1946, his first year as mayor, David Lawrence was not able to focus on his Republican Renaissance. Instead, he was forced to respond to "a . . . steel strike, two coal strikes, a 115-day walkout at Westinghouse, a 53-day hotel shutdown, several bus strikes, and an assortment of 81 other work stoppages."[73] During the twenty-six-day steel strike that winter, 125,000 Pittsburgh steelworkers quit work and steel production fell to 3 percent of capacity. During the fifty-nine-day coal strike that spring 56,000 UMW miners walked out and steel production subsequently dropped to 29 percent of capacity.

Then, in November 1946, the coal miners struck again and, *Newsweek* reported, "For the fourth time in 1946, the urban symbol of American preeminence in heavy industry was being paralyzed by strike . . . This time, Pittsburgh . . . the citadel of King Coal and the steel capitol of the world . . . was even worse off than last spring . . . Already, Pittsburgh's steel industry, first as always to feel a coal strike, was closing down . . . It was only a matter of time before Pittsburgh's aluminum, glass, electric, and other industries would go the way of the 350 coal mines and the 35 steel mills in the area.

"As if the Pittsburgh area hadn't enough worries, Mayor Lawrence had another of his own. Some 5,000 city employees were demanding wage hikes ranging from 18 and a half to 75 percent. While the fires that powered Pittsburgh's industry were being banked, the city's firemen, asking 25 percent raises, threatened the City Council: 'If you don't give the right answer, we'll take other means.'"[74] This was in addition to a twenty-seven-day general strike which turned Pittsburgh into a ghost town.

These examples of working class militancy illustrated, of course, workers' economic concerns. More importantly, they illustrated a level of such intense and broadly based class solidarity, that its like has not been witnessed in the half century since. This militant solidarity brought not just Pittsburgh, but the nation to a standstill a number of times in the immediate post-war years and forced working class concerns to the top of the nation's domestic agenda.

****

Throughout the war, wages had been frozen at the pre-war low level mandated by the "Little Steel Formula." With the end of the war and wage controls, workers were eager to catch up. The result was not only, in terms of numbers, the largest strike wave America has ever witnessed, before or since, but also a strike wave bigger than anything ever witnessed in Europe, including the British General Strike of 1926. "In the year after V-J Day, over five million workers hit the picket line, and by the end of January 1946, the industrial core of the economy was virtually at a standstill as the auto, steel, electrical and packinghouse workers were simultaneously on strike."[75]

By the end of 1946, almost 5,000 strikes had broken out. The largest were in steel, auto, oil-refining, meatpacking, and electrical appliances, but in six cities from coast to coast, from Oakland, California, to Rochester, New York, and Pittsburgh in-between, city-wide general strikes shut down everything. The class war was once more on America's front pages.

To an extent World War II had muted the class war. War-time wage and price controls had restricted a traditional goal of the labor movement, higher wages. At the same time, rationing had limited available goods for purchase.

Nevertheless, advertisers were already whetting people's appetites for the unlimited tidal wave of goods the end of the war promised to bring. Thus, "Even before the cross-channel invasion of 1944, the advertising industry had its largest budget in history and had begun to prepare the public for post-war goods . . . The potential market was vast. At the time of Pearl Harbor, the liquid assets of individuals came to $50 billion; by the end of 1944 that figure had reached a record $140 billion. The National Association of Savings Banks conducted a survey of depositors that showed 43 percent eager to spend their savings for 'future needs,' 20.6 percent more precisely for homes and their accoutrements, 9 percent for automobiles. The Office of Civilian Requirements in June 1944 announced that eleven appliances led the list on Americans' post-war plans for buying, with washing machines first, followed by electric irons, refrigerators, stoves, radios, vacuum cleaners, electric fans, and hot water heaters. Those items, advertisers had claimed throughout the war, constituted the American way of life."[76]

For 12 million G.I.s and for millions more of blue collar workers on the homefront, a shining image of post-war America had taken root during the industrial marathon of all-out production and full employment needed to win the war. It would be an America devoid of Great Depression scarcities and deprivation, devoid of economic insecurity and anxiety. America would become a Utopia composed of "a little white house in the suburbs where a young wife wearing a pretty blue dress and an anniversary bracelet would greet her veteran husband every evening with slippers to change into from his Johnston and Murphy shoes, with a Scotch whiskey highball and a sirloin steak, all within the efficient antiseptic environment created by electric appliances that cooked the meals, did the housework, kept out the cold or heat, and left the couple free to listen to their radio . . . that was the decent, uninspired picture, for thousands of Americans, of their post-war world."[77] A Ford, they were promised, was in their future. They could be sure if it was Westinghouse. They were in good hands with Allstate.

It would also be a Utopia for an emerging new consumer the marketers anticipated. In September 1944, a new magazine hit the stands, destined to prosper as the bible of teenage girls for the next half century: *Seventeen*. It was the world's first magazine pitched exclusively to teenagers and its cover promised it would be all about, "Young fashions & beauty, movies & music, ideas & people."

As the war economy began to convert to meet the consumer demands of a booming peace economy, President Harry Truman, who had inherited the presidency following the death of Franklin Roosevelt, was receptive to dismantling the war-time wage and price controls as quickly as feasible in order to return to a market economy and meet the pent-up demand for spending.

However, to do so too quickly would also bring a wave of inflation, as producers raised prices to profit from surging demand. Therefore, he moved cautiously, attempting to maintain for the time being price controls as a lid on inflationary pressures. Then he began to lift rationing, beginning with gasoline. In order to put more money in people's pockets, he also signed into law a six billion dollar tax cut. But he was ultimately unable to persuade Congress to maintain price controls and so, in June 1946, all price controls except those on rent were lifted.

The result was exactly as feared. Inflation spiralled skyward. The inflation rate for that year, 1946, was a fearsome 18.2 percent and food prices alone rose more than 25 percent between 1945 and 1947.

Workers responded by demanding higher wages. Management stonewalled. Strikes had been raging throughout the nation already, as massive layoffs had quickly taken place following the cancellation of orders for war material. This had brought about the very unemployment situation the labor movement had feared peace would bring. Even among those yet working, the end of overtime and war-inspired high wages cut income by up to 30 percent, just at the time workers were anticipating a "peace dividend." Now, faced with spiraling inflation, those strikes spread and escalated.

Many CIO leaders, such as Walter Reuther of the UAW, had visionary plans for the future which went far beyond higher wages and better working conditions. However, this 1945-46 strike wave was above all fueled by rank and file outrage at the continuing opulence of a wealthy class, and the righteous perception that they, too, after the sacrifices of the war, deserved a little of the good life.

The sense of "equality" and "fairness" already noted among Pittsburgh workers certainly seemed to be a prime catalyst among the industrial heartland's steelworkers as they voted to strike. "A week or so before we took the strike vote," said one steelworker, "one of the Pittsburgh papers ran a story about a big party one of the . . . [steel] executives gave for his daughter." He and his buddies added up the cost of the girl's party and discovered that her night of fun cost more than the annual wages of the five of them combined. "That sort of stuff made us realize, hell, we *had* to bite the bullet [and strike] . . . the bosses sure didn't give a damn for us."[78]

But, as far as the bosses of such firms as Westinghouse, General Motors (GM), and Ford were concerned, the time had come to reassert the managerial control they felt had been lost due to New Deal and wartime gains on the part of labor. They, too, felt the time had come to renew the still unresolved class war. It was just such enthusiasm for combat on the part of both labor and management which contributed to the magnitude of the showdown that fall.

Thus, when Walter Reuther led 320,000 GM workers out on November 21, 1945, neither side was eager to compromise. GM had already begun moving out of Detroit in order to get away from the UAW. In the plants still in Detroit, it had no desire to welcome labor's demands.

Meanwhile, Reuther articulated even broader goals than just more wages for his members. He wanted the labor movement to be the vanguard in reshaping the entire post-war world, both economically and socially. The time had come at last, he felt, for radical measures.

For instance, he did indeed want higher wages for GM workers, as high as 30 percent. But, rather than passing on the cost of such wage increases to the consumer in the form of higher auto prices, Reuther wanted them to come out of the huge profits he contended GM had made during the war. Higher wages would then boost consumption, which would boost production, which would lower per unit cost, making for more company profits. Thus, everyone could win, company, workers, and consumers.

GM felt that this demand encroached upon traditional managerial decision-making powers and rejected it. The reason GM management gave was that they could not afford the pay increases the UAW wanted.

Reuther didn't believe them and demanded that they "Open the books!" and prove it. Instead, GM rejected Reuther's demand for open access to financial data, as well as his broader demands for union representation in all company decisions. That would have been too much power-sharing with their workers.

Instead, GM offered wage increases of about 20 percent, a level the United Steelworkers and the United Electrical Workers had already accepted for their members. As Reuther kept his membership out on strike for weeks after other industrial unions had settled, criticism within his own ranks joined the criticism from without. GM worsened the situation by stonewalling and refusing to concede on even the most trivial point.

In mid-March 1946, after four months on strike, Reuther was forced to accept GM's terms. The UAW would get more money, but it would not get a say in managerial decisions. The final result was that GM and other major employers reasserted their control over workplace decisions. When Truman lifted price controls three months later, corporations were soon able to pass along the wage increases to their consumers in the form of higher prices.

Thus was launched the modern pattern of upwardly spiralling wages and prices which has continued down to our own day as the primary inflationary engine of the American economy. Thus, also, was the pattern set for corporate decisions concerning such things as investment and de-investment to be made by management alone. This would have devastating consequences in the 1970s, 1980s, and beyond, when corporations abandoned, first, America's industrial heartland, and then abandoned America itself for cheaper, more pliable workers overseas.

But workers had won as much as they could at the time. And what they won were, nevertheless, signal victories. Not only had they gained significant wage increases, but the unions had entrenched their positions within the economy and, by doing so, prevented a replay of the post-World War I near-destruction of the labor movement. "Unlike the great steel strike of 1919-20 or the sit-down strikes of 1937, the postwar strikes posed little threat to the very existence of the unions. The specter of hundreds of thousands of mass production workers laying down their tools, manning the picket lines, and attending the countless union meetings at which strike details were relayed gave impressive testimony to the permanence and strength of the new dispensation in labor relations emerging from the 1930s."[79]

"An Injury to One . . . "

But not all of the strikes which were a part of this strike wave were about wages. Throughout this period—and even later—strikes were also called in the name of class solidarity. As late as 1950, for example, 16,000 steelworkers at Bethlehem Steel's Lackawanna, New York, plant walked out in support of one man, a welder, who'd been fired for leading wildcat strikes.[80]

The city-wide general strikes of 1946 were also about class solidarity. Three general strikes in Rochester, New York, Oakland, California, and Pittsburgh are illustrative of the class solidarity which was powerful enough to mobilize blue collar workers and send them to the barricades from coast to coast.

On May 16, 1946, the Rochester City Manager fired 489 Department of Public Works employees who were attempting to organize a union. Conflict escalated until culminating in a two-week city-wide general strike which erupted on May 28. As the unions for all city workers and local organized labor rallied to the defense of the Public Works employees and shut Rochester down, the municipal administration caved in. It granted the Public Works employees everything they demanded: all the fired workers were rehired without prejudice, wages were increased, and fringe benefits were added. Most importantly, the municipal administration agreed to recognize the right of the Public Works employees to join a union of their own choosing and to bargain collectively.[81]

The city-wide general strike in Oakland was also over union recognition and respect for the rights of workers. In October 1946, the 400 members of the AFL affiliated Department and Specialty Store Employees Union employed at the Hastings' and Kahn's department stores struck to force recognition of their union. Supported by the local Teamsters and other AFL unions, the striking employees threw picket lines around the stores.

On December 1, scab drivers crossed the picket lines to deliver twelve truckloads of goods to the Kahn's store. This crossing of the picket lines was made possible by the small army of 250 Oakland police who escorted the trucks. The next day, December 2, enraged at this intervention in a private dispute by the city administration, and in solidarity with the besieged department store workers, the Oakland Central Labor Council called for a general strike.

And the very next day, December 3, over 100,000 workers belonging to 142 unions jammed into the streets of Oakland, shutting down municipal services and most businesses and industries in the city. When the municipal administration promised to respect the rights of workers in the future, the general strike ended. The strike against the department stores continued on as a private dispute.

But because of such manifest anti-labor actions on the part of the mayor of Oakland and the City Council, the Oakland labor movement organized a political campaign the following May 1947, to place five of its people on the nine-person City Council. The labor campaign demanded municipal neutrality in all labor disputes, the repeal of anti-picketing and anti-handbill ordinances, the restoration of rent control, the repeal of the sales tax, more equitable tax assessments, and respect for civil rights.

Against this challenge, the incumbents called upon the voters of Oakland to reject "CIO communism." They were unsuccessful. Four of labor's five candidates won election to the Council, with the fifth losing by less than a thousand votes.[82]

The Pittsburgh general strike was also launched by the call of class solidarity. It had begun as a serious, though contained, strike by its workers against the city's electricity provider, Duquesne Light Company. Now that the war was over, Duquesne's workers wanted wage increases, just like everyone else.

The workers were represented by a "company union"—the "Independent Association of Employees of Duquesne Light Co. and Affiliated Companies."[83] This union had no formal ties to the Pittsburgh labor movement, as it was affiliated with neither the AFL nor the CIO nor even the Pittsburgh Central Labor Union. The Duquesne management had encouraged the formation of the 3,200-member independent union in 1937, "thus hoping to keep out A.F.L. and C.I.O., which were sniffing at the door." In 1939, George L. Mueller was elected the union's president.[84]

In September 1945, Mueller presented Duquesne's president, Pressly H. McCance, with a demand from his members for a 37 percent wage increase. McCance countered by offering 7 percent. Fruitless negotiations continued until February 9, 1946, at which point Mueller issued a strike notice. This strike threat came as a surprise for two reasons. First, there was a no-strike clause in the union's contract with the company. Second, utility strikes were virtually unheard of in America because of an unofficial ban on them by all concerned due to the importance of public utilities. Nevertheless, the strike was to begin three days later, February 12, and would cut off all but emergency electrical power throughout Allegheny and the adjacent Beaver Counties.

Faced with this unprecedented crisis, Mayor Lawrence asked the U.S. Secretary of Labor to seize control of the power company, to no avail. "Federal officials . . . doubted whether the strikers would return to the power stations if the plants were taken over by the Government."[85] He then requested an emergency $25,000 appropriation from City Council to deal with the impending catastrophe, ordered all police and firemen to work over-time, prepared to hire an additional 1,000 auxiliary policemen to deal with the anticipated chaos, and called union and company officials to meet in his office with government mediators.

When neither company nor union budged, Lawrence appealed to the public to repudiate the union's action and pressure it into calling off its strike. Lawrence went on radio station KQV the morning of February 11 to plead with and threaten the union, which he attempted to isolate by pointing out that it was "neither CIO nor A.F. of L." "I cannot believe that people whom we know," he said, "people who are part of our community, people who are one with us, will plunge our city into darkness—risk the lives of people near death's door in our hospitals, menace the mother going down into the valley of shadows so that life can come into the world. I simply cannot believe it of the good people—the good citizens—the good neighbors whom we know as workers in our public utility system." He appealed to the union to keep the lights on in Pittsburgh, but, if they did not, "Whatever may take place we will protect the health, the safety, and the welfare of all the people of Pittsburgh."[86]

The next morning, the union struck on schedule. In that morning's pre-dawn hours, a desperate Lawrence called Mueller to his office to meet with as many influential and persuasive people as he could assemble, including AFL and CIO union officials, state and federal labor mediators, County Commissioner John J. Kane, and the Rev. Charles Owen Rice, who was at that time also the Pittsburgh area federal Rent Control Director. Mueller remained adamant.

But even God had declared, "Let there be light," Father Rice reminded him.

"God doesn't run the independent union," Mueller replied.[87]

Lawrence again appealed to President Truman to seize control of the power company, which Truman again refused to do.

Then the union bowed to the increasing pressure and called off the strike, returning to negotiations with the company. The media hailed the end of the short strike as a major triumph for Lawrence's powers of persuasion. It also increased his aura of independence from the labor movement, further proof that he wasn't "labor's boy," as he had not pressured the company to give in, only the union. The city's business elements saw this as a welcome development by a Democratic mayor, but the labor movement saw it as decidedly unwelcome. This dual perception was soon heightened.

Viewing the union as defanged, Duquesne Light stonewalled and negotiations dragged on unproductively between the company and the union. Indeed, despite intense community pressure to do so, Pressly McCance, President of Duquesne Light, now refused to meet with union representatives.

Lawrence called McCance to his office the morning of February 24 and, after a marathon harangue, got McCance's agreement to submit to arbitration. Mueller quickly followed suit.[88]

A negotiated arbitration agreement which neither side liked, giving the workers an 18-cents-per-hour wage increase, was approved by the union membership in early March. On April 13, Mueller announced that negotiations would begin on a new contract in August.[89]

In the meantime, Duquesne Light exacerbated things by announcing that it intended to phase out its construction division, which the workers felt they could not allow. That June the union submitted its proposals for a new contract to the company. Included were, "a 20-percent wage increase, additional holidays with pay, proposals for a profit-sharing plan which would benefit both workers and consumers, and a master contract to cover the Duquesne Co. and its 12 affiliated subsidiaries—about 30 demands in all."[90]

Duquesne Light Co. again refused to negotiate, and that August, as promised, Mueller issued a new strike deadline for early September.

The Lawrence administration then sought a "novel experiment," a court injunction forbidding the utility strike.[91] One of the victories workers had won with the Little New Deal had been the Anti-Injunction Act of 1937, which severely curtailed the use of court injunctions to halt strikes during labor-management disputes. The Republican Thermidor of 1938, however, had done what it could to dismantle the Little New Deal. One of its successes had come in 1939 when the state legislature restored the power to Common Pleas judges to issued injunctions in labor disputes. Now the Democrat Lawrence availed himself of that anti-labor Republican law.

One minute before the strike was to begin, the courts issued Lawrence's requested injunction. Mueller scorned the injunction as a "scrap of paper," as did his membership. "Signs appeared on union bulletin boards telling the members to attend the injunction hearing as defendants,"[92] and, at a mass meeting on September 21, the workers voted 1,035 to 309 to reject arbitration, to attend en masse any scheduled court hearings, and to strike at 9:30 a.m. on September 24.[93]

As far as organized labor in Pittsburgh was concerned, David Lawrence had crossed the line. His invocation of the injunction had escalated the confrontation into a government attack upon all workers everywhere. At an emergency meeting of the Pittsburgh Central Labor Union Executive Board on September 12, the Board members expressed "a definite fear of the consequences of the Injunction to organized labor and unanimity in the opinion that the Central Labor Union should opposed the Injunction."

At a meeting of the entire PCLU that night, the body passed a unanimous resolution declaring that, "We . . . abhor and oppose the issuance of injunctions in any labor dispute. We . . . will without hesitation use all our resources to prevent the issuance of injunctions that will affect the welfare of organized labor."[94] The injury to the Duquesne Light Co. workers they viewed as an injury to all workers.

At another emergency meeting on September 20, the PCLU Executive Board formulated a statement to the media which highlighted their feeling of grievance which had been inflamed by Lawrence's injunction. The Board felt the use of the courts against "us" was a violation of basic American rights to which they were entitled. Indeed, it just wasn't *fair*. "It most certainly is un-American to take away from Labor by force or subterfuge the right to strike," the Board declared. "Labor has never condemned or criticized any other group's efforts to improve their enjoyment of life, liberty, and the pursuit of happiness as guaranteed by the Constitution, neither do we believe that our efforts should be restricted when we are operating under the laws prescribed by our State, National, and Local Governments.

"It must be understood that Labor is a part of the citizenry of every community. As have all other citizens, they have suffered . . . at the hands of utilities, politicians, anti-religious, anti-American, unfair employers, unfair prices for commodities, and all of the unfairness that can be imposed upon a people in any Community, City, or State in America. We do not believe there is a fair-minded person anywhere who will disagree with this statement."[95]

Meanwhile, in defiance of Lawrence's injunction, the strike against Duquesne Light began as scheduled September 24th. "Night travelers to Pittsburgh had the unnerving experience of coming into a city illuminated largely by candles. And the farther they went into the dimmed-out city, the deeper grew the sense of having strayed into some darker century or into that ice age projected by the gloomier prophets of industrial paralysis . . . No streetcars and few busses were running. A picket line tie-up of coal trucks knocked out the central steam plant heating most of the big downtown buildings and department stores, restaurants, and other businesses closed down for lack of light and heat. Office workers hitch-hiked in and out of town as best they could, climbed long flights of dark stairs to work, huddled in coats and sweaters in stone cold offices . . . Pittsburgh appeared more than ever a city under siege."[96]

The strike affected not just Pittsburgh, but the entire region, as it "virtually closed down the commercial and industrial life of an area inhabited by nearly 2,000,000 persons . . . All but two of the 131 companies in an industrial association reported that they were forced to close their plants."[97] "All but a handful of Pittsburgh's hundreds of restaurants were shut. Department stores were shut. All but a few office buildings were shut. Water supply in surrounding townships dwindled. Transportation facilities were crippled. Some 100,000 people were out of work. Mayor Lawrence admitted that he could no longer guarantee the continuing health and safety of his city."[98]

On September 25th, the state Democratic Party adopted a motion condemning the use of injunctions to settle labor disputes. Nevertheless, that same day Lawrence asked a three-judge panel composed of one Democrat and two Republicans for a permanent injunction against the strike.

While considering this request, the judges demanded that Mueller apologize for spurning the earlier injunction as a "scrap of paper." Standing in the court before more than 1,500 of his union members, while a thousand more milled around outside the City-County Building on Grant Street, Mueller refused.

The two Republican judges retaliated by immediately sentencing Mueller to a year in prison for contempt of court. As the police led Mueller out of the courtroom to jail, the judges then threatened to arrest the union's entire nine-member executive committee if the strike was not called off the next day. The Rev. Charles Owen Rice, who was in attendance, described the resulting chaos as "a mob scene."[99]

At 2:30 that same afternoon an enraged PCLU Executive Board held an emergency meeting to discuss the events. Much opposition to the court's actions was voiced. "Brothers Smith and Morgan, of the Street Railways, Division 85 . . . stated that their people were ready to stop work because Mueller . . . was put in jail."[100]

Many other workers were also instantly ready to strike in solidarity with the embattled electrical workers. Over 700 Bell Telephone employees staged an immediate protest rally and "Labor leaders talked darkly of a general strike."[101]

"At this point, unions affiliated with the A.F.L. and C.I.O. in Pittsburgh, neither of which had been too sympathetic to Mueller's independent group beforehand, saw a vital principle at stake. To protest the jailing of a strike leader . . . these unions struck or threatened to strike almost every important unionized place of employment in the community."[102]

What followed indeed turned "Pittsburgh into a ghost town as [the strike] escalated from a utility strike into a general strike."[103] "Sympathy strike action developed, [8,000] employees of the Jones & Laughlin Steel Corp. [South Side] going out in sympathy on the second day of the stoppage. Several manufacturing plants of the Westinghouse Electric Corp. closed when [13,000] workmen refused to operate with power generated by the Duquesne Light Co. The Amalgamated Association of Street, Electric Railway, and Motor Coach Employees (AFL) called out their members as a 'protective measure,' stating that threats had been made against the men operating trolleys with 'struck power.' This halted trolley service. Shortly thereafter bus service was withdrawn upon order of the drivers' union."[104]

The day after Mueller was sentenced to prison, thousands of Pittsburgh workers marched on the Grant Street City-County Building where Lawrence had his office, loudly demanding Mueller's release. The Rev. Charles Owen Rice attempted to calm the angry workers. Chanting "Free Mueller, jail Lawrence," the workers shouted him down and forced him to abandon the futile effort.

"It was horrible," a shocked Father Rice later told an interviewer. "I thought I could talk to them, but there were Mueller's friends out there who were like locusts. They were screaming furiously."[105] Indeed, the labor priest recalled with revulsion that the angry workers even spat upon him.[106]

"Alarmed by the raging bear they had by the tail, Pittsburgh city officials presented to the jailed Mueller a company proposal for settling the strike." Mueller was released from jail and escorted by the police to a hastily called meeting of his membership to present the company's newest offer. "[T]he meeting voted to entertain no settlement proposal until the injunction was dissolved. The strike continued . . . and the sympathetic strike action spread," while the police returned Mueller to jail.[107]

"By Thursday morning [September 26th], the city knew it was licked. Solicitor [Anne X.] Alpern asked the court to dismiss the injunction and release Mueller." Faced with a city in darkness and an escalating labor rebellion, the Republican judges agreed to both requests. "Triumphantly borne off on the shoulders of his followers, Mueller capped his victory with an order to picket trolley barns and power stations. That night, pickets stopped six trucks which were delivering coal to one of the power plants. By Friday . . . the city was all but paralyzed . . . At the end of the week, the strike was still on, the city still hamstrung."[108]

The solidarity strikes continued as negotiations resumed once more between Duquesne Light and its workers. Over 100,000 Pittsburgh workers were now striking in solidarity with the independent union.[109] Backing for the strike continued from Pittsburgh's bus and streetcar drivers, even in defiance of their national leadership, who felt that the release of Mueller had defused the situation. "Over the protests of their national officials, the operators voted to refuse to go through picket lines established at car barns by the power-plant strikers."[110]

As negotiations stalled, "The union members held steadfast through nearly a month of concentrated abuse. Their side got very little hearing. Many sins against journalism went into building up the anti-Mueller legend . . . [But] Several citizen committee attempts to promote back-to-work movements or recruit volunteer strikebreakers were miserable failures."[111]

By then, the Pittsburgh strike had taken on larger importance, as the national media was quick to point out. "Wave of utility strikes threatens now that unwritten ban against them has been broken," warned *Business Week*. "An important utility strike was virtually unknown in this country until the Duquesne employees walked out last month . . . the implications of a utility stoppage were considered to be so intensely anti-social that all parties to disputes involving power had always been induced to make some peaceful settlement of their differences. Then the Duquesne strike actually occurred and . . . This week the C.I.O. Utility Workers Union struck the Warren Division of the Ohio Public Service Co. in support of demands for an 18 cent hourly wage boost. Warren and Niles, Ohio, were put on reduced power rations and a business blackout of the Pittsburgh type appeared imminent. Threats of future strikes were also voiced against the Virginia Electric & Power Co. and New York City's Consolidated Edison Co. Clearly the Duquesne strike, whatever its eventual outcome, is becoming a landmark. Unless the situation is changed by law, the power companies can no longer expect any more immunity from serious labor trouble than other key industries."[112]

But it was not just the precedent of a utility strike which was unsettling to the national media. Even more disturbing was the demonstrated impotence of the courts and government to counter what they saw as labor run amok. "The . . . citizens of Greater Pittsburgh," cried *Newsweek*, "found out last week that a labor union was stronger than its city government," not comprehending that it was not the light company union, but the citizens of Greater Pittsburgh who had proven themselves stronger than David Lawrence's city government.[113]

And, while Pittsburgh's workers had seen the issue as being whether the law could be "unfairly" used as a club to batter down workers when they presented their just demands, *TIME* magazine warned that Pittsburgh workers, "had defied the city and the courts and demonstrated that labor recognizes no exceptions whatsoever—even the public's welfare—to its right to strike."[114]

The Duquesne Light Co. strike "was of such overriding importance," said *Business Week*, "that everything else on the labor front seemed insignificant by comparison. It was not the economic implications of the Pittsburgh strike . . . which made it so momentous. It was the question of law, and of the law's limitations in safeguarding the public interest, which was raised so insistently . . . the problem so starkly exposed was fundamental; given the degree of unionization which we now have, can the power of the courts prevail in asserting the public interest against a group interest which can command economic forces of sufficient magnitude?"[115] The question now before the nation, continued *Business Week,* was "whether government is able to force an ending to a labor dispute, no matter how vitally the public interest is affected?"[116]

Because of these anti-labor interpretations of the conflict, many in the national media saw the Duquesne strike as a watershed in the American public's attitude toward the labor movement, with crucial political and legal ramifications. "The Duquesne strike's example of the impotence of the judicial process in the face of a determined, disciplined body of organized labor," predicted *Business Week,* "may prove to be a turning point in the thinking of those searching for an effective mechanism to prevent strategic strikes."[117]

U.S. News & World Report concurred: "A small group of strikers now has shown how easy it is to choke off the industrial life of a large, modern city. An independent union of power-plant employees in Pittsburgh has provided a dramatic example for members of Congress who have been advocating a law to prevent strikes in public utilities. The walkout has increased considerably the chances of restrictive labor legislation being enacted by the next Congress."[118]

This statement would soon prove prophetic.

On October 18, Mueller was summoned to Washington, D.C., to appear before the House Un-American Activities Committee to answer charges of being a Communist agent.[119] Father Rice, a militant anti-Communist himself and still seething from being spat upon, also began charging that the strike was Communist influenced.[120]

Public sympathy was also waning as, "In the fourth week of George L. Mueller's power strike, the nation's tenth city was not exactly ghostly. It was just ghastly. Pittsburghers hitchhiked to work . . . skipped up and down stairs, brought their lunch (few restaurants were open), shivered through a shortened work day, then bummed a ride home. Statisticians guessed that . . . the strike had cost about $400,000,000 in wages and lost business."[121]

Faced with charges of being Communist agents and the difficulty of maintaining a long strike in the face of increasing public resentment, the light company workers reluctantly decided to compromise. Twenty-seven days after the power strike began, the union voted on October 21 to accept binding arbitration and the strike ended.

The Second Thermidor

The post-war strike wave, of which the Pittsburgh general strike was part, galvanized and mobilized the Republican base as never before. Two weeks after the settlement of the Duquesne Light strike, in the November 1946, elections, voters in Pennsylvania and across the nation reacted to the 1945-46 strike wave by defeating Democrats high and low. It was a repeat of the Thermidorian election of 1938, which had also put Republicans in office in the wake of the massive 1937 strike wave. In Pennsylvania, where the state Democratic Party had adopted a platform plank condemning anti-strike injunctions in labor disputes, voters swept two-term U.S. Senator Joseph Guffey out of office and buried the Democratic gubernatorial candidate, with both losing by over half a million votes.

Democrats fared just as poorly at the national level, as Republicans took control of both the U.S. Senate and the House of Representatives, increasing their numbers by twelve additional seats in the Senate and fifty-five in the House. Thus, for the first time since 1930, the Republicans controlled Congress. Of the eleven incumbent Democratic Senators running for re-election outside the still "Solid South," seven were defeated. Over 40 percent of the non-southern Democratic House seats were lost and the Republicans picked up twenty-five non-southern governorships. It was a rout.

With the first chance since 1930 to roll-back labor's gains, the new Republican-controlled Congress quickly showed its hatred for anything associated with the New Deal, which it viewed as little better than Communism. "Bring on your New Deal, Communistic and subversive groups," John Bricker, the newly-elected Republican Senator from Ohio had thundered during his campaign. "If we can't lick them in Ohio, America is lost anyway."[122]

As a major New Deal constituency, organized labor became a primary target for such hatred. "Increasingly hostile to the unions, which had become ever more open in their identification with the Democratic Party, GOP leaders resolved anew to restrict organized labor. Certain of support from a strong contingent of conservative southern Democrats, the Republicans made labor legislation a priority for the incoming Eightieth Congress."[123]

Foremost on the agenda of restrictive labor legislation was a revision of the 1935 Wagner Act. What eventually emerged was the Taft-Hartley Act of 1947, named after co-sponsorers Robert A. Taft (R-OH) in the Senate and Fred A. Hartley (R-NJ) in the House.

Taft-Hartley restructured the character and functions of the National Labor Relations Board in order to make it less of an advocate of organized labor and more of a theoretically neutral arbiter between labor and management. While collective bargaining was still allowed, the amendment provided for decertification elections whereby members in a particular location could disassociate themselves from their current union representative. It also made possible more management agitation among workers against the union. It outlawed solidarity strikes, wildcat strikes, mass picketing, secondary or supportive boycotts, and union political campaign contributions. It also gave individual states the right to legislate certain areas of labor relations, such as the right to forbid a closed (union) shop in a particular state. Finally, it required all union officers to sign loyalty oaths, affidavits affirming that the officials were not members of the Communist Party.

Of course, the Taft-Hartley Act was closely followed and debated in the Steel Valley as it wound its way through Congress in 1947. Because of that,

The McKeesport Junto, a civic organization composed of local businessmen and employers which hosted debates on topical issues, invited two freshmen Congressmen, both just-elected members of the House Committee on Education and Labor, to debate the legislation in McKeesport on April 21, 1947.

The new Congressmen, one a Republican from California and one a Democrat from Massachusetts, rode up from Washington together on the overnight train to Pittsburgh. They flipped a coin to see who got the preferred lower bunk in the Pullman sleeping car. The Democrat won.

However, the Democratic Congressman, twenty-nine-year-old John F. Kennedy, who opposed Taft-Hartley, did not win at the McKeesport debate. His pro-Taft-Hartley Republican opponent, thirty-four-year-old Richard M. Nixon, argued that, "The public was happy with labor on VJ Day, but in the years since, we have seen a shift in public opinion."

Certainly public opinion among his businessmen listeners was with Richard Nixon that day. Coming as a surprise to no one, Nixon recalled later that he felt the audience of 100 McKeesport businessmen gathered in the Penn McKee Hotel "tended to be on my side," agreeing with him that labor had won too much. It was time to clip labor's wings. He left the Steel Valley victorious in the first Kennedy-Nixon debate.[124]

And the conservative coalition of Republicans and Southern Democrats was also victorious in Congress. It not only passed Taft-Hartley into law, the coalition now had the numbers to also marshal a two-thirds majority to override the president when Truman vetoed it.

Organized labor objected strenuously to every aspect of what it called the "slave labor law"—the anti-strike provisions, the attacks on union security, the anti-Communist disclaimers. Repeal of the act thus became a rallying cry for the labor movement and a focus around which to organize in 1948 for renewed class war.

A Fair Deal for Workers

The class war in America reached its peak in 1948, with the electoral class cleavage reaching the highest levels ever recorded. That year workers (aligned more closely than ever with the Democratic Party) and WASP reaction (aligned as ever with the Republican Party) faced each other along battle lines drawn more sharply than ever before. The class war was intensified by the Republican-controlled 80th Congress. Not only did it pass anti-labor legislation such as the Taft-Hartley Act, but it also enacted a far-reaching tax cut for the wealthy, which President Truman vetoed.

In the midst of these ever-more bitter conflicts between the Republican and Democratic parties, the Democratic Party fractured three ways.

When he inherited the presidency upon Roosevelt's death in 1945, Harry Truman had also inherited FDR's former vice president, Henry Wallace, as a member of his Cabinet. However, the two drifted further and further apart in the immediate aftermath of World War II, especially when it came to foreign policy. These differences came to a head in September 1946, when Wallace made a speech deemed by powerful Republicans in Congress as too conciliatory toward the Soviet Union. In order to quell the firestorm and deny Republicans yet another issue as November's mid-term elections approached, Truman fired Wallace.

His dismissal, however, only seemed to free Wallace to become even more critical of the Truman Administration, accusing it of betraying the New Deal legacy. Thus, sentiment for some kind of "progressive" political insurgency by the left wing of the Democratic Party began to crystalize around Wallace all during 1947. Just after Christmas of that year, Wallace made it official: He would challenge Truman in the 1948 presidential election as the standard bearer of a new third party, the Progressive Party.

Meanwhile, unhappy with both the liberal aspects of New Deal democracy and increasing acceptance of black aspirations within the Democratic Party, conservative Southern Democrats began their Long March out of the Democratic Party.

Under Truman's leadership, the Democratic Party had become even more supportive of black hopes than it had been under Roosevelt. Truman had appointed a civil rights commission to investigate the status of black Americans and to make policy recommendations. In February 1948, Truman took the commission's report, *To Secure These Rights*, to Congress, delivering the first presidential message in the nation's history to focus only on civil rights. In addition, northern Democratic legislators introduced bills making lynching a federal crime and establishing the anti-discrimination Fair Employment Practices Commission as a permanent body. Republicans and like-minded Southern Democrats ensured neither was reported out of committee.

Increasingly worried by the direction the national party was taking, South Carolina Governor Strom Thurmond warned the Truman Administration that, "the South was no longer in the bag."[125] At a meeting of the Southern Governors' Conference, Thurmond called together a gathering of sympathetic colleagues to pressure the Administration to walk softly on the civil rights issue. In March, seven of those governors, including Thurmond, called upon white Southern Democrats to vote in the November election only for candidates who opposed civil rights for blacks.

When the Democratic nominating convention opened in Philadelphia that June, civil rights had become an unavoidably divisive issue. Liberal Northerners, led by Minnesota Senate candidate Hubert H. Humphrey, succeeded in adding a statement to the party platform praising the civil rights proposals advocated by Truman during his February speech to Congress.

For many white Southern Democrats, this was the final straw. The entire Mississippi delegation stormed out of the convention in protest, followed by half the Alabama delegation. The Alabama delegates who left the convention declared that they had been instructed "never to cast their vote for a Republican, never to cast their vote for Harry Truman, and never to cast their vote for any candidate with a civil rights program such as adopted by the convention." They had also been instructed to bolt the convention if it adopted a civil rights plank and so, "We bid you goodbye!"[126]

Shortly after the Philadelphia convention, 6,000 disgruntled Southern Democrats from thirteen states met in Birmingham, Alabama, to launch a new political party. With Confederate battle flags flying in a revivalistic atmosphere, these "Dixiecrats" nominated South Carolina Governor Strom Thurmond for president and Mississippi Governor Fielding Wright for vice president as the candidates of the new States Rights Party. Their hope was to win enough Southern votes in the electoral college to hold the balance of power, and thus persuade the Democratic Party nationally to see the error of its civil rights ways and repent.

In the meantime, Truman threw down the gauntlet. He would not be bullied and if he would win, he would win without the likes of the Dixiecrats. In July he issued Executive Orders forbidding racial discrimination in federal employment and racially integrating the armed forces.

Mississippi Senator James Eastland thundered to a Memphis rally in September that, if Truman won in November, "our traditions and our culture will be destroyed and mongrelized by the mongrels of the East."[127]

Thus, the Republicans smelled victory. Not only was the Democratic Party splintered into three factions, with the "Solid South" slipping away and the "progressive" left running their own candidate, but Roosevelt was dead. The astounding loyalty of the working class which elected Roosevelt to the White House four times was thought to be a personal loyalty to the man, himself. And now that man was gone. And a man who'd never actually been elected president stood in his place. After years in the wilderness, the Republicans felt they would soon return to power.

Everyone who knew anything agreed with them. The prestigious Gallup and Roper Polls predicted Democratic disaster and all the pundits foretold a rescinding of the New Deal.

Harry Truman ignored them and embarked on his "Give'em Hell" campaign across America. Frank K. Kelly accompanied him as his speech writer. Kelly told me that Truman was met everywhere by huge and enthusiastic crowds. In one city where Truman was mobbed by jubilant supporters, Kelly remarked to a policeman standing next to him that such a massive outpouring of support made it hard for him to believe that Truman was going to lose. "Aw, they're just coming to say 'Goodbye' to Harry," the officer told him. Kelly refused to believe his eyes and agreed with the officer.

But, to the surprise of Truman's speech writer, and everyone else, Truman won. It wasn't even close. Truman beat the Republican candidate, Thomas E. Dewey, by over two million popular votes and by 303-189 in the electoral college.

Meanwhile, Wallace and Thurmond each won a little over one million votes each, with Wallace gaining no votes in the electoral college and Thurmond capturing four Southern states and thirty-nine Southern electoral votes which otherwise would most likely have gone to Truman. The Democrats also took back control of Congress, winning a stunning 263-171 margin in the House and a comfortable 54-42 margin in the Senate. Instead of a rescinding of the New

Deal, there would be a continuation of the New Deal. And, as attuned to what workers wanted as Roosevelt had been, Truman dubbed this continuation, "The Fair Deal."

As it turned out, the Dixiecrats had misjudged their power, both within the Democratic Party and within the national electorate. The enduring New Deal majority, based upon such constituencies as organized labor and blacks, would survive without rabid Southern Democratic segregationists.

Thus, white Southern Democrats began to feel increasingly alienated from a national Democratic Party which had shown it could win without them. In some respects, therefore, 1948 was much like the election of 1860. In that election, Abraham Lincoln became the first president in American history to be elected without carrying a single Southern state. That meant that the new-born Republican Party—which had swept the North and California on a platform calling for the "containment" of slavery—was under no constraints to heed Southern voters. One could be elected without racist Southern votes. So, too, could a president be elected in 1948 without catering to Southern racism.

What that meant in 1860 was that the racist South left the United States, resulting in the Civil War. What it meant after 1948 was that racist white Southerners began to leave the Democratic Party, resulting in another kind of civil war.

This was because the complexion of the New Deal constituency was changing. Black voters, for one, were becoming more salient. "A part of the New Deal coalition since 1936, blacks made a massive migration toward the Democrats in party identification in 1948. Four years earlier . . . figures showed that 40 percent of black voters identified as Democrats and 40 percent as Republicans; in 1948 those figures shifted to 56 percent and 25 percent, respectively. This overwhelming Democratic loyalty among blacks would hold for at least the next four decades."[128]

Because of this, and because of increased support for civil rights by the national party, Southern whites were beginning to question their long-held allegiance to the Democratic Party. As of yet, however, they had nowhere else to go. As evidenced by the instructions to the Alabama delegation to the Philadelphia convention, they could not yet bring themselves to vote for the party of Lincoln, a legacy of Civil War defeat. In 1948, therefore, large numbers of them turned their backs on both major parties to vote "Dixiecrat."

But in the 1950s the appearance of an aggressive civil rights movement among Southern blacks—and a national Democratic leadership increasingly sympathetic to this movement—caused Southern white Democratic voters to look more favorably upon the Republican Party. In the 1952 presidential election, the Republican, Dwight D. Eisenhower, came within a mere 5,000 votes of winning South Carolina. In 1956, Eisenhower actually did win Louisiana, as it went Republican for the first time since the end of Reconstruction.

That same year, Virginia Senator Harry F. Byrd, running for president as a segregationist independent, ran a strong second behind the Democrat Adlai Stevenson in South Carolina. In the close presidential race of 1960 between

Kennedy and Nixon, Byrd, running again, won all of Mississippi's eight electoral votes. Meanwhile, Richard Nixon, the losing Republican presidential candidate, was only 10,000 votes behind John F. Kennedy in South Carolina.

After 1960, taking notice of this trend and at the urging of Nixon, the Republican Party adopted a "Southern Strategy" designed to welcome racist Southern whites into its ranks. This strategy began to produce fruit in the 1964 presidential election. In 1948, running on a racist platform, Strom Thurmond had carried the states of Louisiana, Mississippi, Alabama, and South Carolina. In 1964, running on the "Southern Strategy," Republican presidential candidate Barry Goldwater carried the very same states, while adding Georgia. Indeed, outside of his own state, Arizona, which he won by only 1 percent of the vote, these five Southern states were the *only* states Goldwater carried. It helped that Senator Goldwater had voted against the Civil Rights Act of 1964. Southern whites knew where he stood on the race issue.

In the 1968 presidential election, the Democrats again failed to carry any of these five once solidly Democratic Southern states. South Carolina again voted Republican, while Louisiana, Mississippi, Alabama, and Georgia again voted for a racist third party candidate, Alabama Governor George Wallace.

But, support for Wallace's third party candidacy was merely the final stepping stone out of the Democratic Party and into the Republican Party for white Southerners. By the 1980s and 1990s, Republican Party leaders—such as House Speaker Newt Gingrich of Georgia and Senate Majority Leader Trent Lott of Mississippi, Governor Jeb Bush of Florida and his brother, Governor George W. Bush of Texas—came from the former Confederacy. The South had become the backbone of the resurgent Republican Party as that party—once the northern party which had won the Civil War against the South—transformed itself into an overwhelmingly white Southern party. Thus, the winds of change which began to reshape the South in the 1948 presidential election had finally completed their work.

In addition to an increased black vote, however, Truman's victory in 1948 was also made possible because labor was still on the march. Membership in CIO-affiliated unions, for one example, climbed by almost a million in the decade between 1944 and 1953.[129] This was despite the CIO expulsion of many member unions—such as its third-largest affiliate, the United Electrical Workers (UE)—for alleged Communist domination during this same period.

Truman also won because these still-marching workers, largely (though not wholly) ethnic Catholics, were continuing to vote Democratic in ever increasing numbers. For example, in the 1928 presidential election, Catholic New Yorker Al Smith did not even carry his home state. Indeed, the only two states north of the Mason-Dixon Line to go Democratic were heavily Catholic Rhode Island and Massachusetts. But the Catholic Democratic vote, even in these states, was concentrated in large cities, such as Boston and Cambridge. Outside the cities, the states remained Republican—so much so, in fact, that Republican Henry Cabot Lodge, Jr., could still beat Boston's Democratic Mayor James Michael Curley for a seat in the U.S. Senate in 1936.

But Catholics continued to make gains. In 1948 the Democratic vote reached new record highs in eleven Boston wards due to a "Catholic outpouring" which reflected "the heavy Catholic vote in other parts of the country." In the same 1948 election, eight Italian-Americans nationwide were elected to Congress, twice as many as in any previous election.[130] Because of this increasing Catholic vote, the Democrats finally won their first majority in the Massachusetts House of Representatives with the 1948 elections. When he was sworn into office in January 1949, State Representative Thomas P. "Tip" O'Neill, from the blue collar district of Irish Catholic North Cambridge, became the first Democratic Speaker of the Massachusetts House since the Civil War.

It was just such a continuing "Catholic outpouring" which made possible Truman's victory in 1948. Indeed, more Catholics voted for Harry Truman in 1948 than for any previous Democratic presidential candidate, including Franklin D. Roosevelt and Al Smith. Truman's 1948 vote in heavily Catholic St. Paul, Minnesota, for instance, was about 10 percent higher than FDR's had been in 1944.[131]

This astonishing and still-increasing loyalty to the Democratic Party by Catholic blue collar workers was overlooked by the political pundits who predicted a Republican landslide in 1948. But it was also missed by the left-liberals—in and out of the unions—who backed Henry Wallace's Progressive Party bid for the presidency that year. Strom Thurmond and his racist-reactionary Southern Dixiecrats may have deserted the Democratic Party; left-liberal Progressives may have deserted the Democratic Party; but the Democratic Party was still the party of the workers, and the workers remained loyal to their party.

"[A]s of the 1940s," Robert Zieger reminds us, "working people were . . . heavily oriented toward the Democratic party. While the party was not a labor party and while its candidates avoided appeals to class consciousness, public opinion experts regularly reported high percentages of working-class identification with the Democracy. Indeed, in the immediate post-World War II decade, American workers often voted as heavily for Democratic candidates as did British working-class citizens for the Labour party in the United Kingdom. Thus, the loyalty of American workers to the Democratic party . . . was simply a fact of life.

"In 1940, John L. Lewis himself had urged workers to join him in repudiating Roosevelt and the Democratic Party. Their refusal to do so and their ringing endorsement of FDR held a profound lesson for labor's political operatives. As the liaison between organized labor and the Democratic Party became tangled and frustrating through the late 1940s, some leftists began to think of it (in socialist commentator Mike Davis's phrase) as 'a barren marriage,' but in reality *it was American workers, and not the labor movement, who had long before become wedded to the Democracy.*"[132]

It was this working class loyalty to "their" party—despite defections on the Democratic Party's left and right wings—which made all the difference in 1948, as Henry Wallace, like John L. Lewis before him, soon learned. As FDR's vice president after 1940, as well as head of the administration's Board of Economic Warfare, Wallace had become closely aligned with the labor movement and, especially, the CIO. With others in the Roosevelt Administration becoming increasingly caught up in winning the war, Wallace stood out more and more as one of the few still fanning the flame of New Deal social reform. It was Wallace, therefore, who became the principal administration champion of the CIO's "Economic Bill of Rights," while others in the administration ignored it.

Not only was Wallace labor's true tribune, his vision of a social democratic transformation of the post-war world also appealed to workers. Typical of his thoughts was his address to 20,000 auto workers at the Detroit State Fairgrounds on July 25, 1943, where he was introduced by UAW-CIO President R.J. Thomas as, "the architect and crusader for a new world." Vice President Wallace then went on to call for a "war-proof post-war world pledged to enlightenment of all peoples, 'full production and full employment' and cooperation with other nations to enforce international justice and security."

In volatile words he then attacked "small but powerful groups which put money and power first and people last . . . Some call them isolationists, some reactionaries, and others American Fascists . . . [These] defeatists who talk about going back to the good old days of Americanism (after the war) mean the time when there was plenty for the few and scarcity for the many, or the days when Washington was only a way station in the suburbs of Wall Street," but following the war, "nothing will prevail against the common man's peace in a common man's world."[133]

Incendiary sentiments such as these had won him an enthusiastic labor following. Thus, at the 1944 convention of the CIO in Chicago, CIO and USWA President Philip Murray introduced Wallace to the lustily cheering delegates with the words, "We love him because he is like us—*a common man.*"[134]

Philip Murray and CIO-PAC President Sidney Hillman also exhorted the Democratic Party's delegates to support Wallace's re-nomination at the party's convention in July 1944. So did powerful elements within the Pennsylvania Democratic Party, such as the two U.S. Senators, Guffey and Meyers.

But the same views which had moved Murray to declare that "We love him" had also alienated Wallace from other powers within the party, not the least President Roosevelt himself. FDR indicated lukewarm support for his vice president and acceptance, instead, of Senator Harry Truman of Missouri, the protege of early Roosevelt supporter Thomas Pendergast in Kansas City.

Other Wallace opponents included Southern conservatives and bosses of big city machines, career politicians who felt threatened by Wallace's social democratic leanings. These included such figures as Mayor Ed Kelly of Chicago, who was also the Democratic National Committee (DNC) Chairman, Mayor Frank Hague of Jersey City, the DNC Vice Chairman, and the influential Edward H. Flynn of the Bronx.

Wallace's opponents also included David Lawrence of Pittsburgh, once again chairman of the Pennsylvania Democratic Party and a member of the party's National Committee, the latter a position he would hold the rest of his life. The opposition of these big city political bosses was enough to deny Wallace the party's vice presidential nomination in 1944, but Lawrence was himself able to deliver to Truman only twenty-four of the seventy-two votes of the pro-Wallace Pennsylvania delegation he theoretically controlled.

As a consolation prize, Roosevelt appointed Wallace his Secretary of Commerce. Even in this, Wallace encountered opposition from party bosses. However, indicative of Wallace's continuing support in the Pittsburgh labor movement was the Central Labor Union's response. On February 1, 1945, the PCLU adopted a resolution introduced by Executive Board member Nick Lazari of the Hotel and Restaurant Employees Alliance, Lo. 237, supporting Wallace's nomination as Commerce Secretary. Intended to be a letter to their Congressional delegation, the PCLU resolution declared, "The American people are very cognizant . . . of the stand taken by [an] unholy combination of reactionaries of both parties . . . against Mr. Wallace's realistic people's program, the best guarantee of job security, free enterprise, peace and prosperity for generations to come. We, of organized labor, are vigorously and unequivocally supporting our President's appointment of Mr. Wallace . . . [for the] security and welfare of the American people as a whole. Therefore, we urge you, Mr. Senator . . . to stand by the side of the American people, who are the greatest treasury of our Republic."[135]

However, despite the popularity of Wallace in the Pittsburgh labor movement, he was not able to retain its support when he broke with the Democratic Party the following year. On September 10, 1946, the PCLU Executive Board, of which Nick Lazari was a member, received a resolution from Painters Lo. 1103 in Mentor, Ohio, supporting Wallace's third-party presidential bid. "The philosophies of the late president, Franklin D. Roosevelt, have not been carried out by President Truman," the Ohio painters declared. Therefore, they requested that the Pittsburgh Central Labor Union join them in supporting Henry Wallace as the next President of the United States. The Executive Board refused to do so, as did the general membership of the PCLU.[136]

This coolness of labor leaders toward Wallace's third party effort was reflective of what the rank and file also felt. The loyalty of the average worker for the Democratic Party was dramatically evident when Henry Wallace, their erstwhile champion, campaigned in union strongholds.

At the Detroit Fairgrounds in 1943, UAW President R.J. Thomas had hailed Wallace before a crowd of 20,000 enthusiastic UAW members as, "the architect and crusader for a new world."

But, in 1948, "When Henry Wallace came campaigning into Detroit, Chrysler Seven [UAW Local 7] was having its first strike in ten years. Wallace tried to join the picket line, but was jeered off. I was told of one elderly union member who had been indifferent to the campaign until several workers started sporting Wallace buttons. 'Give me one of those Truman buttons,' he demanded angrily of his shop steward."[137]

As with Detroit workers, so with East Pittsburgh workers. In East Pittsburgh the largest and strongest union at the massive Westinghouse plant dominating the town was Local 601 of the United Electrical Workers (UE), a local led by Communist sympathizers. The Communist Party endorsed and worked for the election of Henry Wallace in 1948. Local 601 officers, therefore, tried hard to convince their otherwise loyal "followers" to abandon the Democratic Party in favor of Wallace. Instead, Truman received almost 25 percent more votes in East Pittsburgh that year than Roosevelt had received in 1944.[138]

Unlike UE, most of organized labor was quite aware of how the rank and file felt, and therefore threw its people and treasure behind Truman's campaign. These unions concentrated their efforts in heavily industrialized states such as California, New York, West Virginia, Indiana, and Michigan, where the organizational links between labor and the party were already strong. The resulting unexpected Democratic victory has entered myth and legend as due to Truman's unstinting "Give'em Hell" campaign. Truman himself acknowledged the truth when he said, "labor did it."[139]

Truman carried with him into office a Democratic majority in both the Senate and the House, capturing seventy-five new House seats and nine new Senate seats. This Democratic President and Congressional majority outlined and then implemented major segments of social legislation which came to be known as the "Fair Deal." This 1949-1950 Fair Deal Congress was the most liberal Congress since 1938 and produced more "New Deal-Fair Deal" legislation than any Congress between 1938 and Johnson's Great Society of the mid-1960s.

The Fair Deal, along with labor's political triumph in 1948, signalled that post-World War II America would not experience a repeat of the post-World War I debacle, in which a red scare and political repression crushed the labor movement and the democratic aspirations of American workers. "A generation earlier, the very spirit of Wilsonian New Freedom had been buried deep in the debris of reaction following world war. Not so with the New Deal."[140]

During the interim, the political landscape had undergone a tectonic shift, which Truman built upon. True, he was not able to repeal Taft-Hartley, obtain civil rights legislation, or implement health care insurance and educational funding, all of which he sought.

But what his Fair Deal accomplished in less than two years in a single Congress was impressive. "This was the Congress that enacted the comprehensive housing program, providing generously for slum clearance, urban redevelopment and public housing; the Congress that put through the major revision of social security, doubling insurance and assistance benefits and greatly—though not universally—extending coverage. This was the Congress that reformed the Displaced Persons Act, increased the minimum wage, doubled the hospital construction program, authorized the National Science Foundation and the rural telephone program, suspended the 'sliding scale' on price supports, extended the soil conservation program, provided new grants for planning state and local public works and plugged the long-standing merger loophole in the Clayton Act ... Moreover, as protector, as defender, wielder of the veto against encroachments on the liberal preserve, Truman left a record of considerable success—an aspect of the Fair Deal not to be discounted."[141]

Some have argued that these gains came not so much because of any perceptible *organizational* influence by unions on New Deal and Fair Deal labor and social policy, which was negligible, but because of Democratic sensitivity to what common working class *voters* wanted. Because of their numbers and because of their militancy and solidarity, politicians were forced to respond favorably to the workers' hopes and aspirations.[142]

Direct policy input, however, is not the sole measure of the influence labor unions had on the Roosevelt-Truman administrations, as unions also played vital roles in fundraising and in providing workers for Democratic campaigns. Thus, Democratic leaders had to be responsive to official union concerns, as well as to the more generalized hopes and aspirations of their shared working class constituency.

Meanwhile, in Pittsburgh's Mon Valley, steelworkers continued to dominate the politics of the towns as the 1940s became the 1950s. Elmer Maloy declined to run for a third term as burgess (mayor) of Duquesne in 1945, but only because he said he'd accomplished all he'd set out to do. The town's politics remained firmly in the hands of the people who first put him in office in 1937. The union was secure. Working class ethnics were no longer second class citizens. Social welfare programs were being implemented.

In Clairton, John J. Mullen, now a leading USWA official, did run for and was re-elected to a third term as the town's burgess in 1945, an office he would retain throughout the Fifties. By the time Truman was sworn into office for a new term in January 1949, the burgess of Homestead and ten of the borough's sixteen officials were all steelworkers in the local mill. Additionally, "Compared with 1936 more than twice as many Italian names answered the 1951 legislative roll calls in Pennsylvania, New Jersey, New York, Connecticut, Rhode Island and Massachusetts—the six states with the heaviest Italo-American concentrations."[143]

The ethnic working class was at last accepted to full citizenship in America, and Workers' Democracy remained secure in the industrial heartland.

Notes

1. "What's Itching Labor?" *Fortune,* November 1942, Vol. 26, 101, no authors listed.

2. "What's Itching Labor?" 102. Unfortunately, the anonymous authors do not elaborate on what they mean by, "a controlled economy."

3. "What's Itching Labor?" 228. "Being played for a sucker" seems to be the language of a market consciousness. One is "played for a sucker" when the other side forces or tricks you into a bad deal.

4. "What's Itching Labor?" 232, for all preceding paragraphs dealing with "favorites." There also appears to be some evidence at around this time that those who were less well off economically were also supportive of civil liberties, which would correspond with this emphasis upon "equality" and a "fair shake" we find among Pittsburgh workers. In a *Fortune* magazine national survey reported in its February 1940 issue, the question was asked: "Do you think that in America anybody should be allowed to speak on any subject any time he wants to, or do you think there are times when free speech should be prohibited or certain subjects or speakers prohibited?"

The survey respondents were divided into two categories, "Prosperous" and "Poor." While 47.5 percent of the "Prosperous" felt there should be total freedom of speech for anybody, on any subject, at any time, even more of the "Poor," 52.1 percent, felt this way.

Meanwhile, while a majority of the "Prosperous," 51.6 percent, felt there should be some subjects or speakers prohibited, only 38.7 percent of the "Poor" could go along with this. Survey reproduced in "Gallup and Fortune Polls," *Public Opinion Quarterly,* June 1940, 350.

5. Stephen S. Rosenfeld, "The Korean War, Remembered," *The Pittsburgh Post-Gazette,* July 30, 1993.

6. "What's Itching Labor?" 236.

7. Robert H. Zieger, *American Workers, American Unions, 1920-1985,* The Johns Hopkins University Press: Baltimore, 1986, 63.

8. Zieger, *American Workers, American Unions,* 64.

9. Information on Duquesne and Aliquippa comes from *The Pittsburgh Press,* October 15, 1940, 1.

10. Quoted in Zieger, *American Workers, American Unions,* 64.

11. *The Pittsburgh Press,* November 23, 1940. While this was a "wildcat" action and not an official union initiative, it no doubt reflected a union objective: The creation of a union shop with full recognition of the union as bargaining agent for all employees and dues checkoff.

12. Mike Davis, *Prisoners of the American Dream: Politics and Economy in the History of the U.S. Working Class,* Verso: London, 1986, 74.

13. Zieger, *American Workers, American Unions,* 64. The actual number of strikes was a little higher than this, 4,314, of which 2,138 were solely for union recognition. The previous year, 1940, there had been only 2,493 total strikes in the country, of which 1,243 were for union recognition. Only the year 1937 witnessed more strikes during this period, 4,720, of which 2,728 were for union organization. See *Historical Statistics of the United States, Colonial Times to 1957,* U.S. Dept. of Commerce, 99, table 3, Industrial Conflicts, 1930-1942.

Even though these figures were elevated, they represent about half the total number of strikers (with a much smaller workforce) in 1919 and less than half of the total for the twelve months after VJ Day, 1945-46.

14. *The Pittsburgh Press,* May 7, 1941.

15. *The Pittsburgh Press,* May 7, 1941. Again, the goal was no doubt a "union shop" in the mines.

16. Curtis Miner, *Forging A New Deal: Johnstown and the Great Depression, 1929-1941,* Johnstown Area Heritage Association: Johnstown, Pa., 1993, 77. The Johnstown and Bethlehem NLRB elections in these very pro-union plants probably give a more accurate idea of the division of rank-and-file opinion toward the union (75 percent and 80 percent pro-union) than the isolated coal mining enclaves where minority holdouts could be more easily coerced into 100 percent unionism.

17. Zieger, *American Workers, American Unions,* 65.

18. *The Pittsburgh Press,* September 16, 1941.

19. Zieger, *American Workers, American Unions,* 67. Rank-and-file activism was crucial to gaining the NLRB election, but Ford's acquiescence was also influenced by

intensified government pressure and the belief that government contracts would be a lucrative source of profits in what was quickly developing into a war economy.

20. Zieger, *American Workers, American Unions*, 68.

21. *The Pittsburgh Press*, May 29, 1941.

22. *The Pittsburgh Press*, August 19, 1941.

23. *The Pittsburgh Press*, August 26, 1941.

24. *The Pittsburgh Press*, October 1, 1941.

25. *The Pittsburgh Press*, September 23, 1941.

26. *The Pittsburgh Press*, June 20, 28, 1941.

27. *The Pittsburgh Press*, August 29, 1941.

28. *The Pittsburgh Press*, October 30, 1941.

29. *The Pittsburgh Press*, December 9, 1941. After the bombing of Pearl Harbor on December 7, this strike was postponed "indefinitely."

30. *The Pittsburgh Press*, July 11, 1941.

31. Zieger, *American Workers, American Unions*, 73.

32. *The Pittsburgh Press*, November 18, 1941.

33. *The Pittsburgh Press*, November 20, 1941.

34. *The Pittsburgh Press*, November 21, 1941.

35. *The Pittsburgh Press*, November 22, 1941.

36. *The Pittsburgh Press*, February 26, 1942.

37. *The Pittsburgh Press*, March 18, 1944.

38. Nelson Lichtenstein, *Labor's War at Home: The CIO in World War II*, Cambridge University Press: New York, 1982, 80-81.

39. *The Pittsburgh Post-Gazette*, November 5, 1941.

40. *The Pittsburgh Post-Gazette*, November 5, 1941.

41. Zieger, *American Workers, American Unions*, 75.

42. Minutes of the Pittsburgh Central Labor Union, September 1, 1942, in the holdings of the Pittsburgh Typographical Union, Lo. No. 7, Archives of Industrial Society, University of Pittsburgh. Hereafter, "Minutes of the PCLU."

43. Minutes of the PCLU, September 17, 29, 1942. Just as their "National Unity"program called for an end to racial discrimination, so, too, did the PCLU call for an end to sexual discrimination. At the October 15 meeting, a representative of the National Woman's Party appeared before the body and asked them to endorse Alice Paul's Equal Rights Amendment to the U. S. Constitution. The membership so voted to endorse the ERA. Among other things, the resolution they adopted declared, "When we say the 'Brotherhood of Man,' we mean the Brotherhood of Man includes woman." Minutes of the PCLU, October 15, 1942.

44. Minutes of the PCLU, October 27, 1942.

45. Minutes of the PCLU, November 5, 1942.

46. Minutes of the PCLU, November 18, 19, 1942.

47. Minutes of the PCLU, October 7, 1943.

48. Zieger, *American Workers, American Unions*, 115.

49. Minutes of the PCLU, April 14, 1943, *The Pittsburgh Post-Gazette*, November 7, 1941.

50. Minutes of the PCLU, April 14, 1943.

51. Minutes of the PCLU, April 15, 1943.

52. Minutes of the PCLU, April 26, 1943.

53. Minutes of the PCLU, December 21, 1944.

54. Minutes of the PCLU, October 7, 1943.

55. Minutes of the PCLU, November 4, 1943.

56. *Steel Labor,* monthly newspaper of the United Steelworkers of America, November 1944, back cover.

57. Minutes of the PCLU, August 11, September 7, 1944.

58. Minutes of the PCLU, September 20, 1944.

59. Minutes of the PCLU, September 13, 1944.

60. *Steel Labor,* November 1944, 2, 5.

61. *The New York Times,* June 14, 1944.

62. *The New York Times,* November 8, 1944, 1.

63. David Dempsey, "Not Today's Wage, Tomorrow's Security," *The New York Times Magazine,* August 7, 1949, 10+ for the following material on Henry Mikula.

64. See Roy Lubove, *Twentieth Century Pittsburgh: Government, Business and Environmental Change,* University of Pittsburgh Press: Pittsburgh, 1969, especially chapter 6, "The Pittsburgh Renaissance: An Experiment in Public Paternalism."

65. *The Pittsburgh Post-Gazette,* November 7, 1941.

66. See John F. Kain, "The Distribution and Movement of Jobs and Industry," in James Q. Wilson, Ed., *The Metropolitan Enigma: Inquiries into the Nature and Dimensions of America's "Urban Crisis,"* Harvard University Press: Cambridge, 1968, 2-39; and Richard P. Nathan and Charles Adams, "Understanding Central City Hardship," *Political Science Quarterly,* No. 91, 1976, 47-62.

67. See Jon C. Teaford, *The Rough Road to Renaissance: Urban Revitalization in America, 1940-1985,* The Johns Hopkins University Press: Baltimore, 1990.

68. *The Pittsburgh Post-Gazette,* April 20, 1945.

69. As the Pittsburgh Renaissance was one of the first major attempts to address postwar urban decline, the origins of Lawrence's plans would seem to be of great interest.

However, no one who has written about this period has supplied a satisfactory answer or, indeed, seems even to have thought about it much. Lawrence himself, of course, is dead and so cannot tell us. With no basis other than a guess for his assertion, Michael P. Weber speculated it was because Lawrence wanted "to broaden the party's traditional New Deal coalition." See Michael P. Weber, *Don't Call Me Boss: David L. Lawrence, Pittsburgh's Renaissance Mayor,* University of Pittsburgh Press: Pittsburgh, 1988, 208.

Roy Lubove, author of *Twentieth Century Pittsburgh,* the foremost history of the Pittsburgh "Renaissance," also had no idea as to the origins when I put this question to him in a conversation on August 25, 1994. Lubove speculated on the spot that it was probably Jack Robin's idea, though there is no evidence for this other than the fact that Robin became Lawrence's Executive Secretary after Lawrence was elected. Robin had also been Executive Secretary to Cornelius Scully and had written some speeches for Lawrence toward the end of the war. At the time Lawrence was considering running for mayor, Lawrence asked for Robin's advice. Robin encouraged him to run for patronage reasons—it was important for the party not to lose control of city jobs.

But there is no evidence Robin gave Lawrence the idea for the Renaissance. See the interview with Jack Robin conducted by Robert Pease, September 20, 1972, unpaginated, and Michael Weber's interview with Robin, 18, both on file at the Archives of Industrial Society, University of Pittsburgh.

Lubove ended our conversation by saying he'd ask Weber where Lawrence got the idea the next time he saw him. I have no idea if he did. Lubove died February 17, 1995, before I was able to take this up with him again.

70. Pittsburgh election returns, 1941, 1945, Allegheny County Bureau of Elections, Pittsburgh City-County Building.

71. Inaugural address, January 7, 1946, David L. Lawrence file, Allegheny Conference on Community Development.

72. George Sessions Perry, "The Cities of America: Pittsburgh," *The Saturday Evening Post,* August 3, 1946, 46.

73. Frank Hawkins, "Lawrence of Pittsburgh: Boss of the Mellon Patch," *Harper's,* August 1956, 55-61.

74. "Strike, Shutdown, Poverty; Strike, Shutdown, Poverty—That's Been the Cycle in Pittsburgh Throughout This Year," *Newsweek,* December 9, 1946, 24-25.

75. Davis, *Prisoners of the American Dream,* 86.

76. John Morton Blum, *V Was for Victory: Politics and American Culture During World War II,* Harcourt Brace Jovanovich: New York, 1977, 100.

77. Blum, *V Was for Victory,* 104-105.

78. Quoted in Zieger, *American Workers, American Unions,* 102.

79. Zieger, *American Workers, American Unions,* 104.

80. Bruce Lambert, "Vincent Copeland, 77, Is Dead; Led Anti-War Protests in 1960's," obituary in *The New York Times,* June 10, 1993.

81. See David Lee Hardisky, "The Rochester General Strike of 1946," unpublished Ph.D. dissertation, University of Rochester, 1983.

82. See Marilynn S. Johnson, "Mobilizing the Home Front: Labor and Politics in Oakland, 1943-1951," paper presented at the Organization of American Historians annual meeting, Anaheim, California, 1993.

83. The "company union" description is found in "Duquesne Light Co. Dispute," *Monthly Labor Review,* October 1946, 593.

84. "George Does It," *TIME,* October 7, 1946, 23.

85. "Union's Power to Cripple City: Pittsburgh Case as Sample of What Even Small Independent Can Do," *U.S. News & World Report,* October 11, 1946, 37.

86. *The Pittsburgh Post-Gazette,* February 12, 1946.

87. *The Pittsburgh Sun-Telegraph,* October 12, 1946.

88. *The Pittsburgh Press,* February 21-25, 1946.

89. *The Pittsburgh Post-Gazette,* February 26, 1946; *The Pittsburgh Sun-Telegraph,* April 14, 1946.

90. "Duquesne Light Co. Dispute," 593.

91. "Union's Power to Cripple City," 37.

92. Charles Owen Rice, "Pittsburgh's Power Strike: A company union finally succeeds in standing on its own feet," *The Commonweal,* November 8, 1946, 90.

93. See Charles Owen Rice Papers, Archives of Industrial Society (AIS), University of Pittsburgh, Box No. 10.

94. Minutes of the PCLU, September 12, 1946.

95. Minutes of the PCLU, September 20, 1946.

96. *Fortune,* February 1947, 69-70.

97. "Union's Power to Cripple City," 37.

98. "George Does It," 24.

99. Ronald L. Filippelli interview with Charles Owen Rice, The Pennsylvania State University United Steelworkers of America Oral History Project, April 5, 1967, 6.

100. Minutes of the PCLU, September 25, 1946.

101. "LABOR: Power in Pittsburgh," *Newsweek,* October 7, 1946, 32.

102. "Strike That Can Make History," *Business Week,* October 5, 1946, 92.

103. Hawkins, "Lawrence of Pittsburgh: Boss of the Mellon Patch," 55.

104. "Duquesne Light Co. Dispute," 594.

105. Interview with Michael P. Weber, July 17, 1982, on file at the Archives of Industrial Society, University of Pittsburgh, 8.

106. Filippelli interview with Rice, 6.

107. "Strike That Can Make History," 93.

108. "LABOR: Power in Pittsburgh," 32.

109. *The Pittsburgh Post-Gazette,* October 21, 1946.

110. "Union's Power to Cripple City," 38.

111. Rice, "Pittsburgh's Power Strike," 91.

112. "Pittsburgh Looks to Lewis," *Business Week,* October 12, 1946.

113. "LABOR: Power in Pittsburgh," 31.

114. "George Does It," 23.

115. "Strike That Can Make History," 92-93.

116. "Pittsburgh Looks to Lewis."

117. "Strike That Can Make History," 93.

118. "Union's Power to Cripple City," 37.

119. *The Pittsburgh Post-Gazette,* October 18, 1946.

120. Ronald L. Filippelli interview, 6.

121. "Ghost Town," *TIME,* October 28, 1946, 25.

122. Quoted in Gary W. Reichard, *Politics as Usual: The Age of Truman and Eisenhower,* Harlan Davidson, Inc.: Arlington Heights., IL, 1988, 18.

123. Zieger, *American Workers, American Unions,* 109.

124. Johnna A. Pro and Matthew P. Smith, "McKeesport debate was first of many Nixon visits," *The Pittsburgh Post-Gazette,* April 23, 1994, A6; Larry King's column, "1960 election wasn't first loss to JFK," *USA Today,* April 23, 1994. Also, see *The Pittsburgh Press,* October 21, 1960.

125. Quoted in Reichard, *Politics as Usual,* 34.

126. Quoted in Irwin Ross, *The Loneliest Campaign: The Truman Victory of 1948,* Greenwood Press: Westport, Conn., 1968, 1977, 127.

127. Quoted in Reichard, *Politics as Usual,* 36.

128. Reichard, *Politics as Usual,* 42.

129. See Lichtenstein, *Labor's War at Home,* 80, table 1, "Membership of the ten largest CIO affiliates." Despite this growth in overall numbers, however, it was slower than the growth in the labor force, and so union membership, while larger, actually declined as a percentage of the workforce.

130. Samuel Lubell, *The Future of American Politics,* Third Edition, Revised, Harper & Row: New York, 1965, 76, 203.

131. Lubell, *The Future of American Politics,* 201, 213.

132. Zieger, *American Workers, American Unions,* 118. Emphasis added.

133. "Peace Initiative Urged by Wallace on America Now; For 'Common Man' he asks Full Production, Employment and Security; With Democracy For All," *The New York Times,* July 26, 1943, 1.

134. Quoted in, *Facts to Fight With for Wallace and the New Party: A Fact Book for Wallace-Taylor Workers,* published by the National Wallace for President Committee, New York, 1948, 60.

135. Minutes of the PCLU, February 2, 1945.

136. Minutes of the PCLU, September 10, 19, 1946.

137. Lubell, *The Future of American Politics,* 175.

138. Lubell, *The Future of American Politics,* 201, 213.

139. Zieger, *American Workers, American Unions,* 119.

140. Richard E. Neustadt, "From FDR to Truman: Congress and the Fair Deal," in Allen F. Davis and Harold D. Woodman, Eds., *Conflict and Consensus in Modern American History,* Sixth Ed., D.C. Heath & Co.: Lexington, Mass., 1984, 398.

141. Neustadt, "From FDR to Truman," 386-387, 398. Truman fought very hard, but unsuccessfully, to implement a national health care program analogous to what the Labour government in Great Britain had been able to create after World War II. Part of this program, guaranteed medical care for retirees in the form of Medicare, was signed into law by Democratic President Lyndon Johnson on July 30, 1965. Appropriately, Johnson signed the law establishing Medicare in Independence, Missouri, Truman's home, signifying continuity of the struggle over successive Democratic administrations.

142. This is the argument, for instance, of Murray Edelman, "New Deal Sensitivity to Labor Interests," in Milton Derber and Erwin Young, Eds., *Labor and the New Deal,* University of Wisconsin Press: Madison, 1957, 189-190.

143. Lubell, *The Future of American Politics,* 77.

Chapter 11

No Retreat, No Surrender, 1949-1960

Referendum on the Republican Renaissance

Mayor David Lawrence had disenchanted Pittsburgh workers even before he was elected mayor. Once in office, he did much to confirm their suspicions of the Democratic boss. His actions during the 1946 Duquesne Light Co. strike alienated many of the city's labor groups, as well as ordinary workers. His wooing of the city's business elites for his renovation plans seemed a betrayal of his own roots. And the actions he took to implement his "Renaissance" bred a major rival in the form of City Councillor Edward Leonard, an official of Plasterer's Local No. 31 and the Pittsburgh Building Trades Council, whom Lawrence had appointed, at the PCLU's behest, to one of the two "labor seats" on the Council when a vacancy occurred in 1939.

After Lawrence took office in 1946 he established the practice of presiding over an informal meeting of the City Councillors every Monday morning. The purpose of this was to outline the game plan for that week's legislative action in the formal Council meeting. This was similar to the practice he'd established in the Earle Administration as the ringmaster of the Democratic legislators. Leonard, however, refused from the first to attend Lawrence's agenda-setting meetings.

Leonard's independent streak became more noticeable after Lawrence launched his Renaissance campaign. Leonard particularly opposed Lawrence's decision to ban the use of cheap but smoky bituminous coal for home use. Pittsburgh was then legendary as the "Smoky City," and not only because of the belching steel mill smokestacks. Virtually every home was heated by coal-burning hearths. As part of his campaign to clean up the city's air, Mayor

357

Lawrence wanted Pittsburghers to start burning less smoky, more expensive, anthracite coal.

Councillor Leonard waged a relentless opposition to this campaign, both before and after the Council passed it into law. Leonard contended that the Mayor's smoke control crusade could be easily afforded by the wealthy, but it was a terrible hardship for the working class. And by making the change, he contended, the city's largest coal company, the Mellon-owned Consolidation Coal, would get even wealthier by taking more money out of the pockets of workers. Local newspapers were deluged by letters in support of the Councillor, and anti-Lawrence sentiment among the city's workers began to coalesce around Edward Leonard.[1]

Leonard was among four Councillors up for re-election in 1948. As the election season got underway, he stepped up his campaign against the smoke control program and, because of this, directed most of his fire against its author, Mayor Lawrence, rather than against his putative, but now insignificant, Republican opponents. That November, Councillor Leonard proved to be the city's best vote getter, topping the ticket. Obviously, he'd struck a chord in the Pittsburgh electorate.

As the spring of 1949 unfolded, many in the Pittsburgh labor movement turned to Councillor Leonard as a champion who might unseat Mayor Lawrence in the September Democratic mayoralty primary. In a resolution passed May 5, 1949, the city's AFL-affiliated Pittsburgh Central Labor Union (PCLU) called upon Councillor Leonard to run against the Mayor and urged a united labor coalition to topple Lawrence. To this end, they called upon all CIO locals, the United Mine Workers, local teamsters, the Railroad Brotherhoods, and all other labor organizations to rally behind the "draft Leonard" movement.[2]

In addition, local union presidents began to personally plead with Leonard to run. This seemed to be a genuine draft initiative, as Leonard backed off from the endorsement and praised the mayor as the Democratic standard bearer.

Nevertheless, by mid-June the pressure to run bore fruit. At a fund-raising rally in the blue collar Democratic bastion of Ward 12, the Lincoln-Lemington neighborhood next door to Leonard's own East Liberty, the Councillor blistered "Davey" Lawrence for defecting from labor's cause and for his collaboration with the class enemy.

"When Lawrence set up a labor-management group," Leonard charged, "he didn't consult me or councilman Tom Gallagher, both labor men or CIO men, or County Commissioner John J. Kane . . . [Instead] He has become a valuable servant of the financial and industrial dynasty that has dominated the economy and political life of the community for three generations. He is a prisoner of the royal family of high finance. Under the guise of cooperation he helped big business capture both political parties. In secret sessions in their counting houses they determine the policies of his administration. A coalition of Daveycrats and conservative Republicans detoured the Democratic program from its liberal course."[3]

The gauntlet had been flung. Many in the labor movement were cheered to find their designated champion no longer reluctant. Three days after Leonard issued this indictment, Mayor Lawrence sent a congratulatory telegram to a banquet honoring PCLU President John Dorsey for his sixty-three years in the labor movement. The banquet erupted in a storm of jeers and boos as the Mayor's telegram was read to the local labor leaders. As a PCLU officer, Leonard was present. No doubt the hostility his colleagues expressed toward the mayor made an impression. The next month, July, Leonard formally announced his campaign to unseat the mayor.

But Davey Lawrence still controlled the city's Democratic Party apparatus, and he ordered all party functionaries to bail as if their lives depended upon the outcome. In addition, he spared no effort to repair his bridges to the labor movement.

Since, as a plasterer, Leonard was a member of an AFL craft union, his base of support appeared to be in the AFL-affiliated Pittsburgh Central Labor Union. Therefore, Lawrence turned to CIO President Philip Murray for an endorsement. As former president of the United Steelworkers, which was headquartered in Pittsburgh, Murray still lived in the city and had much influence among the region's steelworkers.

Murray gave Lawrence the requested endorsement. In return, Lawrence had to name a Murray man, Patrick Fagan, to fill a vacancy on the Council left by the death of Councillor Joseph McArdle. Pat Fagan was the former Pittsburgh district director of the United Mine Workers, Murray's old union, and was the popular president of the CIO-affiliated Steel City Industrial Union Council.

Lawrence promised to do so. And so it was done. And the word came down from USWA headquarters that all good CIO men were to support David Lawrence for re-election in the up-coming Democratic Party primary.

With the CIO officially backing him, and with David McDonald, who'd replaced Murray as president of the United Steelworkers, campaigning for him, Lawrence began wooing other elements of the Pittsburgh labor movement. Just before the September primary he obtained the endorsements of the local Teamsters, the Railroad Brotherhoods, and scattered AFL representatives.[4]

Then he wangled the ultimate labor endorsement. For the big Labor Day extravaganza at the Allegheny County Fair in South Park, Davey Lawrence brought in the biggest gun of all, President Harry S. Truman. President Truman owed Lawrence, as the mayor had helped maneuver Truman onto the national ticket at the 1944 Democratic national convention when Lawrence and other city bosses dumped Wallace.

A Labor Day crowd of 100,000 Pittsburgh workers witnessed Lawrence ride into the park grounds surrounded by Secret Service agents and sandwiched between President Truman and County Commissioner John J. Kane, all three waving cheerfully to the throng. Truman then addressed the mass of humanity, urging all good union members and Democrats to support Lawrence in the primary as one of the "greatest Democrats of our day."[5]

And so Lawrence pulled it off. He beat Leonard in the primary by 75,838 votes to 53,205, but he lost seven wards entirely and ran behind three of the five party-endorsed candidates for City Council. Lawrence's strongest wards were the city's richest and least ethnic wards: Squirrel Hill, Shadyside, Stanton Avenue, white collar parts of Oakland.[6] In these wards, Lawrence beat Leonard by as much as four to one. The mayor also did well in black wards, such as the Hill District and Manchester on the North Side.

Meanwhile, Leonard carried his native East Liberty. Also, despite the endorsement of the mayor by CIO President Philip Murray and USWA President David McDonald, Leonard carried and did his strongest in four South Side wards heavily populated by CIO steelworkers at the local J & L plant, Wards 16, 17, 18, and 31. By one measure, these particular CIO wards were the most class conscious wards, not only in Pittsburgh, but in the entire nation. Between 1940 and 1954 these wards ranked among the strongest "labor wards" in America in terms of the percentage of their vote these CIO voters gave to Democrats.[7]

Wards 16 and 17 also were the "most foreign" wards in the city, with the highest concentration of ethnics, mainly Poles and Lithuanians. Additionally, "By 1930, and throughout the entire decade, these wards were the lowest rental areas in the city. In 1934 the Seventeenth and the Sixth [Polish Hill] ranked among the five wards with the greatest unemployment in the city. By 1940 all three were among the top 40 percent of wards with individuals on the WPA payroll; the Sixth and Seventeenth Wards were also among the four wards housing the greatest proportion of laborers."[8]

In 1928 Wards 16 and 17 had also gone for Al Smith when Pittsburgh was still a Republican town. In 1924 these wards had gone heavily for Robert LaFollette for president on the "Progressive-Socialist" ticket. Before that, they had voted for Socialist Eugene V. Debs. And it was here, among the most loyal CIO-Democratic voters in America, that Democratic mayor and party leader David Lawrence did his worst, losing them outright to the AFL plasterer.

The voting in this 1949 primary election was a mirror image of the pattern set by the coming of the New Deal to Pittsburgh in 1932. In that presidential election, FDR, the Democratic standard bearer, did his best in the South Side Wards 16 and 17, while he lost Squirrel Hill and Shadyside to the Republican Hoover.

Now, Squirrel Hill and Shadyside—the richest and least Catholic wards in the city—were the best wards for the Catholic Democratic standard bearer, while his worst wards were the South Side wards—the poorest and most Catholic in the city. Just ten months before, in November 1948, Squirrel Hill had voted Republican for Tom Dewey over Harry Truman. In 1949, it was still voting "Republican," only this time for David Lawrence instead of Tom Dewey. Meanwhile, Lawrence was rejected by the most militant CIO rank and file, rejected by the most ethnic and most Catholic wards, rejected by the most "Democratic" wards in the city.

Nevertheless, with the backing of President Truman, the CIO leadership, and the support of the city's most affluent voters, Lawrence had won. Having proved his political clout, he would never again face such a strong contender. Lawrence himself viewed this "dramatic primary" as a referendum on his plans to remake the city according to his own vision. "Since that time," he said, there has been "no political challenge . . . The victory . . . had been the signal for a concentrated attack on the entire range of community problems. It was Pittsburgh's breakthrough."[9]

Edward Leonard seems to have been chastened by his defeat, as was the Central Labor Union. But it must have been a bitter defeat. Although, as loyal Democrats, both Leonard and the PCLU endorsed Lawrence for the general election in November, Lawrence made public before the election that he had spurned the PCLU's request for representation on the urban development agencies which would soon realize his Renaissance vision. Labor was to have no voice in the physical reorganization of the city.[10] But, David Lawrence was now the official Democratic Party candidate and the labor movement had nowhere else to go.

Edward Leonard, for his part, chose to go back to his union. He decided not to run for re-election in the next Council election and stepped down to become a high official in, and later president of, the International Plasterers' Union.

After taking his new oath of office in January 1950, David Lawrence immediately set to work with his business allies to remake Pittsburgh. The Renaissance was underway.

Season of the Witch

At the same time that David Lawrence was launching his Republican Renaissance building plans, the Republicans launched another enterprise in Pittsburgh. This was a Red witch hunt of Communists, who were suspected of being the master manipulators of the industrial heartland's easily-led working class, and the cause of all the turmoil in the region.

Initially, the Communist Party had targeted the Pittsburgh region for high-priority agitation following the 1929 Stock Market Crash. As I pointed out in chapter 7, the Communists played a hand in organizing and leading the first Allegheny County Hunger March in June 1931.[11] They also established Unemployed Councils and generated something of a following in the steel town of Ambridge, where they played a role in the big labor confrontation there in 1932.[12]

However, as I also mentioned, the Communists themselves admitted they were having trouble putting down roots in much of the Steel Valley. But, it was not just the mill towns of the Steel Valley in which the Communists were failing. They confessed they were inactive even on Pittsburgh's Polish South Side, perhaps the most volatile and class conscious neighborhood in the city.[13]

Given the status of the region's industrial workers as an oppressed population, and the collective saviour of humanity, destined to usher in the millennium, a good Marxist might presume that they would be more "radical," more "revolutionary," and seek to overthrow American society rather than struggle to become part of American society.

But, as I've demonstrated, there is no evidence in the language or actions of the mass of "proletarians" in the industrial heartland to support these presumptions. The workers did not speak in terms of "the proletariat" or "socialism" and vehemently denied they were "reds." Indeed, most Pittsburgh-area workers were not only passionately patriotic, but also aggressively anti-Communist.

Nevertheless, conditions had changed dramatically for the industrial heartland's working class. It had moved from the periphery to the center of things, from powerlessness to power. I. W. Abel, later president of the USWA, recalled his days as a mill hand in Canton, Ohio, during the 1930s, recalled when the steelworkers had been beaten down and subjugated. "They [the corporations] had arsenals beyond imagination. They [the congressional LaFollette investigations of 1937] revealed how the corporations controlled our local police. They showed how they controlled the sheriffs' offices and, of course, how they controlled the governor of the state of Ohio, who used the troops against us."[14]

But when Phil Murray—head of the USWA and the CIO—died in November 1952, all of Pittsburgh came to a stop to mourn his passing. The man who died was not the local hero of a despised and cast aside people, he was the chieftain of a mighty movement, a power to be reckoned with, which commanded the allegiance of multitudes in Pittsburgh alone.

As Murray's funeral mass was being said in St. Paul's Cathedral on Fifth Avenue in the Oakland section of Pittsburgh, head church of the region's Catholic diocese, "at a prearranged moment in hundreds of steel mills, foundries, and other places of work of his beloved steelworkers, tens of thousands paused from their labor for a minute to pay tribute. It was a measure of the man that such an event could take place, an acknowledgement of stature that even the hard-nosed steel mill owners had to defer to for the occasion."[15]

But such respect and allegiance by "tens of thousands" of Pittsburgh-area workers was a frightening spectacle to many, and not just "hard-nosed steel mill owners." Thus, as David Lawrence put into motion his Republican Renaissance and Phil Murray was buried, the labor movement in Pittsburgh faced a police challenge which marshalled both local and federal power against it.

In response to the continuing intensity of class feeling and class conflict in Pittsburgh—and mistakenly suspecting Communists to be behind it all—the federal government and the local judiciary launched a massive Communist witch hunt. But, while destroying many careers and lives and dominating newspaper headlines, it had negligible impact upon the underlying political loyalties of Pittsburghers.

The workers of Pittsburgh voted Democratic not because Communists told them to, but because they perceived the Democratic Party as "their" party. And they continued to pledge their allegiance to their unions and their union leaders, such as Phil Murray, not because of sectarian Leftist ideology, but because men such as Phil Murray had led them out of the shadows and into the American Promised Land.

Thus, in an era of loyalty oaths and pledges of allegiance to flag and country, Pittsburgh workers continued to honor the leaders of their unions and to swear their political allegiance to the party of labor, the Democratic Party.

****

Witch hunts for the Communists who were presumed to be leading gullible workers astray were not new to the post-war period. They had been afoot even in the Thirties. By the spring of 1940, a congressional committee was at work trying to ferret out the suspected Communists who created and were responsible for labor militancy in the Pittsburgh area. The committee called several Pittsburgh radicals to its hearings, most of whom defied the committee. On March 27, 1940, the committee recommended criminal contempt charges against George Powers, secretary of the Communist Party in Western Pennsylvania, because Powers refused to answer their questions about party membership in the Pittsburgh region.[16]

A week later, Philip Frankfeld, an organizer of the early 1930s Unemployed Committee of Pittsburgh, was held in contempt of Congress because he refused to answer the committee's questions about his activities.[17]

But such early pre-war witch hunts had little impact on the political power balance. Labor was still on the march and political liberalism was still ascendant. In that November's presidential elections, as we have seen, Roosevelt and the Democrats swept labor's strongholds in Western Pennsylvania with unprecedented numbers and class politics was at an all-time high.

Immediately after the war's end, Left populism remained apparent in popular culture. Indicative of this are films such as Capra's *It's A Wonderful Life* (1946) and his *State of the Union* (1948), as well as the non-Capra *Crossfire* (1947) from RKO.

The latter was based upon the Richard Brooks novel, *The Brick Foxhole*, which dealt with the murder of a homosexual soldier by a homophobic fellow soldier. Changing the homosexual to a Jewish war hero, the movie starred Robert Ryan as the Jew-hating G.I. murderer, tracked down by detective Robert Young. Instead of emphasizing the detective aspect, however, the film focussed on the reason for the crime, anti-Semitism, which allowed Robert Young to label the hatred which leads to such violence as "un-American."

But by 1948, the Cold War had begun and with it a chilling of the cultural climate at home. That was the year the Hollywood Blacklist of suspected Communists and fellow travellers began. That was the year the "Hollywood Ten"—including Dalton Trumbo and John Howard Lawson, two of Hollywood's most talented screenwriters—were indicted for contempt for failing to testify before Congress about their possible Communist backgrounds and associates.

Popular author Howard Fast, then a member of the Communist Party, recalled that, "I was terrorized, my kids were threatened. I expected it. I had nothing to hide. The real terror was among people who had something to hide. Those people—I could walk down the street and meet three people I had known for years, and they would all walk past me pretending not to see me for fear for what would happen to them if they said hello."[18]

Indicative of this change was 1948's *The Iron Curtain*, the first of a cycle of anti-Communist films which would soon pour out of Hollywood. From 20th Century-Fox, *Iron Curtain* starred Dana Andrews and Gene Tierney as a Russian couple who defect to America. That same year Republic put out *The Red Menace* in which an innocent war vet is duped by the Commies.

On September 14, 1949, MGM released *The Red Danube,* a heavy-handed film starring Angela Lansbury, Janet Leigh, Peter Lawford, Ethel Barrymore, and Walter Pidgeon. Set in 1945 Vienna, it portrayed the pitiful plight of Soviet refugees pursued by Soviet agents and forced to return behind the Iron Curtain. The next day, September 15, Howard Hughes' RKO opened *I Married a Communist,* starring Robert Ryan. Only the previous year RKO had released *Crossfire* with Ryan. Eager to repudiate such liberal tendencies, RKO now featured Ryan as an all-American opponent of a Communist labor leader.

Indeed, according to Hollywood, it now appeared that all labor leaders were actually Communists in disguise. Hollywood had never portrayed either workers, strikes, or organized labor in very many movies. When such were portrayed, though, it was usually unsympathetically. The turbulent Thirties would have seemed an ideal time for topical films dealing with labor unrest, yet only a handful appeared.

One of the first was *Black Fury,* released in 1935. The movie was based upon a script by prominent Pittsburgh judge and author Michael Angelo Musmanno, who had investigated mining conditions in Pennsylvania. The original story dealt with a 1929 strike in the coal mines during which a miner had been beaten to death by Pennsylvania's infamous Coal and Iron Police. The original script "was a hard-hitting indictment of the coal mining industry. It begins with a list of mining disasters and bloody strikes dating back to the turn of the century . . . The script goes on to describe a plot by the mine owners to break their contract with the workers in order to take advantage of depressed wage levels. They hire a detective agency which sends in an agent to infiltrate the union and create a strike. This enables the owners to charge the union with breaking its contract and allows them to import scabs protected by the iron and coal police. The cruelty of the police, who are nothing more than uniformed thugs, leads to a confrontation with the strikers in which 35 people are killed including a ten-year-old boy."[19]

After going through the Hollywood meat grinder, the completed film bore little resemblance to the pro-worker story Judge Musmanno wrote. "In the new version, the company's labor relations are generally favorable and it is no longer the owners who are interested in breaking the contract. Instead, we are presented with an industrial detective agency that foments strikes in order to hire out guards and strike-breakers to management. The agency sends a man in to stir up unrest, but even here the script is careful to avoid any mention of the real problems that existed in the mining industry. The agent limits his attack on the company to peripheral complaints unlikely to excite any Depression-era audience. "For a time, the agent is thwarted by the head of the local union who reminds his members that 'things ain't as bad as they used to be, and they're gettin' better all the time.'"[20]

Eventually, however, the agent is successful in provoking a strike. The intelligent and benevolent mine president declares that, "We tried to play ball

. . . by granting them everything we reasonably could." A court clears the way for the hiring of strike-breakers, protected by the scheming detective agency. "But even at this point, the company exhibits compassion for the workers as the president warns the agency to avoid any abuse or mistreatment of the strikers."[21] Eventually, all is revealed as a misunderstanding and the company and strikers rejoice and go back to work together. Fade to black.[22]

A similar transformation was wrought on Richard Llewellyn's best-selling 1940 novel, *How Green Was My Valley.* The novel "told the story of the gradual disintegration of a Welsh family and the disappearance of their way of life against the background of a troubled coal industry."[23]

Darryl F. Zanuck, head of 20th Century-Fox, bought the film rights and then vetoed the faithful first script his screen adapter produced. He felt his writer had produced what he called "a labor story and a sociological problem story instead of a great human, warm story about real living people." He also objected to the portrayal of the mine owners who were seen as "nothing but villains with mustaches. That might have been all right a little while ago, but I'll be damned if I want to go around making the employer class out-and-out villains in this day and age." He claimed the script was an attack on the English capitalist class similar to Steinbeck's *The Grapes of Wrath,* about which nobody "gives a damn."[24]

Thus, the film became a neutered and nostalgic story of the "common people" in which "All that was left of anything hinting of labor militancy were two brief scenes ultimately amounting to two minutes of screen time." The bosses were portrayed favorably, the radicalism of the workers virtually disappeared, and labor unrest hardly existed, as the novel's major strike "all but disappears . . . We know nothing about the issues that triggered the strike, how the strike was conducted, or for that matter, how the strike was resolved."[25]

The career of director King Vidor is itself indicative of the arc film making went through during this period. In 1934 Vidor wrote and directed *Our Daily Bread*, along with *The Grapes of Wrath,* one of the most socially conscious big budget films to come out of the Thirties. Produced independently of the studio system, *Our Daily Bread* was criticized as Communist propaganda because of its optimistic faith in the common sense of the common people.

The film followed an idealistic city couple who inherited an uncultivated farm. Welcoming other displaced families to their acreage, they took part in the birth of a utopia built upon the barter system, shared labor, and equality for all. The anarchist utopia which was joyously created was offered up as the obvious solution for national economic recovery.

A decade later, however, Vidor seems to have lost his faith in the common sense of the common man. In King Vidor's 1944 *An American Miracle,* we find such docile and mind-befogged workers that they beg the boss' son to be their spokesman. Vidor wanted the story, based on his own idea, to be a paean to the capitalists "who made this country what it is and will save it."

And indeed it was such a paean, as the story was told as the heroic life of a captain of industry who worked his way up—like Henry Ford—to head his own automobile company. At a climactic scene when a delegation of workers file into the directors' board room to present their case, it is Teddy, the boss' son, who presents the case for the sheepish workers.

"Teddy informs the board that the workers have no intention of telling management how to run its business. 'In fact,' he concedes, 'most of us are willing to admit that we are not good enough to be where you are.' All the workers want is to be just part of the team and one way of accomplishing this is through a union." Swayed by his son's reasonable request, the tolerant father allows the formation of a union.

"Once again we are presented with workers who are incapable of managing their own affairs . . . And although Teddy talks about a partnership between management and labor, the film makes it clear that the strength of the American economy lies in the ingenuity and hard work of its captains of industry."[26]

A similar view was presented the next year in 1945's *Valley of Decision*. Based on the novel by Marcia Davenport, it was set in the Pittsburgh iron industry during the 1870s and was the seventh highest grossing film of the year. Both the novel and the film are about a love story across class lines set in Pittsburgh's Steel Valley, the "Valley of Decision."

In the film, Greer Garson plays the Irish Catholic working class girl who throws her lot in with the Protestant iron-mill owning family for whom she goes to work as a maid. Gregory Peck is the owner's son who loves her and who eventually takes over the family business from his crotchety old father, Lionel Barrymore. Although Garson's misguided brother attempts to stir up trouble among the workers against Barrymore and son, Gregory Peck is so reasonable, so understanding, so benevolent, that the trouble-maker is soon isolated and all ends happily.

Interestingly, though both the novel and the movie purport to portray Pittsburgh labor relations in the decade of the 1870s, neither makes the slightest reference to the cataclysmic railroad strike of 1877. This strike turned Pittsburgh into a massive battleground and was not only one of the biggest things which ever happened in Pittsburgh, but part of the greatest labor upheaval anywhere on earth for the entire century between 1800 and 1900.

After 1945, however, Hollywood was a little more willing to portray labor strife. Only now it was the Communists who were stirring up the otherwise happy workers, around the country and in Pittsburgh. The Steel City, thought to be a center of powerful and influential Communist labor leaders, was portrayed as a battleground in Hollywood pictures—as indeed it was in real life, though not with the protagonists Hollywood portrayed.

Pittsburgh, declared David Caute, was "The violent epicenter of the anti-Communist eruption in postwar America . . . From 1947 onward the press was pumping anti-Communism into every artery of Pittsburgh. From April 11 until April 30, 1948, the Scripps-Howard *Pittsburgh Press* published the names, addresses and places of employment of about one thousand citizens who had signed [Henry] Wallace nominating petitions. At the great Westinghouse plant a campaign conducted by Father Charles Owen Rice and the Association of Catholic Trade Unionists, vigorously supported by the priests from their pulpits, culminated in a victory for the anti-Communist IUE-CIO, led by James B. Carey, over the pro-Communist United Electrical Workers [UE].

"Hearst's *Pittsburgh Sun-Telegraph*, the *Pittsburgh Post-Gazette* and other local papers joined in the witch hunt by blazoning the names, addresses and employers of the red termites across their pages. Nearly one hundred people lost their jobs in short time, notably at U.S. Steel, Etna Steel, and the Crucible Steel Company." Union members were expelled and perhaps 200 people were hounded out of town.[27]

The federal government made Pittsburgh a focus of its attention because of the very militancy of the local labor movement, a militancy presumably fomented by Communists. In addition, it seemed anti-Communist efforts might actually be successful in the Pittsburgh region because of the religious and ethnic background of Pittsburghers. "In heavily Catholic Pittsburgh," for instance, "the repression of the church in eastern Europe by Soviet-initiated Communist regimes engendered an especially emotional response. Anxiety soon turned into overt hostility as American Catholic leaders in defense of their religion denounced 'Christ-hating Communists . . . men who as their God know only Satan and Stalin.'"[28]

Much of this anti-Communist crusade in Pittsburgh was under the leadership of Judge Blair F. Gunther and Harry Alan Sherman, the organizers and leaders of Americans Battling Communism (ABC), "a local group whose membership included some of Pittsburgh's most prominent citizens."[29] Judge Gunther, who would later be elected to the State Supreme Court, was a powerful figure in the Pennsylvania Republican Party, while Sherman was a former Assistant District Attorney who focussed much of his activity on the UE locals at Westinghouse, which he termed, "a labor front for the activities of the Communist Party."[30]

The irony of all this furor, however, is that even J. Edgar Hoover acknowledged that the Communist presence in Pittsburgh, and even Pennsylvania as a whole, was miniscule, with only 2,875 Communist Party members in all of Pennsylvania as of June 1950, according to the FBI's own figures.[31] In addition, the small number of Communists in the industrial heartland had virtually no support or influence among the region's industrial workers. In truth, Republicans, the business elite, and legal agencies had absolutely no idea what motivated Pittsburgh's workers and why they were angry, aggressive, and class conscious. So they turned to the most obvious scapegoat.

And so the anti-Communist hysteria continued for a decade. In November 1953, the U.S. Senate sent Senator John M. Butler to Pittsburgh to conduct hearings on continuing Communist influence in the United Electrical Workers locals in Pittsburgh and Erie. "The subpoena of John W. Nelson, an official of UE's Local 506 at the Erie plant of General Electric, was the bugle call for a new wave of mass firings. Pittsburgh was the worst area for 'run-outs.' On March 30, 1954, Westinghouse dismissed Thomas J. Fitzpatrick, former president of UE Local 601, and Frank Pazio, former UE business agent in East Pittsburgh.

"In January 1955, Westinghouse Electric in Pittsburgh dismissed five workers named as Communists before McCarthy's Permanent Subcommittee on Investigations. It was two months later when the black Communist leader

Benjamin Davis, Jr., was taken straight to Pittsburgh county jail on his release from a federal penitentiary, to serve a sixty-day sentence for contempt handed down to him when he testified as a defense witness for [Steve] Nelson."[32]

Indeed, the legal persecution of Communist leader Steve Nelson was a centerpiece of the anti-Communist hysteria in Pittsburgh. In fact, Nelson, under another name, was portrayed in a major Hollywood film of the period in the act of murdering someone, virtually the one "crime" the courts never actually accused him of. The film was the 1951 Warner Brothers release, *I Was A Communist for the FBI*.

By 1951 the ideological battle lines had become hardened and this Warner Bros. film agreed with prevailing sentiment by presenting Pittsburgh as the storm center of America's domestic ideological war. The director was Gordon Douglas, who directed thirty "Our Gang" comedies during the Thirties, including *Bored of Education,* which won an Oscar in 1936 for best one-reel film. Douglas broke into feature films in 1940 when he directed Laurel and Hardy's comedy *Saps at Sea.* Unfortunately, *I Was A Communist for the FBI* was no comedy.[33]

Told in an almost documentary style (indeed, it was nominated for an Academy Award for Best Documentary), the film was the story of Matt Cvetic, "a simple Pittsburgh steelworker" who attends a meeting of the "Pittsburgh Steel Union and discovers it is a hot-bed of communist sympathizers."[34]

The Communists in the film are portrayed as cynical vermin who will tell any lie in an effort to destroy all that is American. They denigrate intellectuals, teachers, and the ordinary workers who believe in them, but " . . . save their most savage remarks for people of liberal political leanings. They sarcastically explain that such well-meaning 'bleeding hearts' can easily be exploited to cause economic problems because of their belief in causes like the civil rights movement. Negroes in particular are depicted as being an easy mark, as well as laborers and union members—especially those who would under any circumstances consider a strike."[35]

In one compelling scene, the Steve Nelson character sends Communist thugs with lead pipes wrapped in Yiddish newspapers to beat into silence union officers trying to end a Communist instigated strike at a Pittsburgh steel mill.

Matt Cvetic, played by Frank Lovejoy, turns out to be an FBI informer who gains the confidence of his comrades and rises in their ranks. As a trusted member, he attends a lavish Communist Party banquet "in a plush hotel suite, where they stuff themselves on caviar and guzzle bottles of expensive wine. But when Cvetic complains to one of the ringleaders that this is a far cry from the dedicated speeches which brought him into the organization, the man snaps back: 'This is the way we're *all* gonna live after we take over the country!' The implication, of course, is that communism—besides being an incorrect approach to the problems of America and the world—lacks even the saving grace of sincerity, as its leaders are cynically living off the work of those naive fools who labor for their cause."[36]

The world premiere of this film was at Pittsburgh's downtown Stanley Theater on April 19, 1951, the anniversary of the day the first shots were fired in the American Revolutionary War at Lexington and Concord. Mayor David

Lawrence attended the film's premiere and declared April 19 to be "Matt Cvetic Day" in Pittsburgh at a special luncheon held in Cvetic's honor at the William Penn Hotel. It turned out that Matt Cvetic was an actual Pittsburgher. Following the luncheon, a parade formed in front of the Allegheny County Courthouse on Grant Street, where a state sedition trial just happened to be in progress against local Communists Andrew Onda and Jim Dolsen.[37]

I Was a Communist for the FBI became a successful radio serial in 1952-53 with well-known Hollywood actor Dana Andrews portraying Matt Cvetic. This paved the way for a popular 1953-56 TV series which told a similar story. Entitled *I Led Three Lives,* the TV series starred Richard Carlson, who also starred in many science fiction and horror films in the 1950s, most notably 1954's *Creature from the Black Lagoon.* The series was based on the best-selling autobiography of the same title by Herbert Philbrick. The TV show was approved by the FBI and FBI Director J. Edgar Hoover even reviewed the scripts.

Narrated by Philbrick's character and told in a documentary style, it always opened with the announcer telling the viewer that this was the "fantastically true story of Herbert A. Philbrick, who for nine frightening years did lead three lives," that of an ordinary family man working in advertising, a secret Communist Party member of which even his wife knew nothing, and FBI informant.

It seems that in the 1940s, Philbrick had joined the Massachusetts Youth Council, which he thought was a peace group. Learning that it was a Communist front organization, he went to the FBI. In turn, the FBI convinced him to stay in the organization and recruited him as their internal spy. Over the years Philbrick rose to become a top member of the New England section of the Communist Party, feeding the FBI information all the while. It was his information which was credited with the arrest and imprisonment of the top eleven New England Communists when the organization was eventually outlawed.[38]

And so, like Herb Philbrick, Matt Cvetic, the hero of *I Was a Communist for the FBI* who launched this genre, was also real. Further, Cvetic and Steve Nelson were not only reel life antagonists, but real life antagonists, as well. They were at the center of what David Caute called, "Hell in Pittsburgh."

Steve Nelson, claims Caute, was "The red bogeyman of the Pittsburgh area."[39] Born Stephen Mesarosh, he was a carpenter who had attended the Moscow Lenin School, had been a Communist Party leader in Pennsylvania's anthracite coal district, and had served as the last leader of the Abraham Lincoln Brigade in the Spanish Civil War. While fighting with those American volunteers for the Spanish Republic against Franco's fascist military rebellion, he had been wounded. By 1948 he was back in Pittsburgh as the chairman of the region's Communist Party.

Nelson's troubles began in late February 1950, when Matthew Cvetic testified for six days before the U.S. House Un-American Activities Committee (HUAC) as a friendly witness. Cvetic was an emotionally unstable alcoholic who had joined the Pittsburgh local of the Communist Party at the urging of the FBI. Since 1937 Cvetic had worked as a placement interviewer at a Pittsburgh branch office of the U.S. Employment Service. According to the FBI agent in charge of the Pittsburgh office, the Bureau had long been concerned about "Communists" who worked at the Employment Service and "who exert a tremendous influence over . . . policies and personnel." Cvetic, therefore, was one of several informants contacted by the FBI to keep "an eye open for Communists infiltrating our war plants," which Cvetic agreed to do in April 1941.[40]

Cvetic began attending Communist Party meetings and rallies, became a vocal supporter of Communists at work and elsewhere, and aided in finding party members jobs they otherwise would not have gotten due to his position at the Employment Service. By February 1943, he had become a party member himself. For the next seven years, he served as a low-level party functionary and paid FBI informer. In early 1950 he surfaced and began to testify against his erstwhile comrades and their infiltration of the Pittsburgh labor movement, particularly UE Local 610 at Westinghouse, and most particularly the activities of local Communist leader Steve Nelson.

Cvetic's testimony before HUAC came at an emotional crest of the witch hunt hysteria. As Daniel Leab reminds us, "His testimony came only a few months after the nation's second largest labor organization, the Congress of Industrial Organizations, purged itself of various Communist-influenced unions (including its third largest affiliate, the UE, which had over 500,000 members); it took place just weeks after the conviction of Alger Hiss for perjury; and it followed only days after Senator Joseph McCarthy had burst onto the national scene with his conflicting statements about Communists working in the State Department," a charge McCarthy leveled near Pittsburgh in a speech in Wheeling, West Virginia.[41] Cvetic's accusations thus garnered maximum publicity, especially back home in Pittsburgh where ABC leaders Gunther and Sherman were using Cvetic's testimony to fuel their local anti-Communist crusade.

On August 31, 1950, a local judge and ABC member named Michael Angelo Musmanno—the same Musmanno who had authored the novel upon which the film *Black Fury* was based—got into the act by leading a raid, with Matt Cvetic in tow, on Steve Nelson's Communist Party headquarters. Musmanno was a contradictory figure. He had championed the case of Sacco and Vanzetti, had supported the New Deal, and viewed himself as a friend of labor.

Yet, as a young man, he had studied law in Mussolini's Fascist Italy, from whence he wrote a letter to the *Pittsburgh Press* praising "the heroic work of the Fascisti in driving Bolshevism from the country when the Fascisti began their purification of Italian soil."[42] Evidently, he considered his raid on Pittsburgh's Communist Party headquarters part of the same "heroic work" of "driving Bolshevism from the country."

In the party's Grant Street office across from the County Court House, Musmanno seized a pile of papers, some of which he later turned over to HUAC. Clutching these, he hurried to the office of another Allegheny County judge to request a warrant for Nelson's arrest, as well as those of Andrew Onda and Jim Dolsen, under the Pennsylvania state sedition law. This law had been passed in 1919 to deal with the Great Steel Strike of that year. These actions catapulted Musmanno into the public spotlight, which was exactly where he wanted to be, as he was at that time running for Democratic lieutenant governor. He didn't win that office, but he would soon be elected to the State Supreme Court for a twenty-year term, along with his friend and fellow ABC jurist, Blair Gunther.

Meanwhile, the trials of the three Pittsburgh Communists began the next year. First, Andrew Onda and Jim Dolsen were brought before the bar. "During the trial the local press lampooned the defense and published hearsay accusations linking Nelson to wartime atomic espionage. To encourage the jury a bit . . . United States marshals chose the moment that Onda was making his final statement to the jury to arrest him and Dolsen under the Smith Act . . . On August 31, 1951, Dolsen, the 68-year-old Pittsburgh correspondent of the [Party's] *Daily Worker,* and Onda [director of the Party's activities among steelworkers] were sentenced to twenty years' imprisonment and a fine of $10,000 for a crime—in fact, neither man had done anything at all—that Judge Henry X. O'Brien characterized as 'worse than murder' and comparable to that of the Rosenbergs."[43]

In December 1951, Steve Nelson's postponed sedition trial began, despite the fact that no local lawyer would defend him. The prosecutor was William A. Cercone, a nephew of Musmanno, and Musmanno had appointed as trial judge Harry M. Montgomery, a leading member, like so much of the Pittsburgh judiciary, of Americans Battling Communism. Appearing as a witness to testify against Nelson was ABC member Judge Michael Musmanno himself, who waved the books and magazines he'd seized at Communist headquarters and declared, "I regard these books as more dangerous than any firearms."[44]

Matt Cvetic also testified against Nelson, justifying the depiction of the Steve Nelson character in his film committing a fictitious murder on the grounds that Nelson once told him that "there would be a liquidation of one third of the United States population" after the Communists took over.

On the eve of the jury's verdict, a juror proclaimed his belief in Nelson's innocence in a local bar. "After a thorough beating, he was brought into court painted in iodine, accompanied by detectives, and no longer convinced of Nelson's innocence. Montgomery then handed down not only the maximum sentence of twenty years' imprisonment and a $10,000 fine . . . but also ordered that Nelson should pay the court costs of $13,291, which covered the expenses of Matt Cvetic and his fellow prosecution witnesses."[45]

Nelson was shipped off to brutal years in the Blawnox Workhouse while his appeals worked their way through the judicial system. His state sedition conviction was eventually reversed by the Pennsylvania Superior Court on the grounds that the federal Smith Act superseded the state sedition act. In April 1956, the U.S. Supreme Court upheld this reasoning.

In the meantime, however, Nelson and his comrades had been convicted and sentenced under that same Smith Act, in a trial in which Cvetic again appeared as a prime witness. Because of numerous judicial irregularities, the U.S. Supreme Court granted Nelson and his comrades a new trial in October 1956.

Meanwhile, Matt Cvetic's lucrative career as a professional ex-Communist came crashing down in the summer of 1955 when, on June 10-11, he testified before the Senate Internal Security Subcommittee. The bulk of his testimony this time around concerned the alleged Communist affiliations of former SWOC leader, current USWA official, and current Clairton Mayor John J. Mullen. Along with Elmer Maloy, his friend and fellow SWOC leader, John Mullen had been elected to office in the huge tidal wave of CIO-Democratic municipal victories in 1937.

This time, however, Cvetic's allegations did not go unchallenged, as Mayor Mullen also testified before the committee and put an end to Cvetic's career. Mayor Mullen "systematically and convincingly contradicting the allegations. Subsequently, the Department of Justice formally 'disapproved the use of Cvetic as a witness in Government prosecution.'"[46]

Following this debacle, in June 1957, the federal government decided to drop the Smith Act charges against Nelson and his comrades, in which Cvetic's testimony would have been crucial. The strong opposition of labor and political leader John J. Mullen was the waterbreak against which the Pittsburgh witch hunt finally broke and then began to recede.

By the late Fifties the hysteria had lost most of its power and influence, although Judge Musmanno, HUAC, the Senate Internal Security Subcommittee, the American Legion, and the VFW would all join forces in the early Sixties for one last witch hunt. This time it was against Dr. Robert Colodny, a professor of history at the University of Pittsburgh. Colodny was revealed to have been wounded fighting for the Republic as a member of the Abraham Lincoln Brigade during the Spanish Civil War. But by the Sixties, the times they were a-changin' and, after much sound and fury, Robert Colodny remained on the history faculty at Pitt, finally retiring in the 1990s.

In the final analysis, despite the decade's parade of charlatans and Communists, the headlines about witch hunters and their victims which dominated this period, little of it penetrated beneath the surface to touch the underlying political loyalties of American voters. Indeed, few even cared greatly about the spectacle of the age. In one national survey in the early 1950s, fewer than 1 percent of those interviewed volunteered Communism as something they worried about. Rather, it seemed the witch hunt was conducted by conservative elites—as in Pittsburgh where judges like Musmanno led the crusade as founders of Americans Battling Communism. Simply, "The poll data did not suggest a mass political uprising over the question of communism."[47]

And why should there have been one? Most people realized Communist influence was insignificant and irrelevant to their real world of work and politics. Thus, during the 1952 presidential election, polling data indicated that "less than 3 percent expressed concern over Communists in government—fewer than referred to the Point Four program."[48] Instead, those who supported the witch hunt were conservatives who opposed New Deal and Fair Deal liberalism anyway. The isolated and vulnerable Communists were just a convenient whipping boy, and the Red Scare was just the latest cudgel with which to belabor the opposition.

Meanwhile, liberals, Democrats, union members, and the working class in general opposed the hysteria and cleaved as strongly as ever to their political loyalties. Especially among working class voters, "The evidence does not suggest that the Communist issue preoccupied the lower classes, or that they were using that issue to vent general grievances about their position in society."[49]

This may be one reason that red-baiting crusades were not as immediately successful among many unionists as labor leaders assumed they would be. In the spring of 1949, for instance, the United Steelworkers, which had joined the CIO hierarchy's anti-Communist crusade, launched a war on a number of unions which actually did have Communists among their leadership. One of these was the Mine, Mill, and Smelter Workers.

Locals of Mine, Mill in Bessemer and Red Mountain, Alabama, were particular targets of a vicious campaign. Through violence, intimidation, and appeals to anti-Communism, the USW was able to win a decertification election at the Red Mountain Mine, Mill local—but only by 463 votes out of nearly 5,000 cast. Indeed, Mine, Mill's 2,000 black members were virtually unanimous in voting for continued membership in Mine, Mill. Similarly, "In Montana and Connecticut, the Steelworkers found that even campaigns of virulent red-baiting could not dissuade copper miners and brass workers from demonstrating their loyalty to Mine, Mill."[50]

The United Auto Workers had similar difficulty in raiding locals of Farm Equipment (FE), a farm implement union with "Communist" tendencies. And in Erie and Pittsburgh, a savage battle to destroy the United Electrical Workers also met with mixed success. Pittsburgh's labor priest, Rev. Charles Owen Rice, had joined the campaign against "Communist" Local 610 of UE, which represented workers at Union Switch and Signal in nearby Turtle Creek and Westinghouse Air Brake Co. (WABCO) in the similarly nearby Wilmerding. A "Red" majority had won overwhelmingly in union elections there in October 1947, despite a relentless attack upon them by Rev. Rice in his newspaper columns.

"By the close of the year, it was clear to Rice that what had to be done in both locals was to convince members that communism was not only an issue, but *the* issue that overrode all others, even those of traditional bread-and-butter unionism. He had been selling this line in his column for years, but the membership obviously had not been buying."[51]

Similarly, UE workers elsewhere were not buying Rice's anti-communism, as he complained that "Sharon, Erie, Fairmont, and Wilmerding have all been won by the Reds" in union elections in late 1949. Indeed, the workers in Erie, Pennsylvania, voted "Red" by a three-to-one margin, despite the fact that Rice and his colleagues "had given it all they had, had driven hundreds of miles, and harangued hundreds and thousands of union members that communism in the UE was *the* issue. But they had not succeeded in winning the majority of members to their viewpoint, at least not so far as evidenced in union elections for local control."[52]

In fact, there was less "Communism" here than charged. In chapter 7, for example, I reported the experience of Erie UE member Thomas Brown. Tom Brown, a General Electric worker in Erie, had helped found the "Leftist" United Electrical Workers union there. He recalled that, later, "In the 1940s, when we got so big and powerful, a 'Red-scare' came into the picture. They dragged us through all the mud and slime and everything they could think of. What they did to the electrical workers from the Atlantic to the Pacific you could never replace. Many guys went to their graves condemned. They crucified the guys . . . I went through that Red smear. I know what it was like. Christ, you come out of church on a Sunday morning and the priest would say, 'Hey, you still with the Red union? Why don't you think it over?' . . . this stuff of trying to be Communists was from people who were out of their minds. None of us were Communists."⁵³

Eventually, the UE locals in Sharon and Fairmont would be ousted by their CIO-sponsored rival, the International Union of Electrical Workers (IUE), but UE Local 610 in Wilmerding and the Erie UE local would both be left alone after 1949, unassailable bastions of supposed "Red" unionism.

Meanwhile, victory in a three-year crusade led by Rice and others against UE Local 601 at the Westinghouse plant in East Pittsburgh (during which Rice persuaded HUAC to come to town to hold public interrogations of his union antagonists) "remained nearly as elusive as ever." Eventually, however, Local 601 was disenfranchised in favor of the CIO's IUE. "It is important to recognize, however, that their victory [Rice's and the CIO] had not come through the union ballot box . . . It had come instead via an authoritative pronouncement from CIO headquarters . . . [as part of their] secede-and-purge tactics." This was despite Rice's earlier belief that, "The business of purges is the last resort of desperate men."⁵⁴

There is no reason to believe such purges made many converts among unionists, however, and they certainly did not alter fundamental political allegiances. A breakdown of those who supported or opposed the witch hunt illustrates the enduring political attitudes of both sides. "[P]erhaps the single most important characteristic of supporters of McCarthy in the national opinion polls was their party affiliation; Democrats opposed McCarthy, and Republicans supported him. In April 1954, Democrats outnumbered Republicans more than two to one among those having an unfavorable opinion of McCarthy . . . Totaling support for McCarthy in a series of Gallup Polls in the early 1950s reveals that 36 percent of the Democrats favored McCarthy while 44 percent opposed him. The comparable Republican figures were 61 percent for and 25 percent against . . . The total percentage point spread by party was 44 points. In these polls . . . no other single division of the population (by religion, class, education, and so forth) even approached the party split.

"Similarly, in October 1954, respondents were asked whether they would be more or less likely to vote for a candidate endorsed by McCarthy. The strong Republicans split evenly, the strong Democrats were five to one against the senator, and the weak and independent Democrats divided four to one against McCarthy."⁵⁵

Perhaps not surprisingly, support for Senator McCarthy also closely paralleled conservative and liberal attitudes toward the political and economic questions of the time. On a host of foreign policy issues, McCarthy supporters held "right-wing preferences," while economic conservatives also disproportionately supported him. Polls which revealed antagonism toward strikes, federal health care, and liberalism in general also revealed greater support for McCarthy among those who held these views.

Meanwhile, "union membership significantly increased the opposition to McCarthy among laborers" and "The anti-business, pro-labor group was more anti-McCarthy than any other group." Thus, polling data at the time "locates McCarthy's roots in existing political cleavages."[56]

These political cleavages—besides being along party and class lines—were also along another fault line with which we have by now become familiar: The rural vs. urban breakdown. Even in Wisconsin, the state which sent McCarthy to the senate, public opinion polls and voting returns revealed that his support was among farmers in rural counties, while urban workers voted against him. An electoral map of Wisconsin would show heavy Democratic voting in Milwaukee, Madison, and other urban areas, with McCarthy's support coming from the rural counties of the state. Thus, rural Republicans, primarily the "traditional right wing of the midwestern Republican Party," constituted a major element in McCarthy's popular following. "Here was a group to whom McCarthy was a hero. He seemed to embody all their hopes and frustrations. These were the militants in the McCarthy movement. They worked hardest for him and were preoccupied with his general targets. To them, communism was not the whole story; their enemies were also the symbols of welfare capitalism and cosmopolitanism."[57]

Yet even in the Midwest, "this appeal had its greatest impact upon activists and elites, not upon the rank and file voters. And while McCarthy mobilized the Republican right wing, he did not change its traditional alliances. This was not a 'new' American Right, but rather an old one with new enthusiasm and new power." Thus, while the McCarthyite witch hunt destroyed many lives and careers and chilled the nation's political atmosphere, it was not because he led a new mass movement which had won the hearts and minds of the urban working class. "In so far as McCarthy challenged political decisions, political individuals, and the political fabric, he was sustained *not by a revolt of the masses* so much as by the actions and inactions of various elites."[58]

Despite all the sturm und drang of the witch hunts, an Inquisition conducted and supported by Republican-leaning elites, none of it touched bedrock political loyalties. There was no winning of hearts and minds during the period, least of all among workers. "We know from our national surveys that the proportions of the electorate identifying themselves as Democrats or Republicans did not change throughout the eight years of the Eisenhower administration. In 1960, when the candidacy of Mr. Eisenhower was no longer a consideration, the vote swung strongly back toward the 'normal' Democratic majority."[59] Indeed, "From 1952 through 1964, the proportion of strong Democratic and Republican party identifiers fluctuated in a narrow range between 36 percent and 40 percent."[60]

The witch hunt, then, in Pittsburgh and nationally, was irrelevant to political realities. It was a drama full of sound and fury, signifying nothing. It was a storm whipping the surface of the ocean, while the tidal currents swept on underneath, unroiled and unaltered.

Democratic Ascendancy

These tidal currents were the social changes of all those decades since the turn of the century enumerated in chapter 3. It wasn't the Communist Party which was the cause of working class militancy and political upheaval in America at this time. It was the reality of working class life, intersecting with the beliefs workers cherished most dearly. It was these realities, and these beliefs, which had brought on the twenty years of upheaval. It was these realities and these beliefs which had permanently changed America.

And, at the beginning of the 1950s, certain things in American economic and political life had changed so much that Republicans dared not repudiate them once they came into office. One of these was the belief that the government had a responsibility to insure the economic security of the body politic.

In 1931 President Hoover had rejected government's power to do anything about the economy, declaring that some people "have indomitable confidence that by some legerdemain we can legislate ourselves out of a world-wide depression. Such views are as accurate as the belief that we can exorcise a Caribbean hurricane."[61]

The experience of the Great Depression proved that economic conditions were not manifestations of God's will, but of human activity. As such, politicians were henceforth held responsible for the economy. Thus, the Employment Act of 1946 established a permanent Council of Economic Advisors to the President to keep him abreast of economic developments and advise him on means to keep the economy healthy.

Thus, when campaigning for the presidency in 1952, Republican candidate Dwight D. Eisenhower came to Pittsburgh and pledged to Pittsburgh's workers that, "Never again shall we allow a depression in the United States . . . [As soon as we] foresee the signs of any recession and depression . . . the full power of private industry, of municipal government, of state government, of the Federal Government will be mobilized to see that that does not happen. I cannot pledge you more than that."

He reiterated his Pittsburgh pledge to the people of Yonkers, New York, where he said that he had "repeated this particular pledge over and over again in the United States" and that he and his party were "dedicated to this proposition."[62] (Even with this "Pittsburgh pledge" and with his great personal popularity, however, Eisenhower lost Allegheny County in the 1952 election and barely won Pennsylvania, 2,415,789 votes to Adlai Stevenson's 2,146,269.)[63]

In addition, contemporary social observers at the end of the 1930s had felt that "the spirit of the age" was "progressing . . . [toward] fuller economic equality," but this was more than just the "spirit of the age."[64] Economically, a "Great Leveling" indeed took place in America between 1935-50, the only period in our history during which income distribution was so altered. The share of the national income "earned" by the top 20 percent of all American families during these years declined by 12 percent. At the same time, the share of the bottom 20 percent increased by 17 percent. The distribution of mean family income reflected the same changes. The mean income for the bottom 60 percent of families increased between 75 percent-80 percent, while the mean for the top 20 percent increased only 33 percent.[65]

This "Great Leveling" was accompanied by an intensity of blue collar class consciousness which astounded contemporary sociologists. Writing in 1949, one of them flatly declared that, "Americans have become class conscious, and a part of them, calling themselves the working class, have begun to have attitudes and beliefs at variance with traditional acceptances and practices."[66]

In the same year, Daniel Bell interpreted President Truman's pronouncement that Americans as a whole had "rejected the discredited theory that the fortunes of the nation should be in the hands of a privileged few" as symbolic of the fact that America had been dramatically transformed by an "Un-Marxist Revolution" since the beginning of the Great Depression.[67]

Politics are the result of social change. Thus, in Pennsylvania, once the most safely Republican state in the nation, such profound socio-economic changes were reflected in the increased viability of labor's party, the Democratic Party, throughout the 1950s. "[S]ince the realignment of the 1930s," for instance, "both parties have contested every statewide office in Pennsylvania as a matter of course . . . In the period 1956-62 there have been 840 general election contests for the Pennsylvania House of Representatives. Of these, all but six, or 0.7 percent, have been contested by both major political parties. No Pennsylvania State Senate seat has been uncontested during this period."[68]

This Democratic Party dominance was made possible because, even during the entire period of the 1950s Red Scare, Democratic Party voter registration continued to gain on Republican registration. Again, changes in Pennsylvania reflect the national trend. In successive gubernatorial elections during this period, Republican vote totals steadily fell, while Democratic totals steadily rose (table 7). Republican voters, it would seem, were more apathetic than Democrats on election day, a reversal of current patterns. And, by 1960, Democratic registration at last outnumbered Republican registration in the state as a whole for the first time.

Table 7
Pennsylvania Party Registration and Gubernatorial Vote,
1946-1956

Year	Party Registration		Gubernatorial Vote	
	GOP	Democratic	GOP	Democratic
1946	2,737,279	1,854,080	1,828,462	1,270,947
1948	2,864,029	1,810,517	....	....
1950	2,772,778	1,930,916	1,796,119	1,710,355
1952	3,130,078	2,136,511	....	....
1954	2,995,971	2,088,857	1,717,070	1,996,266
1956	2,897,307	2,450,396	....	....

Source: Edward F. Cooke and G. Edward Janosik, *Guide to Pennsylvania Politics*, Greenwood Press: Westport, Conn., 1957, Tables 3 and 4, p. 13, 15.

A major reason Pennsylvania became more politically competitive over the course of the late Forties and Fifties was because the New Deal finally triumphed in Philadelphia. In 1951 the city belatedly experienced its own "mini-realignment" and elected Democrat Joseph S. Clark, Jr., as mayor.

Democratic strength had been steadily gaining in this Republican bastion throughout the Thirties and Forties. Indeed, in the 1950 municipal elections, Democrat Richardson Dilworth had upset the Republican machine for the first time in the twentieth century by winning the city treasurer post. His surprise upset catapulted him to the Democratic gubernatorial nomination in 1950 and, though he lost the state by 85,764 votes, this obscure municipal office holder carried both Pittsburgh and Philadelphia.

Nevertheless, although voting Democratic nationally and in state elections, "This great metropolitan city had remained loyal to the Republican Party [in local elections] even during the peak years of Democratic popularity in the Thirties and Forties. Philadelphia was one of the few urban areas in the entire country which had not come under Democratic control. In 1951, and again in 1955, a revitalized Democratic organization, under new leadership, swept to victory. The other great metropolitan area, Allegheny County, strongly Democratic since 1932, turned out larger Democratic pluralities."[69]

Based upon these increasing Democratic margins of victory in Allegheny County, and Philadelphia's delayed mini-realignment, Democrats again took control of the state in the 1954 elections. Not only did the Democrats elect George M. Leader as Governor, they also elected Pittsburgher Genevieve Blatt as Secretary of Internal Affairs. Blatt thus became the first woman ever elected to any statewide office in Pennsylvania history.

Additionally, the Democrats elected a majority of Pennsylvania's U.S. Representatives, took control of the state House of Representatives for the first time since 1940, and came within two seats of capturing the State Senate. George Leader's margin of victory in Pittsburgh was 58,000; in Allegheny County 87,000; and in Philadelphia 121,000; for a statewide victory margin of almost 300,000 votes. It was the biggest Democratic victory since Earle had been elected Governor exactly twenty years before.

Nor was this 1954 Democratic surge solely a Pennsylvania phenomenon, as Democrats also pulled off victories in other crucial Northern industrial states, including New York and Minnesota. Indeed, that year Democrats did not lose a single one of the ten governorships they held, and they picked up eight new governorships formerly held by Republicans.

In the 1956 election, President Eisenhower won Pennsylvania big in his re-election bid—but his coattails weren't long enough to re-elect the incumbent Republican U.S. Senator, James H. Duff, who'd been governor until moving to the Senate in 1950. Instead, former Democratic Mayor Joseph S. Clark, Jr., of Philadelphia, became the new U.S. Senator. "Though Clark's margin of victory was slight (18,000 compared to Eisenhower's 600,000), it was a political phenomenon in light of the Republican landslide."[70]

In 1957 David Lawrence won an unprecedented fourth term as mayor of Pittsburgh. This made him a high-profile contender for the gubernatorial nomination in 1958. Not that he wanted it. He remained convinced that no Catholic could ever be elected statewide in Pennsylvania.

But Governor George Leader was running for the U.S. Senate and the Democratic power brokers deadlocked on a gubernatorial candidate. When Richardson Dilworth, now mayor of Philadelphia, withdrew as a possible candidate, the most logical choice was the recently re-elected mayor of the state's other big Democratic stronghold, Pittsburgh. So, party hierarchy unanimously endorsed David Lawrence for the nomination and he reluctantly accepted it.

To his surprise, David Lawrence carried the state by 76,000 votes in the 1958 election, coming out of Pittsburgh with a 68,000 vote majority and winning Philadelphia by 175,000 votes. He thus became the first Democrat in Pennsylvania history to follow a Democrat into the governor's seat, as well as Pennsylvania's first Catholic governor.

However, the Republicans retained their two seat majority in the State Senate and the Democrats lost two seats in the state House of Representatives, giving the Republicans a 106 to 104 margin. Additionally, George Leader lost the Senate race to Republican Hugh Scott.

By 1958, then, political power in Pennsylvania had become not only polarized into an enduring urban-rural pattern, but had stabilized into a permanent standoff. The Republicans usually won about two-thirds of the state's sixty-seven counties, the overwhelmingly rural ones, while the Democrats retained a firm grip on the state's more populous urban and industrial counties. The electoral balance was about equal. For instance, in three of the four state elections between 1952 and 1958, the elections were so close that victors could not be discerned until all votes had been counted. In those three elections, Democrats won two of the close contests.

Additionally, in the Democratic strongholds of Pittsburgh and Allegheny County, Democratic strength remained virtually unchanged throughout the Fifties, despite being the focus of an intense federal crusade which attempted to roll back labor militancy. In spite of the Red witch hunts of the Fifties, however, labor's party remained firm in its claim upon the allegiance of Pittsburgh's working class voters. Indeed, between 1950 and 1958, Democratic Party registration in Pittsburgh increased from 59.4 percent to 59.8 percent of all registered voters, while Allegheny County communities outside Pittsburgh showed an almost imperceptible decrease in Democratic registration from 53.5 percent to 53.2 percent. Third class cities in the county, meanwhile, increased Democratic registration from 52.3 percent of all voters to 60.2 percent in the same period, though with a decreased population.[71]

Also, the relative strength of the two major parties remained unchanged throughout the Fifties. In 1950, for example, Allegheny County produced 13.7 percent of the state's Republican vote, 15.8 percent of the state's Democratic vote, and 14.8 percent of the total vote for the state. In 1958 the percentages were virtually identical, with the county producing 13.8 percent of Pennsylvania's Republican vote, 15.9 percent of the state's Democratic vote, and 14.8 percent of the state's total vote. No converts were won anywhere along the political spectrum.[72]

Perhaps most revealing of all, however, is when we look at party loyalty at the ward level. When we do so (table 8), we find that neither the Red witch hunt nor even President Eisenhower's vaunted personal popularity could shake working class allegiance to the Democratic Party in Pittsburgh's strong labor wards. Even Ike was buried alive in these wards during his "crusade" of 1952.

Table 8

Democratic Vote Percentage
in Selected Strong Pittsburgh Labor Wards, 1940-1954

Ward	1940	1944	1948	1950	1952	1954
6 (Polish Hill)	85	84	83.7	79.7	79.1	83.0
16 (South Side)	76	78	77.6	68.5	71.4	77.4
24 (North Side)	---	59	61.8	54.3	54.3	60.0
31 (Hays-Lincoln Pl.*)	62	62.8	56.4	55.4	63.6	---

Source: James Caldwell Foster, *The Union Politic: The CIO Political Action Committee*, University of Missouri Press: St. Louis, 1975, Tables 1948D, 1952B, 1954E, pp. 217, 220, 225.
*Ward 31 is south of the Mon adjacent to Homestead and Munhall.

The percentage of Pittsburgh's working class voters pulling the Democratic lever in 1954, after the worst of Pittsburgh's Red witch craft hysteria, after the popular Ike had retired Harry Truman's Fair Deal, indeed, after both Truman and Roosevelt had left the stage, was virtually identical to the percentage voting Democratic a decade before, when FDR ran for re-election in the middle of World War II, and only very slightly less than in 1948, when class polarization of voting reached its historic all-time high levels. Neither John L. Lewis, the death of Roosevelt, the Progressive Party, the departure of Truman, a popular war-hero president, or Red Scare purges had weakened working class allegiance in the industrial heartland to the party of the workers, the Democratic Party.

Deadlock Confirmed

Thus, the Red witch hunt, despite the mesmerizing spectacle and flash, despite the attention paid to it by both contemporary commentators and later historians, did nothing to affect the nation's political alignments over the course of the 1950s, nor the underlying class basis of the nation's politics. As Samuel Lubell noted in the 1950s, "The ward returns in our major cities reveal no discernible break in the habit of voting according to economic status. If here and there Democratic ardor is plainly less intense than in 1936 or 1940, the basic line of class division remains."[73]

Nor was there a diminution in the drive for political power on the part of ethnic Catholic Democrats. For instance, "Compared with 1936 more than twice as many Italian names answered the 1951 legislative roll calls in Pennsylvania, New Jersey, New York, Connecticut, Rhode Island and Massachusetts—the six states with the heaviest Italo-American concentrations."[74]

Nor did eight years of a popular Eisenhower presidency (1953-1961) result in any basic change in the proportions of the electorate who identified themselves as either Democratic or Republican. Indeed, beneath the Eisenhower landslides of the Fifties—more attributable to his personal popularity than to his political philosophy—there was a quiet Democratic consolidation of the nation's political fault lines which went on apace. "In the 1954 congressional elections the nation's Democrats, although they turned out less well than Republicans in minor elections, still fashioned a solid majority of votes cast. The fall of 1958 witnessed a Democratic landslide. Even in 1956, 'underneath' Eisenhower's towering personal margin, a Democratic popular vote majority exceeding that which Kennedy won in 1960 appeared at other levels of the ticket."[75]

Hence, the New Deal political realignment continued to consolidate itself during the 1950s, in other Northeastern industrial states as well as Pennsylvania. One of these states was Massachusetts, where one example at the local level illustrates the political reality. Middlesex County is an eastern Massachusetts county including and stretching from Cambridge up through Lawrence and Lowell to the New Hampshire border. In the 1958 state elections, Edward J. Sullivan, a Cambridge Irish Catholic, became the first Democrat ever to be elected Middlesex County Clerk of Courts. Republicans were never able to retake the office and in 1994, thirty-six years later, Edward J. Sullivan was re-elected the Clerk of Courts for Middlesex County yet once more with 70 percent of the vote. His six-year term of office took him to the year 2000.

At the federal level, in the 1954 mid-term elections the Republicans lost the artificial majority in the U.S. House of Representatives they'd acquired with the popular landslide for Eisenhower in 1952. Those two years, 1952-1954, along with their brief tenure in the majority following the 1946 Second Thermidor elections, were the only times they would ever hold the House majority for half a century. Although that seemingly permanent minority status changed after the November 8, 1994 mid-term elections, nevertheless on September 17, 1994, the House Republicans experienced their 14,500th day as a minority party, a record unparalleled in American history. In the period between Presidents Lincoln and Eisenhower, neither party—not even in the long Republican ascendancy before the Great Depression—had ever been in the minority for more than sixteen consecutive years.

The political changes which matured in the Fifties, then, were of historic proportions. In election after election between 1952 and 1960, during the Eisenhower presidency, "national samples of the American electorate have indicated a preference for the Democratic Party by a margin approaching 60-40."[76] The fiery furnace of the Great Depression had welded America's working class to the Democratic Party, and the Fifties had not changed that reality.

The Last New Deal Election

By 1960, continuing urban working class loyalty to the Democrats boded well for John F. Kennedy in his quest for the presidency. Where the Republicans had claimed thirty governorships in 1930, they could boast of only sixteen in 1960. In that same thirty year span, Republicans controlled Congress for a mere four years. Throughout the Eisenhower years, total Republican polling strength declined nationally from 49 percent in 1950 to 47 percent in 1954 to 43 percent in 1958. In the Congress convening as Eisenhower left office, Democrats outnumbered Republicans two to one in the Senate and three to two in the House of Representatives. Despite Eisenhower's tenure in the White House, the Fifties had been a lost decade for the Republicans.[77]

Nevertheless, Kennedy's victory over Richard Nixon that year was one of the closest in American political history, as Kennedy won by only 113,000 votes out of almost 70 million cast, a margin of only 0.2 percent. And, while Democrats consolidated their control over the Congress, the congressional coalition of Republicans and conservative Southern Democrats which had first coalesced in Congress in the 1938 Republican Thermidor remained strong. The Presidential contest of 1960, then, was fought along political fault lines mapped out thirty years before and served to confirm the political deadlock which had solidified in the Forties and Fifties.

It was, however, the last national election which would be fought along those fault lines. Although Kennedy held the Democratic "Solid South," white Protestant Southerners in worrisome numbers defected to Nixon because of Kennedy's support for civil rights. As the Sixties unfolded, Southern defections would mount and new social issues would demand attention, shattering the basis of the class politics which had dominated the nation for thirty years.

For many, race rather than class became the defining issue, and on this matter many whites who comprised the Democratic New Deal base found the party lacking. After 1964, for example, no Democratic presidential candidate would ever again win a majority of the white vote. The 1960 presidential contest, then, was the last New Deal election.

****

David Lawrence was, above all else, a career politician whose view of politics had been shaped during his long years of exile when the Democratic Party was a vestigial organ on the Pennsylvania body politic. Thus, he always thought of his party as a minority party, long after it had come to dominate Pittsburgh and Allegheny County. He never truly comprehended the magnitude and nature of the electoral realignment which had taken place around him. The political landscape had been permanently transformed by an earthquake, but he didn't have a map to the new terrain, nor trust the solidity of the new contours.

For this reason, he consistently underestimated his own constituency's strength and routinely appealed to the no-longer-majority Republican electorate for support. This was a major reason why he opposed Tom Kennedy, the Secretary-Treasurer of the UMWA and Lt. Governor during the "Little New Deal," for the gubernatorial nomination in 1938. He was convinced a Catholic—especially a pro-labor Catholic—could not win the office. In 1945, he doubted that he, himself, would be a good candidate for mayor of Pittsburgh because of his religion.

And in 1954 he again rejected Tom Kennedy as the party's gubernatorial candidate because of Kennedy's religion. Indeed, Lawrence felt no Democrat could win in that first election after Eisenhower's 1952 landslide victory. For this reason, Lawrence and the party leaders chose a sacrificial lamb to run for governor. This token candidate was George Leader, an obscure first term State Senator.

As it turned out, George Leader went on to win easily.

Then, in 1958, after twelve years as mayor of Pittsburgh, the party drafted Lawrence as its gubernatorial candidate. This was over his strenuous objections, as Lawrence was convinced his Catholicism would make it impossible for him to be elected.

Instead, Lawrence won comfortably. Surveys later discovered that his religion had helped in counties with a significant Catholic population and was irrelevant in counties with low or moderate numbers of Catholics.[78]

But, in 1960, David Lawrence opposed the presidential candidacy of John F. Kennedy for the same reason. Like Lawrence, Kennedy was an Irish Catholic, and Lawrence was still under the fallacious impression that he'd almost failed to be elected governor in 1958 due to his religion and, "Having just come through that I figured, well, hell, he'll lose Pennsylvania, sure."[79]

But, yet once more, Lawrence was out of step with Pennsylvania Democrats, who now outnumbered the state's Republicans. All of his strongest efforts to take a totally uncommitted delegation to the party's nominating convention failed. An unexpected write-in primary vote of 180,000 for Kennedy and similarly surprising victories in district primary elections across the state resulted in Kennedy winning half of Pennsylvania's eighty-one delegates before the convention even convened.

That November, while running a close race against Nixon nationally, Kennedy won big in Pennsylvania, the state Governor Lawrence was "sure" he'd lose. Catholic bastions gave him over a quarter of a million votes and Philadelphia and Allegheny Counties alone gave him almost half a million votes, swamping the Republican hinterlands.[80]

In most particulars, the national vote in 1960 broke down along now-familiar divisions. For instance, of the forty-one major urban centers, Kennedy swept twenty-seven. Outside of the South, the bulk of Democratic voters were Catholic and, as might be expected of a Catholic candidate, Kennedy also swept 80 percent of the Catholic vote.

It helped, of course, that Kennedy was Roman Catholic, but perhaps not as much as it seemed. Since the New Deal realignment, Catholics tended to vote Democratic anyway and in the 1958 elections, 70 percent of Catholic voters voted

Democratic. Throughout the Fifties, in fact, only about 20 percent of Catholic voters considered themselves to be Republican.[81]

This was to Kennedy's great benefit in Pennsylvania, where in 1960 Democrats, who were mostly Catholics, at long last out-numbered Republicans in statewide registration. This became evident when Kennedy toured the state in a motorcade which drew nearly a million enthusiastic on-lookers. In a sense, Kennedy's victory in Pennsylvania was a Catholic victory. He lost the "least Catholic" rural counties worse than did Stevenson four years earlier and made only small gains over Stevenson's vote in the "moderately Catholic" counties. But this was irrelevant compared to his victory margins in the state's urban, industrial, Catholic heartland. In addition, the huge Catholic vote reversed the Republican majority in the State House and erased the Republican State Senate majority in favor of a 25-25 tie.[82]

And the old Democratic New Deal coalition not only remained alive and well at the state level, it continued to color the local politics of Pittsburgh, where the "labor vote" could still be counted on to elect "labor candidates." In a special City Council election that year, labor lawyer J. Craig Kuhn was elected to fill "labor's seat" on the City Council. Kuhn, who'd gained a reputation as a champion of labor not only by defending the United Mine Workers union but also individual workers, went on to serve the entire decade of the 1960s on the Pittsburgh City Council, finally resigning in December 1970—by which time he was Acting City Council President and Chairman of the Finance Committee.[83]

But when Kuhn left the City Council in 1970, however, so, too, did the idea of an identifiable "labor seat." Amy Ballinger, who'd been active in Pittsburgh labor circles since the Thirties, replaced him on the City Council that year, and would serve until 1976. But her tenure was never seen as filling "labor's seat" on the Council, and she was most remembered for supporting the adoption of cable TV in Pittsburgh.

When Ballinger retired in 1976, her seat was filled by Sophie Masloff, a Jewish grandmother from Squirrel Hill. However, Masloff had worked her way up since the Thirties in the Democratic Party hierarchy, and her religion was seen as irrelevant. The idea of there being an identifiable "Jewish seat" on the Council ended when City Councillor Edgar Michaels retired in 1973. He was replaced at that time by the Irish Catholic William Coyne.

The decade of the Sixties had dissolved the New Deal coalition upon which the Democrats had built their house, both nationally and in Pennsylvania. New fault lines were forming, new constituencies were mobilizing. The New Deal social order was in decay. At the height of its power, David Lawrence's Democratic machine created the Nationalities Committee as a liaison to the myriad ethnic groups which normally voted Democratic. The party's Nationalities Committee faded from the scene in the late Sixties.

A close analysis of the Pittsburgh electorate for the presidential election of 1972 and the Pittsburgh city election of 1973 confirmed the end of New Deal politics. In those elections, the "New Immigrant" groups were no longer over-represented in the local Democratic Party. Instead, only Pittsburgh's black population was disproportionately Democratic, comprising 21 percent of the city's population, but 27 percent of the Democrats to only 4 percent of the Republicans.[84] In the 1972 presidential election, "Democratic candidates received their greatest shares of the two-party vote from blacks and their smallest shares from whites . . . The figures also show a rare uniformity in the mean percentages of votes received from white ethnic groups by each candidate. The only real contrast is in the percentage received from blacks versus the percentage received from whites."

Thus, even in Pittsburgh, perhaps the most "New Deal" city in the nation, "The data we have presented here accord with the impression that traditional ethnic politics is declining in Pittsburgh. The contrasts between white ethnic groups with regard to party support and party voting appear to be considerably smaller than the over-all contrast between blacks and whites regarding these phenomena . . . the data are suggestive of a potential loss for the Democrats of traditional ethnic supporters like Italians and Irish; the data also suggest a developing white-versus-black polarization among the parties."[85]

Getting away from party labels, that same 1972 election also included a non-partisan election of eleven members to the Pittsburgh Home Rule Commission, for which a multicultural field of forty-two candidates ran. In looking at this election, too, "ethnicity played an important role only for those candidates who were otherwise unknown to the voters."[86]

The next year, 1973, Mayor Pete Flaherty's victory in the spring primary provided more evidence of decline. It was evident from the vote analysis that his victory was based upon the erosion of the old New Deal loyalties and the rise of the new politics of race. The party endorsed black City Councillor George Shields for re-election. He went down in defeat in the primary, while his four endorsed white Councillors all won election with nearly equal numbers of votes.

Meanwhile, the Irishman Pete Flaherty scored impressive vote totals in Italian areas. These outcomes suggested that, "except for race, ethnicity is unimportant in determining voting choice for well-known candidates" in Pittsburgh.[87]

****

When David Lawrence retired as governor in 1962, he was replaced by wealthy, Yale-educated, Protestant, Republican, William Scranton. Republican Scranton had demolished Philadelphia's Democratic Mayor Richardson Dilworth by almost half a million votes and carried sixty-two of the state's sixty-seven counties. It was a major Republican landslide in the midst of President John F. Kennedy's presidency.

Times had changed in Pennsylvania.

Times had changed in Pittsburgh.

It was the end of the New Deal Era.

Notes

1. *The Pittsburgh Press, The Pittsburgh Post-Gazette, The Pittsburgh Sun-Telegraph,* February 3-10, 1948.

2. See the AFL Central Labor Union resolution reprinted in *The Pittsburgh Press,* May 6, 1949.

3. *The Pittsburgh Press,* June 22, 1949.

4. *The Pittsburgh Post-Gazette,* September 1, 1949.

5. *The Pittsburgh Post-Gazette,* September 2, 1949.

6. For example, in 1930 Shadyside, Ward 7, had the city's largest proportion of native whites, 59.4 percent, while Squirrel Hill, Ward 14, had the lowest percentage of people on WPA payrolls, 1.1 percent, and the lowest percentage of laborers in its workforce, 1.6 percent, with Shadyside close behind in these categories. See Bruce M. Stave, *The New Deal and the Last Hurrah: Pittsburgh Machine Politics,* University of Pittsburgh Press: Pittsburgh, 1970, 49, Map 7; 48, Map 6, and 47, Map 5.

7. See James Caldwell Foster, *The Union Politic: The CIO Political Action Committee,* University of Missouri Press: St. Louis, 1975, Tables 1948D, 1952B, 1954E, 217, 220, 225.

8. Stave, *The New Deal and the Last Hurrah,* 40-41.

9. Lawrence quoted in Stefan Lorant, *Pittsburgh: The Story of an American City,* Doubleday: Garden City, New York, 1964, 402.

10. *The Pittsburgh Post-Gazette,* October 18, 20, 21, 1949.

11. Joe Dallet, "The Steel Workers Fight for Unemployment Relief," *Labor Unity,* December 1932, 13. *Labor Unity* was the "official organ" of the TUUL.

12. Dallet, "The Steel Workers Fight," 14, 13.

13. Dallet, "The Steel Workers Fight," 15.

14. Quoted by Russell W. Gibbons in, "I. W. Abel: a legendary figure in the history of the steel industry," *The Pittsburgh Post-Gazette,* August 20, 1987.

15. Gibbons, "I. W. Abel."

16. *The Pittsburgh Press,* March 28, 1940.

17. *The Pittsburgh Press,* April 4, 1940.

18. Fast made this comment in a 1987 *Washington Post* interview also reported by Woodene Merriman, "Reviving McCarthy days," a review of Fast's book, *The Pledge, The Pittsburgh Post-Gazette,* October 26, 1988, 17.

19. Francis R. Walsh, "The Films We Never Saw: American Movies View Organized Labor, 1934-1954," *Labor History,* Vol. 27, No. 4, fall 1986, 565.

20. Walsh, "The Films We Never Saw," 567.

21. Walsh, "The Films We Never Saw," 568.

22. Musmanno's original story was finally published as a novel in 1966 by Fountainhead Publishers of New York.

23. Walsh, "The Films We Never Saw," 570.

24. Zanuck's comments quoted in Walsh, "The Films We Never Saw," 571.

25. Walsh, "The Films We Never Saw," 572-73

26. Walsh, "The Films We Never Saw," 577-78.

27. David Caute, *The Great Fear: The Anti-Communist Purge Under Truman and Eisenhower,* Simon & Schuster: New York, 1978, 216-217.

28. Daniel J. Leab, "Anti-Communism, the FBI, and Matt Cvetic: The Ups and Downs of a Professional Informer," *The Pennsylvania Magazine of History & Biography,* Vol. 115, No. 4, October 1991, 550.

29. Leab, "Anti-Communism, the FBI, and Matt Cvetic," 555.

30. Leab, "Anti-Communism, the FBI, and Matt Cvetic," 555.

31. J. Edgar Hoover, "FBI Reveals How Many Reds Live in Your State," *Look,* August 1, 1950, 69. Presumably, these numbers included the paid FBI informers, such as Matt Cvetic, working inside the Communist Party, who numbered 1,500 nationwide by 1956.

32. Caute, *The Great Fear,* 222.

33. See his obituary in *The New York Times,* October 2, 1993.

34. Douglas Brode, *The Films of the Fifties,* The Citadel Press: Secaucus, N.J., 1976, 62.

35. Brode, *The Films of the Fifties,* 62.

36. Brode, *The Films of the Fifties,* 62.

37. Caute, *The Great Fear,* 219-220.

38. See his Associated Press obituary in *The Pittsburgh Post-Gazette,* August 18, 1993.

39. Caute, *The Great Fear,* 217.

40. Leab, "Anti-Communism, the FBI, and Matt Cvetic," 542.

41. Leab, "Anti-Communism, the FBI, and Matt Cvetic," 540.

42. Caute, *The Great Fear,* 218.

43. Caute, *The Great Fear,* 219.

44. Caute, *The Great Fear,* 219.

45. Caute, *The Great Fear,* 220.

46. Leab, "Anti-Communism, the FBI, and Matt Cvetic," 576.

47. Michael Paul Rogin, "Alienated Grownups: McCarthyism as Mass Politics," in Allen F. Davis and Harold D. Woodman, Eds., *Conflict and Consensus in Modern American History,* Sixth Ed., D.C. Heath & Co.: Lexington, Mass, 1984, 411-412.

48. Rogin, "Alienated Grownups," 429.

49. Rogin, "Alienated Grownups," 430.

50. Robert H. Zieger, *American Workers, American Unions, 1920-1985,* Johns Hopkins University Press: Baltimore, 1986, 133.

51. Patrick J. McGeever, *Rev. Charles Owen Rice: Apostle of Contradiction,* Duquesne University Press: Pittsburgh, 1989, 117.

52. McGeever, *Rev. Charles Owen Rice,* 123.

53. Thomas Brown in John Bodnar, *Workers' World: Kinship, Community, and Protest in Industrial Society, 1900-1940,* The Johns Hopkins University Press: Baltimore, 1982, 155, 156.

54. McGeever, *Rev. Charles Owen Rice,* 127.

55. Rogin, "Alienated Grownups," 420-21.

56. Rogin, "Alienated Grownups," 421-22.

57. Rogin, "Alienated Grownups," 431, 433.

58. Rogin, "Alienated Grownups," 433-434. Emphasis added.

59. Angus Campbell, "Voters and Elections: Past and Present," in Stephen V. Monsma and Jack R. Van Der Slik, Eds., *American Politics: Research and Readings,* Holt, Rinehart, and Winston: New York, 1970, 497.

60. Walter Dean Burnham, "The End of American Party Politics," in Walter Dean Burnham, Ed., *Politics/America: The Cutting Edge of Change,* Van Nostrand Co.: New York, 1973, 131.

61. Quoted in Carl N. Degler, "The Third American Revolution," in Allen F. Davis and Harold D. Woodman, Eds., *Conflict and Consensus,* 370.

62. Quoted in Degler, "The Third American Revolution," 370-371.

63. See Edward F. Cooke and G. Edward Janosik, *Guide to Pennsylvania Politics,* Greenwood Press: Westport, Conn., 1957, table 4, 15.

64. Gustavus Myers, *The Ending of Hereditary American Fortunes,* Julian Messner: New York, 1939, 381.

65. Herman P. Miller, *Income of the American People,* John Wiley: New York, 1955, 109-12. Jeffrey G. Williamson and Peter H. Lindert, *American Inequality: A Macroeconomic History,* Academic Press: New York, 1980, 82-92.

66. Richard Centers, *The Psychology of Social Classes: A Study of Class Consciousness,* Russell and Russell: New York, 1961, originally 1949, 218. For more recent sociological research which reached the same conclusion, see Mary R. Jackman and Robert W. Jackman, *Class Awareness in the United States,* University of California Press: Berkeley, 1983.

67. Daniel Bell, "America's Un-Marxist Revolution," in Reinhard Bendix and Seymour Martin Lipset, *Class, Status and Power: A Reader in Social Stratification,* The Free Press: New York, 1953, 163, 172.

68. Walter Dean Burnham, "The Changing Shape of the American Political Universe," *The American Political Science Review,* Vol. 59, No. 1, March 1965, 21, fn No. 39.

69. Cooke and Janosik, *Guide to Pennsylvania Politics,* 14.

70. Cooke and Janosik, *Guide to Pennsylvania Politics,* 15.

71. Edward F. Cooke, "Patterns of Voting in Pennsylvania Counties, 1944-1958," *Pennsylvania History,* Vol. 27, No. 1, January 1960, 81, fn 7.

72. Cooke, "Patterns of Voting in Pennsylvania Counties, 1944-1958," table 2, 80.

73. Lubell, *The Future of American Politics,* 206.

74. Lubell, *The Future of American Politics,* 77.

75. Philip E. Converse, Angus Campbell, Warren E. Miller, and Donald E. Stokes, "Reaffirming the Stalemate: Stability and Change in 1960," in Allen F. Davis and Harold D. Woodman, Eds., *Conflict and Consensus,* 473.

76. Converse, et al., "Reaffirming the Stalemate," 474.

77. Emmet John Hughes, "The Politics of Stasis: A Word on Eisenhower," in Allen F. Davis and Harold D. Woodman, Eds., *Conflict and Consensus,* 443-444.

78. See William J. McKenna, "The Influence of Religion in the Pennsylvania Elections of 1958 and 1960," *Pennsylvania History,* No. 29, October 1962, 407-419, and Daryl R. Fair, "The Reaction of Pennsylvania Voters to Catholic Candidates," *Pennsylvania History,* No. 32, July 1965, 305-315.

79. Interview with David L. Lawrence by Stefan Lorant, December 14, 1963, 59, Archives of Industrial Society, University of Pittsburgh.

80. McKenna, "The Influence of Religion," 416.

81. Converse, et al., 477.

82. McKenna, "The Influence of Religion," 416.

83. See his obituary by Lawrence Walsh, "Ex-Councilman J. Craig Kuhn, 73; Fought for Workers," *The Pittsburgh Post-Gazette,* September 1, 1994, C-9.

84. Michael Margolis and George H. Foster, "Ethnicity and Voting," in Roy Lubove, Editor, *Pittsburgh,* New Viewpoints: New York, 1976, 251.

85. Margolis and Foster, "Ethnicity and Voting," 254, 252.

86. Margolis and Foster, "Ethnicity and Voting," 254.

87. Margolis and Foster, "Ethnicity and Voting," 257.

Chapter 12

All That is Solid Melts into Air

A new America was coming into existence in the Fifties, bringing with it vast social transformations. In the wake of World War II's devastation, America—which, as early as the 1880s, had already become the world's biggest industrial power[1]—stood alone as the only major industrial nation to emerge unscathed. America was also politically stable in a world roiled by post-war turmoil in Europe and national liberation struggles in the colonial Third World.

This combination gave the United States undisputed military, economic, and political hegemony over all of the non-Communist world. America reaped vast economic benefits from this status and entered into a period of unprecedented and widespread affluence and prosperity. The American socioeconomic system seemed to most to be not only the best in the world, but the best in the history of the world. Success was its own vindication. There seemed to be no viable alternative. Even more than in the wake of World War I, American corporate capitalism luxuriated in a seemingly all-powerful cultural hegemony.

This phenomenal economic growth changed the entire culture. Poverty for most had been the norm up until this time. A majority of Americans, for example, could never afford to own their own homes until the late 1950s. Home ownership became the American norm only in 1960, by which time three out of every five families owned their own dwelling.[2]

Thus, for the first time in our national history, the years after World War II brought prosperity, not just for the lucky few, but on a mass scale. In real dollar terms (adjusted for inflation), the Gross National Product more than doubled between 1929-1953. Likewise, blue collar wages doubled in real dollar terms in the twenty year span of 1945-65. In terms of income, blue collar workers essentially became middle class over the course of the Fifties and early Sixties.[3]

One result of this mass-based prosperity was a car in every garage. Five million cars were sold in 1949, breaking the pre-Depression record year of 1929. Production and sales climbed throughout the 1950s and 1960s. By the early 1970s, there were two cars for every three Americans.[4]

There was a subsequent decline in the use of mass transit. Even by 1960 the impact of this transition was evident. According to that year's report of the Committee for Economic Development, "Between 1950 and 1958 transit riding in American cities fell from 17.2 billion to 9.7 billion rides per year, a drop of 43 percent. More and more people are getting to work or shopping by car."[5]

The car, in turn, along with cheap energy supplies and government subsidies, made possible the explosive growth of a new American nation called "Suburbia." "Of 13 million dwelling units erected in non-farm areas from 1946 through 1958," the Committee for Economic Development tells us, "approximately 11 million, or 85 percent, have been located outside of central cities."[6]

In the thirty years from 1940-1970 there was an increase of 56 million people living in these suburbs. This figure represents *almost twice* the *total* number of immigrants who flooded into America in the entire century between 1820 and 1920. That immigrant flood had been part of the largest mass movement of people in the history of humanity, and it had transformed America into a different country. The creation of the "nation" of Suburbia in the thirty years after 1940 dwarfed that earlier immigration tide.[7]

And it, too, transformed America into a different country. A "nation" with 56 million people is larger than most European countries, even large ones such as France. And this new nation was built from scratch, along with all its infrastructure—roads, bridges, hospitals, water filtration plants, homes, schools, sewers—in only thirty years. A daunting task, swiftly accomplished, bringing even greater economic growth in its wake. Not only did blue collar building trades boom, but Suburbia also needed an entire nation's worth of service workers to keep it functioning smoothly.

Suburbia thus became the heart of American society. The new national culture became that of dispersed automobile-based mass consumption. All that is today identifiably "American" to the rest of the world—vast highway networks, shopping malls, fast food franchises, et cetera—came to dominate not only the physical, but also the cultural landscape at this time. Between the mid-1950s and the late 1970s, America built 22,000 suburban shopping malls.

Meanwhile, lavish federal highway funding guaranteed there would be new roads to connect the suburbs to the cities, while the lack of investment in public transportation meant that buses and trains were insufficient in themselves to service this new suburban nation. Increasingly, Americans became encased in their mobile isolation chambers, as cars were needed to reach work, the marketplace, and leisure centers.

The unintended consequence of this residential and transportation dispersal and isolation was the destruction of "community" as America knew it. The old urban cultural forms, based on tight-knit, ethnic, urban, working class communities, dissolved in the acid of the new society. For most large cities in America's traditional Northeastern industrial heartland, 1950 marked the peak of their population. The last half century has brought steady population declines throughout what came to be known as "the Rust Belt." Pittsburgh for instance, once one of the ten largest cities in America, has lost more than half its population since 1950. In place of the close "urban villages" of old, America became a nation of strangers, anonymous neighbors, alienated suburbanites, and declining central cities.

This transformation had serious social consequences. One of them was the post-war "Baby Boom" brought about by unprecedented prosperity. The American birth rate had fallen by 50 percent from 1880-1940. After 1945, however, the birth rate leaped by 25 percent and remained high throughout the 1950s.

This fueled mushrooming suburban school populations and, by the 1960s, the "youth culture" of the exploding numbers of college students—many of them the first in their families to attend college. Raised in affluence and with drastically different worldviews from their parents, these children of the Fifties, the grandchildren of the ethnic immigrants I have written about, would become the young rebels of the Sixties.[8]

Another cloud on the horizon was the status of women. The Fifties decade is now seen through highly gendered filters as either a lost Eden of "Ozzie and Harriet" domesticity or an era of proto-"Stepford Wives" indoctrination and female subordination. Both home sales and family sizes boomed as women married younger and their husbands brought home larger paychecks. For social conservatives, the result was welcomed as a highly gendered utopia in which the sexes knew their proper places—a paradise conservatives have been trying to replicate ever since.

For Fifties' homemakers (and future feminists) like Betty Friedan, however, the resulting "feminine mystique" of suburban female domesticity masked a viciously anti-female national culture based on male supremacy. This sexist national culture resulted in private nightmares for millions of isolated, depressed, and bitter women trapped in a suburban purdah. Indeed, the very ideal of the free-standing single-family suburban house conjures up images of isolation from neighbors and community.[9]

Yet, even as the dominant ideology of the era was one of complacent and happy domesticity, female workforce participation continued to rise, especially for middle-class and married women. The new nation of Suburbia needed workers, lots of them, and its insatiable demand pulled women out of their homes in record numbers. The workforce participation rate for married women tripled and the rate for mothers doubled.

That internal contradiction alone introduced tremendous strains into traditional patriarch-oriented families in which the male was seen as the sole breadwinner—with consequent authority. But this growing female workforce participation also took place in a context of continued occupational sex segregation. These increasing numbers of working women were channelled into low-paying "women's work," such as nursing, secretarial, and clerical jobs. For them, there was rising frustration over society's economic restrictions on their lives.[10] All of these factors contributed to the anger which found expression in the late Sixties explosion known as "the Women's Movement."

Yet another consequence of the Fifties socioeconomic transformation was racial polarization. As whites fled the cities, "people of color" moved in. The 1960 Report of the Committee for Economic Development recalled that, "An historic function which the central city continues to perform is that of reception center for low-income migrants from outside the region. A steady stream of people from the rural South and Puerto Rico has replaced earlier migrations from abroad as the chief source of unskilled and semiskilled labor in urban centers."[11]

These blacks and Hispanics, who didn't have the money to flee to Suburbia, were left in the cities. But, it wasn't lack of money alone that kept then in urban centers. Federal housing policies also legitimized racially discriminatory lending standards, exclusionary suburban developments, and restrictive covenants, thereby subsidizing "white flight" to the suburbs.

Hazelwood, home to a giant Jones & Laughlin steel mill, was a typical ethnic working class neighborhood in Pittsburgh. Taking advantage of higher, unionized wages, and federal housing policies available to them, the white steelworkers who lived in that neighborhood quickly left it for the suburbs during the Fifties and Sixties. As one remaining resident told me, "The steelworkers left Hazelwood long before steel did." The same was true throughout the Steel Valley, as white steelworkers deserted Homestead, Braddock, Clairton, Duquesne, Aliquippa, Monessen, McKeesport—and Pittsburgh neighborhoods like Hazelwood. All are now overwhelmingly black communities.

Thus, "In a 1967 survey, labor leaders discovered that almost 50 percent of their membership lived in suburbs, including an astounding 75 percent of those under 40 years of age. The teeming neighborhoods of the vast industrial cities, with their union halls, saloons, social clubs, and traditions of solidarity and cultural cohesion, gave way to new, transient, fragmented patterns of life." [12]

The "middle-class welfare" which subsidized this "white flight" thus also undergirded substantial wealth accumulation in the form of white-owned suburban property. State policy makers, banks, realtors, and the construction industry abetted this creation of affluent white suburban neighborhoods, where credit profiles operated like electric fences, red-lining and zoning Suburbia off from an increasingly ghettoized inner-city black populace.

And, with the white middle class moving out and their populations dropping, the economic base of the cities eroded and tax revenues dried up. Cities became poorer and fell into decay and fiscal crisis, as the needs of their remaining populations rose at the same time that urban revenues fell.

"White flight" to the suburbs therefore created two nations: white and wealthy Suburbia and the dark and decaying cities, segregated from each other and mutually hostile. The bill came due in the Sixties, as that decade erupted into urban riots, black revolts, and social rebellion.

The "white" social rebellion took two forms, that of the youth revolt and the Women's Movement. Both of these groups discovered that "the personal is political" and that what they had assumed were private problems actually masked vast social distortions best faced collectively.

And both were met with great hostility by the white, male, ethnic, working class, which could not understand the changes transforming the America they knew beyond recognition.

****

In describing the breakdown of old social bonds under the impact of the Industrial Revolution, Karl Marx and Friedrich Engels said in 1848 that the newly-created society was characterized by "Constant revolutionizing of production, uninterrupted disturbance of all social conditions, everlasting uncertainty and agitation . . . All fixed, fast-frozen relations, with their train of ancient and venerable prejudices and opinions, are swept away, all new-formed ones become antiquated before they can ossify. All that is solid melts into air."[13]

And so it was true of the New Deal Era. The conditions and circumstances which brought it into existence, with its "train of ancient and venerable prejudices and opinions," were swept away.

Solidarity does not come from an act of will, does not result from an attitude, from merely saying, "comrade" or "brother." Nor does solidarity arise automatically out of the workplace, as Marxist dogma preaches. Solidarity is created by ties of mutual obligations and responsibilities. Labor historians such as Herbert Gutman, Alan Dawley, Eric L. Hirsch, and others, have emphasized the importance in the nineteenth century of close-knit ethnic communities, characterized by dense webs of kin, neighborly, and friendship ties, high levels of social and political organization, and with much insulation from "mainstream" culture as prerequisites for working class political mobilization.[14] This was no less true for the twentieth century. And such social webs of mutualism were created and nurtured by the nature of life and work in the industrial heartland just before and during the New Deal Era. And with similar resulting working class political mobilization.

But these tight-knit ethnic villages of related families gave way to a crabgrass frontier of anonymous suburbs. Blue collar factories with clearly demarcated class lines of "us" and "them," boss and worker, gave way to ambiguous service jobs where the class lines were not so clearly drawn. Largely male and white workforces composed of fathers and sons, uncles and nephews, in-laws and neighbors, gave way to workforces composed of strangers who were both male and female, white, black, and brown.

Today, then, the social web has frayed and, with it, the force of solidarity. Solidarity with one's fellow worker is easier when that fellow worker is also white and male and engaged in a similar job. It is easier when one's fellow worker is also one's neighbor, one's fellow church member, one's fellow fraternal society member, one's father, uncle, son, brother, or brother-in-law.

Solidarity is not as easy when one's fellow worker is of a different race or sex and engaged in a job different from one's own. It is not as easy when one's fellow worker is a stranger who commutes from a different town and is unknown outside of work. In such situations, isolation is more likely than solidarity and class consciousness fades. In such situations, it is easier to see the differences between workers—race, sex, religion, residence, job description, et cetera—all the things which keep them apart. And powerless. It is harder to see what they all have in common, and what would make them powerful if they saw it: They are all workers, and all thus share the same class membership.

We now live in a society in which community of all kinds has declined to such a point that we are all "bowling alone." It is not a recent phenomenon. The social web has been fraying for over half a century. Indeed, beneath the surface world of Red Scares and political spectacle, the signs were becoming evident to astute post-war social observers even in the Fifties. Already by the 1950s, for example, social commentator Vance Packard noted that we were becoming "a nation of strangers."

And, as the tight, cohesive, ethnic, working class, urban villages dissolved away, so did the socioeconomic basis of class politics—the sources of solidarity which had made possible a Workers' Democracy. It was thus these socioeconomic changes which ended the New Deal Era and brought our current world into existence.

All that is solid melts into air.

Notes

1. See chart on worldwide distribution of industrial production in Nelson Lichtenstein, Susan Strasser, and Roy Rosenzweig, *Who Built America? Working People and the Nation's Economy, Politics, Culture, and Society, Vol. 2, Since 1877,* Worth Pub.: New York, 2000, 321.

2. Lichtenstein, et al., *Who Built America?* 593.

3. See "The Post-War Economic Boom," in Lichtenstein, et al., *Who Built America?* 570-576.

4. Lichtenstein, et al., *Who Built America?* 570.

5. Report of the Committee for Economic Development, in Charles N. Glaab, Ed., *The American City,* Dorsey: Homewood, Ill., 1963, 461-473.

6. Report of the Committee for Economic Development, 461-473.

7. See "Suburban America," in Lichtenstein, et al., *Who Built America?* 591-595. The roots of Suburbia, of course, go back much further than the post-World War II era, beginning to grow as early as the 1850s. See, e.g., Sam Bass Warner, Jr., *Streetcar Suburbs: The Process of Growth in Boston, 1870-1900,* 2nd Ed., Harvard University Press: Cambridge, 1978; Jon C. Teaford, *City and Suburb: The Political Fragmentation of Metropolitan America, 1850-1970,* Johns Hopkins University Press: Baltimore, 1979.

The two acknowledged classic histories of the suburbanization process are Kenneth T. Jackson, *Crabgrass Frontier: The Suburbanization of the United States,* Oxford University Press: New York, 1985 and Robert Fishman, *Bourgeois Utopias: The Rise and Fall of Suburbia,* Basic Books: New York, 1987. Both books pinpointed the political and economic forces and racial tensions driving suburban growth. Two newer books by Yale professor Dolores Hayden reconceptualize the historical development of suburbia and its more recent transformation. They are *Building Suburbia: Green Fields and Urban Growth, 1820-2000,* Pantheon: New York, 2004, and *A Field Guide to Sprawl,* Norton: New York, 2004.

8. Lichtenstein, et al., *Who Built America?* 572.

9. This is not a caricature. For a recent overview of the women's movement which does, indeed, present this picture of the Fifties, see Ruth Rosen, *The World Split Open: How the Modern Women's Movement Changed America,* Viking: New York, 2000.

10. See Alice Kessler-Harris, *In Pursuit of Equity: Women, Men and the Quest for Economic Citizenship in 20th-Century America,* Oxford University Press: New York, 2001.

11. Report of the Committee for Economic Development, 461-473.

12. Robert H. Zieger and Gilbert J. Gall, *American Workers, American Unions: The Twentieth Century,* The Johns Hopkins University Press, Baltimore: Maryland, Third Edition, 2002, 183-184.

13. Karl Marx and Frederick Engels, *The Communist Manifesto,* International Publishers: New York, 1948, 1986, 12.

14. Herbert Gutman, *Work, Culture, and Society in Industrializing America,* Vintage Books: New York, 1973, 1977; Alan Dawley, *Class and Community: The Industrial Revolution in Lynn,* Harvard University Press: Cambridge, 1976, 2000; Eric L. Hirsch, *Urban Revolt: Ethnic Politics in the Nineteenth-Century Chicago Labor Movement,* University of California Press: Berkeley, 1990.

Chapter 13

The Crucible of Freedom

In November 1940, a few days after President Franklin D. Roosevelt's third-term victory, Samuel Lubell visited the United Auto Workers (UAW) Chrysler Local No. 7 in Detroit. "The scene was one of belligerent activity," he recalled. "Bulletin boards bristled with photographs of police clubbing strikers and of tear gas riotings. When the union's educational director heard that I was analyzing the election for the *Saturday Evening Post*, he stiffened suspiciously and seemed about to have me thrown out. Then, he began boasting freely of how class conscious the auto workers were and how ready they were to vote Roosevelt a fourth or a fifth term. He wore a lumber jacket. With his feet on his desk and a buzzer by his hand, he looked the very picture of newly arrived power."[1]

Eight years later, in November 1948, shortly after Harry Truman's presidential victory, Lubell revisited Chrysler Local No. 7. "The same photographs of Franklin Roosevelt and Frank Murphy hung on the wall," he said, "but it was hard to believe that it was the same place. The strike photographs had come down from the bulletin boards and had been replaced by idyllic snapshots of the union's annual outings and sporting events. An honor roll listed fifty-nine union members who had been killed in the war. Nearby stood a cabinet filled with loving cups and other trophies won in city-wide UAW tournaments . . . In 1940 the flavor of the local was one of street barricades and sit-down strikes; eight years later it was almost like a lodge hall. Not only Chrysler Seven but the whole American labor movement has undergone a striking transformation in recent years . . . the dynamic near-revolutionary surge, which doubled union membership from 1935 to 1938 and which brought such industrial giants as General Motors and U.S. Steel to the bargaining table, is now gone. The labor dynamo has slowed down . . . The inner mechanics of Reuther's own union today resemble more closely the momentum of a bureaucracy than the trampling of a new social movement . . . the urgent sense of grievance, so evident even fifteen years ago, is gone . . . [What we see is the] ebbing of labor's political vitality."[2]

The same transformation was repeated everywhere else in the labor movement. In 1946, for example, the United Steelworkers of America self-published a book entitled *The First Ten Years,* edited from its Pittsburgh headquarters by Vincent Sweeney, one of the original founders of the union. It, too, documented a militant birth of the union and a placid present of bowling leagues and picnics, bathing beauty contests and prosperous union locals in steelworker communities.[3]

Lubell lamented this transformation and the fact that "the urgent sense of grievance, so evident even fifteen years ago [i.e., in 1933], is gone . . . " Evidently, he wanted workers to continue feeling aggrieved, perhaps because they had not yet accomplished the goals he had in mind for them.

In this, Lubell was not so different from many labor historians, political radicals, and Marxist intellectuals who, instead of seeking to know the actual hopes and dreams of ordinary workers, have instead projected their own hopes and dreams for the working class onto workers. And, because workers did not fulfill the hopes and dreams of these political radicals and labor historians, some of them have argued that what happened in the Thirties and Forties was the betrayal, co-optation, and suppression of a radical workers' movement by triumphant "corporate liberalism," and that the militant grassroots working class political mobilization of the era brought only minor and disappointing "short-lived gains."[4]

Such views are part of a widely-accepted tradition of radical historiography which sees the New Deal Era as a period of radicalism betrayed and subdued. By affiliating with the Democratic Party, for instance, they say that labor's "radical" voice was stilled. As organized labor lost the ability to articulate an alternate vision to corporate capitalism, class issues faded from the national agenda. Mike Davis is representative of Marxist historians who argue along these lines.

There were several culprits, Davis says: Internal divisions among the workers; "accepting the discipline of the Cold War mobilization;" "the gradual bureaucratization of the new industrial unions;" and a "Barren Marriage" to the Democratic Party resulting from a "New Deal capture of the labor movement." Thus, "By relying on backroom lobbies and campaign support for the Democrats . . . the CIO leadership willingly conceded the last vestiges of its political independence and demobilized the rank-and-file militancy." For this reason, the "forty years of marriage between labor and the Democrats have produced a politically dispirited and alienated working class."[5]

Others, such as Joshua B. Freeman, have additionally cited the Cold War as a contributor to the demise of New Deal militancy.[6] The international Cold War against Communism was also a domestic "Cold War Against Labor," as the labor movement of the time was perceived to be tinged with Communism.[7] This resulted in a coerced yet nevertheless self-imposed post-war purge of Communists and other radical leaders from the CIO, and organized labor in general.

For example, in 1949 the militant Pacific Coast-based International Longshoreman and Warehouseman Union, led by ex-Wobbly Harry Bridges, was expelled from the CIO when it refused to purge itself of Communist officials. The United Electrical Workers (UE) was also expelled for similar reasons and faced workplace incursions from the rival International Brotherhood of Electrical Workers, backed by the labor movement itself in an effort to destroy UE. With the most "class conscious" element of its leadership decimated, these historians claim, the organized working class was less able to resist the cultural and political impact of a forty-five-year-long Cold War against Communism. Combined with such things as a union bureaucracy, which stifled shop floor activism, argues Nelson Lichtenstein, the Cold War generated "a passive and atomized consciousness among large sections of the industrial working class."[8]

At the same time, they say, there were dramatic changes in industrial relations which contributed to working class political demobilization. In a sense, they argue, a New Deal "Devil's Bargain" had been struck between labor and management in which workers and their unions consciously and voluntarily traded a large measure of class militancy for an equally large slice of the American Pie. In exchange for job security, higher wages and increased employee benefits, organized labor abandoned its claim to share in management decisions. Confrontation over anything other than "bread and butter" issues was deemed illegitimate by both sides. "Business unionism" replaced social vision.

This voluntary dismissal of class conflict helped create a political culture of social passivity and political acquiescence among blue collar workers and their unions, blurring class identities and encouraging them to feel they shared common interests with management.[9] The potentially "revolutionary" New Deal thus ended in merely bolstering corporations and the capitalist state.[10]

The Wagner Act and the Social Security Act are cited by others as prime examples of how the revolutionary potential of the workers was betrayed and subdued, ending in the further entrenchment of capitalism. Frances Fox Piven and Richard A. Cloward, for instance, claim that the "guaranteeing of a minimum standard of subsistence" through such measures as unemployment compensation, Social Security, and work relief by the Roosevelt administration was done reluctantly and minimally and only in response to disruptive political actions on the part of workers and the poor. Far from being seen as a "right" by the New Dealers, the public welfare system was viewed as reluctant charity serving capitalist-oriented social control functions. Once these functions had been performed, once workers and the poor had been pacified and "reintegrated" into capitalist society, the system was dismantled as much as possible.[11]

This political reintegration and subordination of the masses worked. The election of 1936 was a landslide for the New Deal. "The years of discontent and disaffection, of protest and possibility, were over; the people had lined up behind the New Deal. What trouble and turbulence persisted were not sufficient to rock the New Deal or to alter its course."[12]

These historians are part of a neo-Marxist tradition which challenges what has been called "corporate liberalism," a political orientation, it is claimed, which has dominated much of American politics. This is also the view of Barton Bernstein. In his pioneering essay, Bernstein argued that there was no beneficent, humane liberalism at work in the New Deal. Roosevelt and his disciples were "doctrinaires of the center" who had no desire to redistribute political or economic power. Rather, they were engaged in a self-consciously deliberate and successful rescue of large-scale corporate capitalism.

True, the people on the bottom benefited somewhat from the backwash of this bailout of the capitalists, but we must not magnify their crumbs. "In moving to social security, guarantees of collective bargaining, utility regulation, and progressive taxation, the government did advance the nation toward greater liberalism, but the shift was exaggerated and most of the measures accomplished far less than either friends or foes suggested."[13]

Additionally, "Not only was the extension of representation to new groups less than full-fledged partnership, but the New Deal neglected many Americans—sharecroppers, tenant farmers, migratory workers and farm laborers, slum dwellers, unskilled workers, and the unemployed Negroes. They were left outside the new order.

"Yet, by the power of rhetoric and through the appeals of political organization, the Roosevelt government managed to win or retain the allegiance of these peoples. Perhaps this is one of the crueller ironies of liberal politics, that the marginal men trapped in hopelessness were seduced by rhetoric, by the style and movement, by the symbolism of efforts seldom reaching beyond words."[14] Thus, the New Deal was a great charade, doling out crumbs, style, and rhetoric, without fundamentally altering the political landscape for most people or addressing their aspirations.

To a large measure, Paul K. Conkin agrees with this assessment.[15] He adds, however, that much more than a dramatic corporate rescue effort was accomplished by the New Deal. For instance, there was not a return to the rampant but unstable corporate capitalism of pre-1929. Rather, while tossing a few plums in the direction of the populace, Roosevelt and his followers created a "welfare state for business" and enabled American capitalism to emerge from the Depression stronger, healthier, wealthier than could have been imagined.

"After the New Deal innovations, entrepreneurs and major producers were increasingly more secure in their property, more certain of high profits, less vulnerable to economic cycles, and more heavily subsidized and more extensively regulated by the federal government, while welfare policies guaranteed at least a minimum of subsistence for those excluded from, or those unable to compete effectively for, the benefits of a capitalist system."[16]

One big problem with these neo-Marxist critiques of "corporate liberalism" is that they demand the existence of a Machiavellian cabal of capitalist manipulators to pull the whole charade off. But, as Theda Skocpol points out, this really doesn't fit the facts of the major New Deal reform efforts at all.

True, corporate capitalism was not seriously challenged during the New Deal, either by Roosevelt or by any other dissident forces. But important and serious changes did take place, principally the transformation of the federal government from "a mildly interventionist, business-dominated regime into an active 'broker state' that incorporated commercial farmers and organized labor into processes of political bargaining at the national level."[17]

Skocpol also investigates the "political functionalism" of Nicos Poulantzas, who argues that an "autonomous state" automatically benefits the capitalist class and operates to the detriment of the working class. This is so because the state is basically a vehicle of system maintenance and capitalism is the system being maintained. Therefore, while they may well be class conscious and active on their own behalf, there is no *need* for capitalists to be class conscious or to act in their own best interests. The state will do it for them.[18]

But the problem with this argument is that, before the New Deal, there really *wasn't* an autonomous federal bureaucracy to act in the interests of the capitalist class. The government was essentially a "state of courts and parties," as Stephen Skowronek has phrased it, especially before World War I, and was physically incapable of intervening systematically in the economy to regulate it for capitalism. Indeed, this was the very reason so many of the members of the NIRA regulatory bodies were drawn from the business world. The state had no personnel of its own to staff such vast watchdog agencies.

Yes, it is true that material conditions improved for workers after the New Deal. For example, in the 1930s, virtually every Italian family in Pittsburgh's Panther Hollow took in boarders to help make ends meet. Camilla Caliendo, for example, remembers that in 1939 her family had five boarders. Each boarder paid five dollars a month for a bed, lunch, and supper. "They bought their own food," she said. "We just had to cook it for them." Sometimes washing the dirty clothes of the boarders was also part of the deal. But, her cousin John Casciato, told me, "Boarders stopped being done after World War II. Everybody started buying their own homes."

They were able to buy their own homes because of many of the changes Democratic administrations had made in their favor, such as the Wagner Act which led to secure and better paying jobs through unionization, and mortgage and educational assistance through the G.I. Bill. "Democrats took care of people," John said. "Out of this Hollow we have a magistrate, police officers, plenty of them, many CPAs, many attorneys, doctors . . . If our parents could only see us. The Democrats were good for everybody."[19]

Such material advances were not mere crumbs. Beyond that, and contrary to what Samuel Lubell and Malcolm Cowley and other Marxist intellectuals have believed, these workers fought for more than just loving cups, bowling leagues, beauty pageants, new Buicks and new homes. They also had a larger social vision—and they also gained much of that larger social vision. This larger social vision was particularly visible in Republican-corporate industrial bastions, such as the Pittsburgh region, which were radically reshaped in the 1930s and 1940s into an enduring stronghold of what Pittsburgh workers called "a workers' democracy."[20]

Some have used the term "industrial democracy," a phrase and concept which once permeated the vocabulary of industrial relations, to mean much the same. According to Joseph A. McCartin, it was this idea—democratizing relations between labor and capital—which workers and their allies fought for after the turn of the twentieth century, not some quasi-socialist goal such as "workers' control" or the explicitly socialist goal of the abolition of capitalism. Examining the National War Labor Board and other such war agencies during World War I, McCartin argues that such agencies endorsed "three things that resonated deeply among working people: their demand for a rule of law in the workplace, their call for a voice in determining the conditions of their work, and their desire to claim their rights as citizens through their labor."[21]

Workers in the industrial heartland also wanted all this—and even more. What they termed a "workers' democracy" proclaimed that workers, too, were human beings deserving of respect, consideration—and equality. Their dream was deeply rooted in the American Dream. Indeed, its roots can be traced back to the Declaration of Independence itself, our founding document which declared that "All men are created equal."

These workers—who were not, at least in the eyes of WASP Americans, "created equal," and so had to fight for equality—interpreted this idea as mandating a society which valued them as "Americans," and as "citizens," even if they were huddled masses from Southern or Eastern Europe; as guaranteeing them civil liberty and political equality; as offering a more level playing field for labor and capital; and, yes, *also* offering them economic security and advancement, the latter being what Lubell, Cowley, and others were able to see most easily.

These workers came out of a past of political subservience, of vast disparities of wealth, and what Daniel DeLeon once called "industrial feudalism." Their creation of a society promising a democratization of labor-capital relations, a more equal chance to prosper, economic security, political rights for workers, and respect for ethnic Americans was therefore a truly radical departure from the past and a genuine reform.

We might therefore call this package of transformations "radical reform." It was not a continuation of old-style top-down elitist Progressivism, nor was it the socialist revolution which some saw as the fated task of the working class, but which was never really in the hearts and minds of American workers. Nevertheless, it was a radical vision which was neither betrayed nor subdued. It created a new political order upon the ruins of a repressive past, as ordinary workers dismantled a feudal remnant which had existed for centuries and, in both politics and economics, created the modern liberal state.

In the process, class politics re-defined the political agenda. For the first time in American history the political universe in the 1930s and 1940s polarized along class lines. Not only did the liberal pro-worker New Deal of President Franklin D. Roosevelt seem to indicate the saliency of class politics at the national level, but class conscious workers and their unions also moved to control local governments at the same time. This transformed grassroots politics and provided the bedrock upon which pro-working class policies at the national level were supported.

The New Deal was thus not something foisted upon befuddled ordinary workers by FDR and co-opting liberal elites, as patronizing Leftists habitually proclaim. Rather, the New Deal was the *creation* of ordinary workers, a *response* to their demands, and both its successes—and its limitations—belonged to them. This new worker-created socio-political order was what put New Deal "Progressive liberals"—people like Senator Robert Wagner, Rexford Tugwell, Henry Wallace, and, yes, even Roosevelt—into power and, to a large extent, defined and determined their radical reform agenda. The New Deal Era was, therefore, not Arthur Schlesinger's "Age of Roosevelt." Rather, it was the "Age of the Common Man."

Political scientists usually study the forest, broad developments at the national level. But an up-close examination of the trees, the small local transformations out of which national developments emerge, often reveals much more about the true nature of those broad national developments. Pittsburgh and its surrounding steel towns in the industrial heartland were major battlegrounds upon which ordinary workers created their New Deal, and it is with their creation of the Steel Valley's "Workers' Democracy" that this radical transformation can be seen most clearly.

But, while the Pittsburgh region was an emblematic working class region during the Thirties, the changes which took place there also took place in the context of larger struggles. The American government is a federal system, and much political power is constitutionally reserved to the individual states. In addition, towns and cities are not independent entities; they are creatures of those same states. Thus, this is not just the story of radical transformation in a single political arena. Rather, it is the story of conflict in multiple arenas—the small Steel Valley mill towns; the larger city of Pittsburgh; Allegheny County, in which both the mill towns and Pittsburgh are located; the Commonwealth of Pennsylvania; and the nation itself. The changes which took place in these different arenas were all interwoven, with one influencing the others.

In some arenas, such as America at large, the only arena Marxist intellectuals usually examine, workers scored major but partial victories. In others, such as the mill towns, workers won everything—and it is here that the shape of the Common Man's hopes and aspirations can be most clearly discerned. Such different victories help explain why many rank and file workers did not react to the Taft-Hartley Act of 1947 with the same alarm felt by some of their national union leaders. As Elmer J. Maloy, a steelworker who became mayor of the Steel Valley town of Duquesne, said when he declined to run for re-election in 1945, the workers had won everything they had set out to win. "All I wanted to do in the first place was to take the place over. The union was strong enough now, so I didn't give a damn."[22]

Abraham Lincoln proclaimed at Gettysburg in 1863 that triumph in the Civil War would bring "a new birth of freedom" to America, a freedom "dedicated to the proposition that all men are created equal." And so it did. Slavery was abolished, a necessary precursor to future struggles and future victories. In addition, the concept of equality gained more political legitimacy as Lincoln, citing the Declaration of Independence, rededicated America to that founding principle.

Marxist intellectuals idealized the industrial proletariat as the collective Messiah who would usher in a classless heaven on earth at the end of history. But American industrial workers never shared such apocalyptic hopes and dreams.

They had their own hopes and dreams. While Marxist intellectuals dreamed of blood and revolution, of the destruction of capitalism and of the millennial dictatorship of the proletariat, workers dreamed of freedom and equality, of justice and democracy, and of an equal opportunity for their children to share in the American Dream.

Marxist intellectuals often disdain such dreams as trivial. But these dreams are not so very different from Martin Luther King, Jr.'s Dream. And his Dream, and his accomplishments, profoundly changed America.

So, too, did the dreams and accomplishments of American workers during the Thirties. Out of the crucible of the industrial heartland, these nameless workers democratized large sectors of the economy. These despised "foreigners" brought political democracy to large portions of the country. And these industrial serfs abolished our feudal past, bringing us closer to the reality of equality for all.

And, by doing so, these common and ordinary people brought about a "new birth of freedom" in America.

Notes

1. Samuel Lubell, *The Future of American Politics*, Harper and Brothers: New York, 1952, 190.

2. Lubell, *The Future of American Politics*, 190-193, 2.

3. Vincent D. Sweeney, *The United Steelworkers of America . . . The First 10 Years*, published by USWA, Pittsburgh, Pa. No date, but 1946. Copy in possession of author.

4. A recent version of this argument is presented by Joshua B. Freeman, who claims that a "hegemonic liberalism" crushed the social democratic aspirations of workers. One of the primary ways this was accomplished was via the anti-Communist witch hunts of the 1950s. These silenced the most effective and class-conscious leaders of the labor movement, leaving unions to drift rudderless toward the "liberal center." Thus, workers were prevented from "winning and wielding social power." Unfortunately, Freeman never presents any evidence of rank and file aspirations for a social democratic transformation, which, in any case, he never clearly defines. See Joshua B. Freeman, *Working-Class New York: Life and Labor Since World War II*, The New Press: New York, 1999.

5. Mike Davis, "The Barren Marriage of American Labour and the Democratic Party," *New Left Review*, 124, 1980, 43-84, later a chapter by the same title in his book, *Prisoners of the American Dream: Politics and Economy in the History of the U. S. Working Class*, Verso: London, 1986, 52-101. Citations on 96, 53, 99, 101.

6. See Joshua B. Freeman, *Working-Class New York*.

7. See Ann Fagan Ginger and David Christiano, Eds., *The Cold War Against Labor*, Studies in Law and Social Change, No. 3, Meiklejohn Civil Liberties Institute: Berkeley, Cal., 1987.

8. Nelson Lichtenstein, *Labor's War at Home, The CIO in World War II*, Cambridge University Press: New York, 1982, 244. See, also, his discussion of the impact this had on "deradicalizing" UAW leader Walter Reuther in the post-war period, 85-89, as well as his "From Corporatism to Collective Bargaining: Organized Labor and the Eclipse of

Social Democracy in the Postwar Era," in Steve Fraser and Gary Gerstle, Eds., *The Rise and Fall of the New Deal Order, 1930-1980*, Princeton University Press: Princeton, N.J., 1989, 122-152.

9. See, for instance, David Brody's arguments along these lines, "The Uses of Power I: Industrial Battleground," and "The Uses of Power II: Political Action," in *Workers in Industrial America: Essays on the Twentieth Century Struggle*, Oxford University Press: New York, 1980. In addition, see Ronald Radosh, "The Corporate Ideology of American Labor Leaders from Gompers to Hillman," in James Weinstein and David W. Eakins, Eds., *For a New America: Essays in History and Politics*, Random House: New York, 1970, 151-152; and Melvyn Dubofsky, "Not So 'Turbulent Years': A New Look at the American 1930s," in Charles Stephenson and Robert Asher, Eds., *Life and Labor: Dimensions of American Working-Class History*, State University of New York Press: Albany, 1986, 205-223.

Emerging labor law also played a role in limiting labor's possibilities. On this, see Karl E. Klare, "Judicial Deradicalization of the Wagner Act: The Origins of Modern Legal Consciousness, 1937-1941," *Minnesota Law Review*, 65, 1978, 265-339; and Christopher Tomlins, *The State and the Unions*, Cambridge University Press: New York, 1985, 99-316.

10. See Barton J. Bernstein, "The New Deal: The Conservative Achievements of Liberal Reform," in Bernstein, ed., *Towards A New Past: Dissenting Essays in American History*, New York: Vintage, 1967.

11. Frances Fox Piven, and Richard A. Cloward, *Regulating the Poor: The Functions of Public Welfare*, Vintage: New York, 1971, xiii.

12. Piven and Cloward, *Regulating the Poor*, 100.

13. Bernstein, "The New Deal," 275.

14. Bernstein, "The New Deal," 281.

15. Paul K. Conkin, *The New Deal*, New York: Thomas Y. Crowell Co., 1967.

16. Conkin, *The New Deal*, 23. Other historians who have contributed to this interpretation of the New Deal Era include Ronald Radosh, "The Myth of the New Deal," in Radosh and Murray Rothbard, Eds., *The New Leviathan: Essays on the Rise of the American Corporate State*, New York: Dutton, 1972, 146-187, and, more recently, Colin Gordon, *New Deals: Business, Labor, and Politics in America, 1920-1935*, New York: Cambridge University Press, 1994.

17. Theda Skocpol, "Political Response to Capitalist Crisis: Neo-Marxist Theories of the State and the Case of the New Deal," *Politics & Society*, Vol. 10, No. 2, 1980, 171.

18. See Nicos Poulantzas, *Political Power and Social Classes*, Verso: London, 1975.

19. Interview with Camilla Caliendo and John Casciato by Eric Leif Davin, May 24, 1996.

20. This phrase was used by the Pittsburgh Central Labor Union (PCLU)—the congress of all AFL unions in the city—in a resolution welcoming and endorsing the 1937 national convention in Pittsburgh of the Peoples Congress for Democracy and Peace. The PCLU endorsed whatever "actions that Congress might take to further advance progressive labor legislation *and the cause of a workers' democracy*." Pittsburgh Central Labor Union Minutes, November 16 and 18, 1937, in the holdings of the Pittsburgh Typographical Union, Lo. No. 7, Archives of Industrial Society, University of Pittsburgh. Emphasis added.

21. Joseph A. McCartin, *Labor's Great War: The Struggle for Industrial Democracy and the Origins of Modern American Labor Relations, 1912-1921,* University of North Carolina Press: Chapel Hill, 1997, 95.

22. Elmer J. Maloy Interview, United Steelworkers of America Papers, Historical Collections and Labor Archives, Pattee Library, Pennsylvania State University Libraries, 36.

Bibliography

Academic Journal Articles

Allen, Howard W., and Erik W. Austin. "From the Populist Era to the New Deal: A Study of Partisan Realignment in Washington State, 1889-1950," *Social Science History,* 3, 1979.

"American Institute of Public Opinion—Surveys, 1938-1939," *Public Opinion Quarterly.* October 1939.

Bell, Rudolph M. "The Transformation of a Rural Village: Istria, 1870-1972," *Journal of Social History,* No. 7, spring 1974.

Berg, Gordon. "The Workingmen's Party—A First in Labor Politics," *Worklife,* No. 1, March 1976, 23-26.

Beaver Valley Labor History Journal, Vol. 1, No. 2, June 1979.

Bernstein, Irving. "John L. Lewis and the Voting Behavior of the C.I.O.," *Public Opinion Quarterly,* June 1941.

Bicha, Karel Denis. "Liberalism Frustrated: The League for Independent Political Action, 1928-1933," *Mid-America,* 47, 1966, 19-28.

Billington, Monroe, and Cal Clark, "Catholic Clergymen, Franklin D. Roosevelt, and the New Deal," *Catholic Historical Review,* 79, 1993.

Bloom, Jonathan D. "Brookwood Labor College: The Final Years, 1933-1937," *Labor's Heritage,* Vol. 2, No. 2, April 1990, 24-43.

Bodnar, John. "Immigration and Modernization: The Case of Slavic Peasants in Industrial America," *Journal of Social History,* No. 9, 1975, 44-71.

Bronner, Edwin B. "The New Deal Comes to Pennsylvania: The Gubernatorial Election of 1934," *Pennsylvania History,* Vol. 27, No. 1, January 1960.

Brown, Richard J. "John Dewey and The League for Independent Political Action," *Social Studies,* 59, 1968, 156-161.

Burnham, Walter Dean. "The Changing Shape of the American Political Universe," *The American Political Science Review,* Vol. 59, No. 1, March 1965.

———. "The End of American Party Politics," *Trans-Action,* 7, December 1969, 12-23.

Cerullo, John and Gennaro Delena. "The Kelayres Massacre," *The Pennsylvania Magazine of History and Biography,* Vol. 107, No. 3, July 1983.

Cobb, William H. "From Utopian Isolation to Radical Activism: Commonwealth College, 1925-1935," *Arkansas Historical Quarterly,* 1973, 32, 132-147.

Cohen, Lizabeth. "Reflections on the Making of *Making a New Deal,*" *Labor History,* Vol. 32, No. 4, fall 1991.

Coode, Thomas H. and John D. Petrarulo. "The Odyssey of Pittsburgh's Father Cox," *The Western Pennsylvania Historical Magazine,* Vol. 55, No. 3, July 1972.

Cooke, Edward F. "Patterns of Voting in Pennsylvania Counties, 1944-1958," *Pennsylvania History,* Vol. 27, No. 1, January 1960.

Cravens, Hamilton. "The Emergence of the Farmer-Labor Party in Washington Politics, 1919-1920," *Pacific North West Quarterly,* 57, 1966, 148-157.

Davin, Eric Leif, and Staughton Lynd. "Picket Line and Ballot Box: The Forgotten Legacy of the Local Labor Party Movement, 1932-1936," *Radical History Review,* No. 22, winter 1979-80, 43-63.

———. "Blue Collar Democracy: Class War and Political Revolution in Western Pennsylvania, 1932-1937, *Pennsylvania History,* Vol. 67, No. 2, spring 2000.

Dwyer, Richard. "Workers' Education, Labor Education, Labor Studies: An Historical Delineation," *Review of Educational Research,* 47, winter 1977, 179-207.

Fair, Daryl R. "The Reaction of Pennsylvania Voters to Catholic Candidates," *Pennsylvania History,* No. 32, July 1965, 305-315.

Flynt, Wayne. "Florida Labor and Political 'Radicalism,' 1919-1920," *Labor History,* No. 9, 1968, 73-90.

Foner, Eric. "Why is There No Socialism in the United States?" *History Workshop,* No. 17, spring 1984, 57-80.

Foster, George. "Peasant Society and the Image of Limited Good," *American Anthropologist,* No. 67, April 1965, 293-315.

"Gallup and Fortune Polls," *The Public Opinion Quarterly,* September 1940.

Gallup, George, and Claude Robinson. "American Institute of Public Opinion— Surveys, 1935-38," *The Public Opinion Quarterly,* July 1938.

Greenberg, Irwin F. "Philadelphia Democrats Get a New Deal: The Election of 1933," *The Pennsylvania Magazine of History and Biography,* April 1973.

Hays, Samuel P. "The Politics of Reform in Municipal Government in the Progressive Era," *Pacific Northwest Quarterly,* 55, October 1964.

Heineman, Kenneth J. "A Catholic New Deal: Religion and Labor in 1930s Pittsburgh," *The Pennsylvania Magazine of History & Biography,* Vol. 118, No. 4, October 1994.

Howlett, Charles F. "Brookwood Labor College and Work Commitment to Social Reform," *Mid-America,* 61, 1979, 47-66.

———. "Brookwood Labor College: Voice of Support for Black Workers," *Negro History Bulletin,* 45, 1982.

Keller, Richard C. "Pennsylvania's Little New Deal," *Pennsylvania History,* Vol. 29, No. 4, October 1962.

Key, Jr., V. O. "The Future of the Democratic Party," *Virginia Quarterly Review,* Vol. 28, No. 2, spring 1952.

———. "A Theory of Critical Elections," *Journal of Politics,* Vol. 17, No. 1, February 1955.

———. "Secular Realignment and the Party System," *Journal of Politics,* Vol. 21, No. 2, May 1959.

Klare, Karl E. "Judicial Deradicalization of the Wagner Act: The Origins of Modern Legal Consciousness, 1937-1941," *Minnesota Law Review,* 65, 1978.

Kornhauser, Arthur W. "Attitudes of Economic Groups," *The Public Opinion Quarterly,* April 1938.

Leab, Daniel J. "Anti-Communism, the FBI, and Matt Cvetic: The Ups and Downs of a Professional Informer," *The Pennsylvania Magazine of History & Biography,* Vol. 115, No. 4, October 1991.

Lovin, Hugh. "The Fall of the Farmer-Labor Parties, 1936-1938," *Pacific North West Quarterly,* No. 62, January 1971.

———. "Toward A Farmer-Labor Party in Oregon, 1933-1938, *Oregon Historical Quarterly,* Vol. 76, No. 2, June 1975.

———. "The Persistence of Third Party Dreams in the American Labor Movement, 1930-1938," *Mid-America,* No. 58, October 1976.

———. "The Ohio Farmer-Labor Movement in the 1930s," *Ohio History,* No. 87, Autumn, 1978.

———. "The Farmer-Labor Movement in Idaho, 1933-1938," *Journal of the West,* Vol. 18, No. 2, April 1979.

———. "The Automobile Workers Unions and the Fight for Labor Parties in the 1930s," *Indiana Magazine of History,* No. 77, 1981.

———. "CIO Innovators, Labor Party Ideologues, and Organized Labor's Muddles in the 1937 Detroit Elections," *The Old Northwest,* No. 8, fall 1982.

Lynd, Staughton. "The Possibility of Radicalism in the Early 1930s: The Case of Steel," *Radical America,* Vol. 6, No. 6, November-December 1972.

McKenna, William J. "The Influence of Religion in the Pennsylvania Elections of 1958 and 1960," *Pennsylvania History,* No. 29, October 1962, 407-419.

Morgan, Alfred L. "The Significance of Pennsylvania's 1938 Gubernatorial Election," *The Pennsylvania Magazine of History and Biography,* April 1978.

Nathan, Richard P. and Charles Adams. "Understanding Central City Hardship," *Political Science Quarterly,* No. 91, 1976, 47-62.

Nelson, Daniel. "The CIO at Bay: Labor Militancy and Politics in Akron, 1936-1938," *The Journal of American History,* No. 71, December 1984.

Oestreicher, Richard. "Urban Working-Class Political Behavior and Theories of American Electoral Politics, 1870-1940," *The Journal of American History*, Vol. 74, No. 4, March 1988.

Patterson, James T. "A Conservative Coalition Forms in Congress," *The Journal of American History*, 52, March 1966, 757-772.

Pivar, David J. "The Hosiery Workers and the Philadelphia Third Party Impulse, 1929-1935," *Labor History*, winter 1964.

Pratt, William C. "Socialism on the Northern Plains, 1900-1924," *South Dakota History*, 18, spring/summer 1988, 1-35.

Robinson, James W. "The Expulsion of Brookwood Labor College from the Workers' Education Bureau," *Labour History* [Canberra, Australia], No. 15, 1968, 64-69.

Rose, Jim. "'The Problem Every Supervisor Dreads': Women Workers at the U.S. Steel Duquesne Works During World War II," *Labor History*, Vol. 36, No. 1, winter 1995.

Shapiro, Stanley. "'Hand and Brain': The Farmer-Labor Party of 1920," *Labor History*, 26, summer 1985, 405-422.

Shover, John L. "The Emergence of a Two-Party System in Republican Philadelphia, 1924-1936," *The Journal of American History*, Vol. 60, No. 4, March 1974.

Seidman, Joel. "Organized Labor in Political Campaigns," *The Public Opinion Quarterly*, October 1939.

Skocpol, Theda. "Political Response to Capitalist Crisis: Neo-Marxist Theories of the State and the Case of the New Deal," *Politics & Society*, Vol. 10, No. 2, 1980.

Spencer, Thomas T. "'Labor is with Roosevelt!' The Pennsylvania Non-Partisan League and the Election of 1936," *Pennsylvania History*, Vol. 46, No. 1, January 1979.

Van DeWater, Peter E. "The Workers' Education Service," *Michigan History*, 60, 1976, 99-113.

Walsh, Francis R. "The Films We Never Saw: American Movies View Organized Labor, 1934-1954," *Labor History*, Vol. 27, No. 4, fall 1986.

Weber, Michael, John Bodnar, and Roger Simon, "Seven Neighborhoods: Stability and Change in Pittsburgh's Ethnic Community, 1930-1960," *The Western Pennsylvania Historical Magazine*, Vol. 64, No. 2, April 1981.

"The Workingmen's Party of California, 1877-1882," *California Historical Quarterly*, No. 55, 1976.

Zieger, Robert H. "The Career of James J. Davis," *Pennsylvania Magazine of History and Biography*, 97, 1974, 67-89.

Archives

Allegheny County Democratic Committee Headquarters, David L. Lawrence Speech Folder, Publicity File.

Allegheny County Employment Records, 1930-35, City-County Building, Pittsburgh.

American Federation of Labor Papers, 1935 Office Files of President William Green, AFL-CIO, Washington, D. C.

Cox Papers, James. Campaign Diary of Father James Cox, 1932, Historical Archives of the Diocese of Pittsburgh.

Gallagher File, Thomas J. Pennsylvania Division, Carnegie Library of Pittsburgh.

Gomrick Collection, Charles G. Archives of Industrial Society, University of Pittsburgh.

Maloy Papers, Elmer J. In the possession of his daughter, Jean Striegel.

Pennsylvania Federation of Labor Papers, Election Materials, Labor's Non-Partisan League, Historical Collections and Labor Archives, Pattee Library, Pennsylvania State University Libraries, State College, Pennsylvania.

Pennsylvania Historical and Museum Commission, Department of Justice Papers, Board of Pardons, Clemency File, R. G. 56.

Pittsburgh Central Labor Union Minutes. In the holdings of the Pittsburgh Typographical Union, Lo. No. 7, Archives of Industrial Society, University of Pittsburgh.

Rice Papers, Charles Owen. Archives of Industrial Society, University of Pittsburgh.

Roosevelt Papers, Franklin D. Franklin D. Roosevelt Library, Hyde Park, New York.

United Steelworkers of America Papers, Historical Collections and Labor Archives, Pattee Library, Pennsylvania State University Libraries, State College, Pennsylvania.

Books

Abrahamson, Mark. *Urban Enclaves: Identity and Place in America,* St. Martin's Press: New York, 1996.

Alford, Robert. *Party and Society,* Rand McNally: Chicago, 1963.

Anderson, Elin L. *We Americans,* Harvard University Press: Cambridge, 1938.

Barr, Andrew. *Drink: A Social History of America,* Carroll & Graf: New York, 1999.

Beers, Paul. *Pennsylvania Politics: Yesterday and Today,* Pennsylvania State University Press: University Park, Pa., 1980.

Beik, Mildred Allen. *The Miners of Windber: The Struggles of New Immigrants for Unionization, 1890s-1930s,* Pennsylvania State University Press: University Park, Pa., 1996.

Bell, Daniel. "America's Un-Marxist Revolution," in Reinhard Bendix and Seymour Martin Lipset, *Class, Status and Power: A Reader in Social Stratification,* The Free Press: New York, 1953.

————. "The Capitalism of the Proletariat: A Theory of American Trade-Unionism," in *The End of Ideology: On the Exhaustion of Political Ideas in the Fifties*, rev. ed., The Free Press: New York, 1960.

Bell, Thomas. *Out of This Furnace*, University of Pittsburgh Press: Pittsburgh, 1941, 1976.

Bernstein, Barton J. "The New Deal: The Conservative Achievements of Liberal Reform," in Barton J. Bernstein, Ed. *Towards A New Past: Dissenting Essays in American History*, New York: Vintage, 1967.

Blum, John Morton. *V Was For Victory: Politics and American Culture During World War II*, Harcourt Brace Jovanovich: New York, 1977.

Bodnar, John. *Workers' World: Kinship, Community, and Protest in an Industrial Society, 1900-1940*, The Johns Hopkins University Press: Baltimore, 1982.

————. Roger Simon, and Michael P. Weber. *Lives of Their Own: Blacks, Italians, and Poles in Pittsburgh, 1900-1960*, University of Illinois Press: Urbana, 1982.

Bradley, Sculley, Richmond Croom Beatty, and E. Hudson Long, Eds. *The American Tradition in Literature, Vol. 2*, W.W. Norton & Co.: New York, 1956.

Brinkley, Alan. *Voices of Protest: Huey Long, Father Coughlin, and the Great Depression*, Random House: New York, First Vintage Books Edition, August 1983.

————. *The End of Reform: New Deal Liberalism in Recession and War*, Alfred A. Knopf: New York, 1995.

Brinton, Crane. *The Anatomy of Revolution*, Vintage Books: New York, 1938, 1952, 1965.

Brode, Douglas. *The Films of the Fifties*, The Citadel Press: Secaucus, N.J., 1976.

Brody, David. *Steelworkers in America: The Nonunion Era*, Harvard University Press: Cambridge, Mass., 1960; Harper & Row: New York, 1969.

————. *Labor in Crisis: The Steel Strike of 1919*, J. B. Lippincott Co.: New York, 1965.

————. *Workers in Industrial America: Essays on the Twentieth Century Struggle*, Oxford University Press: New York, 1980.

————. "Workers and Work in America: The New Labor History," in James B. Gardner and George Rollie Adams, Eds. *Ordinary People and Everyday Life: Perspectives on the New Social History*, The American Association for State and Local History: Nashville, Tenn., 1983.

Brooks, Robert R.R. *As Steel Goes, . . . Unionism in a Basic Industry*, Yale University Press: New Haven, 1940.

Brophy, John. *A Miner's Life*, University of Wisconsin Press: Madison, 1964.

Burke, Robert E. *Olson's New Deal for California*, University of California Press: Berkeley, 1953.

Burner, David. *The Politics of Provincialism*, Alfred A. Knopf: New York, 1967.

Burnham, Walter Dean. *Critical Elections and the Mainsprings of American Politics*, W.W. Norton: New York, 1970.

———. Ed. *Politics/America: The Cutting Edge of Change,* Van Nostrand Co.: New York, 1973.

———. *The Current Crisis in American Politics,* Oxford University Press: New York, 1982.

Burns, James MacGregor. *The Crosswinds of Freedom,* Vintage Books: New York, 1990.

Campbell, Angus. "Voters and Elections: Past and Present," in Stephen V. Monsma and Jack R. Van Der Slik, Eds. *American Politics: Research and Readings,* Holt, Rinehart, and Winston: New York, 1970.

Cantor, Milton, Ed. *American Working Class Culture: Explorations in American Labor and Social History,* Greenwood Press: Westport, Conn., 1979.

Carter, Paul A. *The Twenties in America,* Thomas Y. Crowell Co.: New York, 1968.

Caute, David. *The Great Fear: The Anti-Communist Purge Under Truman and Eisenhower,* Simon & Schuster: New York, 1978.

Centers, Richard. *The Psychology of Social Classes: A Study of Class Consciousness,* Russell and Russell: New York, 1949, 1961.

Chalmers, David M. *Hooded Americanism: The History of the Ku Klux Klan,* Duke University Press: Durham, N.C., 1987.

Cohen, Lizabeth. *Making a New Deal: Industrial Workers in Chicago, 1919-1939,* Cambridge University Press: Cambridge, England, 1990.

Conkin, Paul K. *The New Deal,* Thomas Y. Crowell Co.: New York, 1967.

Converse, Philip E. , Angus Campbell, Warren E. Miller, and Donald E. Stokes, "Reaffirming the Stalemate: Stability and Change in 1960," in Allen F. Davis and Harold D. Woodman, Eds. *Conflict and Consensus in Modern American History.*

Cooke, Edward F. and G. Edward Janosik, *Guide to Pennsylvania Politics,* Greenwood Press: Westport, Conn., 1957.

Cowley, Malcolm. *The Dream of the Golden Mountains: Remembering the 1930s,* The Viking Press: New York, 1980.

Coy, Patrick G., Ed. *A Revolution of the Heart: Essays on the Catholic Worker,* Temple University Press: Philadelphia, 1988.

Cumbler, John T. *Working-Class Community in Industrial America,* Greenwood Press: Westport, Conn., 1979.

Daugherty, Carroll R. , Melvin G. de Chazeau, & Samuel Stratton. *The Economics of the Iron and Steel Industry,* Bureau of Business Research, 1937.

Davin, Eric Leif. "The Very Last Hurrah: The Defeat of the Labor Party Idea, 1934-1936," in Staughton Lynd, Ed. *"We Are All Leaders": The Alternative Unionism of the Early 1930s,* University of Illinois Press: Urbana, 1996.

———. "The Labor Party Movement of the 1930s," in Ronald Hayduk and Immanuel Ness, Eds. *The Encyclopedia of Third Parties in America,* M. E. Sharpe Publications: New York, 1999.

Davis, Allen F., and Harold D. Woodman, Eds. *Conflict and Consensus in Modern American History,* Sixth Ed., D.C. Heath & Co.: Lexington, Mass., 1984.

Davis, Allison, et al. *Deep South: A Social Anthropological Study of Caste and Class,* University of Chicago Press: Chicago, 1941.

Davis, Mike. *Prisoners of the American Dream: Politics and Economy in the History of the U. S. Working Class,* Verso: London, 1986.

Dawidowicz, Lucy S. *The War Against the Jews, 1933-1945,* Bantam Books: New York, 1976.

Dawley, Alan. *Class and Community: The Industrial Revolution in Lynn,* Harvard University Press: Cambridge, 1976.

De Caux, Len. *Labor Radical: From the Wobblies to CIO, A Personal History,* Beacon Press: Boston, 1970, 1971.

Degler, Carl N. "The Third American Revolution," in Allen F. Davis and Harold D. Woodman, Eds. *Conflict and Consensus in Modern American History.*

DeVault, Ileen. *Sons and Daughters of Labor: Class and Clerical Work in Turn-of-the-Century Pittsburgh,* Cornell University Press: Ithaca, 1990.

Donahoe, Bernard F. *Private Plans and Public Dangers: The Story of FDR's Third Nomination,* University of Notre Dame Press: Notre Dame, Indiana, 1965.

Douglas, Paul H. *The Coming of A New Party,* McGraw-Hill: New York, 1932.

Dubofsky, Melvyn and Warren Van Tine, *John L. Lewis: A Biography,* Quadrangle-The New York Times Book Company: New York, 1977.

————. "Not So 'Turbulent Years': A New Look at the 1930s," in Charles Stephenson and Robert Asher, Eds. *Life and Labor: Dimensions of American Working Class History,* State University of New York Press: Albany, 1986.

Edelman, Murray. "New Deal Sensitivity to Labor Interests," in Milton Derber and Erwin Young, Eds. *Labor and the New Deal,* University of Wisconsin Press: Madison, 1957.

Farley, James A. *Behind the Ballots: The Personal History of a Politician,* Harcourt, Brace & Co.: New York, 1938.

Fast, Howard. "An Occurrence at Republic Steel," in Isabel Leighton, Ed. *The Aspirin Age, 1919-1941,* Simon & Schuster: New York, 1949.

Fine, Nathan. *Labor and Farmer Parties in the United States, 1828-1928,* Rand School: New York, 1928.

Fine, Sidney. *Sit-Down: The General Motors Strike of 1936-1937,* University of Michigan Press: Ann Arbor, 1969.

Fink, Leon. *Workingmen's Democracy: The Knights of Labor and American Politics,* University of Illinois Press: Urbana, 1983.

Fishman, Robert. *Bourgeois Utopias: The Rise and Fall of Suburbia,* Basic Books: New York, 1987.

Fitch, John A. *The Steel Workers,* The Russell Sage Foundation, 1910, University of Pittsburgh Press: Pittsburgh, 1989.

Foner, Philip S., Ed. *We, the Other People: Alternative Declarations of Independence by Labor Groups, Farmers, Woman's Rights Advocates, Socialists, and Blacks, 1829-1975,* University of Illinois Press: Urbana, 1976.

Foster, James Caldwell. *The Union Politic: The CIO Political Action Committee,* University of Missouri Press: St. Louis, 1975.

Fraser, Steve, and Gary Gerstle. *The Rise and Fall of the New Deal Order, 1930-1980,* Princeton University Press: Princeton, N.J., 1989.

Freeman, Joshua B. *Working-Class New York: Life and Labor Since World War II,* The New Press: New York, 1999.

Gallaher, Jr., Art. *Plainville Fifteen Years After,* Columbia University Press: New York, 1961.

Gallup, George, in Judah L. Graubart and Alice V. Graubart. *Decade of Destiny,* Contemporary Books, Inc.: Chicago, 1978.

Gallup Political Almanac for 1946, American Institute of Public Opinion, Princeton, N.J.

Gans, Herbert J. *The Urban Villagers: Group and Class in the Life of Italian-Americans,* The Free Press: New York, 1962.

Gatell, Frank Otto, Paul Goodman, and Allen Weinstein, Eds. *The Growth of American Politics, Vol. II, Since the Civil War,* Oxford University Press: New York, 1972.

Gerstle, Gary. *Working-Class Americanism: The Politics of Labor in a Textile City, 1914-1960,* Cambridge University Press: New York; Cambridge, England, 1989.

Gieske, Millard L. *Minnesota Farmer-Laborism: The Third-Party Alternative,* University of Minnesota Press: Minneapolis, 1979.

Ginger, Ann Fagan, and David Christiano, Eds. *The Cold War Against Labor,* Studies in Law and Social Change, No. 3, Meiklejohn Civil Liberties Institute: Berkeley, Cal., 1987.

Glaab, Charles N., Ed. *The American City,* Dorsey: Homewood, Ill., 1963.

Glasco, Laurence. "Double Burden: The Black Experience in Pittsburgh," in Samuel P. Hays, Ed. *City at the Point: Essays in the Social History of Pittsburgh,* University of Pittsburgh Press: Pittsburgh, 1989.

Goldfield, Michael. *The Color of Politics: Race and the Mainsprings of American Politics,* The New Press: New York, 1997.

Gordon, Colin. *New Deals: Business, Labor, and Politics in America, 1920-1935,* Cambridge University Press: New York, 1994.

Greenstone, J. David. *Labor in American Politics,* Alfred A. Knopf: New York, 1969.

Greenwald, Maurine Weiner. "Women and Class in Pittsburgh, 1850-1920," in Samuel P. Hays, Ed. *City at the Point: Essays on the Social History of Pittsburgh,* University of Pittsburgh Press: Pittsburgh, 1989.

Gregory, G. H., Compiler and Editor, *Posters of World War II,* Gramercy Books: New York, 1993.

Guffey, Joseph F. *Seventy Years on the Red-Fire Wagon,* privately printed, 1952.

Gutman, Herbert G. *Work, Culture, and Society in Industrializing America: Essays in American Working-Class and Social History,* Vintage Books: New York, 1977.

Harrington, Michael. *Socialism,* Saturday Review Press: New York, 1972.

Harris, Chester. *Tiger at the Bar: The Life Story of Charles J. Margiotti,* Vantage Press: New York, 1956.

Hartz, Louis. *The Liberal Tradition in America: An Interpretation of American Political Thought Since the Revolution,* Harcourt, Brace & World, Inc.: New York, 1955.

Hayden, Dolores. *Building Suburbia: Green Fields and Urban Growth, 1820-2000,* Pantheon: New York, 2004.

————. *A Field Guide to Sprawl,* Norton: New York, 2004.

Heineman, Kenneth J. *A Catholic New Deal: Religion and Reform in Depression Pittsburgh,* Pennsylvania State University Press: University Park, Pa., 1999.

Hillquit, Morris, and Matthew Woll, *Should the American Workers Form a Political Party of Their Own?* Rand School: New York, 1932.

Hirsch, Eric L. *Urban Revolt: Ethnic Politics in the Nineteenth-Century Chicago Labor Movement,* University of California Press: Berkeley, 1990.

Hollingshead, August. *Elmtown's Youth,* John Wiley Sons, Inc.: New York, 1949, rev. ed., 1975.

Holt, Michael Fitzgibbon. *Forging a Majority: The Formation of the Republican Party in Pittsburgh, 1848-1860,* Yale University Press: New Haven, 1969.

Huber, Raphael M., Ed. *Our Bishops Speak: National Pastorals and Annual Statements of the Hierarchy of the United States, 1919-1951,* Bruce: Milwaukee, 1952.

Hughes, Emmet John. "The Politics of Stasis: A Word on Eisenhower," in Allen F. Davis and Harold D. Woodman, Eds. *Conflict and Consensus in Modern American History.*

Hughes, Langston. "How About It, Dixie?" in *Jim Crow's Last Stand,* Race and Culture Series No. 2, Negro Publication Society of America: New York, 1943.

Irvine, E. Eastman, Ed. "Estimated United States Population, July 1, 1943," *The World Almanac and Book of Facts for 1947, The New York World-Telegram,* New York, 1947.

Issel, William. *Social Change in the United States, 1945-1983,* Schocken Books: New York, 1985.

Jackman, Mary R. and Robert W. Jackman. *Class Awareness in the United States,* University of California Press: Berkeley, 1983.

Jackson, Kenneth T. *Crabgrass Frontier: The Suburbanization of the United States,* Oxford University Press: New York, 1985.

Jacques, Jr., Charles J. *Kennywood: Roller Coaster Capital of the World,* Vestal Press Ltd.: New York, 1982.

Jeffries, John W. *Testing the Roosevelt Coalition: Connecticut Society and Politics in the Era of World War II,* The University of Tennessee Press: Knoxville, 1979.

Jones, Alfred Winslow. *Life, Liberty, and Property,* Temple University Press: Philadelphia, 1941.

Jones, Mother. *The Autobiography of Mother Jones,* Charles H. Kerr & Co.: Chicago, 1925, 1972.

Kain, John F. "The Distribution and Movement of Jobs and Industry," in James Q. Wilson, Ed. *The Metropolitan Enigma: Inquiries into the Nature and Dimensions of America's "Urban Crisis,"* Harvard University Press: Cambridge, 1968.

Kane, John J., and George Rankin, Jr. *Your Future in Allegheny County,* North River Press: New York, 1947.

Keller, Richard. *Pennsylvania's Little New Deal,* Garland Publications: New York, 1982.

Kessler-Harris, Alice. *In Pursuit of Equity: Women, Men and the Quest for Economic Citizenship in 20th-Century America,* Oxford University Press: New York, 2001.

Key, Jr., V. O. *Politics, Parties, & Pressure Groups,* Thomas Y. Crowell: New York, 1964.

Klein, Philip, et al., *A Social Study of Pittsburgh: Community Problems and Social Services of Allegheny County,* Columbia University Press: New York, 1938.

Klein, Philip, and Ari Hoogenboom, *A History of Pennsylvania,* New York, 1973.

Klejment, Anne, and Alice Klejment, *Dorothy Day and "The Catholic Worker": A Bibliography and Index,* Garland Publications: New York, 1986.

Kleppner, Paul. *Who Voted? The Dynamics of Electoral Turnout, 1870-1980,* Praeger Publishers: New York, 1982.

Klinkner, Philip A., with Rogers M. Smith. *The Unsteady March: The Rise and Decline of Racial Equality in America,* University of Chicago Press: Chicago, 1999.

Ladd, Jr., Everett Carll and Charles D. Hadley. *Transformations of the American Party System,* W.W. Norton: New York, 1975.

Lazarsfeld, Paul, et al., *The People's Choice: How the Voter Makes Up His Mind in a Presidential Campaign,* Duell, Sloan, & Pearce: New York, 1944.

Leighton, Isabel, Ed. *The Aspirin Age, 1919-1941,* Simon & Schuster: New York, 1949.

Lens, Sidney. *The Labor Wars: From the Molly Maguires to the Sitdowns,* Anchor Press/ Doubleday: Garden City, New York, 1974.

Leuchtenburg, William, E. *The Perils of Prosperity, 1914-1932,* University of Chicago Press: Chicago, 1958.

———. *Franklin D. Roosevelt and the New Deal, 1932-1940,* Harper & Row: New York, 1963.

Levinson, Edward. *Labor on the March,* Harper & Bros.: New York, 1938.

Lichtenstein, Nelson. *Labor's War at Home, The CIO in World War II,* Cambridge University Press: New York, 1982.

———. "From Corporatism to Collective Bargaining: Organized Labor and the Eclipse of Social Democracy in the Postwar Era," in Steve Fraser and Gary Gerstle, Eds. *The Rise and Fall of the New Deal Order, 1930-1980,* Princeton University Press: Princeton, N.J., 1989.

———. Susan Strasser, and Roy Rosenzweig, *Who Built America? Working People and the Nation's Economy, Politics, Culture, and Society, Vol. 2, Since 1877,* Worth Pub.: New York, 2000.

Lorant, Stefan. *Pittsburgh: The Story of an American City,* Doubleday: Garden City, New York, 1964.

Lorwin, Lewis L. *The American Federation of Labor,* The Brookings Institution: Washington, D.C., 1933.

Lubell, Samuel. *The Future of American Politics,* Harper and Brothers: New York, 1952.

———. *The Future While It Happened,* W.W. Norton & Co.: New York, 1973.

Lubove, Roy. *Twentieth Century Pittsburgh: Government, Business and Environmental Change,* University of Pittsburgh Press: Pittsburgh, 1969.

Lynd, Robert S. and Helen Merrell Lynd, *Middletown in Transition,* Harcourt, Brace, & World: New York, 1937.

McCartin, Joseph A. *Labor's Great War: The Struggle for Industrial Democracy and the Origins of Modern American Labor Relations, 1912-1921,* University of North Carolina Press: Chapel Hill, 1997.

McDonald, David J. *Union Man,* E.P. Dutton & Co., Inc.: New York, 1969.

McElvaine, Robert S., Ed. *Down & Out in the Great Depression: Letters from the "Forgotten Man,"* University of North Carolina Press: Chapel Hill, 1982.

McGeever, Patrick J. *Rev. Charles Owen Rice: Apostle of Contradiction,* Duquesne University Press: Pittsburgh, 1989.

McKibbin, Ross. *Class and Cultures in England, 1918-1951,* Oxford University Press: New York, 1998.

Maclean, Nancy. *Behind the Mask of Chivalry: The Making of the Second Ku Klux Klan,* Oxford University Press: New York, 1994.

Magda, Matthew S. *Monessen: Industrial Boomtown and Steel Community, 1898-1980,* Pennsylvania Historical and Museum Commission: Harrisburg, 1985.

Manchester, William. "FDR Thunders," in *A Sense of History: The Best Writing from the Pages of American Heritage,* American Heritage: New York, 1985.

Margolis, Michael, and George H. Foster, "Ethnicity and Voting," in Roy Lubove, Ed. *Pittsburgh,* New Viewpoints: New York, 1976.

Martin, George. *Madam Secretary, Frances Perkins,* Boston: Houghton Mifflin, 1976.

Marx, Karl, and Frederick Engels, *The Communist Manifesto,* International Publishers: New York, 1948, 1986.

Miller, Herman P. *Income of the American People,* John Wiley: New York, 1955.

Miller, William D. *A Harsh and Dreadful Love: Dorothy Day and the Catholic Worker Movement,* Liveright: New York, 1973.

———. *Dorothy Day: A Biography,* Harper & Row: San Francisco, 1982.

Miner, Curtis. *Forging A New Deal: Johnstown and the Great Depression, 1929-1941,* Johnstown Area Heritage Association: Johnstown, Pa., 1993.

Mowry, George E. *The Urban Nation: 1920-1960,* Hill and Wang: New York, 1965.

Musmanno, Michael Angelo. *Black Fury,* Fountainhead Publishers: New York, 1966.

Myers, Gustavus. *The Ending of Hereditary American Fortunes,* Julian Messner: New York, 1939.

Neustadt, Richard E. "From FDR to Truman: Congress and the Fair Deal," in Allen F. Davis and Harold D. Woodman, Eds. *Conflict and Consensus in*

Modern American History, Sixth Ed., D.C. Heath & Co.: Lexington, Mass., 1984.

Oestreicher, Richard. "Working-Class Formation, Development, and Consciousness in Pittsburgh, 1790-1960," in Samuel P. Hays, Ed. *City at the Point: Essays on the Social History of Pittsburgh,* University of Pittsburgh Press: Pittsburgh, 1989.

Orren, Karen. *Belated Feudalism: Labor, the Law, and Liberal Development in the United States,* Cambridge University Press: Cambridge, 1991.

Park, Robert E. "The City," in Robert E. Park, Ernest W. Burgess, and Roderick D. McKenzie, Eds. *The City,* University of Chicago Press: Chicago, 1967, originally published 1925.

Parmet, Herbert S., and Marie B. Hecht. *Never Again: A President Runs for a Third Term,* The Macmillan Co.: New York, 1968.

Piehl, Mel. *Breaking Bread: The Catholic Worker and the Origin of Catholic Radicalism in America,* Temple University Press: Philadelphia, 1982.

Piven, Frances Fox and Richard A. Cloward. *Regulating the Poor: The Functions of Public Welfare,* Vintage: New York, 1971.

Polenberg, Richard. *One Nation Divisible: Class, Race, and Ethnicity in the United States Since 1938,* The Viking Press: New York, 1980.

Pollak, Katherine H., and David J. Saposs. *How Should Labor Vote?* Brookwood Labor College Publications: Katonah, New York, 1932.

Poulantzas, Nicos. *Political Power and Social Classes,* Verso: London, 1975.

Powers, George. *Cradle of Steel Unionism: Monongahela Valley, PA,* Figueroa Printers, Inc.: East Chicago, Ind., 1972.

Radosh, Ronald. "The Corporate Ideology of American Labor Leaders from Gompers to Hillman," in James Weinstein and David W. Eakins, Eds. *For a New America: Essays in History and Politics,* Random House: New York, 1970.

———. "The Myth of the New Deal," in Ronald Radosh and Murray Rothbard, Eds. *The New Leviathan: Essays on the Rise of the American Corporate State,* New York: Dutton, 1972.

Reichard, Gary W. *Politics as Usual: The Age of Truman and Eisenhower,* Harlan Davidson, Inc.: Arlington Heights., IL, 1988.

Reichley, James. *The Art of Government: Reform and Organization Politics in Philadelphia,* New York, 1959.

Rees, Laurence. *World War II Behind Closed Doors,* Random House: New York, 2009.

Reuther, Victor. *The Brothers Reuther and the Story of the UAW: A Memoir,* Houghton Mifflin: Boston, 1976.

Reynolds, David. *Rich Relations: The American Occupation of Britain, 1942-1945,* Random House: New York, 1994.

Rice, Stuart A. *Farmers and Workers in American Politics,* Columbia University Press: New York, 1924.

Robbins, Hayes. *The Labor Movement and the Farmer,* Harcourt Brace: New York, 1922.

Roberts, Nancy L. *Dorothy Day and the "Catholic Worker,"* State University of New York Press: Albany, 1984.

Rogin, Michael Paul. "Alienated Grownups: McCarthyism as Mass Politics," in Allen F. Davis and Harold D. Woodman, Eds. *Conflict and Consensus in Modern American History,* Sixth Ed., D.C. Heath & Co.: Lexington, Mass., 1984.

Rosen, Ruth. *The World Split Open: How the Modern Women's Movement Changed America,* Viking: New York, 2000.

Rosenman, Samuel I., Ed. *The Public Papers and Addresses of Franklin D. Roosevelt,* Random House: New York, 1938-1950.

Ross, Irwin *The Loneliest Campaign: The Truman Victory of 1948,* Greenwood Press: Westport, Conn., 1968, 1977.

Schlesinger, Jr., Arthur M. *The Age of Roosevelt: The Crisis of the Old Order: 1919-1933,* Houghton Mifflin Co.: Boston, 1957.

————. *The Politics of Upheaval,* Houghton Mifflin Co.: Boston, 1960.

Schultz, Bud, and Ruth Schultz, Eds. *It Did Happen Here: Recollections of Political Repression in America,* University of California Press: Berkeley, 1989.

Shumsky, Neil Larry. *The Evolution of Political Protest and the Workingmen's Party of California,* Ohio State University Press: Columbus, 1991.

Shorter, Edward, and Charles Tilly. *Strikes in France, 1830-1969,* Harvard University Press: Cambridge, 1974.

Sims, Patsy. *The Klan,* Stein and Day: New York, 1978.

Stave, Bruce M. *The New Deal and the Last Hurrah: Pittsburgh Machine Politics,* University of Pittsburgh Press: Pittsburgh, 1970.

————. "The Great Depression and Urban Political Continuity: Bridgeport Chooses Socialism," in Bruce M. Stave, Ed. *Socialism and the Cities,* Kennikat Press: Port Washington, New York, 1975.

Stedman, Murray S., and Susan W. Stedman, *Discontent at the Polls: A Study of Farmer and Labor Parties, 1827-1948,* Columbia University Press: New York, 1950.

Stegner, Wallace. "The Radio Priest and His Flock," in Isabel Leighton, Ed. *The Aspirin Age, 1919-1941,* Simon & Schuster: New York, 1949.

Stokes, Thomas L. *Chip Off My Shoulder,* Princeton University Press: Princeton, N.J., 1940.

Stoughton, Judith L. *Proud Donkey of Schaerbeeck: Ade Bethune, Catholic Worker Artist,* North Star Press: St. Cloud, Minnesota, 1988.

Stryker, Roy Emerson, and Nancy Wood, *In This Proud Land: America 1935-1943 as Seen in the FSA Photographs,* Galahad Books: New York, 1973.

Sundquist, James L. *Dynamics of the Party System,* The Brookings Institution: Washington, D.C., 1973.

Sweeney, Vincent D. *The United Steelworkers of America... The First 10 Years,* booklet published by the USWA, Pittsburgh, 1946.

Teaford, Jon C. *City and Suburb: The Political Fragmentation of Metropolitan America, 1850-1970,* Johns Hopkins University Press: Baltimore, 1979.

———. *The Rough Road to Renaissance: Urban Revitalization in America, 1940-1985,* The Johns Hopkins University Press: Baltimore, 1990.

Thompson, E. P. *The Making of the English Working Class,* Vintage Books: New York, 1963.

Tomlins, Christopher. *The State and the Unions,* Cambridge University Press: New York, 1985.

Valelly, Richard M. *Radicalism in the States: The Minnesota Farmer-Labor Party and the American Political Economy,* University of Chicago Press: Chicago, 1989.

Van Gelder, Robert, Ed. *The Stephen Vincent Benet Pocket Book,* Pocket Books: New York, 1946.

Wade, Wyn Craig. *The Fiery Cross: The Ku Klux Klan in America,* Simon and Schuster: New York, 1987.

Walkowitz, Daniel J. *Worker City, Company Town,* University of Illinois Press: Urbana, 1978.

Warner, Jr., Sam Bass. *The Private City,* University of Philadelphia Press: Philadelphia, 1968.

———. *Streetcar Suburbs: The Process of Growth in Boston, 1870-1900,* 2nd Ed., Harvard University Press: Cambridge, 1978.

Warner, W. Lloyd, and Paul S. Lunt. *The Social Life of a Modern Community,* Yale University Press: New Haven, 1941.

———. *The Status System of a Modern Community,* Yale University Press: New Haven, 1942.

Weber, Michael P. *Don't Call Me Boss: David L. Lawrence, Pittsburgh's Renaissance Mayor,* University of Pittsburgh Press: Pittsburgh, 1988.

West, James (pseud. of Carl Withers). *Plainville, USA,* Columbia University Press: New York, 1947.

Whitman, Alden. *Labor Parties, 1827-1834,* International Publishers: New York, 1943.

Williamson, Jeffrey G., and Peter H. Lindert. *American Inequality: A Macroeconomic History,* Academic Press: New York, 1980.

Winkler, Allan M. *Home Front U.S.A.: America During World War II,* Harlan Davidson, Inc.: Arlington Heights, Ill., 1986.

Work Projects Administration, Writers' Project. *These Are Our Lives: As Told by the People and Written by Members of the Federal Writers' Project of the Works Progress Administration in North Carolina, Tennessee, and Georgia,* University of North Carolina Press: Chapel Hill, 1939; W.W. Norton & Co.: New York, 1975.

———. Writers' Project. *New York City Guide,* Oxford University Press: New York, 1939.

———. *Pennsylvania: A Guide to the Keystone State,* Oxford University Press: New York, 1940.

Zieger, Robert H. *American Workers, American Unions, 1920-1985,* The Johns Hopkins University Press: Baltimore, 1986.

Dissertations and Academic Papers

Altenbaugh, Richard. "Forming the Structure of a New Society Within the Shell of the Old: A Study of Three Labor Colleges and Their Contributions to the American Labor Movement," Ph. D. dissertation, University of Pittsburgh, 1980, *Dissertations Abstracts International* 41, 565-A.

Chamovitz, Marcia. "The San Rocco Celebration of Aliquippa: An Italian Saint in an American Setting," seminar paper, History Department, University of Pittsburgh, 1977.

Draham, Ann Marie, et al. "People, Power, and Profits: The Struggle of U.S. Steel Workers for Economic Democracy, 1882-1985," unpublished manuscript, n.d.

Foy, Martha E. "The Negro in the Courts: A Study in Race Relations," Ph.D. dissertation, University of Pittsburgh, 1953.

Hardisky, David Lee. "The Rochester General Strike of 1946," Ph.D. dissertation, University of Rochester, 1983.

Hays, Samuel P. "The Welfare State and Democratic Practice in the United States Since World War II," paper presented at a history conference at the University of Pittsburgh, 1992.

Johnson, Marilynn S. "Mobilizing the Home Front: Labor and Politics in Oakland, 1943-1951," paper presented at the Organization of American Historians annual meeting, Anaheim, California, 1993.

Maddalena, Lucille A. "The Goals of the Bryn Mawr Summer School for Women Workers as Established During its First Five Years," Ph.D. dissertation, Rutgers University, 1979, *Dissertation Abstracts International,* 40, 76-A.

Miller, James E. "The Negro in Pennsylvania Politics, with Special Reference to Philadelphia, Since 1932,"Ph.D. dissertation, University of Pennsylvania, 1945.

Onochowski, Stanley M. "Community History," undergraduate paper, University of Pittsburgh, March 18, 1971.

Serene, Frank H. "Immigrant Steelworkers in the Monongahela Valley: Their Communities and the Development of a Labor Class Consciousness," Ph.D. dissertation, University of Pittsburgh, 1979.

Shrake, II, Richard W. "Working Class Politics in Akron, Ohio, 1936: The United Rubber Workers and the Failure of the Farmer-Labor Party," M.A. thesis, University of Akron, 1974.

Simmons, Ruth Louise. "The Negro in Recent Pittsburgh Politics," M.A. thesis, University of Pittsburgh, 1945.

Steed, Karen L. "Unionization and the Turn to Politics: Aliquippa and the Jones and Laughlin Steel Works, 1937-1941," graduate seminar paper, University of Pittsburgh, 1982.

Warren, Wilson. "Behind the Radical Veil of an Unemployed Organization: An Examination of Working-Class Consciousness During the Great Depression," graduate seminar paper, University of Pittsburgh.

Weber, Michael P. "Ethnicity and the Democratic Political Machine in Pittsburgh, 1930-1960," paper delivered at the annual convention of the Organization of American Historians, 1991.

Wong, Susan I. "Workers Education, 1921-1951," Ph.D. dissertation, Columbia University, 1976.

Wood, Robert W. "Community History," undergraduate paper, University of Pittsburgh, March 18, 1971.

Interviews

Brooks, Evelyn. By Eric Leif Davin and Anita Alverio, 1980.

Brown, Thomas. In John Bodnar, *Workers' World: Kinship, Community and Protest in an Industrial Society, 1900-1940,* The Johns Hopkins University Press: New York, 1982.

Brozek, Stanley. In John Bodnar, *Workers' World.*

Caliendo, Camilla. By Eric Leif Davin, May 24, 1996.

Casciato, Charles. By Eric Leif Davin, May 24, 1996.

Casciato, John. By Eric Leif Davin, May 24, 1996.

Czachowski, Ray. In John Bodnar, *Workers' World.*

Czelen, John. In John Bodnar, *Workers' World.*

DeAndrea, Vincent. By Eric Leif Davin, April 6, 1999 and January 8, 2002.

Del Turco, Domenic. In John Bodnar, *Workers' World.*

DeSenna, Louis. By Eric Leif Davin and Karen L. Steed, November 23, 1980.

Doratio, "Rocky." In *Crashin' Out: Hard Times in McKeesport,* prepared by the McKeesport Oral History Project, Mon Valley Unemployed Committee, Pittsburgh, August 1983.

Fagan, Patrick. By Alice M. Hoffman, Historical Collections and Labor Archives, Pattee Library, Pennsylvania State University, State College, Pennsylvania, September 24, October 1, 1968, August 8, 1972.

Filipe, Dee. By Eric Leif Davin and Anita Alverio, 1980.

Gottlieb, Peter. Curator of the United Steelworkers of America Papers, Historical Collections and Labor Archives, Pattee Library, Pennsylvania State University Libraries, State College, Pennsylvania. By Eric Leif Davin, October 5, 1988.

Kelly, Frank K. By Eric Leif Davin.

Kelly, John B. In Edwin B. Bronner. "The New Deal Comes to Pennsylvania: The Gubernatorial Election of 1934," *Pennsylvania History,* Vol. 27, No. 1, January 1960.

Law, James. In Michael P. Weber, *Don't Call Me Boss.*

Lawrence, David L. By Stefan Lorant, December 14, 1963, Archives of Industrial Society, University of Pittsburgh.

Lubove, Roy. By Eric Leif Davin, August 25, 1994.

Luketich, Tom. In John Bodnar, *Workers' World.*

McGuigan, Phil. In *Crashin' Out.*

Maloy, Elmer J. United Steelworkers of America Papers, Historical Collections and Labor Archives, Pattee Library, Pennsylvania State University Libraries, State College, Pennsylvania.

Mullen, John J. United Steelworkers of America Papers, Historical Collections and Labor Archives, Pattee Library, Pennsylvania State University Libraries, State College, Pennsylvania.

Rice, Charles Owen. Interviewed by Ronald L. Filippelli, The Pennsylvania State University United Steelworkers of America Oral History Project, April 5, 1967.

Rice, Orville. In John Bodnar, *Workers' World.*

Rudiak, Joe. In John Bodnar, *Workers' World.*

Smolinski, Louis. In John Bodnar, *Workers' World.*

Stackhouse, Paul. By Eric Leif Davin, October 3, 1995.

Striegel, Tom. By Eric Leif Davin, June 6, 1989.

Weber, Michael P. July 17, 1982, Archives of Industrial Society, University of Pittsburgh.

Zahorsky, Mike. By Eric Leif Davin and Karen L. Steed, November 23, 1980.

Zahorsky, Michael. In John Bodnar, *Workers' World.*

Magazine Articles

Alsop, Joseph, and Robert Kintner. "The Guffey, Biography of a Boss, New Style," *The Saturday Evening Post,* March 26, 1938.

———. "The Guffey, The Capture of Pennsylvania," *The Saturday Evening Post,* April 16, 1938.

Bliven, Jr., Bruce. "Pennsylvania Under Earle," *The New Republic,* August 18, 1937.

Blumenthal, Sidney. "Reinventing Lincoln," *The New Yorker,* November 14, 1994.

Breasted, Mary. "The Eveready Mayor," *Pittsburgh,* July 1992.

Bulletin Index. November 11, 1937.

———. September 19, 1940.

Business Week. October 5, 12, 1946

Commons, John R. "Wage-Earners of Pittsburgh," *Charities and the Commons,* Vol. 21.

Commonwealth: The Magazine of Pennsylvania. "Pennsylvania Votes for Governor," November 1946.

Dahir, Mubarak S. "Oakland Writ Large," *Pitt Magazine,* June 1998.

"Duquesne Light Co. Dispute," *Monthly Labor Review,* October 1946.

Fitch, John A. "A Man Can Talk in Homestead," *Survey Graphic,* Vol. 25, No. 2, February 1936.

Fortune. February 1947.

Frank, Stanley. "Labor Answers the G.I.," *Collier's,* October 13, 1945.

"George Does It," *TIME,* October 7, 1946.

"Ghost Town," *TIME*, October 28, 1946.

Hawkins, Frank. "Lawrence of Pittsburgh: Boss of the Mellon Patch," *Harper's*, August 1956.

Hicks, Jimmie. "Frank Capra," *Films in Review*, September-October 1992.

Hoover, J. Edgar. "FBI Reveals How Many Reds Live in Your State," *Look*, August 1, 1950.

"Justice for All," *Life Celebrates 1945*, July 5, 1995.

Kelly, Michael. "The Man of the Minute," *The New Yorker*, July 17, 1995.

Kiger, Patrick J., "Ethnic Roots: The Melting Pot Myth," *Pittsburgh Magazine*, October 1983.

Labor. September 9, 1944.

Laidler, Harry W. "Toward a Farmer-Labor Party," *Industrial Democracy*, Vol. 5, No. 11, February 1938.

Lambert, Craig. "Cantos and The Stem Christie," *Harvard Magazine*, January-February 1995.

LIFE Celebrates 1945. "Justice for All," June 5, 1995.

Literary Digest. November 17, 1934.

Lubell, Samuel. "Post Mortem: Who Elected Roosevelt?" *The Saturday Evening Post*, January 25, 1941.

McIntosh, Roderick J. "Listening to the Mill: Growing up in the Shadow of 'The Steel,'" *Archaeology*, November-December 1999.

Mendelson, Abby. "Bloomfield," *Pittsburgh Magazine*, June 1980.

———. "Invisible Boundaries," *Pittsburgh Magazine*, April 1989.

———. "In Allentown," *Pittsburgh Magazine*, January 1991.

Miller, Guy V. "Pennsylvania's Scrambled Politics," *The Nation*, May 14, 1938.

Newsweek. November 17, 1934.

———. October 7; December 9, 1946.

"Pennsylvania Votes for Governor," *Commonwealth: The Magazine of Pennsylvania*, November 1946.

Perry, George Sessions. "The Cities of America: Pittsburgh," *The Saturday Evening Post*, August 3, 1946

Plagens, Peter. "Norman Rockwell Revisited," *Newsweek*, November 15, 1999.

Rice, Charles Owen. "Pittsburgh's Power Strike: A company union finally succeeds in standing on its own feet," *The Commonweal*, November 8, 1946.

Sam Clark's Red Ink: Volleys of Truth, September 1934.

Schlesinger, Jr., Arthur M. "Not the People's Choice: How To Democratize American Democracy," *The American Prospect*, March 25, 2002.

Sprigle, Ray. "Lord Guffey of Pennsylvania," *The American Mercury*, November 1936.

"Union Mayor, Union Town," *Friday*, December 27, 1940, Vol. 1, No. 42.

"Union's Power to Cripple City: Pittsburgh Case as Sample of What Even Small Independent Can Do," *U.S. News & World Report*, October 11, 1946.

"What's Itching Labor?" *Fortune*, November 1942.

Newspaper Articles

Aliquippa Gazette. April 3, 1936.

Aliquippa News. November 19, December 10, 1941.

American Guardian. September 18, 1936, 1.

Associated Press. "Bethlehem Steel Sets Closing Timetable; 1,700 To Lose Jobs," *The Tribune-Review,* (Pittsburgh) October 15, 1994.

Barcousky, Len. "Bethlehem: Stronger Than Steel," *The Pittsburgh Post-Gazette,* March 3, 1996.

Batz, Jr., Bob. "Memories Flow from Rivers of Steel," *The Pittsburgh Post-Gazette,* April 1, 1998.

Belko, Mark. "Competition Bending Kanes," *The Pittsburgh Post-Gazette,* October 11, 1999.

Blair, Peter. "Iron Heritage and Steel Dreams," *In Pittsburgh Newsweekly,* October 20-26, 1994.

Cloonan, Anne. "Italian Immigrants Found a Home in Greensburg's Hilltop Neighborhood," *The Pittsburgh Post-Gazette,* May 1, 2002.

Cohan, Jeffrey. "Pittsburgh says, 'Grazie'-Annual parade honors Columbus, Italy," *The Pittsburgh Post-Gazette,* October 8, 2000.

Costa, Peter. "A Conversation with Morris Fiorina," *Faculty of Arts and Sciences Gazette,* Harvard University, spring 1993.

Dallet, Joe. "The Steel Workers Fight for Unemployment Relief," *Labor Unity,* December 1932.

Dawson, Pat. "East Pittsburgh Spans a Century of Ups and Downs," *The Pittsburgh Post-Gazette,* August 24, 1995.

Dempsey, David. "Not Today's Wage, Tomorrow's Security," *The New York Times Magazine,* August 7, 1949.

Dispatch. York, Pennsylvania, May 14, 1934.

Dubrovsky, Anna. "The Ties That Bind," *The Pittsburgh Post-Gazette,* July 25, 1996.

Duquesne Times. November 7, 1941.

Eagle. Reading, Pennsylvania, October 23, October 30, 1934.

Evans, Patrick. "Black in the Old Days," *In Pittsburgh,* January 31-February 6, 1990.

Frankowski, Stanley Anthony "Sluggo." "My Lawrenceville," *The [Lawrenceville] Observer,* October 1994.

Gazette & Daily. York, Pennsylvania, May 2, 1934.

Gibbons, Russell W. "I. W. Abel: a legendary figure in the history of the steel industry," *The Pittsburgh Post-Gazette,* August 20, 1987.

Ham, Cliff. "Window on the Past: Picture Provides a Look Back," *Oakland,* August 1994.

Homestead Daily Messenger. September 2; November 6, 1912.

———. November 5, 1920.

———. November 5, 1924.

———. June 17, 1933.

―――. Letters to the Editor, October 1, 2, 3, 7, 8, 9, 19, 27, 30; November 4, 1936.

―――. September 2, 1941.

Holusha, John. "Farewell to a Mill That Shaped the Modern City," *The New York Times,* October 21, 1995.

ITU News. May 1937.

Kapsambelis, Niki. "In Pittsburgh, Homes Are Seen as Family Heirlooms," *The Pittsburgh Tribune-Review,* October 10, 1998.

Kilborn, Peter T. "A Pennsylvania City Prepares for Life after Steel," *The New York Times,* December 6, 1994.

King, Larry. "1960 Election Wasn't First Loss to JFK," *USA Today,* April 23, 1994.

Klinkner, Philip A. Interviewed by Peter Monaghan, *The Chronicle of Higher Education,* November 19, 1999.

Kosterlitz, Eleanor Gedunsky. "Bates Street Memories," *Oakland,* May 1992.

Kovacic, Kristin. "Being Pittsburgh," *The Pittsburgh Post-Gazette,* March 24, 1999.

Lambert, Bruce. "Vincent Copeland, 77, Is Dead; Led Anti-War Protests in 1960's," *The New York Times,* June 10, 1993.

Lippmann, Walter. "Today and Tomorrow," nationally syndicated column, March 25, 1937.

Lowry, Patricia. "Paesani in Pittsburgh," *The Pittsburgh Post-Gazette,* September 29, 1998.

―――. "Saving St. Nicholas," *The Pittsburgh Post-Gazette,* October 10, 2000.

McCaffrey, Kate. "Bloomfield Cobbler for 66 Years," *The Pittsburgh Post-Gazette,* August 19, 2006.

McKay, Jim. "Under Its Editor Courier Grew to be Nation's Top Black Paper," *The Pittsburgh Post-Gazette,* February 6, 1995, B1.

―――. "A Leader in Area's Labor Movement," Paul Stackhouse obituary, *The Pittsburgh Post-Gazette,* December 18, 1997.

McKeesport Daily News. January 4, 1938.

Malcolm, Wade. "Oakland Cobbler who 'Saved Soles' for 75 Years," *The Pittsburgh Post-Gazette,* June 30, 2005.

Martin, William T. "Pittsburgh Figures on 1933 City Voting," *The New York Times,* December 4, 1932.

Martinez, Andres. "WW II Posters Attract Baby Boomers," *The Pittsburgh Post-Gazette,* August 13, 1995.

Merriman, Woodene. "Reviving McCarthy Days,"*Pittsburgh Post-Gazette,* October 26, 1988.

New York Times. January 17, 1932.

―――. November 5, 1933.

―――. July 19; October 21; November 6, 1934.

―――. May 16, 17; September 10; October 16, 1938.

―――. November 6, 1940.

―――. July 26, 1943.

———. June 14; November 8, 1944.

———. April 29, 1985.

———. October 2, 1993.

———. "The Infamous 'Protocols of Zion' Endures," Week in Review, July 26, 1987.

O'Neill, Brian. "Fading Footsteps: Cobbler Sees Changes in Oakland During 60 Years," *The Pittsburgh Press,* February 21, 1990.

———. "Cobbler's Life Leaves Behind Footprints," *The Pittsburgh Post-Gazette,* September 27, 1999.

Ostendorf, Kristen. "Leo Sokol: Steelworker, Cartoonist," *The Pittsburgh Post-Gazette,* March 21, 1999.

———. "Women Mine Memories from Life in a Coal Patch," *The Pittsburgh Post-Gazette,* August 19, 1999.

"Pennsylvania Democrats and Mr. Lewis," *Philadelphia Evening Ledger,* March 12, 1938.

Philadelphia Inquirer. May 16; November 6, 1934.

Philadelphia Record. September 1; November 4, 1934.

———. March 18, 29; April 1, 7, 8, 12, 20; May 10, 17; September 3, 5, 11, 17, 18, 21; October 1, 4, 25; November 8, 1938.

Pitts, Tiffany. "It's Hard to Heel to Retirement Living: Oakland Cobbler Shutters his Shop After 68 Years," *The Pittsburgh Post-Gazette,* June 22, 1998.

Pittsburgh Courier. October 8, 1932.

———. September 16; November 11, 18, 1933.

———. February 3, 1934.

Pittsburgh Post-Gazette. September 4, 5, 14, 15, 16, 1931.

———. March 11, 14, 15, 17, 18, 19, 28, 29; April 13; October 20; November 9, 1932.

———. February 20; September 1, 6; November 3, 8, 10, 1933.

———. October 11, 1934.

———. November 4, 5, 1936.

———. November 3, 1937.

———. November 9, 1938.

———. November 1, 6, 7, 1940.

———. April 20, 1945.

———. February 12, 26; October 18, 21, 1946.

———. February 3-10, 1948.

———. June 27, 1985.

———. August 18, 1993.

——— "Breakfast With . . . Michael Keaton," October 18, 1999.

Pittsburgh Press. February 5, June 1, November 15, 1888.

———. January 21, 1931.

———. January 6, 1932.

———. Letter to the Editor from "A Disgusted Republican," August 31; editorial, September 22; October 26, 1933.

———. June 9; July 18; October 2, 21; November 7, 9, 1934.

———. February 7, 11, 19, 24, 26, 27; March 7, 16, 1935.

———. July 6; October 1, 3, 1936.

———. May 18; October 8, 1938.

———. June 23, 30, 1939.

———. March 28; April 4; October 9, 12, 15, 27; November 6, 23, 1940.

———. May 7, 29; June, 20, 28; July 11; August 19, 26, 29; September 16, 23; October 1, 30; November 5, 7, 18, 20, 21, 22; December 9, 1941.

———. February 26, 1942.

———. March 18, 1944.

———. February 21-25, 1946.

———. February 3-10, 1948.

———. May 6; June 22; September 1, 2; October 18, 20, 21, 1949.

———. October 21, 1960.

Pittsburgh Sunday Post. August 4, 11, 1912.

Pittsburgh Sun-Telegraph. August 25, 1933.

———. January 30; September 5, 1934.

———. February 11; October 7, 1935.

———. April 14; October 12, 1946.

———. February 3-10, 1948.

Pittsburgh Sun-Times. October 23, 1933.

Pro, Johnna A., and Matthew P. Smith. "McKeesport debate was first of many Nixon visits," *The Pittsburgh Post-Gazette,* April 23, 1994.

Record. Wilkes-Barre, Pennsylvania, October 5, 26, 31, 1934.

Reddig, Julie A. "Steel plant inspires trail of history," *The Pittsburgh Post-Gazette,* October 11, 2000.

Roddy, Dennis B. "Rita Wilson Kane, Her Longtime Alter Ego, Was Shoulder To Lean On," *Pittsburgh Post-Gazette,* February 3, 1993.

Rosenfeld, Stephen S. "The Korean War, Remembered," *The Pittsburgh Post-Gazette,* July 30, 1993.

Rotstein, Gary. "Panther Hollow's Demise is Feared," *The Pittsburgh Post-Gazette,* March 15, 1993.

Royko, Mike. *The Pittsburgh Post-Gazette,* August 28, 1996.

Sammons, Jeffrey L. Letter to the Editor, *The New York Times,* August 7, 1987.

Saunders, K. A. "Proud Traditions Keep Neighbors Close," *Oakland,* September 1998.

Scranton *Times.* November 6, 1934.

Shogan, Robert. "50 Years On, FDR Legacy Largely Intact," *Los Angeles Times* story reprinted in *The Pittsburgh Post-Gazette,* April 13, 1995, A-5.

Simonich, Milan. "Learning a Lesson from Aliquippa Schools," *The Pittsburgh Post-Gazette,* December 21, 1997.

———. "The Lessons of World War II," *The Pittsburgh Post-Gazette,* November 11, 1999.

Soloman, Rev. S. H. Letter to the Editor, *The Homestead Daily Messenger,* September 19, 1936.

Steel Labor. United Steelworkers of America, November 1944.

Thomas, Lillian. "The Tiny Town That Fought the Klan," *The Pittsburgh Post-Gazette,* April 11, 2004, F-1.

Times. Scranton, Pennsylvania, September 4, 1934.

Union Press. Vol. 1, No. 4, September 8, 1937; No. 10, No. 11, October 29, 1937.

"Vital Facts—Countries of Origin of Leading Foreign Born Groups in Pittsburgh," *Federator,* 19, June 1944.

Walsh, Lawrence. "Ex-Councilman J. Craig Kuhn, 73; Fought for Workers," *The Pittsburgh Post-Gazette,* September 1, 1994.

Walters, Gardner J. Letter to the Editor, *Pittsburgh Post-Gazette,* November 18, 1997.

Warnick, Mark S. "FDR's Legacy on the Hill," *The Pittsburgh Press,* October 9, 1990.

Weisberg, Deborah. "Pupils Gather Tales to Weave Narrative of Bloomfield's History," *The Pittsburgh Post-Gazette,* June 15, 2000.

Welch, William M. "'A Sea Change' in Character of the House," *USA Today,* November 9, 1994.

Young, Marguerite. "Ruffner Led Vigilante Committee," *The Union Press,* No. 10, October 20, 1937.

Official Reports and Other Documents

Allegheny Conference on Community Development. Inaugural address, January 7, 1946, David L. Lawrence file.

Allegheny County Department of Elections, Pittsburgh election returns, 1941, 1945.

———. Preliminary Street List for 1996, Pittsburgh Ward 4, District 15, January 16, 1996.

Ambridge, Pennsylvania, Statistical Abstract of, 1952.

American Institute of Public Opinion, Survey 87, June 14, 1937.

Black, Bertram J. and Aubrey Mallach. "Population Trends in Pittsburgh and Allegheny County, 1840-1940," Federation of Social Agencies of Pittsburgh and Allegheny County, April 1944.

Colored Democratic [Pennsylvania] State Campaign Committee, "The Story of the New Deal and the Negro," 1938.

Communist Party, Pittsburgh Branch. "Gov. James Kept His Promises... To the Bankers! Put Out the Bonfire! Unite to Win the 1939-1940 Elections!" pamphlet.

Congress of Industrial Organizations. *Proceedings of the First Constitutional Convention of the Congress of Industrial Organizations, Held in the City of Pittsburgh, Pennsylvania, November 14 to November 18, 1938, Inclusive.*

Epstein, Abraham. *The Negro Migrant in Pittsburgh,* University of Pittsburgh School of Economics: Pittsburgh, 1918.

Ferri, Kathleen. "Braddock and Penn Ave., Turtle Creek, PA," painting in collection of Westmoreland County Museum of Art, Greensburg, Pennsylvania.

Gompers, Samuel. *Should A Political Labor Party Be Formed?* pamphlet, American Federation of Labor, 1918.

Legislative Journal, Commonwealth of Pennsylvania, 1935.

Moyers, Bill. on the NBC Evening News, April 11, 1995.

National Tube Co. Historical Notes, "Summary of Three Strikes," September 19, 1935, Box 3061, L4061, 91:6, 8, Archives of Industrial Society, University of Pittsburgh.

National Wallace for President Committee. *Facts to Fight With for Wallace and the New Party: A Fact Book for Wallace-Taylor Workers,* New York, 1948.

Ninth Industrial Directory of the Commonwealth of Pennsylvania, 1938.

Pennsylvania Manual, 1935-1936, 1939.

Proceedings of the First Constitutional Convention of the Congress of Industrial Organizations, Held in the City of Pittsburgh, Pennsylvania, November 14 to November 18, 1938, Inclusive.

Rice, Charles Owen. WWSW radio broadcast, May 15, 1937, Box 27, Rice Papers, Archives of Industrial Society, University of Pittsburgh.

————. "Utica Textile Workers Organizing Committee," radio address, WIBX, Utica, New York, July 19, 1938, Box 27, Rice Papers.

Report of the Anthracite Coal Industry Commission, Murelle Printing Co.: Harrisburg, Pa., 1938.

Robinson, J. Carter. Report of State Department of Labor Placement Secretary for Pittsburgh's Hill District office, to Forrester B. Washington, Director, State Department of Labor's Negro Survey, December 1924.

Seidman, Joel. *A Labor Party for America?* pamphlet, Education Department, United Automobile Workers of America, Detroit, 1937.

United States Department of Commerce, *Historical Statistics of the United States, Colonial Times to 1957,* Industrial Conflicts, 1930-1942, U.S. Government Printing Office, Washington, D.C.

Westmoreland Museum of Art, "Valley of Work," Pittsburgh Art Exhibit Teacher's Packet, Greensburg, Pennsylvania.

Workers School. "Training for the Class Struggle," announcement of classes for 1926-1927, New York, 1926.

Works Progress Administration. "The Employment Situation in the Pennsylvania Anthracite Region," Washington, D.C., 1935.

Index

About the Author

Eric Leif Davin, Ph.D., teaches American Labor History at the University of Pittsburgh. He won the 1997 Eugene V. Debs Foundation Literature Prize for his essay, "The Very Last Hurrah: The Defeat of the Labor Party Idea, 1934-1936." He is also the author of *American Labor History Made Easy!*

Breinigsville, PA USA
02 April 2010
235449BV00004B/2/P

9 780739 122389